Appellate Practice

in the
United States

Appellate Practice

in the
United States

Robert L. Stern

The Bureau of National Affairs, Inc., Washington, D.C.

Library of Congress Cataloging in Publication Data

Stern, Robert L.
  Appellate practice in the United States.

  Includes index.
  1. Appellate procedure—United States. I. Title.
KF9050.S75   347.73'8   81-1963
ISBN 0-87179-352-0   347.3708   AACR2

International Standard Book Number: 0-87179-352-0
Printed in the United States of America

Preface

Two years ago, just as the Fifth Edition of Stern and Gressman's *Supreme Court Practice* was being completed, Howard S. Primer, then associated with the American Bar Association and now the administrator of the courts of the State of Washington, suggested to me that there was no book describing appellate practice in the United States and that I should undertake to prepare one. After some thought and inquiry, and after obtaining the consent of my partners at Mayer, Brown & Platt to my devoting substantial time to such a project, I concluded that I should make the effort.

I began with knowledge of the practice in the federal and Illinois appellate courts derived from many years of experience in the Solicitor General's office of the United States Department of Justice and in private practice in Chicago. I have also been a member of the Advisory Committee which drafted the Federal Rules of Appellate Procedure in the 1960s and the Illinois Supreme Court Rules Committee. Participation in the work of committees of the American Bar Association's Appellate Judges Conference and its Task Force on Appellate Procedure, as well as the Federal Judicial Center's Study Group on the Case Load of the Supreme Court, made me familiar with the problems facing appellate courts throughout the United States. This experience was supplemented by examination of the rules of the other forty-nine states in the course of writing this volume. As explained more fully in the Introduction, subtitled What This Book Covers and What It Doesn't, I was thus enabled to describe and analyze most, but by no means all, of what lawyers must know to handle appeals throughout the country.

I have been aided in this project by many lawyers, judges and appellate court administrators, including approximately

100 lawyers who were good enough to respond to a survey on how they prepared for oral argument.

I am grateful to my partners for contributing my time and some of their resources to the preparation of the book. My colleagues Douglas A. Poe, Richard L. Jacobson, Michele Odorizzi, Gary T. Johnson and Stephen M. Shapiro (now an Assistant to the Solicitor General) were good enough to review the whole text and make valuable suggestions. Their backgrounds as law clerks with the United States Supreme Court and the courts of appeals provided a helpful perspective. The project would have been substantially more difficult without the aid of Janice B. Bentley, the firm's librarian, Bobby Towns, assistant librarian, and the other members of the library staff, and also of Timothy Pyne, librarian for the American Judicature Society. I am especially appreciative of the help of Rosemarie Horan, my secretary, who suffered through, revised and corrected draft after draft. She knows that anything I—or for that matter any other lawyer—write isn't finished until it finally appears in print, and she will be happy and relieved when this does.

My editor Louise Rosenblatt took over when the manuscript was submitted to The Bureau of National Affairs, Inc., as she did for the last edition of *Supreme Court Practice,* and I continue to be thankful for her invaluable assistance.

ROBERT L. STERN

Chicago
May 1981

Acknowledgments

Grateful acknowledgment is extended to the following for permission to reprint excerpts from copyrighted material:

American Bar Association, FEDERAL RULES OF CIVIL PROCEDURE AND PROCEEDINGS OF THE INSTITUTE ON FEDERAL RULES (1938).

American Bar Association, MODEL CODE OF PROFESSIONAL RESPONSIBILITY, as amended (1980).

American Bar Association, STANDARDS RELATING TO CRIMINAL APPEALS (1969).

American Bar Association Commission on Standards of Judicial Administration, STANDARDS RELATING TO APPELLATE COURTS (1977).

American Bar Association Task Force on Appellate Procedure, EFFICIENCY AND JUSTICE IN APPEALS: METHODS AND SELECTED MATERIALS (1967).

Bazelon, D., *New Gods for Old: "Efficient" Courts in a Democratic Society*, 46 New York University Law Review 653 (1971).

Blair, P., *Appellate Briefs and Advocacy*, 18 Fordham Law Review 30 (1949).

Burger, W., *Annual Report on the State of the Judiciary*, 62 American Bar Association Journal 443 (1976).

Carrington, P., Meador, D., and Rosenberg, M., JUSTICE ON APPEAL, West Publishing Co. (1976).

Carson, R., *Conduct of the Appeal—A Lawyer's View*, in A CASE ON APPEAL, 4th edition, American Law Institute (1967).

Cooper, F., *Stating the Issue in Appellate Briefs*, 49 American Bar Association Journal 180 (1963).

Currie, G. R., *Appellate Courts Use of Facts Outside of the Record by Resort to Judicial Notice and Independent Investigation*, 1960 Wisconsin Law Review 39.

Davis, J. W., *The Argument of an Appeal*, 26 American Bar Association Journal 895 (1940).

Fitzgerald, H., and Hartnett, D., *Effective Oral Argument*, in THE PRACTICAL LAWYER, Vol. 18, No. 4, American Law Institute (1972).

Godbold, J., *Twenty Pages and Twenty Minutes—Effective Advocacy on Appeal*, 30 Southwestern Law Journal 801 (1976).

Goodrich, H., *A Case on Appeal—A Judge's View*, in A CASE ON APPEAL, 4th edition, American Law Institute (1967).

Harlan, J., *What Part Does the Oral Argument Play in the Conduct of an Appeal?*, 41 Cornell Law Quarterly 6 (1955).

Jackson, R., *Advocacy Before the Supreme Court: Suggestions for Effective Case Presentations*, 37 American Bar Association Journal 801 (1951).

Johnedis, D., *Massachusetts' Two-Court Appellate System in Operation*, 60 Massachusetts Law Quarterly 77 (1975).

Korn, H., *Civil Jurisdiction of the New York Court of Appeals and Appellate Divisions,* 16 Buffalo Law Review 307 (1967).

Leflar, R. A., INTERNAL OPERATING PROCEDURES OF APPELLATE COURTS, American Bar Foundation (1976).

Louisell, D., and Degnan, R., *Rehearing in American Appellate Courts,* 44 California Law Review 627 (1956).

Marvell, T., and Kuykendall, M., *Appellate Courts—Facts and Figures,* 4 State Court Journal 9 (No. 2, Spring 1980).

Mitchell, W., *Book Review,* 64 Harvard Law Review 350 (1950).

Pittoni, M., BRIEF WRITING AND ARGUMENTATION, 3rd edition, The Foundation Press, Inc. (1967).

Prettyman, E. B., *Some Observations Concerning Appellate Advocacy,* 39 Virginia Law Review 285 (1953).

Prettyman, E. B., Jr., *Supreme Court Advocacy: Random Thoughts in a Day of Time Restrictions,* in LITIGATION, Vol. 4, No. 2, American Bar Association Section of Litigation (1978).

Rall, O., *The Use of Visual Aids in Courts of Review,* 52 Northwestern Law Review 90 (1957).

Rutledge, W., *The Appellate Brief,* 28 American Bar Association Journal 251 (1942).

Schaefer, W., *Appellate Advocacy,* 23 Tennessee Law Review 471 (1954).

Sobieski, J., *The Theoretical Foundations of the Proposed Tennessee Rules of Appellate Procedure,* 45 Tennessee Law Review 161 (1978).

Strunk, W., and White, E. B., THE ELEMENTS OF STYLE, 3rd edition, Macmillan Publishing Co., Inc. (1979).

Tate, A., Jr., *The Art of Brief Writing: What a Judge Wants to Read,* in LITIGATION, Vol. 4, No. 2, American Bar Association Section of Litigation (1978).

Wallace, J. C., *Wanted: Advocates Who Can Argue in Writing,* 67 Kentucky Law Journal 375 (1978).

Wasby, S., Marvell, T., and Aikman, A., VOLUME AND DELAY IN STATE APPELLATE COURTS: PROBLEMS AND RESPONSES, National Center for State Courts (1979).

Wilkins, R., *The Argument of an Appeal,* 33 Cornell Law Quarterly 40 (1947).

Contents

Introduction. What This Book Covers and What It Doesn't 1

1. The Appellate Courts and How They Function . 5

   1.1   The Relationship Between Appellate Court Administration and Appellate Practice 5
   1.2   Historical Background 6
   1.3   The Structure of American Appellate Courts 7
   1.4   Original Jurisdiction of Appellate Courts .. 12
       (a)   Jurisdiction 12
       (b)   Procedure 15
   1.5   Appeals as a Matter of Right or Discretion. 18
   1.6   The Appellate Explosion 22
   1.7   The Effect on the Right to Argue Orally... 23
   1.8   The Effect on Petitions for Review........ 26
   1.9   Internal Operation of the Courts—Law Clerks and Staff Attorneys 27
   1.10 Problems of the Two-Tiered System— Avoiding Duplication of Work........... 30
       (a)   Using the Same Briefs in Intermediate and Supreme Courts—Advantages and Disadvantages 30
       (b)   Supreme Court Screening Prior to Hearing Below 33

2. Before the Appeal Is Taken 37

   2.1   The Need for Raising in Lower Courts the Points to Be Presented on Appeal 37
   2.2   Should a Case Be Appealed?............. 41

2.3   Should New Counsel Be Brought In on
Appeal?.................................   44
2.4   Standing to Appeal.....................   49
(a)   Appellant Must Have Been a Party
Below...........................   49
(b)   Appellant Must Be Aggrieved by the
Decision Below...................   51

**3. What Orders Are Appealable—The Finality
Doctrine and Exceptions**   52

3.1   The General Principle That Appeals May
Be Taken Only From Final Judgments or
Orders.................................   52
3.2   Exceptions to the Finality Doctrine—In
General...............................   54
3.3   Interlocutory Appeals as a Matter of Right.   56
3.4   Judgment Final as to Some but Not All of
the Claims or Parties   58
3.5   Review of Interlocutory Orders as a Matter
of Discretion...........................   59
(a)   The Federal Standards   59
(b)   State Deviations From the Federal
Standards........................   61
(c)   Application to Both Courts or Only to
the Reviewing Court   65
(d)   Conclusiveness of Trial Court's
Refusal to Certify..................   67
(e)   Review of Interlocutory Orders of
Intermediate Appellate Courts.......   69
3.6   Judge-Made Exceptions to the Finality Rule   69
3.7   The Extraordinary Writs   73
3.8   Contempt   78

4. The Taking of an Appeal From the Trial Court .   80

4.1   Background   80
4.2   The Initial Jurisdictional Documents   81
4.3   Service of the Notice of Appeal   85
4.4   Fees..................................   87
4.5   Papers to Accompany the Initial Document   88
(a)   The Bond for Appeal...............   88

		(b)	Designations of the Record; Ordering of Transcript	88
		(c)	Assignment of Errors	89
		(d)	Information Statement	90
	4.6		Time to Appeal	93
	4.7		Cross-Appeals and Cross-Petitions	97
		(a)	Additional Time for Cross-Appeals	97
		(b)	When a Cross-Appeal Is Necessary	99
	4.8		Docketing the Appeal	103
	4.9		Appeals Requiring Leave of Court	106
	4.10		Appeals Involving Constitutional Questions Where the Government Has Not Previously Been Made a Party	106
	4.11		Stays, Bonds and Supersedeas	107
		(a)	Security for Costs on Appeal	107
		(b)	Stays and Supersedeas Bonds	109
	4.12		The Record and Transcript	111

5.			**Appeals to the Highest Court When There Is an Intermediate Appellate Court**	112
	5.1		In General	112
	5.2		Granting Review by Majority or Minority Vote	114
	5.3		Appeal as of Right to a Supreme Court From a Trial Court	116
	5.4		Appeal as of Right to a Supreme Court From an Intermediate Appellate Court	119
		(a)	Specific Subjects	119
		(b)	General Categories Not Based Upon Particular Subject Matter	120
		(c)	Procedure	121
	5.5		Bypassing the Intermediate Appellate Court	122
	5.6		Review on Certification by the Intermediate Appellate Court	126
		(a)	Certification Before Decision Below	126
		(b)	Certification After Decision Below	129
	5.7		Review on Application of a Party After Judgment in the Intermediate Appellate Court	130
		(a)	The Documents to Be Filed	130

(b) The Time for Seeking Discretionary
Review 135
(c) Grounds for Granting Review 137
(d) Content of the Petition or Application
for Review 142
5.8 The Brief in Opposition to the Petition. . . . 148
5.9 Comparative Analysis of the Methods of
Review by the Highest Court 150
(a) Discretionary Jurisdiction 150
(b) Certification by the Intermediate
Court 151
(c) Appeals to Highest Court as of Right. 152
5.10 Certificate to State Supreme Courts by
Courts of Other Jurisdictions 154

6. Records, Appendices and the Like 156

6.1 An Overall View 156

Preparation of the Original Record

6.2 The Content of the Record 159
6.3 The Transcript or Report of Proceedings . . 163
6.4 Procedure Where Proceedings Are Not
Transcribed 170
6.5 Agreed Statement of Facts 172
6.6 Preparation and Transmission of the
Record by the Trial Court Clerk 172

Making Additional Copies of the Record

6.7 The Need for Duplication in General 176
6.8 Judicial Efforts to Reduce the Length of the
Duplicated Parts of the Record 179
6.9 The Number of Copies to Be Duplicated . . 183
6.10 Method of Reproduction of Records 187
6.11 Should the Pertinent Evidence Be Narrated
or Quoted Verbatim 190
6.12 How to Prepare the Portions of the Record
to Be Duplicated 197
6.13 When to File the Appendix—The Deferred
Appendix System 200
6.14 Records in the Highest Court of a
Two-Tiered Appellate System 205
6.15 Recommendations 207

7. Brief Writing 209

7.1 Types of Briefs 209
7.2 Importance of Briefs.................... 210
7.3 The Status or Function of the Particular
     Appellate Court........................ 214
     (a) Differences Between Briefs and
          Petitions in Intermediate and Supreme
          Courts 214
     (b) Use of Intermediate Appellate Court
          Briefs in a Supreme Court 216
7.4 The Time Schedules for Writing and Filing
     Briefs................................. 219
7.5 Allowing Time for Revising, Rewriting and
     Checking............................... 224
7.6 The Maximum Page Length 226
7.7 Preparation for Writing 230
7.8 Writing Good English—In General 233
7.9 References to Parties in Covers, Captions
     and Text............................... 240
7.10 Headings............................... 243
7.11 The Organization of Briefs—In General ... 244
7.12 The Cover of the Brief.................. 246
7.13 Indexes, and Points and Authorities....... 249
7.14 The Beginning of the Brief—Arrangement
     of the Preliminary Items................ 251
7.15 The Nature of the Proceeding........... 256
7.16 Jurisdictional Statement 257
7.17 Statutes Involved....................... 259
7.18 Statement of the Questions Presented..... 261
7.19 Restrictive Effect of the Statement of
     Questions Presented.................... 268
7.20 The Statement of Facts 270
7.21 Summary of Argument.................. 276
7.22 The Argument Part of the Brief—
     Arrangement and Selection 280
     (a) Arguing Factual as Well as Legal
          Issues 281
     (b) Selection of Points to Argue......... 282
     (c) The Arrangement of Points 286
7.23 Putting Yourself in the Position of the
     Judge................................. 289

7.24	Inaccuracy, Overstatement, Lack of Candor, Personalities		291
7.25	The Handling of Cases—The Importance of "Why"		295
7.26	Authorities Other Than Cases		301
7.27	Overruling; Dissenting and Concurring Opinions		303
7.28	Quotations		305
7.29	Forms of Citation		309
	(a)	United States Supreme Court Cases	310
	(b)	Other Federal Court Cases	312
	(c)	State Court Decisions	313
	(d)	Dates	314
	(e)	Words Showing Case History	314
	(f)	Names of Cases	315
	(g)	Rehearings	316
	(h)	Statutes	316
	(i)	Legislative Material	316
	(j)	Books and Articles	317
7.30	Facts Outside the Record—Mootness, Brandeis Briefs and Judicial Notice		317
7.31	*Supra*'s, *Infra*'s and Footnotes		323
7.32	The Conclusion		326
7.33	Answering Briefs		327
7.34	Reply Briefs		331
7.35	Supplemental Briefs and Statements		333
7.36	*Amicus* Briefs		335
7.37	Physical Form—Methods of Reproduction		344
7.38	Number of Copies of Briefs		345
7.39	Checking for Errors in Text and Citations		348
7.40	Serving and Filing Briefs		352
8.	**Oral Argument**		358
8.1	The Importance of Oral Argument		358
8.2	How to Obtain Oral Argument		365
8.3	Who Should Argue		368
8.4	The Time Allowed for Oral Argument— Parties and *Amici Curiae*		369
8.5	When the Case Will Be Heard and When Counsel Should Arrive		373

8.6   The Order of Argument—Opening and
        Closing 376
8.7   Number of Counsel—Multiple Parties 379
8.8   How to Prepare for Argument and Argue.. 383
        (a) Becoming Familiar With the Material . 384
        (b) Rough Outline of Points—The
             Process of Selection 387
        (c) Preparing in Detail................. 388
        (d) Rehearsing........................ 396
8.9   Style of Speaking—and Dressing 398
8.10   Physical Arrangements for Arguing 401
8.11   The Substance of the Oral Argument—In
        General.................................. 402
8.12   Selection of Points to Argue and Omit—
        Arrangement of the Argument 407
8.13   Opening the Argument—The Nature of the
        Case and the Issues.................... 409
8.14   The Statement of Facts 413
8.15   Charts, Maps, Diagrams, Pictures, Physical
        Evidence................................ 418
8.16   Argument of the Issues 419
        (a) The Importance of Reasons and
             Principles......................... 419
        (b) The Use of Cases.................. 421
        (c) Other Types of Authorities.......... 423
        (d) Reading and Quoting 423
        (e) Answering Questions............... 426
8.17   Concluding Peroration 432
8.18   Appellant's Rebuttal 433
8.19   Appellee's Answering Argument.......... 437
8.20   Client in the Courtroom 441

9. **Rehearings and Mandates** 443

9.1   Rehearings in General 443
9.2   Reasons for Granting Rehearing.......... 447
9.3   Time for Filing Petitions for Rehearing.... 454
9.4   The Contents of the Petition............. 458
9.5   Responses to Petitions for Rehearing 461
9.6   Rehearings in Banc..................... 464
9.7   Successive Petitions for Rehearing 470
9.8   Issuance of the Mandate 472

10.   The Decisional Process   475

10.1   Reading Briefs in Advance of Argument . . .   475
10.2   Conferences Before Argument   477
10.3   Conferences After Argument.   480
10.4   The Assignment of Opinions.   481
10.5   Types of Decision   483
10.6   Publication of Opinions   486
10.7   Ability to Cite Unpublished Opinions   489

11.   Motion Practice   491

11.1   In General—Emergencies.   491
11.2   Classes of Motions   493
11.3   What Must Be Filed; Contents of Motion . .   495
11.4   Filing and Service of Motions   497
11.5   Form and Number of Copies.   498
11.6   Responses to Motions.   499
11.7   Oral Argument   500

Appendix. Forms.   503

Appendix A.   Petition for Leave to Appeal From
State Intermediate Appellate Court
to State Supreme Court.   504

Appendix B.   Answer to Petition for Leave to
Appeal From State Intermediate
Appellate Court to State Supreme
Court.   514

Appendix C.   Brief on the Merits in a State
Supreme Court   523

Index.   541

Introduction

What This Book Covers
and What It Doesn't

The volume by Eugene Gressman and me on *Supreme Court Practice* stated in its Preface that its object was to set forth "to the extent possible everything that a lawyer would want to know" about handling a case in the United States Supreme Court. This book dealing with appellate practice generally in the United States cannot claim to go that far. Inasmuch as the latest (1978) edition of *Supreme Court Practice* covering only one court ran to 935 pages of text, an effort to deal with the practice in all the federal appellate courts and the 51 state and District of Columbia appellate systems in similar depth would have been impossible for the author, and probably for the readers as well.

A less imposing work, however, can cover most of what the practicing lawyer or the law student needs to know, and also enable the procedures in the various jurisdictions to be compared. My activities on committees which drafted both the federal and Illinois appellate rules and on committees of the bar and bench concerned with appellate problems throughout the nation have taught that the procedures and principles are in broad perspective very much the same, that the differences are less significant than the similarities.

As might be expected, since many jurisdictions have similar historical backgrounds and traditions and face the same problems, there is not room for vast variation in methods of taking appeals, obtaining and reproducing the transcripts and other parts of the record for the appellate court, petitioning for discre-

1

tionary review, writing briefs and preparing oral arguments. In many respects the federal rules and those of many of the states are similar and often identical. What differences there are among the jurisdictions, apart from such matters as the precise number of days allowed for the filing of different papers or the number of copies to be filed, in general fall into a small number of patterns. The scope of this book permits discussion of the patterns but not necessarily of each variation.

This book will therefore not describe all the details of practice in any particular appellate court. It does not cite or refer to the rules or practice of each state on each point; in the main it will give only illustrative examples. There will, however, be an attempt to cover those procedures which are commonly employed in numbers of jurisdictions, including the United States Supreme Court and the United States courts of appeals, and an effort will also be made to call attention to novel practices in individual states which may be of interest or value elsewhere.

The object will be not only to describe but to compare, often critically, procedures in the various jurisdictions, in the belief that this in itself will be useful, perhaps not as much to practicing lawyers as to judges and judicial administrators. For little seems to be known in many states as to how problems are handled in other jurisdictions (except for the federal), and cross-fertilization of ideas may lead to improvements.

Of course, no book such as this can make it unnecessary for an appellate practitioner to become familiar with the statutes and rules, and if necessary the case law, governing the court to which his appeal must go. For there can be no assurance that on any point the requirements of any jurisdiction will be mentioned, and certainly not in detail. In addition, statutes and rules are frequently changed, and the careful lawyer must keep his knowledge up-to-date.

Lawyers should also be aware that in many jurisdictions, including the federal, the rules are not always uniform for even all the appellate courts on the same level. Different intermediate appellate courts often supplement in different ways the general rules for the jurisdiction, as do many of the United States courts of appeals in varying degrees.

As I can attest from personal experience, even the fact that one may have participated in the drafting of a court's rules or written about them does not mean that the rules need not be reread when one begins work on an appeal. *A fortiori,* reading, or even memorizing (and few readers will go that far), this book will not adequately substitute for reading the rules themselves. For neither the lawyer's memory nor this volume, nor any other, can be certain to convey all the details which will be relevant in any given case, and conformity to the details of the rules is essential to keeping out of trouble.

Apart from an occasional mention, no attempt has been made to deal with the case law or statutes of the various states. That might have produced a better book, but it would have required encyclopedic treatment which would have far outlasted the temporal capacity of the author. Since readers would still have had to examine the authorities in the particular jurisdiction both to be positive of completeness and to keep up-to-date, the tremendous amount of additional work did not seem worth the effort.

The book concentrates on the main line of civil appeals from lower courts. The procedure for appeals from administrative officials or bodies is usually the same or similar. As to most matters, but not all, criminal appeals are also handled in the same way, or at least similarly. The variations in the criminal practice, however, are generally not discussed. Nor is the practice and procedure in appeals from courts having jurisdiction over small claims or minor offenses.

The large part of the book which deals with the writing of briefs and the presentation of oral arguments, however, applies to all types of appeals.

The reader will notice more frequent reference to the practice in the federal appellate courts and Illinois than to other states. Although I have examined the appellate rules[1] (but not the statutes or the cases) of all the states as of 1978 or 1979, I lived through the preparation of the Federal Appellate Rules and the Illinois rules for many years and undoubtedly have more of a feeling for the reasons underlying them. On the whole, though not in all respects, I believe they are sensible rules, though not necessarily better than those in all other jurisdictions. In particular, Tennessee, Wisconsin and Pennsylvania have rewritten their rules in the last year or two after painstaking study, in which they have perhaps jumped from the foot to the head of the parade in modern rule-making.

---

[1] Unless otherwise indicated, references to the rules of any state or court are to the rules governing practice in the appellate courts.

Despite the above caveats, it is believed that the general similarities in the appellate practices of most state and federal courts are sufficient to make this work useful to lawyers, judges and appellate administrators throughout the country.

1

The Appellate Courts
and How They Function

1.1 The Relationship Between Appellate Court Administration and Appellate Practice

What lawyers must and should do in appellate courts can best be understood if they know how and why those courts function as they do. Thus, the differences between an ordinary brief and a petition for review or certiorari become intelligible in the light of the reasons for a two-court appellate structure and of the work load confronting the highest court. The way in which a record or appendix must be prepared for an appellate court, the number of copies required, and the time when it must be filed reflect the use the judges will make of it. How a brief should be written depends on what function it serves, and on how much and what the judges, staff attorneys or law clerks reading it know about the record as well as the law. How a case should be argued, and even whether it will be argued, depends upon the extent to which the judges, or some of them, have read the briefs or record prior to the argument (and how much time they can devote to such reading), the time allowed for arguing, and the proclivity of the judges to question counsel at length. All of this may depend to a large extent on the size of the court's work load.

Knowledge of the structure of the appellate courts in a jurisdiction and, to some extent, of the courts' internal workings

5

will accordingly provide a useful prologue to the treatment of procedural problems and requirements.

1.2   Historical Background

Appellate practice in the United States did not of course begin in 1789 with the adoption of the Constitution. Prior to the Declaration of Independence each colony had a judicial system. The highest appellate tribunal, however, was not a colonial supreme court but the Privy Council in London. The colonies, or some of them, had their own councils, but, following the British model, these often were composed of the King's (or governor's) advisers and not of judges or even lawyers. Appeals from trial courts often called merely for new trials by other trial judges in superior trial courts, not by true courts of appeal. Pennsylvania and Maryland, however, had a supreme court and a court of appeals.[1]

Between 1776 and 1789 most of the independent states created their own appellate structures, usually a supreme court.[2] And Congress acting under the Articles of Confederation established a United States Court of Appeals to hear appeals from the state courts in cases of capture of vessels at sea, so that a uniform body of law would govern that then important subject.[3]

These appellate tribunals antedating the Constitution drew on the British practice as the source of their appellate procedures. Lawyers were familiar with writs of error in actions at law and appeals in chancery. Appeal by writ of error, directing that the record be sent to an appellate court to be examined for error, historically was a new proceeding rather than continuation of a case begun in a lower court. A petition for allowance of the writ and a formal order of a judge granting the petition were accompanied by an assignment of errors and a citation notifying the other parties that the case was to come before the appellate court. The bill of exceptions combined a statement of the exceptions or errors with the pertinent portions of the rec-

---

[1] J. Goebel, HISTORY OF THE SUPREME COURT OF THE UNITED STATES, Vol. 1, ANTECEDENTS AND BEGINNINGS TO 1801, pp. 13–46 (1971).

[2] F. N. Thorpe, FEDERAL AND STATE CONSTITUTIONS, COLONIAL CHARTERS AND OTHER ORGANIC LAWS OF THE STATES, TERRITORIES AND COLONIES (1909).

[3] Goebel, *supra* note 1, at 150, 169–182.

ord as submitted to and approved or "settled" by the trial court. Since this was before the days of typewriters and shorthand reporting, the testimony was summarized or abstracted on the basis of the notes or memories of counsel and the trial judge. In contrast to the action at law, the appeal in equity was not regarded as a new proceeding but as a removal to a higher court for retrial on the old record below and evidence taken *de novo* if necessary.[4]

These procedures survived for many years in the state and federal courts. They did not disappear in the United States Supreme Court until 1954. And some remnants, or at least the terminology, still exist in a few of the states.

A number of state courts had, however, adopted a simplified appellate process, as did the portion of the Federal Rules of Civil Procedure adopted in 1938 (Rules 72–76) dealing with appeals. Before and after those provisions were superseded in 1967 by the Federal Rules of Appellate Procedure (hereinafter sometimes referred to as the Federal Appellate Rules), many of the states were either adopting the federal procedure in whole or in part or modernizing their own. The federal rules and the many state procedures that are identical or similar to them in many respects constitute the only single body of appellate practice familiar to lawyers throughout the nation. Accordingly, the treatment of the various aspects of appellate procedure in this book will use those procedures as a starting point, and then deal with significant differences in the rules and practices of the states, some of which do not seem to have caught up with the federal improvements and some of which may have gone beyond them.

1.3 The Structure of American Appellate Courts

Article III of the United States Constitution provides for "one Supreme Court" and for "such inferior Courts as Congress may from time to time ordain and establish." The inferior

---

[4]B. Shipman, COMMON LAW PLEADING, pp. 537–539 (3d ed., 1923); J. Sobieski, *The Theoretical Foundations of the Proposed Tennessee Rules of Appellate Procedure,* 45 Tenn. L. Rev. 161, 168–172 (1978); R. Pound, APPELLATE PROCEDURE IN CIVIL CASES, pp. 80–84 (1941); E. Sunderland, *A Simplified System of Appellate Procedure,* 17 Tenn. L. Rev. 651 (1943). At one time a jury whose judgment was overturned by a second, larger jury was subject to "attaint" (imprisonment and forfeiture); a reversed judge could get off with a fine, or even defend his judgment in a duel. Sobieski, *supra* at 170–171.

courts originally set up consisted of district courts in each state and of circuit courts composed of both Supreme Court Justices and the district judges.[5] In the main the Justices riding circuit sat as trial judges, though they had appellate authority over the district judges in some types of cases. Often the trial court would be composed of a Justice and a district judge.

At the beginning two Supreme Court Justices rode circuit in each of the three large circuits into which the nation was divided. Subsequently, the country was divided into separate circuits for each Justice. Riding circuit in those days consisted of traveling long distances on horseback or in a horse-drawn vehicle, or by boat where that was feasible. The chore of covering by such means circuits consisting of a number of states was, as might be expected, not attractive to established and sometimes elderly lawyers of renown. The Justices first protested as early as 1792, and the unattractiveness of the job induced John Jay, the first Chief Justice, to resign in 1795 to run for Governor of New York and to refuse to accept a reappointment to the Court in 1801.[6] This led to the appointment of John Marshall. Not until long into the next century, after the Supreme Court's own case load became heavy, did Congress begin to reduce the Justices' duty to ride the circuits; indeed, some of it even survived the creation of the courts of appeals in 1891, and endured until 1911.[7]

In the 1840s, the Supreme Court's own case load combined with the circuit riding caused the Justices to suggest the need for an intermediate appellate court.[8] As with many other efforts at judicial reform, support for this proposal was not immediately overwhelming. Only after the Supreme Court fell three years

[5]Combining trial and appellate authority in the same body of judges was similar to the English practice and also to that followed in a number of states well into the Nineteenth Century. S. Wasby, T. Marvell and A. Aikman, VOLUME AND DELAY IN STATE APPELLATE COURTS: PROBLEMS AND RESPONSES, pp. 43, 63 (National Center for State Courts, 1979).

[6]1 C. Warren, THE SUPREME COURT IN UNITED STATES HISTORY, pp. 88–89 (1922); I. Dilliard, *John Jay* in 1 L. Friedman and F. Israel, THE JUSTICES OF THE UNITED STATES SUPREME COURT, 1789–1969, pp. 3–21 (1969).

[7]G. Casper and R. Posner, THE WORKLOAD OF THE SUPREME COURT, p. 18 (American Bar Foundation, 1976).

[8]See C. Swisher, HISTORY OF THE SUPREME COURT OF THE UNITED STATES, Vol. V, THE TANEY PERIOD, 1836–1864, pp. 280–283 (1974). An Act "to provide for the more convenient organization of the Courts of the United States," which, *inter alia,* created six three-judge circuit courts with appellate jurisdiction, was enacted during the last days of the Adams Administration, but repealed early in the Jefferson Administration. Act of February 13, 1801, c. 4, 2 Stat. 89; Act of March 8, 1802, c. 8, 2 Stat. 132.

behind in its work in 1890[9] did Congress respond in 1891 by establishing the circuit courts of appeals.

By this time several of the states had already created intermediate appellate court systems.[10] Although at the beginning the same judges could sit as both trial and appellate judges, as in the federal system, by 1847 some of the judges in the New York trial court of general jurisdiction were sitting in General Term in panels of three to review trial court decisions. By the 1870s these tribunals had evolved into the Appellate Division of New York's confusingly misnamed un-supreme "Supreme Court," which is in reality a trial court the decisions of which are reviewable by the Appellate Division and then by the New York Court of Appeals. Even now the judges of the four Appellate Divisions in theory are members of the Supreme Court, although they do not try cases.

Thus, by 1891 the concept of an intermediate appellate court system was no longer strange to the lawyers in the country, and this may have helped make Congress more receptive to the establishment of the circuit courts of appeals. As the various states grew in population and volume of litigation, more and more adopted intermediate appellate court systems, which greatly increase the number of cases which the appellate courts can handle and also make appellate courts more accessible to litigants in various parts of a state.[11] A number of these courts were created in the last 10 years.[12]

As of 1980, 33 states had or had just authorized intermediate courts;[13] 17 did not. Of the 23 states which, according to the Census Bureau estimates for 1980,[14] had populations of 3.6 million or more, all but two have established intermediate

---

[9]F. Frankfurter and J. Landis, THE BUSINESS OF THE SUPREME COURT: A STUDY IN THE FEDERAL JUDICIAL SYSTEM, pp. 86–257 (1927).

[10]New Jersey, New York, Ohio, Missouri, Texas, Illinois, Louisiana. The New Jersey court was created in 1704. E. Curran and E. Sunderland, *Organization and Operation of Courts of Review*, in THIRD REPORT OF JUDICIAL COUNCIL OF MICHIGAN (1935); VOLUME AND DELAY, *supra* note 5, at 51.

[11]M. Osthus and M. Stiegler, STATE INTERMEDIATE APPELLATE COURTS, pp. 2–3 (American Judicature Society, 1980).

[12]Alaska, Arkansas, Hawaii, Idaho, Iowa, Kansas, Kentucky, Massachusetts, Wisconsin.

[13]Alabama, Alaska, Arizona, Arkansas, California, Colorado, Connecticut, Florida, Georgia, Hawaii, Idaho, Illinois, Indiana, Iowa, Kansas, Kentucky, Louisiana, Maryland, Massachusetts, Michigan, Missouri, New Jersey, New Mexico, New York, North Carolina, Ohio, Oklahoma, Oregon, Pennsylvania, Tennessee, Texas, Washington, Wisconsin. The jurisdiction of the intermediate courts in various states is summarized in Osthus and Stiegler, *supra* note 11, at 26–45.

[14]U.S. Department of Commerce, Bureau of the Census, preliminary figures for 1980.

courts. Virginia, the fourteenth in population, with a 1980 population of 5,346,000, and Minnesota, the twenty-first, with 4,077,000, have not; as might be expected, proposals to create such courts have been made in those states.[15] Of the 10 states with estimated 1980 populations between 2 million and 3.6 million, eight have intermediate appellate courts,[16] while two do not.[17] Of the states with smaller populations, Alaska (for criminal cases), Hawaii, Idaho and New Mexico have or have just created intermediate appellate courts.

Missouri, Washington and Oregon divide their highest courts into two departments, even though they also have intermediate appellate courts. Cases heard by one of the departments can be reheard by the entire supreme court *en banc* on appropriate occasions, such as where there might be a conflict between the divisions or when the matter is of great public importance or when the department's decision was not by a majority of the full court. The Minnesota and Mississippi supreme courts usually sit in panels of three, but *en banc* if the panel is not unanimous, or if any Justice in Mississippi so requests or any two Justices in Minnesota. However, all nine Justices vote in every case in Minnesota, and in Mississippi if a written opinion is handed down; some but not all Mississippi *per curiam* decisions are by the three-judge panel alone.[18] The Nebraska and North Dakota constitutions have unusual requirements for five votes out of seven and four out of five, respectively, before a state law may be held unconstitutional.[19]

Pennsylvania has two intermediate appellate courts, the Commonwealth Court for civil government cases and the Superior Court for other cases, both civil and criminal. Texas and Oklahoma have separate courts of last resort for criminal appeals.[20] The Texas Court of Criminal Appeals has had "by far the greatest caseload of the supreme courts not aided by inter-

---

[15]Letter of Feb. 21, 1979, from State Court Administrator of Minnesota (filings doubled between 1972 and 1978); G. Lilly and A. Scalia, *Appellate Justice: A Crisis in Virginia?*, 57 Va. L. Rev. 3 (1971).

[16]Arizona, Arkansas, Colorado, Connecticut, Iowa, Kansas, Oklahoma, Oregon.

[17]Mississippi and South Carolina. In addition to Minnesota and Virginia, Mississippi, Nevada, Utah and the District of Columbia are considering the establishment of such courts. T. Marvell and M. Kuykendall, *Appellate Courts—Facts and Figures*, 4 State Court J. 9, 10–11 (No. 2, Spring 1980).

[18]See Minnesota Appellate Rule 135, and Minnesota cases in 293 N.W.2d; Mississippi Rule 35, *Russell* v. *State*, 312 So.2d 422, 425 (Miss. 1975), and Mississippi cases in 385 So.2d.

[19]Nebraska Const. Art. V, §2; North Dakota Const. Art. IV.

[20]Texas Const. Art. 5, §§1, 5; Oklahoma Const. Art. 7, §4.

mediate courts," over 4800 cases in 1978.[21] Its nine judges now usually sit in panels of three. A constitutional amendment requiring all criminal appeals except death cases to be first routed to the intermediate courts of appeals "as prescribed by law," which is expected to result in discretionary review by the Court of Criminal Appeals, was approved by the Texas voters at the November 1980 election.[22] South Carolina by statute (1979 Acts Nos. 164, 194; South Carolina Code, §§14-8-10, 14-8-200, 210) created a similar court with exclusive appellate jurisdiction over criminal cases and post-conviction proceedings (except for capital cases, which go directly to the Supreme Court, and that Court's constitutional authority to issue writs). After the state Supreme Court invalidated parts of the Act (*State ex rel. Riley* v. *Martin,* 262 S.E.2d 404 (1980)), a new statute postponed the functioning of the Court of Appeals until after the General Assembly elected its judges and provided funds for its operation, or October 1, 1981, whichever is later. Section 16, Act of June 10, 1980. Alabama and Tennessee, recently joined by Alaska, also have separate criminal courts of appeals whose judgments are reviewable on certiorari in the state supreme court.[23]

The supreme courts of a number of states employ a rotating or rolling panel system in order to decrease the number of cases which each judge must hear, or, conversely, to increase the number of cases which the same number of judges can dispose of. The rotating panel usually consists of four or five judges out of seven or nine, or three out of five.[24] The decision of such a panel is that of a majority of the entire court if a majority of the full court concurs. If not, then the case customarily will be referred to the entire court for a rehearing *en banc.* In some states

---

[21]T. Marvell and M. Kuykendall, *Appellate Courts—Facts and Figures,* 4 State Court J. 9, 10–11 (No. 2, Spring 1980).

[22]The proposed constitutional amendment filed with the Texas Secretary of State, May 31, 1979, to become effective, if approved, Sept. 1, 1981, is Senate Joint Resolution No. 36.

[23]Alabama Appellate Rule 39, Alabama Code, §§12-3-14, 12-3-16 (1975); Tennessee Code Ann. §16-452; Alaska Stat. Sec. 22.07.020–.030 (Supp. 1980).

[24]The states in which the supreme courts often sit in panels are Alaska, Colorado, Connecticut, Delaware, the District of Columbia, Florida, Iowa, Massachusetts, Minnesota, Mississippi, Nebraska, New Mexico, Oregon and the Texas Court of Criminal Appeals. The Connecticut court usually sits in panels of five out of six justices. As indicated above, in Mississippi and Minnesota three of the nine justices hear the arguments. In Mississippi the three-judge panel decides some cases but many are decided by the entire court; in Minnesota all nine justices vote in all cases. See T. Marvell and M. Kuykendall, *Appellate Courts—Facts and Figures,* 4 State Court J. 9, 13, 35 (No. 2, Spring 1980); G. Lilly and A. Scalia, *Appellate Justice: A Crisis in Virginia?,* 57 Va. L. Rev. 3, 22–26, 39–42 (1971).

this system is authorized by constitution or statute, but in others it has been created by the court itself in reliance upon the provision that five or a majority of the judges constitute a quorum. The rotating panel system not only avoids the disadvantages of permanent panels, which would be more likely to reach conflicting results, but also saves a considerable amount of judicial time. As long as it is accompanied by the policy of holding a rehearing before the full bench when less than a majority of the full court concurs in the result, or when a case is of major importance, the device would seem to be a beneficial one for an overloaded court.

Intermediate appellate courts almost always sit in panels of three, except for the five-judge panels of the New York Appellate Divisions, the five-judge Iowa Court of Appeals and Alabama Court of Criminal Appeals, and the six-judge Arkansas Court of Appeals which sit *en banc.* [25] The seven-judge Superior Court of Pennsylvania, which previously sat *en banc,* announced in 1978 that because its case load was exceeding 3,000 cases per year all appeals would be heard by three-judge panels.[26] Pennsylvania's Commonwealth Court decides on its own initiative or on request of either party whether argument shall be before a panel of at least three judges or *en banc.* Rule 3713. The Georgia 10-judge Court of Appeals must, under the governing statute (Georgia Code, §24-3501), sit *en banc* whenever one judge dissents from a division's decision, as well as if a majority of the division or of the court so agrees.

1.4 Original Jurisdiction of Appellate Courts

(a) Jurisdiction

The function of appellate courts, of course, is to review the decisions of other courts, not to decide cases in the first instance themselves. In some circumstances, however, appellate courts

---

[25]The Arkansas constitutional amendment (No. 58), approved in 1978, authorized the creation of "a Court of Appeals and divisions thereof," and the authorizing statute provides (Arkansas Stat. Ann. §22-1203) that the Court of Appeals "en banc or any panel thereof may sit in any county seat." Although division of the court into panels would appear to be thus authorized, the court now sits *en banc.* This seems to be contemplated by Arkansas Supreme Court Rule 29(6), which includes as a ground for Supreme Court review by certiorari that a case "was decided in the Court of Appeals by a tie vote," not that there was a conflict among Court of Appeals decisions. Presumably the Supreme Court may authorize the Court of Appeals to sit in panels if the case load becomes sufficiently great. The shifting of many types of cases to the Supreme Court's exclusive jurisdiction in 1980 by amendments to Rule 29(1) indicates that this may soon be necessary. See Sec. 5.3, *infra.*

[26]Order of May 9, 1978, following Pennsylvania Rule of Appellate Procedure 3511.

exercise original jurisdiction and decide cases which have not first been heard in lower courts.

Best known is the authority vested in the United States Supreme Court by Article III, Sec. 2, of the Constitution, as implemented by §1251 of 28 U.S.C.[27] The Supreme Court has original and exclusive jurisdiction over controversies between states. This jurisdiction is most commonly exercised in cases involving disputes between the states as to boundaries and the use of interstate waters. The Supreme Court has original but *not* exclusive jurisdiction over suits by the United States against a state, by a state against the United States if the United States has consented, and by a state against the citizens of other states or aliens. The Court also has similar concurrent jurisdiction, which is rarely exercised, in actions or proceedings in which "ambassadors, other public ministers, consuls or vice consuls of foreign states are parties."[28]

Only one state, Arizona, follows the federal analogy and gives its Supreme Court original and exclusive jurisdiction over cases between counties "concerning disputed boundaries and surveys thereof or concerning claims of one county against another." Arizona Const. Art. VI, §5(2). In Illinois and Nebraska the supreme courts have original jurisdiction over cases relating to revenue.[29] Nebraska adds civil cases in which the state is a party and election contests involving state officers apart from legislators.[30] The Iowa Supreme Court has original jurisdiction to review apportionment plans for the General Assembly.[31]

Seven states—Alabama, Colorado, Maine, Massachusetts, New Hampshire, North Carolina and Rhode Island—in similar language require that the supreme court shall provide the legislature (and in some states either branch thereof) and the governor (and in some states the executive counsel) with the court's opinion "upon important questions of law and upon solemn

---

[27]The cases involving the Supreme Court's original jurisdiction under §1251 have been reviewed and collected in R. Stern and E. Gressman, SUPREME COURT PRACTICE, Chap. 10 (5th ed., 1978); 17 C. Wright, A. Miller and E. Cooper, FEDERAL PRACTICE AND PROCEDURE: JURISDICTION, §§4042–4054 (1978); *The Original Jurisdiction of the United States Supreme Court,* 11 Stan. L. Rev. 665 (1959); C. Wright, FEDERAL COURTS, Sec. 109 (3d ed., 1976); H. Hart and H. Wechsler, THE FEDERAL COURTS AND THE FEDERAL SYSTEM, pp. 242–308 (2d ed., P. Bator, P. Mishkin, D. Shapiro and H. Wechsler, 1973); Annotations to 28 U.S.C.A. §1251.

[28]Section 1251 was amended in 1978 to substitute concurrent for exclusive Supreme Court jurisdiction over suits against "ambassadors, other public ministers and consuls." Act of September 30, 1978, Sec. 8, 92 Stat. 810. See S. Rep. No. 1108, 95th Cong., 2d Sess. 6, reported in 3 U.S. Code Cong. & Admin. News 1946 (1978).

[29]Illinois Const. Art. VI, §4, and Rule 381; Nebraska Const. Art. V, §2.

[30]Nebraska Const. Art. V, §2.

[31]Iowa Const. Art. III, §36.

occasions." Article III, §8, of the Michigan constitution adds to the language quoted:

> "as to the constitutionality of legislation after it has been enacted into law but before its effective date."

Delaware, Florida and South Dakota provide that the supreme court shall give advisory opinions only to the governor.[32] These authorizations appear in the state constitutions, except that the practice is statutory in Alabama and Delaware and judge-made in North Carolina.[33] Such advisory opinions not rendered in any judicial proceeding would be outside the jurisdiction of judicial systems limited, as is the federal, to cases and controversies.[34]

Both state and federal appellate courts have jurisdiction to issue writs "in aid of their respective jurisdictions and agreeable to the usages and principles of law," to use the language of the controlling federal statute (28 U.S.C. §1651). Such ancillary authority would in all likelihood be found to exist as a matter of history and common law even in the absence of explicit constitutional or statutory language.[35] Both supreme and intermediate appellate courts have such power.

Although applications for the writs—principally mandamus, prohibition, certiorari and habeas corpus—are in one sense original proceedings in the appellate court, they almost invariably follow proceedings in a lower court to which the petitioner for the writ is objecting. Indeed, the appellate court would usually dismiss the application if relief available below had not first been sought. Often the judge below is the respondent, although many rules permit him not to appear as a party and to leave the matter in the appellate court to be handled by counsel for the parties before him; his failure to appear is not to be taken as an admission of the facts alleged (e.g., Federal Appellate Rule 21; Delaware Rule 43; Illinois Rule 381(d); Pennsylvania Rule 1513). The petition for a writ is often an effort to obtain review of an otherwise unappealable order. See Sec. 3.7, *infra,* which deals with the use of the writs—or in some states of similar remedies under less technical names—to obtain interlocutory review.

---

[32]Delaware Code Ann. tit. 10, §141; Florida Const. Art. 4, §1(c); South Dakota Const. Art. V, §5.

[33] Comment, *The State Advisory Opinion in Perspective,* 44 Fordham L. Rev. 81, 82 (1975).

[34]*Ibid.* In eight states the advisory opinion provisions have been discontinued.

[35]Pennsylvania Rule 3309 refers to the powers historically preserved for its Supreme Court as the "King's Bench" powers, a title with a wonderful historical flavor but not otherwise very illuminating for younger lawyers.

In all of these various circumstances, the appellate court is in substance reviewing the decision of a lower court even though the proceeding before it takes the form of a new case. The appellate court is thus in substance exercising appellate, not original, jurisdiction. *Marbury* v. *Madison,* 1 Cranch (5 U.S.) 137 (1803), established that the United States Supreme Court lacked constitutional jurisdiction to issue writs when it was not in substance acting in an appellate capacity. A few state constitutions authorize their supreme courts to issue writs of mandamus or habeas corpus addressed to public officers other than judges, and writs of *quo warranto* to determine who has title to public office.[36] This would not be permissible under the theory of *Marbury* v. *Madison* if the state supreme court could act only in an appellate capacity.[37]

In some states the supreme court may directly review decisions of state administrative commissions.[38] Such review may be an exercise of appellate jurisdiction if the agency's action can be regarded as judicial; otherwise, the court would be exercising original jurisdiction. Cf. *Prentis* v. *Atlantic Coast Line Co.,* 211 U.S. 210, 225–226 (1908); *Federal Radio Commission* v. *Nelson Bros. B. & M. Co.,* 289 U.S. 266, 274–278 (1933).

(b) Procedure

The procedure in original cases, including those involving writs, is flexible. In some jurisdictions, including the United States Supreme Court—in cases coming within its original jurisdiction (Rule 9) but no longer in suits for extraordinary writs (Rule 27)—and Illinois, the complaining party commences an original proceeding by filing a motion for leave to file the initial complaint or petition.[39] The proposed pleading must be attached, as should any pertinent records from other courts or other documentary material. In the United States courts of appeals and other state courts the petition or application for a writ need not be accompanied by an unnecessary motion for leave to file what is ordinarily filed along with the motion.[40] In some jurisdictions the court takes no action until the adverse party has

---

[36]Arkansas Const. Art. 7, §§4–5; Florida Const. Art. 5, §4; Wyoming Const. Art. 5, §3.

[37]Cf. *United States* v. *Rice,* 327 U.S. 742, 747 (1946).

[38]Idaho Const. Art. 5, §9; Texas Const. Art. 5, §3-b.

[39]United States Supreme Court Rule 9.3; Illinois Rules 381–382.

[40]E.g., Federal Appellate Rule 21; Arkansas Rules 16, 17; Delaware Rule 43; Wisconsin Rule 809.51.

had an opportunity to file an opposing paper.[41] This should be an argument as to why leave to file should be denied, and, like an opposition to a petition for certiorari or leave to appeal, this document should include the reasons why the proposed case has no merit. In other jurisdictions the court decides, on the basis of the plaintiff's submission alone, whether the defendant should be called upon to answer.[42] The leave-to-file procedure is a method of screening in advance by the appellate court to determine whether the case is substantial enough to be permitted to continue. That can, however, just as easily be accomplished on the basis of the petition itself. This was recognized by the United States Supreme Court in 1980 when it abandoned its leave-to-file requirement for extraordinary writ cases.

On either of the above bases, the court, with or without acting on the motion for leave to file, determines what course the case should then follow. It may deny either the motion for leave to file or the petition, which, of course, would end the proceeding. It may require that process—summons and complaint—issue to other parties. The court may order further written or oral presentation on the motion for leave to file, or on the merits of the case. United States Supreme Court Rule 9.6 provides generally that "additional pleadings may be filed, and subsequent proceedings had, as the Court shall direct." Many states have similar provisions.[43] Illinois Rule 382(b) describes the procedures in more detail:

> "The court may dispose of the case on the papers filed or may order further briefing or may order oral argument on the motion for leave to file or on the complaint or on the pleadings or on the pleadings supplemented by pertinent documentary evidence, or may call for additional evidence and for briefs and arguments after such evidence has been received. If the court determines that disputed issues of material fact must be resolved on the basis of oral testimony, it may appoint a judge or retired judge of any Illinois court to take testimony and to report his findings of fact and recommendations to the Supreme Court."

Thus, if no additional evidence is needed, the appellate court handles the case like an ordinary appeal, disposing of it on the

---

[41]United States Supreme Court Rules 9.5, 27.5; Arkansas Rule 16; Pennsylvania Rule 1515 (if a factual issue).

[42]Federal Appellate Rule 21(b); New Hampshire Rule 11(6); Tennessee Rule 10; Wisconsin Rule 809.51. In Montana the Supreme Court will hear applications for writs upon one hour's prior notice to the chief justice, with 15 minutes allowed for the oral presentation. Montana Rule 17(c) and (e).

[43]Tennessee Rule 10 (Advisory Committee Comment); Wisconsin Rule 809.51.

basis of briefs or briefs plus oral argument, as it deems appropriate.

If oral testimony is called for, the appellate court can hear it itself, as the United States Supreme Court did several times in the 1790s.[44] Oklahoma authorizes the Supreme Court exercising its original jurisdiction to conduct a jury trial *en banc* or before one judge. As a practical matter, the choices are between appointing a special master, who may or may not be a judge or retired or senior judge, or deciding that the case should first be heard by a trial court. The United States Supreme Court has usually designated senior federal judges as masters, but recently has found them too busy with their own courts' work; accordingly it is now beginning to turn to retired state judges, professors or practicing lawyers. Under Arkansas Rule 17 the state Supreme Court appoints a master, while under Wyoming Rule 20 the Supreme Court may direct any state district judge to conduct a hearing at any county seat in the state.

In Illinois "only issues of law will be considered" in original actions seeking mandamus, prohibition or habeas corpus, or relating to revenue. Rule 381(a). That means that cases presenting issues of fact must come through the regular trial and appellate structure. Disputed issues of fact will, however, be heard by a specially appointed judge or retired judge in cases involving legislative redistricting, under Rule 382(b).

Utilizing a master or special hearing officer instead of a regular trial court has little advantage when evidence must be taken, particularly when the master is or was a trial judge. It is probably more expensive for the government and the parties, who must pay the master's fees (unless he is already on a government payroll as a judge or retired judge). Whether it takes more or less time depends on the state of the calendar of the trial court before which the case might be brought, as compared to the length of time which would be necessary before a master. Masters' proceedings as well as trials can be prolonged. The case might also have to come to the highest court through an intermediate appellate court, though perhaps that could be skipped.

The fact that the court may select a master has one advantage, however. It can appoint a judge or a lawyer on the basis

---

[44]The original files in the Clerk's Office reveal that three jury trials were held in the Supreme Court during this period. See *The Supreme Court—Its Homes Past and Present,* 27 A.B.A.J. 283, 286 (1941); *Georgia v. Brailsford,* 3 Dallas (3 U.S.) 1 (1794).

of his recognized competence, and thus can have more assurance that the proceeding will be handled with skill. In addition, for lengthy and/or complex proceedings, the appointment of a master relieves pressure on overburdened trial judges who would otherwise hear the matter.[45]

Most rules do not specify in any detail the procedure to be followed in original cases. If they can be treated as appeals and disposed of on the basis of a written record, briefs and oral argument, the rules governing ordinary appeals can readily be applied. To the extent that pleadings or evidence are called for, trial court procedure would be more appropriate; there would be no reason to establish special trial procedures for this type of case alone. Arkansas Rules 16 and 17 sensibly so provide; where the jurisdiction of the Supreme Court "is in fact appellate," the rules governing appeals are generally made applicable, while in other original cases the procedure is to "conform to that prevailing in the chancery court." Illinois Rules 381 and 382 contain a similar differentiation between original actions which are in substance appellate and those which are new proceedings. The latter are governed by the rules applicable to cases in the circuit court "whenever appropriate." United States Supreme Court Rule 9.2 similarly states that

> "The form of pleadings and motions in original actions shall be governed, so far as may be, by the Federal Rules of Civil Procedure, and in other respects those Rules, where their application is appropriate, may be taken as a guide to procedure in original actions in this Court."

The procedure governing petitions for extraordinary writs, which serve an appellate function, is modeled on that for petitions for certiorari. Rule 27. The "where appropriate" limitation in these rules manifests the appellate court's reservation of power to order whatever procedure it determines will be most suitable for the particular case.

1.5   Appeals as a Matter of Right or Discretion

In the federal courts and in almost every state an appeal as of right is allowed from final judgments, either to the highest court where there is no intermediate appellate court or to the

---

[45]In exceptional circumstances, trial judges may be appointed as masters. See, for example, Federal Rule of Civil Procedure 53.

intermediate court. See Sec. 3.1, *infra*. The principal exceptions are cases involving small amounts or minor offenses, which often are heard in courts lower than the trial court of general jurisdiction. In some jurisdictions decisions in such cases are not appealable to any court; in others they may be appealed to the general trial court, or a panel thereof, either for review or trial *de novo*. Appellate review of specified types of interlocutory orders is also permitted as a matter of right and of other interlocutory orders as a matter of discretion, exercised by the trial court, the appellate court or both. The types of orders that are appealable are discussed at greater length in Chapter 3, *infra*.

Only Virginia, West Virginia and New Hampshire, which have no intermediate appellate courts, do not provide for an appeal as of right from final judgments in the trial courts of general jurisdiction. This means that in those states the losing party is not always entitled to a decision by an appellate court as to whether the adverse decision below was right or wrong.

In Virginia and West Virginia a petition for leave to appeal is filed with the supreme court of the state. In Virginia a panel of three justices of the court (one or more of whom will hear oral argument if requested) and in West Virginia the full court decide whether leave shall be granted. But in both states, the appeal will be heard by the full court if the panel or the court believes that the decision below was erroneous,[46] and perhaps also if the court thinks the issues sufficiently important. The differences between disposing of appeals in this way and the customary full treatment are that in Virginia the determination to hear is by a panel, not the court (although the appeal will be taken for review if one of the three thinks there was error below), and that appellant's presentation of argument is expected to be less than a full brief. West Virginia calls for a separate "note of argument" to accompany a formal petition for appeal, which sounds like substantially less than a full brief on the merits. Apart from these factors, denial of leave is in effect a summary affirmance on the merits but without oral argument before the

---

[46] "*McCue* v. *Commonwealth*, 103 Va. 870, 1008, 149 S.E. 623, 632 (1905). The justices indicate that this standard still prevails. The Appellate Justice Staff saw no evidence to the contrary, although the statistics indicating a decline in the percentage of petitions granted gave rise to an inference that the standard of review has changed. *See* Lilly & Scalia, *Appellate Justice: A Crisis In Virginia?*, 57 *Va. L. Rev.* 3, 12–15 (1971). In fact, this decline in percentage may be attributable to a larger number of frivolous appeals." G. Lilly, THE APPELLATE PROCESS AND STAFF RESEARCH ATTORNEYS IN THE SUPREME COURT OF VIRGINIA, p. 24 (National Center for State Courts, 1974).

court, and is not very different from what many other courts do in dispensing with argument when they determine from the briefs that the appeal presents no substantial question. See Sec. 8.1, *infra*.

The New Hampshire procedure for "declination of acceptance orders" defined in Rule 3 clearly constitutes an exercise of discretion to deny review apart from the merits, although all but the first of the grounds for denying review[47] ("when the issues involve only the application of well-settled rules of law to a recurring fact situation") suggest agreement with the decision below. But such an order is defined in Rule 3 to mean that

> "The supreme court does not deem it desirable to review the issues in a case, as a matter of sound judicial discretion and with no implication whatever regarding its views on the merits."

The New Hampshire court apparently bases its determination whether to review or not on the notice of appeal and the various documents required to be attached to it. These include the decision below, requests for findings, motions challenging the decision, and memoranda supporting and opposing a motion to set aside the verdict. Appellant must also state the nature of the case and the questions raised, and provide a list of cases supporting the appellant's position. This material to some extent should present the arguments supporting appellant, but not as effectively as in a coherent, organized brief. Not many cases which would have been reversed are likely to be denied review in New Hampshire, although this can only be conjectural for an outsider. Nevertheless, New Hampshire seems to be the only American jurisdiction in which the decisions of trial courts of general jurisdiction[48] are not subject to review as of right on the merits. This runs counter to the "imperative"[49] underlying the appellate structures of this country and many others that a litigant should have a remedy against the possibly arbitrary or erroneous rulings of a one-man court.

Appeal as of right from an intermediate court to the highest

---

[47]The other grounds for declining to review are: "the issue asserted is whether the evidence is sufficient, and it clearly is; or disposition of the case is clearly controlled by a prior holding of this court or of a higher court, and no reason appears for questioning or qualifying that holding; or the case is accompanied by an opinion of the lower court or of the administrative agency that identifies and discusses the issues presented, and the supreme court approves the reasons and conclusions in the opinion."

[48]Not infrequently, cases involving small amounts or minor offenses are not appealable.

[49]See P. Carrington, D. Meador and M. Rosenberg, JUSTICE ON APPEAL, pp. 132–133 (1976).

court was initially permitted in the federal courts after 1891 and in some of the state systems. But the 33 states which have intermediate appellate courts now all follow the present federal practice of giving the highest court discretion, though with some limitations and exceptions, to determine the cases which it will hear.[50] In these jurisdictions a petition or application requesting the review of any decision of the intermediate court may be filed in the highest court. As explained more fully in Chapter 5, the principal grounds for granting the petition, though phrased in different ways, are in substance the same: the existence of a conflict between the decision sought to be reviewed and decisions of other intermediate courts or the highest court, the general public importance of the questions presented, and how strongly the court feels about reversing the error below.

Some states use such general standards as the "public interest or the interests of justice" (Massachusetts); "gravity or importance" (Georgia); "special and important reasons" (Pennsylvania); whether review "is desirable or in the public interest" (Maryland). Such general criteria, or more specific language, allow the court to take into account the merits of the appeal—how shocking the decision below appears to be. Others use more specific categories, such as whether the case involves constitutional questions (Alabama) or affects a class of public officers (Alabama, Florida). In Texas, the existence of a conflict and the merits are mentioned as factors to be considered but the public importance of the question is not. The factors considered by a supreme court in determining whether to review a decision of an intermediate appellate court thus differ from those to be argued in an ordinary brief on the merits, even though there may be some overlap. See Sec. 5.7(c), *infra.*

A few categories of cases are appealable as a matter of right to the highest court from the trial court or from the intermediate appellate court. The intermediate court may also certify particular cases or questions of law to the highest court either before or after argument, and the highest court may take cases from the intermediate court before argument either on its own motion or application of a party. Some state supreme courts have used the power last mentioned not only for reasons pertaining to the particular case but also for reasons of judicial administration,

---

[50]In Iowa and Oklahoma all appeals are taken first to the supreme court, which transfers cases to the court of appeals as it deems appropriate. The supreme court subsequently may review the court of appeals' decision on a discretionary basis.

such as when the intermediate courts are more overburdened than the supreme court. These varying routes to the highest court of a jurisdiction, which differ among the states, are described in detail in Chapter 5, *infra*.

1.6 The Appellate Explosion

The accepted model for fair appellate procedure, which was generally followed in the United States without question for many years, was that[51]

(1) A party had a right to appeal to one appellate court, at least from an adverse final judgment;

(2) He was entitled to present his arguments to the appellate court both in written briefs and orally;

(3) The appellate decision-making process reflected both the individual thinking of each judge and the effect of consultation among the judges; and

(4) The court disclosed the reasoning underlying its decisions.

These fundamental elements of the appellate process are being impaired, however, as a result of the rapid increase in the number of cases taken to the appellate courts in recent years.

In the United States Supreme Court the number of cases filed skyrocketed from 1181 in the 1950 Term to 3939 in 1975; it has remained stable in the last several years.[52] In the United States courts of appeals, the number of cases filed in the 11 circuits combined was approximately 1600 in 1924, 3900 in 1960, 11,662 in 1970, and 20,219 in 1979.[53] Thus, the number quintupled in 19 years, during which the number of judges increased only 25 percent, from 78 to 97. The Act of October

---

[51]P. Carrington, D. Meador and M. Rosenberg, JUSTICE ON APPEAL, pp. 7–11 (1976); American Bar Association Commission on Standards of Judicial Administration, STANDARDS RELATING TO APPELLATE COURTS, Sec. 3.10, p. 15 (1977); A. Hellman, *Central Staff in Appellate Courts: The Experience of the Ninth Circuit*, 68 Cal. L. Rev. 937, 937-938 (1980).

[52]These statistics are from those compiled by the Clerk's Office. See also G. Casper and R. Posner, THE WORKLOAD OF THE SUPREME COURT, Tables 1.1 and 2.1, pp. 3, 12 (American Bar Foundation, 1976); *Report of the Study Group on the Case Load of the Supreme Court* (Federal Judicial Center, 1972), reprinted in 57 F.R.D. 573, Tables I and II, pp. A1–A2, at 613–614. The figures include paid cases, *in forma pauperis* cases and original cases. The most recent and thorough analysis appears in A. Hellman, *The Business of the Supreme Court Under the Judiciary Act of 1925: The Plenary Docket in the 1970's*, 91 Harv. L. Rev. 1709 (1978). See 49 U.S.L.W. 3050 (1980).

[53]ANNUAL REPORTS OF THE DIRECTOR OF THE ADMINISTRATIVE OFFICE OF THE UNITED STATES COURTS, Table B-1, up to 1979; P. Carrington, *Crowded Dockets and the Courts of Appeals: The Threat to the Function of Review and the National Law*, 82 Harv. L. Rev. 542, 543 (1969).

20, 1978, Pub. L. No. 95-486, 92 Stat. 1635, 28 U.S.C. §44(a), added 35 new circuit judges. This will still leave the number of judges only 60 percent over what it was in 1960, despite the fivefold increase in the number of cases.

The situation in the state appellate courts is substantially the same. In most states the number of appeals filed increased from 50 to 400 percent in recent years (see table, p. 24). A study by the National Center for State Courts of the number of majority opinions issued by state supreme courts without discretionary jurisdiction concludes that nationwide the number of appeals has doubled between the 1950s and 1975, but that in many intermediate appellate courts the number has tripled.[54] State supreme courts with discretionary jurisdiction are better able to control their work load, even if the number of applications for review increases substantially, since they can limit the number of cases they hear on the merits.[55]

This appellate explosion has been much more rapid than the rate of expansion of the business of the trial courts. It has not been limited to criminal cases, which have sometimes been regarded as primarily responsible for the increase in appellate business. As in the federal courts, the number of state appellate judges has not kept up with the work load, and that has had a significant effect upon the operation of the courts.

1.7 The Effect on the Right to Argue Orally

The most obvious effect of the appellate explosion is on the right to oral argument. In many state courts and most of the federal circuits, oral argument is no longer permitted when preliminary examination of a case indicates to the judges that it would not serve any useful purpose, usually because the appeal raises no substantial question. Argument may also be deemed unnecessary in cases where the appellee's position is hopeless, or even where the briefs on both sides are complete and sufficient.[56] In the Fifth Circuit, which had been the most overburdened of the federal courts of appeals, fewer than one half of the appeals are heard orally.[57]

---

[54]VOLUME AND DELAY, *supra* note 5, at 13–16.
[55]*Id.* at 20; and see table, *infra.*
[56]P. Carrington, D. Meador and M. Rosenberg, JUSTICE ON APPEAL, p. 22 (1976).
[57]The 1978 legislation (28 U.S.C. §44(a)) added 11 judges to the Fifth Circuit. Whether these judgeships will affect the court's present practice with respect to oral argument cannot yet be foretold. Effective October 1, 1981, the Circuit was divided into the Fifth and Eleventh Circuits by Pub. L. No. 96–452, Oct. 14, 1980.

State*	Year	Cases Filed	Year	Cases Filed
California				
Supreme Court	1967–68	2939	1977–78	3881
Courts of Appeal	1967–68	6411	1977–78	13,618
Colorado				
Supreme Court	1967–68	574**	1977–78	854
Court of Appeals	1969–70	373	1977–78	1119
Florida				
Supreme Court	1967	1081	1977–78	2586
District Courts of Appeal	1967	2934	1977–78	9480
Idaho				
Supreme Court	1967	206	1978	323
Illinois				
Supreme Court	1967	720	1977	1139
Appellate Court	1967	1402	1977	4381
Louisiana				
Supreme Court	1965	469	1978	2450
Court of Appeal	1971	1455	1979	2664
Michigan				
Supreme Court	1969	544	1978	1636
Court of Appeals	1969	1959	1977	5724
New Jersey				
Supreme Court	1968–69	531***	1978–79	1218****
Appellate Division	1964–65	1121	1978–79	4774
New York				
Court of Appeals	1973	1947****	1978	3040
Appellate Division	1965	3967	1975	7429
Ohio				
Supreme Court	1974	336	1978	404
Court of Appeals	1974	5503	1978	7546
Oklahoma				
Supreme Court	1969	644	1977	1326
Court of Criminal Appeals	1966	272	1977	893
Pennsylvania				
Supreme Court	1973	740	1977	823
Superior Court	1973	2670	1977	3700
Commonwealth Court	1973	1804	1977	2664
Texas				
Supreme Court	1968	655	1977	1007
Court of Criminal Appeals	1968	811	1977	3267
Courts of Civil Appeals	1968	1133	1977	1969

*Available figures published by the judicial administrations of a number of states, obtained from the American Judicature Society, provide an adequate sampling. The figures for the New Jersey and New York Appellate Divisions are from VOLUME AND DELAY, *supra* note 5, at 15.

**Before Court of Appeals created.

***Number of cases disposed of, based in part on vols. 52–54 of New Jersey Reports.

****Number of cases disposed of.

A recent tabulation for states with available statistics showed that 90 percent of the cases are decided without oral argument in the Arkansas Supreme Court, "almost all" in the Indiana Courts of Appeals, about half in the Alabama Court of Appeals, the Iowa Court of Appeals, the New Jersey Appellate Division and the Pennsylvania Superior Court, "many" in the Florida and Louisiana supreme courts, and from 20 to 30 percent in the Iowa, New Mexico and Pennsylvania supreme courts, the New York Appellate Division and the New Mexico Court of Appeals.[58]

The justification for eliminating oral argument is to save time for overburdened courts. See Sec. 8.1, *infra.* But it does not save much time in view of the devices used to curtail, or even eliminate, oral argument in easy or unimportant cases. Earlier in Supreme Court history arguments taking a number of days were not uncommon, but later the time was reduced to one hour per side and then, in 1970, to 30 minutes. Few courts now allow more than 30 minutes per side for argument, except by special permission in the most complex cases. See Sec. 8.4, *infra.* A screening process often limits the simpler cases to 15 minutes per side or even less. Often, when the judges are all convinced after hearing appellant that his case has no merit, they tell the appellee that he need not argue at all. In the Second and Seventh Circuits, such cases are frequently decided from the bench, with an oral statement of reasons.[59]

The effect of the increase in the work loads of appellate courts is thus of more than mere academic or historical interest to appellate counsel. They should have in mind, in preparing for an appeal, that in some courts the first hurdle their briefs must meet is to persuade the court that the case has enough merit to be heard orally, a function not dissimilar to the burden of per-

---

[58]T. Marvell and M. Kuykendall, *Appellate Courts—Facts and Figures,* 4 State Court J. 9, 14, 36 (No. 2, Spring 1980).

[59]In Arizona the Supreme Court rarely allows oral argument when the case has been argued orally in the Court of Appeals (although it does hear several types of cases which have not been argued in that court). This policy rests upon its commitment to the legislature, when the Court of Appeals was created, that a two-tiered appellate system would not increase the burden upon the parties or their counsel. The effect, however, is to deprive the parties of what elsewhere is generally regarded (except, in varying degrees, for the simplest or least substantial cases) as an essential element of the appellate process. See STANDARDS RELATING TO APPELLATE COURTS, *supra* note 51, at Sec. 3.35; P. Carrington, D. Meador and M. Rosenberg, JUSTICE ON APPEAL, p. 17 (1976). This practice, combined with the Supreme Court's unwillingness to permit the parties to file briefs in addition to those filed in the Court of Appeals (see Sec. 1.10(a), note 68, *infra*), leaves the procedure in the Arizona Supreme Court further than any other from the generally accepted ingredients of a fair appeal.

suading a supreme court to take a case in the exercise of its discretionary jurisdiction. Compare Sec. 5.7(c), *infra.* Counsel should be aware that, depending on the size of its case load, an appellate court may dispose summarily not only of frivolous appeals but also of others which the judges do not find very difficult. If the case lends itself to such treatment—and many appeals will not—the brief should, in addition to arguing the merits, give the reasons why the questions are important enough for the court to hear, and that means, if possible, important to more than the parties to the case.

Even more obvious is the significance to the advocate of the little time which is now allowed for oral argument. Except in the simplest cases, counsel is likely to find compression of the argument he would like to present into the time allowed a painful as well as a painstaking process—and all the more so if he endeavors to leave one third of the time for answering questions, which as a practical matter is necessary in many courts. But counsel who does not prepare his argument with such considerations in mind is likely to have a rude awakening.

More detailed treatment of these problems is left to the chapters on briefing and arguing. It is important, however, that lawyers be aware of not only the limitations imposed on them but also the reasons why the courts find it necessary to impose such restrictions.

1.8   The Effect on Petitions for Review

The need for tailoring petitions for review to the guidelines followed by a supreme court in determining what cases it will hear has frequently been described in relation to the United States Supreme Court's certiorari practice.[60] With state supreme court dockets also rapidly mounting, lawyers should be aware that in most states the need for showing importance or lack of uniformity, as well as error below, is equally essential when the highest court of a state is asked to review the decision of an intermediate appellate court. Counsel should, of course, ascertain the practice in this respect in his own jurisdiction. The strictness with which a court applies these well-nigh universal standards for discretionary review may depend to a large extent

---

[60]E.g., R. Stern and E. Gressman, SUPREME COURT PRACTICE, Chap. 4, particularly pp. 254–264, and Chap. 6, pp. 467–471 (5th ed., 1978).

on the burden of its case load. In the United States Supreme Court the effect has been to reduce the percentage of petitions for certiorari granted from approximately 20 to about 6. The percentages are usually higher in the states, for example: Ohio, 8.4; California, 9; Iowa, 10; New York and Tennessee, 12; Texas, 14; Illinois, 15; and Oklahoma, 18.5.[61] Furthermore, only with awareness of what the chances of success are, as well as of the factors which a court considers, can a lawyer intelligently advise his client as to whether filing a petition in the highest court will be worth the cost and the effort.

1.9 Internal Operation of the Courts—Law Clerks and Staff Attorneys

The manner in which appellate courts do their work has also been evolving. Counsel should be aware of the changes, even though such knowledge may not produce any noticeable difference in the way a case should be presented, except with respect to the restrictions on oral argument referred to above.

As has been noted, appellate courts not only decide cases on the merits but also often screen cases to decide how each case should be handled. The expanding work load precludes giving every case the full panoply of briefing, oral argument for what the lawyer thinks is a reasonable time, and a fully explanatory opinion. Every case need not be handled in the same way. Many appeals, particularly in the indigent criminal category, where the cost of appeal is borne by the state and does not serve as a disincentive to the defendant, have little or no substance. Other appeals also may present no difficult problems requiring detailed analysis of the record or of the authorities. Conversely, other cases require considerable time to understand and decide, either because they are close enough to require much study and research, or because they are complex and hard to analyze and comprehend.

General recognition of this diversity has led to the unsurprising conclusion that less appellate time is needed for some cases or classes of cases than for others, and that the work load problem must be approached with this in mind. The result has

---

[61]Figures are from those published by the judicial administrations of the various states, obtained from the American Judicature Society.

been that in overburdened appellate courts, cases go through a process of screening to determine whether each case warrants less than the full judicial treatment and, if so, how much less.

Up until quite recently judges did their own work, with help in many courts from their individual law clerks who customarily were chosen from among high-ranking law school graduates. In some courts the number of such clerks per judge has grown from one to two, and now even to three or four in the United States Supreme Court. In addition, most of the federal courts of appeals and a number of state appellate courts have begun to use staff attorneys who work for the court as a whole.[62] Although many of them may not, when first hired, be older or more experienced than the judges' clerks, their tenure is not limited to the one or two years for which the latter are usually employed.[63] It is desirable and customary that at least the supervisory or senior staff attorneys have had experience either on the job or as working lawyers. These attorneys often assist in, or initiate, the screening process, but their contribution is often more important than "screening" would seem to imply.

There is no uniformity in how these attorneys are used. They may assist in scheduling arguments, dealing with motions, and helping the court generally, without undertaking analysis of each case and legal research or writing. In the Seventh Circuit, for example, the circuit executive, who performs functions else-

---

[62]See D. Meador, APPELLATE COURTS, STAFF AND PROCESS IN THE CRISIS OF VOLUME (National Center for State Courts, 1974); P. Carrington, D. Meador and M. Rosenberg, JUSTICE ON APPEAL, pp. 46–55 (1976); American Bar Association, Task Force on Appellate Procedure, EFFICIENCY AND JUSTICE IN APPEALS: METHODS AND SELECTED MATERIALS, pp. 129–140 (1977), which concludes with a three-page bibliography on the subject. The total number of attorneys per appellate judge, including both law clerks and staff attorneys, generally is only one or two, but in the California, Louisiana and Pennsylvania supreme courts and the Pennsylvania Superior Court, it ranges from 4 to 4.7. T. Marvell and M. Kuykendall, *Appellate Courts —Facts and Figures*, 4 State Court J. 9, 14, 33, 37 (No. 2, Spring 1980). This practice is described and analyzed at length, with particular reference to the Ninth Circuit, in a recent article by Professor Arthur D. Hellman, for two years Supervising Staff Attorney for that court, *Central Staff in Appellate Courts: The Experience of the Ninth Circuit*, 68 Cal. L. Rev. 937 (1980).

[63]In California and a few other states many appellate judges now use career clerks, or, more accurately, lawyers who serve for long periods of time and not merely a year or two after law school. J. Oakley and R. Thompson, *Law Clerks in Judges' Eyes: Tradition and Innovation in the Use of Legal Staff by American Judges*, 67 Cal. L. Rev. 1286, 1293–1295 (1979). This interesting and informative article is an abridgment of portions of the authors' book, *Law Clerks and the Judicial Process*, published by the University of California Press in 1980. It studies in depth the use of law clerks in the state and federal courts in California, as affected by the "burden of bloated caseloads." Hellman, *supra* note 62, at 950-952, favors the use of recent law graduates for one or two years, largely because he believes able lawyers would not be willing to remain in such positions on a career basis.

where handled by staff attorneys, assists the chief judge in determining whether and how much time each case should be allowed for argument.

In other courts, such as the Michigan Court of Appeals and the California Courts of Appeal, a member of the staff will initially study the briefs and the record. He or she will prepare a memorandum which will state the issues and how the case arose, summarize the facts, impartially analyze the arguments and authorities, and sometimes recommend not only how the case should be handled further but how it should be decided. On the basis of this memorandum, as well as the briefs and the record, the judges determine whether oral argument is desirable and for how long. They can and often do use the attorney's memorandum as the draft or the framework for the explanatory opinion which the court issues in deciding the case.[64] In some courts, such as the Illinois Appellate Court, the staff director selects for such staff treatment only those cases that are thought not to warrant oral argument, although the court, of course, is not bound by his appraisal.

The staff analysis for screening purposes is designed to aid the court in determining not only whether a case shall be argued, and for how long, but also what kind of opinion—summary or complete—the case merits. The staff memorandum, in theory at least, is not meant to serve as a full opinion authored by an individual judge. But there is nothing to prevent a judge from using it as such if he is hard pressed or disinclined to hard work, or if he believes that it does the job adequately. More often the memorandum is used as the basis of a shorter *per curiam* or memorandum opinion, when the case presents little difficulty.

Undoubtedly such staff work greatly assists the judges and enables them to decide a greater number of cases more expeditiously. The danger is that a memorandum which is handed to the judge and contains the very type of analysis which the judge would ordinarily do for himself, or have his own clerk do subject to his personal supervision and advice, may have the effect of substituting the staff attorney for the judge as the actual decider of the case. The fact that the judge reviews the memorandum, and has the record and briefs before him, means that the ultimate decision of course is his. But judges, like other men, partic-

---

[64]The practice in the California courts is described in Oakley and Thompson, *id.* at 1300–1301, 1303–1304.

ularly but not necessarily when they are overburdened, may be inclined to take the easy way. This might not be harmful if the staff attorney's work is as good as or superior to what the judge himself could turn out under the pressure of time; appellate judges are not always selected or elected because of superior legal scholarship. But the responsibility of judging has been placed upon the judges themselves, whose experience is presumed to make them more knowledgeable and wiser than the younger attorneys who work for them.

This description of the use of staff attorneys, which varies from court to court and from judge to judge, does not lead to the easy conclusion that appellate advocates should write their briefs or do any of their other work differently because of it. One cannot know in advance that judges or particular judges or staff attorneys or law clerks will react differently to particular methods of briefing. Too much depends upon unpredictable personal factors. But lawyers should be aware, for what it is worth, that the judges themselves may not spend a great deal of time on each case or read the briefs fully and carefully, and that they may be writing primarily for an audience consisting of young lawyers, albeit able ones, who, for better or worse, may not have the same experience and backgrounds as the judges themselves.

1.10 Problems of the Two-Tiered System—Avoiding Duplication of Work

A two-tiered appellate system is warranted only where a single appellate court cannot keep up with the task of reviewing all of the appeals from the trial courts in its jurisdiction. The creation of an intermediate court has been opposed, in Virginia and elsewhere, on the ground that having a case proceed through two courts will be more expensive in time and money.[65] This is true, of course, if counsel must, when the higher court agrees to hear the case, go through two rounds of briefing and oral argument, at their clients' expense.

(a) Using the Same Briefs in Intermediate and Supreme Courts—Advantages and Disadvantages

Some states have provided that if review is granted by the highest court, the briefs filed in the intermediate court shall also

---

[65]G. Lilly and A. Scalia, *Appellate Justice: A Crisis in Virginia?*, 57 Va. L. Rev. 3, 46 (1971).

serve as the briefs in the highest court. See Sec. 7.3(b), *infra*. In some of these jurisdictions additional briefs may be filed only if leave of court is obtained for good cause shown; in others, the parties have the right to file such briefs if they wish to. The principal cost of the second appeal under such systems will be the cost of reproducing, for a court composed of a larger number of judges, extra copies of the briefs below, and also of the appendix or reproduced portions of the record below if that is necessary. There will also be lawyers' fees for a second oral argument, which should, of course, cover the time needed for preparation. If oral argument is not allowed in the highest court, the cost of the second appeal may be very slight.

Completely to deprive parties of the right to oral argument or briefing addressed to the court which finally decides an appeal would not be consistent with the generally accepted standards for the wise administration of appellate courts.[66] "Oral argument should never be discouraged routinely and should be denied only if the court is convinced that the contentions presented are frivolous or that oral argument would not otherwise be useful."[67]

Compulsory reliance on the briefs filed in the lower appellate court may also prevent the best, or even an adequate, presentation to the highest court. A lower court is bound by a supreme court's rulings, dicta or even intimations to a greater extent than is the supreme court itself; the latter can be more responsive to arguments that will limit, modify or even overrule what it had previously held or said. The brief written for a supreme court may give greater emphasis to arguments of policy and to judicial and nonjudicial authority elsewhere. If every brief in the lower appellate court were written as if it were also prepared for the supreme court, it might unnecessarily go into matters to which the lower court could give little weight. The additional work required would entail additional research, thought and writing. And since most appeals are for many reasons not taken to the highest court—although which ones will be cannot reliably be foretold—the effect of this extra work and cost for the mass of cases in the lower court might greatly increase the cost of briefing overall.

Another reason why a different brief may be desirable in the

---

[66]See STANDARDS RELATING TO APPELLATE COURTS, *supra* note 51, at Secs. 3.30, 3.35; P. Carrington, D. Meador and M. Rosenberg, JUSTICE ON APPEAL, pp. 16–18 (1976).
[67]STANDARDS RELATING TO APPELLATE COURTS, *supra* note 51, at Sec. 3.35.

highest court is that the decision of the intermediate court will often have added a new ingredient to what both the parties and the high court must consider. Unless the decision below says little more than "affirmed" or its equivalent, there will be additional reasoning for the appellant to meet. Even though the issues may be the same as those presented in the briefs below, the treatment often should be modified in the light of what the court below has said. An appellant unable to challenge the precise reasoning of the court below may be under a severe handicap.

Furthermore, inability to file a new brief in the highest court will make impossible the improvement of the brief below by the same counsel, by new participants from his own law firm or by fresh counsel, often with special expertise, brought in from outside. Cases are likely to receive more thorough consideration when they reach a *supreme* court. To preclude this possibility is detrimental not only to the party but to the court. Counsel is unlikely to move to file a new brief, or the court to grant a motion, on the ground, however truthful, that he or other lawyers can do a better job than he or other counsel did below.

At present, Arizona,[68] Massachusetts, New Jersey, New Mexico and Washington require use of the petition for review and the briefs below without more unless the court otherwise directs or permits. The Wisconsin Supreme Court permits or requires additional briefs on a case-by-case basis, but usually leaves it up to the parties. Kansas, explicitly, and Texas and California, implicitly, provide for use of the petition for leave to appeal (plus the briefs below) as the brief on the merits in whole or in part but do not prohibit additional briefs. In Illinois such use of the petition is optional; the filing of an additional brief is permitted but not required. Pennsylvania gives counsel the option of filing an additional or supplemental brief, or neither.

---

[68]The Arizona procedure is unique in that the petition for rehearing in the Court of Appeals not only is a prerequisite to seeking Supreme Court review but constitutes the memorandum supporting the motion for hearing in the Supreme Court. In order to keep faith with its commitment to the legislature that adding an intermediate appellate court would not increase the work required in any case (see Sec. 1.7, note 59, *supra*), the Supreme Court rarely allows a new brief to be filed in addition to those filed in the Court of Appeals. Thus, the only occasion for focusing an argument on the reasoning of the Court of Appeals is the petition for rehearing in that court. But that ambivalent document is expected to be, and usually is, a short explanation both of why the Court of Appeals opinion overlooked something of significance and why the case is important enough for Supreme Court review. Thus it often does not provide an adequate opportunity for dealing with the merits of the issues decided adversely to appellant by the Court of Appeals. See Sec. 5.7(a), *infra*.

See Sec. 7.3(b), *infra*. Making complete reliance on a prior brief or briefs optional with counsel has the advantage of making filing a new brief unnecessary when counsel has nothing to add, while still permitting an additional brief, supplemental or otherwise, when counsel believes that for any reason it will make an improved presentation. This enables a party to avoid the cost of an additional brief but does not preclude him from filing such a brief if he so desires. That would seem to be the best compromise taking into account the competing considerations.

(b) Supreme Court Screening Prior to Hearing Below

Five states avoid a double appeal by having their supreme courts screen all appeals before they are heard by either appellate court.

In Iowa and Oklahoma the governing law requires that all appeals from the trial courts be taken to the state supreme court. That court then has discretion to transfer to the state court of appeals the cases it does not wish to retain. Iowa Supreme Court Rule 401 provides that the Supreme Court may transfer any case in which it does not have exclusive jurisdiction, and that it shall retain constitutional questions, life sentences and cases involving conflicts of decision or substantial questions requiring prompt determination by it, cases appropriate for summary disposition and cases involving lawyer discipline. In general, cases "which involve substantial questions of enunciating or changing legal principles shall be retained," but not those which merely apply "existing legal principles."

The Oklahoma rules embody no standard directly limiting the Supreme Court's discretion in retaining or transferring cases, but Rule 3.2 provides that, within 10 days after the filing of an appellee's brief, any party in a case which had been transferred to the Court of Appeals may move that the Supreme Court retain it because it presents a matter of first impression, seeks overruling of controlling precedents or "presents a question of constitutional law or . . . of substantial public interest."

Idaho and Hawaii have recently created courts of appeals which will operate under the same system.[69]

---

[69]Under the Hawaii Act of May 25, 1979, the Chief Justice of the Supreme Court or his designee from the Supreme Court or the intermediate appellate court shall assign each appeal filed in the Supreme Court either to that court or the intermediate appellate court within 20 days of the filing deadline for the last brief, but the Supreme Court may

The Massachusetts Supreme Judicial Court screens all appeals as a matter of discretion and judicial administration. "The genius of the new two-court appellate system is that, with minor exceptions, either court can hear or decide any case."[70] Two justices are enough to transfer a case from the Appeals Court to the Supreme Judicial Court for direct review (Rule 11), although three votes are needed to grant an application for review after an Appeals Court decision. All or a majority (of a panel) of the Appeals Court may also certify an appeal to the Supreme Judicial Court for direct review, but this is seldom done.

The only guidelines mentioned in the Massachusetts rule are those for applications by parties for direct review. Under Rule 11 the questions presented should be constitutional (state or federal), of first impression or novel, or "of such public interest that justice requires a final determination by the full Supreme Judicial Court." Whether or not an application for review has been filed, a Supreme Court staff lawyer reviews the briefs and records in the Appeals Court and makes a recommendation to a three-judge committee of the supreme court as to which cases should be heard directly by it. As a practical matter, the Supreme Judicial Court accepts for direct review cases it believes it would be likely to accept for review after hearing below, thereby minimizing "the risk of delays caused by double appellate reviews." It also may accept whatever cases are needed to provide for "an equitable distribution of the appellate workload."[71] This procedure has resulted in the court hearing many more cases on direct review on its own motion (142 in 1978–

---

reassign any case to itself. The criteria to be considered, among others, are the importance of the questions presented, a conflict in appellate decisions, the existence of a state or federal constitutional question or a question as to the validity of a state statute, county ordinance or agency regulation, and a sentence of life imprisonment. Hawaii Rev. Stat. §§602-5(8), (9), 602-6. The Court of Appeals is to consist of three judges. §602-12.

The Idaho Court of Appeals consists of three judges, but the Supreme Court may also assign retired district or appellate judges as needed. The Court of Appeals has jurisdiction to hear cases assigned to it by the Idaho Supreme Court, which shall not assign cases invoking its original jurisdiction nor cases in which capital punishment is imposed. Upon motion of a party or its own motion, either the Court of Appeals or the Supreme Court may transfer appeals back to the Supreme Court. In assigning cases to the Court of Appeals, "the Idaho supreme court shall give due regard to the workload of each court, to the error review and correction functions of the court of appeals, and to the desirability of retaining for decision by the supreme court those cases in which there is substantial public interest or in which there are significant issues involving clarification or development of the law." Idaho Code §1-2406, as amended, effective July 1, 1981.

[70]D. Johnedis, *Massachusetts' Two-Court Appellate System in Operation*, 60 Mass. L.Q. 77, 78 (1975). Mr. Johnedis is Legal Assistant to the Supreme Judicial Court.

[71]*Id.* at 80.

1979) than on applications of parties filed both before and after decision by the Appeals Court; during 1978–1979 it granted 39 out of 68 applications for direct review but only 25 out of 152 for review after the decision below. This system assures expedited hearing and prompt authoritative decision of the most important issues, balances the work load as between the two appellate courts and avoids double appellate review except in a small number of cases.

The Iowa and Oklahoma systems are doubtless designed to achieve the same objectives. In Iowa the number of applications for review of Court of Appeals decisions granted in 1977, 1978 and the first 10 months of 1979 was 10, 21 and 12. The Oklahoma Supreme Court granted review of fewer than 40 Court of Appeals decisions per year from 1973 to 1977; during those years its filings increased from 762 to over 1100 and the number transferred to the Court of Appeals rose into the 400s. Oklahoma Report on the Judiciary (1976 and 1977).

The Iowa, Oklahoma and Massachusetts systems avoid the time and expense of briefing and arguing an appeal in two courts except in the small number of cases which their supreme courts accept for review after decision by the intermediate courts. The number is small primarily because the supreme courts retain or transfer to themselves the cases deemed to raise questions important enough for review by the highest court on examination of the questions presented to the trial courts and on the initial appeal. A supreme court would be less likely to accept for subsequent review a case which it found not important enough for it to hear in the first place. The relatively few cases which a supreme court then takes after decision below are those in which that decision either clearly presents an important question or a conflict for the first time, or which for some other reason strikes the supreme court as in need of review and perhaps reversal.

It should not be assumed that the preliminary screening process does not take substantial supreme court time. An intelligent examination of the papers in a court below to determine whether a case should be heard initially by a supreme court or an intermediate court should take as long as examination of a petition for certiorari, opposing brief and the opinion below. Some cases would take a little time and others a substantial amount.

The Massachusetts Supreme Judicial Court seems able to

handle the burden, however, and Massachusetts is the eleventh most populous state. In 1978–1979, 1500 appeals (with some overlap) were filed in the Supreme Judicial Court and the Appeals Court. The supreme courts of Iowa and Oklahoma, states with smaller populations, had similar case loads. In 1979, the Iowa Supreme Court transferred 377 out of 1507 cases docketed to the Court of Appeals. In 1977, the Oklahoma Supreme Court transferred 353 out of 1320.[72] Whether supreme courts in states with larger appellate case loads can review even cursorily all the appeals to the intermediate appellate courts may well be doubted; only experience can determine where the numerical line should be drawn. Certainly the United States Supreme Court could not review all of the over 20,000 appeals now taken to the United States courts of appeals. Indeed, a much less drastic proposal to authorize the Supreme Court to transfer cases of intermediate national importance to a national court of appeals has gotten nowhere.[73]

The above analysis leads to the conclusion that many states with intermediate appellate courts could use the preliminary screening method for avoiding the delays and costs of two tiers of appeals for the great majority of cases. To do so they would not have to sacrifice any of the essential elements of fair appellate procedure—the right to present an argument addressed to the issues before the court both in writing and orally, and the obligation of the court to render a collegial decision which explains the reasons for its conclusions.[74]

------

[72]In Oklahoma 893 cases were filed in the Court of Criminal Appeals.

[73]Commission on Revision of the Federal Court Appellate System, STRUCTURE AND INTERNAL PROCEDURES: RECOMMENDATIONS FOR CHANGE, pp. 32–34 (1975).

[74]Professors Lilly and Scalia suggest that Virginia use the transfer method to avoid a double appeal in the absence of "judicial impropriety" or "flagrant abuse" impairing the right to "a fair and impartial review." G. Lilly and A. Scalia, *Appellate Justice: A Crisis in Virginia?*, 57 Va. L. Rev. 3, 22–26, 39–42 (1971). This overlooks the possibility that the intermediate court's decision might in itself present a novel question of importance not initially presented to the Supreme Court. And it might still be subject to the vehement objections made to proposals to allow a new federal intermediate appellate court to operate free of at least discretionary review by the highest court. The literature is listed in G. Casper and R. Posner, THE WORKLOAD OF THE SUPREME COURT, Tables 1.1 and 2.1, pp. 3, 12 (American Bar Foundation, 1976); R. Stern and E. Gressman, SUPREME COURT PRACTICE, Sec. 1.16 (5th ed., 1978).

2

Before the Appeal Is Taken

2.1 The Need for Raising in Lower Courts the Points to Be Presented on Appeal

The preparation of, or at least for, an appeal should begin long before a case reaches an appellate court. For the appeal may be lost long before it is taken. I am not, of course, referring to the substantive defects or weaknesses which may make any case impossible to win. But even the most meritorious case will fail on appeal if the questions sought to be presented to the appellate court were not properly raised in the trial court or are not adequately presented in the record brought before the reviewing court.

The governing principle is that a party is not entitled to claim that the court below erred in deciding a case when the basis for the assertion of error was not called to that court's attention so as to give that court an opportunity to avoid the alleged mistake.[1] On occasion, courts depart from this principle for "plain" or "jurisdictional" errors, but counsel cannot count on that.[2]

When the point must be raised below will depend upon its nature and the circumstances under which it arises. A contention

---

[1]See E. Horvitz, *Protecting Your Record on Appeal,* LITIGATION, Vol. 4, No. 2, p. 34 (American Bar Association Section of Litigation, 1978).

[2]Washington Rule 2.5 allows the appellate court to review claims not raised below if they relate to the jurisdiction of either court, "failure to establish facts upon which relief can be granted, and manifest error affecting a constitutional right." The last two exceptions open wide gaps in the general rule.

going to the merits is most appropriately raised in the complaint or other pleading, or by motion to dismiss or strike, or for summary judgment, or in a pretrial conference when the issues are framed. Some defenses such as "lack of jurisdiction over the person, improper venue, insufficiency of process, or . . . of service of process" (Federal Rule of Civil Procedure 12(h) (1)) may be waived if not made in a motion or responsive pleading. On the other hand, a challenge to the court's jurisdiction over the subject matter may be made at any time. (Rule 12(h) (3).)

Objections to rulings admitting or excluding evidence should be made at the time of the ruling, with a statement of reasons. When evidence is excluded, the objection should be accompanied by an offer of proof, in order to provide a basis for arguing that the error was substantial and prejudicial. The offer should state as precisely as possible what the witness would have said if permitted to testify. To avoid having to make repeated objections raising the same question, the trial court should be asked to allow an objection to apply to an entire line of testimony without the need for repetition.

Objection must be made, of course, to instructions to the jury believed to be erroneous or to failures to give requested instructions. An objection should be made to misconduct of opposing counsel, or even of the court itself, at the time such conduct occurs. A motion for a new trial on such a ground may also be appropriate. In some states a motion for a new trial is a prerequisite to raising on appeal questions relating to errors at the trial, either for all cases, most cases or cases tried by jury.[3] In nonjury cases objection should be made to allegedly erroneous findings submitted by an opponent or made by the court, or to the court's failure to make essential findings.

Of special importance in state court cases which counsel may wish eventually to take to the United States Supreme Court is the need for properly raising in the state court any federal question which might warrant Supreme Court review on appeal from or certiorari to the state court.[4] The question raised not only must be substantial but also must be raised in the state judicial system at the proper time, so that the state court's failure

---

[3] E.g., New Jersey Rule 2:10-1 (jury, weight of evidence); Tennessee Appellate Rule 3(e) (jury). The Texas requirement for such a motion in jury cases was repealed in 1978. Texas Rule 324.

[4] See R. Stern and E. Gressman, SUPREME COURT PRACTICE, Secs. 3.25–3.30 (5th ed., 1978).

to deal with it may not be attributed to any failure to comply with state procedural requirements. This means that the litigant must conform to the state's procedures, which often require that the federal question be raised in the trial court, and perhaps even in the pleadings. Obviously, the safest course is to raise the point at the outset, in the pleadings if possible, to continue to raise it whenever appropriate, and to build the record in the state court thereafter with the federal question in mind. As one experienced commentator has stated:

> "if you are about to commence litigation [in a state court] in which there may be involved, then or ultimately, a question arising under the Constitution or laws of the United States, you must raise the federal question at the outset and not as an afterthought after you have lost below. By that time you are almost always too late . . . unless you build the record in your state litigation so that you *do* make a federal case out of it, you not only do not have a rosy chance of review, you don't have any chance at all."[5]

If the point cannot be foreseen at the outset, but unexpectedly or otherwise comes into the case at a later stage, as when the state court decision goes off on an unexpected tack, it should be raised as promptly as possible, certainly within any time limits specified by the state law.[6] And, of course, the issue must also be pressed in the state appellate courts. The object is to give the state judicial system full opportunity to consider the federal question and perhaps to avoid it before Supreme Court review is requested.

Except in the rare instance in which the final state opinion injects a federal question into the case for the first time, presentation of the issue initially in a petition for rehearing is not regarded as sufficient. An actual ruling on the merits of the federal question by the highest state court (not a mere denial of rehearing), even if the point is first raised on a petition for rehearing, will satisfy the Supreme Court's requirements, but careful counsel certainly cannot dare rely on anything as unlikely as that.[7]

The careful trial lawyer will in normal course follow the procedures suggested above. It may be too much to ask that he keep the possibility of appeal on every point in the forefront of

[5]F. Wiener, *Wanna Make a Federal Case Out of It?*, 48 A.B.A.J. 59, 60, 62 (1962).
[6]R. Stern and E. Gressman, SUPREME COURT PRACTICE, Sec. 3.27 (5th ed., 1978).
[7]*Id.* at Secs. 3.27–3.28.

his mind at every stage of the trial process. But he should at least be fully aware of the necessity for preserving the right to challenge any errors of the courts below if there is any possibility that the case will be appealed. If new counsel is brought in to handle the appeal, one of his first chores must be to determine whether the issues have been adequately presented in a court or courts below. This, of course, applies to new points which had not been urged by prior counsel. But unless the new lawyer enters the case while there is still time to present the issues in those courts, there may be nothing he can do to correct a failure in that respect.

All questions to be raised on appeal not only must have been properly presented below but must appear in the written record before the appellate court, which means both that they must appear in the record in the trial court and that the relevant parts of that record be transmitted to the reviewing court. There is no difficulty as to this if all that need be said on a point is contained in papers filed in the trial court, such as pleadings, motions, responses thereto, affidavits, and briefs or memoranda.[8] When a question is only presented orally, or when oral proceedings are relevant, a typewritten transcript is needed. When proceedings were not reported or available, the rules customarily permit the reconstruction of the oral proceeding by "the best available means," including the recollection of counsel or the court (e.g., Federal Appellate Rule 10(c)), or even "holding hearings if necessary" (Illinois Rule 323(c)).[9] Indeed, before the days of court reporters, records could only be reconstructed by such means.

Unfortunately, the absence of a verbatim transcript is difficult to overcome. If counsel can anticipate the problem and cannot, perhaps for pecuniary reasons, arrange to have a reporter present, he should try to use a tape recorder, or even a stenographer from his law office, or anyone who can take notes rapidly.

The need for a transcript may extend beyond the testimony and the accompanying remarks of the court and counsel. What

---

[8]Briefs and memoranda of counsel are usually not regarded as part of the record to be transmitted to the appellate court. But counsel should make sure that they are included when they are needed to prove that an issue has been presented to a lower court.

[9]See Sec. 6.4, *infra;* and R. Stern, *The Record and Abstract or Excerpts,* ILLINOIS CIVIL PRACTICE AFTER TRIAL, Sec. 7.8 (Illinois Institute for Continuing Legal Education, 1976).

is said during conferences in chambers, pretrial conferences, the selection of the jury (the voir dire), and colloquies with the court not heard by the jury may in some cases have a significant relationship to a point to be raised on appeal. The instructions to the jury and any discussion thereof are often of vital importance. On occasion, even counsels' arguments to the court or jury will be relevant. If counsel can anticipate even the possibility that any of this may raise an issue to be considered on appeal, he should endeavor to have such proceeding reported, or recorded in some way, so that it can be incorporated in the appellate record.

Once the necessary material is filed in the trial court, which means in its clerk's office, counsel for appellant must be sure that it is transmitted to the appellate court. Often this will be done by the clerk of the trial court, but counsel is still responsible. In many jurisdictions the entire record is sent up in the absence of a stipulation to omit unnecessary items. In other jurisdictions specific designation by the parties of the items desired is required. See Sec. 6.2, *infra.* Whichever method is used, the process is not difficult.

Thereafter, most jurisdictions require that the items counsel deems important enough for the appellate judges to read should be incorporated in a duplicated portion of the record— variously called record, appendix, abstract, excerpts, etc.— which appellant files with the reviewing court, usually along with his brief. See Secs. 6.7–6.13, *infra.* In most jurisdictions, all papers filed in the reviewing court are deemed part of the record before that court, even though not reproduced, so that failure to reproduce particular items is not fatal. And if any items are omitted from the record as transmitted, for any reason, the omissions may be corrected pursuant to stipulation of the parties or order of the trial court or reviewing court.[10]

2.2 Should a Case Be Appealed?

The fact that a case can be appealed does not mean that it should be. Fortunately for the judicial system, most cases are not taken to appellate courts, which could not possibly handle them if they were. And many should not be. On the average perhaps about 70 percent of the civil cases appealed as of right are

---

[10]E.g., Federal Appellate Rule 10(e); Illinois Rule 329.

affirmed.[11] The percentage is greater for criminal cases, in which indigent defendants provided with counsel free of charge lack a financial incentive not to appeal cases of little merit.[12] The proportion of reversals is greater in cases decided on the merits by supreme courts which exercise discretion as to the cases they should review. For such courts are much more likely to accept for review decisions which they deem improperly decided below than those which they would be likely to affirm. Thus although the United States Supreme Court granted only about 7 percent of all the 3943 applications for review during the 1978 term, it affirmed in only 30 percent of the certiorari cases disposed of by full opinion.[13]

In determining whether to take an appeal, the first and most important consideration is obviously the likelihood of obtaining a reversal. Determining this can be little more than an educated guess. As indicated in Sec. 2.3, *infra,* the guess is more likely to be accurate if made by, or with the aid of, an attorney other than the aggrieved lawyer who tried and lost the case, although many such lawyers do, usually by conscious effort, manage to retain their objectivity.

A second factor is the importance financially or otherwise of what is involved. In some situations, of course, the effect of a case upon the client, the industry, the business community or the government may give an issue importance greatly exceeding the amount directly involved. But many cases just do not involve

---

[11]Statistics as to affirmances and reversals are not commonly published, and are then sometimes difficult to classify or interpret. The percentage of reversals or modifications in the Tennessee Court of Appeals in 1978 was approximately 30; in the Texas Court of Civil Appeals in 1977, 33. Those courts hear only civil appeals. Judge Milton Pollack wrote in 1968 that the proportion of reversals in civil appeals to the New York appellate courts and the Court of Appeals for the Second Circuit ranged from 17 to 22 percent, excluding modifications. M. Pollack, *The Civil Appeal,* in COUNSEL ON APPEAL, p. 35 (1968).

[12]The proportion of reversals or modifications (including affirmances in part as modifications) in the Tennessee Court of Criminal Appeals in 1978 was 13 percent; in the Oklahoma Court of Criminal Appeals, 18 percent in 1976.

[13]*The Supreme Court, 1978 Term,* 93 Harv. L. Rev. 278 (1979). A recent study "indicated that 16 state supreme courts over a 100-year period, in deciding 5133 cases, had a reversal rate of 38.5%; for criminal cases, the reversal rate was 35.6%." *Godfrey* v. *Georgia,* 446 U.S. 420 (1980) (Mr. Justice White, dissenting, citing Note, *Courting Reversal: The Supervisory Role of State Supreme Courts,* 87 Yale L.J. 1191, 1198, 1209 (1978)). The Note and the supporting survey conclude that reversals are more likely when a supreme court exercises discretion as to which cases it will take from an intermediate appellate court (pp. 1200–1202) and less likely in criminal cases (pp. 1209–1210). The figures reported in the survey, however, reveal that these differences were considerably less than might have been expected. The more recent statistics referred to in the preceding notes suggest that the results over the 100-year range of the survey may not be the same as for the overloaded appellate courts of today.

enough money to warrant an appeal. Court fees, cost and security bonds, and the preparation and duplication of records and briefs will almost invariably run to at least a few hundred dollars, and usually a great deal more. Counsel fees will make the cost significantly higher unless a party acts as his own lawyer (which is regarded as highly unwise even if he is a lawyer), or because of indigence or otherwise does not have to pay a lawyer, or has one on a contingent basis. For an appeal takes, or should take if properly prepared, a substantial amount of lawyer time for research, studying the record, and thinking, in addition to briefing and arguing. If the appeal is successful, some of the costs can usually be charged to the other party, and where special statutes permit so can the legal fees, but seldom can a party be positive that he will achieve a reversal.

Only in simple cases—and such cases are not likely to be appealed—is it easy to tell where these factors in combination lead. Since the cost of appealing will normally exceed $500, apart from counsel fees, an appeal to recover that amount is seldom worth taking even if the party is sure of winning, unless the costs and fees themselves will be recoverable. Contrariwise, costs of $10,000 would not discourage appealing a million dollar case with a 10 percent chance of winning.

Lawyers must frequently decide whether to appeal cases which they believe are likely to be lost. That is not in itself a sufficient reason for refusing to appeal. An appeal is entirely proper if the argument to be presented is a reasonable one, with no unanswerable hole in it. This is so even if the lawyer recognizes that the odds are against him, though he will usually not want to appeal unless he believes he has a reasonable chance of success. In the exceptional situation where all the authorities are against him, an appeal may still be appropriate if (as would seldom be true) a lawyer can reasonably argue that they should no longer be followed and has some reason to believe the appellate court may agree. But there should be some rational basis for the argument which must be made. The standard should be the same in criminal cases, but I am not sure it is. See *Anders* v. *California*, 386 U.S. 738 (1967).[14] Apart from that, a lawyer

---

[14]Defendant may always appeal, but appointed counsel may withdraw if he finds the case "wholly frivolous" and submits a brief written as an "active advocate," not as an *amicus curiae*, referring to anything in the record that might arguably support the appeal. If the court finds any point "arguable," and "therefore not frivolous," it must provide counsel to argue the appeal. 386 U.S. at 744.

should not accept or present an appeal unless he believes a respectable argument can be made. This is the essence of Ethical Consideration 7-4 of the American Bar Association's *Code of Professional Responsibility,* which reads:

> "The advocate may urge any permissible construction of the law favorable to his client, without regard to his professional opinion as to the likelihood that the construction will ultimately prevail. His conduct is within the bounds of the law, and therefore permissible, if the position taken is supported by the law or is supportable by a good faith argument for an extension, modification, or reversal of the law. However, a lawyer is not justified in asserting a position in litigation that is frivolous."

Needless to say, appeals should not be taken merely to harass one's adversary, or solely as a bargaining device to force a better settlement, or otherwise to delay a final decision.[15] Doubtless appeals are often taken for those purposes, although such appeals seldom reach the stage of oral argument. But for a lawyer to take a "frivolous legal position" is contrary to professional ethical standards, and nonetheless so because of the difficulty of insuring that such standards are adequately enforced.

2.3   Should New Counsel Be Brought In on Appeal?

Whether or not new counsel should be brought in after trial to handle an appeal is a subject on which there is considerable difference of opinion.[16] A recent study of one state supreme court showed that in only 45 percent of the cases did the same attorney carry the case all the way through. Most of the switching occurred in criminal cases, but in civil cases over a third of the brief writers had not been at the trial.[17] The following discussion relates to cases in which the lawyers are employed by the parties. Criminal cases in which they are appointed to represent indigent defendants present different problems, often complicated by the fact that an issue which can be raised on appeal is

---

[15]W. Harte and S. Karasik, *Preliminary Considerations,* ILLINOIS CIVIL PRACTICE AFTER TRIAL, Secs. 3.8–3.9 (Illinois Institute for Continuing Legal Education, 1976).

[16]See American Bar Association Commission on Standards of Judicial Administration, STANDARDS RELATING TO APPELLATE COURTS, p. 42 (1977); F. Wiener, BRIEFING AND ARGUING FEDERAL APPEALS, pp. 380–394 (1967); Harte and Karasik, *supra* note 15, at pp. 3–14; H. Levy, HOW TO HANDLE AN APPEAL, pp. 201–226 (Practising Law Institute, 1968).

[17]T. Marvell, APPELLATE COURTS AND LAWYERS: INFORMATION GATHERING IN THE ADVERSARY SYSTEM, p. 53 (1978).

the incompetence of defendant's counsel at the trial.[18] As to criminal indigent cases, the plans adopted for the federal courts under the Criminal Justice Act (18 U.S.C. §3006A) and the special rules of the states should be consulted.

Whether a new lawyer should be brought in for the appeal is usually a question for the trial lawyer himself to resolve, since the idea is not likely to occur to legally unsophisticated clients who may not know that trial and appellate work may call for different talents and experience. On the other extreme is the corporate counsel who, in retaining outside lawyers, is likely to be fully aware that trial and appellate expertise are not necessarily the same or combined in the same lawyer.

There would seem to be obvious reasons why calling in a new lawyer for an appeal would be unwise and indeed foolish. He would start off unfamiliar with the case, in contrast to the complete familiarity of the attorney who tried it. He would presumably need much more time to read the record than the lawyer who had lived and worked through the trial, even though the latter might also have to review the record before writing the appellate brief. The trial lawyer might better appreciate and remember the nuances as well as the substance of the evidence. If the issues had been thoroughly briefed for the trial, as sometimes happens and sometimes does not, the trial lawyer would not have to start from scratch in order to get the authorities into his head as well as into his brief.

If the lawyer in private practice brought in on appeal was compensated on a basis related to the number of hours he

---

[18]American Bar Association, STANDARDS RELATING TO CRIMINAL APPEALS, Sec. 2.2, p. 47 (1969), states that trial counsel, whether retained or court appointed, should continue to represent a convicted defendant to advise on whether to appeal and throughout the appeal unless new counsel is substituted or trial counsel is permitted by the appellate court to withdraw "in the interests of justice or for other sufficient cause." The accompanying Commentary notes that some appellate courts routinely assign trial counsel to handle the appeal, but that most do not, the choice often depending merely on the tendency to use lawyers who regularly appear in the appellate court. Chief Justice Burger has urged the appointment of trial counsel, but Chief Judge Bazelon and Judge Leventhal of the Court of Appeals for the District of Columbia Circuit favor new counsel "in part because of the overriding virtues they found in fresh appellate counsel, versed in appellate practice. Holmes v. United States, 383 F.2d 925 (D.C. Cir. 1967)." *Id.* at 51. Compare W. Burger, *The State of the Federal Judiciary,* 57 A.B.A.J. 855, 858 (1971), with D. Bazelon, *New Gods for Old: "Efficient" Courts in a Democratic Society,* 46 N.Y.U. L. Rev. 653, 667–668 (1971), which emphasizes the unsurprising fact that "trial counsel will almost never explicitly urge that his client was deprived of the effective assistance of counsel." This and other material relating to the appointment of counsel in criminal appeals is compiled in APPELLATE JUSTICE: 1975, Vol. III, CRIMINAL JUSTICE ON APPEAL, pp. 97–106 (P. Carrington et al., eds., 1975). See also Comment, *Ineffective Counsel's Last Act—Appeal,* 1979 Ariz. State L.J. 595.

worked on the case, as he usually would be in the absence of a contingent fee arrangement or an indigent client, the additional time needed for him to prepare would be reflected in his fees.[19] The need for more time might also have the effect of delaying the appeal if the new lawyer was able to obtain an extension from the court.

Other factors, however, should be balanced against these reasons for retaining the trial lawyer for the appeal. Most important, perhaps, because it is independent of the comparative abilities of the individual lawyers, is the greater objectivity which a lawyer who did not try the case can bring to an appeal. The lawyer who lost is often too easily persuaded that all rulings adverse to him were completely erroneous, or even outrageous. Appellate judges will not start off with this bias, and neither will a new lawyer whose appraisal of the case, at the beginning at least, is more likely to coincide with that of the judges who are also seeing the case afresh. He will therefore be better able to advise as to the chances of winning the appeal and also as to which arguments, if any, are likely to be persuasive:

> "The appeals specialist views the case precisely as does the appellate court, through the little square window of the record, so to speak, and not as something viewed from the great outdoors. The trial man's mind cannot free itself of matters which entered in during preparation for trial but which did not get into the record."[20]

Such advice may be invaluable in determining whether an appeal should be taken. Consulting a different lawyer (who may, of course, be a member of the same firm) at this stage of the case will often be extremely important, even if he is not given complete or primary responsibility for the appeal.

Appellate advocacy also requires abilities and techniques different from those needed at the trial. The personality and approach which will be successful before a jury is not necessarily the best for persuading a panel of judges:

> "[T]he style of oratory a trial man develops, through his constant appeal to a jury less learned than himself, is out of place in an appellate court. A calm, conversational style is there appropriate; and his hearers' learning exceeds his own, or at least he should conduct himself as though it did."[21]

---

[19]This would not be true as to a lawyer for a government or other agency who receives a fixed salary. But the extra time would still be paid for by his employer.

[20]Judge Paxton Blair, *Appellate Briefs and Advocacy*, 18 Ford. L. Rev. 30, 46–47 (1949), quoted in F. Wiener, BRIEFING AND ARGUING FEDERAL APPEALS, p. 386 (1967).

[21]*Ibid.*

The emotional approach which may work with a jury is likely to antagonize or amuse sophisticated judges:

> "Generally, however, the objective approach of the appellate advocate is more effective and more efficient. Appellate specialists are more familiar with the appellate rules, procedures, and the many applicable precedents in the appellate courts. Their presentation is more direct and less time consuming. Their ability to answer effectively the questions propounded during oral argument often spells the difference between sustaining one's position and being reversed."[22]

> "[T]here is merit in the separation of responsibilities, mainly for the reason that the effective trial lawyer is all too often not an effective appellate pleader and *vice versa.*"[23]

On the other hand, the same experienced attorney also thought that

> "there are times when the appellate lawyer, working from a cold record, loses some of the color of the case or tends to isolate issues without sufficient emphasis on the whole factual picture."[24]

Apart from the above, the appellate lawyer should to some extent be a generalist in the law, who will be aware of and able to discuss analogous situations with the judges. A trial lawyer's main job, on the other hand, is to concentrate on the facts of a case. The appellate lawyer in these days of heavy appellate dockets usually has 30 minutes or less not only to present his argument but to answer questions from the bench. He must have the ability to condense a case, to concentrate on one or two critical issues, factual or legal, and to discuss the law with the judges if necessary.

Furthermore, a lawyer who has the intangible feel of a particular court in which he has frequently appeared also has an advantage if the judges know they can rely on his ability and integrity.

The above statement of the reasons for bringing in new counsel to handle an appeal does not mean that this is advisable for every appeal. Whether it is or not will depend on the nature of the case and the comparative legal skills of the lawyers being considered. The advantages must be weighed against the possible differences in time and cost referred to earlier.

---

[22]Statement of then United States Attorney Oliver Gasch, as quoted in Wiener, *supra* note 20, at 386.

[23]Statement of former Assistant Attorney General Charles K. Rice, quoted in Wiener, *supra* note 20, at 384.

[24]*Ibid.*

The lawyer who tried the case may himself be an experienced appellate advocate or a legal scholar capable of making an excellent appellate argument. Or he may be an ordinary trial lawyer of no particular competence outside of his specialty. Even if he is capable, he may be so busy trying cases that he cannot devote the necessary time, which includes time for thinking, to the appeal. If he is a senior partner, whether he tried the case or not, he may be too busy on other matters to undertake the necessary study and preparation. The position or stature of a lawyer will be of no help if he has not taken the time thoroughly to familiarize himself with the case before he gets up to argue. Obviously he should not take over the argument unless he can become fully prepared.[25]

When all is said and done, most important is the comparative abilities of the lawyers. One lawyer may be better than another because of innate ability or more experience in appellate work or more familiarity with the particular court. Argument by different counsel is warranted if it brings in a lawyer who is *better* qualified to argue the appeal, taking into account the factors referred to above.

All this, of course, is very difficult for a lay client to determine. This might not be true for corporate clients who deal with and select outside litigators through their own in-house lawyers. And, of course, governmental agencies whose large legal staffs include appellate sections are in a different category. In other situations the client must usually rely on the lawyer or firm that tried the case for advice, which obviously has its difficulties since most trial lawyers like to argue their own appeals and may not recognize the limits of their own capacities. If the trial lawyer is affiliated with a firm, he may have an appellate specialist or a more experienced or objective colleague within the organization to turn to for advice. He will often have sense enough to do this on his own. Nevertheless, in large offices most appeals are probably handled capably by the lawyers who try the cases, although some may be turned over to appellate experts. A seasoned trial lawyer who enjoys working with people may prefer to stay in the trial courts, and to turn his appeal over to a colleague with perhaps more scholarly inclinations who enjoys working with books and written records.

---

[25]See Sec. 8.3, *infra*, which quotes H. Goodrich, *A Case on Appeal—A Judge's View*, in A CASE ON APPEAL, pp. 24–25 (ALI-ABA, 1967).

When the trial lawyer has no colleague to consult, it is often too much to expect him to bring in an appellate expert. But many lawyers in various areas of the law do recognize their own deficiencies and bring in outsiders whom they believe to be superior in particular fields. This innate integrity of most members of the bar should to a large extent operate in the same way for the trial lawyer confronted with an appeal. Or he may merely recognize that his trial work keeps him too fully occupied to undertake adequate preparation of the appeal.

The best solution in many cases is to combine the advantages of familiarity with the trial with appellate expertise and objectivity by adding an appellate expert to the litigating team if one has not been in on the case from the beginning. Only cases of some magnitude may be able to afford such additional staffing, particularly if it is necessary to go outside a single law firm. But the process of consultation between lawyers who have been and who have not been immersed in the case produces many advantages and often the best results, no matter which of them ends up doing the arguing.[26]

Preferably the decision as to who argues should be based upon an understanding between the lawyers as to what is best for the client. The client, of course, has a right to decide the matter himself and perhaps should if he is sufficiently knowledgeable.

2.4 Standing to Appeal

A person wishing to appeal must have been (a) a party to the proceeding below; and (b) aggrieved by the decision below, or a part of it. In the vast majority of cases this presents no problem. The potential appellant has been a party and has no doubt that he has been a loser—that in some respect the judgment below was adverse to him, either by ordering him to act or by denying him some of the relief he requested.

(a) Appellant Must Have Been a Party Below

In the rare instance in which a person who has not been a party below has a practical need to appeal, he should endeavor to become a party by moving for leave to intervene. Obviously,

---

[26]"Where the trial lawyer participates with expert appellate counsel in the preparation of the brief and argument, the client receives the best of both worlds." Harte and Karasik, *supra* note 15, at pp. 3–14.

this should be attempted as early in the case as possible and certainly before the entry of the judgment in the trial court. If it must be attempted thereafter, the effort should first be made in the lower court; only in the most unusual circumstances should it be made for the first time in the reviewing court. *United States* v. *Imperial Irrigation Dist.,* 559 F.2d 509, 520-524, 543-544 (CA 9, 1977), affirmed on this ground *sub nom. Bryant* v. *Yellen,* 447 U.S. 352 (1980), illustrates the proper procedure when such circumstances arise. After an adverse judgment, the United States, which had been the plaintiff in the district court, refused to appeal. Affected persons who had supported the Government's position as *amici* thereupon moved in the district court for leave to intervene after the judgment for purposes of appeal. The district court's denial of their motion, an appealable order in itself, was then reversed by the court of appeals.

Unless good reason for not attempting to intervene at an earlier stage can be shown, neither court is likely to grant such relief after judgment. On at least two occasions, however, intervention has been allowed in the United States Supreme Court. *Banks* v. *Chicago Trimmers,* 389 U.S. 813 (1967), 390 U.S. 459 (1968); *Hunter* v. *Ohio ex rel. Miller,* 396 U.S. 879 (1969). In those cases, the parties whose interests were actually adversely affected by the decision below had been represented in the lower court by another party (a government official) who did not intend to seek Supreme Court review. In such circumstances it would have been highly unfair to preclude review at the instance of the aggrieved party, as the Government admitted in the *Banks* case, and intervention in the Supreme Court was accordingly allowed.[27]

Other appellate courts appear to follow the same principle.[28] On rare occasions they allow intervention after judgment in the trial court. "One reason . . . is so that the intervenor can prosecute an appeal that the existing party has determined not to take." Even on appeal "there are a few cases in which intervention has been allowed."[29]

---

[27]In *Banks,* the Court granted the motion to intervene and the petition for certiorari, decided the case on the merits, and reversed, but without anywhere explaining its ruling on intervention. 389 U.S. 813 (1967), 390 U.S. 459 (1968). In *Hunter* intervention was granted, but certiorari denied. 396 U.S. 879 (1969). The facts pertaining to the intervention issue in both cases appear in the petition filed in the *Hunter* case, which is printed in R. Stern and E. Gressman, SUPREME COURT PRACTICE, Sec. 20.38, pp. 1056–1065 (5th ed., 1978).

[28]In the *Hunter* case, however, intervention had previously been denied by the Ohio Supreme Court. *Id.* at 1061.

[29]7A C. Wright and A. Miller, FEDERAL PRACTICE AND PROCEDURE, Civil Sec. 1916, pp. 582–584 (1972).

An *amicus curiae* in the court below is not a party and therefore cannot appeal. He can, however, apply for leave to file an *amicus* brief in the reviewing court if a party appeals. See Sec. 7.36, *infra.*

(b) Appellant Must Be Aggrieved by the Decision Below

To have standing to appeal, a party must have lost something in the court below; the judgment in that court must in some respect be adverse to his position. The determination of standing in this context is relatively simple, to be made by comparing the judgment with the party's pleading or prayer for relief or other pertinent statement of position. A party is aggrieved not only if all of his claims are rejected, or if he is ordered to do something to which he objected, but also if he only obtains a part of what he prayed for. If a plaintiff sues for $100,000 in damages and obtains a judgment for $90,000, he has standing to appeal for the difference, as has a defendant who persuades the court to reject most but not quite all of the relief sought by the plaintiff.

The issue differs from the question whether a party has standing to sue or seek relief in the first place, although, of course, the considerations may overlap. That is a broad subject, with constitutional overtones in the federal courts at least, since a party who is not aggrieved—that is, injured in some way, however slightly—is also likely to lack standing to institute a "case" within the meaning of the Case and Controversy Clause of Article III of the Constitution. The meaning of standing in that sense is beyond the scope of this book.[30]

The principle that the winning party cannot bring a case to a higher court has one narrow exception in the United States Supreme Court as well as a number of state supreme courts in the same circumstances. After an appeal has been taken by the losing party to the intermediate appellate court, either party may then petition the highest court to grant review at any time before judgment below on the ground that the case is of exceptional public importance and in need of an authoritative and expeditious decision. See Sec. 5.5, pp. 125–126, *infra.*

---

[30]A large and growing body of law on that subject is reviewed in 13 C. Wright, A. Miller and E. Cooper, FEDERAL PRACTICE AND PROCEDURE, §§3529–3535 (1975); 6A J. Moore, FEDERAL PRACTICE, ¶¶57.11–57.15 (1974); C. Wright, FEDERAL COURTS, pp. 42–50 (3d ed., 1976); R. Stern and E. Gressman, SUPREME COURT PRACTICE, Sec. 3.35 (5th ed., 1978).

3

What Orders Are Appealable—
The Finality Doctrine and Exceptions

3.1 The General Principle That Appeals May Be Taken Only From Final Judgments or Orders

The fact that a case may ultimately be appealable does not mean that every preliminary order can be taken to an appellate court. The general rule in most jurisdictions is that only final judgments are reviewable,[1] with the substance of any prior order which still remains significant at the end of the trial being reviewable along with the judgment.[2]

Although this principle is now embodied in many statutes, rules and decisions, it stems from the English rule at common law (but not in equity) extant long before the Constitution. It was first embodied in the federal structure by three sections of the Judiciary Act of 1789,[3] and in some state laws before that.[4] In the United States the statutory exceptions which have long

---

[1]Often with an exception for cases involving small amounts. See Sec. 1.5, *supra*.

[2]F. James and G. Hazard, CIVIL PROCEDURE, pp. 669–672, 680–684 (2d ed., 1977); 15 C. Wright, A. Miller and E. Cooper, FEDERAL PRACTICE AND PROCEDURE, §§3905–3919 (1976); C. Wright, FEDERAL COURTS, §§101–102 (3d ed., 1976); 9 J. Moore, FEDERAL PRACTICE, ¶¶110.06–110.30 (2d ed., 1975); J. Sobieski, *The Theoretical Foundations of the Proposed Tennessee Rules of Appellate Procedure*, 45 Tenn. L. Rev. 161, 217, n. 308 (1978), and authorities cited therein.

[3]1 Stat. 72 (1789), §§21, 22, and 25. The difference between law and equity in England seems to have resulted from the practice in equity where a Master initially merely took depositions and submitted them with his recommendations to the Chancellor, who would issue all orders, interlocutory or final.

[4]Virginia Act of (May) 1779 (c.22, 10 Stat. Large 89, 101); Maryland Act of 1785 (c.72).

been recognized in most jurisdictions for such equitable functions as the granting or denying of temporary injunctions or the appointment of receivers have had both a historical and a pragmatic justification.

At least two reasons underlie limiting appeals to final judgments. Usually a party is not seriously aggrieved or injured until a case is finally decided; the cost and annoyance of litigating are regarded as necessary and normal incidents of the judicial process, and do not count. Of greater significance is the feared delaying effect of allowing appeals from preliminary orders. Even the fastest appeals usually take a number of months. A trial might often be impeded while trial court rulings are under consideration by a reviewing tribunal, and if no stay were granted pending appeals from one or more orders dealing with preliminary matters, there might be a need to repeat different aspects of the lower court litigation. As stated by the Supreme Court, speaking through Mr. Justice Frankfurter:

> "Congress from the very beginning has, by forbidding piecemeal disposition on appeal of what for practical purposes is a single controversy, set itself against enfeebling judicial administration. Thereby is avoided the obstruction to just claims that would come from permitting the harassment and cost of a succession of separate appeals from the various rulings to which a litigation may give rise, from its initiation to entry of judgment. To be effective, judicial administration must not be leadenfooted. Its momentum would be arrested by permitting separate reviews of the component elements in a unified cause."[5]

The taking of a number of appeals from different orders in the same case would only be confusing; appellate courts in busy jurisdictions could easily be overloaded, as has occurred in New York where a great many interlocutory orders are appealable.[6]

In most cases and in most circumstances the rule accomplishes its purposes and is unobjectionable. Immediate and separate appeals should not be allowed from rulings made during a trial, in part because the final judgment usually follows closely after the trial. And when the trial follows shortly after the institution of the case, or when the trial is short and uncomplicated, it makes much more sense to let the case proceed to its conclu-

---

[5]*Cobbledick* v. *United States,* 309 U.S. 323, 325 (1940), quoted with approval in *Coopers & Lybrand* v. *Livesay,* 437 U.S. 463, 467, n. 8 (1978), and *Firestone Tire and Rubber Co.* v. *Risjord,* 449 U.S. _____ (1981).
[6]H. Korn, *Civil Jurisdiction of the New York Court of Appeals and Appellate Divisions,* 16 Buffalo L. Rev. 307, 330 (1967).

sion and then allow a single appeal raising all the questions than to permit separate appeals from separate prejudgment orders. Undoubtedly most cases fall within these categories, although in many metropolitan jurisdictions where the trial courts are overloaded with work even such cases may take months or years.

On the other hand, if the trial will not take place until long after the pleadings are filed because of the state of the calendar or the nature of the case, some interlocutory appeals may expedite rather than retard the litigation. Complex cases involving long discovery often fall in this category. Furthermore, in such cases particular pretrial orders, such as those allowing or denying temporary injunctions, bail, changes of venue, class actions, or the use of alleged privileged testimony, may often have serious and continuous effects which cannot be remedied on appeal from the final judgment long in the future. An appeal from a denial of a motion to dismiss, which by its very nature is not a "final" order, might be disposed of before the case would be tried in normal course, so that what the appellate court decides or says might make the trial completely unnecessary or give guidance as to how it should be conducted. In such circumstances appeal from an interlocutory order may well put the litigation on the right track, or prevent irreparable injury, or resolve an issue separable from the merits so as to avoid the loss of a right or privilege.[7] This can often speed up rather than delay otherwise prolonged litigation. Awareness of these countervailing considerations has produced general agreement in recent years that

> "(1) no type of order other than a final judgment is invariably of such importance that it should be appealable of right, and (2) almost any type of order can be, under certain circumstances, an appropriate occasion for corrective action through appellate review."[8]

3.2   Exceptions to the Finality Doctrine—In General

General recognition that invariably prohibiting appeals from non-final orders would often be unfair to a party and not justified by the needs of effective judicial administration

---

[7]C. Crick, *The Final Judgment as a Basis for Appeal,* 41 Yale L.J. 539, 553 (1932).
[8]F. James and G. Hazard, CIVIL PROCEDURE, p. 681 (2d ed., 1977). See also Sobieski, *supra* note 2, at 217–220.

has produced many exceptions to the final judgment rule. Indeed, many years ago it was said that the final judgment rule caused more litigation than it prevented.[9] The volume of litigation on the subject has certainly not diminished since then.[10] There is both a diversity of exceptions among the various jurisdictions and confusion as to the scope of the exceptions in particular jurisdictions, including the federal courts.[11]

In New York, the exceptions may have largely swallowed the rule. The Commentaries to §5701 of the New York Civil Practice Act and Rules, which section allows appeals as of right from any interlocutory order which, *inter alia,* "involves some part of the merits" or "affects a substantial right," conclude that "almost anything can be appealed to New York's intermediate appellate court," the Appellate Division. These two provisions "betwixt them both . . . come close to licking the platter clean," although a lawyer should still check the cases since "there are a few instances in which orders have [still] been held unappealable."[12]

Other states do not go that far, although a few others do use criteria of similar breadth. In Minnesota "orders involving the merits or some part thereof" are appealable (Supreme Court Rule 103.03(d)); in Arizona a party may seek interlocutory review by filing a special action in the reviewing court. That is a remedy which supersedes the extraordinary writs and other means of seeking such review. There are no specific standards, so that the appellate courts have broad discretion to grant review when they think it warranted, but in fact they do so extremely sparingly. It does not appear that these broad statements have been construed so as to allow most, or indeed many,

---

[9]C. Crick, *The Final Judgment as a Basis for Appeal,* 41 Yale L.J. 539, 553 (1932).

[10]As of 1979, the United States Code Annotated contained 607 pages of annotations to the statutes (28 U.S.C. §§1291, 1292) which embody the finality rule and the exceptions thereto.

[11]The authorities are collected in the material cited in note 2, *supra.*

[12]See 7B McKINNEY'S CONSOLIDATED LAWS OF NEW YORK, CIVIL PRACTICE AND RULES, §5701, pp. 573, 577 (1978). Professor Harold L. Korn, an authority on New York practice, wrote in 1967: "It is generally recognized that this broad authority for appeal as of right from almost every kind of intermediate determination is a prime source of delay and expense in litigation and imposes an undue burden on the Appellate Divisions. Nevertheless, the proposal of the CPLR revisers to eliminate the broad catchall language met with substantial opposition from some segments of the bar." H. Korn, *Civil Jurisdiction of the New York Court of Appeals and Appellate Divisions,* 16 Buffalo L. Rev. 307, 330 (1967). There has been no significant change in the New York law since 1967.

interlocutory orders to be appealed. In Minnesota few interlocutory appeals are allowed, and then only in extraordinary circumstances.

In several states the trial court may "reserve" questions of law for the appellate court, which means that it is certifying them to the appellate court before deciding them itself. In Connecticut this can be done only with the consent of the parties. Connecticut Practice Book, §§3133-3134 (1978).

The final judgment requirement is usually embodied in a statute or rule of court, where it is followed either by a list of specific exceptions or by standards for the court to follow in determining whether to authorize interlocutory appeals, or both.[13]

3.3 Interlocutory Appeals as a Matter of Right

The first class of exceptions lists particular categories of interlocutory orders from which appeals can be taken as of right. In the federal system, the courts of appeals have jurisdiction to review interlocutory orders granting, modifying, continuing, or denying injunctions, appointing receivers or refusing to wind up receiverships or to take steps to accomplish the purposes thereof, determining rights and liabilities in admiralty cases in which appeals from final decrees are allowed, and judgments in patent cases which are final except for accounting.[14] Under the Classified Information Procedures Act of October 15, 1980 (Pub. L. 96-456, 49 U.S.L.W. 188), the United States may take an interlocutory appeal in a criminal case from an order authorizing the disclosure of classified information within 10 days after the order if the criminal trial has not commenced; if an appeal is taken during trial, the court of appeals shall, if necessary without briefs or written opinion, hear argument within four days after the required adjournment of the trial, and decide the case within four days thereafter. How this

---

[13]Sobieski, *supra* note 2, at 219–222.

[14]28 U.S.C. §1292(a); 16 C. Wright, A. Miller, E. Cooper and E. Gressman, FEDERAL PRACTICE AND PROCEDURE, §§3920–3936 (1977); C. Wright, FEDERAL COURTS, §102, p. 512 (3d ed., 1976). Prior to the enactment of 28 U.S.C. §1293, in Section 236(a) of the Bankruptcy Reform Act of 1978 (92 Stat. at 2667), interlocutory appeals could often be taken in bankruptcy cases. The law governing bankruptcy appeals before and after the 1978 Act and its effective dates is discussed in the text and pocket part of §3926 in FEDERAL PRACTICE AND PROCEDURE, which finds the meaning of the new statute not at all clear.

novel method of expediting interlocutory appeals will work will be of interest.

Most state courts are governed by similar provisions as to injunctions[15] and receiverships.[16] Other exceptions cover orders requiring payment of money or the immediate delivery of property,[17] certain types of orders in probate,[18] tax[19] and partition[20] litigation, and orders terminating parental rights.[21] In a number of states, orders granting or denying new trials or certain types of new trials are appealable either as a matter of right, as in Florida, Idaho, Iowa, New York, Pennsylvania and Washington, or by leave of the appellate court, as in Illinois.[22] Orders changing or refusing to change the place of trial are reviewable in Nevada.[23] Nevada also has an unusual rule (3A(b)(5)) that a denial of summary judgment may not be reviewed on appeal but may on mandamus (as to which see Sec. 3.7, *infra*). Florida permits review of nonfinal orders only in some of the above situations and also for orders determining venue, jurisdiction of the person, the issue of liability in favor of a party seeking affirmative relief, and the right to immediate monetary relief or child custody in domestic relations matters. Florida Rule of Appellate Procedure 9.130(a). In criminal cases the state is often allowed to appeal from orders suppressing evidence where the practical effect is to terminate the case and the defendant has not been placed in double jeopardy by the appeal.[24] This list of exceptions is not complete; each jurisdiction's rules and case law should, of course, be consulted.

---

[15] Alabama, Arkansas, California, Florida, Georgia, Illinois, Indiana, Kansas, Maryland, Montana, Nevada, Oklahoma, Pennsylvania, Texas, Virginia.

[16] Alabama, Arizona, Arkansas, California, Georgia, Idaho, Illinois, Indiana, Iowa, Kansas, Maryland, Montana, Nevada, Oklahoma, Pennsylvania, Texas.

[17] California, Florida, Illinois, Indiana, Kansas, Maryland, Montana, Nevada, Virginia.

[18] California, Idaho, Montana, Texas.

[19] California, Kansas.

[20] Montana, Nevada, Pennsylvania, Texas.

[21] Illinois, Washington.

[22] New York Civil Practice Laws and Rules, §5701(a)(2), 4402–4404; Korn, *supra* note 12, at 333–336; Washington Appellate Rule 2.2(a)(9); Idaho Rule 11; Iowa Rule 1(a); Florida Rule 9.110, 9.130(a)(4); Illinois Rule 306; Pennsylvania Appellate Rule 311(a)(5) (granting).

[23] See Nevada Rule 3A(b)(2).

[24] E.g., 18 U.S.C. §3731; Washington Rule 2.2(b); Florida Rule 9.140(c) and Committee Note. In November 1980, an amendment to the Texas constitution was approved permitting appeals in similar circumstances. Under Colorado Rule 4.1, the state's notice of appeal must be filed within 10 days of the entry of the order complained of, the state's brief within 10 days after the filing of the record in the Supreme Court, the appellee's brief within 10 days thereafter, and the reply brief within 5 days.

3.4   Judgment Final as to Some but Not All of the Claims or Parties

Rule 54(b) of the Federal Rules of Civil Procedure, as well as the rules or statutes of many states,[25] provides that the trial court "may direct the entry of a final judgment as to one or more but fewer than all of the claims or parties only upon an express determination that there is no just reason for delay and upon an express direction for the entry of judgment."[26] Although such a judgment does not terminate the entire litigation, the United States Supreme Court regards the rule as consistent with the final judgment statute because such orders are in fact final as to particular parties or claims. *Sears Roebuck & Co.* v. *Mackey,* 351 U.S. 427, 435–437 (1956). Certification under provisions like Rule 54(b) would seem appropriate when ultimate determination of the remainder of the case in the trial court both will involve separable issues and will take considerable time, and when there is good reason for not delaying the appeal as to the matters disposed of. *Curtiss-Wright Corp.* v. *General Electric Co.,* 446 U.S. 1 (1980). If the remainder of the case is soon to be decided, however, there is little to be gained by allowing the case to be divided for purposes of appeal.

The two Supreme Court decisions cited above recognize that under the federal rule the district court's certification is not conclusive; it is reviewable in the court of appeals for "abuse of discretion." See also *Brunswick Corp.* v. *Sheridan,* 582 F.2d 175, 183 (CA 2, 1978). Judge Friendly stated in the *Brunswick* case that Rule 54(b) orders "should be used only in the infrequent harsh case" where there is "some danger of hardship or injustice through delay which would be alleviated by immediate appeal." The rule should not be invoked when the issues still to be tried are intertwined with the supposedly "separable" issue already decided. Subsequently in *Curtiss-Wright* the Supreme Court emphasized the "substantial deference" to be given the district court's assessment; "the task of weighing and balancing the contending factors is peculiarly for

---

[25]E.g., Arizona, California, Idaho, Illinois, Texas. Missouri Rule 81.06 spells out in more detail when an order issued after a separate trial of some of the claims is appealable.

[26]See 10 C. Wright, A. Miller and E. Cooper, FEDERAL PRACTICE AND PROCEDURE, §2654 (1976); C. Wright, FEDERAL COURTS, pp. 506–507 (3d ed., 1976).

the trial judge." 446 U.S. at 10, 12. In that case, where the trial court had provided a carefully considered statement of reasons, the Supreme Court held that the court of appeals should have accepted the district court's ruling. The trial court's certification, which gives the order deciding part of the case the status of a final judgment, begins the running of the time to appeal and makes the order *res judicata* if not reversed. 10 C. Wright and A. Miller, *Federal Practice and Procedure,* §2661 (1976); 6 J. Moore, *Federal Practice,* ¶54.42 (2d ed., 1976). It therefore may push the losing party into taking an immediate appeal from the certified order. Each party should carefully consider, before requesting a certification, whether this will be strategically wiser than waiting to see what happens to the rest of the case.

3.5 Review of Interlocutory Orders as a Matter of Discretion

In some states (such as Florida and Colorado) interlocutory appeals may be taken only where authorized as a matter of right, as described in Sec. 3.3, *supra.* In the federal system and many of the states, however, the courts have discretion to authorize interlocutory review in accordance with prescribed standards. These standards are applied either by the trial court in the first instance and then by the reviewing court, or by the reviewing court alone. They are phrased in various ways, but in general they relate to the urgency of immediate review, whether it will expedite and not retard the completion of the litigation, and the importance and doubtfulness of the question as to which review is sought.

(a) The Federal Standards

The most common provision for appeals from nonfinal orders appears in the Federal Interlocutory Appeals Act of 1958 (28 U.S.C. §1292(b)), and similar statutes or rules of a number of states.[27] Section 1292(b) permits interlocutory appeal when the district judge entering an interlocutory order certifies "that

---

[27]Alabama (only to Supreme Court in cases within its "original appellate jurisdiction"), Idaho, Illinois, Kansas, Michigan, New Mexico, Pennsylvania, Rhode Island, Tennessee, Vermont. Colorado, which in general follows the federal practice, omits §1292(b).

such order involves a controlling question of law as to which there is substantial ground for difference of opinion and that an immediate appeal from the order may materially advance the ultimate termination of the litigation." The appellant must file a petition for leave to appeal in the court of appeals within 10 days after the trial court's certificate explaining why the standards for interlocutory review have been met and why the appeal should be heard. Adverse parties have seven days to answer.[28]

As stated in the House Committee Report supporting the enactment of the Interlocutory Appeals Act, such a certification by the trial court of

> "the case as appropriate for appeal serves the double purpose of providing the Appellate Court with the best informed opinion that immediate review is of value, and at once protects appellate dockets against a flood of petitions in inappropriate cases. . . . [A]voidance of ill-founded applications in the Courts of Appeals for piece-meal review is of particular concern. If the consequence of change is to be crowded appellate dockets as well as any substantial number of unjustified delays in the Trial Court, the benefits to be expected from the amendment may well be outweighed by the lost motion of preparation, consideration, and rejection of unwarranted applications for its benefits."[29]

The trial court certification brings the interlocutory order before the appellate court, but does not require the latter court to hear the appeal. As stated by Mr. Justice Stevens for the Supreme Court in *Coopers & Lybrand* v. *Livesay,* 437 U.S. 463, 475 (1978):

> "even if the District Judge certifies the order under § 1292 (b), the appellant still 'has the burden of persuading the court of appeals that exceptional circumstances justify a departure from the basic policy of postponing appellate review until after the entry of a final judgment.' *Fisons Ltd.* v. *United States,* 458 F.2d 1241, 1248 (CA7 1972). The appellate court may deny the appeal for any reason, including docket congestion."

The Interlocutory Appeals Act was designed "to meet the recognized need for prompt review of certain nonfinal orders" (*id.* at 474) which do not fall within categories readily definable in advance.

---

[28]Federal Rule of Appellate Procedure 5(a). The time limits differ in some of the states. E.g., Illinois (14 days for each party).

[29]H.R. Rep. No. 1667, 85th Cong., 2d Sess. 6 (1958).

(b) State Deviations From the Federal Standards

A number of states which provide for discretionary inter-locutory review deviate from the §1292(b) pattern in one or more respects:

(1) The guiding standard is phrased differently;
(2) The application is made only to the reviewing court and not initially to the trial court; and
(3) Application may be made to the reviewing court even if the trial court refuses to certify.

The states which depart from the 1292(b) standards do so in varying degrees. Some use the federal language with minor or major modifications.

Illinois Supreme Court Rule 308 follows the federal model but omits the word "controlling" because:

> "The meaning of 'controlling' has not been clear, despite many cases on the point, and experience has shown that sometimes an important question of law that only arguably could be said to be controlling should be heard on appeal without awaiting final judgment."[30]

To certify that determination of an important question as to discovery, privilege, venue or class action status, for example, would be "controlling" in the litigation as a whole was frequently difficult unless "controlling" was construed so broadly as to be practically meaningless. As might be expected, the federal courts differ as to how this provision should be applied, and its presence in the federal statute is more confusing than helpful.

Oklahoma (12 Oklahoma Stat. §952(b)(3), Oklahoma Rule of Appellate Procedure 1.50) incorporates the second 1292(b) requirement that the trial court must certify "that immediate appeal may materially advance the ultimate termination of the litigation." It omits the need for a controlling and doubtful question of law. The state Supreme Court then has discretion whether to accept the appeal.

Many of the states add to the factors which must be consid-ered under §1292(b) irreparable injury to appellant if appellate review must await final judgment.[31] Thus, the standard embod-

---

[30]Committee Comments to Illinois Supreme Court Rule 308.
[31]New Jersey Rule 2:2-2 authorizes interlocutory appeals to the Supreme Court by leave of court when necessary to prevent irreparable injury and in death cases.

ied in Indiana Rule 4(B)(5) requires a finding by both trial and appellate courts that:

> "(a) the appellant will suffer substantial expense, damage or injury if the order is erroneous and the determination thereof is withheld until after judgment, or (b) the order involves a substantial question of law, the early determination of which will promote a more orderly disposition of the case, or (c) the remedy by appeal after judgment is otherwise inadequate."

Clause (b) embodies the substance of §1292(b), but (a) and (c) emphasize irreparable injury and the inadequacy of the ordinary remedy of appeal after judgment. Significantly, the three clauses are in the disjunctive; a finding of any one of them is sufficient. Michigan Rule 806.3(1)(a)(ii) adds two alternative grounds to those mentioned in §1292(b): a showing "that the matter is either of major significance to the jurisprudence of the state or that the decision is clearly erroneous and appellant will suffer substantial harm by awaiting final judgment before taking appeal."

A number of other states include irreparable injury as a factor to be considered,[32] or substantial alteration of the status quo.[33] Alaska Rule 24 then provides that even in such circumstances review is discretionary and to be allowed

> "only where
> 1. The order is important enough to deviate from normal appellate procedure and require immediate attention,
> 2. the policy of finality is outweighed by a claim that justice in the case demands immediate review of a non-appealable order, or
> 3. the trial court has so far departed from the accepted and usual course of judicial proceedings or sanctioned such a departure as to call for exercise of the Supreme Court's power of supervision and review."[34]

Other states employ broad general language which gives the courts wide discretion either as the controlling standard or as an alternative with somewhat more specific criteria. Georgia allows review of interlocutory orders when they are "of such importance that immediate review should be sought" (Georgia

---

[32]E.g., Alaska Rule 23.

[33]Washington Rule 2.3.

[34]Paragraph 3 is taken almost verbatim from United States Supreme Court Rule 17.1 indicating the factors which will be considered in passing upon a petition for certiorari.

Code 6-701). In Maine and Massachusetts[35] the test is whether the matter ought to be determined by the appellate court "before any further proceedings are taken" below. In South Dakota the test is whether justice will be served by deciding the appeal before a final determination below (South Dakota Comp. Laws 15-26-1). Iowa Rule of Appellate Procedure 2 provides for review of any interlocutory ruling upon a finding by the Supreme Court or a justice that the ruling "involves substantial rights and will materially affect the final decision and that a determination of its correctness before trial on the merits will better serve the interests of justice."

Delaware Rule 42, after referring to the trial court's order as determining "a substantial issue and establish[ing] a legal right" and specifying criteria of importance (such as novelty, conflict and constitutionality), adds the alternative factor whether the immediate appeal will terminate the litigation or otherwise serve considerations of justice. Iowa Rule 2 refers to similar considerations, but with a conjunctive "and" rather than the disjunctive "or."

Washington Rule 2.3 allows interlocutory review as a matter of discretion if the trial court "has committed an obvious error which would make further proceedings useless" or a "probable error" which "substantially alters the status quo," or so far departs "from the accepted and usual course" of a judicial proceeding or sanctions such departure by lower courts or agencies as to call for action by the appellate court. This both serves the same purpose as §1292(b) and supersedes the extraordinary writs. See Sec. 3.7, p. 76, *infra*.

Some of the above standards for allowing review of nonfinal orders appear to be very broad, some omit relevant considerations and some are complicated. This does not necessarily mean that they do not work satisfactorily. That would depend on how the courts apply them, whether strictly or liberally. A completely flexible system, with no standards which limit the court's discretion, such as Arizona's special action practice (see p. 55, *supra*),

---

[35]Maine Rule 72 and Massachusetts Ann. Laws, Chap. 231, Sec. 111. In both states the trial court "reports" the question to the appellate court, or the aggrieved party may petition. Maine and Vermont also permit the trial court, with the agreement of the parties, to report prior to judgment any question of law to the supreme court if the question is of sufficient importance or doubt, and its disposition would in at least one alternative finally dispose of the action. Maine Rule 72(2); Vermont Rule 5(a). Vermont Rule 5(b) is the equivalent of 28 U.S.C. §1292(b).

may function as well as or better than when a court's discretion is limited by specific standards, so long as it does not result in a flood of unwarranted applications which burden the appellate courts even if only a few are granted. How different standards operate in practice can only be determined by studies in depth of both the statistics as to judicial work load and the reaction of the bench and bar in each jurisdiction.

Two recent formulations state the reasons why interlocutory review should be allowed in language specific enough to be meaningful to judges and lawyers, and yet broad enough to allow ample room for judicial discretion. In 1977, the American Bar Association approved the *Standards Relating to Appellate Courts* proposed by a commission composed of many distinguished judges and lawyers. Section 3.12, p. 29, which was immediately taken almost verbatim into Wisconsin Rule 809.50 (1978), represents "a synthesis" both of the federal practice "and the corresponding rules of a number of the states." It provides for review at the discretion of the appellate court on a showing

> "that review of the judgment or order immediately rather than on an appeal from the final judgment in the case or proceeding will materially advance the termination of the litigation or clarify further proceedings therein, protect a party from substantial and irreparable injury, or clarify an issue of general importance in the administration of justice."

This formulation differs from §1292(b) in adding protection "from substantial and irreparable injury" and clarification of an issue of general importance. It also makes the factors listed alternative grounds for immediate review by substituting "or" for "and." It omits the limitation to "controlling question of law as to which there is substantial ground for difference of opinion," although the word "clarify" more broadly embodies the same concept of uncertainty in the existing law. New Hampshire Rule 8, adopted in 1979, combined the language of §1292(b) with the last three classes of the *Appellate Standards* quoted above and in the Wisconsin rule.

Shortly thereafter, in 1979, new Tennessee Rule of Appellate Procedure 9(a) spelled out substantially the same factors but in greater and perhaps more helpful detail, as follows:

> "In determining whether to grant permission to appeal, the following, while neither controlling nor fully measuring the courts' discretion, indicate the character of the reasons that will be considered: (1) the need to prevent irreparable injury, giving

consideration to the severity of the potential injury, the probability of its occurrence, and the probability that review upon entry of final judgment will be ineffective; (2) the need to prevent needless, expensive, and protracted litigation, giving consideration to whether the challenged order would be a basis for reversal upon entry of a final judgment, the probability of reversal, and whether an interlocutory appeal will result in a net reduction in the duration and expense of the litigation if the challenged order is reversed; and (3) the need to develop a uniform body of law, giving consideration to the existence of inconsistent orders of other courts and whether the question presented by the challenged order will not otherwise be reviewable upon entry of final judgment. Failure to seek or obtain interlocutory review shall not limit the scope of review upon an appeal as of right from entry of the final judgment."

These criteria proposed by the *Appellate Standards,* Wisconsin and New Hampshire, on the one hand, and Tennessee, on the other, both of which rest on a study of the practice throughout the country,[36] best describe the factors which should guide courts in determining whether to allow interlocutory appeals.

(c) Application to Both Courts or Only to the Reviewing Court

Many jurisdictions, including the federal, condition interlocutory review on a certificate by the trial court to the appellate court that the order in question satisfies the prescribed standards.[37] The reviewing court then exercises its own discretion independently, presumably applying the same standards but without being restricted to them, as the Supreme Court recently declared in the *Coopers & Lybrand* case (437 U.S. 463), quoted at p. 60, *supra.*

In other jurisdictions the party seeking review applies directly to the reviewing court to allow the interlocutory appeal.[38] The latter system is simpler; it avoids the need for filing two applications in two different courts which may apply different standards. It also avoids requiring the trial court to undertake the difficult task of objectively evaluating and determining the appealability of its own ruling. On the other hand, having the trial court sift out the "ill founded" applications lessens the

---

[36]As to the theory underlying the new Tennessee rules, see Sobieski, *supra* note 2, at 220–226.

[37]Delaware, Georgia, Illinois, Indiana, Maine, Oklahoma, Tennessee.

[38]Alaska, Arizona, Iowa, South Dakota, Utah, Wisconsin.

burden on the appellate courts which might result if they were required to pass upon all applications for discretionary interlocutory review in the first instance.

Whether an appellate court will be unduly burdened without such a preliminary screening by the court below will depend not only on the work load in the particular jurisdiction but also on the extent to which counsel are likely to abide by the limitations imposed by judicial interpretation of the state's standards. The experience under the Wisconsin standard quoted in the preceding section was that not too many unwarranted applications were filed and that the system was working quite well without requiring preliminary trial court certification.

In general, certification by the trial court should not be required except when necessary to protect the reviewing court against a flood of unwarranted applications. But this "exception" may encompass most of the state appellate courts as well as the federal courts of appeals. It may not be a coincidence that few of the more populous states dispense with the certificate from the trial court. The experience of New York, which freely allows interlocutory appeals (see p. 55, *supra*), may prove the wisdom of the other jurisdictions in this respect.

No matter how the standards for discretionary review are formulated, the procedure whereby the matter is presented to the appellate courts is very much the same. Where leave of the trial court as well as the appellate court is required, as in the federal courts and in many of the states, the trial court must be persuaded to enter a certificate, order or other document containing the necessary findings. A petition or application for permission to appeal is then filed in the appellate court with the certificate or order attached, usually within 10 days after the entry in the trial court of the order being appealed or the certificate of appealability, whichever is later. If leave need be obtained only from the appellate court, the petition or application should be filed in that court within the specified number of days after the entry of the order below.[39] In either event, enough copies should be filed to provide each member of the appellate court with a copy, along with proof of service. The opposing party then has a specified number of days to respond, seven under Federal Rule of Appellate Procedure 5(b), South Dakota

---

[39]E.g., South Dakota Rule 5; Wisconsin Rule 809.50. Both allow 10 days.

Rule 5(3) and Tennessee Rule 9(d), and 10 under Wisconsin Rule 809.50.

If permission to appeal is granted, the appellant files the cost bond, usually required within 10 days, and pays the required fees. In general, the date of granting leave to appeal is the date from which the time for further steps, such as the preparation of the record, is to run. The application for leave to appeal, or the grant thereof, does not stay proceedings in the trial court unless the trial court or the appellate court, or a judge thereof, so orders.

(d) Conclusiveness of Trial Court's Refusal to Certify

The §1292(b) technique makes the trial court's determination *not* to certify conclusive; it is not made reviewable in any way.[40] See *Coopers & Lybrand* v. *Livesay,* 437 U.S. 463 (1978). That approach has the obvious disadvantage of committing to the trial judge the determination as to whether his own ruling is to be subject to immediate appeal—which sometimes may in practical effect mean subject to any review at all. While some judges may be happy to pass the buck upstairs, others may not be entirely objective in deciding whether their own rulings are sufficiently doubtful to warrant further review. Presumably for this reason the American Bar Association's *Standards Relating to Appellate Courts* and Professors James and Hazard's treatise on *Civil Procedure* have proposed a procedure

> "in which the trial judge can indicate whether he believes interlocutory appeal would be appropriate with regard to a particular order, but in which his adverse view in this respect would not foreclose the appellate court from granting review."[41]

This would have the advantage of not giving an obdurate trial judge power absolutely to preclude an immediate appeal from his ruling, and "would seem to represent a better balance of the practical considerations that should govern allowance of interlocutory review in contemporary procedural context."[42]

The *Appellate Standards* similarly recommends (Sec. 3.12, pp. 28–29):

---

[40]As to the use of the extraordinary writs to review otherwise unappealable orders, see Sec. 3.7, *infra.*

[41]F. James and G. Hazard, CIVIL PROCEDURE, p. 684 (2d ed., 1977).

[42]*Ibid.*

"The most desirable combination is to provide that, in every case where interlocutory review is sought, the lower court should give its opinion whether such review is appropriate, but that its determination should not bind the appellate court. Such an arrangement would give the appellate court the benefit of the lower court's view of the matter, but reserve the ultimate decision to the appellate court."

Three states, Delaware, Idaho and Vermont, permit submissions to their supreme courts of applications to review interlocutory orders after the trial court has refused to grant a certificate. In these states the applicant has 30, 14 and 5 days, respectively, to file an application setting forth the reasons why interlocutory review should be allowed. The disadvantage of this modification of the §1292(b) system is that it might subject the presently overloaded appellate courts in the more populous states to a mass of unworthy petitions to review interlocutory orders. That only states with small populations and presumably no appellate overload have permitted what is in substance an appeal from the trial court's refusal to certify may not be a coincidence.

A proposed amendment to §1292(b) would permit a court of appeals to hear an interlocutory appeal if it finds "that an appeal is required in the interest of justice and because of the extraordinary importance of the case," even though the district court has refused to authorize the appeal.[43] Some safety valve against arbitrary action by the trial judge would seem to be desirable unless the result clearly would be to overburden the reviewing court. That result might be avoided if the appellate courts made it clear that they would overturn the trial court's refusal to certify only in rare and exceptional circumstances of abuse of discretion, and if the petitions to the appellate court were kept short enough—perhaps by a 5- or 10-page limitation —so as not to require much judicial time. Whether the bar would heed the appellate courts' reluctance to accept such applications, and not file many which were unwarranted, would be the critical question. Analysis of the experience in the states which now allow applications to the reviewing court, and also in more populous states if any would be willing to try the system proposed by the *Appellate Standards*, might demonstrate whether the otherwise more desirable system is administratively feasible.

---

[43]Section 201 of S. 678 and S. 1477, S. Rep. No. 96-304, 96th Cong., 1st Sess. 7 (1979).

(e) Review of Interlocutory Orders of Intermediate Appellate Courts

In the federal system and most states with two tiers of appellate courts, an interlocutory order of a trial court which has been reviewed by an intermediate appellate court is subject to review in the higher court. The supreme court's discretionary authority is not limited to final orders. Accordingly, the ordinary route of petition for certiorari or leave to appeal may be utilized.

The fact that an order is interlocutory is a factor counting against the exercise of discretion in favor of review, but it is not a jurisdictional barrier. See Illinois Rule 315(a). Frequently when there is good reason review is granted of nonfinal orders, such as a ruling of the intermediate court reversing a trial court's dismissal of a complaint. Such cases may present important questions of law, e.g., *Estelle* v. *Gamble*, 429 U.S. 97 (1976); *United States* v. *General Motors Corp.*, 323 U.S. 373, 377 (1945).[44] Under New Jersey Rule 2:2–5, however, the judgment of the Appellate Division on an interlocutory appeal shall not be appealable to the Supreme Court unless it is dispositive of the action.

3.6 Judge-Made Exceptions to the Finality Rule

The above exceptions to the final judgment rule, which appear in statutes or rules of courts, are supplemented by others that are judge-made. In the federal courts a large body of law has interpreted the statutory word "final" as including many orders which do not terminate the litigation. Although these decisions literally constitute "interpretations" of the statutory language, even the Supreme Court refers to them as establishing "exceptions" to the finality rule. See *United States* v. *MacDonald*, 435 U.S. 850, 854 (1978); *Coopers & Lybrand* v. *Livesay*, 437 U.S. 463, 467 (1978).

These decisions have been concerned with the concept of finality under both §1291 of 28 U.S.C., which gives the courts of appeals jurisdiction over appeals from "final decisions" of the district courts, and §1257, which authorizes the Supreme Court to review "final judgments or decrees rendered by the highest

---

[44]See also R. Stern and E. Gressman, SUPREME COURT PRACTICE, Sec. 4.19 (5th ed., 1978).

court of a State in which a decision could be had." Both lines of cases reflect "the pragmatic approach that we have followed . . . in determining finality" (*Cox Broadcasting Corp.* v. *Cohn,* 420 U.S. 469, 486 (1975)). They emphasize that the statutory language is to be given a "practical rather than a technical construction" (*Cohen* v. *Beneficial Industrial Loan Corp.,* 337 U.S. 541, 546 (1949); *Abney* v. *United States,* 431 U.S. 651, 658 (1977)). In the *Cox* case, the Court stated that there were "at least four categories" of cases in which the Court has reviewed state court decisions under §1257 even though "additional proceedings [were] anticipated in the lower state courts" (420 U.S. at 477).[45]

In subsequent cases the Court has recognized the collateral order exception articulated in the *Cohen* case as identifying the following factors which were significant in giving the phrase "final decision" in §1291 a practical or pragmatic construction:[46]

> "First, the District Court's order had fully disposed of the question of the state security statute's applicability in federal court; in no sense did it leave the matter 'open, unfinished or inconclusive' [337 U.S. at 546]. Second, the decision was not simply a 'step toward final disposition of the merits of the case [which would] be merged in final judgment'; rather, it resolved an issue completely collateral to the cause of action asserted. *Ibid.* Finally, the decision had involved an important right which would be 'lost, probably irreparably,' if review had to await final judgment; hence, to be

---

[45]These categories were (420 U.S. at 479–483):

(1) Those cases "in which there are further proceedings—even entire trials—yet to occur in the state courts but where for one reason or another the federal issue is conclusive or the outcome of further proceedings preordained."

(2) Cases "in which the federal issue, finally decided by the highest court in the State, will survive and require decision regardless of the outcome of future state-court proceedings."

(3) Cases "where the federal claim has been finally decided, with further proceedings on the merits in the state courts to come, but in which later review of the federal issue cannot be had, whatever the ultimate outcome of the case."

(4) Cases "where the federal issue has been finally decided in the state courts with further proceedings pending in which the party seeking review here might prevail on the merits on nonfederal grounds, thus rendering unnecessary review of the federal issue by this Court, and where reversal of the state court on the federal issue would be preclusive of any further litigation on the relevant cause of action rather than merely controlling the nature and character of, or determining the admissibility of evidence in, the state proceedings still to come. In these circumstances, if a refusal immediately to review the state-court decision might seriously erode federal policy, the Court has entertained and decided the federal issue, which itself has been finally determined by the state courts for purposes of the state litigation."

[46]As the Court summarized the rule in *Cohen* (337 U.S. at 546):

"This decision appears to fall in that small class which finally determine claims of right separable from, and collateral to, rights asserted in the action, too important to be denied review and too independent of the cause itself to require that appellate consideration be deferred until the whole case is adjudicated."

effective, appellate review in that special, limited setting had to be immediate. *Ibid.*" *Abney* v. *United States,* 431 U.S. 651, 658 (1977); *United States* v. *MacDonald,* 435 U.S. 850, 855 (1978).

Shortly thereafter in *Coopers & Lybrand* v. *Livesay,* 437 U.S. 463, 468 (1978), the Court, through Mr. Justice Stevens, relying on *Abney* and *MacDonald,* stated that

> "To come within the 'small class' of decisions excepted from the final-judgment rule by *Cohen,* the order must conclusively determine the disputed question, resolve an important issue completely separate from the merits of the action, and be effectively unreviewable on appeal from a final judgment."

Firestone Tire and Rubber Co. v. *Risjord,* 449 U.S. _____ (1981), which again reviews the authorities, emphasizes the narrowness of this exception.[47]

None of the cases explicitly suggests that the collateral order exception of the *Cohen* case, which came up from a federal court of appeals under §1291, differs from the exceptions categorized in *Cox Broadcasting* and other cases taken from state courts to the Supreme Court under §1257. Nevertheless the pragmatic approach has resulted in giving special weight, in construing §1257, to considerations of federalism and the special need for ensuring that effective Supreme Court review of state court decisions on federal questions is not impeded, or federal statutory or constitutional policy obstructed; these factors would not apply to §1291 cases. So long as emphasis is placed on obtaining the best practical result in the individual case, the Court's pragmatic approach appears to have generally operated reasonably. But the cost of such an open-ended approach which pays little heed to the statutory language—"final judgments" and "final decisions"—could be to stimulate many unjustified appeals or attempts to appeal which would undermine the underlying policy against piecemeal review.[48]

---

[47]The difficulty in applying this rule is illustrated by the recent holding of a closely divided Second Circuit *en banc* that orders denying motions to disqualify counsel are not appealable but orders granting such motions are. *Armstrong* v. *McAlpin,* 625 F.2d 433, 437, 440 (CA 2, 1980), vacated and remanded, 449 U.S. _____ (1981), which cites conflicting decisions in other circuits. In *Firestone Tire and Rubber Co.* v. *Risjord,* 449 U.S. _____ (1981), the Supreme Court agreed as to the unappealability of orders denying motions to disqualify (as to which 10 circuits had divided evenly), but (in n. 8) reserved judgment as to orders granting motions to disqualify.

[48]"Although well-established rules of appealability might at times cause an action to be determined unjustly, slowly, and expensively, they have nonetheless the great virtue of forestalling the delay, harassment, expense, and duplication that could result from multiple or ill-timed appeals. The great value of the final judgment rule may be that it combines generally effective review with guides sufficiently clear to prevent most of the

Coopers & Lybrand v. *Livesay, supra,* an attempt to appeal to a federal court of appeals under §1291, relied largely on the fact that in enacting §1292(b) Congress had established a flexible means of differentiating between those interlocutory orders which should and should not be appealed prior to the entry of the final judgment; *Livesay* held that orders disallowing class actions were not appealable, even though limiting a case to a few plaintiffs with only a nominal financial interest instead of a large class would in substance sound its "death knell." The practical dilemma there facing the plaintiffs might well have led the Court to the opposite conclusion. The case may thus foreshadow at the least an unwillingness to expand the collateral order exception, in recognition of the congressional understanding that §1292(b) provides the necessary escape hatch from the inflexibility of the finality statutes strictly construed.

Section 1292(b), however, applies only to federal civil appeals, not to criminal appeals to the courts of appeals under §1291 or to appeals to the Supreme Court from state courts under §1257. Flexibility is available in the last two categories of cases[49] only through continued resort to the exceptions which the Court has read into the concept of finality. A number of these cases, including the *Cohen* case itself (337 U.S. 541 (1949)), antedate the enactment of §1292(b) in 1958, and possibly for that reason the principles governing the three types of cases have thus far been the same. The recent decisions suggest, however, that the Court may be more rigid in its interpretation of finality under §1291, where §1292(b) may provide the needed flexibility at least in civil cases, than under §1257, where federal-state relationships are properly regarded as significant.[50] The

great waste that could result from protective appeals and litigation over appellate jurisdiction. Earnest pursuit of a 'practical approach' could quickly destroy this accomplishment." 15 C. Wright, A. Miller and E. Cooper, FEDERAL PRACTICE AND PROCEDURE, §3913, p. 523 (1976).

[49]*Abney* v. *United States,* 431 U.S. 651, 658 (1977); *United States* v. *MacDonald,* 435 U.S. 850, 855 (1978); and *Helstoski* v. *Meanor,* 442 U.S. 500 (1979) were criminal cases. *Abney* held that an order denying a pretrial motion to dismiss an indictment on double jeopardy grounds was appealable under the collateral order doctrine, but *MacDonald* refused to extend *Abney* to a pretrial order denying a defendant's speedy trial claim. *Helstoski,* in denying mandamus, stated that appeal from dismissal of an indictment to enforce the commands of the Speech or Debate Clause of the Constitution would have been appropriate.

[50]This difference in approach is illustrated by the Court's treatment in recent decisions of *Gillespie* v. *United States Steel Corp.,* 379 U.S. 148 (1964). *Gillespie,* in order to resolve "an unsettled issue of national significance" as to the exclusivity and coverage of a federal statute, had extended the *Cohen* collateral order exception to an order which was not at all collateral, but was fundamental to the further conduct not only of the particular case but of litigation generally on the same subject. That "trouble inheres in

failure of Congress to modify § 1257, which contains the original 1789 language, may be attributable to lack of dissatisfaction with the pragmatic approach which the Supreme Court has followed in interpreting it, to mere inertia, to the failure of anyone to call the matter to the attention of the legislators, or to difficulty in applying the § 1292(b) technique to appeals coming to the United States Supreme Court from state courts.

3.7 The Extraordinary Writs

The extraordinary writs of mandamus, prohibition and certiorari also are means whereby review is obtained of some types of interlocutory orders. Since they take the form of new proceedings filed in the appellate court, they are in one sense an exercise of that court's original jurisdiction, as described in Sec. 1.4, *supra*. In substance, however, they are almost always means of obtaining review of otherwise unappealable orders. The procedure in such cases is as described in Sec. 1.4(b), *supra*.

Historically, mandamus and prohibition were writs used to compel an inferior court or official to perform a nondiscretionary duty,[51] or to confine a court to a lawful exercise of its prescribed jurisdiction. Mandamus was a prayer for an affirmative order; prohibition for a negative one. Since most issues can be framed either affirmatively or negatively, this line was not strictly observed, and most cases seemed to have been characterized as mandamus.[52]

The common law writ of certiorari orders a lower court to certify a record to a higher court for review. Although the discretionary statutory writ of certiorari issued by the Supreme Court

---

Gillespie" was soon noted by leading commentators. 6 J. Moore, FEDERAL PRACTICE, ¶54.43(5) (2d ed., 1975); C. Wright, FEDERAL COURTS, pp. 511–512 (3d ed., 1976); 15 C. Wright, A. Miller and E. Cooper, FEDERAL PRACTICE AND PROCEDURE, §3913 (1976). Subsequently, in *Livesay,* which like *Gillespie* was an appeal from the lower federal courts under §1291, the Court seemed to have effectively devitalized *Gillespie* as an authority, noting that if that case "were extended beyond [its] unique facts . . . §1291 would be stripped of all significance" (437 U.S. at 477, n. 30). Two years later in *American Export Lines, Inc.* v. *Alvez,* 446 U.S. 274 (1980), a §1257 case from a state court, the plurality opinion of four Justices, including Mr. Justice Stevens who had written *Livesay,* twice cited *Gillespie* with approval, emphasizing that "the federal issue, finally decided by the highest court in the State, will survive and require decision regardless of the outcome of future state-court proceedings," and that it would be less costly for the Court to decide the question then than to send the case back with those issues undecided.

[51]The writs could be used against governmental or corporate officers as well as lower courts.

[52]Mandamus is also used to compel a lower court to comply with the mandate of a higher court (*In re Sanford Fork & Tool Co.,* 160 U.S. 247, 255 (1895); *United States* v. *United States District Court,* 334 U.S. 258, 263 (1948)).

of the United States and other supreme courts was doubtless derived from this common law writ, they are not to be confused and do not serve the same function.

With respect to lower courts, the writs were used to compel compliance with mandatory requirements and were often described as a means of correcting jurisdictional error. Such errors often occur early in a litigation, as when a right to trial by jury is denied,[53] when a court is exercising a jurisdiction committed by Congress to another court or to an administrative agency,[54] or when one court exceeds its power in transferring a case to another.[55] The writs in such circumstances were in substance means of reviewing otherwise unappealable interlocutory orders.[56] Indeed, one of the prerequisites to issuance of a writ was a showing that no other means of obtaining relief, such as appeal through the usual channels, was available. *Helstoski* v. *Meanor*, 442 U.S. 500 (1979).

The federal courts, however, have not confined themselves to "an arbitrary and technical definition of 'jurisdiction' " (*Will* v. *United States,* 389 U.S. 90, 95 (1967); *Kerr* v. *United States District Court,* 426 U.S. 394, 402 (1976)). Indeed, on occasion, the line between lack of jurisdiction and abuse of discretion became very faint.[57] In recent years the Supreme Court, concerned that the writs might breach too widely the rule banning interlocutory appeals (*Will, supra* at 96; *Kerr, supra* at 403), has retreated in the direction of the original lack-of-power approach, pointing out in *Will* v. *United States,* 389 U.S. at 98, n. 6:

> "Courts faced with petitions for the peremptory writs must be careful lest they suffer themselves to be misled by labels such as 'abuse of discretion' and 'want of power' into interlocutory review of nonappealable orders on the mere ground that they may be erro-

---

[53]*Beacon Theatres* v. *Westover,* 359 U.S. 500, 511 (1959).

[54]*Ex parte Northern Pacific Railway Co.,* 280 U.S. 142 (1929); *Matter of National Labor Relations Board,* 304 U.S. 486 (1938); *United States Alkali Association* v. *United States,* 325 U.S. 196 (1945).

[55]*Hoffman* v. *Blaski,* 363 U.S. 335 (1960); *Van Dusen* v. *Barrack,* 376 U.S. 612, 615 (1964).

[56]This is recognized in Montana Rule 17(a), which states:

"The institution of such original proceedings in the supreme court is sometimes justified by circumstances of an emergency nature, as when a cause of action or a right has arisen under conditions making due consideration in the trial courts and due appeal to this court an inadequate remedy, or when supervision of a trial court other than by appeal is deemed necessary or proper."

[57]E.g., *LaBuy* v. *Howes Leather Co.,* 352 U.S. 249 (1957). Whether *LaBuy* still has authority is now doubtful. See *Will* v. *Calvert Fire Insurance Co.,* 437 U.S. 655, 665, n. 7 (1978).

neous. 'Certainly Congress knew that some interlocutory orders might be erroneous when it chose to make them nonreviewable.' "

See also *Will* v. *Calvert Fire Insurance Co.,* 437 U.S. 655, 665, n. 7 (1978). The Court has reemphasized "that the writ will issue only in extraordinary circumstances" and

> "that the party seeking issuance of the writ have no other adequate means to attain the relief he desires, . . . and that he satisfy 'the burden of showing that [his] right to issuance of the writ is "clear and indisputable." ' "58

Subsequently, reiterating these limitations, the Court held that mandamus may "rarely, if ever" be used to review "a trial judge's ordering of a new trial." *Allied Chemical Corp.* v. *Daiflon, Inc.,* 449 U.S. _____ (1980).

The difficulty in determining where the Court will draw the line is demonstrated by the *Calvert Fire Insurance* case in which four Justices found that Judge Will's "decision to defer proceedings because of concurrent state court litigation" was a discretionary matter not subject to mandamus (437 U.S. at 665). Four Justices described his action as "depriving *Calvert* of a federal court determination of a legal issue within the exclusive jurisdiction of the federal courts" (*id.* at 677), and the ninth Justice concurred with the first four on different grounds (*id.* at 667–668).

In sum, the writs are occasionally usable in the federal courts to review interlocutory orders in certain circumstances: when a lower court exceeds its power, when no other adequate remedy is available and when the court thinks the matter is of substantial importance.59

A few of the states, notably California, treat writs more hospitably as an accepted method of providing interlocutory review. In California, "the writ is ordinarily allowed whenever

---

58*Kerr* v. *United States District Court,* 426 U.S. at 403. But see *United States* v. *Denson,* 603 F.2d 1143 (CA 5, 1979, *en banc*), holding that if a district court exceeds the scope of its judicial authority, the aggrieved party should be granted the writ almost as a matter of right, and that the district court should not have suspended execution of sentence and placed defendants on probation.

596 J. Moore, FEDERAL PRACTICE, ¶54.43(5), p. 953 (2d ed., 1975), criticizing *Gillespie* (see Sec. 3.6, note 50, *supra*), recognizes that "there comes a point when mental honesty balks in transforming an interlocutory order into a 'final' order"; Moore suggests that the remedy is to use the extraordinary writs instead. That technique for accomplishing the same result would not "pervert" a statute, but it would strain the historical understanding of the purpose and function of the writs, and thereby lead to confusion and misunderstanding. To start afresh, as some states have done, with standards that reflect the factors which justify interlocutory appeals is a better approach to the problem.

the question presented is either of great practical importance in a particular case," as when great hardship would result to the petitioner if he could not appeal until after the final judgment, or "of general importance as a matter of procedural law."[60] In Missouri, where the statutes permit interlocutory appeals in only a few situations, the appellate courts grant writs when the result will be "attractive," which presumably means fair and just.[61] Other states, such as Arizona, Pennsylvania, Tennessee, Vermont and Washington, accomplish substantially the same result by abolishing the writs, at least in name, and establishing a new remedy for reviewing otherwise unappealable orders previously reviewable by a writ or under one of the more modern procedures permitting review of interlocutory orders. In Arizona, the new flexible remedy is called "special action"; in Washington, "discretionary review." Tennessee Rule 10 provides for filing an "application for extraordinary appeal" addressed to the discretion of the appellate court to be exercised

"(1) if the lower court has so far departed from the accepted and usual course of judicial proceedings as to require immediate review, or (2) if necessary for complete determination of the action on appeal as otherwise provided in these rules. The appellate court may issue whatever order is necessary to implement review under this rule."

In Vermont a complaint showing that no adequate remedy is otherwise available may be filed in the Supreme Court or with a justice thereof.

Pennsylvania Appellate Rules 1501–1502, 1511–1513 abolish the writs and also actions for declaratory judgment against government officials and substitute a petition for review of governmental action. The governmental agency (including a lower court) is the respondent unless it is in fact disinterested, in which case the real parties in interest are to be named as respondents.

The effect of such provisions is to eliminate the historical, often technical, restrictions on the use of particular writs, and either to leave the court with unfettered discretion to do what seems right, as in Arizona, or to substitute general standards which concentrate on the practical reasons why allowing review before termination of a case is reasonable in the circumstances,

---

[60]F. James and G. Hazard, CIVIL PROCEDURE, p. 682 (1977).
[61]See D. Tuchler, *Discretionary Interlocutory Review in Missouri: Judicial Abuse of the Writ?*, 40 Missouri L. Rev. 577 (1975).

as in Washington Rule 2.3 quoted in Sec. 3.5(b), *supra*, p. 63. The latter course would be more helpful to the bar, and probably also to other judges.

The application should state the pertinent facts and supporting reasons and be accompanied by copies of any relevant orders or opinions below and other essential parts of the record, and also, if necessary, by affidavits. The judge below is usually the respondent, but in many jurisdictions he need not answer if he does not choose to, but may leave the defense to the opposing parties below. E.g., Delaware Rule 43; Pennsylvania Rules 1513–1516. This is the preferable procedure, since the controversy is really between the original parties and not with the judge. The appellate court may either deny the application without more, request the filing of an answer or briefs, set the case for oral argument or dispose of the proceeding in whatever manner seems appropriate. This is the usual procedure for dealing with applications for writs.

Lawyers must, of course, study the case law in their own jurisdictions to determine to what extent mandamus and the other writs, or substitutes therefor, can be used to obtain appellate review of interlocutory orders. Most jurisdictions, however, are still likely to heed the Supreme Court's admonition in *Kerr* v. *United States District Court,* 426 U.S. 394, 402–403 (1976), that

> "mandamus actions such as the one involved in the instant case 'have the unfortunate consequence of making the [district court] judge a litigant, obliged to obtain personal counsel or to leave his defense to one of the litigants [appearing] before him' in the underlying case. *Bankers Life & Cas. Co.* v. *Holland, supra,* at 384–385, quoting *Ex parte Fahey, supra,* at 260. More importantly, particularly in an era of excessively crowded lower court dockets, it is in the interest of the fair and prompt administration of justice to discourage piecemeal litigation. It has been Congress' determination since the Judiciary Act of 1789 that as a general rule 'appellate review should be postponed . . . until after final judgment has been rendered by the trial court.' *Will* v. *United States, supra,* at 96; *Parr* v. *United States,* 351 U.S. 513, 520–521 (1956). A judicial readiness to issue the writ of mandamus in anything less than an extraordinary situation would run the real risk of defeating the very policies sought to be furthered by that judgment of Congress."

The unreasonableness of strict adherence to the finality statutes in many situations has induced some courts to stretch almost beyond recognition the meaning of the concept of jurisdiction which has been the traditional guideline to the issuance of extraordinary writs, just as the courts have done with such seemingly simple statutory words as "final judgment" or "final decision." The characterization of "the use of extraordinary writs for interlocutory review" as "little less than a perversion of the concept of 'jurisdiction' "[62] even more aptly applies to the interpretation of the statutory word "final" in §§1257 and 1291 to embody the exceptions to finality enumerated in *Cox Broadcasting Corp.* v. *Cohn,* 420 U.S. 469 (1975), and other cases.

Judge-made law in such circumstances, when judges are understandably prone to differ as to how far they can go in disregarding established legal principles or legislative language, is likely to substitute a wavering line of case-by-case law for a standard upon which litigants can rely with some certainty. There would seem to be little excuse for confusion and uncertainty as to such procedural matters as when and how decisions can be appealed. This result can be avoided by the formulation of standards in statutes or rules along the lines proposed in the *Standards Relating to Appellate Courts* or the recent Tennessee rules described in Sec. 3.5(b), *supra.*

3.8 Contempt

A hazardous route for obtaining interlocutory review is deliberately to disobey a nonappealable order and to invite the trial court to impose a sanction for contempt of court which would constitute a separate appealable order. Resort to such a stratagem would be feasible only when the party or lawyer risking punishment could count on leniency because the purpose was to obtain a prompt appellate ruling before the client suffered severe irreparable injury, or when the result of obeying the order would be serious enough to justify running the risk of substantial punishment.

The general rule is that violation of a court order is punishable as contempt even if the order was erroneous; the proper way to attack an order is by appeal, not disobedience. *United States* v. *United Mine Workers,* 330 U.S. 258, 293 (1947); *Maness* v. *Meyers,* 419 U.S. 449, 458–459 (1975); *Walker* v. *Birmingham,* 388 U.S. 307, 313 (1967); 17 Am. Jur.2d *Contempt* §§42–47 (1964). This rule may not apply in some circumstances if the

---

[62]F. James and G. Hazard, CIVIL PROCEDURE, p. 682 (2d ed., 1977).

lower court lacks jurisdiction to issue an order (*In re Green,* 369 U.S. 689 (1962)), but the difficulty in guessing what errors will be deemed jurisdictional makes reliance on this avenue of review dangerous indeed.[63]

A prominent example of such a tactic is Attorney General Bell's refusal to disclose to plaintiffs, in a suit against government officers for damages, the identity of informers to the FBI. When the district court ordered the disclosure of the names, the Government initially sought review both under the collateral order exception to §1291 (see Sec. 3.6, pp. 70–72, *supra*) and through an extraordinary writ authorized by §1651, the All Writs Act. The Second Circuit concluded that only "extraordinary circumstances" or "abuse of discretion" would warrant review of interlocutory discovery orders in the absence of a certification under §1292, and accordingly denied review. *In re United States,* 565 F.2d 19, 22–23 (CA 2, 1977). Thereafter, the Attorney General, believing that the public interest in criminal law enforcement would be seriously impaired if the identity of informants had to be revealed, and that the Second Circuit's adherence to the finality requirement meant that there was no other means for obtaining appellate review before the disclosure of identity, refused to comply with the district court's ruling requiring disclosure in order to obtain a contempt order which could be appealed. He explained that he would, of course, comply with any final appellate determination. The district court thereupon found him in contempt and refused a stay pending appeal, but a stay was granted by a circuit judge, and the finding of contempt was then set aside by the Second Circuit.[64]

Needless to say, such a means of obtaining review of an interlocutory order should only be used *in extremis,* both because the outcome in terms of penalty or sanction cannot be predicted and may be very unpleasant and because no lawyer or party wants to deliberately place himself in the position of disregarding the order of a court.

---

[63]See Annotation, 12 A.L.R.2d 1059 (1950). Professor Wright suggests that the Supreme Court's cases can be reconciled, as establishing "that the validity of an order can be challenged in a contempt proceeding for violation of the order only if there was no opportunity for effective review of the order before it was violated." C. Wright, FEDERAL COURTS, p. 61 (3d ed., 1976).

[64]*Socialist Workers Party* v. *Attorney General,* 458 F. Supp. 895 (S.D. N.Y. 1978), contempt order vacated, 596 F.2d 58 (CA 2, 1979), cert. denied, 444 U.S. 903 (1979). The proposal to allow courts of appeals to hear interlocutory appeals without leave of the trial court (see Sec. 3.5(d), note 43, *supra*) was designed to overcome the Second Circuit's prior decision in this case.

4

The Taking of an Appeal
From the Trial Court

4.1 Background

The taking of an appeal has been converted from a very complicated process to one of the simplest. The practice followed in the federal courts before the United States Supreme Court approved the Federal Rules of Civil Procedure in 1938, and in the Supreme Court itself until its rules were drastically revised in 1954, was an unbelievably cumbersome way of notifying the courts that an appeal was being taken. And the history in the state courts was not dissimilar.

In the federal courts, the appellant was required to submit to the judge of the court from which he was appealing a petition for allowance of appeal, a formal order allowing the appeal, an assignment of errors and a citation.[1] Each of the above papers was to be submitted to the judge, or a judge, of the lower court,

---

[1]The citation was a misleading and useless anachronism. Its function was to notify appellee that the appeal had been taken. But, as used in the United States Supreme Court, it admonished appellee " 'to be and appear in the Supreme Court of the United States' on the day specified and to 'show cause, if any there be, why the judgment rendered against the said appellant . . . should not be corrected, and why speedy justice should not be done to the parties in that behalf.' Inexperienced or timid counsel might well read this admonition as an order to appear in Washington on the day specified or suffer dire consequences, and on one occasion counsel from as far away as California actually appeared in person. In fact, the citation is not intended to compel appellee to do anything, and the words are both meaningless and deceptive." R. Stern and E. Gressman, SUPREME COURT PRACTICE, p. 211 (1st ed., 1950).

preferably the judge who had heard the case. The petition prayed that the judge allow the appeal, and a formal order of allowance was to be attached for his signature. Since appeal was a matter of right, allowance in the main was, or should have been, automatic; if the lower court judge would not sign the order, it could be submitted to an appellate judge.[2]

4.2 The Initial Jurisdictional Documents

The initial jurisdictional documents formerly required have been superseded in most courts, state and federal, for most appeals as of right, by a simple notice of appeal, which merely gives notice that the appellant appeals to the named appellate court from the judgment or a described portion thereof entered on a particular date. The notice usually bears the caption of the case in the trial court. A typical form would be as shown on the following page.

The notice of appeal is the only step necessary to "the validity of the appeal," as Federal Appellate Rule 3(a) and some of the state rules specifically declare. In some states the document bears a different name, but the substance is about the same. It is called a "notice of intent to appeal" in South Carolina, an "appeal" in Connecticut, a "claim of appeal" in Michigan, an "order of appeal" in Maryland and a "petition in error" in Oklahoma. North Carolina Rule 3(a) gives appellant the option of giving oral notice in open court when judgment is entered, with the clerk noting the appeal on the docket sheet, or of filing a written notice of appeal within 10 days after entry of judgment; most appellants do the former. Alabama Rule 3(a) contains a similar provision for criminal appeals. Under Colorado Rule 4(c) the notice of appeal in a criminal case is treated as a request for the appointment of counsel. Vermont Rule 3(b) makes a notice unnecessary when the defendant has been sentenced to death or life imprisonment.

Some states (e.g., New Jersey) require that the name of the judge in the trial court and the names of all counsel and

---

[2]A similar system survived in Tennessee prior to the adoption of the Tennessee Rules of Appellate Procedure in 1979. See J. Sobieski, *The Theoretical Foundations of the Proposed Tennessee Rules of Appellate Procedure*, 45 Tenn. L. Rev. 161, 168–169, 185 (1978).

IN THE [NAME OF TRIAL COURT]
CASE NO. 79–104:

NOTICE OF APPEAL

A.B., Plaintiff-Appellee	) Appeal to the Appellate Court,
	) First District, from the Circuit
v.	) Court of Zeno County, Hon.
C.D., Defendant-Appellant	) Adam Smith, presiding.

Notice is hereby given that C.D., defendant above named, hereby appeals to the (Name of Appellate Court) from the (final judgment or an identified part thereof or the order, describing it) entered in this action on the _____ day of _____.

(S) _____
Attorney for C.D.

_____

(Address)

_____

(Phone Number)

Date _____

---

parties be included in the notice. Minnesota also requires counsel's telephone number. This information is of interest to the appellate judges and of obvious value to the clerk's office. The Oklahoma petition in error contains the items usually found in a notice of appeal plus a brief description of the nature of the case and the decision appealed from, the points of law to be urged, and a brief outline of the relief sought. Oklahoma Rule of Civil Appellate Procedure 1.16. New Hampshire calls for a large amount of additional information for which other states require a separate information statement, and also the attachment of the documents showing the basis for the ruling below and the parties' contentions. Compare form of notice of appeal attached to the New Hampshire Supreme Court rules with Sec. 4.5(d), *infra.*

In most jurisdictions only one copy of the notice of appeal is required to be filed. In some, however, additional copies must be filed to enable the clerk to serve the other parties or the reporter or to file in the appellate court. E.g., Alabama Rule 3(a), (d); Vermont Rule 3(d). A note to the federal rule requests the appellant to furnish the clerk with that number of copies (see p. 85, *infra.* Connecticut requires three copies plus the number needed for service. In Oklahoma four copies must be filed in the Supreme Court and one in the trial court. New Hampshire Rule 5 requires 15 copies, the same as the number for briefs, but the notice includes portions of the record which elsewhere are customarily found in the appendix to appellants' briefs.

Under Texas Rules 354 and 363, appeal is taken by filing a bond for costs on appeal (usually for $500), but a notice of appeal if no bond is required. Indiana Appellate Rule 2(a) requires that a motion to correct errors first be filed in the trial court; the appeal is initiated by filing a "praecipe designating what is to be included in the record" within 30 days of the court's ruling on the motion.

In most jurisdictions the appellant's notice of appeal or equivalent document must be filed with the clerk of the trial court. Notice to the trial court is essential to inform that court that an appeal has been taken from its ruling, to enable it to act on applications for supersedeas or stay, and to enable the clerk to begin to prepare the record for transmission to the reviewing court.

In recent years many jurisdictions have become aware that it is desirable also to notify the reviewing court at the same time. Accordingly, many states now require that a copy also be transmitted to the court to which the appeal is taken. A 1979 amendment to Rule 3(d) of the Federal Appellate Rules contains a similar requirement that a copy of the notice of appeal and the docket entries be transmitted by the district court clerk to the clerk of the court of appeals. In many states the trial court clerk is required to send a copy of the notice to the clerk of the appellate court.[3] In a few states, however, appellant must file the notice in the appellate court as well as in the trial

---

[3]Alabama, Alaska, California, Colorado, Connecticut, Georgia, Illinois, Kentucky, Minnesota, Missouri, Montana, North Dakota, Ohio, Tennessee, Utah, Vermont, Virginia, Washington.

court.[4] One purpose of this in New Jersey is to enable the trial judge to state or amplify the reasons for his decision if he has not already done so. New Jersey Rule 2:5-1. Pennsylvania Rule 1925 also requires the lower court to file a statement of the reasons for its ruling if it has not already done so.

Whether imposing this responsibility upon the trial court clerk reflects a belief that the clerk will be more reliable than appellant's counsel, a desire not to complicate the latter's task or to create confusion as to which filing constitutes the taking of the appeal for jurisdictional purposes, or simply inertia is anyone's guess. Although filing in the trial court should be sufficient for jurisdictional purposes, there would seem to be no good reason why the appellant should not also transmit a copy of the notice of appeal to the appellate court as well. Proof of such filing or transmission could be submitted to the clerk of the trial court along with the filing with him of the notice, or shortly thereafter. Such a procedure would relieve the trial court of a ministerial function without imposing any significant additional burden upon appellant's counsel.

Either procedure makes available to the appellate court information as to the cases which are coming before it and enables it to control their progress and the condition of its docket. The appellate court has ultimate responsibility for insuring that records, transcripts and briefs reach it without undue delay. It can more readily police the performance of these functions, as well as perform its other duties, if an identifying document is on file showing that the case has been appealed to it. See Sec. 4.8, *infra.*

Under the practice still followed in many appellate courts, such information is not available until the appeal is docketed in the appellate court by filing the record (including the notice of appeal) and paying the required fee some time—often many months—after the notice of appeal has been filed in the court below. There is no reason, however, why the appellate court should not be notified before the end of the relatively long period needed for preparing and filing the record.

---

[4]Delaware, Michigan, New Hampshire, New Jersey, Oklahoma (in Supreme Court), Wisconsin. In Delaware the clerk of the Supreme Court sends a copy to the trial court. Delaware Supreme Court Rule 7. Filing may be with the clerk in any of the three counties or the Supreme Court. Rule 10(d). Other papers may be served on each judge individually, with notice to the clerk.

The filing of a timely notice of appeal is generally said to transfer jurisdiction over a case to the appellate court and to divest the trial court of jurisdiction except as to matters in aid of the appeal and of timely motions for reconsideration (as to which see Sec. 4.6, p. 96, *infra*). The theory of this judge-made rule and the exceptions to it are reviewed (as to the federal courts) in 9 J. Moore, *Federal Practice,* ¶203.11 (2d ed., 1980).

4.3 Service of the Notice of Appeal

In the United States courts of appeals (Federal Appellate Rule 3(d)) and many of the states,[5] the clerk of the trial court is required to transmit copies of the notice of appeal to the other parties to the case by mailing them either to counsel or to a party not represented by counsel. In some states a copy must also be served on the reporter responsible for transcribing the oral proceedings below, with a designation of the parts of the record to be transcribed.[6] In a criminal case appealed by counsel on behalf of the defendant, the clerk also serves a copy on the defendant himself. (Federal Appellate Rule 3(d).) This imposes on the clerk the chore of making copies of the notice, ascertaining from his files or from appellant the names and addresses of the other parties to the case, enclosing the notices in envelopes, and mailing them to the parties. In Vermont, appellant is required to furnish the clerk with enough copies. In other states, the clerk may ask appellant to furnish the needed additional copies. The Note attached to the form of notice of appeal appended to the Federal Appellate Rules as Form 1 stated that

> "Counsel for the appellant is requested to furnish the clerk of the district court with a sufficient number of copies of the original notice to permit the clerk to serve a copy on each party other than the appellant."

In other states and in the United States Supreme Court (Rule 10.2), the notice of appeal must be served by the appellant. In most of these states proof of such service must be filed with the trial court clerk at the same time as the notice of ap-

---

[5]Alabama, Arizona, Arkansas, Kentucky, Missouri, Montana, North Dakota, Ohio, Rhode Island, Vermont.
[6]Idaho Rule 17(H); Oregon Rule 2.05(k).

peal.[7] The latter system has the disadvantage that at the time of service appellant may not know and cannot tell the parties being served the precise date upon which a mailed notice will be filed. That date can be noted on a copy of the notice served by the clerk, as Federal Appellate Rule 3(d) and the state rules modeled upon it require. Apart from that, there appears to be no good reason for placing the burden of serving the notice upon the trial court clerk rather than upon appellant. The failure of many states and the federal rules applicable to the United States courts of appeals, but not to the United States Supreme Court (although both were promulgated by the Supreme Court at about the same time), to require notices of appeal to be served in the same way as other papers may be a matter of tradition or inertia and not a considered preference.[8]

Illinois Supreme Court Rule 303(d) provides for service by the appellant on all other parties both of the notice of appeal and notice of the date of filing no later than seven days *after* the filing, with proof of such service to be filed with the clerk within seven days of service, and adds that "[n]o action shall be taken until it is filed." This both relieves the clerk of the burden of serving all other parties to all appeals and informs the other parties of the date of filing the appeal before any other action is taken. It best avoids the disadvantages of other methods of serving the notice of appeal. Tennessee's 1979 Rule 5(a) contains a similar provision, which also requires appellant to serve a copy on the appellate court clerk together with the names and addresses of all parties or their counsel. Pennsylvania Rule 906 requires appellant to send a copy to the judge below and the court reporter if evidence need be transcribed.

---

[7]Delaware, Idaho, Illinois, Iowa, Kansas, Michigan, Minnesota, Nevada, New Mexico, North Carolina, Oklahoma, Oregon, Pennsylvania, South Dakota, Utah, Wisconsin. In Minnesota, service of the notice constitutes the taking of the appeal; the notice must be filed with the trial court clerk within five days, with the fee and the cost bond. In Wisconsin the filing of the notice of appeal constitutes a certification that the notice has been served on the other parties. This is the rule for the service of all papers, under the Wisconsin Rules of Civil Procedure. Vermont Rule 25(c) is similar.

[8]The explanation of why the trial court clerk serves the notice of appeal but not other documents may be historical. Appeals, or some kinds of appeals, were regarded as new actions in the appellate court, so that the initial document was regarded as having the status of a summons in a case filed in the trial court. Summonses and complaints are customarily served upon defendants by the sheriff or marshal in the belief that this provides greater assurance that the defendants will actually receive the papers—even though fictitious or "sewer" service by such officials is not unknown. But there is no reason to think that court clerks are more careful than counsel or that a notice of appeal mailed by a court clerk will be more likely to be received than when delivered or mailed by an appellant's lawyer.

Perhaps a criminal defendant not represented by an attorney—if there still are any after *Gideon* v. *Wainwright*, 372 U.S. 335 (1963), and its statutory and other progeny—cannot be counted on to serve the prosecuting attorney. But with counsel now available to indigent defendants through the initial appeal, this is also highly improbable. With that possible exception, there does not seem to be any compelling reason for not having a notice of appeal, like all other appellate documents, served by the appellant instead of by the court clerk.

4.4 Fees

In civil cases the appellant is customarily required to pay a docketing fee for taking an appeal. In the United States courts of appeals the docketing fee prescribed by the Judicial Conference is $65.[9] In addition, under 28 U.S.C. §1917, a $5 fee must be paid the district court clerk for filing the notice of appeal. In the United States Supreme Court, the fee for docketing an appeal or petition for certiorari is $200, plus $100 more if oral argument is permitted.[10] The amount varies in the different states.[11] These fees need not be paid by persons who qualify as indigents or are otherwise exempted by law, such as governmental bodies, agencies or officers.

In many jurisdictions the fees must be paid to the clerk of the appellate court when the case is docketed in that court,[12] which usually means when the record is filed in that court. Others require the fee to be paid to the clerk of the trial court[13] when the notice of appeal is filed there. The clerk of the trial court then forwards the fee to the clerk of the appellate court.[14] This seems to be the modern trend, reflected in the recent revision of the Federal Rules of Appellate Procedure. Prior to July 1, 1979, those rules required the appellant's fee to be paid when the record was filed in the court of appeals. New Rule 3(e) provides for payment of the required fees to the clerk of the district court at the time of the filing of the notice of appeal.

---

[9]E.g., Seventh Circuit Rule 26(1).
[10]See Supreme Court Rule 45. The 1980 revision of the rules doubled the prior fees.
[11]E.g., $20—Idaho, Missouri, Nebraska; $25—Oklahoma, Oregon, Wisconsin, Wyoming; $30—Arizona; $50—California. In Oregon, *respondent* must pay a fee of $15.
[12]E.g., Alabama, Alaska, Arizona, Colorado, Illinois, Kansas, Kentucky, New Hampshire.
[13]E.g., California, Connecticut, Minnesota, Pennsylvania, Wisconsin.
[14]E.g., California, Minnesota, Pennsylvania, Wisconsin.

In the few jurisdictions where no additional time is allowed to cross-appeal (see Sec. 4.7, *infra*), a few extra days for paying the fee by the initial appellant would be appropriate, so that he can withdraw his appeal without cost if he learns that no appeal is being taken by another party. Alabama permits the fee to be paid within 14 days after the filing of a notice of appeal, which would take care of this.

4.5   Papers to Accompany the Initial Document

Some states require that other papers be filed with the notice of appeal or other initial document.

(a)   The Bond for Appeal

Some states (Connecticut, North Dakota, Texas) require the bond for costs on appeal to be filed with the notice of appeal, as did the federal courts of appeals before the 1979 revision of the Federal Rules of Appellate Procedure. As to the substance of this requirement, see Sec. 4.11(a), *infra*.

(b)   Designations of the Record; Ordering of Transcript

In some states the designation of the portions of the record which the appellant believes to be relevant to the appeal must be filed with the notice of appeal[15] or within a short time thereafter.[16] In Connecticut, Idaho, Michigan and North Dakota the notice must be accompanied by proof or acknowledgment that the transcript (if any is needed) has been ordered from the court reporter. In most jurisdictions, however, these steps may be taken a prescribed number of days after the filing of the notice of appeal. The requirements with respect to filing the record and the transcript, and for reproducing additional copies of the relevant or essential parts thereof, are described at greater length in Chapter 6, *infra*. In many jurisdictions, including the federal (see Federal Appellate Rule 10(b)(3)), if the appellant does not include the entire transcript in the record, he must

---

[15]Alaska, Arkansas, Connecticut, Delaware, Georgia, Idaho, Nebraska, Oklahoma, Oregon, Washington. In Indiana the designation (praecipe) is the equivalent of the notice of appeal. Indiana Appellate Rule 2.
[16]See Sec. 6.2, p. 163, *infra*.

serve appellee with a statement of the issues he intends to present on the appeal.

(c) Assignment of Errors

An assignment of errors had been one of the numerous documents long required for the taking of an appeal. Since errors not listed could not subsequently be raised, counsel were careful to include every possible point, stated in every possible way, and the assignments were frequently long, overlapping and repetitive. Thereafter, only the relatively few issues deemed meritorious after research and more careful consideration were included in the briefs.

The original purpose, of course, had been both to give appellee notice of the points he must meet on the appeal and to advise the appellate court of the questions to be considered. Recognition that the long list of assignments filed in advance of the appellant's brief was deceptive in those respects and did not actually present the points which appellants would argue led to its elimination from most modern appellate systems.[17] The statement of the questions presented at the beginning of the brief gives the appellee and the appellate court sufficient notice. See Sec. 7.18, *infra.*

A few states still require an assignment of errors or its equivalent at some stage of the proceeding. The "motion to correct errors" to be filed with the trial court under Indiana Rule 2 before appealing is in substance an assignment of errors, though addressed to the trial court in time to perform the function of a petition for reconsideration. In Georgia, under Rules 24–3614 and 4514, an "enumeration of errors" must be filed in all cases not more than 20 days after docketing. North Carolina Rule 10(c) requires the assignments to appear at the conclusion of the record on appeal; each assignment is to be followed by a list of all the exceptions on which it is based, identified by number and record reference. As indicated in the preceding subsection and at greater length in Sec. 6.3, *infra*, under Federal

---

[17]Connecticut recently abolished the assignment of errors, but substituted a "preliminary statement of the issues to be presented," which could be amended as of right up to the time of filing the brief. Connecticut Practice Book, §3012. This resembles the similar requirement in some information statements, as described in the following subsection.

Appellate Rule 10(b)(3) and the rules of many states a statement of the issues must be filed by the appellant at the time he submits his designation of the portion of the transcript to be included in the record if less than the entire transcript is called for. As indicated in the following subsection, the information statement required by an increasing number of jurisdictions also frequently must include the issues presented.

(d)   Information Statement

The American Bar Association's *Standards Relating to Appellate Courts* recommends (Sec. 3.13(c), p. 31) that

> "An appellant should be required upon filing the notice of appeal to complete a form supplied by the appellate court setting forth information necessary to facilitate processing the appeal."[18]

A number of appellate courts now require the appellant to file with the notice of appeal or shortly thereafter an information statement, variously described as "docketing statement" (new Illinois Rule 303(g), Wyoming Rule 2.03, Tenth Circuit Rule 8),[19] "civil appeal statement" (Washington Rule 5.5), "statement of appeal" (Kentucky Rule 76.06) and "skeleton transcript" (New Mexico Rule 6(a)), containing facts which will assist the reviewing court in classifying and administering the appeal.[20] In New Hampshire the information is to be included in the notice of appeal as shown on the prescribed form. The Oklahoma petition in error and the Oregon notice of appeal call for much of the same information, including the points to be raised. To be stated are such things as the critical dates of the judgment below and any postdecision motion for reconsideration or the like and any order entered thereon, the jurisdictional basis for appeal to the particular appellate court, the substance of the judgment below and the relief sought, the facts as to cross-appeals, bonds, bail,

---

[18]See also American Bar Association Task Force on Appellate Procedure, EFFICIENCY AND JUSTICE IN APPEALS: METHODS AND SELECTED MATERIALS, pp. 43–44, 46–47, 73 (1967).

[19]Fifth Circuit Rule 11.4 provides for a joint docketing statement in proceedings for the review of orders of the Federal Energy Regulatory Commission which shall list the issues to be raised, and any other review proceedings pending in any other court as to the same order, and append copies of the order to be reviewed.

[20]In New York such a statement is to be prefixed to the record. New York Civil Practice Act, §5531. In Minnesota such a statement must be filed prior to the prehearing conference now required in all civil cases. Supreme Court of Minnesota Order of September 10, 1976, prescribing prehearing conference procedures (addendum to Minnesota Rule of Civil Appellate Procedure 133.02).

stay, reasons to advance the hearing, whether oral argument is requested or waived, and the names, addresses and telephone numbers of all parties and their attorneys and the court reporter. In some states the other parties have a specific number of days to respond. In Washington they must file, within seven days, their answers, correcting errors, presenting any additional issues and making any necessary modifications.

These statements serve a number of purposes. The information as to the names of the parties and of all affiliated corporations, such as Fourth Circuit Rule 17 and Illinois Rule 303(g) now require, will enable the judges of the appellate court to determine whether they should disqualify themselves from the particular case. See *Standards Relating to Appellate Courts*, p. 35; amended United States Supreme Court Rule 28.1 (Nov. 21, 1980). Prior appeals in the same litigation, related cases and pending cases raising the same questions should be identified to enable the court to determine whether several cases should be heard together or assigned to the same panel. Identifying the type of action and the issues can also help in this respect.

The facts bearing on the status of the record should be set forth. New Mexico Rules 6(a)(6) and 7(f) require that the appellant file certificates of the clerk and the reporter that the clerk's record and the reporter's transcript have been ordered with "satisfactory arrangements" for payment. The new Illinois form calls for not only the identity of the reporter and his address and phone number but the approximate duration of the proceeding to be transcribed. The *Standards Relating to Appellate Courts* recommends (p. 35) that the statement include

> "a certificate by the appellant that the preparation of the record has been duly requested of the court reporter and trial court clerk.[21] A party to an appeal should be authorized to request the appellate court to exercise special supervision of preparation of a record that is unusually extensive."

Some rules do and some do not require the information statement to contain a concise statement of the material facts, the questions presented on the appeal and the supporting au-

---

[21]Illinois Rule 303(g) requires such a certificate. The First District Appellate Court also "requires the appellant's attorney to list the dates of the proceedings to be transcribed, and the names of the court reporters who will transcribe them," and to obtain the signature of the supervising court reporter showing that an appropriate deposit or indigency order has been received. This aids the court in determining whether delays are caused by court personnel. M. Bennett, *The New and Amended Illinois Supreme Court Rules and Appellate Practice in the First District Appellate Court,* 62 Chi. Bar Rec. 20, 24 (1980).

thorities (but without additional argument). The Wyoming rule requires that the statement include each of these items; the Tenth Circuit calls for the questions and the material facts.[22] The form suggested in *Efficiency and Justice in Appeals* (p. 44) would also include them "if the court is in fact going to use [such information] for some preliminary or screening purpose."

The *Standards Relating to Appellate Courts* (p. 36) states that "[t]he information form should not require reference to the questions or authorities to be presented on appeal, for if it does the litigants will feel obliged to regard it as a preliminary brief" —or, I add, as the equivalent of the earlier assignment of errors. To avoid this difficulty, at least in part, the Tenth Circuit rule prefaces its enumeration of the items to be included in the docketing statement with the following admonition:

> "Rule 8(b). The docketing statement is used by the Court in making a calendar assignment pursuant to local Rule 10.[23] The docketing statement is not a brief and should not contain argument or procedural motions. Although the appellant or petitioner is not limited to the issues presented in the docketing statement, effort should be made to include all the issues which will be presented to the Court."

New Hampshire Rule 16(3)(a) permits the raising of questions in the brief not listed in the notice of appeal so long as they are presented by the record.

The form of docketing statement prescribed in Illinois' new (1979) Rule 303(g) calls for a brief (usually checked-off) indication of the general subject of the case (e.g., contract, personal injury, domestic relations) and of its nature and the result below (with reasons for an expedited schedule, if requested), and a "General Statement of Issues Proposed to be Raised," to which is added the important qualification:

> "Failure to include an issue in this statement will not result in the waiver of the issue on appeal."

Disclosure of the nature of the case, the issues, the critical facts and even the principal authorities relied on should aid in classifying the appeal for a number of purposes. Such disclosures permit classification of the case with related cases or assignment to a particular panel familiar with the subject, and

---

[22]Rule 8(c)(4)(5).

[23]Under Tenth Circuit Rule 10 the chief judge assigns each case to one of three calendars for briefing and arguing.

provide knowledge useful in determining whether the issues can be simplified or the case settled in a pretrial conference and whether and how long oral argument should be allowed or whether summary disposition is appropriate. Bennett, *supra* note 21, at 22. It may also enable the appellate court to take steps to expedite the completion of the record and the scheduling of briefs and oral argument. Preparation of such statements on court-approved forms should not be difficult for counsel, and it may be extremely helpful to the appellate court in these and other respects. This modern innovation is a means whereby appellate courts can improve their administration if appeals are brought before them when or soon after they are initially filed.

Many appellate courts obtain some of the information appearing in information statements through the notice of appearance which counsel are often required to file with or shortly after the docketing of the case or the filing of the first document in the appellate court. E.g., Third Circuit Rule 9; Fifth Circuit Rule 5; Seventh Circuit Rule 5(a). This identifies counsel by name, address, and telephone number and also preferably firm name, and in addition gives the name of the party or parties represented. Obviously, in his own interest counsel should apprise the clerk of the appellate court of this information as soon as possible after the appeal is taken whether or not a rule so requires. Under 1980 Seventh Circuit Rule 5(b) the appearance must be accompanied by a "certificate of interest" naming all attorneys who have appeared or are expected to appear in the case, the party or *amicus* represented and any parent corporation.

4.6 Time to Appeal

The time for taking appeals from judgments in civil cases to the United States courts of appeals and to the appellate courts in approximately 30 of the states is 30 days (Utah, one month), usually computed from the day of entry of the judgment below. In South Carolina the time runs from the date of receiving notice of the judgment; in Missouri, from the time the judgment becomes final (usually 30 days later, after post-trial motions are due); and in California, from the date of mailing or of serving notice of the entry of judgment, whichever is earlier.[24]

---

[24]A third alternative in California is 180 days after entry of the judgment, if earlier.

The time allowed, when other than 30 days, appears in the following list:

10 days—Mississippi, Missouri, North Carolina, South Carolina;
15 days—Wyoming;
20 days—Connecticut, Michigan, Rhode Island;
42 days—Alabama, Idaho;
45 days—New Jersey;
60 days—California, South Dakota;
90 days—Minnesota, North Dakota, Wisconsin.

In Virginia the notice of appeal must be filed in 30 days (Rule 5:6), but the appellant has three months to file his petition for appeal (Rule 5:24). The Federal Appellate Rules, Massachusetts and Montana allow 60 days if the government or an officer or agency is a party. Less time is allowed in some states for interlocutory appeals.[25]

In many states the time in criminal cases is the same. Federal Appellate Rule 4(b) allows only 10 days for appeals by criminal defendants but 30 days by the Government, and a number of states follow this pattern. Michigan and Minnesota, however, allow more time in criminal cases, 60 days in Michigan and 180 in Minnesota.[26]

These periods govern the filing of the notice of appeal or equivalent document. The first day counted is the day after the judgment is filed in the lower court. If the period ends on a Saturday, Sunday or holiday, days on which the clerks' offices are usually closed, the time is extended to the next day on which the office is open.[27] In the United States Supreme Court, the Clerk's Office remains open on Saturday morning, so that papers can be filed in that Court on Saturday. Rule 1.2.

In some states but not all, the trial court or appellate court may extend the time for taking appeals for specified or unspecified periods. In the United States Supreme Court, for the

---

[25]E.g., Alabama, Delaware, New Jersey.

[26]Wisconsin Rule 809.30(1) provides that in felony cases defendant shall file his notice of appeal or motion seeking post-conviction relief within 30 days of service of the transcript, that the trial court shall act on the latter within 60 days or it shall be deemed denied, and that defendant shall file his appeal from the judgment of conviction and the order on post-conviction relief within 10 days of the latter. The appeal will, thereafter, be governed by the civil appeals rules. This procedure for combining appeals from the conviction and the post-conviction order is designed to speed up the ultimate disposition of criminal cases.

[27]Hawaii, Kentucky, New Mexico, North Dakota, South Carolina.

few cases which still come to that Court by direct appeal, no extension of time for the filing of a notice of appeal may be granted, even though a 60-day extension may be obtained for the filing of the more significant jurisdictional statement, as it can for civil petitions for certiorari.[28] Since a notice of appeal is simpler to prepare than a motion for extension of time, ordinarily there would be little need for obtaining an extension. If counsel is in doubt whether to appeal, he can file a notice out of abundance of caution and withdraw it or dismiss the appeal if necessary thereafter.

Some flexibility is desirable, however, when unexpected circumstances interfere with timely filing. Federal Rule of Appellate Procedure 4(a)(5), as revised in 1979, provides for an extension "upon a showing of excusable neglect or good cause"; the application must be filed before or no later than 30 days after the expiration of the prescribed time. Any extension granted shall not go beyond the 30 days "or 10 days from the date of entry of the order granting the motion, whichever occurs later." If the motion is filed before expiration of the prescribed time, it may be *ex parte,* but otherwise notice must be given to other parties. The primary purpose of this provision is to deal with emergencies which cannot be foreseen, such as death or sudden illness of counsel, a post-office strike or other failure, snow storms, floods, or other disasters which prevent a document from reaching the clerk's office in time. In view of the ease of preparing a notice of appeal, extensions were not thought necessary for the ordinary anticipatable excuses, such as the pressure of work or another case. A number of states have similar provisions,[29] which allow all of the flexibility needed as a practical matter. In some, however, the only excuse recognized is failure to know of the entry of the judgment. (Kansas Stat. Ann. §60-2103.) The problem of postal delay can be avoided by allowing the date of mailing to count as the date of filing, as a number of courts, including the United States Supreme Court, now do for briefs. That Court's Rule 28.2 applies to all documents to be filed with its Clerk, including Jurisdictional Statements in direct appeals but not the notices of appeal to be filed in the lower court. See Sec. 7.40, *infra.*

---

[28]Supreme Court Rules 11.4, 12.2, 20.2; 28 U.S.C. §2101(c). In criminal cases the time for applying for certiorari may be extended 30 days.

[29]E.g., Colorado Rule 10.4(a); Kentucky Rule 73.02(b). Nevada, however, rejected the federal type of extension as "unnecessary and undesirable." (Note to Nevada Rule of Appellate Procedure 4.)

Either as a matter of statute, rule or common law,[30] the time does not run during the pendency of a timely petition for rehearing or reconsideration, or a motion for judgment notwithstanding the verdict, or to amend a judgment or findings of fact or for a new trial. The time begins to run again after the lower court's action on such a petition or motion. In 1980 the Supreme Court of the United States held that a motion for a new trial on some issues rendered nonfinal the trial court's disposition of all issues and therefore extended the time to appeal. *Washington* v. *Confederated Tribes,* 447 U.S. 134, 149, n. 24 (1980). To the same effect see Supreme Court Rules 11.3 and 20.4. Federal Appellate Rule 4(a)(4), as revised in 1979, makes it clear that "a notice of appeal filed before the disposition of any of the above motions shall have no effect," and that a new notice of appeal must be filed from the order disposing of the motion, though without additional fees. Even without such an explicit rule, this sensible procedure should be followed.

Even in the absence of a timely petition or motion to change the judgment below, the time to take an appeal begins to run anew if the lower court actually changes the judgment—at least in a significant respect—as the result of an untimely petition or motion or otherwise. Indeed, if the lower court affirmatively allows an untimely petition or motion to be filed and considers its merits—instead of simply denying it—the effect will be to toll the time for taking an appeal in the United States Supreme Court.[31]

Whether, to have such an effect, a change in the judgment must relate to the part of the judgment from which the appeal is taken is not clear. Perhaps inconsistently with *Confederated Tribes, Federal Trade Commission* v. *Minneapolis Honeywell Co.,* 344 U.S. 206 (1952), held that the time to appeal from a completely separate and unchanged part of a judgment will not be tolled. A different result was reached when the two parts of the judgment were found to be "inextricably linked." *United States* v. *Adams,* 383 U.S. 39, 41–42 (1966).

Notices of appeal or equivalent papers indicating that an appeal has been taken are sometimes filed before the entry of the appealable judgment or order in the lower court. This oc-

---

[30]E.g., Federal Appellate Rule 4(a)(4); Kansas Stat. Ann. §60-2103; Kentucky Rule 73.02; Maine Rule 73. See *United States* v. *Healy,* 376 U.S. 75, 77–78 (1964); *Communist Party* v. *Whitcomb,* 414 U.S. 441, 445–446 (1974). Virginia, however, permits an extension only when the judgment is modified.

[31]*Bowman* v. *Loperena,* 311 U.S. 262, 266 (1941); R. Stern and E. Gressman, SUPREME COURT PRACTICE, p. 399 (5th ed., 1978).

curs most frequently when the trial court has orally announced
its decision or embodied it in a written opinion or ruling which
is to be followed by formal entry of the order or judgment. The
orthodox treatment of such appeals is to dismiss them because
of the absence of an appealable order. That means that a fresh
appeal must be taken as soon as the order or judgment is actually entered.

A few states[32] and a 1979 modification of Federal Appellate
Rule 4(a)(2) make the filing of a second notice of appeal unnecessary. In those jurisdictions a premature notice of appeal is
to be regarded as filed immediately after the appealable judgment or order has been noted, either on the same day or the
next day. This avoids proceedings to dismiss the appeal, opinions dealing with that inconsequential and unnecessary issue,[33]
and the need for taking an appeal identical with the first except
for the date of the judgment or order appealed from. As the
Tennessee and federal rules recognize, such provisions do not
apply when a post-trial motion extending the time to appeal is
filed after the notice of appeal; in that circumstance, the prior
notice of appeal becomes ineffective.[34]

4.7 Cross-Appeals and Cross-Petitions

(a) Additional Time for Cross-Appeals

The rules of most states, the Federal Appellate Rules and
the rules of the Supreme Court of the United States, as recently
revised, allow any party other than the original appellant an
additional number of days after the filing of the first notice of
appeal to file his own notice of appeal. If filed by the opposing
party, this is called a cross-appeal or cross-petition.[35] Fourteen

---

[32]California Rule 2(c); Kansas Rule 2.03; Missouri Rule 81.05; Ohio Rule of Appellate
Procedure 4; Tennessee Rule 4(d); Washington Rule 5.2(g); Wyoming Rule 2.01.

[33]Cf. *Foman* v. *Davis*, 371 U.S. 178 (1962).

[34]The courts of appeals seem to be in conflict as to whether any effect can be given
a notice of appeal filed after the filing of a post-trial motion. *Century Laminating, Ltd.* v.
Montgomery, 595 F.2d 563 (CA 10, 1979), cert. granted, 444 U.S. 897 (1979), writ
dismissed as improvidently granted, 444 U.S. 987 (1979). The conflicting decisions are
cited in the Tenth Circuit opinion.

[35]When both parties have appealed, the problem is presented as to which is to be
deemed the appellant with respect to the briefing schedule and the right to open and
close the oral argument. In the federal courts of appeals (Federal Appellate Rule 28(h))
and some states the plaintiff below is treated as the appellant. In other states the first
party to appeal is (Connecticut, Iowa). This is always subject to rearrangement by
"stipulation" or court order, usually so as to insure that the principal loser below is
treated as the appellant. In some states this is determined on a case-by-case basis by the
court or a court official.

days is allowed by Federal Appellate Rule 4(a)(3), 30 days by Supreme Court Rules 12.4 and 19.5. Most of the states allow from 5 to 30 days,[36] though some allow no extra time. A few states, on the other hand, permit the appellee to raise any issues in his brief without filing a separate or cross-appeal at all.[37] Illinois Rule 303(a) allows 10 days to cross-appeal to the Appellate Court, but Rule 318(a) makes cross-appeals unnecessary in appeals "by whatever method from the Appellate Court to the Supreme Court." Any party "may seek and obtain any relief warranted by the record on appeal."

If any separate appeal at all is required where no additional time is authorized, as under Oklahoma Court of Appeals Rule 1.18, a party who does not wish to appeal unless his opponent does must file his appeal within the time prescribed for appeals generally. This is not particularly difficult if only a notice of appeal must be filed in time, since that document is simple to prepare and can, if necessary, be withdrawn or the appeal dismissed by the cross-appellant, if the other party fails to appeal. If, however, a fee must be paid or record designated or filed at the same time as the notice, the taking of the cross-appeal becomes more burdensome. And if, as in the United States Supreme Court before its 1980 rules revision,[38] the jurisdictional document is not merely a notice of appeal but a petition for review or similar paper, which requires careful preparation, the filing of a cross-appeal or petition unnecessarily without waiting to see if the opponent files his own petition can be expensive and costly, at least if the lawyers are to be paid for their work.

If any separate appeal is required, allowing additional time for the taking of an appeal by any other party has advantages for both parties and the court. Often a party who has not prevailed in every respect is nevertheless willing to accept a ruling below if his opponent does, but not otherwise. If the latter appeals from a portion of the judgment, the former may wish to be able to challenge other portions of the ruling below in the appellate court. If the deadline for filing his appeal is the same as for his opponent, he is faced with several unsatisfactory alternatives:

---

[36]Five days—Iowa; 10 days—Connecticut, Illinois, Indiana, Kentucky, Maryland, Utah (from designation or stipulation of record); 14 days—Idaho, Pennsylvania, Washington; 15 days—Delaware; 20 days—Michigan; 30 days—Wisconsin.

[37]Indiana, Nebraska, Tennessee.

[38]Until the 1980 revision, the United States Supreme Court's rules allowed no additional time to cross-petition or cross-appeal.

(1) He can wait to see if his opponent appeals. If, as many lawyers do, the latter acts at the last moment, the cross-appellant may not have time to file his cross-appeal unless he or a member of his staff waits at the clerk's desk with a notice of appeal ready to file until expiration of the opponent's time to appeal, or any extension thereof.

(2) He may ask his opponent whether he intends to appeal or to let him know when he makes up his mind. But some lawyers do not fully trust their adversaries, sometimes with reason, and, apart from that, may not wish to tip their hands before they have to. And opponents may not finally decide until the last minute.

(3) He can proceed to file an appeal without waiting until the last minute, and then withdraw it if the opponent has not appealed.

For the lawyer who dares not risk relying entirely on what his adversary tells him as to the latter's intent to appeal, these alternatives require the preparation and even the filing of unnecessary papers, as well as perhaps even an undignified vigil at the clerk's office until the time for the opponent to file has expired. For the court it means that unnecessary papers may be filed and perhaps withdrawn, which may necessitate wasteful motions and court orders as well as paperwork by the clerk's office. All of this can be avoided if a cross-appeal is allowed to be filed after the initial appeal, as most jurisdictions now permit.

(b) When a Cross-Appeal Is Necessary

A lawyer often has doubts as to whether a cross-appeal is necessary. The trial court may have decided the case wholly or partly in his favor, but rejected some of his contentions or not mentioned them. Suppose he wins on everything but interest, costs or attorney's fees? Or obtains a judgment for 95 percent of the amount prayed for, and the defendant appeals?

The general rule, followed by the federal courts and most states, is that a party must file a separate appeal or cross-appeal if he seeks to change the judgment below or any part thereof.

> "Unless he takes a cross appeal . . . the appellee may not attack the decree with a view either to enlarging his own rights thereunder or of lessening the rights of his adversary, whether what he seeks is to correct an error or to supplement the decree with

respect to a matter not dealt with below. But it is likewise settled that the appellee may, without taking a cross-appeal, urge in support of a decree any matter appearing in the record, although his argument may involve an attack upon the reasoning of the lower court or an insistence upon matter overlooked or ignored by it."[39]

This principle makes sense since it does not require a party to appeal when he is satisfied with what the court has ordered. He need not—indeed he cannot—appeal merely because of dissatisfaction with what the court has said or not said, or how it has reasoned, if there is no part of the court's order to which he objects. On the other hand, a party may without a cross-appeal present any argument in support of the judgment challenged by his adversary even if the court below has rejected or not dealt with the contention.[40]

A cross-appeal is necessary with respect to each separate claim or part of a judgment, even for such incidental items as interest, costs and attorney's fees.[41] A cross-appeal may be necessary to challenge the same provision of the judgment as is involved in the initial appeal. If a defendant attacks a judgment for $100,000 because it is too high or not warranted at all, the plaintiff must file a cross-appeal if he wants the appellate court to hold that the amount was too low, and that he is entitled to more. A single sum may embody awards as to a number of claims, each of which would require a separate appeal.

In the federal courts, exceptions to the governing doctrine appear in the case law, although sometimes without recognition that the court is creating an exception, or any statement of reasons for doing so. Thus, without explanation, appellees have been barred in the absence of a cross-appeal from raising defenses of improper venue[42] or statute of limitations.[43] The Supreme Court has also held that a cross-appeal is necessary when

---

[39]*Massachusetts Mut. Life Ins. Co.* v. *Ludwig*, 426 U.S. 479, 480–481 (1976); *United States* v. *American Ry. Exp. Co.*, 265 U.S. 425, 435 (1924). See also R. Stern and E. Gressman, SUPREME COURT PRACTICE, Sec. 6.34 (5th ed., 1978); R. Stern, *When to Cross Appeal or Cross Petition—Certainty or Confusion?*, 87 Harv. L. Rev. 763 (1974).

[40]See R. Stern and E. Gressman, SUPREME COURT PRACTICE, Sec. 6.34 (5th ed., 1978); 5 Am. Jur.2d *Appeal and Error*, pp. 153–154 (1962).

[41]9 J. Moore, FEDERAL PRACTICE, ¶204.11(3) (2d ed., 1980).

[42]*United States* v. *American Ry. Exp. Co.*, 265 U.S. 425, 435 (1924), explaining *Peoria and Pekin Ry. Co.* v. *United States*, 263 U.S. 528, 536 (1924).

[43]*Alaska Industrial Board* v. *Chugach Electric Association*, 356 U.S. 320, 324–325 (1958); *Tallman* v. *Udall*, 324 F.2d 411, 417–418 (CA DC, 1963), rev'd on other grounds, 380 U.S. 1 (1965).

the rationale of an argument would entitle a nonappealing party to more than the judgment gave him, even though he was not asking for anything more and was willing to accept the judgment as entered.[44] Whether a case falls within this category will frequently be not at all clear, so that cautious attorneys might often appeal unnecessarily. These unexplained exceptions have trapped able lawyers who were unaware of them. At least when no additional time is allowed for a cross-appeal, they impose unnecessary burdens of appealing on a party satisfied with the judgment below. The distinctions between the situations thus treated as exceptions and cases following the general rule do not warrant a difference in result. Adherence to the general doctrine is desirable not only because it makes better sense but also because it avoids confusion and unfairness.[45]

The more recent Supreme Court decisions seem to be moving in this direction,[46] but it is not at all clear that the exceptions referred to have been abandoned. Cautious counsel should, therefore, act accordingly and consider whether filing a conditional cross-appeal or cross-petition might be advisable. *Helstoski* v. *Meanor,* 442 U.S. 500 (1979).

All of these complications can be avoided if cross-appeals are never required and all questions can be presented by any party once a notice of appeal has been filed. "The result of eliminating any requirement that an appellee file his own notice of appeal is that once any party files a notice of appeal the appellate court may consider the case as a whole."[47] The reporter for the Commission which drafted the new Tennessee rules justified dispensing with a notice of cross-appeal on the

---

[44]For example, in *Strunk* v. *United States,* 412 U.S. 434 (1973), the court of appeals, after finding that defendant had been denied a speedy trial, reduced but did not vacate his sentence. His petition for certiorari contended that the sentence should have been vacated entirely. The Government, though willing to accept the short reduction in sentence ordered by the court of appeals, sought unsuccessfully to support the sentence as reduced on the ground that the defendant had not been denied a speedy trial, and therefore that the judgment of conviction should not have been reversed. For other holdings that a cross-appeal is necessary in such circumstances, see *Mills* v. *Electric Auto-Lite Co.,* 396 U.S. 375, 381 (1970); *NLRB* v. *International Van Lines,* 409 U.S. 48, 52 (1972); *Brennan* v. *Arnheim & Neely, Inc.,* 410 U.S. 512, 516 (1973); *NLRB* v. *Express Publishing Co.,* 312 U.S. 426, 431–432 (1941).

[45]See R. Stern and E. Gressman, SUPREME COURT PRACTICE, Sec. 6.34 (5th ed., 1978); R. Stern, *When to Cross Appeal or Cross Petition—Certainty or Confusion?,* 87 Harv. L. Rev. 763 (1974).

[46]*United States* v. *New York Telephone Co.,* 434 U.S. 159, 166, n. 8 (1977); *United States* v. *ITT Continental Baking Co.,* 420 U.S. 223, 226–227, n. 2 (1975); *Scherk* v. *Alberto-Culver Co.,* 417 U.S. 506, 525 (1974)(dissent); R. Stern and E. Gressman, SUPREME COURT PRACTICE, Sec. 6.34, pp. 482-486 (5th ed., 1978).

[47]Comment to Tennessee Rule of Appellate Procedure 13(a) (1979).

ground that a notice of appeal is not intended to inform the parties of the issues or arguments; that is left to the later brief writing stage.[48] The purpose of the notice of appeal is "to declare in a formal way an intent to appeal," to inform the parties that the case is to go to the appellate court.[49] The first noticed appeal does that.

The new Tennessee rules differ from those of most other jurisdictions, including the federal, in requiring the notice of appeal to designate only the "judgment from which relief is sought" (Tennessee Rule 3(f)), and not in addition the "part thereof appealed from" (Federal Rule of Appellate Procedure 3(c)) if the appeal is from less than the whole judgment. This reflects the theory underlying the elimination of cross-appeals that more information as to the issues when an appeal is taken will not be helpful until the refinement of the questions argued in the briefs.

Whether cross-appeals should be abolished as inconsistent with the general theory of leaving specification of the issues to the briefs should depend on whether knowing in advance the parts of a judgment the parties want reviewed will be helpful or subject to the same defects as the former assignment of errors. Specific reference to the parts of a judgment to be challenged would seldom, however, present any serious problem. Judgments are usually not so complicated as to make such a recital difficult, or to induce parties to list a great many items which they might abandon at the briefing stage. And knowledge of the parts of the judgment involved in the appeal will also be helpful in designating the material to be included in the record or appendix, as well as in giving the other parties earlier notice of the points they should prepare to meet.

Eliminating the cross-appeal would, of course, avoid the confusion resulting from authorities such as the Supreme Court cases discussed above, which in my view unreasonably depart from the general doctrine as to when a cross-appeal is required. Nevertheless, my own conclusion is that requiring a cross-appeal to identify the parts of the judgment an appellee intends to challenge is on the whole more helpful than harmful. However, the cross-appeal should be permitted to be filed after appellant files his notice of appeal.

---

[48]Sobieski, *supra* note 2, at 191–192.
[49]*Ibid.*

4.8 Docketing the Appeal

Traditionally an appeal is "taken" when a notice of appeal or similar document is filed in the court which had entered the judgment appealed from. The appeal is "docketed" in the reviewing court when the record is filed in that court and the docket fee paid.[50] The case is then given a number in the appellate court. In lieu of the record itself, a certificate that the record is ready for transmission is also sufficient under the rules of a number of appellate courts which permit the record to be retained in the lower court for use by counsel in preparing briefs.[51] This is still the practice in many states.

The significance of docketing was not merely that the case was placed on the docket of the appellate court. In most cases docketing gave the appellate court its first notice that the case had been appealed to it.[52] This was therefore the point when the appellate court customarily assumed jurisdiction over the case. The date of filing the record was also the time from which the period for the filing of appellant's brief was computed. There is no necessary connection, however, between those objectives and the delivery of the record to the appellate court, as the rules of a number of courts now recognize.

Many state rules and the Federal Rules of Appellate Procedure as revised in 1979 now require that a copy of the notice of appeal be transmitted to the appellate court by the appellant or the court below at the same time as or shortly after it is filed in the lower court. See Sec. 4.2, *supra.* This enables the appellate court to be made immediately aware of the appeal and to be in a position to supervise it from the beginning.[53] The fee for the

---

[50]These fees need not be paid by persons who qualify as indigents or are otherwise exempted by law, such as governmental bodies, agencies or offices. See Sec. 4.4, *supra.*

[51]See Sec. 6.6, *infra.*

[52]In some cases preliminary motions for extensions of time, stays or other matters might have brought a case to the attention of the appellate court before the case was docketed.

[53]This does not necessarily mean that the trial court has lost all of its jurisdiction, although there is considerable uncertainty as to its remaining powers in the absence of specific indication by the appellate court. See Sec. 4.2, *supra;* 9 J. Moore, FEDERAL PRACTICE, ¶203.11 (2d ed., 1980). In the main the trial court may deal with such matters as settling the record, preserving the status quo (supersedeas, stays, bonds, bail), determining indigency, and other issues ancillary to the appeal. Pennsylvania Rule 1701(b) enumerates the powers retained by the lower court after an appeal has been taken. In addition to the above, the lower court may enforce unstayed orders, reconsider pursuant to timely application, authorize the taking of depositions or the preservation of testimony, and proceed as to parts of the case not involved in the appeal.

The Washington Rules of Appellate Procedure define the time when the appellate court "accepts review" as when the notice of appeal is filed in the trial court

appeal is paid at that time to the clerk of the trial court who transmits it to the clerk of the appellate court. Under this system a case is docketed in the appellate court when that court receives its copy of the notice of appeal.[54]

Revised Federal Appellate Rule 3(d), for example, provides that after the clerk of the district court has received the notice of appeal, he

> "shall transmit forthwith a copy of the notice of appeal and of the docket entries to the clerk of the court of appeals named in the notice."

Revised Rule 12(a) then provides:

> "Upon receipt of the copy of the notice of appeal and of the docket entries, transmitted by the clerk of the district court pursuant to Rule 3(d), the clerk of the court of appeals shall thereupon enter the appeal upon the docket."[55]

Tennessee Rule 5(c) and Illinois Rule 303(f), both also as revised in 1979, are substantially identical. See also Ohio Rule of Appellate Procedure 11; North Dakota Rule 12. In Illinois a docketing statement must be filed in the Appellate Court within 14 days of the filing of the notice of appeal, as indicated in Sec. 4.5(d), *supra.*[56] Pennsylvania Rule 907(b) requires the clerk to notify the parties, the trial court clerk and the administrator of

---

from a decision appealable as of right, or when the appellate court grants a motion for discretionary review. Rules 6.1–7.3. Although the appellate court retains overriding powers, Rule 7.2 enumerates various subjects over which the trial court may still exercise authority. To the extent that such a listing eliminates doubt, it should be helpful.

[54]In Montana, the trial court clerk mails a copy of the notice of appeal to the Supreme Court, but the appellant may pay the fee within the time allowed for transmission of the record. The case is docketed when the fee is paid, or if no fee need be paid, at or before the time of filing the record. Rules 4, 11.

[55]In order to protect a party whose counsel is confused as to where the notice should be filed, revised Federal Appellate Rule 4(a)(1) adds:

"If a notice of appeal is mistakenly filed in the court of appeals, the clerk of the court of appeals shall note thereon the date on which it was received and transmit it to the clerk of the district court and it shall be deemed filed in the district court on the date so noted."

[56]Tennessee Rule 5(c), like Federal Appellate Rule 12(a) and the rules of many other states, provides that

"An appeal shall be docketed under the title given to the action in the trial court, with the appellant identified as such; but if such title does not contain the name of the appellant, his name, identified as appellant, shall be added to the title."

The caption should accordingly entitle the case as "*Minnie School,* plaintiff-appellee v. *Lotta Doe,* defendant-appellant." In the United States Supreme Court and some state appellate courts, however, the appellant's name always comes first.

the number of the case in the appellate court. Connecticut Practice Book §3094 requires the trial court clerk to state the names of counsel on the file sent to the Supreme Court.

Wisconsin 1978 Rule 809.10-809.11 requires that the filing fee be deposited with the trial court clerk when the notice of appeal is filed, that at the same time appellant send a copy of the notice of appeal to the clerk of the appellate court, and that within three days the trial court clerk forward to the court of appeals the fee, a copy of the notice and a copy of the trial court's docket entries; when these are received the clerk of the court of appeals shall docket the appeal.

In the United States Supreme Court, where the record need no longer be filed until the Court accepts a case for oral argument, a case is placed on the docket when appellant or petitioner pays the docket fee and files 40 copies of his jurisdictional statement or petition for certiorari. Rules 12.3 and 19.3.

Each of these systems achieves the purpose of subjecting the appeal to the appellate court's supervisory authority shortly after the notice of appeal or its equivalent is filed. E.g., New Jersey Rule 2:9-1. This does not mean, of course, that the time for filing appellant's brief cannot continue to commence with the day the compilation of the record is completed. For the availability of the record is often essential for the lawyers while preparing the briefs. This is not true in every case, either because the record is short and the facts not disputed or because counsel already has copies of all the important record papers. Nevertheless, the date the preparation of the record is completed by the trial court clerk may still provide the best single starting point for the briefing process.

The New Hampshire Supreme Court's 1979 Rule 12 goes further in having the court immediately take over the administration of the appeal. As has been noted, the form for the notice of appeal, which is filed in both the trial court and the Supreme Court, calls for the submission of a substantial volume of information about the case, including the questions, the authorities relied on, the copies of rulings and memoranda of law, contracts, and similar documents. The parties are then to await an order from the clerk which shall set forth the dates for filing the record, briefs, and appendices (see Sec. 7.4, *infra*) and holding oral argument, direct attendance at a prehearing evaluation conference (see Sec. 10.2, *infra*), or decline to accept review (see Sec. 1.5, p. 20, *supra*).

4.9   Appeals Requiring Leave of Court

The notice of appeal is, and should be, the only jurisdictional document necessary when an appeal is taken as a matter of right from the trial court either to an intermediate or supreme appellate court. Only when, as occurs in direct appeals to the United States Supreme Court, the right to such an appeal is often in doubt or the court uses the preliminary document to determine whether to hear argument may an explanation of the jurisdictional basis for the appeal or even the merits of the case at the initial stage be worthwhile.[57]

In many situations leave of court must first be obtained before the first appellate court has jurisdiction over the appeal. As shown in Sec. 3.5, *supra,* many jurisdictions, including the federal, specify generally that appeals may be taken from all or particular types of interlocutory orders upon the granting of leave by the trial court, or both courts.[58] Leave may also be necessary for an appeal to an appellate court from a superior trial court which has authority to act as a reviewing court for decisions of an inferior tribunal, such as a justice of the peace or a magistrate. The subject of discretionary appeals from intermediate appellate courts to supreme courts is considered in Chapter 5.

The taking of any of these types of discretionary appeals requires the filing of an argumentative document explaining why the court should hear the appeal, and not merely of a notice of appeal. In some jurisdictions both a notice and a petition or application for leave are required, but in most only the latter. The statutes and rules governing such appeals in the various jurisdictions should be examined to ascertain the time limits and other requisites for taking such appeals.

4.10   Appeals Involving Constitutional Questions Where the Government Has Not Previously Been Made a Party

Federal Appellate Rule 44 provides that a party who challenges the constitutionality of a federal statute in a case in which

---

[57]See also Illinois Rule 317, with respect to appeals as of right from the Appellate Court to the Supreme Court.

[58]Some states require leave to appeal from orders granting a new trial. E.g., Illinois Rule 306.

the United States or an agency or officer thereof is not a party shall notify the court of the existence of the constitutional question, and that the court should thereupon certify such fact to the Attorney General who, under 28 U.S.C. §2403(a), may then intervene as a matter of right. Under §2403(b) the same procedure is to be followed with respect to a state attorney general if the validity of a state statute is drawn in question.

A number of states have similar laws or rules, designed to insure that the state government has an opportunity to participate in litigation as to the constitutionality of a state law when it is not named as a party. Some of the states follow the simpler procedure of having the party directly notify the attorney general of the existence of a constitutional question. E.g., Alabama Rule 44; Pennsylvania Rule of Appellate Procedure 521. The Pennsylvania rule then provides that the Attorney General may be heard on the constitutional question without formal intervention; if he files a brief, the Commonwealth shall be deemed an intervening party.

Pennsylvania Rule 522 then adds a parallel provision for challenges to the constitutionality of a rule of court. Notice is then to be given to the Court Administrator of Pennsylvania, who shall have the same right as the Attorney General under the preceding section. The accompanying Note explains that "the purpose of this rule is to prevent the recurrence of situations" in which the Attorney General had failed to defend a rule of the Pennsylvania Supreme Court. "It is anticipated that the Court Administrator will coordinate with the appropriate rules committee" in defending the rule.

4.11 Stays, Bonds and Supersedeas

An appellant in a civil case is faced with the need for posting two types of bonds or other security: a bond to cover the costs of the appeal, and a supersedeas bond or other security if he wishes to stay enforcement of the judgment from which he is appealing.

(a) Security for Costs on Appeal

In civil cases in many state courts, as in the federal courts of appeals prior to the 1979 rules revision, the appellant must post a bond for costs on appeal, to be borne by him if his appeal is unsuccessful. These costs usually include the filing fees for docketing the appeal and the cost to the clerk of preparing and transmitting the record, including the transcript, as well as the cost to the losing party of transcribing and printing the necessary copies of briefs, appendices and records. (E.g., United States Supreme Court Rule 50.) The costs are eventually to be borne by the party losing the appeal.

Many jurisdictions do not require the posting of a security bond for costs on appeal in every case. The 1979 revision of Rule 7 of the Federal Rules of Appellate Procedure eliminated the requirement of a $250 bond or equivalent security for costs on appeal in civil cases generally, and substituted the simple provision that

> "The district court may require an appellant to file a bond or provide other security in such form and amount as it finds necessary to ensure payment of costs on appeal in a civil case."

This means in substance that unless an appellee has reason to believe that appellant will not be able to pay the costs on appeal, and brings the matter to the court's attention by motion, no security need be posted. The earlier, more orthodox rule was abandoned both because the $250 amount was hopelessly out of date and any other specific figure would have been completely arbitrary, and because security was unnecessary in most civil appeals. The bond on appeal was also eliminated from the Kentucky rules in 1978. See Kentucky Rule 73.05.[59] These recent abandonments of the required security bond on appeal suggest that either generally or in many states there really is no need for it.

Indigent parties and governmental bodies or officials are usually exempted from these requirements, although Federal Appellate Rule 39 permits the recovery of costs against the United States or an agency or officer thereof when "authorized by law." See 28 U.S.C. §2412. Some states also exempt executors, administrators, trustees and other fiduciaries from having to put up security for costs.

The amount which the appellant must post in advance as a security bond for costs is usually prescribed by rule or statute,

---

[59]Illinois Rule 364 allows an appellee "upon the filing . . . of an affidavit that any appellant is not a resident of this State or is insolvent and that no bond for costs has been filed" to have a rule "entered against the appellant to show cause why the appeal should not be dismissed." Since Illinois does not require the filing of a bond for costs, a more sensible rule would merely permit the appellee in the circumstances indicated to move that appellant post such a bond, leaving the appeal to be dismissed only if appellant fails to do so.

although the amount may be changed by the trial court. In state courts the amount varies. E.g., Wyoming—$100; Arkansas and Nevada—$250; Utah—$300; Arizona, Connecticut, Minnesota, South Dakota, Tennessee and Texas—$500; Alaska—$750. These amounts may be more or less than the costs eventually to be paid; they are almost certain to be less when the record or transcript to be duplicated is of substantial length.

The bond or equivalent security customarily is a security bond posted by a bonding company, although cash or other types of security may also usually be posted. A separate bond for costs need not be posted when the supersedeas bond or other security presented to obtain a stay pending appeal also covers the costs on appeal, as often will be the case.

(b) Stays and Supersedeas Bonds

An appellant often, but not always, wishes to stay enforcement of the adverse judgment below pending the final decision by the appellate court or courts. A defendant against whom a judgment for money damages or an injunction has been entered will often seek a stay pending appeal. On the other hand, an unsuccessful plaintiff would have nothing to stay except perhaps a defendant's collection of costs against him.

When the judgment sought to be stayed is for money, the posting of a bond in the amount of the judgment is normally deemed adequate security. A number of jurisdictions provide an automatic stay in such cases if the appellant files a bond in that amount. A few prescribe a larger amount, ranging from 115 to 200 percent of the amount of the judgment.[60] Such a bond is known as a supersedeas bond.

In other jurisdictions, including the federal courts and Illinois, the amount must be determined or approved by the court, which means the trial court in the first instance, with resort to the appellate court or a judge thereof if either party is dissatisfied with the trial court's ruling. (E.g., Federal Appellate Rule 8; Illinois Rule 305.) When there is no doubt that the bond submitted conforms to the practice in the particular court, approval by the clerk is often sufficient. Illinois went so far in 1971 as completely to eliminate the term "supersedeas," in the belief that the phrase "stay of judgment pending appeal" would be

---

[60]Florida—115 percent; Pennsylvania—120; Iowa—125; Alabama—150 up to $10,000, 125 over that; Oklahoma—200.

more intelligible to the substantial portion of its citizenry not familiar with the Latin language.

The purpose of requiring a bond is to enable the other party to recover the amount to which he is entitled without another lawsuit. Federal Appellate Rule 8(b) accordingly provides:

> "If security is given in the form of a bond or stipulation or other undertaking with one or more sureties, each surety submits himself to the jurisdiction of the district court and irrevocably appoints the clerk of the district court as his agent upon whom any papers affecting his liability on the bond or undertaking may be served. His liability may be enforced on motion in the district court without the necessity of an independent action. The motion and such notice of the motion as the district court prescribes may be served on the clerk of the district court, who shall forthwith mail copies to the sureties if their addresses are known."

When a different kind of stay is needed, such as a temporary injunction pending appeal, a motion must be submitted to a judge (although in Maryland the filing of the order for appeal operates as a stay in certain types of non-money cases (Rule 1016)). The judge is required to condition the granting of relief on the filing of a bond or such other security or term as he determines to be just. (Federal Appellate Rule 8; Illinois Rule 305.) Michigan Rule 808 provides that a stay must be conditioned on a suitable bond.

Although both the trial and the appellate courts have authority to issue stays, the general and approved practice is for the application first to be submitted to the trial court. Federal Rule of Appellate Procedure 8(a) provides:

> "Application for a stay of the judgment or order of a district court pending appeal, or for approval of a supersedeas bond, or for an order suspending, modifying, restoring or granting an injunction during the pendency of an appeal must ordinarily be made in the first instance in the district court. A motion for such relief may be made to the court of appeals or to a judge thereof, but the motion shall show that application to the district court for the relief sought is not practicable, or that the district court has denied an application, or has failed to afford the relief which the applicant requested, with the reasons given by the district court for its action. The motion shall also show the reasons for the relief requested and the facts relied upon, and if the facts are subject to dispute the motion shall be supported by affidavits or other sworn statements or copies thereof. With the motion shall be filed such parts of the record as are relevant. Reasonable notice of the mo-

tion shall be given to all parties. The motion shall be filed with the clerk and normally will be considered by a panel or division of the court, but in exceptional cases where such procedure would be impracticable due to the requirements of time, the application may be made to and considered by a single judge of the court."[61]

When obtaining a stay is important to appellant, the necessary steps should be commenced even before the filing of the notice of appeal. In some jurisdictions, the supersedeas bond must be filed with the notice. The arrangement with the surety company and the drafting of the motion papers should be undertaken as soon as a party knows that he intends to appeal and that a stay will be desired, so that all documents needed can be filed along with the notice or immediately thereafter.

The provisions for a supersedeas in a number of states are elaborate and differ from each other in numerous details. The lawyer must therefore examine the statutes and rules of his jurisdiction. In general, however, the substance of the practice in the various jurisdictions is similar to what has been briefly summarized here.

4.12 The Record and Transcript

The appellant must, either by the time of filing the notice of appeal or within a few days thereafter, take the first steps toward having the record prepared for use in the appellate court. This customarily consists of advising the clerk, the court reporter and also the opposing parties of the portion of the papers on file in the trial court (the record) or of the testimony to be, but usually not yet, transcribed by the court reporter (the transcript) which he wants included in or omitted from the record. In the federal courts and many states, the entire record below constitutes the record on appeal unless the parties stipulate as to what may be omitted, and the appellant must designate the relevant portions of the reporter's transcript within 10 days of the notice of appeal (Federal Appellate Rule 10(a)). As stated on p. 88, *supra,* in some states designation must accompany or precede the notice of appeal.[62] See Sec. 4.5(b), *supra.* This subject is treated in detail in Chapter 6, *infra.*

---

[61]Illinois Rule 305(b)(2) is almost identical.

[62]Alaska, Arkansas, Connecticut, Georgia, Idaho, Nebraska, Oklahoma, Oregon, Washington.

5

Appeals to the Highest Court When There Is an Intermediate Appellate Court

5.1 In General

As shown in Chapter 1, Sec. 1.3, *supra,* most states have created a two-tiered appellate structure generally similar to the federal. Although 17 states still have only one appellate court, a supreme court, they contain less than 15 percent of the population of the United States. Thus, by far the largest part of the litigation in the country arises in states with two tiers of appellate courts, with problems and procedures similar to those in the federal system.

Most of these states follow the same general pattern. Cases are appealed as a matter of right to the lower or intermediate appellate courts, which in most jurisdictions are called the courts of appeals;[1] I shall follow that usage here. In almost all of these states, as well as in the federal system, appeals in the vast majority of cases may be taken to the supreme court[2] only by permission of that court. In New York the highest court reviews only questions

---

[1] In Illinois the intermediate court is the Appellate Court, in Maryland the Court of Special Appeals, in Massachusetts the Appeals Court, in Connecticut the Appellate Session, in New York and New Jersey the Appellate Division, and in Pennsylvania the Superior Court and the Commonwealth Court.

[2] In New York the highest court is the Court of Appeals and the same is true in Maryland. In Massachusetts and Maine it is the Supreme Judicial Court, and in West Virginia, the Supreme Court of Appeals.

of law unless the intermediate court has made new findings of fact. New York Civil Practice Act, §5501(b).

The word "taken" embodies two separate concepts. In general it means that the highest court agrees to take jurisdiction over the appeal and to decide the case on the merits; its refusal to grant leave to appeal is not a decision on the merits but a ruling that the case does not satisfy its standards for further review. "Taking" the case may also mean that the highest court agrees to hear oral argument.

In Texas, if the Supreme Court finds that it has jurisdiction over an appeal, a nondiscretionary determination, it exercises discretionary authority only as to whether it will hear oral argument. It need not do so if it agrees with the judgment below. If it agrees entirely with the Court of Appeals, its order of "refusal" has the effect of an affirmance, and leaves the decision below with precedential value. If the Supreme Court is not satisfied in all respects, its order reads "Refused: no reversible error," which means that no error required reversal but that the opinion below does not have precedential value. See Texas Rule 483; Texas Civil Stat. Ann. arts. 1728, 1821.

The Texas procedure for *all* appeals to its Supreme Court resembles the practice in the United States Supreme Court for appeals to that Court as of right in contrast to petitions for certiorari.[3] If the Supreme Court has jurisdiction over the appeal, it first decides whether to hear oral argument, but its disposition of the case without oral argument is on the merits. A summary affirmance or dismissal for want of a substantial federal question is binding on other courts if they can figure out what the Supreme Court meant to affirm.[4]

The other state supreme courts heading a two-tiered appellate structure, like the United States Supreme Court, exercise discretionary authority to determine what cases they will hear and decide on the merits, and most cases come before them on appeals by the losing party. All cases coming to those supreme courts do not, however, follow the most common route. Some

---

[3]Indeed, the Texas practice is not very different from that in Virginia and West Virginia, in which the single appellate court reviews the case preliminarily on the merits to decide whether oral argument will be worthwhile, or from that in some of the United States courts of appeals. See Sec. 1.7, *supra.*

[4]See *Hicks* v. *Miranda,* 422 U.S. 332 (1975); *Washington* v. *Yakima Indian Nation,* 439 U.S. 463 (1979); *Illinois State Board of Elections* v. *Socialist Workers Party,* 440 U.S. 173, 181 (1979), and cases therein cited; R. Stern and E. Gressman, SUPREME COURT PRACTICE, Secs. 4.28–4.31 (5th ed., 1978).

classes of cases come by direct appeals as a matter of right from the trial court, and others by appeal as of right from the intermediate court of appeals.

Furthermore, in the federal system and in many states, the highest court on its own initiative or on application of a party may order that the court of appeals be bypassed before argument, and that a case, or in some states even a group or class of cases, be transferred to the supreme court. In some states the court of appeals, before or after decision, may certify particular cases or particular questions in a case to the supreme court. Or that court may take a case after decision in the court of appeals on its own initiative as well as on application of a party.

Each of these routes to the highest court is not available in every state. Some have been adopted in some jurisdictions and some in others. These different approaches will be discussed below, roughly in the order in which they may enter into the litigation. This will leave for treatment in depth at the end of the chapter the route most commonly used, the petition for certiorari or leave to appeal after decision of the intermediate appellate court, followed by a comparative analysis of the different methods of determining what cases a highest court should decide.

5.2   Granting Review by Majority or Minority Vote

An unusual feature of discretionary review by the Supreme Court in the federal system and in some states is that it may be granted by less than a majority of the court. This is occasionally authorized by a state constitution, statute or rule, but more often it is merely a practice or policy which the court follows.

The most prominent example of this practice is the Rule of Four which the United States Supreme Court has long applied as a matter of its own policy in determining whether to grant petitions for certiorari: The votes of four out of nine Justices are sufficient to grant review. "The whole philosophy of the 'rule of four' . . . is that any case warranting consideration in the opinion of such a substantial minority of the Court will be taken and disposed of." *Ferguson* v. *Moore-McCormack Lines,* 352 U.S. 521, 560, 564 (1957) (opinion of Mr. Justice Harlan for the Court). "It is a working rule devised by the Court as a practical mode of determining that a case is deserving of review, the theory being that if four Justices find that a legal question of general importance is raised, that is ample proof that the question has such importance." *Id.* at 529 (dissenting opinion of Mr. Justice Frankfurter). Although not based on "a command of Congress" (*ibid.*), the rule embodies a "promise to Congress," when the Court's certiorari jurisdiction was greatly expanded in 1925, "to let the vote of four justices bring up any case here on certiorari." *Harris* v. *Pennsylvania R. Co.*, 361 U.S. 15, 18 (1959) (concurring opinion of Mr. Justice Douglas).[5]

The Supreme Court follows the same practice in deciding whether an appeal should be argued orally or disposed of summarily. *Ohio ex rel. Eaton* v. *Price*, 360 U.S. 246, 247 (1959).

A few state courts have adopted the same policy in determining whether to grant discretionary review. By statute, rule or guideline, Maryland, Massachusetts, New Jersey, Oregon and Wisconsin provide for the granting of review by three of the seven justices.[6] In Pennsylvania two votes out of seven and in Connecticut two out of six are sufficient.[7] Tennessee Rule 11(e) provides for granting of an application for review by the Supreme Court "if two members [out of five] are satisfied that the application should be granted." In Texas three out of nine justices are enough for the granting of a writ of error.

Most states, however, require a majority vote to grant review, so far as can be ascertained from reading the rules of court and the state constitutions. In Illinois a majority vote of the Supreme Court is required to review a judgment of the Appellate Court. Somewhat anomalously, however, "the Supreme Court or a justice thereof" may order that an appeal filed in the Appellate Court shall be transferred to the Supreme Court if "the public interest requires prompt adjudication" by that court. Illinois Rule 302(b). Thus, a single justice may authorize the unusual procedure whereby the Supreme Court takes an appeal directly from the trial court without awaiting decision by

---

[5]Mr. Justice Douglas' opinion in the *Harris* case quotes the supporting legislative history. See also Mr. Justice Burton, *Judging Is Also Administration*, 21 Temple L.Q. 77, 84–85 (1947), 33 A.B.A.J. 1099, 1164 (1947); J. Leiman, *The Rule of Four*, 57 Columbia L. Rev. 975 (1957); R. Stern and E. Gressman, SUPREME COURT PRACTICE, pp. 346–349 (5th ed., 1978); 16 C. Wright, A. Miller, E. Cooper and E. Gressman, FEDERAL PRACTICE AND PROCEDURE, pp. 512–516 (1977).

[6]Maryland Ann. Code—Courts and Judicial Proceedings, §12-203; Massachusetts Rule of Appellate Procedure 27.1(e); New Jersey Rule 2:12-10; Oregon Rule 10.15; Wisconsin Guideline. Massachusetts Rule 27.1(e) also permits a majority of the judges of the Appeals Court or of the panel deciding the case to grant review. Rule 11(f) permits two justices of the Supreme Judicial Court or a majority of the judges of the Appeals Court to grant direct appellate review before judgment in the Appeals Court.

[7]Connecticut Practice Book, §3146; Pennsylvania Rule 1121.

the Appellate Court, but a majority vote is necessary to review the Appellate Court in the ordinary case.

In most jurisdictions a supreme court's refusal to review an intermediate court's decision is not to be regarded as an affirmance or as any expression of opinion on the questions raised. The United States Supreme Court has so stated on many occasions.[8] Colorado Rule 35 and Georgia Rule 24-4536 embody the same principle. It is believed that most of the other states take the same view. Kentucky Rule 76.20(9)(a) provides, however, that "if the motion is denied the decision shall stand affirmed." And as to Texas, see Sec. 5.1, *supra*.

5.3   Appeal as of Right to a Supreme Court From a Trial Court

Appeal may be taken directly from the trial court to the supreme court as a matter of right without going through the intermediate appellate court in specified classes of cases in a number of jurisdictions. The most common classes are death sentences (Arkansas, Florida, Illinois, Indiana, Kentucky, Missouri, New Jersey, North Carolina, Washington), and also sentences to life imprisonment (Arkansas, Missouri, North Carolina), 30 years or more (Arkansas), 20 years or more (Kentucky) and 10 years or more (Indiana).

Cases involving constitutional questions are to be taken directly to the highest court in Arkansas, Florida, Missouri and Texas (if injunctive relief is sought). The statutes providing for three-judge district courts and direct appeals therefrom to the United States Supreme Court in suits to enjoin the enforcement of state or federal statutes on grounds of federal unconstitutionality (28 U.S.C. §§2281, 2282) were repealed in 1976 (90 Stat. 1119). But Congress has not yet repealed—though a bill to do so is pending—the statute (28 U.S.C. §1252) providing for direct appeal to the Supreme Court when any federal court, including a district court of one or three judges, has held a federal statute unconstitutional in a civil action in which the United States or any agency, officer or employee thereof is a party.[9] Illinois, Indiana, Kansas, Missouri and Washington also allow

---

[8]*Brown* v. *Allen*, 344 U.S. 443, 489–497 (1953); *Hughes Tool Co.* v. *Trans World Airlines*, 409 U.S. 363, 365–366, n. 1 (1973); R. Stern and E. Gressman, SUPREME COURT PRACTICE, Sec. 5.7 (5th ed., 1978); but cf. *United States* v. *Kras*, 409 U.S. 434, 443, 460–461 (1973).

[9]R. Stern and E. Gressman, SUPREME COURT PRACTICE, Secs. 2.5, 2.10 (5th ed., 1978).

direct appeals to the highest court when a trial court has held a state or federal statute to be unconstitutional. In Arkansas the state Supreme Court's exclusive appellate jurisdiction was at first defined by rule to include cases involving the constitutionality or construction of statutes, ordinances, administrative and court rules, the review of orders of important commissions, election cases, criminal penalties of more than 30 years and petitions for writs and post-conviction relief. In 1980, in order to keep the new Court of Appeals from being overloaded, the Arkansas Supreme Court added interlocutory appeals and appeals in usury, product liability, tort, deed and will construction, and oil, gas and mineral right cases, as well as, for the last half of 1980, criminal cases with sentences of over 10 years.[10]

The Florida constitution, as amended in 1980, authorizes, when provided by statute, direct appeal to the Supreme Court from final orders "in proceedings for the validation of bonds or certificates of indebtedness" and from action of statewide agencies (which means the Public Service Commission) relating to rates and service of electric, gas and telephone utilities. Florida Const. Art. 5, §3(b)(2)(1980); Rule of Appellate Procedure 9.030(a)(1)(B), 381 So.2d 1371 (1980). Missouri provides for direct appeals in cases involving the construction of revenue laws and title to office (Missouri Const. Art. III); and Washington, in cases involving the issuance of writs against state officers as well as where the appellate decisions are inconsistent or the issue is of great public importance (Rule of Appellate Procedure 4.2). In Illinois workmen's compensation cases to review orders of the Industrial Commission go directly from the circuit court to the Supreme Court (Rule 302(a)).

The procedure for taking these appeals from a trial court to a supreme court is usually the same as to an intermediate appellate court, by notice of appeal. But where, as under the Washington rule just referred to, there may be doubt as to whether the case comes within the class, a statement explaining why direct review is proper must be filed.

This is the procedure for all appeals (not certiorari cases) to the United States Supreme Court. In addition to the constitutional cases already referred to, appeals may be taken in government suits to enforce the antitrust laws if the trial court has found that "immediate consideration of the appeal by the Supreme Court is of general public importance in the administra-

---

[10]Arkansas Supreme Court Rule 29.

tion of justice," a provision not invoked since the passage of the statute in 1974 (15 U.S.C. §29(b)). Appeals to the Supreme Court are also taken from three-judge district courts, but with the repeal of most of the principal statutes authorizing such courts, they are now required only in major reapportionment cases (28 U.S.C. §2284(a), as revised in 1976) and under several provisions of the Civil Rights Act of 1964, the Voting Rights Act of 1965, the Regional Rail Reorganization Act of 1973 and the Presidential Election Campaign Fund Act of 1971. Few cases have arisen or are likely to arise under these surviving three-judge court statutes.[11]

The procedure in all appeals to the United States Supreme Court is to file a notice of appeal in the trial court, which is simple enough, and at the same time a deceptively titled "Jurisdictional Statement" in the Supreme Court, which is not. A small portion of that document is ordinarily sufficient to explain why the Supreme Court has jurisdiction over the case by way of appeal as of right; the major part should argue why the questions presented are substantial enough to warrant full briefing and oral argument on the merits.[12] What is wanted is a combination of a short but persuasive brief on the merits with a showing that the case has public importance and, because of both factors, warrants oral argument.

In Iowa and Oklahoma all appeals from trial courts are taken to the supreme court, although there is an intermediate court of appeals. In Iowa a notice of appeal is filed and in Oklahoma a petition in error (described in Sec. 4.2, *supra*). The supreme court then decides which cases should be retained and which transferred to the court of appeals. In Oklahoma any party may move that the Supreme Court retain the case because of substantial public interest, as well as for other specified reasons. Court of Appeals Rule 3.2. In each state the decision of the court of appeals is subject to discretionary review by the supreme court. Hawaii and Idaho have recently adopted the same system. See Sec. 1.10(b), *supra*.

Although in Massachusetts most appeals are filed in the Appeals Court and not the Supreme Judicial Court, the latter court presently screens them before argument to determine in

---

[11]The subject of direct appeals to the Supreme Court under these statutes is considered at length in R. Stern and E. Gressman, SUPREME COURT PRACTICE, Secs. 2.9–2.16, pp. 70–136 (5th ed., 1978).

[12]United States Supreme Court Rule 15. See R. Stern and E. Gressman, SUPREME COURT PRACTICE, Chap. 7 (5th ed., 1978).

which court they should be heard. The substantive result is thus not very different from that in Iowa and Oklahoma. A Supreme Court staff lawyer reviews the briefs and records in the Appeals Court, and makes a recommendation to a three-judge committee of the Supreme Judicial Court as to which cases should be heard directly by it even without an application.[13] This procedure has resulted in the court hearing many more cases on direct review on its own motion (142 in 1978–1979) than on applications of parties filed both before and after decision by the Appeals Court. This is a highly unusual method of exercising discretionary jurisdiction, perhaps attributable to the newness and work load of the Appeals Court as well as to the willingness of the Supreme Judicial Court to retain full responsibility for the appeals in important cases. It enables those cases to be decided more promptly and authoritatively than if they had to go through both appellate courts. Such a system would be in the public interest for other supreme courts which have the time for it. See Sec. 1.10(b), *supra.*

5.4 Appeal as of Right to a Supreme Court From an Intermediate Appellate Court

Some specified subjects or categories of cases decided by the intermediate appellate courts do not fall within the highest court's discretionary authority to determine what cases it will hear and decide. These cases, like those from the trial courts just discussed in the preceding section, are appealable to the highest court as a matter of right. They are defined either in terms of specific subject matter or of general standards which the highest court is to apply.

(a) Specific Subjects

As was true for direct appeals from the trial courts, death sentences and constitutional questions are the classes of cases for which appeals as of right are most frequently prescribed. In Alabama, review on certiorari is automatic when there has been a death sentence (Rule 39); in Ohio, leave to appeal is unnecessary in such cases. Appeals as of right are authorized for cases involving constitutional issues in Ohio and New York; in New

---

[13]Two votes are enough to bypass the Appeals Court either on the Supreme Court's own motion or on application, although three votes are required *after* an Appeals Court decision.

Jersey and North Carolina, if there is a substantial constitutional question; in North Carolina, to review an order of its Public Utility Commission in a rate-making case (Gen. Stat. §7A-30); in Florida, if the District Courts of Appeal have declared invalid a state statute or constitutional provision; and in Illinois and Kansas, if the constitutional question arises for the first time as a result of the action of the appellate court. In the latter states, if the statute had been held unconstitutional by the trial court, the appeal would have gone directly to the supreme court and not to the lower appellate court at all.[14]

In the federal system, appeals as of right to the United States Supreme Court from the courts of appeals are authorized when the latter courts have held a state statute unconstitutional (28 U.S.C. §1254(2)) or a federal statute unconstitutional in a civil proceeding to which the United States is a party (28 U.S.C. §1252).[15] Appeal, and not merely discretionary review by certiorari, also may be taken to the United States Supreme Court from a judgment of the highest state court to which a case may be taken which holds a federal statute or treaty unconstitutional or a state law valid as against the claim that it is repugnant to the Constitution, treaties or laws of the United States. 28 U.S.C. §1257(1)(2). Few appeals are taken under any of these provisions except the last, which does present the Supreme Court with a large number of contentions, mostly insubstantial, that state laws violate the federal Constitution. And most of these appeals are dismissed summarily for failure to present a substantial federal question.[16] Proposals have been made to abolish these appeals as of right and to transfer such cases to the Supreme Court's discretionary jurisdiction in order to relieve that Court of some of its tremendous work load. See Sec. 5.9(c), *infra.*

(b)   General Categories Not Based Upon Particular Subject Matter

Other states permit appeals as of right in circumstances not dependent upon the subject matter of the particular case. In

---

[14]E.g., Illinois Rule 302(a); Kansas Stat. Ann. §60-2101.

[15]In addition, an expedited appeal to the Supreme Court as of right lies when a court of appeals has answered certified questions as to the constitutionality of the Federal Election Campaign Act of 1971 (2 U.S.C. §437(h)).

[16]The scope and application of these federal statutes and the problems which have arisen under them are considered at length in Chapters 2, 3, 4, 5 and 7 of R. Stern and E. Gressman, SUPREME COURT PRACTICE (5th ed., 1978).

New York an appeal to the highest court lies if there has been either a dissent in the Appellate Division or a reversal or substantial modification of the trial court's judgment by the Appellate Division on a question of law (New York Civil Practice Act, §5601(a)); this provision is responsible for a substantial portion of the Court of Appeals' work load. New Jersey (Rule 2:2-1) and North Carolina (Gen. Stat. §7A-30) also permit an appeal as of right when there has been a dissent in the intermediate appellate court. In Washington there must be *both* a dissent and a reversal of the trial court (Rule 13.2). Texas Article 1953 makes the fact of dissent below a ground which the Supreme Court may consider in deciding whether to review a case.

(c) Procedure

Although an appeal as of right from a lower appellate court may, as in Washington Rule 13.2, be taken by filing a notice of appeal, usually something more is required to demonstrate to the high court that the case probably is appealable as of right. Such a statement of the basis for the court's jurisdiction may be included in an enlarged notice of appeal, as in Ohio (Rule I(B)) and North Carolina (Rule 14), or made in a separate jurisdictional statement filed within 10 days of the taking of the appeal, as in New York (Court of Appeals Rule 500.2). In New York the jurisdictional statement is intended to show the basis for the court's jurisdiction; the relevant documents are to be attached. *(Ibid.)* If, as in the United States Supreme Court and Illinois, the court views the category of appeals "as of right" as including only those cases that present substantial constitutional issues, the jurisdictional memorandum should also include an argument showing substantial merit to the appeal. United States Supreme Court Rule 15; Illinois Rule 317. Also, cf. Ohio Supreme Court Rule II, §3.

In Illinois only a notice of appeal was originally required to be filed to take an appeal as of right. But experience demonstrated[17] that this procedure was often invoked improperly. As a result, Rule 317 was modified to require the appellant to submit a "Petition for Appeal as a Matter of Right" in the same form as a petition for leave to appeal as a matter of discretion, except "that the petition need only contain argument as to why

---

[17]See Committee Comment to Illinois Rule 317.

appeal lies to the Supreme Court as a matter of right. . . ."[18]
Counsel should, however, normally not so limit the petition but
should make it broad enough to cover the possibility that the
court may find that the appeal cannot be taken as a matter of
right. Another reason for going further is that the factors which
will be persuasive in a petition for leave to appeal addressed to
the Supreme Court's discretion will almost invariably also help
induce the court to take the appeal as of right. This means that,
in substance, the form and function of the Illinois petition to
appeal as of right are almost the same as for the ordinary petition for leave to appeal. The Illinois petition thus resembles the
jurisdictional statement in the United States Supreme Court,
which includes most of the features of the petition for certiorari
even though it serves a substantially different function.[19]

5.5   Bypassing the Intermediate Appellate Court

The United States Supreme Court and the supreme courts
of a number of states may exercise their discretion to review
decisions which have been appealed to an intermediate appellate court before the latter court renders a decision. Some of the
supreme courts may enter orders of transfer on their own initiative or on certification of the lower appellate court; all may act
on application of a party.

This bypass procedure is utilized not only because of the
importance of the particular case and a need for expedited decision. A number of states—Indiana, Kansas, Missouri, North Carolina and Washington—specifically provide for consideration of
such administrative factors as the case load burden of the respective appellate courts or the orderly administration of justice. In Arkansas, California and New Jersey the supreme court
has an unrestricted right to transfer in either direction, which
might permit consideration of the same factors.[20] The Arizona
and Massachusetts supreme courts have transferred to themselves classes or large groups of cases to relieve an overloaded

---

[18]*Ibid.*
[19]See R. Stern and E. Gressman, SUPREME COURT PRACTICE, Secs. 7.9–7.10,
7.14 (5th ed., 1978).
[20]In Indiana the Chief Justice may transfer cases among the courts of appeals and the
Supreme Court in order to expedite consideration. Rule 4. Arkansas Supreme Court
Rule 29(7) provides that

"It is the intention of this court by the adoption of this rule to achieve an equalization
of the appellate workload between the Supreme Court and the Court of Appeals. If the
classifications made herein do not achieve this objective, adjustments will be made."

intermediate appellate court.[21] Such wholesale transfer orders are made on the supreme court's own motion or, more likely, after informal discussions with the lower appellate court judges.

The United States Supreme Court is empowered to grant certiorari upon "a petition of any party to any civil or criminal case, before or after rendition of judgment or decree" in the court of appeals (28 U.S.C. §1254(1)); application "to review a case before judgment has been rendered in the court of appeals may be made at any time before judgment" (28 U.S.C. §2101(e)). These provisions have been construed to mean that the case must be *in* the court of appeals before it can be taken to the Supreme Court; not only must a notice of appeal have been filed but the appeal must have been docketed in the court of appeals, in the past by filing the certified record from the district court.[22]

Chief Justice Burger has written that "[a]ny case decided in any district court with a genuine need for swift review by the Supreme Court can be the subject of a petition for certiorari before judgment. No one can point accurately to a case in which the Supreme Court has failed to give expedited review when circumstances warranted that action."[23] But the Court has not regarded many circumstances as justifying expedited review. Supreme Court Rule 18 provides that certiorari will be granted before judgment in the court of appeals

> "only upon a showing that the case is of such imperative public importance as to justify the deviation from normal appellate practice and to require immediate settlement in this Court."

The cases cited as examples involved the constitutionality of important statutes or matters of urgency calling for immediate action, such as a national coal strike or seizure of the steel mills.

---

[21]The Arizona Supreme Court has frequently taken over large numbers of cases from the Court of Appeals for the First District (located in Phoenix) for this reason. The Massachusetts Supreme Judicial Court has taken substantial numbers of cases from the Appeals Court. See Sec. 1.10(b), *supra.*

[22]The above statutory provisions do not in terms require that the *record* be filed in the court of appeals. With the filing of the record no longer a prerequisite to docketing a case in that court (Federal Appellate Rule 12), the jurisdiction of the Supreme Court to take the case should vest when the case is docketed in the court below. Even the filing of the notice of appeal might be sufficient, as it is in Illinois (see Illinois Rule 302(b)); even though that occurs in the trial court, it vests the court of appeals with jurisdiction over the case, and the federal statute does not in terms require "docketing." No case presenting an issue as to this has arisen, and cautious counsel may still be careful to have the record filed when the case is docketed in the court of appeals in order to avoid running into any difficulty.

[23]Chief Justice Burger, *Annual Report on the State of the Judiciary,* 62 A.B.A.J. 443, 444 (1976).

Urgency to the parties has not been deemed sufficient. The Court has also granted certiorari before judgment in the court below when a similar or identical question of constitutional or other importance was before the Court in another case; "importance" in that situation did not have to meet the standard of exceptionality otherwise called for.

The procedure in the states which authorize a petition for review before judgment in the intermediate appellate court is often very much the same as in the United States Supreme Court. The petition for leave may be submitted to a state supreme court any time after notice of appeal has been filed with the intermediate court (as in Illinois Rule 302; Indiana Appellate Rule 4(A)(10)), or any time before the court of appeals places the case on its calendar for consideration (as under Wisconsin Rule 809.60), or within 10 (Kentucky Rule 76.18) or 20 (Kansas Rule 8.02) or 30 (Michigan Rule 852) days of the filing of the notice of appeal (or claim, in Michigan), or within 10 or 15 days after the appeal is docketed in the appellate court (Massachusetts Rule 11; North Carolina Rule 15), or within 10 days after all briefs are filed (New Jersey Rule 2:12-2). In Illinois the petition may be submitted to and granted by the Supreme Court or a single justice thereof. Illinois Rule 302.

The standard in Illinois is whether the case is one "in which the public interest requires prompt adjudication by the Supreme Court." Rule 302(b). In Massachusetts the grounds for a bypass order are that the case presents a novel issue, or a constitutional question, or that such an order would be in the public interest. Rule 11. Michigan requires a showing of merit by appellant plus a substantial question as to the constitutionality of a statute, a legal principle of major significance, a significant public interest involving the state or an officer thereof or a determination that delay in final disposition will cause substantial harm. Rule 852. Kentucky requires a showing of great and immediate public importance;[24] Kansas, of public interest; and Indiana, of "a substantial question of law of great public importance and that an emergency exists for a speedy determination." Indiana Rule 4(A)(10); Kansas Rule 8.01–8.02; Kentucky Rule 76.18. The North Carolina statute (Gen. Stat. §7A-31) is very similar, except that it adds, as alternative grounds, that "the

---

[24]The same standard applies to recommendations for transfer from the Kentucky Court of Appeals. Kentucky Rule 76.18.

work load of the appellate courts is such that the expeditious administration of justice requires certification" or that delay in final adjudication is likely to cause substantial harm. The Wisconsin and Maryland rules set no standard to guide their supreme courts, but it is likely that they will take the same factors into consideration.

These guidelines certainly sound less forbidding than the "imperative public importance" which must be shown under United States Supreme Court Rule 18. That the issue is clearly important enough to require eventual determination by the state's highest court and that the public interest calls for a prompt decision may be sufficient.

The result is that many of the state supreme courts are more liberal than the United States Supreme Court in the granting of petitions which allow the intermediate appellate courts to be skipped.[25] They do not regard this procedure as appropriate only for drastic emergencies, but as available whenever there is a good reason for a prompt decision by the highest court. Their greater liberality in contrast to the United States Supreme Court may be attributed to their having a smaller case load.

The procedure in applying for review before decision by the lower appellate court is much the same as in applying for review after decision. A petition or application must be filed setting forth the reasons why the review is called for. In general the petition should stress the same factors as would influence a supreme court to grant certiorari or review in any case (see pp. 137–142, *infra*), but with emphasis on what makes the case especially important and requires decision as speedily as possible, or in any event more rapidly than the normal course of appellate review.

In the United States Supreme Court and a number of states,[26] the procedure for bypassing the intermediate appellate court has one novel feature. The request or application may be made by the *winning* party below as well as the loser. The latter must first have taken an appeal to the intermediate appellate court, which requires docketing the appeal in that court. See Sec. 3.8, *supra.* After that has been done, however, either party

---

[25]In the year ending August 31, 1979, the Massachusetts Supreme Judicial Court allowed 39 applications for direct review (bypass of Appeals Court) out of 68, and took 142 cases on its own motion before hearing below. See Sec. 1.10(b), *supra.*

[26]Colorado Rule 50(b); Illinois Rule 302(b); Indiana Appellate Rule 4(A)(10); Kansas Rule 8.02; Michigan Rule 852.

may request that the appeal be transferred to a higher court.[27] In the usual appellate situation to allow the winner to appeal from a decision in his favor, from which the loser was not appealing, might well present an issue as to the existence of a continuing justiciable case or controversy. But no such problem can arise when the practical effect of a request for immediate decision by the highest court is merely to transfer an appeal by a loser from one appellate court to another. See Sec. 2.2(b), *supra.*

5.6   Review on Certification by the Intermediate Appellate Court

In a number of states as well as the federal system, the intermediate appellate court may certify a case or particular question to the highest court of the jurisdiction. The certificate may issue before or after decision by the intermediate court.

(a)   Certification Before Decision Below

The United States courts of appeals and the Court of Claims are empowered by statute to certify "any question of law" in any "case as to which instructions are desired" to the Supreme Court for binding instructions. 28 U.S.C. §§1254(3), 1255(2). In cases coming from a court of appeals—but not the Court of Claims—the Supreme Court has the alternative of requiring the "entire record to be sent up for decision of the entire matter in controversy." Certificates to obtain instructions issue before decision in the lower court.

A few states also provide for certification by the intermediate appellate court before decision. In Kansas the test is the public interest and whether there is a need for expedition (Rule 8.101-8.102). Under Arkansas Supreme Court Rule 29(4), adopted in 1979 when the state Court of Appeals was created, the Court of Appeals must find that the case is within the exclusive jurisdiction of the Supreme Court (see Sec. 5.3, *supra*) or "involves an issue of significant public interest or a legal princi-

---

[27]The federal statutory language (28 U.S.C. §1254(a)) permitting a writ of certiorari to be granted "upon a petition of any party to any civil or criminal case" would seem to allow petitions by successful parties in all cases and not just those in which a petition was sought before judgment in the intermediate court. No case has been found, however, in which a victorious party was enabled to take an appeal in the first instance.

ple of major importance." In contrast to the practice under the federal statutes, most of these procedures seem to contemplate that such certification obligates the state supreme court to decide the issue certified to it, although the language of some of the controlling statutes or rules does not appear to be explicit as to this.[28] Wisconsin Rule 809.61 and Arkansas Rule 29(4), however, permit the supreme court to refuse to take jurisdiction over appeals certified to it by the court of appeals. See also Hawaii Rev. Stat. §602-59. In Texas the Court of Appeals may certify questions before decision, but only when the Supreme Court may not review the case by writ of error, which is seldom. The Supreme Court has discretion to refuse to hear certified cases, very few of which are submitted to it.

A 1980 amendment to the Florida constitution provides that the Supreme Court in its discretion may review orders and judgments "certified by the district court of appeal in which the appeal is pending to require immediate resolution by the Supreme Court, and:

"(i) to be of great public importance, or
"(ii) to have a great effect on the appropriate administration of justice throughout the state."

Florida Const. Art. 5, §3(b)(5); Florida Rule of Appellate Procedure 9.030(a)(2)(B), 381 So.2d 1372 (1980). The District Court of Appeal may certify "on its own motion or upon suggestion of a party." The suggestion must be filed within 10 days of the filing of a notice of appeal, shall not exceed five pages, and shall contain both an explanation of why the appeal satisfies the above constitutional requirements and a certificate of counsel expressing his belief that it does, "based on a reasoned and studied professional judgment." Other parties may respond within 5 days. The District Court of Appeal need not rule on the suggestion. If the Supreme Court accepts jurisdiction, the prior time limits for the filing of papers remain in effect except that papers to be filed thereafter shall be filed in the Supreme Court, and the District Court of Appeal record shall be transmitted to the Supreme Court. Florida Rule of Appellate Procedure 9.125, 381 So.2d 1384–1385 (1980).

Although a reading of the federal statutes on certification would seem to leave to the lower court the question of what

---

[28]Connecticut §3135A; Georgia Code Ann. §§24-3638, 4541; Kansas Rule 8.02; Louisiana Rule XI; Massachusetts Rule of Appellate Procedure 11(f); New Jersey Rule 2.12-2.

cases are to be certified and reviewed, the Supreme Court regards the certification route as a possible device for undermining its discretionary authority to limit its review to cases which the Court itself deems worthy. As a result the Court has for many years, for one reason or another, been able to dismiss almost all of the cases certified to it without answering the questions submitted. In *Wisniewski* v. *United States,* 353 U.S. 901, 902 (1957), the Court dismissed a certificate presented because different panels of the same court of appeals had disagreed, on the ground that this was not an adequate basis "for invoking so exceptional a jurisdiction of this Court," and further stated:

> "It is also the task of a court of appeals to decide all properly presented cases coming before it, except in the rare instances, as for example the pendency of another case before this Court raising the same issue, when certification may be advisable in the proper administration and expedition of judicial business."

As a result, the certification provision has become practically a dead letter in the federal courts, although not entirely, since the Court has accepted three certified questions in the last 32 years. In the only two such cases since 1946, the Court answered a question as to whether the Governor of Mississippi was entitled to a trial by jury when charged with contempt for violating a desegregation order of the court of appeals (*United States* v. *Barnett,* 376 U.S. 681 (1964)), and also a question whether a senior judge of a court of appeals who has sat on the original panel hearing a case can participate in a rehearing *en banc* (*Moody* v. *Albemarle Paper Co.,* 417 U.S. 622 (1974)).

Apart from the Supreme Court's discretion not to accept certifications, which may find justification in the statutory use of the word "may" in describing what the Court is to do (28 U.S.C. §1254), there are certain statutory requirements which must be met. The statute permits only questions of law to be certified. Supreme Court Rule 24 goes further and declares that the certification shall state "the nature of the cause and the facts on which such question or proposition of law arises" and that the question must be distinct and definite.

These requisites are to be met by the court of appeals, not by the parties or their counsel. It is for the court of appeals to determine, as it sees fit, before or after the presentation of briefs or oral argument, whether a question is to be certified. There is no provision in the rules or statutes for a request or petition for certification. Since the 1980 revision of the Supreme Court rules, the parties have not had to pay any fees. If the Court orders that the case be briefed or argued, the Clerk will obtain the record from the court below. Rule 25.3. The parties may then prepare a joint appendix in the manner prescribed by Rule 30 for other types of cases. See Secs. 6.12–6.14, *infra*. A party may move that the Court dismiss the certificate as improper (*Carolina, Clinchfield & Ohio Ry.* v. *United States*, 266 U.S. 636 (1924)), or may stipulate or make concessions rendering the answers to the certified points unnecessary (*Lederer* v. *McGarvey*, 271 U.S. 342, 343–344 (1926)).

(b) Certification After Decision Below

A few states—Florida, Illinois, Massachusetts, Missouri, New York—provide for certification from the lower appellate court after decision. In Missouri the Court of Appeals may certify a case to the Supreme Court because of its "general interest or importance . . . or for purposes of re-examining existing law" (Rule 83.02). In Connecticut the Appellate Session may certify questions of law deemed "substantial" enough for Supreme Court review (§§3148–3151). Texas Rule 463 provides that if there is a dissent on a material question the Court of Appeals on its own or a party's motion shall certify the point to the Supreme Court. The Florida District Court of Appeal may, after decision, certify to the Supreme Court questions found "to be of great public importance" and "in direct conflict with a decision of another district court of appeal." Florida Const. Art. 5, §3(b)(4)(1980); Florida Rule of Appellate Procedure 9.030(a)(2), 381 So.2d 1371 (1980).

Illinois Rule 316 provides for a certificate by a division of "the Appellate Court that a case decided by it involves a question of such importance that it should be decided by the Supreme Court." A party may, and often does, apply for a certificate of importance either by filing a separate petition therefor or including his request in a petition for rehearing. An application for a certificate may also be filed within 14 days after the court's action on a petition for rehearing. If the Appellate Court grants the certificate, the clerk of that court transmits the record filed in that court with a certified copy of proceedings in that court to the Supreme Court. In Massachusetts a majority of the

Appeals Court or the panel thereof which decided the case may authorize review by the Supreme Judicial Court. Section 5602 of the New York Civil Practice Act provides for appeal to the New York Court of Appeals by permission of the Appellate Division.[29] In Ohio, if the Court of Appeals finds its judgment in conflict with another court of appeals, it may certify the case to the Supreme Court. These certificates of the intermediate appellate courts are in some states sufficient in themselves to obtain review by the supreme courts. In Illinois, where this is true,

> "Certificates of importance are rarely granted. As a general rule, the justices of the Appellate Court prefer to allow the Supreme Court to decide for itself which cases are of sufficient importance to be added to its docket. However, the Supreme Court promulgated Rule 316, presumably intending for it to be used, and such certificates are allowed from time to time."[30]

In Florida, on the other hand, the Supreme Court retains discretionary authority to determine whether or not to accept the certified case.

5.7   Review on Application of a Party After Judgment in the Intermediate Appellate Court

Except in the situations described in the preceding subsections, review by the highest court in the appellate structure of the decision of the intermediate court must be sought by the filing of a petition or application urging the high court to accept the application for review in the exercise of its discretion. The petition or application is filed by a party dissatisfied with the judgment of the intermediate court.

(a)   The Documents to Be Filed

The principal document filed is variously called a petition or application for certiorari[31] or certification,[32] a petition for

---

[29]When the Appellate Division grants leave to appeal, it should define the questions of law to be reviewed and advise as to whether it has made factual findings.

[30]PRACTITIONER'S HANDBOOK FOR APPEALS TO THE ILLINOIS SUPREME AND APPELLATE COURTS, p. 32 (1978).

[31]United States, Colorado, Georgia, Maryland, New Mexico, Tennessee. Florida's 1980 constitutional amendment and the corresponding rule eliminated the word "certiorari," but left the procedure the same. Florida Const. Art. 5, §3(b). Florida Rule of Appellate Procedure 9.120, 381 So.2d 1382 (1980).

[32]Connecticut, New Jersey.

leave to appeal[33] or to allow[34] or to permit[35] an appeal or a hearing,[36] or a petition for review[37] or to transfer.[38] It constitutes both the formal prayer for review and the statement of facts and reasons why the application should be granted. Texas retains the older terminology: petition for writ of error; this is in substance a brief on the merits as well as a petition for review. See Sec. 5.1, *supra.* The number of copies is usually the same as for briefs in the same court, but in Connecticut only nine copies need to be filed, not 55. Connecticut Practice Book §3139 (1978).

In the New York Court of Appeals a short motion for permission to appeal is to be supported by a brief showing the court's jurisdiction, the questions presented and why the questions merit review. Ten copies should be filed, instead of 20 for briefs on the merits. Either party may also submit a copy of his brief below; respondent must file his brief below if he does not submit an answering memorandum. New York Court of Appeals Rule 500.9. In Ohio a short notice of appeal is accompanied by a memorandum in support of jurisdiction which in substance constitutes the petition for leave to appeal, and should include a short treatment of the merits. Ohio Supreme Court Rules I, II. In Arizona the petition for review is merely a formal paper, like a notice of appeal. It must be accompanied by the petition for rehearing in the Court of Appeals, which therefore must be written so as also to serve the quite different purpose of persuading the Supreme Court that the decision below should be reviewed (Arizona Rule 23); it will also be petitioner's only opportunity to supplement his brief below in presenting the merits of the case to the Supreme Court if review is granted. See Sec. 1.10(a), note 68, *supra,* and pp. 134–135, *infra.* In Arkansas a two-page petition for certiorari may be accompanied by the petition for rehearing below. Alabama Rule 39 requires that both a petition for certiorari and an accompanying brief be filed; the petition is to state the grounds for review, while the brief is to be the full brief on the merits, to stand as such if certiorari is granted. Petitioner may, however, file a reply to respondent's brief. See p. 215, *infra.*

---

[33]Illinois, Michigan.
[34]Pennsylvania.
[35]New York.
[36]California.
[37]Kansas, Kentucky, Massachusetts, Oregon, Washington.
[38]Indiana, Missouri.

Florida, Georgia and New Jersey provide for a short preliminary notice or notice of intent to be filed in the court of appeals or in both that court and the supreme court, with a petition for certiorari or its equivalent to be filed subsequently. See Sec. 5.7(b), *infra*.

Many states, like the United States Supreme Court, require the opinions and judgment below to be appended to the petition or application.[39] Under Pennsylvania Rule 1925(c), if no statement of reasons already appears in the record, the court below must file a brief explanatory statement after the petition for allowance of appeal to the Supreme Court has been received.

Some states, unlike the United States Supreme Court's recent practice, require a copy of the record or appendix in the intermediate court to be filed, either by the clerk of that court[40] or by the petitioner.[41] In Texas, the single copy of the record in the Court of Appeals is sent to the Supreme Court, along with three copies of the briefs below, even though the application for writ of error and the reply thereto are also briefs. In Connecticut the Supreme Court clerk makes seven copies of the certified file. Connecticut Practice Book, §3145.

Kentucky and Ohio, however, like the United States Supreme Court, do not want the record transmitted unless and until the high court decides to hear the case, or unless that court orders the record to be transmitted.[42]

The United States Supreme Court required the certified record below to accompany the petition for certiorari until 1970; indeed, up to 1954, at least 10 printed copies had to be filed. By 1970, the expansion of the Court's case load caused the Court to recognize that it seldom looked at any of the record except the judgment and the opinions below, which were required to be attached to the petition. The vast majority of the thousands of records filed each year remained unread, and consumed storage space in the Supreme Court building. The Clerk's Office merely unpacked the record when it arrived, and

---

[39]E.g., United States Supreme Court Rule 21.1(k); Georgia Rule 24-4536(d); Illinois Rule 315; Kentucky Rule 76.20; Louisiana Rule X-4; New Jersey Rule 2:12-7(a).

[40]Connecticut, Georgia, Michigan. Maryland allows the clerk below 60 days to transmit the record.

[41]California, Illinois, New Jersey, New York, Pennsylvania, Tennessee. New Jersey requires nine copies.

[42]United States Supreme Court Rules 19.1, 19.2, 23.2; Kentucky Rule 76.20(4); Ohio Supreme Court Rule II, §9. See R. Stern and E. Gressman, SUPREME COURT PRACTICE, Sec. 6.14 (5th ed., 1978).

then repacked it and returned it to the court below in the vast majority of the cases in which certiorari was denied.

Accordingly, in 1970 the Supreme Court rules were amended to make the filing of the record with the petition unnecessary. Either party is still entitled to request the clerk below to certify the record, but Supreme Court Rule 19.1, as amended in 1980, discourages the making of such requests. They "should not be made as a matter of course but only when the record is deemed essential to a proper understanding of the case by this Court." If possible, the party should include the "essential" portions of the record in the text of his petition or brief in opposition if it really is important that the Justices read it. If a Justice wishes to see the record before voting on the petition, the Clerk will ask the clerk below to transmit the record, or any part of it. Such requests are not infrequent. Either party may also request all or part of the record to be sent up at any time thereafter.

But in the vast majority of cases, the record is not called for unless the Court grants certiorari. When that happens, the Clerk promptly requests the clerk of the court below possessed of the record to transmit it to the Supreme Court. Rule 23.2. No formal writ of certiorari issues unless the lower court refuses to submit the record, as once happened. *In re Summers,* 325 U.S. 561, 562 (1945).

The United States Supreme Court (Rule 19.3) and a number of states—Colorado, Indiana, Michigan, Pennsylvania—require that the filing fee be paid at the time the petition or application is filed. Louisiana requires a separate assignment of errors. Georgia requires a certificate of counsel that the application is contemplated and not prohibited by the rules (Rule 24-4536(i)). In Connecticut and New Jersey counsel must certify that the petition presents a substantial question, is filed in good faith and is not for delay.

In a number of states[43] the filing of a petition for rehearing or reconsideration in the court below is a prerequisite to seeking review in the state's supreme court. In Oregon the petition for review filed in the Supreme Court must also be filed in the Court of Appeal as a petition for rehearing. Rule 10.10. If the Court of Appeal does not change its decision within 10 days, the Su-

---

[43]Alabama, Arizona, Colorado, Georgia, Indiana, Missouri, Oklahoma, Texas, Washington.

preme Court will proceed to pass upon the petition. The purpose of these provisions is to give the lower court an opportunity to respond to the arguments to be presented to the Supreme Court, either by changing its decision or by additional comment if it so desires. This would seem to be theoretically reasonable. But experience teaches that petitions for reconsideration, which attempt to convince judges who have once made up their minds to change their positions, are hardly ever successful. Often there is no sensible reason for presenting again to those judges arguments which may have a reasonable chance for success when addressed to members of a higher tribunal. Making a petition for rehearing a prerequisite to seeking further review thus in most cases is an unnecessary waste of time and effort for both the lawyers and the judges.

Arkansas does not require a petition for rehearing below, but permits such a petition to be attached to the petition for certiorari, which may not be longer than two pages. Accordingly, only through a petition for rehearing may the petitioner for certiorari present more than two pages of supporting argument.

Arizona goes further in merging the required motion for rehearing in the Court of Appeals and the petition for review in the Supreme Court. After rehearing is denied below, the unsuccessful party files in the Supreme Court a formal petition for review, which is not permitted to be argumentative, together with copies of the motion for rehearing filed below as the only statement of reasons why the Supreme Court should hear the appeal.

As suggested in Sec. 1.10(a), *supra,* the Arizona requirement that the petition for rehearing below serve as the petition for review in the state Supreme Court disregards the differences in the functions of the two documents. A petition for rehearing customarily is directed to demonstrating to the lower court that it overlooked something or made a drastic error. A petition for leave to appeal or for certiorari has the broader purpose of convincing the higher court that review is warranted. This goes beyond the merits of the case and deals with matters which are not the business of the lower court, such as the importance of the issues raised. A petition which would be appropriate for one of the two courts would often not be suitable for the other. The hybrid which counsel must now prepare is certainly inapt for the court below, and its focus may not be proper for the higher court either. Nor should counsel be required to waste his time and that of the judges by rearguing to the Court of Appeals questions once fully presented when nothing more can be added. The desirability of insuring that issues have been first presented to that court does not mean that they must be presented twice. Since the judges below who have already decided the case are much less likely to grant rehearing than different judges of the higher court are to grant review, in most cases the only reasonable course will be to subordinate or even disregard the rehearing function of the petition and emphasize the reasons why the Supreme Court should grant review.

When the confusing nature of the surviving document is taken into account, the preparation and filing of an application not appropriate for either court would not appear to be justified by the reduction in the number of papers which counsel must file. It is regrettable that the Arizona Supreme Court believes that this procedure is required by its commitment to the legislature not to allow the creation of an intermediate appellate court to increase the amount of work required of counsel for an appeal.

(b) The Time for Seeking Discretionary Review

The statutes or rules of each jurisdiction prescribe the time during which the petition or application for discretionary review must be filed. The period most frequently chosen is 30 days from the judgment below,[44] which is also the most common time to appeal to other appellate courts. California, Hawaii and Massachusetts allow 10 days.[45] A number of states have adopted 14-,[46] 15-,[47] 17-[48] and 20-day[49] limits. In Georgia the preliminary notice of intent to apply for certiorari must be filed within 10 days after the judgment below, with the petition for certiorari

---

[44]Colorado, Connecticut, Florida, Louisiana, New Jersey, New York, Ohio, Oregon, Pennsylvania, Texas, Washington, Wisconsin. The 1979 Tennessee rules allow 30 days after judgment if no petition for rehearing is filed, but 15 days after denial of a petition for rehearing. Rule 11(b).

[45]In California the appellee has 10 additional days to respond and the Supreme Court 10 days to act before the Court of Appeal's judgment becomes final—unless the Supreme Court grants an extension of time. In Hawaii the Supreme Court "shall" act within 10 days; its failure to accept the application within that period "shall constitute a rejection." No provision is made or time allowed for a response to the application.

[46]Alabama.

[47]Arizona, Maryland, Missouri, North Carolina, Oklahoma.

[48]Arkansas.

[49]Idaho, Indiana, Iowa, Kansas, Kentucky, New Mexico.

to be filed within 30 days of the judgment.[50] In New Jersey and Florida the preliminary notice is to be filed within 20 and 30 days, respectively, of the judgment below with the petition for certiorari or its Florida equivalent to be filed within 10 days thereafter.[51] Only Illinois (56)[52] and the United States Supreme Court (90 days for most cases)[53] allow more than 30 days.

In a number of supreme courts, including the United States Supreme Court since 1980, additional time is allowed for filing a cross-petition. E.g., Pennsylvania Rule 1113; United States Supreme Court Rules 19.5, 20.5. Cf. Sec. 4.7, *supra.*

Generally the petition must be received by the clerk of the supreme court by the due date. Under United States Supreme Court Rule 28.2 (1980), the date of mailing may constitute the date of filing. See Sec. 7.40, *infra.*

The time to petition from a judgment below is almost everywhere tolled by a timely motion for rehearing or reconsideration, or by a substantive change in the judgment below. It begins to run anew after the lower court acts on such a motion or changes the judgment. The governing principle is the same as for appeals from the trial court to the first or only appellate court, as described in Sec. 4.6, note 30, *supra.*

In addition, in most jurisdictions extensions of time can be obtained from the supreme court or a justice thereof. In the United States Supreme Court extensions of up to 60 days may be granted by individual Justices in most cases, and of up to 30 days in federal criminal cases. 28 U.S.C. §2101(c); Supreme Court Rule 20.1. "[E]xcept in the most extraordinary circumstances," such as death or illness of counsel, or a printers' strike, the application for extension must be submitted at least 10 days before expiration of the period sought to be extended. Rule 29.2. Applications for extension filed before the 10-day period may be granted for "good cause." 28 U.S.C. §2101(c); Rule 29. It is unwise to invoke these extension provisions unless the "cause" is very "good." Good causes include serious personal reasons, with other professional engagements falling further down on the scale unless counsel's difficulty is both aggravated

---

[50]Georgia Rule 24-4536.

[51]Florida Rule 9.120; New Jersey Rules 2:12-3, 2:12-7.

[52]Illinois Rule 315(b). The Illinois Supreme Court is now considering reducing this period. The Rules Committee has recommended 35 days.

[53]28 U.S.C. §2101(c). Supreme Court Rule 20.1 now provides that in criminal cases the time is 60 days; before 1980 30 days had been allowed in criminal cases from federal courts and 90 days in criminal cases from state courts.

and unavoidable. Personal convenience, such as vacation schedules, enjoys a very low rating.

The Supreme Court of the United States also frequently allows petitions to be filed tardily when the time limits are prescribed by its own rules and not by statute. The Court has held that time limits such as are contained in its Rule 20 for both state and federal criminal cases are not jurisdictional, that is, binding upon it, and can be waived by the Court.[54] Sometimes the Court grants such extensions or disregards the tardiness of the petition without mention of the point, even without an application or apparent justification. But, of course, a party cannot be sure that the Court will be that lenient to him. Petitions have been denied because they were one day late.

(c) Grounds for Granting Review

The rules of court often enumerate the factors which are to be considered in determining whether review should be granted. Whether the standards are defined broadly or narrowly or not at all, the factors considered are usually the public importance or significance of the case or the questions raised, the existence of conflict with decisions of other courts of the same rank (immediately below the supreme court) or of the supreme court of the state or the United States, and the extent of error or injustice in the result reached by the court below.

Illinois Rule 315(a), which was modeled on United States Supreme Court Rule 17, sets forth factors which most courts consider:

> "The following, while neither controlling nor fully measuring the court's discretion, indicate the character of reasons which will be considered: the general importance of the question presented; the existence of a conflict between the decision sought to be reviewed and a decision of the Supreme Court, or of another division of the Appellate Court; the need for the exercise of the Supreme Court's supervisory authority; and the final or interlocutory character of the judgment sought to be reviewed."

For similar enumerations of grounds for review, see California Rule 29; Colorado Rule 49; Michigan Rule 853; Missouri Rule 83.02–83.03; New Jersey Rule 2:12-4; New York Rule 500.9(a)(2); North Carolina Gen. Stat. §7A-31; Oklahoma Court

---

[54]*Schacht* v. *United States,* 398 U.S. 58, 63–64 (1970); R. Stern and E. Gressman, SUPREME COURT PRACTICE, Sec. 6.1, pp. 389–394 (5th ed., 1978).

of Appeals Rule 3.13; Tennessee Rule 11(a).[55] Other state laws or rules merely refer generally to "gravity and importance" (Georgia Rule 24-4536(j)),[56] "the public interest" or the "interest of justice" (Massachusetts Gen. Laws Ann. ch. 211A, §11), "desirable and in the public interest" (Maryland Ann. Code, Courts and Judicial Proceedings, §12-203), "special and important reasons" (Pennsylvania Rule 1114).[57] Connecticut adds to the customary reasons for review division among the members of the panel of the Appellate Session or inability of the judges to agree upon a common ground of decision. Connecticut Practice Book, §3137. Hawaii refers to inconsistency not only with decisions of the state Supreme Court or the intermediate appellate court but with "federal decisions" generally. Hawaii Rev. Stat. 602-20(b). Where rules or statutes are silent, the same factors are taken into consideration.[58]

More specific categories describe classes which would generally be regarded as important, such as constitutional questions[59] or questions affecting public officers.[60] Several also mention the needs of judicial administration, which means that the work load of the respective appellate courts may be taken into account.[61] In Arkansas, where the Court of Appeals sits *en banc,* a tie vote is a ground for certiorari. Rule 29(6). The general

---

[55]The Wisconsin Supreme Court has issued guidelines as to the court's discretion in granting review, although they are neither "controlling nor limiting." *In re Standards to Review Petitions to Appeal,* Nov. 15, 1978. Review will be granted on the vote of three or more of the seven justices, and "when any one of the following criteria are met":

(A) A significant question of constitutional law is presented.
(B) Need is demonstrated for the court to consider establishing, implementing or changing a policy within its authority.
(C) Decision by the court "will help develop, clarify or harmonize the law," and the case calls for application of a new doctrine, or presents a novel question of statewide impact, or a question of law likely to recur.
(D) The decision below is in conflict with a decision of another court of appeals or of the Wisconsin or United States Supreme Courts.
(E) Although the decision below is in accord with other decisions, they are ripe for re-examination.

The presence or absence of one or more of these factors is not to be taken "as assurance" that review will be granted or denied.
[56]The same subsection provides that in appeals from the Georgia Workmen's Compensation Board, there must be a dissent by three judges below or a conflict among divisions of the Court of Appeals on a question of law.
[57]A note attached to the Pennsylvania rule calls attention to the factors mentioned in the United States Supreme Court rules.
[58]Letter from Mr. Justice Harbison, Supreme Court of Tennessee, with respect to the pre-1979 Tennessee practice.
[59]Alabama Rule 39, Iowa Rule 402(b)(3), Massachusetts Gen. Laws Ann. ch. 211A, §10.
[60]Florida Rule 9.030(a)(2)(iii).
[61]Indiana, Kansas, Missouri, North Carolina, Washington. As to Arkansas, see Rule 29(7) quoted at Sec. 5.5, note 20, *supra.*

authority to transfer cases is also broad enough to permit such matters to be considered.

Although only a few rules include as a factor whether the decision was correct on the merits (Hawaii Rev. Stat. 602.20(b) ("grave errors"); Iowa Rule 402(b)(1); Michigan Rule 853; Texas Rule 469(e), (f)), that would seem to be encompassed in such undefined phrases as "has so far departed from the accepted and usual course of judicial proceedings" (United States Supreme Court Rule 17.1(a)) or "need for the exercise of the Supreme Court's supervisory authority" (Illinois Supreme Court Rule 315(a)) or the other general standards mentioned above. Indeed, the *importance* of reviewing a decision may depend on which way it has been decided. A supreme court may think it much more important to review a lower appellate court's ruling when the decision below seems wrong than when it seems right. If a decision outrages the court's sense of justice, that may be enough to convince it that reversal is important.[62] In Texas and Louisiana denial of review warrants an inference of agreement with the decision below. As to Texas, see Sec. 5.1, *supra.*

Florida, in order to cope with the tremendous and rapidly increasing case load (see table, Sec. 1.6, *supra*), has taken more drastic measures to "limit the Supreme Court's appellate, discretionary, and original jurisdiction to cases that substantially affect the law of the state." Committee Note to Rule 9.030, as revised in 1980, 381 So.2d 1373. In addition to narrowly restricting the Supreme Court's mandatory jurisdiction, the 1980 revision of the judicial article of the state constitution made it clearer than it had been before that the importance of the case or the question presented was not a permissible ground for Supreme Court review in the absence of a certificate of importance from the District Court of Appeal, either before or after decision in that court. The Supreme Court then has discretion as to whether to accept the certified case for review. See Sec. 5.6(a), *supra.* At the same time the state Supreme Court's power to grant discretionary review because of a conflict in appellate decisions was limited to cases in which the conflict was "express" as well as "direct," even though only a "direct" conflict was necessary for the issuance of a certificate by a District Court of Appeal. Compare subsections (b)(3) and (b)(4) of Art. 5, §3, of the Florida constitution as amended. The conflict—or alleged

---

[62]E.g., *Thompson* v. *City of Louisville*, 362 U.S. 199 (1960); *Washington* v. *United States*, 357 U.S. 348 (1958).

conflict—"cases comprised the overwhelming bulk of the [Supreme Court's] caseload and gave rise to an intricate body of case law interpreting the requirements for discretionary conflict review," even permitting review of decisions rendered without opinion. Committee Note to Rule 9.030, 381 So.2d 1374 (1980); Note, *The Erosion of Final Jurisdiction in Florida's District Courts of Appeal,* 21 Fla. L. Rev. 375 (1969). The word "expressly" was also attached to the other bases for discretionary Supreme Court review without a certificate from the District Court of Appeal—decisions declaring a state statute valid (if invalid, a nondiscretionary appeal lies), construing a constitutional provision or affecting a class of state officers.

Error in the decision below is nowhere mentioned as a ground for review. The Florida Committee Note to Rule 9.120 on the preparation of the jurisdictional briefs admonished that (381 So.2d 1383):

> "It is not appropriate to argue the merits of the substantive issues involved in the case or discuss any matters not relevant to the threshold jurisdictional issue. The petitioner may wish to include a very short statement of why the Supreme Court should exercise its discretion and entertain the case on the merits if it finds it does have certiorari jurisdiction."

Whether this will completely preclude the Florida Supreme Court from taking into account, perhaps *sub silentio,* the merits of a ruling below in deciding whether to grant review remains to be seen. The object of the revised Florida system is to constitute the District Courts of Appeal "the courts of last resort for the vast majority of litigants." *Id.* at 1373; Note, *The Erosion of Final Jurisdiction in Florida's District Courts of Appeal, supra.*

Florida's novel system thus eliminates error and limits the existence of a conflict as a basis for review, and also enables the intermediate appellate courts to determine in the first instance which cases have sufficient public importance. That should substantially reduce the number of petitions filed with the Supreme Court. The last mentioned feature resembles in some respects the much criticized proposal to have all petitions for certiorari to the United States Supreme Court screened by a new intermediate court.[63] There is no inherent reason why intermediate appellate courts cannot adequately determine public impor-

---

[63] *Report of the Study Group on the Caseload of the Supreme Court,* pp. 18–25 (Federal Judicial Center, 1972), reprinted in 57 F.R.D. 573 at 590–595. The large body of comment on this report, most of it sharply critical, is cited in R. Stern and E. Gressman, SUPREME COURT PRACTICE, pp. 44–47 (5th ed., 1978).

tance, or sift out those cases which are clearly not important enough. Even though their judgment as to that might not always coincide with that of a supreme court's, it would not necessarily be less reflective of the public interest. A supreme court can protect itself against being overburdened by exercising its own ultimate discretion as to which of the *certified* cases are important enough for it to hear. The Florida experience may determine whether such an approach has the desired effect of reducing the burden on a supreme court without unduly limiting its authority or preventing important issues from being reviewed. The result may be helpful to other jurisdictions in which the highest court has a case load much too large for any one body of men to handle adequately and competently.

The phrasing of the standards which courts follow in determining whether to grant discretionary review does not tell the whole story. For the words used do not indicate how liberally or strictly the standards are being applied—how much importance is enough for a grant, or, for that matter, what "importance" means; how clear a conflict must be, whether the facts must be identical or indistinguishable, whether a conflict in dicta or reasoning is sufficient, whether the conflict must be on an issue of some importance; where error is the decisive factor, apart from other importance, how outrageous must the decision below appear to the high court. Many cases involve several of these factors, and the court's judgment reflects a melding of their persuasive effects.

How a supreme court weighs these factors will undoubtedly be affected by its case load. As shown in Secs. 1.6 and 1.8, *supra,* when 1000 to 1200 petitions per year were filed in the United States Supreme Court, it granted 18 percent, but since the number has exceeded 3600, it has granted approximately 6 percent. Although thirty years ago it was thought that the Court would always grant review when there was a square conflict, that is no longer true. Perhaps the Court still usually grants certiorari if there is a conflict, but the fact that it often does not suggests that even in conflict cases the Court gives weight to the importance of the issues and the egregiousness of the error below.[64] In general, the state supreme courts, which are not so overloaded, do not apply their standards so stringently. The percentage of petitions for review granted in recent years runs from approxi-

---

[64]The subject is treated at length in R. Stern and E. Gressman, SUPREME COURT PRACTICE, Sec. 4.4 (5th ed., 1978).

mately 8 in Arizona, California and Ohio, 10 in Iowa, 11 in New York, 12 in Tennessee, 14 in the Texas Supreme Court, 15 in Illinois, to 21 in the Oklahoma Supreme Court. In the states a conflict in itself is more likely to suffice, the required level of importance is substantially lower and a gross error is more likely to induce the court to take the case.

The differences in percentages translate in some unmeasurable way into the amount of importance or the degree of conflict or error which persuades the particular court to grant review. These numbers are therefore not merely of statistical interest. For they reflect the odds against petitions for review being granted. This is a factor which obviously should be taken into account in determining whether review should be sought, along with such other practical matters as additional attorneys' fees, printing and other costs.

The application of the overall statistical odds to a particular case is, of course, not merely a matter of mathematics. Counsel should, if possible, endeavor, either on the basis of his personal experience or information obtained from other lawyers, to get some idea of how the particular court applies its standards and take that into consideration in deciding whether a petition in the particular case is worth the effort. Can the arguments advanced in support of further review be made to appear respectable to the court so that there is some chance of success? This may come down to whether the petition would satisfy counsel's personal standard of legal respectability.

(d) Content of the Petition or Application for Review

The principal document to be filed by the petitioner or applicant for review is in most jurisdictions the petition or application itself, which contains not only the formal prayer and the facts showing jurisdiction but also the arguments as to why review should be granted. As stated above (pp. 131–132), in a few states (Arizona, Florida, Georgia, New Jersey, Ohio) a formal petition or notice is supplemented by a separate memorandum containing the reasons for granting review. Counsel must, of course, comply with the rules of the particular jurisdiction. In Florida, only a jurisdictional brief "limited solely to the issue of the Supreme Court's jurisdiction and accompanied by an appendix containing a conformed copy of the decision of the district court of appeal, shall be served within 10 days of filing the notice." Rule 9.120(d), 381 So.2d 1382. No brief is permitted, however, when the Supreme Court's jurisdiction rests on certification by the District Court of Appeal "of a question of great public importance or certification that the decision is in direct conflict with a decision of another district court" of appeal (*ibid.*, and Committee Note, 381 So.2d 1384).

In the main, the states either prescribe the form of the application in general terms, adhere to the United States Supreme Court form or leave the matter to counsel. Whether the form is prescribed or not, the substance of this document should be determined by its objective, inducing the higher court to accept the case for further review. To that end the form prescribed by the Supreme Court of the United States for petitions for certiorari tells most reviewing courts what they want to know and enables counsel to present his argument effectively. Unless the state requires a different arrangement, that form, except perhaps as to the placement of the Questions Presented and the listing of parties not named in the caption and affiliated corporations (as to which see paragraph (4), *infra*) may appropriately be followed in other jurisdictions, as it often is.[65] A form appears at pp. 504–513, *infra.*

The substance of the cover is the same as for briefs on the merits. See Sec. 7.12, *infra.*[66] The 1980 Supreme Court rules provide that the covers of petitions for certiorari and jurisdictional statements shall be white and of the responses thereto, light orange. Rule 33.2(b).

Except as indicated or as required by local rule, the following form is recommended.

The petition or application or separate document should contain the following sections (except perhaps for the second):

(1) *Prayer for relief.* The petition should commence with a short prayer that the court grant the petition to review the decision below.

(2) *Citation to opinions below.* The United States Supreme Court rules next call for the citations to the opinions below, if reported, which they usually are not by that time. Most courts do not require this. Where, as in many courts, including the Supreme Court, these opinions must be appended to the peti-

---

[65]In Arizona that would mean that the substance of the petition would be incorporated in the motion for rehearing filed in the Court of Appeals.

[66]Oregon has the unusual provision that the petition's cover should identify the author of the opinion below and how each judge voted.

tion, the citations are merely a convenience to the court and not of much practical importance.

(3) *Jurisdictional basis.* The court will want to know at the beginning the legal basis for its jurisdiction, including the facts which demonstrate that it has jurisdiction over the appeal. This means, at the very least, the dates of the judgment below, of any petition for rehearing and of the order disposing of such a petition. The other facts showing that jurisdictional requisites are satisfied should also be set forth, with a reference to the statutory or other basis for the court's jurisdiction. In most cases this can all be accomplished in a short paragraph.

In cases coming to the United States Supreme Court from state courts, the facts critical to jurisdiction include when and how the federal questions were raised in the state courts and how they were decided, with references to the appropriate parts of the record. If this material is of any length, and if supporting argument is necessary to convince the Court that it has jurisdiction, the jurisdictional facts should be included under a separate heading either by itself or at the most appropriate point in the statement of facts or argument.

(4) *The questions presented for review.* Only the questions set forth will normally be considered by the court. A broad question, however, will include "every subsidiary question fairly included therein" (United States Supreme Court Rule 21.1(a)). This provision of the 1980 Supreme Court rules has transferred the Questions Presented to the very beginning of the petition preceding the tables of contents and authorities. (A list of all parties not named in the caption and of affiliated corporations is to follow the Questions. Rules 15.1(b), 21.1(b), 28.1. See Secs. 7.11 and 7.14, *infra.*) Most courts, however, still have the questions follow the preliminary items mentioned above, which would seem to be where they logically fit. The problems presented by the Supreme Court's new rule are discussed in Secs. 7.14 and 7.18, *infra,* in connection with the same provisions for briefs on the merits. A few jurisdictions still call for a separate assignment of errors or a bill of exceptions; counsel should therefore be careful to observe any such local requirement.[67]

In general, the questions should be prepared in the same way as for briefs on the merits, as to which see Sec. 7.18, *infra.* The significance of the importance of the issues and conflict

---

[67]The new Tennessee rules, effective in 1979, abolished the assignment of errors.

among appellate courts should be kept in mind, however, in a petition for review. For example, instead of stating the question as merely:

"Whether Pennsylvania's Sunday closing law violates the Equal Protection Clause,"

petitioner could begin more effectively:

"Whether the court below, disagreeing with three other circuits, erred in holding that. . . ."

(5) *Statement of facts.* Next should come a concise statement of the facts necessary to the consideration of the questions raised. Facts not significantly relevant to the issues presented should be omitted. As in briefs on the merits, as to which see Sec. 7.20, *infra,* the statement should be an unargumentative fair presentation of the facts which the court should know, including significant facts not helpful to the applicant's position. A good statement can, however, be both unargumentative and persuasive. If his case permits, the capable advocate will marshal the facts fairly, letting them speak for themselves, in a way which will convince the court that the applicant's position is just and should prevail. Opposing facts may be stated in a manner which minimizes their significance.

Counsel should know that at this stage of the case the justices who consider the petition are unlikely to have the record before them or conveniently available, or to examine it carefully even if it is. The United States Supreme Court and a number of states no longer require or desire that the record be filed with the petition for review. See Sec. 5.7(a), *supra.* The court is likely to rely in the first instance on the statement of facts in the opinion below, which customarily must be submitted with or attached to the petition. If, as is almost invariably the case, the petitioner is unhappy with the facts as stated in the adverse opinion below, he must present the facts as he sees them to the court in the petition or supporting memorandum, correcting the opinion below as to significant errors or omissions. Evidence or other material critical to issues in dispute should be quoted in the statement of facts or argument so that the justices can read it verbatim. If such material is too long for inclusion in the text, it should be quoted in a footnote or an attached appendix.

As in any brief, all facts except those which are undoubtedly indisputable should be supported by record references. This is so even though the judges may not or will not have a copy of the record conveniently available when passing on the application for review. They can get it if they want it. And the references in themselves lend credibility to the facts stated, as they should if counsel has done his job fairly and accurately; if he has not, of course, his opponent will demolish him. The record will normally have been paginated for use in the court below. But even if it has not, an item may be cited to the page of the particular document, such as "Complaint, p. 4," "Pl. Ex. 6, p. 7" or "Tr. of Oct. 9, 1979, p. 43."

Counsel should not overlook the necessity for keeping the statement reasonably short. The statement of facts in a petition for review should normally not be as long as in a brief on the merits. Compare Sec. 7.20, *infra.* United States Supreme Court Rule 21.1(g) was amended in 1980 to italicize "concise" in calling for

> "[a] *concise* statement of the case containing the facts material to the consideration of the questions presented."

The dilemma facing the writer of an application for review is that, although an unsuccessful petition is disastrous for the applicant and terminates the case, what the court wants is a document which will enable it to decide in a short time whether to hear the case on the merits, not a full-scale brief. Counsel must balance the danger of omitting something he thinks the court should read against the court's need (often embodied in the rules) for short petitions. See p. 147, *infra.*

(6) *Reasons for granting review.* This is the "Argument" portion of the document, but it may more appropriately be entitled "Reasons for Granting the Petition." For that is what it is; and such a title is more likely to induce counsel to focus on the actual function of the document and not to treat it as an ordinary brief on the merits. This portion of the brief should be a short, concise argument as to why the court should review the decision below, including a discussion of the authorities and legislative material and the pertinent portions of the record.

An introductory paragraph should state in summary form, for example, that:

> "Review should be granted because the decision below is in conflict with _____, and the question as to _____ _____ is clearly an important one, affecting all small busi-

nessmen in the state. In addition, the decision clearly frustrates the language and purpose of Sec. 3333 of the Revised Statutes."[68]

The argument should then emphasize the factors which are always significant in persuading a high court to grant review—importance and conflict—as well as any others referred to in the rules of the jurisdiction. In most cases the petition should deal with the merits in summary but persuasive fashion, inasmuch as the court's reaction to the merits will often affect its decision as to whether or not to grant further review. Such an argument can frequently be combined with the treatment of the *importance* of reversal, or with explaining the reasoning of the conflicting decision, or with showing that the court below departed from the accepted and usual course of judicial proceedings or that the high court should exercise its power of supervision.

Some of the state court rules clearly call for a treatment of the merits. Texas calls for little else (Rule 483), and in Louisiana the incorrectness of the decision below is the principal factor considered. Illinois Rule 315(b) requires that the argument tell "why the decision of the Appellate Court should be reversed."

As indicated in Sec. 5.7(c), pp. 139–141, *supra,* the Florida Supreme Court does not want a discussion of the merits but only "a short concise statement of the grounds for invoking jurisdiction and the necessary facts." Committee Note to Florida Rule 9.120(d) (1977), 381 So.2d 1383.

Such a short statement of the reasons for granting review is all that is possible in the states which drastically limit the length of the petition or application. E.g., Arkansas—2 pages typed, legal size, but petition for rehearing may be attached; Arizona—6 pages; Colorado and Oklahoma—10 pages; New Jersey—15 pages printed, 20 pages typed. The United States Supreme Court imposed no page limit until 1980, when Rule 21.4 limited petitions to 30 printed pages.[69]

The argumentative portion of the petition for leave to appeal or certiorari should not be a full brief on the merits. That would defeat its purpose insofar as the court is concerned, which

---

[68]New Mexico Rule 28(c) requires that preceding the argument, in what is in substance an enlargement of the opening paragraph recommended in the text, the reasons for granting review should be stated in a separate section of the petition, with pertinent quotations from the allegedly conflicting decisions, even though the reasons may be amplified in the subsequent argument.

[69]Sixty-five typed pages are permitted, but the typing must be double-spaced in the same space as is allowed for printing. See Supreme Court Rule 33.3; Sec. 6.10, *infra.*

is to enable the court to decide in a short time whether to hear the case fully without delving too far into the merits. Most courts —though apparently not Texas—want the petitions to be short.

5.8 The Brief in Opposition to the Petition

A large majority of the supreme courts to which an application or petition is made to review the decision of an intermediate appellate court allow the adverse party to file a brief in opposition within a specified number of days. Some of the time limitations are as follows:

5 days — Georgia;
10 days — California, Colorado, Connecticut, Iowa, Kansas, Massachusetts, Missouri, North Carolina, Wisconsin;
14 days — Alabama, Illinois, Pennsylvania;
15 days — Arizona,[70] Maryland, Oklahoma, Tennessee, Texas;
20 days — Florida, Kentucky;
30 days — Ohio, United States.

In New York the opposition must be filed by the return day for the motion for permission to appeal, which is the second Monday after service of the motion. New York Court of Appeals Rule 500.9(a). Although Washington permits a brief in opposition to be filed, its rules set no time limit; presumably counsel ascertains from the Supreme Court clerk when his response must be filed in time for the court to consider it.

The difficulty with 10 days, and even more with 5, is that a number of weekend days could be included, fortuitously varying with the calendar, on which law offices would not be open (even though lawyers might work). Both because of that and in order to allow enough time for writing, 14 or 15 days would seem to be a more reasonable time.

A number of the above states either expressly or by implication indicate that the filing of an opposing brief is not necessary.[71] Indeed, Pennsylvania Rule 1116 states that failure to oppose "will not be construed as concurrence" in the application; the court should, however, be notified that no opposing

---

[70] In Arizona 15 days is allowed to answer the petition for rehearing in the Court of Appeals, which serves as the brief supporting the formal petition for certiorari in the Supreme Court.

[71] Alabama, Illinois, Georgia, Kansas, Pennsylvania, Washington.

brief will be filed. Alabama Rule 39 gives respondent the option of filing an answering brief 14 days after receipt of petitioner's brief (which accompanies the petition) or after the petition is granted.

The rules of six states which provide for petitions (Arkansas, Louisiana, Michigan, Missouri, New Mexico and Oregon) and the Hawaii statute make no mention of an opposing brief at all. Whether this means that none will be received is not certain. New Mexico's Rule 28(e) states that a petition not acted on within 20 days will be deemed denied. Thus, approximately one third of the states in which supreme courts review intermediate appellate courts either do not provide for any brief in opposition or suggest that one is not necessary. This is evidence that many courts find they can dispose of petitions for review on the basis of the petition and the opinion below without any presentation from the other side at all. This is probably true in a large number of cases. My understanding is that when the filing of an opposition is optional, many respondents do not file one.

There are many cases, however, where the court will not get the full picture from the petition and the opinion below. The latter, which will usually support the respondent, may be cryptic or nonexplanatory. An opposing memorandum may be able to demonstrate that the allegedly conflicting decision deals with quite a different situation, or that the case does not present the allegedly important question, or that the petition does not accurately reflect either the record or the law. Such a submission should be helpful both to the respondent and to the court. Only respondent's counsel is in a position to determine in advance whether filing an opposition in his case will be useful. The most reasonable procedure, therefore, would be to give him the choice of filing an opposition or not, with the understanding, preferably made explicit in the rules, as in Pennsylvania, that failure to respond shall not be held against him.

What has been said as to the objectives of the petition for review also should serve as the guiding principle for the parties opposing the petition. The opposing brief should not be merely an argument on the merits of the case, although it should endeavor to show that the decision below is right, or at least not clearly wrong. The appellee or respondent should also try to persuade the court that the case is not important enough to warrant review, and that there is no real conflict of decisions or at least not a conflict of any significance. His task is considerably easier than that of the petitioner, not only because the normal

odds are against a petition being granted but also because the
opinion below, which should be appended to the petition, is
likely to help. In states where the document requesting review
is limited to jurisdictional matters, as in Florida, the opposing
memorandum should be similarly restricted.

The opposing document need not cover any of the items
preliminary to the argument in the petition, unless the respondent is dissatisfied with the petitioner's version of any of them,
as he often will be. But he can limit his statements of the questions presented and of the facts to improving, correcting or
supplementing the petition. He may indeed file a short memorandum stating in a few pages without headings why review
should not be granted, as is sometimes done in the United States
Supreme Court. On the other hand, he may feel that he must
cover each subject completely. He may, of course, rely on the
opinion below to whatever extent seems appropriate.

5.9   Comparative Analysis of the Methods of Review by the Highest Court

The preceding sections have shown that where there are
two tiers of appellate courts, cases may be taken to the highest
court by the following routes:

(1) In the vast majority of cases by a petition to the highest
     court to review the decision of the intermediate court;

(2) By petition to the highest court, or by order of that
     court, before decision by the intermediate court;

(3) By appeal as of right from the trial court to the highest
     court;

(4) By appeal as of right from the intermediate court to the
     highest court;

(5) By certificate of the intermediate court before or after
     it has decided the case, with the states differing as to
     whether the highest court has discretion to accept or
     reject the certificate.

(a)   Discretionary Jurisdiction

The reason for establishing intermediate appellate courts is
that the number of appeals in a state is too great for a single
court to handle justly and efficiently. The creation of a number
of intermediate appellate courts almost inevitably means that a

single supreme court cannot review all of the intermediate decisions which parties will bring to it if appeals as a matter of right could be taken in all cases. There must accordingly be some process for selecting which cases the highest court should hear.

By now almost every state with two tiers of appellate courts follows the pattern of the federal system in leaving the choice primarily to the discretion of the highest court, either by a majority vote or by less than a majority. See Secs. 5.1–5.2, *supra.* As to Florida, however, see pp. 139–141.

There is also general recognition that appeals in cases which are both important and in need of expedition should be able to bypass the intermediate court and be heard directly by the highest court. Here again the highest court itself can best determine which cases should be accorded this special treatment, although Florida makes certification by the intermediate court a prerequisite. Many states might well consider whether they should utilize the Massachusetts technique described in Sec. 1.10(b), *supra,* to eliminate double appeals in most cases and to apportion the appellate work load fairly and efficiently.

In exercising its discretion, both before or after intermediate review, the highest court must take into account the importance of the case or the issues presented in the light of its own work load. The process must be in part comparative, designed to accomplish the purpose of enabling the highest court to give adequate consideration to the cases which it does decide.

(b) Certification by the Intermediate Court

The discretion of the highest court in both of these situations is in general invoked by the losing party below. But some jurisdictions also permit the intermediate court to submit the matter to the highest court by certificate or otherwise. To make such a certificate by the lower court decisive as to whether the higher court should hear the case would be to transfer, at least in part, the exercise of discretion from the latter to each of a number of intermediate appellate courts. They would not be likely to have the same overall perspective as to what the high court can and should be able to hear.

As a result, both supreme courts and lower appellate courts generally recognize that this jurisdiction should be exercised sparingly. Whether because of discouragement from above, as in the federal system, or because of the belief that it is the function of the courts of appeals to decide appeals in the first instance, or both, in most jurisdictions few cases now take the certification route.

This objection to certification by a lower court would not apply, however, if (as in Florida) its certification is not binding on the highest court. Since the recommendation of the intermediate court as to whether further review is warranted is likely to be of value and should be given weight, its submission to the highest court, whether in a document entitled certification or something less imposing, or even in the lower court's opinion, should certainly be permitted. This would still allow the high court, however, to exercise its own full discretion as to whether the appeal should be reviewed.

(c)   Appeals to Highest Court as of Right

Whether and to what extent the highest court should be required to take appeals as a matter of right, without any exercise of discretion, has been a subject of substantial difference of opinion, particularly with respect to the United States Supreme Court. The enormous size of that Court's docket, which reflects the magnitude of its constituency, undoubtedly is responsible for its position that all cases should be subject to its discretionary jurisdiction and not appealable to it as a matter of right.[72] The peculiar problems of the Supreme Court in this connection are treated in a large body of literature,[73] and there is no point to enlarging upon or summarizing that debate here.

In courts not so overburdened, the direct appeal as of right is not necessarily inappropriate or unwise for cases of special importance which the highest court would eventually be bound to decide in any event. Cases in which the death sentence is imposed may fall in that category. If the highest court is required by constitution or statute to decide all such appeals on the merits, there is little to be gained by requiring an intermediate review.

Constitutional cases form the other most common category in which appeals may be taken as a matter of right to the highest

---

[72]See letter of June 22, 1978, supporting S. 3100, 95th Cong., to Sen. De Concini, signed by all the Justices, which appears in full in E. Gressman, *Requiem for the Supreme Court's Obligatory Jurisdiction,* 65 A.B.A.J. 1325, 1328 (1979).

[73]E.g., Gressman, *supra* note 72; *Report of the Study Group on the Case Load of the Supreme Court,* pp. 25–38, 47 (Federal Judicial Center, 1972), reprinted in 57 F.R.D. at 595–605, 611; Chief Justice Burger, *Annual Report on the State of the Judiciary,* 62 A.B.A.J. 443, 444 (1976); Mr. Justice Brennan, *The National Court of Appeals: Another Dissent,* 40 U. Chi. L. Rev. 473, 474 (1973); R. Stern and E. Gressman, SUPREME COURT PRACTICE, Sec. 1.16, pp. 38–51 (5th ed., 1978).

court. Limiting direct appeals to cases in which laws have been held *un*constitutional will avoid burdening the high courts with the many cases in which parties raise insubstantial constitutional objections. Decisions of trial courts holding laws unconstitutional are not very numerous, and there is good reason for having questions of that stature decided authoritatively as promptly as possible.[74]

Often there is need for immediate authoritative determination of the validity of state or local bond issues or certificates of indebtedness. There is, therefore, a good deal of sense to Florida's provision for direct appeals in cases of this sort. Missouri's application of the same principle to the construction—and not merely validity—of the revenue laws is likely, however, to cover a large number of cases, many of which would not warrant immediate review by the highest court.

Reapportionment cases may be deemed important enough for direct review by the highest court as a matter of right, both because of their importance and the need for speedy determination before the next election. Congress preserved the right to direct Supreme Court review of decisions of federal district courts (of three judges) in cases involving the constitutionality of the apportionment of congressional districts or state legislatures. 28 U.S.C. §§2284, 1253. Illinois goes so far as to give its Supreme Court original and exclusive jurisdiction over actions concerning redistricting of the state legislature.

It can be said that obligatory review by the highest court in the first instance is unnecessary in any of the above circumstances, since the supreme courts could be counted upon to accept most of those cases for review as a matter of discretion. Often, of course, they would, but there can be no certainty as to that. And they might often not expedite the proceeding by taking the case before review in the intermediate court; the United States Supreme Court rarely does. Indeed, experience in that Court shows that there can be no assurance that high courts will accept for review all cases of substantial importance, even when there is a conflict in the intermediate appellate courts.[75]

---

[74]Of course, intermediate review might result in reversal of the holding of unconstitutionality and thereby lessen the top court's burden, but, on balance, expediting decision of such issues by the highest court would seem to be advisable.

[75]R. Stern and E. Gressman, SUPREME COURT PRACTICE, Sec. 4.4, p. 266 (5th ed., 1978); Commission on Revision of the Federal Court Appellate System, STRUCTURE AND INTERNAL PROCEDURES: RECOMMENDATIONS FOR CHANGE, pp. 11, 17–19, 76–77, 91–111 (1975), reprinted in 67 F.R.D. at 215, 221–224, 281–282, 298–324.

Commentators on that Court's practice have frequently referred, usually favorably, to its preference for waiting until issues have been more fully explored in the courts of appeals. Consideration of issues by a number of the intermediate courts may indeed be of aid to the highest court, but the process may, and often does, take years. Furthermore, as Mr. Justice Douglas points out in his posthumous autobiography, the Justices sometimes take into consideration in deciding whether to grant review such factors as whether the ultimate decision on the merits by their colleagues might not be to their liking. W. Douglas, *The Court Years,* pp. 94–95 (1980). The interest of a substantial body of the public in much more swift authoritative decision-making on issues of public importance would often seem entitled to greater weight.

There is no reason to believe that only the United States Supreme Court may be influenced by such factors. The possibility of review as a matter of discretion may therefore not always be an adequate substitute for direct review as a matter of right in classes of cases where the public interest demands a quick, final determination.

5.10   Certificate to State Supreme Courts by Courts of Other Jurisdictions

Not infrequently courts in one jurisdiction are required to give effect to the law of another. This sometimes results from application of the principles of conflicts of law, as when suit is brought in one state to recover damages for breach of a contract entered into and performed in another, or for injuries from an accident which occurred in another state. Perhaps more often, the federal courts in diversity cases must follow the state law under the doctrine of *Erie R. Co.* v. *Tompkins,* 304 U.S. 64 (1938).

Often the state authorities leave the state law unclear. In some such circumstances, the federal courts abstain from deciding the state law question until the state courts first pass upon it.[76] But this is usually an unsatisfactory and time-consuming solution to the problem, for it usually requires the commence-

---

[76]See R. Stern and E. Gressman, SUPREME COURT PRACTICE, pp. 101–103 (5th ed., 1978); 17 C. Wright, A. Miller and E. Cooper, FEDERAL PRACTICE AND PROCEDURE, §§4241–4255 (1978); 1A J. Moore, FEDERAL PRACTICE, ¶0.203 (2d ed., 1980); American Law Institute, STUDY OF THE DIVISION OF JURISDICTION BETWEEN STATE AND FEDERAL COURTS, pp. 282–298 (1969).

ment of litigation anew in the state judicial system while the federal case waits, and waits. A better procedure would be for the federal court to be able to certify such questions directly to the supreme court of the state, and obtain an authoritative answer in a relatively short time. *Lehman Brothers* v. *Schein,* 416 U.S. 386, 389–391 (1974).

Florida was the first state to authorize such a procedure, whereby the federal appellate courts could certify state law questions to the state supreme court.[77] Eighteen other states have followed suit,[78] and a uniform state law on the subject has now been drafted.[79] These laws permit questions of law to be certified by the United States Supreme Court or federal courts of appeals. Most also authorize certification by federal district courts.[80] Maryland, Massachusetts, Minnesota, Oklahoma and West Virginia go further, and permit appellate courts of other states also to certify. Maryland and Oklahoma, in addition, empower the state's highest court similarly to certify cases to other supreme courts.[81]

The question has been raised as to whether this procedure involves a state supreme court in the rendering of academic or advisory opinions to other courts which decide the actual case. Such statutes have been sustained in Florida and Maine. *Sun Insurance Office, Ltd.* v. *Clay,* 133 So.2d 735 (Fla. 1961); *In Re Richards,* 223 A.2d 827 (Me., 1976). The state supreme courts are deciding questions in real cases, and their determinations will be accepted as binding. The procedure is a practical way of dealing with the manner in which the courts of one jurisdiction ascertain, as they must in various circumstances, the law of another. Its use should be encouraged.[82]

---

[77] 12 UNIFORM LAWS ANNOTATED, p. 50 (1975), now embodied in Florida Const. Art. 5, §3(b)(6) (1980).

[78] Alabama, Colorado, Georgia, Hawaii, Indiana, Louisiana, Maine, Maryland, Massachusetts, Minnesota, Montana, New Hampshire, North Dakota, Oklahoma, Rhode Island, Washington, West Virginia, Wyoming.

[79] 12 UNIFORM LAWS ANNOTATED, pp. 49–56 (1975).

[80] All of the states listed in note 78, *supra,* except Georgia, Hawaii, Indiana, Louisiana.

[81] Maryland Ann. Code, Courts and Judicial Proceedings, §12-607; Oklahoma Stat. tit. 20, §1609.

[82] The state laws are collected and the subject treated at length in 17 C. Wright, A. Miller and E. Cooper, FEDERAL PRACTICE AND PROCEDURE, §4248 (1978); 1A J. Moore, FEDERAL PRACTICE, ¶0.203[5] (2d ed., 1980).

6

Records, Appendices and the Like

6.1 An Overall View

The function of appellate courts is to review the decisions of trial courts, not to try the cases anew. This means that the record before the trial court becomes the record before the appellate court.[1] In a two-tiered appellate structure, the record before the highest court consists of the trial court record supplemented by whatever was added in the intermediate court of appeals, usually only its opinion and judgment.

The preparation of the record may be, except in the simplest of cases, a time-consuming and costly process. It often is a substantial contributing factor to the length of time required to complete an appeal. The trend in recent years, stimulated in

[1]A novel exception to this almost universal requirement is Washington Rule of Appellate Procedure 9.11, which provides that "[t]he appellate court may only on its own initiative direct that additional evidence be taken [ordinarily by the trial court] before the decision of a case on review if:

"(1) additional proof of facts is needed to fairly resolve the issues on review, (2) the additional evidence would probably change the decision being reviewed, (3) it is equitable to excuse a party's failure to present the evidence to the trial court, (4) the remedy available to a party through post-judgment motions in the trial court is inadequate or unnecessarily expensive, (5) the appellate court remedy of granting a new trial is inadequate or unnecessarily expensive, and (6) it would be inequitable to decide the case solely on the evidence already taken in the trial court."

This may enable a case to be finally adjudicated more rapidly than if a new trial were ordered, to be followed by a new appeal. California Rule 23 is a less sweeping provision permitting the appellate court to take evidence and make findings of fact. As to post-judgment facts capable of ready demonstration relating to such matters as mootness, see Tennessee Rule of Appellate Procedure 14, and Sec. 7.30, *infra*.

part by the general availability of less expensive methods of copying papers, has been toward simplification. As will appear, some courts have gone further in this direction than others.

The process in itself is not, or should not be, complicated. The invariable first step is the assembling in the trial court clerk's office of either all the papers comprising the record in the trial court or the parts which the parties believe to be relevant to the points raised on the appeal. The selection of the relevant items may be by designation of what should be omitted from the record as a whole or what should be included. This may be accomplished by agreement or stipulation—as it should be if possible—or by formal cross-designation. The trial court clerk then assembles the papers comprising the record, arranges them in the proper order with appropriate indices and transmits them to the clerk of the appellate court.

In a number of jurisdictions, approximately one third of the states,[2] nothing more is required after the trial court sends up the original record. In some jurisdictions the clerk below, the appellant or the appellate court or clerk is to prepare one to three additional copies of the record for use by the court or the parties.[3] In most of the states, however, as well as in most of the United States courts of appeals and the United States Supreme Court, additional copies of the record or of the parts deemed important for the judges to read must be prepared, usually by counsel, not the clerk. This may also require agreement or cross-designation by the parties as to what should be included, unless each party is permitted to file its items separately.

These copies are usually filed with or shortly after the briefs, either by the appellant and appellee separately or by the appellant for all parties. In theory this document containing the most important parts of the record is an appendix to the briefs, and in most jurisdictions, including the federal, that is what it is now called. More often than not, however, it is a separate volume—or volumes—of some size containing a substantial part of the record, and the word "appendix" is not very appropriate.

This process of duplicating substantial parts of the appel-

---

[2]See Sec. 6.7, *infra.*

[3]California Rule 10—one additional copy prepared by the trial court clerk for use by the parties; New Mexico Rule 8(a)—appellant shall file three copies; Ninth Circuit Rule 4(f)—one set of record transmitted by clerk below unless court of appeals requests additional copies at appellant's expense.

late record is costly both in money and time. Chief Justice Burger has recently declared in his *Annual Report on the State of the Judiciary, 1980* (66 A.B.A.J. 295, 296–297):

> "A good many experienced lawyers believe—and this belief is shared by many appellate judges—that we have 'gone overboard' on the matter of printing records on appeal. There is not universal agreement on this subject. Some believe that an appellate court must have at least three printed copies of the record. Others believe that the original record is sufficient in the vast majority of cases.
>
> "The Fifth Circuit conducted a 20-month experiment, relying primarily on the original record supplemented by a limited printed appendix covering critical material. This eliminated more than three and one-half million pages of printed records in 20 months. (I am reliably informed this is the equivalent of 450 pulpwood trees.) In this one experiment, the savings to the litigants amounted to more than $1 million in printing costs. It reduced fees for assembling the material. It is not unimportant that it also saved 1,500 linear feet of shelf space in the court.
>
> "This is the type of imaginative experimentation by judges and lawyers which we should encourage and on which we have the co-operation of the bar."

The increasing appellate work load has caused some courts to endeavor to limit the copying to the relatively few parts of the record which call for appellate scrutiny: the opinion and judgment below, the documents which establish the court's jurisdiction (such as a notice of appeal and order denying rehearing), and critical portions of the pleadings and evidence, primarily the parts relating to matters as to which the parties are in dispute. So restricted, the document could be a true "appendix" to a brief, such as the devisers of the appendix system probably had in mind.[4]

Although the methods of bringing the trial court record before the appellate court in general are quite similar, the rules of the various jurisdictions, which deal with the subject at some length, differ in many details, and to some extent in principle. Since this volume cannot give all the details, the litigating attorney must, of course, examine the rules—and in some states the statutes and case law—in his particular jurisdiction. The principal features of the methods of designating and preparing the record are discussed below.

---

[4] See Judge John J. Parker, *Improving Appellate Methods*, 25 N.Y.U. L. Rev. 1, 5 (1950).

Preparation of the Original Record

6.2 The Content of the Record

The record may contain two types of material, which often must be assembled in different ways. The first category consists of the pleadings, motions, orders and other documents filed in normal course with the trial court clerk, which are often described as the clerk's record or the clerk's papers, but sometimes simply as "the record." The second category consists of the transcription of what occurred in the courtroom and is commonly described as the transcript, the transcript of testimony or the report of proceedings, although sometimes the word "transcript" is used to mean the entire record. In some states the designated record or transcript is still called the bill of exceptions.[5] Usually the transcript is not typed until a party decides to appeal, so that it cannot be found in the clerk's office when the case is concluded in the trial court. As to such unfiled material, additional steps beyond a request to the clerk are obviously necessary before it can be included in the record.

This may not be true of exhibits introduced at the trial if they are physically left in the clerk's office, but since they are usually meaningful only in relation to the trial, they are treated as a part of the transcript. Often, however, the lawyers retain exhibits after the trial; counsel should be alert to the need for lodging them with the clerk's office so that they can be transmitted to the court of appeals.[6]

The record, of course, normally includes any opinion, findings, rulings or other statement, written or oral (if transcribed), of the reasons for the actions of the trial judge. Under Pennsylvania Rule 1925(a) when the reasons do not appear of record, the judge shall file a brief statement of reasons upon receipt of the notice of appeal. If he is uncertain as to the basis for the appeal, he may order the appellant to file a concise statement of the matters complained of in the appeal; failure to comply may be considered a waiver of all objections.

In some cases the testimony will have been transcribed and filed before judgment, or be available before the appeal is taken.

---

[5]E.g., Nebraska Rule 7; Texas Rule 372.

[6]See the remarks of Judge Friendly in *United States* v. *Ross,* 321 F.2d 61, 65 (CA 2, 1963), cert. denied, 375 U.S. 894 (1963); 9 J. Moore, FEDERAL PRACTICE, ¶210.04[2] (2d ed., 1980).

In cases involving large sums or pecunious clients, counsel will often order and receive the transcript from the reporter during or immediately after the trial. As a practical matter the clerk's record should include everything filed in his office when the appeal is taken, including testimony and exhibits. For an instruction to the clerk is all that is necessary to incorporate such material in the appeal record, just as it is for the other papers filed with the clerk.

In the majority of appeals, however, the transcript must be obtained from the court reporter after the appeal is taken. The special problems of preparing the transcript are considered separately in Sec. 6.3, *infra.*

Historically, only the portions of the record below designated by the parties were treated as the record before the appellate court. The appellant would file a praecipe, a shorthand Latin word which for lawyers means a designation of the parts of the record to be incorporated in the record on appeal. Appellee could file a counterpraecipe for additional items if he so desired. Material not designated was not part of the record, and could not be referred to by appellate counsel. Since the designation process occurred either at the time of filing the notice of appeal or shortly thereafter, counsel were not always sure at that time of what points they would eventually argue in their briefs. The result was that counsel felt compelled to designate anything which might possibly be relevant, often the entire record.

This is still the practice in a number of states where the record consists of the judgment appealed from, the notice of appeal and other parts of the trial court record listed in designations or praecipes.[7] And this remains true even where the original designation may easily be supplemented or corrected by stipulation or order of the trial or reviewing court.

In determining what should be designated for inclusion in the record—as distinct from a subsequently duplicated appendix containing the material important for the judges to read (as to which see Secs. 6.7–6.12, *infra*)—relevance to the issues raised on the appeal is the proper test. For any judge may, and the judge writing the opinion is likely to, wish to examine everything in the record pertinent to the appeal, and not merely the most critical items. Omitted material may always be added to the record, usually by leave of court, and in some jurisdictions by

---

[7]E.g., Alaska, Colorado, North Carolina.

stipulation. In Nebraska either party may file a supplement without leave (Rule 4(c)).[8]

Some modern rules, such as the Federal Rules of Appellate Procedure, revised Illinois Rule 321, Iowa Rule 10(a), Kansas Rule 3.01, Maryland Rule 1026, Michigan Rule 812, New Hampshire Rule 13, Pennsylvania Rule 1921 and Wisconsin Rule 809.15(1), provide that all the papers and exhibits in the court below constitute the record on appeal. Federal Appellate Rule 10(a) states:

> "The original papers and exhibits filed in the district court, the transcript of proceedings, if any, and a certified copy of the docket entries prepared by the clerk of the district court shall constitute the record on appeal in all cases."

Under Tennessee Rule 24(a), the record consists of all the record filed below unless the parties designate less.

Prior to the 1979 revision of the Federal Rules of Appellate Procedure, Rule 11 provided that the record should be transmitted to the court of appeals within 40 days after the filing of the notice of appeal unless the time was changed by court order. It was up to the appellant to see that this was done. A number of states still adhere to this practice. E.g., Iowa Rule 12. Federal Appellate Rule 11(b) now provides, however:

> "When the record is complete for purposes of the appeal, the clerk of the district court shall transmit it forthwith to the clerk of the court of appeals."

Rule 11(b) makes clear the responsibilities of the reporter and the clerk, and requires the clerk to transmit the record as soon as it is complete. In some courts, such as the Circuit Court of Cook County, Illinois, the clerk's office has been known to have difficulty in locating portions of the record which are supposed to be in its files. Thus, even though the responsibility is the clerk's, experienced counsel are careful to ascertain whether the clerk's office has all the significant documents and to supply any which are missing.

Under Rule 11(b) the documents comprising the record shall be numbered by the clerk and accompanied by a list identifying them and showing the number of each. No designation by the parties is called for. But if appellant orders less than the

---

[8]Mississippi Rule 4 and West Virginia Rule VIII preserve the baffling historical terminology whereby a motion to add to the material in the record is entitled a "suggestion of diminution of record" or "certiorari for diminution of the record."

entire transcript from the reporter, he must notify appellee of the parts ordered, and also of the issues he intends to raise, and the appellee has 10 days to cross-designate additional parts. See Sec. 6.3, *infra.*

The parties may stipulate that parts of the record, presumably the irrelevant parts, may be retained in the trial court, although they remain part of the record and either the court or any party may still request their transmittal. "The parts thus designated shall nevertheless be a part of the record on appeal for all purposes."[9] Federal Appellate Rule 11(f).

This system has several advantages. It removes any doubt as to the availability of any of the record in the appellate court; anything in the record below can be referred to. It eliminates the need for time-consuming designations by the parties who, despite the safety valve of a supplemental correction, want to be sure that nothing of possible value is omitted. It usually takes less clerk and lawyer time to bundle up the entire record and ship it to the appellate court than to go through it page by page to eliminate unneeded items. Such overinclusion costs nothing unless the unnecessary parts have to be duplicated, which they never do.

The rules of some states provide for the omission of two types of material from the record to be transmitted: bulky discovery material[10] which contains matter not in evidence below and lawyers' briefs[11] or memoranda; and miscellaneous unnecessary papers, such as subpoenas, summonses, motions, proof of service, extensions of time and the like, unless, of course, there is a special reason why they have significance in the particular case, as they sometimes do.[12] Where, as under the

---

[9]Illinois Rule 321, as revised in 1979, is similar in making the entire record below the record on appeal, but it adds: "unless the parties stipulate for, or the trial court, after notice and hearing, or the reviewing court, orders less." The material omitted by stipulation or court order thus is not a part of the record and, in contrast to the federal rule, may not be referred to on appeal unless it is reincorporated in the record by stipulation or court order under Rule 329.

[10]Thus, a deposition which has been filed but not offered in evidence is not part of the record before the reviewing court. 9 J. Moore, FEDERAL PRACTICE, ¶210.04[2], p. 16-18 (2d ed., 1980).

[11]In a few states the briefs in the intermediate appellate courts are transmitted to the supreme court. See Secs. 5.7(a), *supra,* and 6.7, p. 178, *infra.*

[12]Tennessee Rule 24(a) thus provides:

"Unless a party otherwise designates in writing, the following papers filed in the trial court shall not be included in the record: (1) subpoenas or summonses for any witness or for any defendant when there is an appearance for such defendant; (2) all papers relating to discovery including depositions, interrogatories and answers thereto, reports of physical or mental examinations, requests to admit, and all notices, motions or orders relating thereto; and (3) any list from which jurors are selected."

federal rule, transmission of the whole record is called for, the parties may stipulate to omit such items. Whether a stipulation is worth the effort will depend in part upon whether the clerk's office thinks it more of a nuisance to find and remove these papers from the record than to leave them in, as to which the deputy clerk in charge of the preparation of records should be consulted. A stipulation to omit may also be desirable when discovery or other irrelevant items are bulky, so that transmission to the appellate court would be an unnecessary burden.

When the parts of the record to be transmitted must be designated, the rules of the various jurisdictions require that the designation be filed either with, or within a few days after, the filing of the notice of appeal. The time allowed ranges from the day of filing the notice of appeal (Alaska, Idaho, North Dakota, Ohio, Oklahoma), 7 days thereafter (Alabama), 10 days (Colorado, Iowa, Montana, Rhode Island), 15 days (Tennessee), 21 days (West Virginia) to 30 days (Florida, New York). In Kansas the clerk has 10 days to compile the documents (excluding the transcript).

6.3 The Transcript or Report of Proceedings

When a transcript of the testimony or other oral court proceedings is necessary and has not previously been prepared, the appellant must promptly initiate steps to obtain it. Several states require him to order the transcript, or the portions he wants, from the court reporter no later than the filing of the notice of appeal;[13] usually this is required at the same time appellant designates the relevant portions. Federal Appellate Rule 10(b)(1) and the rules of a great many states[14] allow 10 days after the notice of appeal. Other states allow 14 or 15 days.[15] Only Washington Rule 9.2 allows as many as 45 days. Federal Rule 10(b)(3) and those of many states, including Washington, allow the other parties 10 days to cross-designate. The United States Courts of Appeals for the First, Sixth and Tenth Circuits,[16] though not purporting to discard the 10-day limit fixed in the Federal Appellate Rules, urge the designation of the desired

---

[13]Arkansas, Connecticut, Idaho, Michigan, Nebraska, New Jersey, North Carolina, Ohio.

[14]E.g., California, Colorado, Iowa, Kansas, Rhode Island.

[15]Illinois, Iowa, Tennessee, Utah.

[16]See Rules 7, 13 and 7(b) of those circuits, respectively.

portions of the transcript *immediately* after filing the notice of appeal, with a warning that failure to comply will be taken into account in any subsequent applications for extensions of time.

Many of the rules contain the provision embodied in Federal Rule 10(b)(3) that "unless the entire transcript is to be included" the appellant shall file and serve with his designation of the parts of the record to be transcribed "a statement of the issues he intends to present on the appeal."[17] The purpose of this is to permit appellee to determine whether the parts of the transcript designated by the appellant adequately reflect the record for the points to be presented on the appeal.[18] If the appellee thinks that they do not, he has 10 days to designate additional parts, which appellant must include.[19] Only if appellant is convinced that this counterdesignation contains a substantial body of material not pertinent to the appeal may he legitimately refuse to order transcription of such parts along with what he has designated, at his initial expense. Federal Appellate Rule 10(b)(3) and Wisconsin Rule 809.16 provide that if appellant does not order the parts designated by appellee, *appellee* shall either order the parts himself or apply to the district court for an order requiring the appellant to do so. Under Pennsylvania Rule 2155 appellee is to pay for such items, subject to judicial allocation after the last briefs are filed. The 1979 Tennessee rule (Rule 24(b)) more reasonably requires that the appellant either agree to "have the additional parts prepared at his own expense or apply to the trial court for an order requiring the appellee to do so." If the appellant finds the appellee's designation objectionable, he should take the initiative in submitting the matter to the court.

The statement of issues if less than all the transcript is ordered by appellant is not to be taken as a jurisdictionally binding assignment of errors or as a limitation on the Questions Presented in appellant's brief, although they will normally be

---

[17]E.g., the rules of Colorado, Iowa, Kentucky, New Jersey, Ohio, Rhode Island, Tennessee, Washington.

[18]In Kentucky a party may file all or part in narrative form, but any party may require questions and answers. Kentucky Rule 75.03. California Rule 7 also permits use of a narrative of the testimony in whole or in part.

[19]In Oklahoma if the appellant asserts that the evidence is insufficient to support the verdict or judgment, he shall serve on the adverse party "a statement specifying the material facts which he alleges were not proved," and the latter shall then have 10 days to designate the evidence he relies upon to prove "the specified facts, at the cost of the appellant." Oklahoma Rule of Civil Appellate Procedure 1.21. This relieves the appellant from the dilemma of having to designate the parts of the record which support a finding appellant claims to be unsupported.

the same.[20] If appellant subsequently argues additional points, an appropriate remedy for an appellee who was misled or prejudiced would be to permit him to supplement the transcript at appellant's expense, or something more drastic if the court finds that appellant has acted willfully or without reasonable cause. *Island Creek Coal Co.* v. *Local Union No. 1827,* 568 F.2d 7 (CA 6, 1977). But the appellate court might regard the inadequacy of the record on the point as reason for refusing to allow appellant to present an additional question.[21] In any event, the unsuccessful party on appeal will eventually pay the costs. Since the transcript is expensive and since neither party can be sure of who will have to pay for it, each party has an incentive to omit the items which are not pertinent to the appeal.

Federal Appellate Rule 10(b)(2) also states what should have been obvious in any event:

> "If the appellant intends to urge on appeal that a finding or conclusion is unsupported by the evidence or is contrary to the evidence, he shall include in the record a transcript of all evidence relevant to such finding or conclusion."

This is merely an illustration of the broader policy "that the appellant may not order only those portions of the transcript that favor his arguments."[22] The new Tennessee rule, proposed by the Tennessee Supreme Court Advisory Commission on Civil Rules, for which Professor Sobieski was the Reporter, sought to make this clear by adding the requirement that appellant must designate "such part of the evidence or proceedings as is necessary to convey a fair, accurate and complete account of what transpired with respect to those issues that are the bases of appeal." Tennessee Rule 24(b). The appellant must order all portions of the transcript, whether favorable or unfavorable, that are relevant to the issues he intends to present for review.

Some rules prescribe when the transcript or report of proceedings should be filed in the trial court. The periods range from 14 days in Pennsylvania from receipt of the notice of appeal (Pennsylvania Rule 1922), which does not seem to be nearly enough unless the reporters are trained to adhere to it, to 90

---

[20]See 9 J. Moore, FEDERAL PRACTICE, ¶210.05[2] (2d ed., 1980); J. Sobieski, *The Procedural Details of the Proposed Tennessee Rules of Appellate Procedure,* 46 Tenn. L. Rev. 1, 42–43 (1978).

[21]*Watson* v. *Button,* 235 F.2d 235 (CA 9, 1956). See also 9 J. Moore, FEDERAL PRACTICE, ¶210.05[2], pp. 10-31–10-32 (2d ed., 1980).

[22]Sobieski, *supra* note 20, at 42. See also 9 J. Moore, FEDERAL PRACTICE, ¶210.-05[1], p. 10-26 (2d ed., 1980).

days in Michigan, Montana, Tennessee and Washington, with most states in between. Revised Federal Rule 11(b) provides:

> "If the transcript cannot be completed within 30 days of receipt of the order the reporter shall request an extension of time from the clerk of the court of appeals and the action of the clerk of the court of appeals shall be entered on the docket and the parties notified. In the event of the failure of the reporter to file the transcript within the time allowed, the clerk of the court of appeals shall notify the district judge and take such other steps as may be directed by the court of appeals. Upon completion of the transcript the reporter shall file it with the clerk of the district court and shall notify the clerk of the court of appeals that he has done so."

These times are subject to substantial extension in the first instance for a specified number of days by the trial court, and thereafter by the reviewing court or a judge thereof. The trend, however, is toward giving the primary responsibility to the appellate court from the time the notice of appeal is filed, in part because "trial court judges are commonly lax in supervising court reporters who are often appointed by the trial judge and serve at his pleasure."[23]

When the time for filing the transcript is prescribed, the record on appeal is to be filed, or ready for filing, in the appellate court either at the same time as or shortly after the transcript is filed. In Illinois, for example, two weeks after that is permitted. Rules 323(b), 326.

A number of states do not fix any date for the filing of the transcript, only for the filing of the record with the reviewing court.[24] This means, of course, that the reporter is to file the transcript no later than a short time in advance of the date for transmitting the record (as to which see pp. 173–174, *infra*); the principal reason for granting an extension of the time for filing the record is to obtain the transcript from the reporter.

Some states, like Illinois and Tennessee, still require the report of proceedings to be submitted to the trial judge for approval (called a certificate of correctness in Illinois)[25] unless

---

[23]American Bar Association, Task Force on Appellate Procedure, EFFICIENCY AND JUSTICE IN APPEALS: METHODS AND SELECTED MATERIALS, p. 14 (1977), quoting from National Center for State Courts, WISCONSIN APPELLATE PRACTICE AND PROCEDURE STUDY, pp. 78–79 (1975).

[24]This was the federal system before the 1979 revision of Rule 11; the record was to be filed in the appellate court within 40 days after the filing of the notice of appeal.

[25]Illinois Rule 323(b); Tennessee Rule 24(e). The Tennessee Advisory Commission proposed to abolish this requirement but the Supreme Court deleted the provision from the proposed rule, though still providing that if the trial court fails to act within 45 days, the transcript shall be deemed to have been approved. J. Sobieski, *An Update of the New Tennessee Rules of Appellate Procedure*, 46 Tenn. L. Rev. 727, 746–748 (1979).

the parties stipulate to dispense with the certificate. Most jurisdictions, including the federal, no longer require this.[26] When the testimony has been transcribed verbatim, the judge's recollection will normally not be nearly as accurate, and he cannot take the time to study the transcript to see if it is entirely correct. There is thus no good reason for requiring the judge to participate in the process except in the rare situation in which the parties disagree seriously as to a particular point. The practice is, of course, different, as well it should be, when the testimony has not been transcribed. See Sec. 6.4, *infra.*

The insistence upon speed in starting the process of obtaining the transcript reflects general recognition that the preparation of the reporter's transcript is one of the bottlenecks of the appellate process. Some areas have an insufficient number of reporters to handle the work. Tape recordings or other methods of electronic recording can then be utilized, although this is not as simple as it sounds. The State of Alaska, which has a dearth of court reporters, out of necessity relies on electronic recording (Alaska Rule 9). A member of the court staff, called a "transcript secretary," must be trained to monitor the recording devices, in part to make sure that the speaker is identified and also to prevent several persons from speaking at the same time.[27] New Mexico Criminal Appellate Rule 209(d) provides for using reporters or tape recorders in criminal cases. If a "recording device approved by the Court Administrator" is employed, the clerk is to send three duplicates of the recording to the appellate court. Louisiana Rule I-9 also provides for electronic recording of the testimony in criminal cases. In Oregon an audio recording may be filed in lieu of a transcript if the appellate court permits. Rules 6.12, 6.55. Rhode Island Rule of Appellate Procedure 10 refers to the "transcript of proceedings or electronic sound recordings thereof." Under Alabama Rule 14, the parties and the trial judge may agree to use electronic recording devices. The product is to be transcribed in the usual way except when

---

[26]Alaska Rule 9(h); Arkansas Rule of Appellate Procedure 6(e); Maryland Rule 1026c; North Carolina Rule of Appellate Procedure 11; Texas Rule 377(d). In Washington the report of proceedings must be submitted to the trial judge, but it is deemed approved if no party objects within 10 days. Washington Rule of Appellate Procedure 9.5(b).

[27]R. Reynolds, *Alaska's Ten Years of Electronic Reporting,* 56 A.B.A.J. 1080 (1970); Appellate Judges' Conference, REPORT OF A SPECIAL COMMITTEE ON INCREASING ADMINISTRATIVE EFFICIENCY THROUGH TECHNOLOGY, pp. 53–56 (1972); Administrative Director of Courts of Alaska, ALASKA'S TRANSCRIPT MANUAL. There has been disagreement as to the desirability of such devices. Cf. Reynolds, *supra;* E. Boyko, *The Case Against Electronic Courtroom Reporting,* 57 A.B.A.J. 1008 (1971); H. Keene, *Another View of Electronic Reporting in Alaska,* 11 Judges J. 4 (Jan. 1972). The court reporters argue that the devices are not as efficient as reporters.

videotape is used, in which case the parties must arrange to provide the appellate court with suitable machines to review the record in that form. Ohio Rule of Appellate Procedure 9 also provides that videotape recording need not be transcribed into written form.

The testimony as recorded by these techniques still must be typed for incorporation in the record, unless the judges are enabled and willing both to listen to or see the recording itself and to readily find any passage in which they are interested.

Even where reporters are available, they often do not have enough typists to prepare the transcripts speedily.[28] Reporters either type the transcripts from their own notes, dictate them on to recording machines themselves for others to type, or give the typists their notes if they use a Stenotype or similar device which provides notes the typist can read. The more the reporter attempts to economize by not using enough typists, or by doing the typing himself or herself when not actually reporting in the courtroom, the more slowly the transcript is produced. The appellate courts are beginning to recognize that the reporters, not the appellants, are responsible for the long times needed to produce the transcripts, either because they are understaffed (perhaps unavoidably in a particular area) or undertake to handle too many cases. As a result a number of states make the reporter directly responsible for promptly preparing the transcript. The recent Texas Rule 376c (1978) subjects him to the supervision of the presiding judge, who, if necessary, shall establish priorities on the order in which the reporter gets his work done.

Some states require appellants to submit affidavits from the reporter in support of applications for more time to file the transcript. Others go further and require the reporter himself to obtain the extension. Wisconsin 1978 Rule 809.16 provides:

> "(4) A reporter may obtain an extension for filing the transcript only by motions showing good cause filed in the court and served on all parties to the appeal.
> "(5) If a reporter fails to file timely a transcript, the court may declare the reporter ineligible to act as an official court reporter in any court proceeding and prohibit the reporter from performing any private reporting work until the overdue transcript is filed."

---

[28]EFFICIENCY AND JUSTICE IN APPEALS, *supra* note 23, at 12.

The accompanying Note explains:

> "The obligation is placed on the reporter rather than the appellant to obtain an extension for filing the transcript as this is a matter not in the control of the appellant. The application for an extension is filed in the Court of Appeals rather than the trial court because of the primary concern of the Court of Appeals with cases pending before it and because of the natural reluctance of the trial judge to deny a request made by his own appointee. The power of the Court of Appeals to impose sanctions upon the court reporter for failing to file a transcript on time is especially recognized. These sanctions were among those recommended in 1971 by a special committee appointed by the Supreme Court to study the problem of delayed transcripts."[29]

New Mexico Rule 8(b) requires evidence or an affidavit from the reporter explaining his work load and priorities. The court may then order transcripts to be filed by a certain date, subject to a penalty for contempt of court if the reporter does not comply.[30] Nevada Rule 13 goes so far as to make the reporters officers of the Supreme Court with a duty to refrain from undertaking too much work. Sanctions may be imposed by the State Court Reporters Board[31] or by contempt of court. This may include the payment of damages to the state or other parties injured by the delay. As to Pennsylvania's imposing responsibility on the trial judge, see Sec. 6.6, p. 176, *infra.*

Technology may provide the solution to the problems of reporting, such as by connecting a Stenotype machine or its tape

---

[29]The Wisconsin study quoted in EFFICIENCY AND JUSTICE IN APPEALS, *supra* note 23, at 14–15, recommended:

"The following sanctions should be applied to court reporters who fail to prepare records within time limitations established by court rule:

"1. Reporters who fail to file transcripts on time should be deemed ineligible to act as official reporters in any court and prohibited from reporting new cases or doing out of court work until they have completed preparation of overdue transcripts.

"2. In order to receive his monthly salary, a court reporter should be required to certify that he has pending no uncompleted overdue transcripts.

"3. A reporter's compensation for transcription should be reduced if the transcript is not delivered to the trial court within prescribed time limits."

National Center for State Courts, WISCONSIN APPELLATE PRACTICE AND PROCEDURE STUDY, pp. 78–79 (1975).

[30]Judges have occasionally been baffled as to how to compel a reluctant (or retired) court reporter to complete a transcription of the record. A technique which other judges have found effective after violation of a court order is to find the reporter guilty of contempt of court and to sentence him to imprisonment with a typewriter until the transcript is completed. This is said to result in very rapid transcription.

[31]Nebraska Rule 7(A) provides that it is the function of the State Court Reporters Association to insure that transcripts are produced even if the initial reporter cannot finish the job.

electronically with an automatic typewriter.[32] Presently available office machines which type at magical speeds already perform work not too different from this. Such equipment is now (1981) available to reporters and governmental agencies. The initial Stenotype recording can be automatically transcribed at high speed, once it is known that the case will be appealed. It then must be translated into readable English by a person familiar with the reporter's personal code; this is not very difficult. After that it can be speedily and automatically retyped into usable form. The cost of the equipment and the translation is said to be less than the cost of ordinary slow typing.[33]

6.4 Procedure Where Proceedings Are Not Transcribed

Many cases are tried in courts where no reporter or other method of recording what is said is available. In the main, these are cases involving small amounts of money which are not worth appealing. Such cases are seldom appealed, although appeals may be more frequent as programs to provide counsel without charge to indigent persons become more widespread.

The problem of how to prepare an appellate record in the absence of a transcript is not, of course, of modern origin. For hundreds of years appeals were necessarily heard on the pleadings and on the judges' notes of the testimony, together with statements prepared by the parties and submitted to the court for approval.[34] The preparation of records on the basis of transcriptions of what was said in court came into existence with the invention of typewriters in the 1870s.

Modern rules of court contain provisions for preparing a record in the absence of a report of proceedings, using in substance the techniques which prevailed in earlier years. The federal rules and those of many states provide that the appellant

---

[32]See Appellate Judges' Conference, REPORT OF SPECIAL COMMITTEE ON INCREASING ADMINISTRATIVE EFFICIENCY THROUGH TECHNOLOGY, pp. 53–56 (1972).

[33]At present such a system is being marketed by the Baron Data Systems of San Leandro, California. It is being used by a number of court reporters throughout the country and in several criminal courts in Texas, California and Georgia. The system and its advantages are described in R. Kleps, *Transcripts by Minicomputer: A Solution for Court Delay,* 67 A.B.A.J. 224 (1981), which states that "there are more than 250 systems in use in the United States, located in every major city, and some 1,100 reporters are producing more than one million transcript pages on those systems each month."

[34]See P. Tone, *New Supreme Court Rule on Expeditious and Inexpensive Appeals,* 53 Ill. Bar J. 18, 19–20 (1964).

shall prepare a proposed report of proceedings "from the best available means, including his recollection." Federal Appellate Rule 10(c). In practice this means that appellant's counsel endeavors to summarize the facts or the evidence as best he can from recollection or notes. This proposed statement is to be prepared and served upon opposing counsel, who may submit objections, amendments or his own version, within a specified time period after being served (10 days under Federal Rule 10(c)). The proposed report or reports are then to be submitted to the trial court for settlement and approval. It is the responsibility of the court to settle, that is to correct, the statement so that it accurately reports the proceedings.

Illinois Rule 323(c) provides that the court may "hold hearings if necessary" to accomplish this objective. The quoted phrase was inserted in the Illinois rule in 1967 in order "to make explicit what was implied"—that the court can, if other means of reconstructing the record are not deemed sufficiently accurate, either recall the witnesses or otherwise have the testimony summarized or repeated under oath.[35] In Tennessee the Supreme Court recently held in *Trice* v. *Moyers,* 561 S.W.2d 153, 156 (Tenn. 1978),

> "that a party is not entitled to a new trial simply on the ground that a stenographic report is unavailable. Instead he must at least make an effort to generate a summary of the evidence that would be adequate for appellate review. Only if a transcript or summary cannot be obtained 'by any practical or feasible means . . . [and only if] the respondent and his counsel are without fault in that regard' should the trial court order a new trial."[36]

The federal rule appears to have been construed in the same way.[37]

"The best advice with respect to this problem is to avoid it if possible. This does not mean that a costly court reporter must be provided for every case. But if counsel believes that there is any likelihood that a case may be appealed, he should either arrange for a reporter or for some other method of having the evidence taken down or digested as it comes in. A tape recorder is one solution; some courts are using such devices now, but where they do not, counsel should provide his own. A stenogra-

---

[35]See Committee Comment to Rule 323(c).
[36]See Sobieski, *supra* note 20, at 46.
[37]9 J. Moore, FEDERAL PRACTICE, ¶210.06 (2d ed., 1980), and cases cited. A new trial was ordered in *United States* v. *Knox,* 456 F.2d 1024 (CA 8, 1972).

pher from the lawyer's office might be able to summarize the testimony reasonably accurately, even though not verbatim. If this cannot be done, counsel himself or a colleague or a friend of the party should try to take reasonably detailed and honest notes as the trial proceeds or during recesses. Any such device is better than recollection a number of days later. A new hearing before the court to revive recollection as to what originally had been said would itself have to be transcribed or taken down in some way, and this might be as expensive as providing for a reporter in the first instance."[38]

6.5 Agreed Statement of Facts

The federal rules and those of many states also provide that the parties may stipulate as to the material facts and file the stipulation in lieu of a record or report of proceedings. Federal Rule 10(d) provides that the parties may agree upon a statement showing how the issues presented by the appeal are raised and were decided, as well as stating the essential pertinent facts. "If the statement conforms to the truth, it, together with such additions as the Court may consider necessary fully to present the issues raised by the appeal, shall be approved by the district court" and certified to the court of appeals as the record on appeal. Federal Appellate Rule 10(d). This procedure is seldom utilized;[39] it would be appropriate when there were no disputed factual questions in the case and the parties were in accord that only questions of law were to be considered by the appellate court. Counsel will normally be able to agree much more easily on what should be included in the record in such a case than to prepare a factual stipulation.

6.6 Preparation and Transmission of the Record by the Trial Court Clerk

After the record, including the report of proceedings, has been assembled in the office of the clerk of the trial court, it is his duty to arrange and index documents and transmit the record to the clerk of the court of appeals. He should arrange the items in the correct order (which usually means chronologically)

---

[38]R. Stern, *The Record and Abstract or Excerpts*, ILLINOIS CIVIL PRACTICE AFTER TRIAL, p. 7–10 (Illinois Institute for Continuing Legal Education, 1976).
[39]9 J. Moore, FEDERAL PRACTICE, ¶210.07, (2d ed., 1980); J. Godbold, *Twenty Pages and Twenty Minutes—Effective Advocacy on Appeal*, 30 Southwestern L.J. 801, 806 (1976).

and number the documents (Federal Appellate Rule 11(b)) or the pages (Illinois Rule 324). Under the federal rule he is to transmit with the record a list of the documents as numbered, identified with reasonable definiteness, but there is no overall consecutive page numbering. See also Wisconsin Rule 809.-15(2). Although generally the clerk must forward only one copy of the record to the appellate court, in some jurisdictions he must transmit several extra copies.[40] In the New York Appellate Division for the First Department, appellant may "subpoena" the record from the trial court clerk for filing in the appellate court (New York First Department Rule 600.5).[41]

The pages of the report of proceedings or transcript will already bear the numbers given them by the reporter. Various techniques are utilized in some states to avoid renumbering those pages. Other parts of the record (the clerk's record) can be numbered "R" and the transcript "Tr." Illinois provides that the clerk shall place the letter "C" (for "Clerk's record") before the numbers of the pages that precede the report of proceedings, while pages which follow the report of proceedings shall be numbered consecutively following the pages of that report. Illinois Rule 324. Many states limit the number of transcript pages to be bound together in one volume to a specified number of pages, from 150 to 400.[42] The Illinois system is simple to prepare and easy to use, since numbered pages are easier to find than parts of numbered documents, and no renumbering of transcript pages is necessary.

In many states[43] the record is to be transmitted to or filed in the reviewing court, or completed but retained below, within 40 days after the filing of the notice of appeal;[44] this was the federal rule before the 1979 revision of Rule 11(a) noted above.

---

[40]E.g., Louisiana Rule I-1.

[41]In New York the equivalent of an information statement is to be prefixed to the record. (New York Civil Practice Act, §5531.) The rules of the Appellate Divisions require that the statement be placed at the beginning of the brief in the Second Department (Rule 670.17(c)) but at the end of the brief in the First Department (Rule 600.10). Cf. Sec. 4.5(d), *supra.*

[42]150 pages—Kentucky; 200—Florida, Mississippi, New Jersey; 215—Louisiana; 250—Montana, Nebraska, South Carolina; 300—California (400 if printed), Idaho (if record over 350); 400—Missouri. In South Carolina, both sides of the paper shall be used if the record is over 100 pages.

[43]E.g., Alaska Rule 9(g); Arizona Rule 11(a)(2); Massachusetts Rule 9; Montana Rule 10(a); Ohio Rule 10; Pennsylvania Rule 1931; Utah Rule 9; Wyoming Rule 3.02.

[44]In Vermont the record "not including the transcript" is to be transmitted within the 40 days. The clerk is to notify all counsel and the Supreme Court clerk when the transcript is filed with it by the reporter. "The appellant shall file the original of the transcript with the clerk of the Supreme Court *at the time of oral argument*" (emphasis supplied), which would seem a little late for the judges, but which in substance means any time after the transcript is completed. Rule 11.

Other states specify periods of from 30 to 90 days,[45] and even longer in Florida, North Carolina and Oklahoma.[46] Some allow the clerk a certain number of days after he receives the transcript of testimony,[47] or specify a shorter number of days when the clerk is notified by the appellant that no transcript is being ordered.[48] In Alaska, New Hampshire, New Jersey, Oregon and Washington the record shall be transmitted when the appellate court requests or orders.[49] Minnesota requires transmission 60 days before oral argument (Rule 111). These times can be and often are extended, and less often contracted, by court order, with extensions granted by the trial court being limited in length.

During the course of the preparation of the federal and Illinois rules in the 1960s, I discovered that after the records were transmitted to the appellate court they were often returned to the lower court (if in a different city) so that they would be available to the parties for use during the preparation of the briefs. In order to eliminate wasteful transportation back and forth, both the federal and the Illinois rules were drafted so as to allow the transmission of a statement showing that preparation of the record had been completed in lieu of sending up the record itself. Federal Rule 11(c) provides for retention of the record in the trial court on stipulation of the parties or order of the court on motion of any party; under the simplified procedure adopted in 1979, which is similar to Illinois Rule 325, the clerk certifies to the court of appeals that the record, including

---

[45]30 days—California Rule 5(d), New York (if no transcript or from settlement of transcript); 60 days—Maryland Rule 825, Rhode Island Rule 11, Texas Rule 386, Virginia Rule 5.8-5.9; 70 days—Idaho Rule 24; 90 days—Indiana Rule 3, Michigan Rule 812.3 (after transcript ordered), Missouri Rule 81.12, New Mexico Rule 8(a), Wisconsin Rule 809.15(4).

[46]Florida Rule 9.110 (110 days); North Carolina Rule 12 (150 days); Oklahoma Rule of Appellate Procedure 1.26 (6 months).

[47]Alabama Rule 11(a)(2) (reporter 56 days to file transcript; clerk 7 days more to transmit); Delaware Rule 9(b) (20 days if no transcript; 10 days after transcribed); Illinois Rule 326 (63 days; or 14 days after report of proceedings received); Tennessee Rule 25(a) (30 days after filing of transcript).

[48]Delaware Rule 9(b).

[49]Alaska Rule 9(g); New Jersey Rule 2:5-4(d); Oregon Rule 6.05; Washington Rule 9.8. New Hampshire Rule 13(2) provides that the record shall not be transmitted to the Supreme Court unless an order, rule or form of that court expressly requires transmittal; the date will usually be set in the scheduling order. See Sec. 4.8, p. 105, *supra*. Rule 15(8) requires that the state or the plaintiff (where the state is not a party) "shall file with the clerk of the supreme court a copy of the transcript immediately after oral argument has concluded or immediately after the case is submitted" on briefs if there is no oral argument. This would seem to mean that the New Hampshire Supreme Court surprisingly finds no need for the transcript until after the argument, which may or may not be true of appellate courts generally.

the transcript or designated parts thereof, is complete for purposes of the appeal. Under Illinois Rule 325, if the appellant so requests, the clerk merely delivers to him a certificate for transmission to the reviewing court stating that the record has been prepared and certified in the form required for transmission. Filing of this certificate is to be considered the filing of the record. The record itself then is to be transmitted immediately after the briefs have been prepared.[50] The rules of many other states are similar.[51]

Other states require transmission of the record only after the final brief has been filed.[52] This is much simpler and is feasible in most courts in which the appellate judges are not likely to look at the record until then.[53]

The above procedure for retaining the record in the trial court presupposes that the trial court clerk's office is more accessible to counsel than the appellate court's, and that the clerk will make the record available to counsel for preparation of the briefs. Where both the trial court and the appellate court are located in the same city or the same building, the reasons of convenience for the retention alternative no longer apply, unless the trial court is more willing than the appellate court to allow counsel to remove the record for use during the preparation of the briefs. Counsel should check with both clerks to ascertain whether in such circumstances there is any need to request retention of the record in the trial court. Not surprisingly, small states like Rhode Island and Delaware have found this retention alternative completely unnecessary. And many not so small states have also failed to adopt it. In such states a request to withdraw the record for use in preparing briefs must be made to the appellate court. See, e.g., Tennessee Rule 25(c).

The duty of seeing that the record gets to the appellate court is imposed upon the clerk of the trial court in some jurisdictions, including the federal (Federal Appellate Rule 11(b)), in

---

[50]Federal Appellate Rule 11(c) states that the appellant shall request the district court clerk to transmit the record upon receipt of the *appellee's* brief "or at such earlier time as the parties may agree or the court may order." No good reason is apparent why the record should not be retained below during the preparation of the appellant's reply brief as well.

[51]Rule 11(c) of Colorado, Iowa and North Dakota; Rule 10(d) of Montana and Ohio; Rule 1932 of Pennsylvania; Rule 4.05 of Wyoming.

[52]Iowa Rule 11(b); Kansas Rule 3.07; Kentucky Rule 75.07; South Dakota Rule 11(1).

[53]If a motion which requires examination of part of the record comes before the appellate court before the entire record is filed, the pertinent parts of the record should be filed by the moving party.

others upon the appellant.[54] In the latter the clerk gives the record to the appellant for transmission to the higher court. The rules stating that the clerk shall "transmit" the record may give him the option of mailing the record, transporting it by other means, such as manual delivery, or giving it to the appellant or his counsel.

Pennsylvania charges the trial judge with responsibility for transmitting the record promptly. Rule 1935 directs the Administrative Office of the Pennsylvania Courts to notify the judge of any delinquency in this respect and where appropriate to report any neglect or refusal to the Judicial Counsel. The reasons for this provision, as shown by the Note to the rule, quoted below,[55] should be of interest to other jurisdictions.

As shown in Sec. 4.8, *supra,* the receipt of the record in the appellate court is in many states the occasion for placing the case on the appellate docket, and the time from which the period for filing appellant's brief is computed. Many jurisdictions now provide for the docketing of the appeal when a copy of the notice of appeal first reaches the appellate court at the same time as or shortly after it is filed in the court below. The briefing schedules, however, still begin to run from the time the record is completely assembled and available.

Making Additional Copies of the Record

6.7 The Need for Duplication in General

Every jurisdiction requires that at least one copy of the original record, either as a whole or in relevant part, be filed with or made available to the reviewing court. This sets the bounds of the case the appellate court must decide. It cannot go beyond the facts, positions and rulings disclosed in the record.

An additional reason for filing the record in the appellate

---

[54]In Illinois the clerk may transmit it directly or through the appellant. Rule 325.
[55]The Note to Pennsylvania Rule 1935 states:

"It is intended that the Administrative Office of Pennsylvania Courts will monitor pending appeals in which the record has not yet been filed to identify those cases where the transmission of the record has not been effected within the prescribed time; and that the Administrative Office on its own initiative will bring the delinquency to the attention of the appropriate judge of the lower court for corrective action. The lower court has direct control over the official court reporter and clerk of the lower court, and it is inappropriate (and not infrequently ineffective) for counsel for the losing party below to be responsible for goading the court reporter to transcribe the notes of testimony, the judge to write an opinion, and the judge and clerk to certify and transmit the record, all within the time provided by these rules."

court is to enable the appellate judges to know, or to ascertain, the contents of whatever parts they wish to read. If there were only one appellate judge, this would be simple enough. The single original filed record could be given or made fully available to him. But this may not be sufficient for courts composed, as all appellate courts are, "of panels of three to nine, and sometimes even more judges. Even then, they could pass the papers around and sometimes they do. But it is not an efficient way of doing court business. Some material is almost certain to be lost and the delay occasioned by successive instead of simultaneous consideration of the material would be unfortunate for all litigants. One of the objectives to be attained by good appellate procedure is reasonable expedition. And that would be defeated by one-copy methods."[56] Judge Goodrich would have limited the bulk and expense of the duplicated material to the portions of the record deemed "essential to the court to read," to decide the questions presented.[57] See Sec. 6.8, *infra*.

Different courts have dealt with the problem in different ways. Many states[58] do not require anything more than a filing of one copy (usually the original) of the record. As shown above, this can consist either of the whole record, of all except those parts which the parties agree to omit or of the portions they designate as pertinent to the questions raised. Some of the federal courts of appeals have abandoned the requirement of an appendix, either in all cases or for defined classes of cases. See Sec. 6.9, *infra*. A number of states—Arizona, Connecticut, Florida, Kansas, Montana, New Hampshire, South Dakota, Tennessee—do not *require* any duplication of pertinent parts of the record, but give a party the option of doing so in an appendix to his brief.[59] Alabama Rule 10 allows use of the deferred appendix system (see Sec. 6.13, *infra*) or the filing of "an addi-

---

[56]Herbert F. Goodrich, *A Case on Appeal—A Judge's View,* in A CASE ON APPEAL, p. 8 (ALI-ABA, 1967).

[57]*Id.* at 8–9.

[58]California, Colorado, Georgia, Hawaii, Indiana, Missouri, Nebraska, Ohio (Court of Appeals), Texas, Wyoming. In some states, such as Ohio, one copy of the record below may be sufficient for the intermediate court but not for the larger supreme court.

[59]The Reporter to the Tennessee Supreme Court Advisory Commission which drafted the 1979 Tennessee rules explained:

"Thus, while it is vitally important for a party to call to the appellate court's attention particular portions of the record essential to appellate review or upon which a party particularly relies, preparation of an appendix is only one means of doing so, and the parties are not required to prepare an appendix if they think that some other method is equally effective."

Sobieski, *supra* note 20, at 80–81. One simple and effective method is to quote the critical items in the brief, if there are not too many of them.

tional photocopy of the record on appeal," while in Idaho, Louisiana, New Mexico and North Dakota two or three copies of the original record must be filed, but nothing more, and in Montana six. In Illinois, Montana and Utah an appendix or abstract need be filed only if the court so orders. On the other hand, some of the jurisdictions which generally require filing additional copies authorize the appellate court to dispense with such duplication either by rule or order in the particular case. See Federal Appellate Rule 30(f); Pennsylvania Rule of Appellate Procedure 2151. The Note to the Pennsylvania rule states that this provision "is new and is included in recognition of the developing trend toward sole reliance on the original record." This is to be encouraged in the interest of providing expeditious and inexpensive appeals, to the extent that the appellate judges do not find their work handicapped by not having enough copies of the record below available.

Although briefs below are usually not regarded as part of the record to be transmitted, in a few states the briefs in the intermediate appellate court are transmitted to the state's supreme court. This of course is necessary where the parties must or may rely on those briefs in the higher court. See Secs. 5.7(a), *supra,* and 7.3(b), *infra.*

The prevalent system in many state and federal courts for many years required the making of a number of copies of the portions of the record designated by the parties. Matters not included were not regarded as a part of the record, and this meant that everything thought to be relevant was copied. The federal rules before 1938 and some states required that the testimony be summarized in narrative form, either by the parties separately or in a single document to which the parties would either agree or obtain court approval. This was often called an abstract. The narrative abstract and verbatim excerpts from the record are compared in Sec. 6.11, *infra.*

In the federal courts in 1938, and in many states, the narrative abstract was superseded by a requirement that portions of the record designated by the parties should be reproduced verbatim in appendices to the briefs, either by appellant and appellee separately, or in a joint appendix filed by appellant but containing the material designated by all the parties. The designations were made prior to the filing of the appellant's brief. It may have been expected that only the essential portions of the record would be designated, and that the appendix would be considerably shorter than the designated record. But in practice the standard applied in designating for duplication was the same as that previously used in designating the record; whatever was relevant to the issues was included. The appendix thus did not differ significantly in size or content from the prior record.

Subsequent experience demonstrated that if the designations could be made when or immediately after the briefs were filed, the parties would be able to focus more precisely on the material pertinent to the points raised and designate considerably less. Duplication of the excerpts thus designated would then be deferred until immediately after the due date of the appellee's brief or the appellant's reply brief. In cases with long records, such a "deferred appendix" was likely to be substantially shorter than were designations made before the briefs were written. See Sec. 6.13, *infra*.

The reproduced portion of the record filed along with or after the brief is still generally called "appendix,"[60] although it usually is a completely separate document of some length not attached to the brief. A few states, employing more accurate terminology, entitled these documents "excerpts from record" (Illinois up to 1979), "extracts from record" (Maryland) and "reproduced record" (Pennsylvania). Several states continue to use the word "abstract," particularly when narration of the testimony is still required or favored. See Sec. 6.11, *infra*. And several states, such as South Carolina and Vermont, still employ such older expressions as "case" or "bill of exceptions."

6.8 Judicial Efforts to Reduce the Length of the Duplicated Parts of the Record

Within the last two decades, as many courts became concerned with their overloaded calendars and with the undue length of the duplicated material, they have endeavored to make the bar realize that only items really important for judges to read need be duplicated, and not everything relevant to the issues presented. Thus, Federal Appellate Rule 30(a) requires that the duplicated appendix shall contain, in addition to the docket entries, relevant portions of pleadings, charges, findings or opinions, and the judgment order or decision in question, "any

---

[60]Minnesota Rule 130 requires an appendix to contain the essential documents with a supplement to contain other material items, including the testimony.

other parts of the record to which the parties wish to direct the particular attention of the court." United States Supreme Court Rule 30.1 is almost identical. The equivalent criterion in Pennsylvania Rule 2175 reasonably allows the opinion below to be omitted if it is appended directly to the brief.

Tennessee Rule 28(a), adopted in 1979, though making the filing of any appendix optional, provides that the appendix shall contain "all parts of the record that must be studied in order to determine the issues presented," and not merely "those parts which support [appellant's] argument."

Wisconsin Rule 809.19(2)(1978) calls for an appendix containing the "relevant docket entries . . . findings or opinion of the trial court, and limited portions of the record essential to an understanding of the issues raised." The Judicial Council Committee's Note expresses more clearly what the rule contemplates. The former "lengthy appendix" and "narrative of testimony" are replaced

> "with the system used in the United States Court of Appeals for the Seventh Circuit. Under this system the original record serves as the primary evidence of what occurred in the trial court. The appendix becomes a very abbreviated document with only those items *absolutely essential* to an understanding of the case. It is designed to be nothing more than a useful tool to the members of the court. The failure to include some item in the appendix has no effect on the ability or willingness of the court to consider any matter in the record. This change, combined with the elimination of the requirement of printed briefs, should reduce the cost of our appeal." (Emphasis supplied.)

Seventh Circuit Rule 12, which at first merely "suggested" that the appendix include the judgments, opinion and findings below, now makes this mandatory, and adds that

> "It is preferred but not required that the appendix also include any other short excerpts from the record, such as essential portions of the pleading or charge, disputed provisions of a contract, pertinent patent drawings or pictures, or brief portions of the transcript, that are important to a consideration of the issues raised on appeal."[61]

The Kansas provision for an optional appendix containing material "of critical importance" (Rule 6.02(f)) and Kentucky's requirement of an appendix containing the judgment and opinion

---

[61]The parties are also given the option of filing a joint appendix in either of the forms described in Federal Rule of Appellate Procedure 30(a), (b), (c).

below which may also include other "helpful" items (Rule
76.12(4)(d)(vi)) are not very different.

The appendix system, whether compulsory or voluntary (as
it now is in a number of states), was designed to limit the quantity of material to be copied.[62] Until it was made clear, however,
that the court could look at record material not included in the
appendix, lawyers not unreasonably reproduced in the appendix everything relevant, so that it was nothing more than a
designated record under another name. This not only was expensive but also gave the judges too much reading matter.

Recent use of such phrases as "essential," "essential to the
justices to read," "calling for the particular attention of the
court," "must be studied" (see p. 180, *supra*) are attempts to
reduce the volume of what is included. It is doubtful, however,
if such general phrases will persuade lawyers that judges really
want to examine the record in detail only as to matters as to
which the parties disagree or perhaps as to a few critical documents which need close examination. Many facts may be significant or essential to an argument but not in dispute between the
parties. If the appellant's brief states something to be a fact, and
the appellee either agrees or does not deny it but assumes its
existence in the course of his own argument, the appellate
judges have no need to verify that fact further, except perhaps
for the opinion writer who can use the original record. The
judges may also want to know what the lower court said on the
point in its judgment, findings, opinion or other statement.

If, as some judges have indicated to me orally, material
which relates to disputed matters and the reasoning of the
court below is what each judge should have conveniently available, the rules should say so more explicitly than they now do.
Appending the judgment, opinion, findings and other statements of reasons by the court below to the appellant's brief
should be compulsory, as it now is in the rules of many supreme courts for cases coming to them from intermediate appellate courts. A rule similar to South Carolina's Rule 4, §4,
which provides that

> "undisputed facts must be stated without testimony, and only the
> testimony as to disputed facts shall be stated, omitting all that is
> irrelevant to the issues to be decided,"

---

[62]See the paper of Judge John J. Parker, *Improving Appellate Methods*, 25 N.Y.U. L. Rev.
1, 6 (1950).

may give counsel more of a guideline to what the judges wish to read. This does not, however, include the types of key documents such as are referred to in the Seventh Circuit's Rule 12. A combination of the substance of these provisions from the South Carolina and the Seventh Circuit rules may well be most satisfactory to appellate judges. For example:

> The appendix must contain the judgment, opinions, findings or other statements showing the action of the courts below and the reasons therefor, and should also contain any excerpts from the pleadings or charge which relate to the questions presented on the appeal, testimony or other evidence pertaining to facts which are in dispute but not to indisputable facts which may be stated in the brief without supporting testimony, and pertinent passages from testimony or any document (such as a contract, will or patent) as to which the precise language may be significant. Excerpts set forth in the brief need not be repeated in the appendix.

Preparation of an appendix is not the only means of providing the judges with a verbatim version of the critical items in the record.[63] Even when the record is otherwise duplicated, many attorneys "quote verbatim from the record in their briefs."[64] There is no reason why such passages should be duplicated twice.

A good lawyer will, regardless of any rule, make sure that such passages are easily available to the judges,[65] preferably in the text of his brief. But if the passages are too long for quotation in text or footnote without breaking the continuity of the brief, he should attach them in an appendix whether required to or not. In most cases where the records are not very long or the issues not numerous, quoting the critical items in the brief will be entirely feasible. In cases of greater magnitude, an appendix may be more appropriate.

In Illinois, where Rule 342 requires the mandatory filing by appellant of an appendix containing the decision below and a

---

[63]Sobieski, *supra* note 20, at 80–81.

[64]See Advisory Commission Comment to Tennessee Rule 28, quoted in Sobieski, *id.* at 80.

[65]Thomas B. Koykka, author of OHIO APPELLATE PROCESS (1972), wrote to me that in Ohio "an additional appendix is not required. However, careful counsel will also usually supply an appendix in which are collected the materials counsel believes are particularly important and which each of the panel of three judges ought to have readily available. Ordinarily, counsel will advise his opposite number of material he intends to incorporate in an appendix and inquire whether there is additional material the opponent may wish included to assist the court. The appendix, however, whether joint or separate, is not required and is utilized only when counsel considers it may aid the court."

few other formal papers, but does not refer to or in terms permit any other appendix, the clerk of the Supreme Court has declined to permit appellee to file an appendix containing other record material, at least in a separately bound volume. Such a document submitted by either party, if limited to items in the record which are critical but too long to incorporate in the text of the brief, would contain precisely those portions of the record which judges would normally want to read verbatim. Its filing, even if not required, should not be discouraged. Only an explicit prohibitory rule should be interpreted as barring the use of such a helpful device.

This suggests that the optional appendix allowable under revised Tennessee Rule 28 is a good solution to the problem, so long as the mandatory items (judgment and reasoning of courts below) are made available to each judge. Specific reference to the alternative of quoting the essential excerpts in the brief might, however, be a slight improvement upon the Tennessee rule.

6.9 The Number of Copies to Be Duplicated

How many copies of the material parts of the record should be made depends upon the use which the judges of the appellate court make of the record. This, of course, is likely to vary from court to court and from judge to judge, and even from case to case. In general, however, the judge who writes the opinion is likely to examine the record in some detail, as many judicial opinions demonstrate on their face. Other conscientious but busy appellate judges may rely on the briefs and the findings or other statement of reasons by the court below, except where the parties are not in agreement. As to the portions of the record relating to such matters, which presumably would be critical in determining the appeal, each judge may want to read them himself. Of course, when the briefs are not adequate, and the court below has not made detailed findings, each of the judges may want to examine the record personally or through law clerks or staff attorneys before as well as after the argument.

How many copies of the record or its critical parts will be needed for the above purposes will also depend on the logistics of the particular court. A single copy would, of course, be enough for the judge who writes the opinion, and indeed that judge is likely to call for the actual record on file rather than to rely on the selected excerpts from it. When the court sits in a single building in which all the judges have permanent offices, the experience of a number of courts suggests that three judges can without serious inconvenience mutually arrange for a single complete record to be available to each of them when desired. One or two more court copies would be sufficient even for a larger court. On the other hand, the judges may be more likely to peruse the record if a copy is more readily at hand for each judge. And as the number of judges goes beyond three or the judges' chambers become more distant from one another, such mutual accommodation becomes more cumbersome. Nevertheless, the seven-judge Supreme Court of Illinois, whose members have chambers in their districts, has recently indicated an ability and willingness to get along with only one copy of the original record in most cases.[66] A number of other courts, however, want a copy available for each judge.

Although the needs of the judges are and should be given primary importance in determining how many copies should be filed, the cost of duplicating additional copies is also entitled to consideration. Reproduction costs are borne by the parties or the losing party, or by the government (which means the public) when a party is unable to pay, as is true in most criminal cases. Prior to the development of modern duplicating processes, printing was the required method for reproducing records, and once the type was set the cost of printing was not substantially greater as the number of copies increased. It did not cost much more to print 30 or 50 copies than a smaller number. Modern methods of photographic reproduction[67] cost much less, but the costs are directly proportional to the number of copies. Thirty copies at 10 cents a page cost 10 times as much as three copies. Although even for a large number the cost is almost certain to be substantially less than for printing,[68] larger numbers still impose substantial burdens on the parties. Thus, no more copies should be required than are actually needed for use by the court.

---

[66]The 1979 revision of Illinois Rule 342 provides that "no abstract of the record on appeal shall be filed unless the reviewing court [so] orders," and eliminates the prior option of filing either excerpts from record or an abstract. Only the abstract survived. See Sec. 6.11, pp. 192–193, *infra.* As of November 1980, the Illinois appellate courts have never ordered that an abstract be filed.

[67]The rules of all but a few courts now permit the duplicated portions of the record to be copied by these methods. See Sec. 6.10, *infra.*

[68]Printing may cost from $14-$35 per page (in Chicago) without allowing for changes in the proof. Making 30 copies by a duplicating process might cost $3.00 a page or more plus the cost of binding.

Records, Appendices and the Like 185

As shown in Sec. 6.7, *supra,* many courts do not require the filing of more than the original record, while a few others permit one or two additional copies of the record without further designation or selection. Above that there is a wide variation from three or four copies in many three-judge appellate courts[69] up to 56 (printed by the clerk and including copies for counsel) in the small state of Connecticut (Practice Book, §3085 (1979)) for its Supreme Court and also the law libraries in the state; this record does not include the evidence, which is left to the brief or an appendix thereto. Often, particularly when the duplicated material is at least in theory regarded as an appendix to the brief, the number is the same as for the brief. In the United States Supreme Court, 40 copies of briefs and appendices must be submitted. Rules 30.1, 35.1. Rules 30(a) and 31(b) of the Federal Rules of Appellate Procedure, however, require 10 appendices and 25 briefs, but some of the circuit rules permit less.[70] The Maryland, Pennsylvania and Wisconsin supreme court rules require 30 copies; Massachusetts, 25; the Michigan Supreme Court, 24; Minnesota, Oklahoma, New York (unless the option of using the whole record is utilized) and Virginia, 20; Iowa, West Virginia and the Ohio Supreme Court (but not the Court of Appeals), 18; and South Carolina[71] and the Illinois Supreme Court, 15.

Some states quite reasonably require fewer copies for the

---

[69]E.g., Alabama, Michigan, New Jersey, Tennessee.

[70]Rule 30(f) of the Federal Appellate Rules permits the courts of appeals by rules applicable to all cases or to classes of cases or by orders in specific cases to allow appeals to be made on the original record with such copies as the court may require. In 1978 the Fifth Circuit amended its rules to dispense with any appendix, but to require the filing of "record excerpts" which would include "the docket sheet; any pretrial order; the judgment or interlocutory order appealed from; any other order or orders sought to be reviewed; and any supporting opinion, findings of fact or conclusions of law filed or delivered orally by the district court." Fifth Circuit Rule 13.1. The Ninth Circuit permits all appeals to be heard on the original record, but requires appellant to file with his brief five copies of "excerpts of the clerk's record," which is to consist only of the pleadings, the motion and response upon which the court entered judgment, if any, any pretrial order, the judgment or order appealed from and any supporting findings or statement of reasons, the notice of appeal, and the trial court docket sheet. Ninth Circuit Rules 4(b), 13(a) (1980). In the Third Circuit, an appendix is not required in habeas corpus or post-conviction challenges to criminal convictions. Under Sixth Circuit Rule 10, when the record is not over 100 pages long, three copies of the record will suffice without an appendix. In the Eighth Circuit, the original record is enough in all criminal and post-conviction proceedings, as well as bankruptcy, social security and *in forma pauperis* cases, and by leave of court. Rule 11. In the Tenth Circuit, an original record is enough except in Class A civil cases where the record is longer than 300 pages; in such cases an appendix should be prepared in accordance with Federal Rule of Appellate Procedure 30, preferably paragraph (c). Tenth Circuit Rules 10 and 11(d) (1980).

[71]In South Carolina, where the duplicated portion of the record is called the "transcript of record," Rule 4, Sec. 2, requires that it include "a certificate by counsel that all irrelevant matter has been deleted" and that "no Transcript of Record will be accepted that does not comply . . . ."

intermediate courts than for the larger supreme courts; the number required is often the number of judges on the appellate court, or that number plus one to provide a copy for the clerk's office.[72] Alabama and Tennessee, each of which has several appellate courts with different numbers of judges, do not specify the number, but sensibly require one copy per judge in Alabama or that number plus one for the clerk in Tennessee. In Alaska, North Carolina and Washington only one copy need be filed; the clerk will make the extra copies needed (customarily 20 copies in North Carolina).

In general, one copy for the clerk's office, one, or at most two if allowance is being made for the judge's law clerk, for each judge, and one for a staff attorney or court administrator if the court utilizes such a person to examine the record should be sufficient, not the larger numbers which in some places are presently required. Even though lawyers writing briefs in other cases in the future may on occasion find it convenient to find copies of the records in all appellate cases in law libraries not too far away, this would not appear to justify imposing upon the parties to all appeals the additional cost of duplicating larger numbers of copies. It is doubtful if more than a few of the records are ever examined by outsiders to the initial litigation, except perhaps for United States Supreme Court cases. As to that Court, several private services have microfilmed the records since 1948. They are available (as of 1978) in microfiche or original form in 155 law libraries throughout the country,[73] including the 23 libraries to which the Supreme Court clerk distributes copies available from the 40 filed by the parties. In view of the availability of the microfiche records, even the Supreme Court might now well require only the numbers actually needed for the Justices, their clerks and the Court's own files.

The number of copies which must be duplicated is larger than the number required to be filed. Counsel should not overlook the need for making additional copies for all other counsel (or parties not represented by counsel) as well as for themselves. Court rules require from one to three, and in a few states even five, copies to be served upon counsel for each other party separately represented. A lawyer will also usually want several

[72]E.g., Alabama, Connecticut, Michigan, New Jersey, Ohio, Tennessee. Most of these states require four copies for the three-judge intermediate courts.
[73]See Appendix C to R. Stern and E. Gressman, SUPREME COURT PRACTICE, pp. 1158–1172 (5th ed., 1978).

copies for his own office, depending on the number of lawyers working on the case, and perhaps one for his client, particularly if the latter has house counsel who supervised or otherwise was active in or closely followed the litigation. Thus, at a minimum four and usually a few more copies should be made in addition to those required for the court.

6.10 Method of Reproduction of Records

For many years the reproduced records were printed. Printing was expensive, but it was required unless the party could qualify as an indigent. Other methods of copying then available, such as mimeographing and carbon paper, were not thought to provide clear enough copies for reading by appellate judges.

Then came what may be called the Xerox revolution, which made copying both much less expensive and simple enough to be performed in lawyers' offices. The machines of Xerox and many competing companies permit the copies to be produced both more quickly and economically than if printed. They also enable the actual typewritten pages of a record to be clearly reproduced by photographic processes without further costly editing of galley and page proofs by counsel. And since the charges for using the new machines, in contrast to printing, are by the page, the cost of producing a small number of copies is proportionally less than for a larger number.

The rules of the vast majority of the states permit the pertinent portions of records (in an appendix, abstract, etc.) to be reproduced either by printing, as was previously required, or, in the words of Federal Appellate Rule 32(a) and many of the state rules, "by any duplicating or copying process which produces a clear black image on white paper." Carbon copies, however, are not permitted "except in behalf of parties allowed to proceed *in forma pauperis.*" A few states still require printing,[74] though not as many as require briefs to be printed, as to which see Sec. 7.37, *infra.* Whether these states have consciously determined that the new processes are inadequate for their judges or have just not gotten around to eliminating an obsolete requirement

---

[74]Arkansas Supreme Court Rule 8; Kentucky Supreme Court Rule 76.12(4)(a) and (d)(vi) (for civil cases in Supreme Court); Michigan Rule 857.1; Minnesota Rule 132.01. In Connecticut an appendix is not mandatory, but an optional appendix containing narrated or verbatim excerpts from the transcripts (if too long for inclusion in the brief itself) may be filed in printed form. Connecticut Practice Book, §§3060 F-M (1979).

is not known. It is clear, however, that the federal rules and those of most of the other states were deliberately changed to take advantage of the efficiency and economy of the new processes. There is no reason to believe that these advantages would be any less or the documents less legible elsewhere.

In the federal courts and most states, letter size paper (8½ by 11 inches) is to be used, and the trend clearly is in that direction. The Judicial Counsel Committee's Notes to the 1978 Wisconsin rules stated that this size "is specified for uniformity and ease of handling," and that "a standard size paper simplifies records management. There is a national trend away from legal size paper." See Notes to Rule 809.19 and 809.81, and a similar comment on Washington Rule of Appellate Procedure 9.2.[75] Some states, such as Pennsylvania, Wisconsin and Maryland, now require that all pages be 8½ by 11 inches whether the text is printed or typewritten.

In Alabama, Arkansas, Colorado, Indiana, Louisiana and Nebraska, however, legal size paper (8½ by 13 or 14 inches) is still required. In Florida, Mississippi and Missouri, either size may be used. Delaware accepts either 13 or 14 inches. Where the size of page permitted is smaller than the size of a document in the record, the latter may have to be reduced in size before or while being photocopied, or retyped on a page of the size allowed. Typed material must be double spaced, except in Kansas which permits single spacing; Washington permits 1½ spacing as well as double spacing. Usually quotations and footnotes may be single spaced, except that Georgia Rule 24-3610 requires even quotations to be double spaced.

The rules usually specify smaller size pages for printed matter. The federal courts, both the Supreme Court and the courts of appeals, and many states require printed pages to be 6⅛ by 9¼ inches. The Supreme Court so requires for all pages, printed or not (Rule 33.1(d)). Arkansas and Illinois require paper 6¾ by 10 inches.

The part of a page which may be used for the typed or printed matter and the margins differs among the states. In the United States courts of appeals, typed matter on letter size pages may not exceed 6½ by 9½ inches (Federal Rule of Appellate Procedure 32(a)). Usable space on printed pages in the courts of appeals cannot exceed 4⅙ by 7⅙ inches. The United

---

[75]The Washington rule requires 8½ by 11 inches generally, but 8½ by 13 inches when the cost is borne by the public.

States Supreme Court now limits all briefs, printed or typed, to "approximately 4⅛ × 7⅛ inches," perhaps in recognition of the fact that most rulers do not measure sixths of inches. Rule 33.1(d). In both courts printed type must be no smaller than 11 point, the size of the type in this book. The Supreme Court rule permits footnotes to be as small as nine-point type; there must be "two-point or more leading between lines" of both text and footnotes.

The rules of the United States Supreme Court, as applied by that Court, greatly impede the use of the newer, less expensive processes. Indeed, Rule 33.1(a) now states that standard typographical printing "is preferred"; presumably commercial off-set or other processes which look exactly like printing would be equally acceptable. The rules on their face are identical with the Federal Rules of Appellate Procedure, which the Supreme Court approved for the United States courts of appeals, in defining printing to include any "process which produces a clear, black image on white paper." Supreme Court Rule 33.1(a). Compare Federal Rule of Appellate Procedures 32(a). But as a practical matter the requirements described above as to the size of the page, the part of the page, and the size type which can be used, and double spacing for typewritten matter handicap the photographic reproduction of the actual pages of a record typed in the usual way. The purpose is to keep all Supreme Court records the same size, so that they can be conveniently stored in libraries.

Although double-space typing satisfies these requirements, it would permit little textual material to appear on the usable portion of the page, and many more pages would be needed,[76] which in itself would substantially increase the cost of photocopying. Single-space typing, on the other hand, is not acceptable because the lines are regarded as not adequately leaded, that is, too close together. Single-and-a-half spacing was acceptable prior to the 1980 rule revision, but no longer is, except in the State of Washington. See Sec. 7.37, *infra.*

Whether correctly or not, the Supreme Court regards its definition of printing as providing for an adequate and less expensive alternative to standard printing; it will not waive its requirements except for parties appearing *in forma pauperis. Snider* v. *All State Administrators,* 414 U.S. 685 (1974).

---

[76]United States Supreme Court Rule 33.3 allows photographically copied (typed) documents to be 110 pages long in contrast to 50 pages printed, and 65 pages in contrast to 30 pages printed.

Insofar as costs are concerned, the charge for making 40 photographic copies for the Court and more for counsel of the many more pages needed to satisfy the Supreme Court's spacing requirements makes photographic copying much more expensive per page than in other courts. This should be taken into account in comparing the costs of photocopying with off-set or regular printing.[77] As a result, it is not surprising that most documents in the Supreme Court are still printed, in accordance with the Court's stated preference.

6.11   Should the Pertinent Evidence Be Narrated or Quoted Verbatim

Whether the reproduced part of the testimony should be placed before the appellate court verbatim or in a shorter digested or narrative abstract is a subject of disagreement, although the verbatim method by now has been adopted in all but a few jurisdictions.

Historically, the federal courts have vacillated as to whether to require the testimonial parts of the original record to be narrated so as to substitute a running narrative for the actual questions and answers. In the Federal Equity Rules of 1912, however, the narrative requirement was somewhat surprisingly reinstated.[78] At that time printing was deemed the only feasible method of reproduction, and the Supreme Court was concerned with the cost of reproducing records of great length and the burden imposed upon the Court of reading all that material. It was then the practice to require the reproduction of all of the record filed with the appellate court. Printing that volume of material was tremendously expensive for the parties and also burdensome for the judges who endeavored to read much of it. The narrative abstract, which eliminated the questions and answers and unnecessary colloquy, was substantially shorter and accordingly required less printing and judicial reading time.

Abstracts were prepared in two ways. Under the Supreme Court's 1912 Rule 75, the appellant would draft the abstract and submit it to the appellee, who would make whatever modifica-

---

[77]The cost of photocopying 50 copies of twice as many pages at 10 cents a page would come to $10.00 for two pages, in comparison to a minimum of $14.00 per page of regular printing.

[78]See E. Griswold and W. Mitchell, *The Narrative Record in Federal Equity Appeals*, 42 Harv. L. Rev. 483 (1929); W. Lane, *Twenty Years Under the Federal Equity Rules*, 46 Harv. L. Rev. 638, 656–658 (1933); F. Stone, *The Record on Appeal in Civil Cases*, 23 Va. L. Rev. 766 (1937); J. Parker, *Improving Appellate Methods*, 25 N.Y.U. L. Rev. 1 (1950).

tions or additions he thought necessary. The parties would then, presumably in conference, attempt to agree, and if not they would submit their respective versions to the trial judge for settlement. This might produce an accurate abstract, but it took a great deal of expensive lawyer time and in some cases that of the trial judge as well. It also served to eliminate a great deal of the flavor from the record.

The other technique, still employed in a few states, and in Illinois when requested by the reviewing court, is for appellant to prepare and file his own abstract, unilaterally, and file it with his brief. If appellee is dissatisfied, he can submit his own abstract, of the same as well as additional parts of the record, along with his brief. This at least eliminates the lawyer and judge time spent trying to obtain agreement. But the preparation of the two abstracts still requires a great deal of lawyer time, and also produces two overlapping and even to some extent conflicting documents instead of a single continuing digest of some reliability. Of greater importance, neither version can be relied upon by the court to be trustworthy, even though most of each one usually would be. Without comparing them with each other and with the record itself—and that would defeat the purpose of the abstract—no judge can be sure which parts are accurate, or which represent deliberate or unconscious partisan bias.

With the availability of the present simple and inexpensive means of duplication, a basic reason for using an abstract instead of actual excerpts from the transcript disappeared. In part for this reason, the federal courts and all but a few states now require that the appendix, excerpts, extracts or reproduced record consist of quoted parts of the record, not a lawyers' digest. The Federal Appellate Rules Committee declared that "[t]he narrative form of testimony has been adversely criticized by the bar, by a considerable section of the bench, and by commentators."[79]

---

[79]Quoted in 9 J. Moore, FEDERAL PRACTICE, ¶210.13[2] (2d ed., 1980). Rule 75(c) of the Federal Rules of Civil Procedure adopted in 1938, which dealt with the record on appeal, specifically provided that the "testimony of witnesses designated for inclusion [in the record] need not be in narrative form, but may be in question and answer form." In explanation of the change, former Attorney General and Chairman of the Supreme Court's Advisory Committee, William D. Mitchell, stated at an institute on the new rules held in Cleveland in July 1938:

"The present practice requires that the testimony of the witnesses shall be placed in narrative form, except such parts as present so critical a turn in the case that the exact words used may be contained in the record. There is an enormous amount of objection to that narrative system. It reduces the size of the record somewhat and perhaps saves in printing bills, but we had collected a mass of specific evidence and specific cases showing that the labor of getting up a narrative statement and agreeing on it and settling

The reporter to the Advisory Commission which drafted the 1979 Tennessee rules explained that if a substantial verbatim recital of the entire proceeding is available, a verbatim transcript is required so as "to have as exact a record as possible of what transpired in the trial court and to avoid the inaccuracies that inevitably attend the preparation of a narrative record."[80] Iowa Rule 15(a) provides that "summaries, abstracts or narratives shall not be used in an appendix" except as part of an agreed statement of the case. Maryland Rule 828 provides for verbatim abstracts unless the parties agree upon a narrative.

A few states make an abstract optional with the parties.[81] In some of those states (Texas, Washington) either party may insist on use of the verbatim record in whole or in part. The Oregon abstract appended to the brief is the same as the usual appendix; the evidence may be either narrated or verbatim, but appellant should abstract or summarize the material not in dispute (Rule 7.25). In Utah the filing of an abstract of the transcript before the brief has been discretionary with the Supreme Court since 1977. Although the narrative form is suggested, verbatim excerpts are acceptable.

The Illinois Supreme Court Rules Committee, in departing from the prior Illinois narrative abstract practice to allow counsel the option of using the quoted passages from the record and not a narration, commented in 1969 (Comment to Rule 342):

> "The important change brought about by this rule is that it permits the appellant to elect to replace the abstract with excerpts from record consisting of the parts of the record which the parties deem it essential for the judges of the reviewing court to read. In the judgment of the Committee, the lawyers' time in preparing an abstract costs the client more than the savings resulting from printing a digest of the relevant testimony instead of the relevant excerpts themselves. The abstract is also an unreliable tool for the judge of a reviewing court, inasmuch as it is prepared by counsel for one side and sometimes cannot be relied upon as a fair narrative of the evidence. In the Federal courts, and in many state courts, actual quotations of the relevant portions of the record are

it, greatly outweighed any saving in printing expense. The Bar of the country seemed to be almost overwhelmingly for abolishing the requirement for narrative statement. And so the court has accepted this rule which makes it unnecessary to prepare narrative statements."

American Bar Association, FEDERAL RULES OF CIVIL PROCEDURE AND PROCEEDINGS OF THE INSTITUTE ON FEDERAL RULES, p. 363 (1938).

[80]Sobieski, *supra* note 20, at 41.
[81]Maryland (if the parties agree), Tennessee, Texas, Washington.

used instead of an abstract. Nevertheless, because many lawyers and judges believe the abstract practice is desirable, especially in certain kinds of cases, the Committee included in the Rule an alternative provision for the filing of an abstract in lieu of excerpts, at the election of the appellant."

The 1969 rule (342(e)(3)) explicitly declared, however, that in preparing an abstract "actual quotations may be used in lieu of a narrative for any portion of the evidence," which means that the verbatim transcript will be available if either party provides it.

In 1979 Illinois Rule 342 was substantially rewritten to eliminate the need for filing either excerpts or abstract unless the reviewing court ordered an abstract, which should be in narrative form, although the above provision permitting the actual use of quotations for any portion of the evidence was retained. In addition, the appellant's brief was required to "include, as an appendix, a copy of the judgment appealed from, any opinion, memorandum, or findings of fact filed or entered by the trial judge, the notice of appeal, and a complete table of contents, with page references, of the record on appeal." The revised Committee Comment stated that

> "The contemplation is that in most instances the appeal will be heard on the original papers. It is provided, however, that the reviewing court may order that an abstract be prepared and filed . . . . Since in most cases there will no longer be either abstract or excerpts, the duty of the parties to make a fair and accurate statement of the facts in their briefs, always important, has become even more so. . . ."

To the extent that the 1979 revision calls for a narrative abstract instead of verbatim excerpts from the record,[82] it is a regressive step counter to the general trend in the federal and state courts and unwise for the reasons stated in the preceding pages. The provision will do little harm, of course, if, as seems to have been expected and has been the case in the short time since the new rule became effective, the reviewing court rarely if ever calls for an abstract, or if the proviso allowing quotation of "any portion" of the evidence is deemed to permit an abstract which uses actual quotations on a large scale. Indeed, if only the portions of the testimony relating to disputed matters need be reproduced (see Sec. 6.8, *supra*), the judges should prefer to read them verbatim and not as digested by counsel.

---

[82]Lawyers had often failed to put the excerpts in intelligible form. See pp. 198–200, *infra*.

North Carolina and South Carolina[83] provide for narrating the undisputed facts without quoting the testimony, but for use of the questions and answers where necessary, which means for disputed items. The Committee Comment on North Carolina Rule 9 recommended that the narrative form should be used for "that which merely lays an undisputed factual context or provides an undisputed factual background," but the question and answer form where "shades of meaning, nuances of expression, and ambiguity of question or response bear obviously upon the sense and credibility of testimony." In North Carolina, if the parties cannot agree as to the classification of a particular testimony as well as the accuracy of the abstract, the dispute is to be settled by the court.[84]

Arkansas, Mississippi and Oklahoma still make an abstract mandatory, but Oklahoma's rules do not specify whether the

---

[83]North Carolina Appellate Rule 9(c); South Carolina Rule 4, §§3, 4.

[84]The thoughtful discussion of the problem in the North Carolina Comment to Rule 9(c), though long, warrants quotation:

"The best possible incorporation of testimonial evidence in a record on appeal would 1) include no more than is minimally required for reviewing errors assigned; 2) set out in narrative summary form that which merely lays an undisputed factual context or provides an undisputed factual background; and 3) set out in question-and-answer form all that wherein shades of meaning, nuances of expression, and ambiguity of question or response bear obviously upon the sense and credibility of testimony. An all-narrative summary undoubtedly obscures the true sense of much critical testimony, tends to encourage inclusion of unnecessary portions, and is exceedingly time-consuming. An all-verbatim transcript inevitably includes long passages of confused questions and answers frequently leading finally to the establishment of purely peripheral fact which, though necessary as context or background, is not really disputed and could be compressed fairly into summary form. Generally speaking, it is obvious that a narrative form is easier for the reviewing court to use, while a verbatim question-and-answer form is easier for counsel to prepare. The problem has been and remains one of accommodation to these conflicting interests and values. This subdivision attempts a new accommodation. Its first sentence continues, for obvious reasons, the traditional requirement that evidence whose admission or exclusion is assigned as error be included in question-and-answer form. The rest of the subdivision involves a limited relaxation of the former flat requirement of narrative form for all other testimonial evidence included. The idea expressed is that this remains the ordinarily preferred and required form, but with the option given to use question-and-answer form where the narrative would obscure particular testimony's true sense. With this option given, it may inevitably become the object of disagreement between counsel during the process of composing the record on appeal. To aid both counsel and any judge required to settle such a dispute as to form, the last paragraph of this subdivision is devoted to a general statement of the considerations properly to be used in determining the fitness of the particular mode in dispute. These are to be brought into play in the normal process, set out in Rule 11, of settling the record—whether by agreement, acceptance through adversarial exchange, or judicial settlement. In this process the appellant will obviously have the first opportunity to choose the form or forms to be used (after having first selected those portions of the total evidence which are to be included in any form). This choice might be exercised informally in a proposal to the appellee for an agreed record on appeal, or in a formal 'proposed record on appeal' served upon the appellee. In the latter situation an appellee might either formally object to the proposed form, or include a different form in his 'proposed alternative record on appeal.' In either case, judicial settlement as to the propriety of the disputed form would then be forced."

evidence may be narrated or verbatim; either is acceptable if supported by adequate record references. The Oregon abstract follows the brief within the same cover but with separately numbered pages. Where possible, for portions of the proceedings not in dispute, a digest or summary should be used, but short excerpts are acceptable. Washington Rule 9.3 gives appellant the choice, but provides that if any party prepares a verbatim report it will be used. Arkansas Supreme Court Rule 9(d), however, requires that the abstract of testimony included in the brief be in condensed form. The Mississippi Supreme Court, in requiring an abstract consisting of "an impartial condensation, without comment or emphasis, of only such material facts in the record as are necessary for the clear understanding of all questions presented" (Mississippi Rule 41), has explained in a foreword by the chief justice that requiring an abstract or abridgment causes attorneys to "show greater concentration as to decisive issues, resulting in better briefs and oral arguments."

In Arkansas and Oklahoma, the rules contemplate that the abstract will be part of the brief;[85] in substance it constitutes an enlarged statement of facts. In Mississippi the abstract may be included in the brief, without being counted in the 50-page limitation. Rule 41. Arkansas and Oklahoma have no page limitations.

The Connecticut rule governing briefs (Connecticut Practice Book, §3060F) requires the treatment of evidence in both Statement and Argument to be in narrative form, although relevant charges to the jury, exceptions thereto and requests to charge are to be included verbatim, as may evidence when necessary to understand a ruling or when counsel believes a narrative will not suffice. But these requirements relate to the brief itself, where, of course, the facts (not each witness's testimony) are ordinarily narrated and quotations should be held to a minimum. No appendix is required, although "an appendix may be used to print or excerpt lengthy exhibits or quotations from the transcripts" (§3060J). This implies that verbatim excerpts are permissible, though the cost of printing them is not recoverable if the substance "could be stated as well in narrative form" (§3060L). Connecticut thus leaves it to counsel to determine what to narrate and what to quote, as does North Carolina, but with emphasis on the brief rather than the appendix.

The approach embodied in the North Carolina and South

---

[85]Arkansas Supreme Court Rule 9; Oklahoma Supreme Court Rule 15.

Carolina rules whereby actual quotations can be used for critical items of testimony but a narrative otherwise has much to recommend it from the viewpoint of the appellate judges. But if, as has been suggested earlier, all that need be reproduced for each judge (as distinct from the opinion writer who can use the entire record on file) are the critical items or those relating to matters in dispute, the judges are not likely to examine the record with respect to matters shown by the brief not to be in controversy. They can and should be able to rely on the briefs for the "undisputed factual context" or "undisputed factual background." The briefs should therefore perform the function of the narrative abstract for those parts of the record for which the actual question and answer form is not essential. And a brief can do this much more effectively than an abstract, for the statement of facts in a brief sets forth the relevant facts in logical or chronological order, in contrast to the usual abstract which digests each witness's testimony in the order in which he appeared and in which the questions were asked and answered. Furthermore, the North Carolina approach does not give sufficient weight to the additional burden in time and money imposed by the preparation of a narrative abstract even for parts of the testimony. Each counsel must attempt to narrate the testimony and then to agree "through adversarial interchange," and, in addition, the burden extends to the trial judge who must umpire all disagreements between the parties as to what shall be narrated and how.

A basic advantage of using actual excerpts from the record is its simplicity. The lawyer must designate the parts he thinks the appellate judges may want to read, or ought to read, but he need not attempt to rewrite them. This saves a substantial amount of lawyer time and client money, and gives the appellate judges an accurate and trustworthy report as to what occurred at the trial. The fact that this may be somewhat longer than the narrative version does not make it more expensive if the time needed to prepare the narrative is taken into account.

For these reasons the large majority of American jurisdictions, state and federal, has been wise to reject the abstract or narrative and to require verbatim quotation of those parts of the record deemed important enough for the appellate judge to read. This does not mean that an individual copy necessarily should be made available to each judge. As indicated in Secs. 6.7 and 6.9, *supra,* in a number of courts only the original record, which, of course, consists of the verbatim testimony, need be filed in the belief that it will be available to the individual judges as needed.

6.12 How to Prepare the Portions of the Record to Be Duplicated

What should be done in preparing the portions of the record to be duplicated (hereinafter called the appendix, as it is in most jurisdictions) is in part prescribed by rule and in part by common sense.[86]

If the appendix is not short enough to be bound in the same document as the brief, it should begin with a cover page like that of the brief. Next should come a table of contents of what the appendix contains, in the order in which the material appears, with reference to the pages of the appendix at which each document begins.[87] It is also helpful to the court to have available a list of the contents of the entire record on appeal, so that a judge may readily find items in the record on file which are not included in the appendix. Federal Appellate Rule 30(d) accordingly requires that the "relevant docket entries" shall be set out following the list of contents. To accomplish the same objective, Illinois Rule 342(a) requires that the table of contents list each item in the record on appeal, whether or not it is duplicated in the appendix.[88] The rules of other states differ in many respects from the above versions.

One or the other or both of these two means of informing the court of the contents of the record and of the appendix— table of contents or docket entries—should be used whether or not the rules so require.[89] The table should describe each document in sufficient detail to indicate its nature, including the date where appropriate. For example, "Complaint, filed October 1, 1978," or "Exhibit 6, letter of October 2, 1978, from

---

[86]In North Carolina the clerk does the reproducing. In Connecticut the Supreme Court clerk prints the pertinent parts of the record, not including the evidence, which are to be covered in the parties' briefs and appendices. Connecticut Practice Book, §§3078, 3087. See note 74, *supra.*

[87]E.g., Federal Rule of Appellate Procedure 30(d).

[88]Under the Illinois rule the table of contents should state the nature of each document, the date of filing or entry where appropriate (as for pleadings, motions, notices and orders), and the names of all witnesses together with the pages on which their direct, cross- and redirect examinations begin. The pre-1979 Rule 342(c)(3) provided that record page numbers of items not included in the duplicated material "shall be enclosed in parentheses in the table or otherwise designated as omitted." This still might be a good idea even where not required.

[89]So far as I know, no rules prohibit the use of such convenient devices.

John Doe to AB Company." As to oral testimony, the table should state the name of each witness and the pages where the direct, cross- and redirect examinations begin. If the page numbers of the record as filed differ from those of the duplicated material, both page numbers should be set out, in separate columns.

The nonevidentiary material, such as pleadings, motions, orders and exhibits, can usually be photographically reproduced, page-for-page, except in Arkansas where printing is still required, and in the United States Supreme Court because of its peculiar rules limiting the portion of the small page which can be used for the written matter. See Sec. 6.10, *supra.*

The transcript of the oral proceedings will customarily be on the size page permitted by the court rules, as to which see Sec. 6.10, *supra.* Many lawyers seem to believe that all they need do to reproduce the testimony is to copy the transcript pages on which appear any of the excerpts which they wish to include. More than this is required, however, if the excerpts are to be intelligible to the reviewing court. Just to copy the pages cited might not indicate the identity of the witness, who was examining him and whether the testimony in question was direct examination, cross-examination or the like. Reproduction of the original transcript page often would not indicate where the significant matter began or ended. A page or a series of pages might begin or end in the middle of a sentence or passage, or the relevant passage might begin or end in the middle of a page or include only a portion of it. The judge, unaware of which part of the page he was supposed to read, would have to go back to the record itself to find the connection with the preceding or following pages.

Although the federal judges do not seem to have been bothered sufficiently by these deficiencies to deal with them explicitly in the Federal Appellate Rules, perhaps because the lawyers in the federal courts are aware of these problems and take steps to avoid them, the experience of the Illinois appellate judges was different. Even though Illinois abolished its verbatim excerpts option in 1979 (see Sec. 6.11, pp. 192–193, *supra*), its efforts to deal with the above problem may be instructive for lawyers in other jurisdictions. Former Illinois Rule 342(c)(5) stated:

> "(5) *Responsibility of Appellant's Attorney.* The appellant's attorney is responsible for making the excerpts understandable and

convenient to use and to that end should include explanatory matter indicating the beginning of the evidence on behalf of each of the parties and the beginning of the direct, cross, and redirect examination of each witness; should omit, mask out, or strike out material that is not pertinent appearing on the first or last of a designated sequence of pages; and should cause the excerpts to be neatly and securely bound, using more than one volume when necessary to make them reasonably manageable."

Experience showed that attorneys often disregarded even this clear a rule, merely copying the entire page on the duplicating machine. As a result, a paper dealing with how to prepare a record attempted to be even more specific:

"The lawyer must omit or mask out or strike out—and that really is not very difficult—the portions of a page which are not significant enough for the judge to read. This is particularly necessary at the beginning and end of the designated pages, when the significant material may begin or end in the middle of the page, and the page may begin or end in the middle of a sentence. At the beginning of the significant material, counsel should be careful to state the name of the witness and of the examining attorney, and also whether the witness is on direct, cross or redirect examination, even if that does not appear on the particular page of the transcript. Of course, this is not necessary when the excerpt is merely a continuation of other testimony which is preceded by the proper identifying headings."[90]

Whether or not rules so require, testimonial material should be duplicated in this way.[91]

Judges are also critical of the length of excerpts because attorneys often include the entire transcript without eliminating

---

[90]R. Stern, *The Record and Abstract or Excerpts*, ILLINOIS CIVIL PRACTICE AFTER TRIAL, pp. 7-23–7-24 (Illinois Institute for Continuing Legal Education, 1976).

[91]For example:

Tr. 234 JOHN D. ROE, CALLED AS A WITNESS BY THE PLAINTIFFS
Tr. 256 CROSS-EXAMINATION BY MR. SMITH
Tr. 279 ~~MR. JONES: I object to that last question, your honor; it calls for a conclusion.~~
~~THE COURT: Where is the conclusion?~~
~~MR. SMITH: Let me rephrase the question.~~
Q. Isn't it true that some of the envelopes referred to were returned to you by the Post Office Department?
A. That's true, some of them came back.
Q. Exactly how many of them came back?
A. Sixteen came back marked by the Post Office "moved away," or "different address."
Q. Were any of those that were returned to you for companies who made payments into the fund?
A. No.
Q. ~~What were the names of the companies?~~
~~Mr. Jones: I object to that, your honor, as irrelevant.~~
~~Mr. Smith: On the contrary, it is very significant and I submit~~

matter, or enough matter, not important or material to the issues raised on appeal. And they also reasonably resent copies which are not duplicated clearly enough to be easily read by elderly gentlemen with tired eyes. The lawyer should make certain that his duplicating equipment produces consistent dark type.

As has been indicated, in most jurisdictions either printing or a photographic duplicating process may be used. Printing undoubtedly produces a more compact and neat document. But it is substantially more expensive than the other processes, how much more depending upon the charges for the various processes and the number of copies to be reproduced. See Secs. 6.9–6.10, *supra*. The attorney should compare the cost of the various processes both in and out of his office.

Despite the additional cost, some attorneys for some clients continue to file printed documents in the belief that they are more convenient for judges to handle and read. And they probably are. But it is doubtful that this will affect the manner in which a case is decided, particularly when rules permitting the use of other methods of duplication have been approved by the appellate judges themselves in order to permit the use of less expensive processes than printing.

6.13 When to File the Appendix—The Deferred Appendix System

The Federal Appellate Rules (with an important exception discussed below) and also the rules of a number of states require the document containing the duplicated portions of the record to be filed by the appellant at the same time as the appellant's brief. The parties either agree on what should be included or make their respective designations within a specified time, such as 10 days for each party, after the filing of the record in the appellate court. Federal Appellate Rule 30(b). The advantage of requiring the appendix or excerpts to be filed so promptly is that the parties, including the appellant himself, are able to cite its pages in their briefs, rather than the pages of the record or the transcript, which would not be so conveniently available to the judges.

A disadvantage of this system, as with the older technique of printing designated portions of the record (see Sec. 6.12, *supra*), is that when the designations of what should be included in the appendix are submitted by the parties before their briefs are written, the parties are not certain which portions of the record will be significant for the appeal and err on the side of over-inclusiveness by designating anything which might possibly be relevant.

The length of many administrative records subject to review in the United States Court of Appeals for the District of Columbia Circuit led to experimentation with a "deferred appendix" system. Each party would make his designations at the time his brief was filed. The appellant would then assemble the material designated by all parties and duplicate it within a short time thereafter, usually at or about the time his reply brief was due. Since the portions of the record significant to the appeal were almost invariably those cited in the briefs, this enabled each party to designate simply by referring to the citations in his brief. The only additional task, when the reference was not meant to refer to an entire page of the record or transcript, was to designate by line as well as by page, and to mask out or delete the portions of the page not intended to be included. See Sec. 6.12, *supra.* The result was both that much less lawyer time was required in making the designations and that much less would be designated, which simplified the record both for the judges and counsel.

Federal Appellate Rule 30(c) as originally adopted in 1967 gave appellant the option of filing the appendix along with his brief or of using the deferred appendix system described above.[92] United States Supreme Court Rule 30.4, as revised in 1980, also embodies the deferred appendix option.

Since having the briefs contain page references to the appendix and not merely to the original record would be helpful to the judges, the federal deferred appendix rules for the courts of appeals and the Supreme Court also permit counsel to file on the due date briefs in typewritten form or page proof with refer-

---

[92]The Advisory Committee's Note to Federal Appellate Rule 30(c) stated: "(c) This subdivision permits the appellant to elect to defer the production of the appendix to the briefs until the briefs of both sides are written, and authorizes a court of appeals to require such deferred filing by rule or order. The advantage of this method of preparing the appendix is that it permits the parties to determine what parts of the record need to be reproduced in the light of the issues actually presented by the briefs. Often neither side is in a position to say precisely what is needed until the briefs are completed. Once the argument on both sides is known, it should be possible to confine the matter reproduced in the appendix to that which is essential to a determination of the appeal or review. . . . When the record is long, use of this method is likely to result in substantial economy to the parties."

ences to the pages of the original record, with leave to substitute briefs in final form with references to the pages of the deferred appendix when it becomes available shortly thereafter. Federal Appellate Rule 30(c) allows 14 days after the appendix is filed for the filing of the briefs in final form, which means that counsel has a number of extra days to complete the mechanical chores of checking and printing or duplicating the brief. United States Supreme Court Rule 30.4(b) allows the brief to be filed 10 days after the filing of the deferred appendix.

A number of states also permit deferral of the filing of the appendix. Iowa Rule of Appellate Procedure 15(c) allows the parties to elect whether to defer the filing of the appendix. Massachusetts Rule of Appellate Procedure 18(c) permits deferral with leave of the appellate court or a single justice. Illinois Rule 342 (before the 1979 revision which abolished the verbatim appendix) adopted the deferred system for all cases;[93] the excerpts from the record were to be filed 14 days after the due date of the appellee's brief, which was the same day as the appellant's reply brief was due. Illinois did not find it necessary to allow additional time for filing briefs with the citations to the deferred excerpts. "In order to permit the briefs to be filed before the portions of the record are designated for duplication, Rule 341, dealing with briefs, provides that the briefs may cite either pages of the record itself or pages of the excerpts or abstract." Committee Comment to Rule 342(a). The Illinois plan avoided the delays which have concerned the federal courts, described in the following paragraphs. Elimination of these provisions in 1979, when Illinois concluded that no duplication of parts of the record was needed in most cases, does not detract from the usefulness of its prior deferral system in other jurisdictions which still require duplication.

The use of the deferred appendix in the federal courts, however, resulted in dissatisfaction because it often resulted in delays of up to several weeks. Undoubtedly the decision whether or not to defer might often be influenced not only by the legitimate reason that deferral would allow counsel to designate after

---

[93]The Illinois Rules Committee Comment to 1969 Rule 342(a) explained: "In order to reduce the amount of material to be duplicated, paragraph (a) provides for designations for duplicating at the time each party files his brief. Experience demonstrates that, if designations must be made before that time, counsel designate every part of the record which might become relevant to be sure not to miss anything. After the briefs are written, counsel know what passages are significant enough for the court to read; normally they will be the passages cited in the briefs. In the Federal Rules of Appellate Procedure (Rule 30(a), (b), and (c)) this system is provided for as an alternative to designation in advance of filing briefs."

the briefs were completed, and thus to designate less, but also by the fact that it would allow a few additional days for completing the briefs. As the result of the belief that some lawyers were taking advantage of the deferred system in order to obtain additional time, Federal Appellate Rule 30(c) was amended in 1970 to limit the right to use that system to where "the court shall so provide by rule for classes of cases or by order in specific cases." The Advisory Committee's Note explaining the amendment stated:

> "The amendment should not cause use of the deferred appendix to be viewed with disfavor. In cases involving lengthy records, permission to defer filing of the appendix should be freely granted as an inducement to the parties to include in the appendix only matter that the briefs show to be necessary for consideration by the judges."[94]

Rule 30(c) thus leaves it to each court of appeals to exercise its own discretion in allowing use of the deferred method. Some of the circuits have expressed divergent views as to whether it should be used.

The District of Columbia Circuit favors the use of the deferred system. It has customarily granted requests for permission to defer, which are made in approximately 20 percent of the cases. It is now considering abandoning the joint appendix requirement in favor of the Fifth Circuit's limited appendix described in the note below. The Fifth Circuit, prior to dispensing with appendices completely in 1978,[95] had stated, in its former Rule 13(b), that "[t]he Court encourages use of this deferred appendix procedure . . . as the best known method for eliminating unnecessary expense of reproduction of the appendix." Judge Godbold had written:

> "A splendid appellate tool, the deferred appendix as provided by Fed. R. App. P. 30(c), was long ignored by practitioners, but it is coming into more use as its potentialities are appreciated. On request the clerk's office of the court of appeals will provide counsel with a procedural manual describing the use of the deferred appendix.
> It is only after writing his brief that the appellate lawyer knows the precise contours of what he needs to include in the appendix. Under the deferred appendix system he uses the original record in writing his brief, then he designates the appendix. This permits

---

[94]48 F.R.D. 482.
[95]Fifth Circuit Rule 13.1 and 13.2 now states that no appendix is required, although four copies of "Record Excerpts" containing the judgment and opinions below and several other documents should be filed. See Sec. 6.9, *supra.*

him to designate at a time when he can, with confidence, specify what is really needed and omit everything else. The advocate's communication with the court is consequently less cluttered, less expensive, and performed with less effort. Moreover, counsel is more likely to concentrate on selecting the critical issues. If he has designated the appendix in advance under rule 30(a) and has reproduced more material than he needs, he tends to labor under the self-induced pressure to address every point that the appendix reveals regardless of its importance to the real issues in the case."[96]

On the other hand, the Tenth Circuit, which in its 1972 Rule 10(b) had regarded the deferred appendix with disfavor, reversed itself in its 1980 Rule 11(d); it now prefers deferring the appendix until after the briefs have been filed, as permitted under Federal Appellate Rule 30(c), "in order to eliminate excessive reproduction of the record and to enable counsel to concentrate on selecting the critical issues."

Under Federal Rule 30(c), as revised in 1970, a party may apply for an order allowing him to use the deferred system, and the court presumably will not object where the record is of the sort for which the deferred system was devised and is most helpful. Deferral is not necessary, however, in short record cases, where prior to the writing of the brief there could be little doubt as to what should be included. The deferred appendix is appropriate "where the portions of a bulky record that need to be printed in the appendix cannot be determined or reduced until the issues have been sharpened in the parties' briefs." Paragraph 7 of Memorandum to Counsel prepared and distributed by the Clerk of the Supreme Court of the United States in 1976.

Supreme Court Rule 30.4 permits deferral "[i]f the parties agree or if the Court shall so order." Thus Court approval is not necessary if the parties agree. The effect of allowing the appendix to be filed 14 days after the answering brief and of then allowing 10 days to file the briefs in final form is that the briefs may not be available to the Justices until shortly before the argument, or even that the argument may have to be postponed.[97] As a result, the Clerk's Office endeavors to dissuade

---

[96]J. Godbold, *Twenty Pages and Twenty Minutes—Effective Advocacy on Appeal*, 30 Southwestern L.J. 801, 806 (1976).

[97]The use of the deferred appendix in the United States Supreme Court is discussed at length in R. Stern and E. Gressman, SUPREME COURT PRACTICE, pp. 652–655, 659–669, 683 (5th ed., 1978).

counsel from using the deferred appendix option except in the types of cases for which it will be helpful in reducing the length of the appendix.[98] There will not be many such cases in the Supreme Court, or for that matter in any supreme court which reviews decisions of an intermediate appellate court, since the appendix designated for the lower court will usually suffice in the supreme court. See Sec. 6.14, *infra*.

Some of the states adhere to the federal deferred appendix system as it existed before 1970. Pennsylvania Rule 2154, which prior to 1979 provided for the use of the deferred appendix except where the appellant desired to have the case ready for argument immediately upon the filing of the last brief, reversed its order of preference. Compare Rule 2154(a) and (b) before and after the 1979 amendment. Under paragraph (a) of the revised rule the designation of the contents of the reproduced record by both parties must precede the filing of the appellant's brief. But paragraph (b), entitled "Large records," permits the designation to be deferred until after the briefs are served "if the appellant shall so elect, or if the appellate court has [so] prescribed by rule of court for classes of matters or by order in specific matters." It had "been argued that in a typical state court appeal, the record is quite small," so that the prior alternative of reproducing the record in conjunction with the preparation of appellant's brief would ordinarily have been followed if the rule had not implied a preference for the deferred method. Explanatory Note to §2154 (1979). The Note explains that the rule was redrafted "to imply that the deferred method is a secondary method particularly appropriate for longer records."

6.14 Records in the Highest Court of a Two-Tiered Appellate System

In general, what has been said above applies to appeals to both intermediate and supreme appellate courts. Obviously if a supreme court directly reviews the decision of a trial court, it is in the same position as the intermediate appellate court would have been.

---

[98]Under Rule 29.4 the Clerk has initial authority to act upon applications for extensions of time to file briefs. This power, combined with the weight which most lawyers give to recommendations of the Clerk of the Supreme Court, means that the Clerk is usually successful in encouraging agreement upon a schedule for the briefs and appendix without resort to the deferred appendix. It is highly unlikely that the Clerk's policy in this respect does not have the approval of the Court.

There is one important difference, however, when the case comes to a supreme court after review in an intermediate court. The full record already will have been filed in the latter court, and in most jurisdictions the duplicated copies of the significant portions of the record will already have been prepared for use in that court. Except in the most unusual circumstances, the higher court only reviews questions decided in the lower. Accordingly, in those jurisdictions all parts of the record which would be of significance in the higher court should already have been included in the duplicated material submitted to the lower. There should thus be no need for counsel to take time for any further designating.

In most states the record in the intermediate appellate court is to be transmitted by that court's clerk to the supreme court either on notification that the petition has been filed in the supreme court or on the request of the petitioner or the supreme court clerk. The clerk need transmit only the material submitted to the intermediate court, together with the opinions and judgments in that court, if the latter have not already been made available to the supreme court by attachment to the petition itself.[99]

Other supreme courts, including the United States Supreme Court, do not want other record material sent up until after review is granted.[100] If counsel should discover additional items he wants the court to consider in connection with the granting of the petition, quoting them in his petition is simpler than redoing or enlarging the record or appendix used below.

This does not necessarily mean that enough copies of the duplicated material will be readily available for use in the higher court. Usually they will not be. In the United States Supreme Court, printing or reproduction in a different form is required by that Court's rules. See Sec. 6.10, *supra.* But even where reproduction is not required for such a reason, unless counsel has had the foresight to order enough copies for filing both in the intermediate court and the higher court, he may have difficulty in procuring sufficient copies for the latter. Although the rules in

---

[99]The United States Supreme Court rules and the equivalent rules in many state supreme courts already require that the opinions and judgments of the intermediate court be attached to the petition for review and that they need not be reprinted as a part of the record. See paragraph 8 of the Clerk's Memorandum referred to on p. 204, *supra.*

[100]See Rule 19.1 and R. Stern and E. Gressman, SUPREME COURT PRACTICE, Sec. 6.14 (5th ed., 1978).

some of the states call upon the clerks of the intermediate courts to aid counsel in providing copies for the higher court, this often is difficult. The clerk may not be able to recover records which have been distributed among the judges and law clerks of his court. And even if he does, invariably a greater number are necessary for the higher court with its larger complement of judges. Thus, it is almost always necessary for additional copies to be made. If only a small number are needed at the time a petition for leave to appeal is before that court, the clerk of the lower court and counsel may be able to put their hands on enough copies.[101] A larger number, which seldom would be available, may be necessary, however, if the petition is granted.

Of course, this problem can be avoided if counsel can foresee at the time the appeal to the intermediate court is taken that the case will then go to the higher court in the future. But except in the most obvious case, this is difficult to predict, particularly in the federal system. The odds in favor of any particular case being accepted for further review are normally too slight to warrant the cost of paying for a large additional number of copies of the pertinent record material. This may not be so when the material is being printed, for the cost of ordering additional copies after the type has once been set is very little, but that is not true for photographic methods of reproduction. On the other hand, to run off additional copies of material so reproduced would cost little if any more than making the additional copies in the first place. This assumes that the same size paper and type can be used in both courts, as seems to be true in all of the appellate systems except the federal where, as indicated above, the United States Supreme Court has special requirements.

6.15 Recommendations

The above comparative analysis leads to the following conclusions:

(1) Appellate courts, particularly of only three judges, should be encouraged to attempt to get along, as a minority now do, with a single filed copy of the entire record below (unless the parties stipulate for less), or of designated pertinent portions.

---

[101]E.g., Illinois Rule 315(d) ("two, or, if available, eight copies" of any abstract filed below).

(2) Where, as in most jurisdictions, the judges believe that the critical parts of the record should be made available to each judge:

(a) Appellant should be required to provide each judge with the judgment, findings, opinion or other explanation by the court or courts below of the reasons for their decisions, either as an appendix to his brief or in a separate document;

(b) Either in the Statement of Facts or Argument (whichever is most appropriate) in his brief, or in a separate appendix, or in an appendix prepared jointly with the other party, appellant should, whether the rules so require or not, quote verbatim the critical portions of the record, which means primarily those which relate to matters in dispute as well as where the precise language used is significant. Other facts pertinent to the issues presented should be summarized in the Statement of Facts. See Sec. 7.20, *infra.* Since the nature and magnitude of a case or the record will determine the most appropriate method of presenting this material to the judges, the appellant should have his choice as to whether a separate appendix of evidentiary material should be prepared. Appellee should, of course, have an opportunity to submit additional material in or with his brief.

(c) The number of copies required to be filed should be no more than necessary for the judges to use. This would normally be one per judge, as Alabama provides, and even better, one per judge plus one copy for the clerk, as called for in Tennessee's 1979 rules. Additional copies should be required for staff attorneys or judges' law clerks if the judges are likely to be studying the material at the same time as the attorneys or clerks. Of course, copies also must be made available for the other parties in the case or their counsel.

7

Brief Writing

The first rule of brief writing—as well as of appellate practice generally—is to read, or reread, the pertinent rules of the court to which the appeal is taken. This is necessary even for experienced practitioners, unless perhaps they have *recently* handled a similar type of appeal to the same appellate court. See Introduction, p. 2, *supra.* But even then a review of the rules as they apply to the new case is advisable.

With respect to brief writing, the rules which must be examined (which may include statutes as well as rules of court) prescribe when notices of appeal, the record and briefs must be filed, the number of copies, the maximum number of pages, the permitted methods of printing or duplication, and the form, organization and contents. These matters are discussed in this chapter, as well as the techniques as to how a good brief should be prepared.

7.1 Types of Briefs

This chapter is concerned with briefs on the merits, not petitions for review or rehearing (which are dealt with in Chapters 5 and 9) or memoranda in support of motions. Much of what is said, however, will apply to those other forms of argumentative writing as well.

The briefs filed by the parties to an appeal usually comprise the appellant's main brief, the appellee's main brief and the appellant's reply brief, though a few jurisdictions make no provision for a reply.[1]

If appellee takes a cross-appeal, his main brief should include the opening argument on the points raised on the cross-appeal. The appellant's answer thereto should be included in his reply brief. Usually appellee will be allowed to file a further reply limited to those points.

Supplemental memoranda or letters may be submitted after the last brief to call the court's attention to new authorities or to facts which might show that the case has become moot or otherwise been affected.

Separate briefs may also be submitted by nonparties as *amici curiae,* usually (though not always) only by leave of court.

Each of these types of briefs is considered in this chapter. A sample form of a brief on the merits in a state supreme court appears at pp. 523–540, *infra.*

7.2 Importance of Briefs

Appellate judges and others have expressed different views as to the value of and the need for the oral argument of appeals. See Sec. 8.1, *infra.* There is little dissent, however, from the proposition stated 25 years ago by that eminent authority on procedural law Judge Charles E. Clark of the Second Circuit that in American appellate practice "a brief is a necessity."[2] "There

---

[1]The State of Washington has a unique rule (10.1(d)) for criminal cases when the defendant is not satisfied with his counsel's brief. It reads as follows:

"(d) *Pro Se Supplemental Brief in Criminal Case.* A defendant in a review of a criminal case may file a brief supplementing the brief filed by the defendant's counsel, but only if the defendant files a notice of intention to file a pro se supplemental brief. The notice of intent should be filed within 30 days after the defendant has received the brief prepared by defendant's counsel, a notice from the clerk of the appellate court advising the defendant of the substance of this section [and related sections], and a form of notice of intention to file a pro se supplemental brief. The clerk will advise all parties if the defendant files the notice of intention."

The defendant has 60 days to file his pro se brief after receiving his counsel's brief and having an opportunity to view the report of proceedings; his brief should be limited to those matters which defendant believes have not been adequately covered in his counsel's brief. Rules 10.2(e), 10.3(d).

This could have the beneficial effect of allowing the appellate court to resolve assertions as to the inadequacy and incompetence of appointed counsel on the first appeal from a conviction instead of in later proceedings.

[2]See Judge Clark's Foreword to M. Pittoni, BRIEF WRITING AND ARGUMENTATION, p. viii (3d ed., 1967). Judge Clark, formerly professor and dean of the Yale Law School, was the reporter for the committee which first drafted the Federal Rules of Civil Procedure in 1938. His contributions to procedural law continued during his tenure as a member of the United States Court of Appeals for the Second Circuit from 1939 to 1963.

must be a brief, to summarize the evidence, to set out record references, to collect citations, to discuss the authorities—to do all that oral argument cannot do and at the same time to buttress and support and substantiate the impression made by oral argument."[3]

Judge Goodrich of the Third Circuit has stated:

"It is hard to overstate the importance of the brief on an appeal. Oral argument will be discussed later. It is important, too. But it is made only once in nearly all instances and it is inevitable that some of its effect will be lost in the interval between the time the argument is made and the court opinion appears. The longer the opinion-writing judge takes to produce an opinion the hazier the points of the oral argument become. And there is nothing which counsel can do to hurry the opinion-writing judge. That will have to be left to his colleagues. But the brief speaks from the time it is filed and continues through oral argument, conference, and opinion writing. Sometimes a brief will be read and reread, no one knows how many times except the judge and his law clerk. . . . Certain it is that the brief is the most important thing about an appeal, although oral argument may be the most fun."[4]

Only in the brief does a lawyer have an opportunity to present the reasons supporting his position in an orderly and comprehensive fashion. The oral argument in most courts and most cases is restricted to 30 minutes or less, which must be shared with judicial inquisitors; indeed, answering judges' questions is one of its principal functions. Seldom will counsel be able to lay out his argument in full with the supporting authorities. That can be done only in the brief. Furthermore, a brief, in contrast to an oral presentation, can be read and reread by the judge. He can compare it with the opposing briefs and verify the record references and authorities at his convenience, in his home, chambers or library. Few judges can remember the details of an oral presentation days, weeks or even months later, but briefs are available until the case is finally disposed of.[5]

A brief is of even greater importance in overburdened appellate courts, which often substantially curtail the time allowed for oral argument or dispense with it altogether. Many courts

---

[3]F. Wiener, BRIEFING AND ARGUING FEDERAL APPEALS, p. 32 (1967).
[4]H. Goodrich, *A Case on Appeal—A Judge's View,* in A CASE ON APPEAL, pp. 10–11 (ALI-ABA, 1967).
[5]In some appellate courts the oral arguments are tape recorded or transcribed for future use by the judges.

determine from the initial examination of the briefs whether the questions raised are substantial enough to justify oral argument and, if so, for how long. Obviously, if no oral argument is permitted—and that will usually not be known until after the briefs are prepared and filed—the brief will be the party's only opportunity to persuade the court to decide in his favor. Furthermore, "in most appellate courts today" in the cases which are argued, "the judges read the briefs prior to oral argument. This means that . . . usually . . . he or she has reached a tentative decision prior to oral argument."[6]

Although the brief is an essential feature of American appellate practice, it was not always so. When the nation was young, modern duplicating processes, such as typewriting, were not even dreamed of. Our British legal ancestors relied, as our present cousins still do, entirely on oral argument. But their arguments are of unlimited duration, in which the pertinent decisions or statutes or portions of the record are read aloud to the court, or read by the judges themselves during the course of the argument. With or without a short consultation on the bench at the close of argument, the opinions are then announced orally by the judges seriatim.[7]

I do not know, and have heard of no studies disclosing, whether the longer oral argument means that the individual judge devotes more or less time to an appeal than under the American system in which each judge hears a short argument, but also spends time on brief reading, consultations off the bench with his colleagues, and perhaps even his own research. It seems to be accepted that, contrary to the American experience, the British courts are not swamped with appeals, for a number of reasons not necessary to discuss here. There have also been suggestions by American lawyers and judges—no Britisher would be so rude—that British barristers and judges are more carefully selected and better trained, and have a less complicated legal system to master. Or it may just be that the principal reason for the British practice is that they have done it that way for hundreds of years. Perhaps even British judges would benefit if they had time to delve into the record and the cases at greater leisure on the basis of a written presentation

---

[6]Judge J. Clifford Wallace, *Wanted: Advocates Who Can Argue in Writing*, 67 Kentucky L.J. 375, 377 (1978).

[7]D. Meador, *English Appellate Judges From an American Perspective*, 66 Georgetown L.J. 1349 (1978).

which they would have time to study before and after the oral hearing.[8]

In the United States, doubts as to the need for two types of argument, written and oral, have often—and more and more, as the appellate case loads become heavier—led judges to eliminate the oral argument, at least for uncomplicated or insubstantial or frivolous appeals. Such cases, and they may comprise a substantial portion or even a majority of the appeals, are likely to be disposed of the same way whichever method of presentation comes first. See Sec. 1.7, *supra.*

There has also been experimentation with reliance on oral argument alone, either by agreement of counsel in actual cases or by an attempt to make use of a comparative testing procedure. A great deal of time can be saved if an appeal can be heard orally and decided shortly after the judgment of the trial court, without allowing time for reproducing a record or preparing briefs. Experiments in Arizona and Colorado[9] indicate that simple cases in which the judges have no need to verify counsel's statements against a transcript or record of any length, or to delve into areas requiring legal research, are likely to be decided the same way with or without briefs. Briefs filed in the trial court were available, however, and the filing of short memoranda not exceeding 20 pages on a 15–15 day schedule after the filing of the notice of appeal[10] was deemed advisable. Delaware Rule 25 also provides for oral argument without briefs or with limited briefs if the parties and the Supreme Court agree, or on order of the court *sua sponte.*

To cull out the cases susceptible of such treatment would require some kind of advance written presentation or oral consultation from which the issues and their difficulty and complex-

---

[8]A by no means worldwide informal inquiry among knowledgeable lawyers discloses that the British system prevails in other parts of the British Commonwealth but not in Canada, and that written appellate arguments are presented and relied on in Brazil, Colombia, France, Italy, Japan, Mexico, Switzerland and West Germany.

[9]E. Jacobson and M. Schroeder, *Arizona's Experiment With Appellate Reform,* 63 A.B.A.J. 1226 (1977).

[10]*Ibid.* There is also the experience of the Colorado Court of Appeals referred to in a letter of June 29, 1978, from Barry Mahoney of the National Center of State Courts:

"Under this program, which is an integral element of the Center's current Appellate Justice Project, civil cases in which there is no evidentiary transcript (or in which the evidentiary transcript is short and is readily available) are assigned to the accelerated docket on the basis of preliminary statements filed by counsel. Counsel may rely on briefs written for the trial court, unless they wish to prepare a new brief. Briefs are subject to page limitations (20 pages) and to time limitations for filing (15 days after notice of appeal for appellant's brief; 15 days after appellant's brief for appellee)."

ity could be determined. Such a procedure would resemble those presently utilized by the courts that determine which cases should be heard orally on the basis of a petition for certiorari or review or a preliminary reading of the briefs on the merits. Although further experimentation along these lines may be expected, it is not likely, in my opinion, that briefing will be eliminated on any large scale. It will still remain the primary means by which an appeal is presented in full and in depth to the appellate court.

7.3   The Status or Function of the Particular Appellate Court

(a)   Differences Between Briefs and Petitions in Intermediate and Supreme Courts

How a brief should be written depends upon its function. All briefs should not be written in the same way. A brief prepared for an appellate court which has ultimate authority over a question should be prepared differently, at least in part, from a brief for a lower appellate court. The Supreme Court of the United States has the last word on federal questions and state supreme courts on state questions. But even the highest court in the land is not supreme as to issues governed by state law, as *Erie R. Co.* v. *Tompkins,* 304 U.S. 64 (1938), attests.

The brief writer must recognize that a lower appellate court is bound to a greater extent by the highest court's prior decisions. It can distinguish them, of course, but must do so on rational grounds which respect their reasoning and implications, unless the supreme court itself has in some way undermined or devitalized its own prior ruling, or unless the lower court has some basis for anticipating that the supreme court will do so. Obviously, a lower court cannot disregard or overrule a supreme court's decision.

A supreme court, on the other hand, can be as free as it wants to be in dealing with what it has previously held or said. Usually, of course, it will adhere to its prior decisions as a matter of *stare decisis.* But arguments which challenge the reasoning of those decisions on such grounds as inconsistency with the trend of modern authority in other jurisdictions, for example, are much more appropriately addressed to, and likely to succeed in, a supreme court than a lower one. This difference in approach is not limited to the propriety of asking that a prior authority be overruled. Only the top court is free to distinguish an earlier decision which it no longer fully approves on narrow factual grounds, or to limit it to its facts, or even just to ignore it.

How such problems should be presented by counsel is a delicate matter in any case in any court. No overall generalization can be very helpful, except that counsel should be aware that the status of the court determines how such problems should be approached.

A petition for certiorari or leave to appeal is also a type of brief. It differs from a brief on the merits primarily in that its principal function is to induce the court to which it is addressed to review a decision below on the merits. As shown in Chapter 5, in almost all cases attainment of that objective requires not only a showing of importance and, if possible, of conflict with other appellate decisions but also a reason to believe that the decision below is incorrect.

The general organization and the principal parts of such petititions and of briefs on the merits are similar. Each should contain a short explanation of the basis for the court's jurisdiction, statements of the questions presented and of the facts, and an argumentative section. Thus, most of what is said in this chapter as to writing briefs applies to the preparation of petitions for review as well.

As stated in Sec. 5.7(a), Alabama requires a petition for certiorari and a brief to be filed simultaneously, with petitioner filing nothing else as his main brief if certiorari is granted. The petition is to state the grounds for review, leaving the merits of the case to be argued in the brief.[11] This means that petitioner must file *more* than a full brief on the merits within the 14 days allowed for petitioning, which would often be quite difficult unless substantial extensions of time are easily obtainable. And he must brief the case fully at that stage even though only a small percentage of the petitions are granted and the court may devote little attention to the argument on the merits. The case will, however, be ready for oral argument and final disposition more speedily than if petitioner's main brief still had to be prepared. Whether this gain in a small proportion of the cases is worth the added burden on all petitioners is questionable.

---

[11]Petitioner may also file a reply to respondent's brief, which may be filed 14 days after petitioner's brief is received or after the court grants review.

In many jurisdictions, the highest court may not, will not or is disinclined to review factual determinations made in the lower courts. This reluctance does not merely reflect the universally recognized advantage which the judge who hears the witnesses has in determining factual questions. In some jurisdictions the highest court is limited by state constitution or statute from reviewing anything but questions of law. In others, the practice of the court, as reflected in its rules or rulings, has the same effect. The underlying reason is that factual issues seldom have the broad significance which warrants review by the highest court after such issues have been once reviewed in the intermediate appellate court. For example, the general practice of the United States Supreme Court is not to "review concurrent findings of fact by two courts below in the absence of a very obvious and exceptional showing of error."[12] To what extent a decision without adequate factual support in the record may be treated as erroneous as a matter of law, as it sometimes is in the federal courts,[13] is a question upon which the law of the particular jurisdiction should be consulted.

(b) Use of Intermediate Appellate Court Briefs in a Supreme Court

In the federal courts and most states with two tiers of appellate courts a new brief is filed in the supreme court after that court agrees to take a case. As stated in Sec. 1.10(a), *supra,* a few states do not require the filing of an additional brief in the highest court when the decision of a lower appellate court is being reviewed. Some do not even permit it, at least without special leave of court. In those states the parties may or must rely on the petition for review or the opposition thereto, sometimes accompanied by the briefs in the lower appellate court. A few states give counsel the option of relying on or supplementing the brief below. Pennsylvania Rule 2138 permits the filing of a completely new brief in the Supreme Court, or of the briefs below, or of the latter supplemented by whatever counsel wants to add.

---

[12]*Graver Mfg. Co.* v. *Linde Co.,* 336 U.S. 271, 275 (1949), and cases cited therein; *Berenyi* v. *Immigration Director,* 385 U.S. 630, 635 (1967); *Branti* v. *Finkel,* 445 U.S. 507, 512 n. 10 (1980); R. Stern and E. Gressman, SUPREME COURT PRACTICE, Sec. 4.14 (5th ed., 1978).

[13]E.g., *Thompson* v. *City of Louisville,* 362 U.S. 199 (1960); *Garner* v. *Louisiana,* 368 U.S. 157, 163 (1961); *Washington* v. *United States,* 357 U.S. 348 (1958); R. Stern and E. Gressman, SUPREME COURT PRACTICE, Sec. 4.15 (5th ed., 1978).

The California Supreme Court always has before it the briefs in the Court of Appeal and the petition for hearing in the Supreme Court. Its rules neither require nor prohibit the filing of additional briefs. In the average case, however, such briefs are not submitted, but they sometimes are in major cases.

In Illinois the parties have the option under Rule 315(g) of allowing the petition for leave to appeal or the opposing answer to stand as the brief on the merits. Each party must notify the other and the Supreme Court as to whether he will do so or will file an additional brief.

In Texas the petition for writ of error is customarily a full blown brief on the merits, although copies of the briefs in the Court of Civil Appeals are always included in the record transmitted to the Supreme Court. Supplemental briefs may also be filed. (Rule 496.)

Kansas Rule 8.03 provides that after review has been granted by the Supreme Court, the case will be heard on the briefs previously filed in the Court of Appeals, but that any party within 30 days may file a supplemental brief, or have 30 days to respond to an opposing supplemental brief. Such a brief "shall not exceed one-half the length permitted for original briefs" (50 pages for the principal briefs).

In Wisconsin, when the Supreme Court grants review, it may require or permit the parties to supply additional briefs (Rule 809.62). The rule does not state whether a party may file such a brief without leave of court, but the usual practice is for the court to leave it to the parties. If no additional briefs are to be filed, the parties should submit 10 copies of the briefs filed in the Court of Appeals.

Massachusetts, New Jersey, New Mexico, Oklahoma and Washington allow the filing of additional briefs in their supreme courts only by leave of court. In Massachusetts the filing of additional or supplemental briefs is quite commonly requested and allowed in important cases.

North Carolina Rule 15(g)(2) requires that a new brief be filed in the Supreme Court after a case has been accepted for review, but Rule 28(d) allows all or part of the argument section of a Court of Appeals brief to be incorporated by reference in the Supreme Court brief. The object is to save a substantial amount of repetition if the case makes that appropriate. Nevada Rule 28, on the other hand, prohibits such incorporation.

In Arizona, the petition for rehearing below must not only serve as the substantive application for leave to appeal to the

Supreme Court but also stand as the only new brief which can be submitted at all. Four additional copies of the briefs in the Court of Appeals shall be filed with the clerk of the Supreme Court if the case is accepted for review. Arizona Rules of Appellate Procedure 22, 23. The peculiar problems which this system creates are discussed elsewhere. See Secs. 1.10(a), note 68, and 5.7(a), *supra.*

Where the brief in the intermediate appellate court or the petition for review may or must serve as the brief on the merits, the writer should be aware that the brief or petition may have to do double duty. For the reasons stated in Sec. 1.10(a), *supra,* briefs should often be written differently for intermediate and supreme courts, and in most states a brief on the merits should also be written differently from a petition for review, which should emphasize the reasons why the higher court should hear the case. See Sec. 5.7(c,d), *supra.* Even more clearly, a petition for rehearing customarily has a much narrower focus than a brief on the merits.

The writer of a lower court brief, petition for review or petition for rehearing which may have to serve as the brief on the merits in a supreme court must write with those two—or in Arizona three—not entirely harmonious functions in mind. That may produce a much longer document than supreme courts usually want in petitions for review. The combination of functions means that the writer of the petition for review or rehearing must conform to the requisites of good brief writing in general, and not merely the requirements for petitions for rehearing (discussed in Chapter 9, *infra*) or for petitions for leave to appeal (discussed in Chapter 5, *supra*).

The desirability of not wasting time and money by requiring the filing of an additional brief which would add nothing to documents previously filed would seem obvious. As indicated, however, the supreme court briefs, lower court briefs, petitions for review and petitions for rehearing serve different, though partly overlapping, functions and often would and should be written differently. Only the lawyer is in a position to determine whether a new brief will more adequately present his client's contentions. He should not be prohibited from deciding this either way, or even required to seek a court's permission, since a court cannot make an intelligent ruling without comparing the first document with the second after the latter has been written.

Accordingly, for the reasons stated in Sec. 1.10(a), *supra,* the best solution to the problem is to give counsel the option of relying on any brief or petition previously filed, as some of the states already do to some extent. Incorporation by reference of major portions of a prior brief, but not scattered pages or sections, should be allowed, as should submitting a supplemental brief containing only additional material. This is in substance provided for in Pennsylvania Rule 2138. Obviously sufficient copies of each document must be made available to the court, perhaps with a new cover, but in any event with some form of statement as to whether counsel is adopting a prior brief or petition in whole or in part or is supplementing it with an additional brief.

7.4   The Time Schedules for Writing and Filing Briefs

The first thing a lawyer responsible for a brief must ascertain is when it must be filed. The number of days available will determine whether research must begin immediately, whether he must work at full speed—that is, days, nights and weekends —or at a more leisurely pace, whether he will have to abandon all other office matters until the brief is completed, and whether, and how many, other lawyers must be brought in to assist in the research and writing. How much time will be needed will, of course, depend on the nature of the case, and also on whether the work will be performed by counsel who tried the case and are familiar with it to begin with, or by different lawyers. See Sec. 2.3, *supra.*

The time limits fixed in most American jurisdictions follow the same pattern. The United States Supreme Court allows 45 days from the allowance of oral argument for the briefs on the merits to be filed by a petitioner or appellant, 30 days for a respondent or appellee, and up to 7 days before the oral argument for the reply brief.[14] The times prescribed for the United States courts of appeals by the Federal Rules of Appellate Procedure are 40, 30 and 14 days, respectively.[15]

As appears from the following list, in most states from 30 to 45 days are allowed for the filing of appellant's brief:[16]

---

[14]United States Supreme Court Rule 35.
[15]Federal Rule of Appellate Procedure 31.
[16]These figures are based on my reading of the state rules in 1978 and 1979. As to the different times fixed by the rules prescribed in the various New York courts, see note 18, *infra.*

20 days—Georgia, Maine, North Carolina, Ohio;
28 days—Alabama;
30 days—Alaska, Arizona, California, Connecticut Appel-
    late Session, Delaware, Indiana, Kansas, Ken-
    tucky, Louisiana, Missouri, New Hampshire, New
    Mexico, South Carolina, Tennessee, Texas, Utah
    (one month);
35 days—Idaho, Illinois;
40 days—Arkansas, Colorado, Maine, Maryland, Missis-
    sippi, Missouri, Nevada, North Dakota, Pennsyl-
    vania, Rhode Island, Vermont, Virginia, Wiscon-
    sin;
45 days—Connecticut Supreme Court, New Jersey, South
    Dakota, Washington;
50 days—Iowa;
60 days—Hawaii, Michigan Court of Appeals, Oregon;
70 days—Florida;
90 days—Michigan Supreme Court.

Thirty days (or one month) are allowed for answering briefs
in 29 states, as well as in the federal appellate courts. Nine states
allow 20 days, with the others scattered from 21 to 60 days, as
shown on the following list:

20 days—Connecticut Appellate Session, Georgia, Louisi-
    ana Court of Appeals, Maine, Mississippi, North
    Carolina, Ohio, Rhode Island, West Virginia;
21 days—Alabama;
25 days—Texas, Virginia;
28 days—Idaho;
30 days—Alaska, Arizona, Arkansas, California, Colorado,
    Connecticut Supreme Court, Delaware, Indiana,
    Iowa, Kansas, Kentucky, Louisiana Supreme
    Court, Maryland, Massachusetts, Missouri, Mon-
    tana, Nebraska, New Hampshire, New Jersey,
    New Mexico, North Dakota, Pennsylvania, South
    Carolina, Tennessee, Utah, Vermont, Washing-
    ton, Wisconsin, Wyoming;
35 days—Illinois;
45 days—Minnesota, South Dakota;
60 days—Hawaii, Michigan, Oregon.

The number of days for reply briefs ranges from 5 to 30 days, with most of the states concentrating at 10, 14, 15 and 20 days, as appears from the following list:

5 days—Rhode Island, West Virginia;

10 days—Mississippi, Nebraska, New Jersey, New Mexico, Ohio, Wyoming;

14 days—Colorado, Idaho, Illinois, Maine, Massachusetts, Montana, North Dakota, Pennsylvania, Tennessee, Vermont, Virginia;

15 days—Arizona, Arkansas, Delaware, Indiana, Iowa, Kansas, Kentucky, Minnesota, Missouri, South Carolina, South Dakota, Wisconsin;

20 days—Alaska, Colorado, Connecticut Supreme Court, Florida, Maryland, Oklahoma;

30 days—Hawaii, Nevada, Oregon, Washington.

A few states make no allowance for a reply brief. See Sec. 7.34, *infra.* In some jurisdictions, including the federal courts, the reply must be filed no later than a specified number of days before the date set for oral argument or before the argument session begins.[17]

The New York Civil Practice Act's tight schedule of 20–15–10 days from the settling of the transcript has been criticized as unrealistic and as usually requiring an extension of time (§5530 and Comment thereto). Perhaps for that reason each of the New York appellate courts has prescribed a different schedule for itself in its own rules.[18]

In a few states shorter times are allowed for interlocutory or criminal appeals,[19] or for appeals to intermediate appellate

---

[17]Federal Rule of Appellate Procedure 31(a) (14 days after appellee's brief but no later than 3 days before argument), United States Supreme Court Rule 35.3 (up to 7 days before hearing), Massachusetts, Oklahoma, Oregon.

[18]The New York Court of Appeals rules give an appellant 60 days to file his brief from the time an appeal is taken and respondent 30 days to answer. New York Court of Appeals Rule 500.3, 500.5.

The Appellate Division, First Department, requires appellant's brief to be filed 50 days before the first day of the term in which the case is noticed for argument. The answering brief is to be filed 20 days before, and the reply within 9 days of service of the answering brief. First Department Rule 600.11(b)(c). In the Second Department the briefs are to be filed 38 and 24 days before the beginning of the term, with 7 days to reply. Second Department Rule 670.20. In the Third Department, the appellant's brief is due 60 days after service of the notice of appeal, with 30 days to answer and 10 days to reply. Third Department Rule 800.9. In the Fourth Department, the schedule is the same, except for 9 days to reply. Fourth Department Rule 1000.5.

[19]In Wyoming, for appeals in "worker's compensation cases." Rule 5.06.

courts. In a few others the time varies depending upon whether or not a transcript of the testimony is filed.

In almost every jurisdiction, the number of days for filing the appellant's brief on appeals as of right is computed from the day the record is filed in the appellate court, or, in the alternative, from the time when the clerk certifies that the record is available for transmission to that court.[20] In a few states the time runs from the filing of the notice of appeal (e.g., Florida)—at least if no transcript has been ordered—or the docketing of the appeal (Iowa, Nebraska, North Carolina), or the later of the notice of appeal (Oregon) or the transcript (Michigan).

In New Hampshire, the times set in the scheduling order (see Sec. 4.8, *supra*) run from the dates of the order or of the filing of the transcript with the Supreme Court clerk, whichever is later, and allow 30 days for each brief "unless special circumstances exist." Supreme Court Rule 12.

When leave to appeal must be granted, as for many appeals from interlocutory orders and most appeals taken from an intermediate appellate court to a supreme court, including petitions for certiorari to the United States Supreme Court, the time for the petitioner's brief on the merits runs from the granting of the petition or application.

The time for filing an appellee's brief, and usually of a reply brief, is measured from the date the prior brief is received (United States Supreme Court Rule 35) or served (Federal Rule of Appellate Procedure 31) or due (Illinois Rule 343). The Illinois computation from the time the prior brief is *due* means that if that brief is filed earlier than its due date, the case is not expedited but more time is made available for the writing of the opposing brief, which makes little sense. An attempt by one party to speed up the appeal by filing his brief ahead of time should not be allowed to be frustrated by his opponent.

Under Federal Appellate Rule 25(a) and similar rules in some of the states, briefs, in contrast to other documents, are deemed served or filed on the day of mailing.[21] Many jurisdictions contain provisions similar to the following in Federal Appellate Rule 26(c):

---

[20]E.g., Federal Rules of Appellate Procedure 31, 11(c), 12(b); Illinois Rules 343(a), 325; Oklahoma Rule of Civil Appellate Procedure 1.55.

[21]E.g., Illinois Rule 373. Illinois Rule 12(c) provides that "service by mail is complete four days after mailing." As to United States Supreme Court Rule 28.2 (1980), see Sec. 7.40, note 234, *infra*.

"Whenever a party is required or permitted to do an act within a prescribed period after service of a paper upon him and the paper is served by mail, 3 days shall be added to the prescribed period."

These rules as to precisely when briefing time begins to run should be carefully checked and followed. See Sec. 7.40, *infra.*

The appellate court or a judge thereof may always shorten or extend the time for filing briefs. The time may be shortened either because the case calls for prompt disposition or because the court's calendar permits a prompt argument. Some courts delegate this authority, at least in the first instance, to the clerk or court administrator.[22] Counsel should endeavor to work out a schedule satisfactory to those officials without bothering the members of the court. In some states counsel can stipulate for one extension of limited duration.[23]

Whether courts are liberal or strict in granting extensions varies among courts and judges, and may depend on how far the particular court is behind in its calendar or whether it is able to hear cases promptly when briefs are filed on time. Courts in large cities are more likely to have large dockets and to fall behind; this understandably may make them more liberal in granting extensions since in such circumstances the additional time for brief writing will not delay the hearing of the case. Some courts make it plain that extensions are disfavored. Georgia Rule 24-3616 states that extensions will not be granted except "for providential cause or its equivalent," which sounds as if only death or serious illness will be adequate. Seventh Circuit Rule 8(a) requires a motion supported by affidavit disclosing any prior extensions; "the affidavit must disclose facts which establish to the satisfaction of the court that with due diligence, and giving priority to the preparation of the brief, it will not be possible to file the brief on time." Generalizations such as that "counsel is too busy" will not be sufficient. Seventh Circuit Rule 8(a) further states:

"Grounds that may merit consideration are:
     "(1) Engagement in other litigation, provided such litigation is identified by caption, number, and court, and there is set forth (a) a description of action taken on a request for continuance or deferment of other litigation; (b) an explanation of the reasons why other litigation should receive priority over the case in which

---

[22]E.g., United States Supreme Court Rule 29.4; Minnesota Rules 110.02(3), 131.011.
[23]E.g., California—60 days; Michigan, Nevada—30 days; South Dakota—15 days.

the petition is filed; and (c) other relevant circumstances including why other associated counsel cannot either prepare the brief for filing or, in the alternative, relieve the movant's counsel of the other litigation claimed as a ground for extension.

"(2) The matter under appeal is so complex that an adequate brief cannot reasonably be prepared by the date the brief is due, provided that the complexity is factually demonstrated in the affidavit.

"(3) Extreme hardship to counsel will result unless an extension is granted, in which event the nature of the hardship must be set forth in detail."

The above factors probably typify those which other appellate courts take into consideration.[24]

In order to determine whether an extension is likely to be granted, and for how long, counsel should check in advance with the clerk's office or with lawyers familiar with the particular court's practice. He can thus ascertain whether reasons other than the extraordinary magnitude of the case, or serious emergencies such as illness of counsel or death in his family, will suffice, and how such excuses as a heavy load of other work (a common affliction among lawyers) or a preplanned vacation are likely to fare.

As a general matter, my experience is that one moderate extension of not more than 30 days is not difficult to obtain if good reason is presented. Beyond that, all that can be surmised is that some courts are strict and that others are not, and that counsel should not press his luck too far. Certainly he should not slow down his preparation until he is certain that an extension will be granted.

7.5 Allowing Time for Revising, Rewriting and Checking

Counsel should be aware that the total number of days allowed by the rules cannot be employed in preparing the first

---

[24]See also Ninth Circuit Rule 13(h), which was recently amended to require a statement of the position of opposing counsel if obtainable, and to authorize the clerk to grant unopposed extensions of up to 28 days if the case has not been calendared for hearing. The Second Circuit has announced that "[u]nless [an] application for extended time is made so that it may be considered before the allotted time has expired, it is evidence of a lack of good faith and, failing extraordinary circumstances, it constitutes neglect which will not be excused." *Gilroy* v. *Erie Lackawanna R. Co.*, 421 F.2d 1321, 1323 (CA 2, 1970). In *Community Coalition* v. *FCC*, 49 U.S.L.W. 2437 (CA DC, Dec. 22, 1980), counsel were chastised for a "cavalier attitude" in filing untimely motions for extensions and disregarding even the time limit as extended.

draft of the brief. Brief writing, like other serious writing, does not consist merely of sitting down, writing out what needs to be said, and filing it in court. Very few writers are capable either of dictating or scribbling a really good first draft. I know that my own often sound good on first reading, but on second, preferably at least a day or two later, a great deal of rewriting and often reorganizing is necessary.

A substantial amount of time should be left for rewriting. The oft quoted paragraph from Strunk and White's *The Elements of Style* explains:

> "*Revise and Rewrite.* Revising is part of writing. Few writers are so expert that they can produce what they are after on the first try. Quite often the writer will discover, on examining the completed work, that there are serious flaws in the arrangement of the material, calling for transpositions. When this is the case, he can save himself much labor and time by using scissors on his manuscript, cutting it to pieces and fitting the pieces together in a better order. If the work merely needs shortening, a pencil is the most useful tool; but if it needs rearranging, or stirring up, scissors should be brought into play. Do not be afraid to seize whatever you have written and cut it to ribbons; it can always be restored to its original condition in the morning, if that course seems best. Remember, it is no sign of weakness or defeat that your manuscript ends up in need of major surgery. This is a common occurrence in all writing, and among the best writers."[25]

Rewriting takes time, though, of course, not nearly as much as writing the first version. It is more productive if there is a gap of a day or two between drafts. This enables the writer to take more of a fresh look than if he moves immediately from one draft to another. An experienced appellate advocate has told me that he finds it helpful to read the draft once for substance and the second time for clarity and style. Having other lawyers, either outside co-counsel or office colleagues, review the draft and make suggestions is also very helpful, since no one is the best critic of his own work. But this also takes time. The greater the number of lawyers who have to agree to a brief, particularly if they are in different law firms representing different clients, the more time becomes necessary, in almost astronomical progression.

A third draft will perhaps come close to final form, that is, as good a brief as the lawyer can produce. But with every read-

---

[25]W. Strunk and E. B. White, THE ELEMENTS OF STYLE, p. 72 (3d ed., 1979).

ing, a lawyer will think of some way to improve the product. The more time available for rewriting, the better the brief will be. This will also allow time for additional research as the need for more authority on particular points is recognized.

Time must also be allowed for checking all citations and record references, for proofreading to catch mechanical errors by the lawyers, the typists and the printer—and everyone makes such errors—and for the printing or duplication. A printed brief will go through galley proof and page proof, each of which must be checked for errors; some are always found. And most lawyers cannot resist improving or even rewriting a brief at these stages.

How briefs should be checked is discussed at greater length in Sec. 7.39, *infra.* The point here is that time must be left for all this. Normally at least three days must be allowed, if the brief is to be printed, between the initial sending of the brief to the printer and filing. Nonprinted briefs, if not too long, can often be duplicated and bound in one day, often in the lawyer's own office.

All of the above leads to the inevitable conclusion that brief writing should start as early as possible, often long before the time specified in the rules begins to run. Certainly the legal research and the examination of the record should commence as soon as a party determines to appeal or learns that his opponent will appeal. A new lawyer should begin preparation as soon as he is brought into the case.

It is much better both for the brief and for the lawyer's nerves and health if he works hard and steadily at the beginning of the available time, leaving adequate time for revision and reproduction, than if he has to finish with a mad rush at the end, as too often happens. If any rule of thumb can be suggested, it would be that the first draft, and better yet, the second, be completed at least a week before the brief must be filed.

7.6 The Maximum Page Length

Before starting to write, a brief writer should know how long a brief is allowable under the rules of the appellate court. He must keep the maximum limit in mind unless he is positive that he can stay within it.

The rules of most jurisdictions specify the maximum number of pages for briefs. Longer briefs may be filed if leave of court is obtained by an appropriate motion. The motion should explain why the number or the nature of the issues or the magnitude or complexity of the case requires a greater number of pages. How willing a court will be to grant such an application will depend on the nature of the case, the number of additional pages requested and the unpredictable reaction of the judge or judges who will pass upon the motion.

No page limitation is imposed by Arkansas, California (if printed, 50 pages if not printed), Georgia, Indiana, Louisiana,[26] Minnesota, the New York Court of Appeals, North Carolina, Ohio,[27] Oklahoma, South Carolina, Texas, Vermont and West Virginia. Undoubtedly those courts, like all others, appreciate short briefs and deplore repetition or unnecessary detail in the handling of facts and cases. Nevertheless, they are willing to leave to counsel the determination of how extensive a treatment the issues in the particular case require. There is good reason for this policy in courts which, like the United States Supreme Court, hear many cases which are of great importance and call for extensive, and indeed exhaustive, research if counsel are to give the court the material it should have. The burden upon the Supreme Court has become so great, however, that its 1980 rules limit principal briefs on the merits to 50 pages and reply briefs to 20 pages[28] (Rule 34.3, .4). An application requesting leave to file a longer brief for good cause may be submitted to the Court or a Justice "but such an application is not favored." Rule 33.4. Such an application must comply with Rule 43 governing motions to individual Justices, "and it must be

---

[26]Louisiana requires an Index and Table of Cases if the brief is over 50 pages long.

[27]There are no page limitations in Ohio except in the Ohio Courts of Appeals for the Eighth and Tenth Districts (Cleveland and Columbus) which limit the principal briefs to 40 and 50 pages, respectively.

[28]The Supreme Court's rules setting maximum length (30 pages) for petitions for certiorari, jurisdictional statements and the responding briefs state that the page limitations may exclude "the subject index, table of authorities, any [required] verbatim quotations [from statutes, treatises, regulations and the like] and the appendices." Rules 15.3, 16.3, 21.4 and 22.2. The rules setting page limitations for briefs on the merits (Rule 34.3—50 pages), reply briefs (Rules 16.5 and 22.5—10 pages; Rule 34.4—20 pages) and *amicus* briefs (Rule 36.1—20 pages) do not exclude the items mentioned above. Since there is no sense to limiting the pages of such items in any briefs and even less to doing so for some types of briefs and not others, this difference was undoubtedly inadvertent. The Court "is unlikely to raise any objection" if counsel excludes the items referred to in computing the numbers of pages in all kinds of briefs. E. Gressman and R. Stern, SUPREME COURT RULES: THE 1980 REVISIONS, p. 6, also printed in 48 U.S. Law Week 3827, 3829 (1980). And indeed, the Clerk's Office is permitting the number of pages to be counted in this way. In addition, no objection has been made to exclusion from the page limitation of the initial page or two containing the Questions Presented and the names of additional parties, which under 1980 Rule 34.1 come at the very beginning of the brief, even before the tables of contents and authorities. *Id.* at 6–7, 3829.

submitted at least 15 days before the filing date of the document in question, except in the most extraordinary circumstances." This may require a change in the habits of lawyers who do not know how long their briefs will be 15 days before they must be filed, as most undoubtedly do not now. Since "cases that have been selected for plenary review by the Supreme Court are likely to be more complex, and certainly more important to the development of the law, than the run of the mill appellate case," the Supreme Court should be lenient in allowing longer briefs. W. Allen and A. Kozinski, *Review of Rules of the Supreme Court of the United States,* 94 Harv. L. Rev. 312, 315 (1980). The new rule, however, reflects a movement in the opposite direction, although it is still too early to tell how the Court will treat applications to permit longer briefs in important cases.

Most jurisdictions now allow briefs to be either printed or typed and duplicated by legible processes. See Sec. 7.37, *infra.* Where the maximum number of pages is specified, a larger number is often permitted for typed briefs than for printed ones,[29] in recognition of the fact that fewer words—approximately 25 percent less by my count, using the most common size of pica type (10 pitch, which means 10 letters per inch)—appear on a double-spaced typewritten page than on a printed page, even though the page used for typewriting is subsantially larger.

That fact is now being challenged, perhaps because typewriters which permit more to be written on the typed page are now available. Typewriters with 12 pitch characters (12 per inch) as well as 10 pitch are now available. That permits 20 percent more to be typed on a page, which is very close to the contents of a page printed in conformance with most appellate court requirements. Dual pitch electric typewriters can be adjusted for either 10 or 12 pitch typing. Lawyers should be aware that they can substantially increase the content of a brief limited to a specified number of pages by making use of this device.

Rule 28(g) of the Federal Rules of Appellate Procedure, which previously provided that "principal briefs shall not exceed 50 pages of typographical printing, or 70 pages of printing by any other process of duplicating or copying," and not exceed 25 or 35 pages for the two types of reply briefs, was changed in 1979 to eliminate the larger number of pages for other duplicat-

---

[29]As to the unusual requirements of the United States Supreme Court, see Rule 33 and Sec. 6.10, *supra.*

ing processes. A large number of states, however, still prescribe 50–70 and 25–35 page limits for principal and reply briefs. A large majority of the states which prescribe maximum limits agree upon 50 pages in one form or another.[30] The 50-page limit in Tennessee Rule 27(i) relates "only to the argument" part of the brief.

The maximum number of pages for principal briefs in the state courts is shown in the following list. Where two numbers appear, the first is for printed briefs, the second for briefs typed and photocopied. The number is the same for the principal briefs of appellants and appellees unless otherwise indicated.

25	— Kentucky Court of Appeals, Virginia (appellee);
30, 50	— Nevada;
35	— Delaware, New Mexico (appellant, argument only);
36, 50	— Virginia (appellant);
40, 50	— Alabama, Wisconsin;
50	— Alaska, California, Connecticut, Florida, Iowa, Kansas, Kentucky Supreme Court, Michigan, Mississippi, New Hampshire, North Dakota, Oregon, Rhode Island, Utah;
50, 60	— Maryland;
50, 65	— New Jersey;
50, 70	— Arizona, Colorado, Montana, some New York Appellate Divisions, Pennsylvania, Wyoming;
50, 75	— Maine, Massachusetts;
54, 70	— Washington (54 if 1 1/2 spaced, 70 if double spaced);
60	— South Dakota;
75	— Idaho;
75, 100	— Illinois;
80	— Hawaii;
90	— Missouri (appellee);
100	— Missouri (appellant), Nebraska (for all briefs filed by a party).

The maximum number of pages for reply briefs in some state courts is shown in the following list. See Sec. 7.34, *infra.*

---

[30]Kansas allows typed material to be single spaced. The State of Washington allows typed material to be 1 1/2 spaced, between single and double space. Either of these techniques permits more text per page.

As above, the first number is for printed briefs, the second for briefs typed and photocopied.

5   — Kentucky Court of Appeals;
10   — Kentucky Supreme Court;
10, 13 — Wisconsin;
12, 15 — Virginia;
15   — Florida, Kansas;
15, 20 — New Jersey;
20   — Alaska, Delaware, Hawaii, New York Appellate Division (Second Department);
20, 25 — Alabama;
20, 27 — Illinois;
25   — Iowa, Missouri, North Dakota, Oregon;
25, 35 — Arizona, Colorado, New York Appellate Division (First Department);
27, 35 — Washington (27 for 1 1/2 spaced, 35 for double spaced).

Counsel should of course check the current rules of his jurisdiction to determine whether the figures given above still prevail.

7.7   Preparation for Writing

Writers on appellate advocacy usually recommend that the first responsibility of the brief writer is to read and digest or summarize the record. But reading a record cold, with no idea of the legal theories involved and the positions taken by the parties, would often be as puzzling and fruitless as researching the authorities without some knowledge of the facts in the case. The significance of facts and law is interrelated, each depending on some knowledge of the other.

Accordingly, before an appellate lawyer undertakes to study either in depth he should find out generally what the case is about. If he has tried the case or participated in the trial or its preparation, this may present no problem except the refreshment of memory if much time has elapsed. New counsel brought in for the brief, however, must start from scratch.

If he is coming in at the second appellate level, he can best learn about the case from the briefs filed in the first appellate court and the court's opinion. If he is coming in after the trial, he can usually obtain an overall picture of the case by reading the opinion, findings and judgment below, or perhaps the charge to the jury, as well as any briefs or memoranda filed by the parties in the trial court. A transcript of the oral arguments in that court may be helpful if one is available. In the absence of these documents, or if they turn out to be uninformative, he should turn to the pleadings. If necessary before, and in any event after, the above steps, he should discuss the case with the trial lawyer or other counsel familiar with it in order to obtain their views as to where the lower court committed reversible error.

Such a preliminary review of the case will provide a reasonably accurate impression of what the case is about, both factually and legally. It should identify, at least tentatively, the principal legal issues likely to be of consequence on the appeal and which may need research either *ab initio* or in greater depth than before. It should also provide a fairly accurate picture of the facts or of the conflicting versions of the facts.

After this has been done, the time has come for the principal brief writer to immerse himself in the record. At the same time, if issues call for further research, as they often do, and if additional legal manpower is available, other lawyers can start work on that phase of the case.

Reading the record means reading all the papers and testimony which will be before the appellate court, except what is clearly irrelevant, such as discovery materials not offered in evidence, the *voir dire* when no error is claimed as to the selection of the jury or other preliminary matters no longer in issue. Some of what is read, perhaps a great deal, will turn out not to be relevant to the issues presented, but one object of examining the record is to determine what issues should be presented, and what portions of the record will be relevant or irrelevant. Study of the evidence may narrow the scope of a legal question, and thus enable the legal research to concentrate on the precise issue which the facts present.

Since few persons will be able to remember the details of a record, even a short one, the reader should prepare a digest of the significant facts (with page references) as he goes along. This formerly required putting pencil to paper and summarizing whatever was pertinent, page by page. These notes could, if legible, then be copied by a typist; if, as in my case, the scribbled notes would not be legible enough for that, they would have to be dictated to a secretary. Both lawyer and secretarial time can now be saved by the use of dictating machines which are commonly available. The reader can dictate into the machine his digest of the record as he reads it, quoting what he thinks necessary. He can speak as rapidly as he wants, because the typist who will eventually transcribe his remarks from the tape or belt can reduce its speed to what the typist can comfortably handle.

When the record is very short, this process may be unnecessary. If a digest of the record has been prepared while the case was in the court below, by the same or a different lawyer, it need not be redone. Unless it was done by the same lawyer *and* he can recall what was in the record, the record itself should be reviewed by the brief writer and (if they are different) the lawyer who is to argue the case, and the prior digest supplemented when necessary, most easily by additional interlined notes.

The digest or notes should then be reviewed so as to enable the various items relating to a single subject to be brought together. They can be identified by notes in the margin, as by a mark of a particular color, letter, number or key word. If there are not too many significant items, a page listing each item with the pertinent record references may be sufficient. For a more voluminous record the material relating to each item may be collected or summarized on a single card or page. This can be done by copying or by the application of scissors and paste to an extra copy of the digest.

This review and analysis of the record often suggests new points of law on which research, or more research, is required. If he has not already done so, the brief writer should outline the argument portion of the brief, at least tentatively, in part to determine whether any further research is required.

It is at this point that the brief writer, if he has not already done so, should read not only the briefs and memoranda prepared for use in the court below and significant authorities cited therein, but conduct any additional necessary research. New points may need to be examined, or prior research expanded in depth or updated. If other lawyers are assisting him, the research should have been undertaken and, if possible, completed while the record was being read.

After all that, the brief writer will be in a position to sit back and think, putting all the factual and legal items together in his mind, and *then* to outline the brief, or at least the argumentative portion. From that outline he can identify the questions to be presented and determine what facts will be relevant. An outline of the Statement of Facts may or may not be necessary, depending on the factual complexity of the case and whether a simple chronological statement can be prepared without a prior outline.

The outline may or may not be in great detail. Often the details of the points will tend to write themselves as writing and continued thinking progress. New ideas frequently occur as one moves from one sentence to another. This may result in departure from the outline and require additional research. But the processes of writing, organizing and research are not completely severable. They are all in flux and subject to reconsideration as different thoughts come to mind until the brief is completed.

The outline of the argument should itself identify the questions to be presented on appeal. The actual phrasing of the questions, however, is best left until after the Statement of Facts and the Argument have been drafted. Where the rules of the particular court require a Summary of Argument, as some courts do (see Sec. 7.21, *infra*), it should also be prepared after the Argument has been written, indeed, as the last thing before the brief is completed. Other preliminary matters, such as short statements of the nature of the case, the jurisdictional facts and references to the statutes involved, can be prepared as the writing of the brief progresses.

Generally, the brief should be written in the order in which its parts will finally appear, except for the Summary of Argument, and sometimes the Questions Presented, as indicated above. But this may not be best for all briefs. If the facts are simply stated and uncontroversial and the legal arguments more difficult and complex, one may draft the latter first, in order to have more time to rethink, or to submit it to others for comment and suggestions. Agreement on the proper legal analysis may aid in deciding what facts should be mentioned, stressed, downplayed or even ignored.

7.8 Writing Good English—In General

Of the three essentials to good brief writing, adequate preparation, clear thinking and good writing, the first has already been discussed. As to the second, no advice can be of much help; the lawyer must use whatever thinking ability he has, whether derived from his genes, his training or his experience, or all three in combination.

The third essential element, writing good clear English, is

a subject which in itself calls for a volume larger than this one. For the same principles which govern good writing in general apply to brief writing, subject to the special need for clarity and precision which characterize all legal writing.[31] "Accuracy and clarity" must be "foremost in legal writing," with accuracy ranking first and clarity encompassing "readability."[32] Paraphrasing a Latin maxim, Professor Miller aptly warns that "[e]ven if you know something, nevertheless, if you cannot express it, you might just as well have been stupid in the first place."[33]

The object should be to write like a good writer, not "like a lawyer"—or, more accurately, not the way uninformed persons, probably including many lawyers, think a lawyer should write. Redundancy, expressing the same thought in many different ways, is likely to be more repulsive than persuasive to the busy appellate judge. Contrary to the belief of some novices, use of expressions they regard as manifesting legal learning, such as "whereas," "hereinafter," "said" and the like, is not called for.[34] They are signs of legal immaturity rather than the contrary.

A good brief should flow simply and smoothly, and should be understandable without difficulty. The style often used for contracts, insurance policies, wills or deeds, statutes or regulations is entirely inappropriate.[35] If a judge has to think hard to determine what is meant, or to reread a paragraph a number of times, the brief has failed to accomplish its purpose, which is to convince an impartial reader by making the case sound as simple as possible at first reading.

The object should be to persuade that the case is easy, that the position of one's client is obviously correct, not that the lawyer is brilliant or clever. An opinion which mentions, always flatteringly, the quality or ability of counsel for one side almost always continues with a "but" explaining why the decision must go the other way.

---

[31] In addition to general works on writing good English, see M. Freeman, GRAMMATICAL LAWYER (ALI-ABA, 1975); G. J. Miller, *On Legal Style*, 43 Kentucky L.J. 235 (1955); R. C. Wydick, PLAIN ENGLISH FOR LAWYERS (1979).

[32] Miller, *supra* note 31, at 240.

[33] *Id.* at 262.

[34] R. Carson, *Conduct of the Appeal—A Lawyer's View*, in A CASE ON APPEAL, p. 69 (ALI-ABA, 1967).

[35] *Id.* at 68. Judge Goodrich has written that the "first virtue" a brief "must have is clarity. Attaining clarity is a painstaking effort. If one thinks clearly, one can write clearly, if he puts enough work into what he writes. There is no reason why one should have to read a sentence in a brief, or anywhere else, three or four times before he understands what it says. Lawyers frequently use long sentences. They would write more clearly and effectively if they would chop those sentences into shorter pieces." Goodrich, *supra* n. 4, at 14.

A lawyer should have learned how to write good English before he enters law school, but often he has not. Rules of grammar or principles of good writing were probably last called to his attention in high school, if at all, when they were not taken seriously and have long since been forgotten. And few if any law schools provide courses or training in English composition, or insist, as they should, that students whose writing is deficient take corrective courses in other departments of the university. After admission to the bar, lawyers seldom attempt to improve their writing, although they may learn from experience and the criticism of colleagues, which they should avidly seek without shame.

This book obviously cannot fill that need. Some of the most common faults, however, may be worth mentioning here, in the belief that once they are called to a lawyer's attention he may recognize them in his own writing, and that such awareness may lead to their avoidance in the future. My experience in writing, reading and reviewing briefs over many years suggests that legal writers tend to repeat the same kinds of errors or unclear expressions or inelegancies, though not, of course, all of them or all of the time or uniformly either by the same person or different persons.

(1) Remember that clarity is essential in writing designed to persuade. For lawyers it is a must, and all other rules must give way to it. Thus, even if repetition of the same word might not be good style, a lawyer may resort to it if essential to a precise understanding of what he is trying to get across.

(2) Perhaps the most common fault of brief writers, even if they are very good lawyers, is to fail to make their writing simple enough for the judge to understand. This is not a matter of grammar or composition. The lawyer who has spent months, weeks or at least days familiarizing himself with all aspects of a case before he starts writing must appreciate that judges may be familiar with general principles of law which frequently come before them, perhaps more so than the lawyer; but that they will know nothing about the facts of each case or often the fine points of the legal issues presented.

Lawyers in such technical areas as tax law, patent law, environmental law and many other fields, particularly those arising under new complex regulatory statutes, often do not recognize how ignorant even the brightest judge may be as to such matters. They are likely to think that a numerical reference to, or a short paraphrase of, Sec. 492(b)(1)(A)(ii) of the

Internal Revenue or any other code or statute will enable the judge to appreciate and understand the point of the case, at least if they quote the language in full in an appendix. Or they may describe scientific or engineering facts—and these often become relevant not only in patent but in pollution, product liability and many other kinds of cases—in a way which is comprehensible only to a graduate of an engineering school or a lawyer who has been steeped in the subject almost long enough to become one.

The brief writer must, therefore, for this reason as well as many others, attempt to put himself in the position of the judge, any judge, since he often may not know in advance who the appellate judges in his case will be. He must keep in mind what that actual or hypothetical judge is likely to know. The brief should explain things so that such a judge can understand without reading anything else, and without spending too much time on it, because most judges do not have much time to spend on each case or brief.

Since a lawyer familiar with a subject in depth will always have difficulty in putting himself in the place of a person who is not, no matter how hard he tries, he may need outside help. An excellent technique is to have one's draft read by another, obviously friendly, lawyer, usually in one's own office, who knows nothing about the case, or even by an intelligent non-lawyer. I recall when I was in the Solicitor General's office mainly handling antitrust, administrative and constitutional matters, my tax colleague, now a distinguished judge, would often bring me a tax brief to see if I could understand it; he thought that if I could, so could the Supreme Court Justice least familiar with tax law. The tax briefs often needed a review of that sort, but the problem obviously is not limited to that subject.

Most judges are supposed to be generalists, not specialists, and even the most brilliant will not be experts in the diverse subjects, changing from hour to hour, which come before them. A brief writer—and, of course, also the oral arguer—should keep that in the front of his mind.

(3) Avoid very long sentences or, for that matter, too many very short ones. Five words will often do. But a series of very short sentences may give a staccato effect and not read smoothly. A change of pace is desirable. Often a writer, including this one, will find that in attempting accurately to express a general thought, he will be adding qualification after qualifica-

tion, which though entirely grammatical and in the right order will end by inserting quite a few lines between the subject and the verb, as the Germans do, and thoroughly confuse the reader —as you probably have been by this sentence. This offense creeps up on you. Though perfectly aware of the problem, I often find such sentences in my first drafts, and hope that they go no further. Do not use many dashes or parentheses; they may encumber the sentence. Commas are better, but do not overdo them either. A semicolon may be better for a long pause. Occasional dashes help to shift gears in a sentence of some length to mark an aside or different thought.

(4) Don't show off. Avoid words that the normally intelligent but not overly intellectual judge would be unlikely to understand. He does not like to have to turn to a dictionary, and probably won't. If you must use technical expressions, try to define them in simple language, if that is possible. Of course, you are writing for lawyers, so that words commonly known to lawyers are entirely proper even if laymen may not understand them. But even some words commonly used or overused or even misused in law review articles, like "parameter," may not be clear except from the context—and looking that word up in three dictionaries, as I have just done, was of little help. The brief writer should want the judge to know what he means.

(5) The pronoun "this" often refers to the preceding sentence or a part of it. Which part frequently is not clear. Keep this in mind and, if necessary, substitute or add a more specific word or phrase, even at the risk of repetition.

(6) The same sort of ambiguity often arises from the word "it," compounded by its use as an indefinite pronoun with no meaning of its own. In "When the brown car crossed the white line and hit the green car, it was not clear if it was going too fast," the two "its" have different meanings, and which car the second "it" refers to is not entirely clear, although it probably is the brown one.

(7) Plural nouns should go with plural verbs. If I added "and so should singular," the reader would not be sure whether singular nouns should go with plural verbs or with singular ones. Avoid that problem, and also make sure that your plurals and singulars go with each other.

Most lawyers are sufficiently educated to avoid such gross violations of this principle as "two dogs was in the car." But they might slip, at least in the first draft, if a long phrase or clause, perhaps suggesting a different number, intervenes between the noun and the verb, such as "the whole team, including the guards and tackles, was in the car." "Were" would be incorrect, but confusion is not difficult. The general rule is that the verb follows the number of the subject of the sentence. Some words create difficulty as to this; such words as "each," "everybody," "nobody," "none" and "either" take the singular verb, at least usually, unless it plainly means more than one. Say "everybody is present," not "are present"; no one or none "is present," not "are."

(8) Dangling participial or other clauses or phrases often cause trouble. At the beginning of a sentence they should refer to the subject of the sentence. You can say "A golfer of renown, he was given the key to the city," not "A golfer of renown, his friends gave him the key to the city."

Participles often are confusing. "While driving to work, the car struck two children" is an example. Since the car was not driving to work, the sentence should be rephrased. A modifying expression should be placed near the words it is supposed to modify.

(9) Spelling. Obviously when one has doubt as to how a word should be spelled, he should go to the dictionary. Often, however, the writer can be wrong without having doubt. Lawyers in particular should avoid such mistakes as putting too many "e's" in "judgment," a "c" in "supersede," or "a's" and "o's" in the wrong place in "analogous." Stenographers and printers, and perhaps even lawyers, sometimes confuse "principle" and "principal," and "precedents" and "precedence," but usually not "presidents."

(10) Try to treat parallel words and phrases the same way. Do not say "cheese, the milk, bread and the oranges were in the ice box." Put "the" before all or none of the words.

Parallel expressions conveying the same idea should be phrased in the same way. Not "John won the first race: the second was won by Jim"; but "John won the first race, and Jim the second." Do not say "The significant elements of writing are simplicity, being accurate, and how to spell," but "simplicity, accuracy and spelling."

(11) Be careful with "as" and "than." Do not say "John can jump as high and faster than Joe," but "as high as and faster than." Too often the "as" after "high" is overlooked.

(12) Keep tenses in a sentence, or even in a series of sent-

ences, the same unless there is good reason for not doing so. Do not say "The reporters were present while the race is going on."

(13) Split infinitives, particularly putting a long adverb between the "to" and the verb, should usually be avoided. Usually "to think rapidly" is better than "to rapidly think." Sometimes, however, they sound better, so that avoiding them may be awkward. If so, go ahead and split.

(14) Most authorities on writing say that the use of "and/or" is to be avoided like poison. But sometimes it saves a lot of other words and is perfectly clear. In such situations, I would not be completely averse to using the expression.

(15) Avoid initials, unless you are sure the reader will know what they signify. Substituting initials for a long name saves lots of space, but, unless the initials are well known (such as S.E.C.), spelling the name out in full at the beginning, and perhaps a few times thereafter, may be desirable. Except for familiar initials, the full name should be followed, at least in the first instance, by "(hereinafter referred to as "X.Y.Z.")."

This problem arises particularly in respect to government agencies. I cannot resist calling attention to Mr. Justice Rehnquist's explanatory apology in *Chrysler Corporation* v. *Brown,* 441 U.S. 281, 286–287, n. 4 (1979). After stating the facts of a case involving the FOIA (Freedom of Information Act), the DLA (formerly the Defense Supply Agency) and the OFCCP (Office of Federal Contract Compliance Programs) which required the submission of AAPs and EEO-1 Reports that may result in reviews and investigations "which culminate" in CRRs and CIRs, he added:

> "The term 'alphabet soup' gained currency in the early days of the New Deal as a description of the proliferation of new agencies such as WPA and PWA. The terminology required to describe the present controversy suggests that the 'alphabet soup' of the New Deal era was, by comparison, a clear broth."

The above suggestions do not, of course, remotely cover the subject of good writing style, good grammar or even good spelling. Conforming to the demands of good English is essential to good brief writing. Although brief writers need not have exceptional literary ability, they should write well enough (1) to express the intended thought clearly and accurately, and (2) to avoid making the reader so conscious of deficiencies in grammar or style as to detract from concentration on the merits of the brief—and that happens.

If a writer has been well trained, either in school or from subsequent experience, good writing is, or should be, a matter of feel or instinct. Recollection of all the rules of grammar is not essential, and perhaps will be very rare. But until one is sure of the accuracy of one's feel for good writing, which may even include understanding when the rules need *not* be followed, the writer must work at his English. Having another person review one's draft is a very helpful method of double-checking, even for the experienced and knowledgeable writer. Many of us can detect errors or awkwardness or inelegancies in others' writing much better than in our own. As to the need for allowing ample time for revising, rewriting, checking and correcting, see Secs. 7.5, *supra,* and 7.39, *infra.*

7.9   References to Parties in Covers, Captions and Text

The parties to a case on appeal are referred to on the cover and in the internal caption at the beginning of the brief, as well as in the text. Most, but not all, appellate courts require that the caption in the appellate court, both on the cover and internally, remain the same as in the trial court, that is, that the plaintiff's name come first, and the defendant's second. If there are numerous parties, only the first, or a few (such as the first three), need be included in the caption, which, if some are omitted, should conclude with *"et al."* to show that there are others. The others should then be listed in text or footnote at the appropriate point at the beginning of the brief, or even ahead of the indexes, as in the United States Supreme Court. See Sec. 7.14, *infra.*

If the title in the court below does not contain the name of the appellant, that should be added, as Federal Appellate Rule 12(a) and the rules of many states require. This could occur if only some of the names of other parties on the same side, but not the appellant's, appear in the caption below, or if the case has previously borne some such title as *"Ex parte* Doe," or "Application of John Smith," or "The Permian Basin Cases," or *"In Re:* Multidistrict Vehicle Air Pollution" to which the parties wisely added *"AMF Inc.* v. *General Motors Corp."*

The status of the parties should be identified by adding it

to the description of the parties in the caption used in the court below, as "A.B. Company, Plaintiff-Appellee," or "C. D., Defendant-Appellant."

The rules in most states and the Federal Rules of Appellate Procedure governing the United States courts of appeals require that the title below be used. In other courts, including the United States Supreme Court, the appellant or petitioner always comes first, except that in the Supreme Court petitions for extraordinary writs are to be captioned *"In re* (name of petitioner)." Rule 27.1. In such courts only the status of each party in that court, as appellant or appellee or petitioner or respondent, need be mentioned.

Some of the state rules explicitly declare that the parties shall be referred to as appellant and appellee,[36] or appellant and respondent,[37] or, in some situations, petitioner and respondent.[38] New Jersey prefers plaintiff and defendant. In most, however, that is a matter of practice. In either event, the rule or practice in the jurisdiction should be followed in describing the parties in the caption.

The advantage of not changing the order of the parties in the caption, even though defendant is the appellant, is that the case can be more easily identified in the files and law books if its title remains the same as it wends its way upward, and perhaps downward and upward again, through various courts. Resort to such clumsy citations as *Jones* v. *Smith,* 192 F. Supp. 793 (E.D. Pa. 1936), affirmed *sub nom. Smith* v. *Maloney,* 263 F.2d 125 (CA 3, 1938), is thereby avoided. On the other hand, always putting the appellant's name first means that the appellate court knows, without more, who is the appellant or petitioner. The first mentioned system seems to be preferred by modern rule makers, and prevails in most appellate courts. The difference is obviously not of world-shaking proportions, and the attorney should, of course, become familiar with the practice in the appellate court to which his case has been appealed.

The above requirements as to the formal identifications of parties in the captions do not mean that the parties should always be so described in the textual discussion in the brief. Where court rules are explicit, they should be followed, at least to the extent of not using any other formal designation. If the

---

[36]E.g., North Carolina.
[37]E.g., California.
[38]Cf. United States Supreme Court Rule 21.

rules call for "appellant" and "respondent," do not refer to the latter as "appellee." Even without a rule, do not call a petitioner an appellant, or vice versa.[39]

Another policy, recognized in many rules, comes into play in writing the text of a brief. Judges, of course, are confronted with a continuous stream of cases, in each of which the parties are appellant and appellee, or petitioner and respondent. A plaintiff may have been either appellant or appellee in the intermediate appellate court, or the reverse, and petitioner or respondent in the highest court. A petitioner before an administrative agency may be petitioner or respondent in a reviewing appellate court and the reverse in the highest court. As a result, Chief Judge Prettyman, formerly of the United States Court of Appeals for the District of Columbia Circuit, has urged—and many other judges agree:

> "Don't keep saying 'appellant' and 'appellee.' By the time the reader gets to the third page he becomes completely confused as to which is which."[40]

The same comment applies, of course, to the terms "petitioner" and "respondent," which may refer to different persons at different stages of the case.

Perhaps not surprisingly, Rule 28(d) of the Federal Rules of Appellate Procedure, recommended and adopted by the Advisory Committee of which Judge Prettyman was the chairman 14 years later, urges that counsel

> "keep to a minimum references to parties by such designations as 'appellant' and 'appellee'. It promotes clarity to use the designations used in the lower court [such as plaintiff and defendant] or in the agency proceedings, or the actual names of parties, or descriptive terms such as 'the employee,' 'the injured person,' 'the taxpayer,' 'the ship,' 'the stevedore,' etc."

Many state rules contain a similar or identical provision.[41] One commentator favors "plaintiff Rice."[42] And even when rules do not so require, brief writers should keep in mind the desirability of following the same policy.

---

[39]The Nevada and California rules contain two helpful definitions: Use of masculine, feminine or neuter genders includes the others (California Rule 40(a); Nevada Rule 1(e)(9)); and references to a party (by any designation) include his attorney (California Rule 40(e); Nevada Rule 1(e)(6)), presumably unless the context otherwise indicates.

[40]E.B. Prettyman, *Some Observations Concerning Appellate Advocacy*, 39 Va. L. Rev. 285, 292 (1953).

[41]E.g., Alabama, Colorado, Illinois, Massachusetts, New Mexico.

[42]M. Pittoni, BRIEF WRITING AND ARGUMENTATION, p. 30 (3d ed., 1967).

The Supreme Court of the United States refers to the parties before it as petitioner or respondent, and the Justices may be sufficiently accustomed to that practice to make it entirely appropriate in briefs submitted to that Court. The same may be true in other appellate courts. Nevertheless, references to the parties in ways which more clearly identify them will probably be easier to follow, even in cases filed in those courts.

7.10 Headings

Most lawyers recognize that headings in the Argument section of briefs should indicate not only the subject to be discussed but also the position taken. Merely to identify the point, as "the question of laches," is not very helpful to the court, and even less beneficial to one's client. Even worse is merely to say "Point I"—and I have seen that done.

What is wanted is a reasonably short sentence stating one's position. This should include a reference to one's basic reasoning or to the critical facts, if that can be done without undue elaboration. For example:

> The plaintiff's claim is barred by laches, since the suit could have been brought 10 years earlier and plaintiff's failure to sue caused defendants to change their position.

The entire sentence is much more informative, and persuasive, than merely the first clause.[43]

Some commentators have advocated "argumentative" headings,[44] which sounds as if the heading should contain more of a summary of the argument to be presented than is suggested above. Others disagree.[45] The word "argumentative" would seem to connote an argumentative load heavier than a one-sentence heading can bear. The illustrations given by the advocates of such headings are, however, similar to the example set forth above. A heading of much greater length is likely to be less persuasive than repulsive, in the sense that the judges would

---

[43]Cf. F. Wiener, BRIEFING AND ARGUING FEDERAL APPEALS, p. 67 (1967).

[44]*Id.* at 67–72.

[45]In reply to Col. Wiener's recommendation of argumentative headings, Judge Godbold observed: "They do nothing for me. Rather I resist the notion that I can be affected to any meaningful degree by the semantics of a heading. Argumentative headings generate counter-arguments, and then the judge must settle this side controversy in his own mind in order to identify the real controversy." J. Godbold, *Twenty Pages and Twenty Minutes—Effective Advocacy on Appeal,* 30 Southwestern L.J. 801, 810, n. 23 (1976).

tend to skim over it, or not read it at all. Judges have told me that long headings are likely to have such an effect. Thus, although headings should be argumentative to the extent suggested above, they should not be expected to constitute a full scale summary of the entire argument.

What has been said applies also to subheadings in the Argument, although they are likely to be shorter since they can concentrate on one point.

If the Statement of Facts in the brief is lengthy and complicated, subject headings may also be helpful there. In that context, however, a subject heading may be appropriate, since the statement is not supposed to be argumentative. Thus, the following type of headings would be suitable:

1. The Negotiations Leading Up to the Contract
2. Terms of the Contract
3. Defendants' Reliance on Plaintiff's Failure to Sue Within the Period of Limitation.

7.11   The Organization of Briefs—In General

The organization of the contents of briefs on the merits is usually prescribed by rule in various degrees of detail, but sometimes left to the lawyers. In the main, the rules in the different jurisdictions are quite similar. They usually require that the topics be arranged so as to make the brief most intelligible to the judges. The customary order of the topics should be followed, even when no rules so require.

The appellant's brief should consist of five principal parts:

(1) The cover and the indexes.
(2) The introductory sections designed to give the court a bird's-eye view of the problem and of the material necessary for comprehending the major sections to follow. These should include, preferably in the following order, unless rules require otherwise, as they sometimes do:[46]

---

[46]The United States Supreme Court rules still require (Rule 34.1(d)) as an opening item the citation to the opinions in the lower courts, even though those opinions are now required to be attached to the petition for certiorari by Rule 21.1(k). Many other courts similarly require the opinions below to be included in or appended to the document submitted. Reference to the citations in such circumstances, although a convenience to the Court, is hardly essential. Counsel nevertheless may wish to include such a simple one-sentence item in order to save a little time for the law clerks of the justice writing the opinion.

(a) A brief description of the nature of the case in a short paragraph.

(b) A statement of the factual and legal basis for the appellate court's jurisdiction, also usually in a short paragraph.

(c) The questions presented to the appellate court.

(d) Where appropriate, a reference to the statutory and constitutional provisions and rules involved in the case (hereinafter referred to as Statutes Involved), quoting the key provisions.

(e) In a few jurisdictions, including the United States Supreme Court but not the United States courts of appeals, a summary of argument. A few states require Points and Authorities instead. See Sec. 7.13, *infra*.

(3) Statement of Facts.

(4) Argument.

(5) A short conclusion, usually formal but also stating the relief requested.

A form of appellant's brief appears in the appendix, pp. 523–540, *infra*.

As will appear, the precise order of these items is not the same in all courts. But the substance is very much the same, for the object is to inform the judges at the beginning of what they will want to know before they start digging into the detailed Statement of Facts and Argument. The United States Supreme Court's 1980 rules revision moved the Questions Presented to the beginning of the brief, to be followed by a list of all parties not mentioned in the caption and all affiliated corporations (unless this appears in a previously filed document, as it usually will in the petition for certiorari or brief in opposition thereto). Rules 28.1, 34.1(a), (b). See Sec. 7.14, *infra*. All this comes ahead of the tables of contents and authorities. The problems of pagination which this arrangement presents when the limitations on the length of briefs are taken into account are considered in Sec. 7.6, *supra*. Sometimes the Questions Presented are to be accompanied by the supporting authorities.

The rules almost invariably provide that the brief for appellee should follow the same form except that, after the indexes, every item prior to the Summary of Argument, or Argument, may be omitted if the appellee is satisfied with what the appellant has said on that subject. Of course, an appellee is seldom so satisfied, except perhaps for the introductory statements of the nature of the case, its jurisdictional base and the statutes involved. The Questions Presented may be satisfactory, but he may still wish to rephrase questions he deems loaded in appellant's favor, as questions often are, or even to assert that questions raised by appellant are not actually presented by the record. And an appellee may also raise additional points based upon the record as grounds upon which the case can be decided in his favor.

An appellee also has the option of submitting no Statement of Facts if he is fully satisfied with that presented by his adversary, which almost never happens, or he may limit his statement to correcting any inaccuracy or omission in the appellant's brief. The latter is sufficient in many cases and is probably what most appellate judges prefer, but often appellees find it advisable to submit a full Statement of the Facts in their own briefs.

Reply briefs are restricted to answering the argument in appellee's brief.

7.12　The Cover of the Brief

The principal feature of the cover of an appellate brief is the caption containing the names of the parties. Whether the names should remain in the same order as in the court below or with the appellant's name first has been discussed in Sec. 7.9, *supra.*

Covers should identify the court to which the appeal is being taken above the names of the parties, as shown on the form appearing on the following page. Immediately above or below the name of the appellate court at the top of the cover should appear the number of the case.[47] The Second Circuit requires that the number of the case appear in the right-hand corner in numbers one inch high.[48]

Below or on the side of the caption the cover should indicate the nature of the proceeding in the appellate court and identify the court from which the appeal is being taken, such as "On Appeal from the Court of Appeals for the Third Circuit," or "Petition for Review of Judgment of the Appellate Court for

---

[47]The number will generally be known to the parties before the first brief on the merits is filed. If it is not, the clerk will stamp the number on the file copies and inform appellant's counsel, who should then advise counsel for the other parties to the case.
[48]E.g., Second Circuit Rule 32.

No. 77–571

APPELLATE COURT OF ILLINOIS
SECOND JUDICIAL DISTRICT

BRUNSWICK CORPORATION,	)
	) On Appeal from the
Plaintiff-Appellant,	) Circuit Court of the 19th
	) Judicial Circuit,
	) Lake County, Illinois
vs.	)
	) Honorable
OUTBOARD MARINE CORPORATION	) Harry D. Strouse, Jr.,
	) Judge Presiding
and RONALD R. ANDERSON,	)
	) [As an alternative, this may
	) appear as indicated
Defendants-Appellees.	) immediately below]

On Appeal from the Circuit Court of the
19th Judicial Circuit,
Lake County, Illinois

Honorable Harry D. Strouse, Jr.,
Judge Presiding

BRIEF FOR PLAINTIFF-APPELLANT

ERWIN C. HEININGER
WILLIAM THOMAS BRAITHWAITE
231 South LaSalle Street
Chicago, Illinois 60604
(312) 782-0600
Attorneys for Plaintiff-Appellant

Of Counsel:
MAYER, BROWN & PLATT
231 South LaSalle Street
Chicago, Illinois 60604
(312) 782-0600

May 11, 1979

the First District." A number of courts also require that the name of the trial judge be stated.[49] The brief should then be identified as "Brief for Appellant" or "Plaintiff-Appellant" or "Appellee" or "Respondent," whichever it may be.

Below this come the names and addresses of counsel representing the party or parties for whom the brief is filed. Telephone numbers should also be added, whether or not required by the rules, in order to facilitate immediate communication from the clerk of the court.[50] At least the first lawyer named should be a member of the bar of the appellate court or the state. The names of other counsel who contributed to the brief may be added[51] whether or not they are members of the bar. A few states require that appellant's cover contain the names and addresses of counsel for *all* parties.[52] Firm names may also be added if desired, though that is not necessary. Clerks' offices have, however, found the firm names sometimes useful when they are attempting to communicate with counsel; this in itself is reason for including them.

The New York Court of Appeals (Rule 500.6) and Third Department Rule 800.8(a) require that the identity of the lawyer who will argue and the time requested appear on the cover. Several of the New York Appellate Divisions specify that such information be placed in the upper right-hand corner. First Department Rule 600.10(d)(1)(ii); Second Department Rule 670.1(g); Fourth Department Rule 1000.6(a)(2).

In a number of jurisdictions, counsel for either party should state on the cover "ORAL ARGUMENT REQUESTED," if it is; or, in Michigan, "ORAL ARGUMENT NOT REQUESTED,"[53] if it isn't.

I also have found it helpful to add the date at the bottom of the cover. This often comes in handy in the future when it is helpful to know just when a brief was filed. A date-stamped copy of the brief and any related papers filed should always be obtained from the clerk, not only for record purposes but for any dispute that might arise as to timeliness of filing or priority of filing when parties may file in different appellate courts.

---

[49]E.g., Illinois, Louisiana, Minnesota, New Jersey, South Dakota.

[50]Telephone numbers are required by the rules of the United States Supreme Court, Indiana, Louisiana, Massachusetts and Oregon.

[51]Except in Kansas, where the name of only one lawyer, plus his firm, is to appear on the cover; the names of other counsel may be added at the conclusion of the brief.

[52]E.g., Idaho, Minnesota, South Dakota.

[53]E.g., Alabama, New York Appellate Divisions of the First and Second Departments, Michigan, Illinois.

When cross-appeals or related appeals are being heard together, the cover should bear the appellate case numbers and the captions of all of the appeals. E.g., Seventh Circuit Rule 9(f)(2). This is the usual practice whether or not embodied in a rule.

The covers of the various briefs should bear different colors, whether or not the rules so require, as many now do though some do not. The rules applicable to the United States courts of appeals and many state courts specify the colors, as does United States Supreme Court Rule 33.2(b) as revised in 1980. Under Federal Appellate Rule 32(a) and a number of state rules[54] the appellant's brief is to be blue, the appellee's red, the reply brief gray and the briefs of intervenors or *amici curiae* green; a separate appendix is to be white. The colors prescribed for United States Supreme Court briefs under its 1980 Rule 33.2(b) are the same, except that reply briefs are to be yellow, the joint appendix tan and United States Government briefs gray, as they traditionally have been. Other states prescribe different colors.[55] Such a specification of the colors for the briefs of the various parties makes it much easier for judges, and also lawyers, to find a particular brief.

Even in courts which do not prescribe the colors for covers, each party should select a color not theretofore used on any brief previously filed, so as to make it easier for the judges and lawyers to tell the briefs apart. Adherence to the federal color scheme would be preferable in such circumstances, since appellate lawyers, and judges who have been appellate lawyers, in such states are more likely to be familiar with it than with any other.

7.13 Indexes, and Points and Authorities

In the federal courts of appeals (under Federal Appellate Rule 28(a)(1)) and under many state rules the cover of the brief is to be followed by a Table of Contents and an Index or Table of Authorities, each with page references.[56] The United States Supreme Court requires all briefs exceeding five pages to have a Table of Contents and exceeding three pages to have a Table of Authorities. Rule 33.5.

The Table of Contents contains all the headings in the brief.[57] The Table of Cases contains the cases in alphabetical

---

[54]E.g., Alabama, Iowa, Maine, Oregon, South Carolina, Wisconsin.

[55]California, Illinois, Indiana, Iowa, Kansas, New Jersey, Virginia.

[56]In a few jurisdictions, the cover is to be followed immediately by the statement of the Questions Presented. See Sec. 7.18, *infra.*

[57]In Oregon there should also be a table for the abstract, which is bound with the brief.

order, and separate tables of statutes and other types of material, such as treatises and articles, often under the heading of "miscellaneous," in alphabetical order as far as feasible. Statutes bearing the same name may be indexed in chronological order if that would be more meaningful.[58] The Table of Contents serves two functions: the combination of headings and page numbers enables the reader quickly to find any part of the brief, and the headings in themselves constitute a short summary of the Argument for judges seeking an initial bird's-eye view of the case.

Some states achieve the same result by requiring a statement of Points and Authorities either at the beginning of the brief or at some specified point before the Argument. The "Points" consist of the headings, to each of which must be appended, usually in order of importance, the authorities cited under that heading in the Argument. The Points are identical with the headings in the Table of Contents. The Authorities are the same as those listed in the usual Table of Authorities except that they are arranged by subject rather than alphabetically.[59]

If the page numbers are given for each heading or point and each authority, as the Kentucky rule requires, the Points and Authorities will contain all of the information found in the Table of Contents and the Index of Authorities. When feasible, in their own interest and that of the court, counsel should add the page numbers at least to the Points even when the rules of the particular court do not so require.[60] Kansas, Mississippi, Oklahoma and South Dakota achieve this result by requiring that the Authorities be appended to each Point in the Table of Contents at the beginning of the brief. The rules of other states place the Points and Authorities in the body of the brief, usually between the

---

[58] The Eighth Circuit calls for a one-page addendum to the Table of Contents summarizing the case and giving the reasons why oral argument should be heard and why the requested time should be allowed.

[59] Arkansas Rule 9(c) permits only the two principal authorities to be cited in support of each proposition. Missouri Rule 84.04(d) requires that all the authorities be cited, but not "long lists," which may present a dilemma for an attorney who has cited a substantial number of authorities in support of a particular proposition.

[60] Some states may not make page references mandatory because of the conditions confronting counsel in small communities who must send their briefs to distant cities for duplication. This problem facing lawyers not located in the large cities was the reason that preliminary indexes with page references were not required in Illinois. These lawyers do not see the brief after they send it to the printer, and do not wish to rely on the printer to fill in the page numbers of the index, even though an experienced printer should be able to do this without difficulty. The need for sending the briefs to distant points for duplication may not survive the substitution of other duplicating processes for printing.

Questions Presented and the beginning of the Statement of Facts.[61] Unless both a Table of Contents and Points and Authorities are required, which would be repetitious, the beginning of the brief, where the judges can more readily refer to them, would appear the most suitable place for the Points and Authorities.

Counsel preparing Points and Authorities will often find that cases are cited for different propositions under the same argument heading. When that happens, citing all of the cases standing for different propositions without explanation would be confusing and meaningless. The remedy is to classify the authorities under subheadings where necessary, even though the subhead is not a heading in the text of the brief. For example, the heading

> Defendants' Conduct Was Not Prohibited by the Contract and the Language of the Contract Controls

might be immediately followed by cases directly on the point in the order in which the lawyer would want the court to read them, that is, the strongest first. Cases cited in support of collateral arguments, such as

> An Ambiguous Contract Should Be Construed Against the Party Who Drafted It,

should be listed separately under such a heading. Cases cited by one's opponent upon which one does not rely but only seeks to distinguish should be cited following an explanatory phrase, such as

> Cases Distinguished.

7.14 The Beginning of the Brief—Arrangement of the Preliminary Items

An appellant's brief should begin by telling the judges what they first want to know about a case of which they are totally ignorant. Courts seem to disagree as to how this can be best accomplished. The differences are not major, since they relate to how the same items on the first few pages, usually the first two,

---

[61]E.g., former Illinois Rule 341(e). In December 1980, the Illinois Supreme Court accepted the recommendation of its Rules Committee that the Points and Authorities, with page numbers added, be shifted to the beginning of the brief.

should be arranged. In general, the items to appear at or near the beginning of the brief are a short statement of the Nature of the Case (which in some places, such as Arizona, is confusingly called the Statement of the Case), a statement of the Jurisdictional Facts, the citations to the Opinions Below, the Questions or Issues Presented (which in Vermont are to follow the Statement of Facts) and the Statutes or Regulations Involved.

As a matter of custom, though not required by rule, the caption on the cover (except for the names of counsel) is repeated at the beginning of the text of the brief, either immediately after the cover or after the indexes. This repetition would seem to serve no useful purpose, even though its absence would look uncouth to lawyers and judges accustomed to it. When briefs are limited to a specified number of pages, devoting most of the first page to the caption reduces what can be included in a brief of maximum length. Duplicating the caption also wastes paper, even though not very much, and slightly increases the cost of printing or other reproduction. In the absence of a rule requiring an internal caption—and I know of none—it might well be deleted, though I am aware that most lawyers lack the temerity to be so innovative.

Unusual but not unreasonable additional items or arrangements include:

(1) The names of all the parties not in the caption should be stated at the beginning of the brief in text or footnote. In the United States Supreme Court this is to follow the Questions Presented, presumably in a footnote, but still ahead of the indexes. Rule 34.1(b). See also Texas Rule 418(a).

(2) So that the judges may determine whether to disqualify or to recuse themselves, the United States Courts of Appeals for the District of Columbia and the Fifth and Ninth Circuits require a section on the inside front cover or first page, *before* the Table of Contents, containing the names of all parties and *amici* who have appeared below, including affiliated corporations (District of Columbia Circuit Rule 8(c)),[62] or of all persons

---

[62]District of Columbia Circuit Rule 8(c):

"**(c) Certificate of Counsel.** In all civil and agency cases a certificate shall be furnished by counsel of record for all private (non-governmental) parties, including specifically all appellants (petitioners) and all appellees (respondents), as well as all (including corporations, associations, partnerships, etc.) who "have an interest in the outcome of the case" (Fifth Circuit Rule 13.6.1; Ninth Circuit Rule 13(e)). A separate amendment to United States Supreme Court Rule 28.1, effective November 21, 1980, requires that the first document (except a joint appendix or *amicus* brief) filed on behalf of a corporation shall list, permissibly in a footnote, all affiliated corporations except wholly owned subsidiaries; reference back to an earlier document is sufficient if the later document, such as a brief, makes the listing "currently accurate." See Sec. 7.11, *supra.* Seventh Circuit Rule 5(b) (1980) requires that the text of the "Certificate of Interest" to be filed with the appearance of counsel or first motion (see Sec. 4.5(d), *supra*) also appear in front of the Table of Contents of each party's main brief. It shall state the name of the party or *amicus* represented, of any parent corporation, and of all law firms which appeared in the district court or are expected to appear in the court of appeals. The certificate may be on a separate page or on the inside of the cover page at the beginning of the brief.

(3) The District of Columbia Circuit, for the purpose of deciding which panel of the court should hear the case, also requires a statement after the "Issues Presented for Review" whether the pending case itself previously has been before any court (Rule 8(b)) and identifying related cases in any court.[63]

---

intervenors and amici, setting forth a complete list of all parties and amici who have appeared below. In cases where a corporation is a party or amicus, the certificate of counsel for that party or amicus shall also list all parent companies, subsidiaries and affiliates of that party or amicus. Such certificate also shall indicate which parties and amici are in support of the appellant (petitioner), which are in support of the appellee (respondent), and which are taking a position apart from those of the appellant (petitioner) and appellee (respondent). This certificate shall be incorporated on the first page of each brief before the table of contents or index. The purpose of this certificate is to enable the Judges of this Court to evaluate possible disqualification or recusal and the time and alignment of parties for oral argument."

Fourth Circuit Rule 17 requires such a disclosure statement to be filed on a special form "at the inception of the case in the Court of Appeals," and Tenth Circuit Rule 8(a) as a part of the docketing statement to be filed within 21 days of the notice of appeal.

[63]District of Columbia Circuit Rule 8(b):

"(b) Contents of Brief. In addition to the requirements of Rule 28, Federal Rules of Appellate Procedure, at the bottom of the statement of issues presented for review, counsel shall indicate whether or not the pending case was previously before this Court or before any other court under the same or similar title and the name and number of such prior case. Counsel shall also indicate any other related cases of which he is aware, either presently pending in this Court or in any other court, or that may be presented

(4) The United States Supreme Court since 1980 requires the brief to begin with the Questions even ahead of the preliminary indexes. Connecticut and South Carolina also place the Questions Presented (not to exceed one page) first. Their rules do not seem to require any Table of Contents or Index of Authorities. Connecticut Practice Book, §3060F (1978); South Carolina Rule 8, §2.

(5) Under New Jersey Rule 2:6-2(c) the brief is to start (after the Table of Contents and Index) with a "concise procedural history" which combines the Jurisdictional Facts and the Nature of the Case. In South Dakota the brief begins (again, after the Table of Contents and Index) with the Jurisdictional Facts.

(6) The Eighth Circuit wants a one-page summary of the case and the reasons for allowing oral argument and the time requested, to follow the Table of Contents.

(7) Wisconsin wants the reasons for oral argument and also why and whether the opinion should be published to appear after the Questions Presented.

(8) The United States Court of Appeals for the District of Columbia Circuit also requires a section preceding the Statement of the Case identifying any party not named in the caption, the judge below, any written or oral opinions, findings, conclusions or rulings of the court below, with citations when available, and page references to the appendix or transcript.[64]

---

to this Court or to any other court in the future. The purpose of this requirement is to enable the Court to determine whether the instant case should be assigned to a particular division of the Court, or to a new division chosen by lot, and to consider what disposition should be made of the case. For the purposes of this Rule: (i) the phrase 'any other court' means any other United States Court of Appeals, or any other court (whether federal or local) in the District of Columbia; and (ii) the phrase 'any other related cases' means cases involving the same parties and the same or similar issues, or involving parties similarly situated and the same or similar issues, as the pending case."

[64]District of Columbia Circuit Rule 8(e):

"**(e) References to Parties and Rulings.** In addition to the requirements of Rule 28, Federal Rules of Appellate Procedure, appellant's brief shall contain a section immediately preceding the statement of the case which shall be headed 'References to Parties and Rulings'. In this section counsel shall make such references as may be feasible identifying any opinion, memorandum, findings and conclusions, or other oral or written ruling in which the court set forth the basis of the order or judgment presented for review by this court. The references shall identify the judge involved and the date of the ruling. The references should also include reporter citations when available, and page references in the appendix of the parties or reporter's transcript.

"If there are any parties to the litigation whose identity is not revealed by the caption on appeal, appellant shall set forth the names of all the parties.

"The foregoing provision shall also apply to petitions for review of rulings and orders of Administrative Agencies."

(9) Pennsylvania Rule 2115, as revised in 1979, calls for the verbatim text of the order or other determination appealed from between the Statement of Jurisdiction and the statement of Questions Involved.

There is good reason for an appellate court to want to be informed as to each of these matters at the beginning of the appellant's brief. Obviously all cannot come first, and the precise order is not of great consequence so long as the court and counsel know what it is. Examples of the arrangements specified in three sets of rules are as follows:

Illinois (typical of many states)	*Federal Rules of Appellate Procedure*	*United States Supreme Court*
Nature of the Proceeding	Tables of Contents and Authorities	Questions Presented
Issues Presented	Issues Presented	Names of Parties
Jurisdictional Facts (for appeals to the Supreme Court)	Nature of the Case and the course of proceedings, at the beginning of statement of facts	Tables of Contents and Authorities Citations of Opinions Below
If necessary, Statutes, etc., Involved	Statutes, etc., Involved (at appropriate place, or end of brief (Rule 28(f))	Jurisdictional Facts and Grounds
Points and Authorities (Here or at beginning of brief. See note 61, *supra.*)		Statutes, etc., Involved

"Despite the sequence literally called for by F.R.A.P. 28(a)," the Court of Appeals for the Seventh Circuit sensibly "prefers that the brief introductory statement of the nature of the case, the course of proceedings, and the disposition in the court below appear before, rather than after, the statement of issues presented for review."[65] Next should come the Jurisdictional Statement of "information relevant to jurisdiction." (Under Seventh Circuit Rule 9(b) this precedes the Statement of the Facts.) This should be followed by the Questions Presented. The Questions Presented will then appear in a more meaningful context. "The reference to the statutes and regulations involved, with quotations of the significant items if they are not too long, should appear immediately after the statement of issues, before the beginning of the statement of facts."[66] This arrangement of the principal preliminary sections, which corresponds closely to that called for by the Illinois and federal rules as well as those of other states, would seem to list the items appellate judges would want to read in the order which is most helpful.[67] I suggest that it be followed except to the extent rules otherwise provide.

7.15　The Nature of the Proceeding

"The Nature of the Proceeding," whether it appears as the opening paragraph of the brief (as I recommend) or of the Statement of Facts, should be a short paragraph which indicates broadly the subject of the case and what happened to it below. If it does not appear at the beginning of the brief (as it will not under the rules of the United States Supreme Court), it should come at the beginning of the Statement of Facts.

Illinois Rule 341(e) contains an appropriate illustration:

> "This action was brought to recover damages occasioned by the alleged negligence of the defendant in driving his automobile. The jury rendered a verdict for the plaintiff upon which the court entered the judgment from which this appeal is taken. No questions are raised on the pleadings."

Another illustration might be:

> "This is a private antitrust suit for damages and injunctive relief in which the defendants are charged with conspiring to fix prices.

---

[65]PRACTITIONER's HANDBOOK FOR APPEALS TO THE UNITED STATES COURT OF APPEALS FOR THE SEVENTH CIRCUIT, p. 30 (1979 ed.).

[66]*Ibid.*

[67]A brief recital of where the opinions and rulings below can be found, either in the reports or the record, the reference to related proceedings in the same and other courts, and identification of the parties for recusal purposes, if such information is deemed important, can be inserted between the introductory statement and the Questions Presented.

After trial the trial judge sitting without a jury entered judgment for defendants and plaintiff appeals."

This is all that is necessary in the ordinary appeal. If the appeal is from an interlocutory order, or an order of an intermediate appellate court from which leave to appeal must be obtained, those facts should also be added as, for example:

> "The trial court denied defendants' motion for a summary judgment, but certified the questions set forth in the Questions Presented as appropriate for review under Sec. 1292(b), and this Court granted leave to appeal."

If in the same proceeding there was a subsequent petition for certiorari or leave to appeal to a supreme court, the following could be substituted for the last clause:

> "The Court of Appeals granted leave to appeal, and reversed the order of the trial court. Defendants' petition for certiorari [or leave to appeal] to this court was granted on October 26, 1979."

7.16 Jurisdictional Statement

Some rules do and some do not require a statement of the basis for the appellate court's jurisdiction, which, in some states, like South Dakota, comes at the beginning of the brief. Even when the appeal is taken as a matter of right to the appellate court from a final judgment, and there is nothing else to be said as to the court's jurisdiction over the subject matter of the case, a statement of the date of the judgment below, of any petition for rehearing, of the order denying or otherwise disposing of the rehearing, and of the notice of appeal will show whether or not the appeal is timely. All that need be said is:

> "This is an appeal from a final judgment of the Circuit Court entered on March 11, 1979. The notice of appeal was filed on March 30, 1979."

If a petition for rehearing was filed, insert:

> "A timely petition for rehearing was filed on March 25, 1979, and denied on April 17, 1979."

Or

> "Rehearing was granted on May 1, 1979, and the judgment on rehearing entered on May 14, 1979."

And, if appropriate:

> "On May 26, 1979, Mr. Justice Jones granted appellant an extension of time to file his notice of appeal to June 24, 1979."

Some types of appeals must satisfy other requirements. Interlocutory and some other orders may be appealable only if they meet certain conditions or if leave of the trial court is first obtained. See Chapter 3, *supra*. Direct appeals or appeals as of right to a supreme court in a two-tiered appellate system are allowable only in specified circumstances. See Chapter 5, *supra*. The appellate court should want to know at the beginning that these jurisdictional requisites are satisfied, and how.

Rule 34.1(e) of the United States Supreme Court requires:

> "A concise statement of the grounds on which the jurisdiction of this Court is invoked, with citation to the statutory provision and to the time factors upon which such jurisdiction rests."

Thus, an appeal from a district court judgment holding a federal statute unconstitutional should state, after the jurisdictional dates:

> "Since the judgment below held a federal statute [naming and citing it] unconstitutional, direct appeal to this court lies under 28 U.S.C. §1252."

(This statement as to jurisdiction is not to be confused with the misnamed Jurisdictional Statement which must be filed in appeals to the United States Supreme Court, but is in substance the equivalent of a petition for certiorari.)[68]

Where there has been an application for discretionary review or certiorari, a short paragraph containing the jurisdictional dates and adding the following is sufficient:

> "The jurisdiction of this court is invoked under 28 U.S.C. §1254(1). Leave to appeal [or certiorari] was granted on January 2, 1979."

The rules applicable to the federal courts of appeals do not contain any requirement as to stating jurisdictional facts. Seventh Circuit Rule 9(b) fills this void as follows:

> "Jurisdictional Summary. The brief of the appellant or petitioner will include, under an appropriate heading, a jurisdictional summary, which will appear before the statement of the case and shall

---

[68] See R. Stern and E. Gressman, SUPREME COURT PRACTICE, Secs. 7.9–7.10 (5th ed., 1978).

include an explanation of the statutory basis for this court's jurisdiction, as well as other information relevant to jurisdiction, such
as whether there has been a certification pursuant to Federal Rule
of Civil Procedure 54(b) or 28 U.S.C. §1292(b)."

In the normal case all that is required under this provision is a
statement of the jurisdictional dates such as is set forth above,
plus:

> "This is an appeal under 28 U.S.C. §1291 from the final judgment
> of the district court."

Missouri Rule 84.04(b), however, requires a statement of "sufficient factual data to demonstrate the applicability of the particular provision" of the constitution.

Even when its rules do not require, or even mention, a
reference to the jurisdictional facts, an appellate court will be
aided by such a brief preliminary statement. This will enable it
to determine at a glance whether it has jurisdiction or whether
there is a jurisdictional problem. A short statement of the crucial
dates and of other facts pertaining to possible jurisdictional
problems following the statement of the nature of the case will
impose no burden on counsel, nor unduly delay judges who are
impatient to get to the Questions Presented. Accordingly, the
rules of court should require the inclusion of such a statement
with respect to jurisdictional facts at the commencement of a
brief, and the lawyer should include such a statement whether
or not the rules so require.

7.17 Statutes Involved

Many rules require, as in the language of Illinois Rule
341(e)(4) (which is very similar to United States Supreme Court
Rule 34.1(f)),

> "[i]n a case involving the construction or validity of a statute,
> constitutional provision, treaty, ordinance, or regulation, the per-
> tinent parts of the provision verbatim, with a citation of the place
> where it may be found, all under an appropriate heading, such as
> 'Statutes Involved.' If the provision involved is lengthy, its citation
> alone will suffice at this point, and its pertinent text shall be set
> forth in an appendix."

This portion of the brief is customarily referred to as "Statutes Involved," even though, of course, this heading should be
modified so as to describe accurately the matter included.

This section of the brief customarily follows the statement

of the Questions Presented, since it can best be understood in that context, and the Statement of Facts and Argument can best be understood with knowledge not only of the Questions Presented but also of the precise language of the controlling statutes or rules.

The Federal Rules of Appellate Procedure do not state where this section of the brief should appear, but they do contain a similar provision in Rule 28(f) which states:

> "If determination of the issues presented requires the study of statutes, rules, regulations, etc. or relevant parts thereof, they shall be reproduced in the brief or in an addendum at the end, or they may be supplied to the court in pamphlet form."

Whether or not rules require inclusion of such a separate section in the brief, appellate judges will need to have the exact language of such legislative material conveniently at hand while they are studying the brief, which means that it should be contained in a portion of the brief which a judge can readily find. Accordingly, whether rules so require or not, such a section should be included in the brief, preferably between the Questions Presented and the Statement of Facts, whenever the case calls for the examination of such material.

The same principle applies when the case turns upon the precise language of other types of documents such as contracts, wills or corporate charters. They should similarly be set forth in the preliminary section of the brief or, if they are too long for that, in an appendix or addendum attached to the brief. How long is *too* long for inclusion in the main body of the brief is a matter upon which the lawyer must use his own judgment. Probably if the text to be quoted is over two or three pages, it should be left to an appendix. When that is done, the section in the body of the brief should give the name and citation of the pertinent statute or regulation and state that the text is printed in the appendix.

It may be unnecessary to include in such a section of the brief the text of such familiar provisions as the Commerce, Due Process and Equal Protection clauses of the United States Constitution, the first sentence of the Sherman Act prohibiting restraints of trade, or other legislative language certain to be known to the reviewing judges. But counsel should err in favor of including text verbatim if he has any doubt as to what falls in that category.

7.18 Statement of the Questions Presented

Judges are aided in reading a brief and understanding a case by a short recital at the beginning of the questions which they are called upon to decide. They can then better appreciate the significance of the material in the Statement of Facts and the Argument. Accordingly, in most jurisdictions, after the opening description of the nature of the case but before the Statement of Facts, the appellant's brief must contain a section listing the questions to be presented on appeal. A few jurisdictions,[69] including the United States Supreme Court in its 1980 Rule 34.1(a), require the questions to be stated at the very beginning of the brief. Some rules indicate that this section should not be more than one or two pages in length,[70] and they seldom exceed the latter limitation.

In a few states no such section is required, in the belief that the Table of Contents or the Points and Authorities, both of which copy the headings of the points in the argument, serve the same function of identifying the issues raised on the appeal, which is largely true. Headings, however, should not focus on stating the questions but on indicating the subject of the following portion of the argument. They may not clearly state the questions which the court is called upon to decide. Furthermore, a number of headings may refer to arguments relating to the same point. A brief raising only a single question which can be stated in one sentence may have pages of headings.

In a few jurisdictions[71] each question must be followed by the authorities which relate to it. In other jurisdictions each question is to be followed by a statement of how the court below

---

[69]Connecticut, New York, Ohio, South Carolina, Washington.

[70]Florida, Mississippi, Nebraska, New Jersey, New York, Oregon (optional), South Carolina. Pennsylvania Rule 2116 states that questions should "not ordinarily exceed fifteen lines, must never exceed one page, and must always be on a separate page," which shall include the answer to each question by the court below. The rule continues: "This rule is to be considered in the highest degree mandatory admitting of no exception." Such an arbitrary rule must often impair the presentation of intelligible questions by intelligent lawyers.

[71]Eighth Circuit Rule 12(d); Iowa Rule 14(a)(3). The Iowa rule adds: "Failure in the brief to state, to argue or to cite authority in support of an issue may be deemed waiver of that issue." Read literally, this would seem to preclude argument of novel questions for which counsel must rely on reasons and principles, not authority. Missouri Rule 84.04(d) requires the points relied on to "state briefly and concisely what actions or rulings of the court are sought to be reviewed" and "why they are claimed to be erroneous," citing "all authorities discussed in the argument" but not including "long lists of citations." There might be some difficulty in reconciling the last two requirements.

answered it.[72] This may be helpful to the judges, although in most instances the question itself and the prior statement of the nature of the case will suggest the answer.

A few states still adhere to the older practice of requiring an assignment or specification of errors; this often resulted in the listing of every possible error which the trial judge could have committed during the course of the trial. Some of these states require both a Specification of Errors and a statement of the Questions Presented;[73] others merely require the former.[74] Georgia requires the separate filing of an enumeration of errors prior to the brief, and again with the brief.[75]

If the errors specified, assigned or enumerated are the questions actually presented to the appellate court, without repetition of the same point in various ways, the difference between them and a statement of the questions presented may be only a matter of form. Each item will begin with "the court below erred in holding that," instead of "whether." Thus, "the court below erred in holding that the Sunday law violates the Equal Protection clause" could also be stated, under the heading Questions Presented, as "whether the Sunday law violates the Equal Protection clause."

To the extent that the errors to be specified or assigned go beyond the issues to be raised in the appeal or restate substantially the same question in a variety of ways, as was formerly customary, they serve no purpose useful to the appellate court. They are not needed to show that appellant brought the point to the attention of the lower court. That is a common but separate requirement which appellant must satisfy, but which is better explained in the Statement of Facts or in the Argument portion of the brief.

The Questions or Issues Presented which most court rules now require thus more accurately describe what the appellate courts want to know at the beginning of appellant's brief, and

---

[72]Michigan, Minnesota, New York, Pennsylvania, South Dakota, West Virginia. Michigan also requires appellant to state how he would answer each question.

[73]Alaska, Hawaii, Indiana, Louisiana, Ohio, Rhode Island, Washington, West Virginia. Mississippi requires the filing as separate documents of assignments of error no later than the due date of appellant's brief (Rule 6), and also, along with the brief, "a brief statement not exceeding two pages, setting forth the nature and purpose of the case, the action of the trial court thereon and the points raised on appeal" (Rule 7(f)).

[74]Nebraska, Virginia.

[75]Failure to file the enumeration is contempt of court. Georgia Code, §§24-3614(a), 3618(a)(2), 4514(a), 4518(a)(2).

there is no need for a statement of both the questions and the errors committed below.

Most rules do not elaborate on what is required beyond calling for "a statement of the issues presented for review." See, for example, Federal Rule of Appellate Procedure 28(a)(2); Illinois Rule 341(e)(2). The rules of the United States Supreme Court, however, describe what is wanted in more detail. The rules governing petitions for certiorari, jurisdictional statements and briefs on the merits (Rules 21.1(a), 15.1(a), 34.1(a)) all define what is wanted as

> "[t]he questions presented for review, expressed in the terms and circumstances of the case but without unnecessary detail. The statement of the questions should be short and concise and should not be argumentative or repetitious. The statement of a question presented will be deemed to comprise every subsidiary question fairly included therein."

For petitions for certiorari and jurisdictional statements, Rules 15.1(a) and 21.1(a) add:

> "Only the questions set forth in the petition [or statement] or fairly included therein will be considered by the Court."

Rule 34.1(a), governing briefs on the merits, adds:

> "The phrasing of the questions presented need not be identical with that set forth in the jurisdictional statement or the petition for certiorari, but the brief may not raise additional questions or change the substance of the questions already presented in those documents. At its option, however, the Court may consider a plain error not among the questions presented but evident from the record and otherwise within its jurisdiction to decide."

The one major exception to these restrictions of a brief to points previously raised by appellant is that a brief on the merits may also include in the Questions Presented, as well as in the Argument, additional points which one knows that the opposing party will argue, with or without a cross-appeal. Often it will be better for appellant to meet such points in his opening brief than to reserve them for a reply brief. See Sec. 7.22(c), p. 288, *infra.*

The more detailed Supreme Court rules on this subject are valuable not because they emanate from the highest court in the land or because they are binding on other courts (which they are not) but because they may be the best explanation of the way all appellate courts, and particularly courts of last resort, want the

Questions Presented to be prepared.[76] The first sentence in Rules 15.1(a) and 21.1(a) is the key as to how Questions Presented should be written. The phrase "expressed in the terms and circumstances of the case" is not, of course, very specific, but it shows roughly what is desired. Thus, "Whether Sec. 495 of the Pennsylvania Code violates the Equal Protection clause" is not very helpful. Changing the question to "Whether Sec. 495 of the Pennsylvania Code, which prohibits automobile dealerships from staying open on Sunday, violates the Equal Protection clauses of the Pennsylvania and United States constitutions" is considerably better. If "but no other retail merchants" is inserted after "automobile dealerships," the real point of the case appears. The last version expresses the question "in the terms and circumstances of the case."

The circumstances may be legal, as in the above example, or factual. It is neither adequate nor helpful to the court or to one's client to state the question as

> "Whether plaintiff's complaint is barred by laches."

It would be much better to say

> "Whether a complaint filed 11 years after suit could have been brought is barred by laches."

The question would get even closer to disclosing the real issue if it included the additional circumstance after the word "brought":

> "long after defendant has expended for other purposes the capital available to perform the contract."

The phrase "without unnecessary detail" means that a question should not be long or complicated. Obviously, all the significant facts in a case need not, cannot and should not be mentioned in a statement of the issues, but only those which are most essential or critical.[77] What is critical may depend upon one's position in the case. The question "Whether requiring children of different races to attend different schools

---

[76]See also F. Cooper, *Stating the Issue in Appellate Briefs*, 49 A.B.A.J. 180 (1963).

[77]The tests suggested by Professor Cooper include stating the issue in terms of the facts of the case and eliminating unnecessary details, which point in opposite directions. *Id.* at 181–183. Obviously judgment must be exercised as to when facts become too detailed. Cooper also insists that the question "must be readily comprehensible on first reading," and "be so drafted that the opposing party will accept it as accurate." These are goals which should be kept in mind even though they may not always be fully attainable.

violates the Equal Protection clause of the Fourteenth Amendment" can be embellished by inserting "which do not give a minority race equal facilities," or "which provide the minority race with facilities equal in all respects." Which, if either, of the above clauses should be added should depend on what the record establishes, and perhaps also on which side of the case the brief writer is on.

Often, no matter how you try to frame the question, the significant "terms and circumstances" are too complex to be covered in an intelligible one-sentence question. The proper technique, then, is to precede the question with a short introductory paragraph stating facts or circumstances which will give meaning to the question or questions which follow.

For example, the laches question could have more effectively been presented as follows:

> "In 1960 defendant refused to perform a contract with plaintiff. In the following years, no claim having been made by plaintiff, defendant used the capital originally available to perform the contract with plaintiff for other purposes. The closest statute of limitations is six years. Plaintiff brought suit for specific performance in 1971.
>
> "The question is whether in such circumstances plaintiff's complaint is barred by laches."

To attempt to combine the above terms and circumstances with a question in a single sentence would not only violate the principles of good English but end up by being very awkward and confusing.

Questions Presented should not be so general as to be meaningless. Questions such as "whether the court below erred in dismissing the complaint" or "in entering judgment for defendant" have not been unknown. "Whether defendant is entitled to due process of law" is not much better.[78] The answer is obvious, but the court knows no more about the real question in the case than it did before.[79]

The cardinal sin is to overload the brief with questions, many of which frequently constitute different ways of framing the same issue. This was more common in the past, when law-

---

[78]Cf. *Seaboard Air Line R. Co.* v. *Watson*, 287 U.S. 86, 91 (1932).

[79]In urging that a question should not state a "self-evident proposition," Cooper illustrates the point with a question stricken from the final draft of an actual brief: "Did the lower court err in declining to follow and apply the rule established by the Supreme Court decisions?" F. Cooper, *Stating the Issue in Appellate Briefs*, 49 A.B.A.J. 180, 183 (1963).

yers who were used to the technicalities of common law pleading and motions thought, perhaps correctly, that the appellate courts would treat Questions Presented in the same way. Apart from that, appellant's counsel must be selective. He must concentrate on the significant issues on which he believes he may be successful. The appellate courts view with disfavor the statement of many questions, in part because they are disinclined to believe that the lower court will have erred on practically everything, even though that occasionally may happen. Most cases present only one, two or three significant questions, although, of course, there are complex cases of such magnitude that this generalization, like all others, cannot be followed. Indeed, some cases may present multiple claims, each one of which may present more than one issue or question. Usually, however, if you cannot win on a few major points, the others are not likely to help, and to attempt to deal with a great many in the limited number of pages allowed for briefs will mean that none may receive adequate attention. The effect of adding weak arguments will be to dilute the force of the stronger ones. The difficult problem of selecting which points should be argued is considered in Sec. 7.22, *infra*.

The second part of United States Supreme Court Rule 21.1(a) provides at least a partial answer to this problem. It declares that the statement of a question "will be deemed to comprise every subsidiary question fairly included therein." This means that the various reasons or theories or facts embodied in an overall question need not be dealt with in separate questions. *Vance* v. *Terrazas*, 444 U.S. 252, 258, n. 5 (1980). Thus, a question such as "whether the court below correctly interpreted prior decisions of the state supreme court" is subsidiary to the issue to which those cases relate, and should not be stated as a separate question apart from the statement of that issue.

The questions must, of course, be stated fairly. But this does not preclude counsel from remembering that he is an advocate for one party. One fair statement of a question may induce a judge to be favorably inclined in one direction, while a different fair statement may produce the opposite reaction.[80] Thus, in the Sunday law example given above, the question may be stated as either,

---

[80]F. Wiener, BRIEFING AND ARGUING FEDERAL APPEALS, pp. 72–81 (1967).

"Is the state Sunday law [citing it] in violation of the Constitution"
or "of the Equal Protection clause of the Constitution?"

or

"Is the state Sunday law, which prohibits only automobile dealers
from opening on Sunday, in violation of the Equal Protection
clause?"

The reader's first reaction to these two questions is probably a
strong "no" to the first, but "not so sure" or even "yes" to the
second. Arguably the first version does not reveal all the circumstances of the case, but it is not inaccurate or misleading.

In the case in which the Supreme Court overruled prior
authority to hold that the insurance industry was in interstate
commerce and regulable under the Sherman Act, *United States
v. South-Eastern Underwriters Association,* 322 U.S. 533 (1944), the
Questions Presented in the appellant's brief were

"(1) Whether the fire insurance business is in commerce.
"(2) Whether the fire insurance business is subject to the constitutional power of Congress to regulate commerce among the
several states.
"(3) Whether, if so, the Sherman Act is violated by an agreement
among fire insurance companies to fix prices and monopolize
trade through boycotts directed at other companies."[81]

That each of these questions ought to be answered "yes" would
seem obvious from the questions. The appellee's brief, however, restricted itself to the one question on which it had a
chance to win, as follows:

"Whether fire insurance in and of itself is interstate commerce
within the meaning of the Sherman Antitrust Act."

This was also a fair and accurate statement of the question. An
equally fair and accurate question would have been:

"Whether the Sherman Act should be construed to punish crimi-
nally the conduct of insurance companies when for almost a century under this Court's decisions, including half a century under
the Sherman Act, the word 'commerce' had consistently been
construed by this Court as not to include the insurance business."

This version would also have been accurate. It would have had
the advantage, to appellee at least, of suggesting that to read
new constitutional principles into the application of the Sherman Act in a criminal case would be grossly unfair to the defen-

---

[81]Question No. 3 has been somewhat abbreviated.

dants, as the three dissenting justices, who had shown themselves otherwise to be strong advocates of a broad interpretation of the Commerce Clause, found themselves impelled to declare.[82]

In short, a question should, if possible, be "subtly persuasive" but not openly argumentative, and certainly not slanted or twisted so as to be vulnerable to challenge by opposing counsel.[83]

7.19 Restrictive Effect of the Statement of Questions Presented

The appellant's Questions Presented have a significance beyond enabling the appellate justices to get a quick preliminary view of the case before them. In various contexts, the issues listed under that heading limit the arguments which will be considered by the appellate court not only in the appeal to which the brief is directed but thereafter.

The general principle is that only points listed in the portion of the brief entitled Issues or Questions Presented are before the appellate court. Other points are deemed waived. Pennsylvania goes further and provides that it will be assumed that appellee is satisfied with appellant's statement of the questions, unless appellee challenges them. Pennsylvania Rule of Appellate Procedure 2112.

This may not present a serious problem in relation to arguments made in the same brief. A lawyer is unlikely to omit from the preliminary statement of the questions points he argues subsequently in the brief. Often, the Questions Presented section is prepared after and based upon the legal argument. But even if it is prepared beforehand, counsel will normally make sure before the brief is completed that none of the arguments actually made under the heading Argument has been omitted from the Questions Presented.

Moreover, a lapse in this respect would on its face be inadvertent, since counsel could not rationally have intended not to present an argument which he does present later on in the same brief. Since no one would have been misled or prejudiced when the argument is actually made in the brief, an appellate court

---

[82]See the opinions of Chief Justice Stone and Justices Frankfurter and Jackson, 322 U.S. at 562, 583, 595.
[83]F. Cooper, *Stating the Issue in Appellate Briefs*, 49 A.B.A.J. 180, 183 (1963).

might well be willing (outside of Georgia, as to which see Sec. 7.18, n. 75, *supra*) to consider questions thus presented even if not contained in the enumerated questions.

The consequences are drastic, however, with respect to the right to raise in a subsequent stage of the case points omitted from prior statements of Questions Presented.

A supreme court will normally refuse to consider questions not raised in the lower appellate court,[84] and it is likely to look first to the Questions Presented in the brief below to find out what issues were there raised.

A higher court is even less likely to decide questions not contained in the Questions Presented in a petition for review or certiorari. With respect to the argument of additional questions in the United States Supreme Court, Mr. Justice Jackson declared in *Irvine* v. *California*, 347 U.S. 128, 129 (1954):

> "We disapprove of the practice of smuggling additional questions into a case after we grant certiorari. The issues here are fixed by the petition unless we limit the grant."[85]

The proper procedure for adding new questions to those stated in a petition is to move to amend the petition.[86] *Costello* v. *United States*, 365 U.S. 265, 284 (1961).

The United States Supreme Court has often recognized exceptions to the above general principles. Jurisdictional issues may be considered whether or not raised by counsel.[87] *United States* v. *Storer Broadcasting Co.*, 351 U.S. 192, 197 (1956); *Gutierrez* v. *Waterman S.S. Corp.*, 373 U.S. 206, 209 (1963). A point actually decided in the lower appellate court may be raised in a supreme court, even if it was not presented in the petitioner's brief below. *Adickes* v. *Kress & Co.*, 398 U.S. 144, 147, n. 2 (1970). When a party was not represented by counsel below, the court will consider questions raised for the first time by appointed counsel. *Pollard* v. *United States*, 352 U.S. 354, 359 (1957).

Appellate courts unpredictably notice "plain error" whether or not raised or even mentioned by counsel, in "appropriate circumstances." *United States* v. *Terrazas*, 444 U.S. 252,

---

[84]E.g., *Youakim* v. *Miller*, 425 U.S. 231, 234 (1976); *California* v. *Taylor*, 353 U.S. 553, 557, n. 2 (1957); *United States* v. *Ortiz*, 422 U.S. 891, 898 (1975).
[85]See also *Dorszynski* v. *United States*, 418 U.S. 424, 431, n. (1974), and cases there cited.
[86]Whether a petition to amend may be filed in the United States Supreme Court after expiration of the time to petition is not certain. R. Stern and E. Gressman, SUPREME COURT PRACTICE, Sec. 6.28 (5th ed., 1978).
[87]*Id.* at 459.

258, n. 5 (1980); *Vachon* v. *New Hampshire,* 414 U.S. 478, 479 (1974); *Cuyler* v. *Sullivan,* 446 U.S. 335 (1980); *United States* v. *Mendenhall,* 446 U.S. 544 (1980). As has been noted, United States Supreme Court Rule 34.1(a) provides that at its option the Court may do so, as it has long been doing, when the unpresented question is "evident from the record and otherwise within its jurisdiction to decide." Courts sometime reach and decide unraised statutory questions because they prefer not to decide the constitutional question which counsel did present. *Fry* v. *United States,* 421 U.S. 542, 545, n. 5 (1975).[88]

On occasion, when the parties did not raise a question because they could not foresee that the Supreme Court was ready and willing to overrule its own prior decisions, which the parties not unreasonably regarded as authoritative, the Court went ahead and decided the question on its own initiative. *Erie R.R.* v. *Tompkins,* 304 U.S. 64 (1938), is perhaps the best known example. See also *Blonder-Tongue Laboratories, Inc.* v. *University of Illinois Foundation,* 402 U.S. 313, 319–321 (1971); *Moragne* v. *States Marine Lines,* 398 U.S. 375, 378–380, n. 1 (1970).

A court's power to depart from the general principle that only the Questions Presented will be considered does not mean that a party can count on this occurring in his case. The wise lawyer will attempt to be sure that questions he may wish to present to any appellate court are raised in all his briefs and petitions for review.

Although in the usual situation an appellant's brief on the merits may not present questions not raised in a petition for review, this does not bar counsel from rephrasing, rearranging, clarifying or otherwise attempting to improve his earlier presentation of a point. And, as previously indicated, an appellant's brief on the merits may add questions raised by other parties in their briefs or memoranda submitted in opposition to the petition for review.

7.20   The Statement of Facts

The Statement of Facts should not be regarded as one of the preliminary portions of a brief, to be prepared somewhat cursorily before the writer gets to the legal argument. The facts

---

[88]*Id.* at 459.

usually determine who will win the case, except in the relatively few cases which turn on bare questions of law. In the words of Mr. Justice Jackson:

"The purpose of a hearing is that the Court may learn what it does not know, and it knows least about the facts. It may sound paradoxical, but most contentions of law are won or lost on the facts. The facts often incline a judge to one side or the other. A large part of the time of conference is given to discussion of facts, to determine under what rule of law they fall."[89]

Chief Judge Kaufman of the United States Court of Appeals for the Second Circuit has sounded the same note:

"Let the narrative of facts tell a compelling story. The facts are, almost without exception, the heart of the case on appeal . . . . The facts generate the force that impels the judge's will in your direction."[90]

Louisiana Supreme Court Justice Albert Tate, Jr., has recently elaborated on the same theme:

"The statement of the facts is regarded by many advocates and judges as the most important part of the brief. In the first place, regardless of how much the judge knows about the legal issues beforehand, he does not know the facts until he reads this statement. Second, law and legal principles are designed to produce fair and socially useful results when applied to *facts*. This fundamental aim of law lurks always in the mind of the judge. If the application of the given legal principle produces a result deemed unfair by the judge, he will wish to study carefully whether indeed the given principle was truly intended to apply to the particular facts before him.

"This initial statement of facts should not be confused with any argument about the facts to be advanced in the subsequent section of the brief. By this initial statement, counsel attempts to state accurately and with reasonable fairness the material facts, without failing to disclose those which are contested. The attempt is to summarize, without too much unnecessary detail, only those facts that are most cogent and persuasive, without omitting unfavorable circumstances, so that the court may understand the basic factual background of the legal issues. Accurate reference to the transcript or appendix should be provided to allow the court immediately to verify counsel's facts as stated. Counsel's selec-

[89]Mr. Justice Robert H. Jackson, *Advocacy Before the Supreme Court: Suggestions for Effective Case Presentations,* 37 A.B.A.J. 801, 803 (1951).
[90]Quoted from Justice Albert Tate, Jr., *The Art of Brief Writing: What a Judge Wants to Read,* LITIGATION, Vol. 4, No. 2, p. 14 (American Bar Association Section of Litigation, 1978).

tion, arrangement, and emphasis of these facts, if without sacrifice of accuracy, may readily suggest to the court how the legal issues presented should be decided."[91]

There is general agreement as to what Statements of Facts should contain. If the nature of the proceeding, and the procedural history of the case, has not been set forth at the beginning of the brief, as preferably it should be (but see Secs. 7.14–7.15, *supra*), it should appear at the beginning of the Statement of Facts.

Apart from that, the Statement should, in the words of Illinois Rule 341(e)(6), "contain the facts necessary to an understanding of the case, stated accurately and fairly without argument or comment, and with appropriate reference to the pages of the record on appeal," or of any appendix or other duplication of pertinent portions of the record.

The Federal Rules of Appellate Procedure (Rule 28(a)(3)) similarly call simply for

> "a statement of the facts relevant to the issues presented for review, with appropriate references to the record."

United States Supreme Court Rule 34.1(g) requires "[a] concise statement of the case containing all that is material to the consideration of the questions presented, with appropriate references" to the appendix. The rules in other jurisdictions are to the same effect.

References to the facts are always to be supported by appropriate record references. This should be to the pages of the appendix or abstract or other duplicated version of the pertinent parts of the record which are available to each judge. If the judges only have access to the original record or copies of it, the pages of that record, including the transcript of testimony, should be cited. The customary symbols are R. __ for record, Tr. __ for transcript, C.R. __ for clerk's record if separate from the transcript, and A. __ for appendix or abstract. South Carolina requires reference to the lines of the transcript on each page, and Colorado and New Jersey require that each page of the record and brief be divided into 10-line or folio units (a folio is 100 words), which should be cited.

If necessary, where record page numbers are not available, reference should be to the pages of the part of the record in-

---

[91] *Ibid.*

volved. E.g., Answer, p. 7; Motion for Judgment, p. 2. See Federal Rule of Appellate Procedure 28(e). The same federal rule also provides that

> "If reference is made to evidence the admissibility of which is in controversy, reference shall be made to the pages of the appendix or of the transcript at which the evidence was identified, offered, and received or rejected."

With respect to exhibits, United States Supreme Court Rule 34.5 provides that "the page numbers at which the exhibit appears, at which it was offered in evidence, and at which it was ruled on by the judge must be indicated, *e.g.* (Pl. Ex. 14; R. 199, 2134)." Even when rules do not so provide, such citation techniques will be helpful to all appellate courts.

The facts which should be stated are those which are relevant to the issues being presented in the appeal, not all the facts of the case. The pertinent facts, and no others, should be set forth fairly, accurately and not argumentatively, although—as will appear below—that is not the whole story. Lawyers probably err more on the side of overinclusion than underinclusion.

Usually appellate judges, like other persons unfamiliar with a factual story, can best follow a factual recitation if the thoughts are stated in chronological order. Sometimes, however, a topical arrangement will be easier to understand, particularly in a complex case with a number of separate topics. Thus, in an accident case, a description of what happened, in the order in which it happened, will best state the facts underlying all the issues, although facts as to jurisdiction or damages may well be stated separately from facts as to liability. In a fraud or SEC case, when a number of different representations are in issue, a separate summary of the evidence relating to each may be preferable.

In the few states—Arkansas, Mississippi, Oklahoma and Oregon—which provide for incorporating in the brief an abstract or summary of the pertinent testimony, a witness-by-witness summary of the testimony is acceptable or even required. In Mississippi the abstract may be included in the brief or filed with it. In some of these states this summary is required to be in narrative form, and in Arkansas and Mississippi in the first person. Oregon does not seem to preclude the use of verbatim questions and answers. Oklahoma permits the abstract to be in either narrative or verbatim form; uncontradicted facts may be stated generally without quoting or narrating the testimony.

Connecticut requires that the summary of the evidence in the Statement be in narrative form[92] rather than verbatim, with quotations only where necessary. Thus, in the last three states the Statements of Facts may not differ very much from those prepared elsewhere. The disadvantages and advantages of the narrative abstract, which most state courts as well as the federal courts have abandoned, are considered in Sec. 6.11, *supra.*

Statements of Facts in an appellant's brief should state all the facts which are material to the issues presented, not merely those which support appellant's position. Not only is this essential to providing the appellate judges with all the facts which they must know in order to decide the questions before them. Of equal importance is the effect upon the judges of counsel's failure to mention the facts which are adverse. For when they do discover the omitted facts, as they invariably will either from an opposing brief or from their own inquiries into the record, they are likely to treat them as of greater significance than if the appellant had mentioned them. In addition, they may well lose their confidence in the integrity of appellant's counsel and this is likely to affect their reaction to everything said in the brief. Most often appellee will pounce upon both the omitted facts and the fact of omission with the result that appellant's failure to mention them will emphasize them rather than the contrary. The benefit to appellant of delaying the court's discovery of the adverse facts by perhaps as much as 30 minutes—until it has read the opposing brief—is thus hardly worth the effort. Practical considerations thus strongly confirm the ethical demand for complete candor in the way in which the facts are described to a reviewing court.

For the same reasons counsel should not overstate or exaggerate. Not only is this improper; it will backfire on him. By the same token, do not merely recite facts without indicating that evidence on a material point is in dispute, if it is, although it is perfectly proper to arrange your statement so as to make the evidence supporting your position seem more trustworthy. Thus, if appellant faces up to the unfavorable facts, he can attempt to minimize their importance, to lessen their sting, by the context in which he places them. But even if this is not possible, the material unfavorable facts must be stated.

The Statement will normally conclude with a description of

---

[92]That means a narrative story of the case, not a narrative of the testimony of each witness, such as Arkansas and Mississippi seem to require.

what the lower court or courts decided. Whether the grounds
for the adverse rulings should be set forth in detail at this point
or subsequently in the Argument will depend upon which seems
preferable for the particular brief. Sometimes the reasoning of
the court below is better dealt with in the Argument where the
appellant can appropriately point out what he believes to be its
defects.

There is more to the effective preparation of a Statement
of Facts than accurately and candidly summarizing the material
parts of the record. As is also true for the framing of the Questions Presented (see Sec. 7.18, *supra*), counsel need not and
should not forget that he is an advocate for one party. The
Statement can perform a vital part of the brief's persuasive function. To the extent that the case permits, and some do not, the
Statement should be so written that judges reading it will want
to decide the appeal in favor of the position advocated in the
brief. At least the Statement should make the most favorable
impression possible and leave the court in as sympathetic a
frame of mind as the facts of the case permit.

Of course, the facts will often make this a lot easier for one
side than the other. In many, if not most, cases, decision is
foreordained by the facts no matter how able the lawyer; he has
to take the facts of his case as he finds them. But the art of brief
writing is to do the best with what one has. And in a surprisingly
large proportion of cases, there are ways of stating the facts
which will support opposing positions without departing from
the maxim that the Statement be a candid and fair recitation of
the facts which are material.

I well remember a draft of a brief prepared for me years ago
by an even younger lawyer. None of the facts were in dispute and
his Statement was accurate enough. Nevertheless, the Statement
in his draft of the brief for appellee left me with an uncomfort-
able feeling, which I finally traced to his having closely followed
the Statement contained in the opposing brief. He justified this
unusual method of brief writing on the ground that the facts
were not in dispute. Rearrangement and different emphasis had
the desired effect of making the facts pull in one direction rather
than in the other. I am sure that that lawyer never made the same
mistake again. The lesson to be learned is that differences in
nuances, emphasis, arrangement and selection (without omitting the unfavorable material) can be very important.

The art of effective brief writing is to reconcile the judges'
need for a fair and adequate statement of the relevant facts, and

no others, with the advocate's desire to state the facts as persuasively for his side as the case permits. This is not impossible. Judges do not object to it; on the contrary, they recognize fair, effective advocacy when they see it. It does not deceive them, but it does focus their attention on the facts which the party deems critical.

A brief writer must be careful, of course, not blatantly to press on the court facts which are legally irrelevant or outside the record which he thinks will appeal to the prejudices of the judges. Judges resent obvious efforts by counsel to appeal to their supposed predilections. Often such matters will come to their attention in any event. But counsel should be aware that he is treading on dangerous ground and approach it with delicacy, if at all.

How the art of advocacy can be invoked in particular cases cannot be described in this volume. But awareness of the problems and permissible techniques should better enable the lawyer both to satisfy the court and to advance the position of his client.

7.21 Summary of Argument

The United States Supreme Court and a few states[93] require that a Summary of Argument precede the Argument. Supreme Court Rule 34.1(h) requires such Summaries in all main briefs on the merits but not petitions for certiorari, jurisdictional statements or reply briefs. The rules of the District of Columbia Circuit (Rule 8(b)) and of the Fifth Circuit (Rule 13.6.2 as amended in 1978) require a summary for all briefs. The Federal Rules of Appellate Procedure and also the rules of Hawaii, Iowa, Ohio and Tennessee provide that "the Argument may be preceded by a summary," which leaves the inclusion of a Summary optional with the brief writer. Wisconsin Rule 809.19(1)(e) requires each point to begin with a "one-sentence summary," which would often seem to call either for an inadequate summary (little more than a heading) or an impossibly long sentence.

The purpose of the Summary of Argument is to give the appellate judges a short bird's-eye view of the Argument. A

---

[93]Colorado, Delaware, Indiana, Minnesota, New Hampshire, Oregon, Pennsylvania. Delaware requires appellee's Summary to admit or deny the propositions in appellant's Summary. In New Hampshire a Summary is not required in a reply brief which is "appropriately divided by topical headings."

judge may read this while he is reading the brief the first time, to give him an overview before he comes to the Argument. Even if he has read the brief, he may use the Summary to refresh his recollection just before or during the oral argument. The Summary may be all the judge will read before the argument. And even worse, it may be the only part of the brief some judges will ever read, either because they find the case simple enough to decide without further study or because they are too overloaded with work, or simply unwilling to work very hard. The opinion writer, at least, is likely to read the entire brief, although the actual writer of the opinion may be an attorney on the staff of the court or of a judge.

Unless the practice of the judges on the court is uniform and known to the bar—and some courts make it known that they do read the briefs before argument—the brief writer is not likely to know how his brief will fare in the above respects. But he should know that the function of the Summary is an important one; indeed, in some cases and for some judges,[94] it may be vital.

The function of the Summary is not merely to state the issues but to persuade. That means, in the words of Supreme Court Rule 34.1(h) and Fifth Circuit Rule 13.6.2, that the Summary "should be a succinct, but accurate and clear, condensation of the argument actually made in the body of the brief. It should not be a mere repetition of the headings under which the argument is arranged."[95] It should be a short narrative argument. "Because the summary of argument if properly prepared is most helpful to the court in following the oral argument and will often render unnecessary the making of inquiries by the court which consume time allowed for argument, counsel are urged to prepare the summary with great care."[96]

---

[94]But not for Judge Goodrich, who wrote:

"The 'Summary of Argument' is not as good a device as theoretically it might be thought to be. If the brief writer must put his various arguments in summary form before they have been made *in extenso* he must necessarily be peremptory in his method of statement. Otherwise he repeats the argument to be made later. Peremptory conclusions on points, before the reader of the brief has had a chance to go along and see how the points are developed, is premature. The statements often raise great doubt and sometimes opposition in the mind of one who is just getting acquainted with the case. It would be better to have the summary of the argument and the conclusion of the brief writer put in one section, following the extensive argument, as a sort of recapitulation of the whole." Goodrich, *supra* note 4, at 12–13.

[95]See also Rule 8(b) of the rules of the United States Court of Appeals for the District of Columbia Circuit, as amended through February 11, 1977.

[96]Quoted from former Rule 17(7) of the United States Court of Appeals for the District of Columbia Circuit. Although the quoted passage no longer survives in the rules, it still indicates the manner in which a Summary of Argument will be helpful to an appellate court.

The Summary of Argument should, of course, be prepared after the Argument it summarizes, which normally would be after the remainder of the brief has been completed. It should follow the order of the points and subpoints of the Argument, using the same numbers and letters but without headings, getting to the heart of the affirmative argument on each point as quickly as possible. It should "go beyond mere assertion,"[97] and include the most persuasive parts of the reasoning in the Argument, though in short form. Sometimes key sentences from the Argument may be taken over without change. That is permissible. More often new, concise, forceful composition, often including phrases from the Argument, is necessary.

Since detailed analyses of facts or cases or legislative history would be too long, they should be summarized. Critical decisions, however, should be cited, and, where necessary, an explanation made as to why they are or are not controlling. Emphasis should be on the most important and persuasive parts of the Argument, factual or legal.

There seldom is space for a rebuttal of all opposing arguments, though the principal points should be covered. The Summary will fail of its purpose if it is too long as well as if it is too condensed.

How long should the Summary be? That will obviously depend on factors which vary with the Argument being summarized. Normally two to three pages should be sufficient. Pennsylvania Rule 2118 provides that the Summary should normally not exceed one page and should never exceed two pages. Fifth Circuit Rule 13.6.2 says that the Summary "should seldom exceed two and never five pages." More may be necessary when the Argument is very long.[98]

When the rules of the particular jurisdiction contain special requirements, such as inclusion of the authorities cited at the end of the Summary for each point, they should, of course, be followed. The Table of Contents or the Points and Authorities required in some jurisdictions to some extent serve the same

---

[97]F. Wiener, BRIEFING AND ARGUING FEDERAL APPEALS, p. 117 (1967).

[98]An examination of the length of Summaries of Arguments in a number of recent briefs filed by the Solicitor General's Office in the United States Supreme Court shows that they averaged 17 percent of the length of the Argument section of the briefs. The average in a similar survey of Solicitor General's briefs written (often by me) many years ago was 9 percent. My obviously biased educated guess is that most judges would find the first figure too high, as the Pennsylvania and Fifth Circuit rules indicate.

purpose. That may be the reason why most jurisdictions do not require Summaries. But the headings or Points, which are the same as the section headings, will not be as persuasive as the summarized narrative argument, although they will be considerably shorter. Thus each technique has advantages and disadvantages over and under the other.

No outsider can say that a Summary of Argument is or is not helpful enough to the judges to be worth the effort or expense. And do not let its short length fool you; writing a good Summary is hard work and may take substantial time, just when counsel thinks that he has finished the brief. As the varying practices of different courts demonstrate, judges have not been of the same view as to the need for a Summary. A Summary would not seem necessary, however, if all the judges of the court read the entire briefs before the argument, or when the Arguments to be summarized (not the entire brief) are in most cases less than 20 or so pages long. Those may be the reasons why most courts do not require Summaries.

In the United States Supreme Court, however, where the issues in the cases which the Court accepts for argument are likely to be of great importance and to require extensive research and analysis, where the briefs are likely to approach or (with permission) exceed the new 50-page limit, and where the Justices may well want their recollections refreshed before oral argument, there is good reason for requiring a Summary.

The following example taken from a recent Supreme Court brief will indicate the proper form for a Summary:

"SUMMARY OF ARGUMENT

"The plain language of Section 14(b) (of the Age Discrimination in Employment Act (ADEA)) sets forth a mandatory prerequisite to the filing of a civil suit in federal court alleging claims of age discrimination. This interpretation is supported by the identity of language between Section 14(b) and the state deferral provisions of Title VII of the Civil Rights Act of 1964, §706(c), 42 U.S.C. §2000e-5 (c), which has consistently been interpreted to require claimants to file charges of discrimination with state authorities before proceeding on the federal level. Further, Section 14(b) is phrased similarly to Section 7(d) of the ADEA which sets forth other procedural requirements uniformly interpreted as jurisdictional prerequisites to the filing of a federal lawsuit.

"The legislative history of the ADEA indicates that Congress desired to structure the Act in a manner that would encourage the settlement of age discrimination claims in the most expeditious fashion possible with formal proceedings being utilized only as a last resort. This purpose is frustrated by the decision of the court below, which held that filing with state authorities is not mandatory and thus increases the likelihood of individual claims of age discrimination ripening into litigation.

"During the Congressional hearings on the ADEA, testimony was offered suggesting that the Act have state deferral provisions modelled after Title VII. This testimony was never disputed or debated but, as noted above, Section 14(b), as it was subsequently enacted, is phrased identically to Section 706(c) and should be interpreted accordingly."

Where the rules of court limit the length of briefs, as most do, the rule makers should recognize that the longer the remainder of the brief, the less space will be left for the Summary of Argument. This is now true of the United States Supreme Court, which since 1980 limits principal briefs to 50 pages. See Sec. 7.6, *supra*. Indeed, if a Summary is made optional, as under the Federal Appellate Rules, the effect may be to discourage counsel from including a Summary at all for the longest briefs, where they will be most helpful. One solution to this problem would be to exclude the Summary of Argument from the page limitation, as the recently amended Rule 8 of the rules of the United States Court of Appeals for the District of Columbia Circuit now provides.[99] To avoid abuse by counsel, this privilege might well be limited to no more than perhaps 10 percent of the length of the Argument.

7.22   The Argument Part of the Brief—Arrangement and Selection

Court rules usually leave counsel free to organize their arguments in the most effective manner. As indicated in the preceding section, Wisconsin Rule 809.19(1)(e) requires the Argument on each issue to begin with a one-sentence summary. North Carolina Rule 28(b)(3) requires each point to begin with a reference to the pertinent assignments of error and exceptions identified by number and page number. Under North Carolina Rule 28(d), portions of the Argument section of briefs filed in the Court of Appeals may be incorporated by reference into briefs filed in the Supreme Court.

---

[99]Rule 8 provides: "The summary of argument shall not be considered part of the brief for purposes of the page limitation imposed by Rule 28(g), Federal Rules of Appellate Procedure."

(a) Arguing Factual as Well as Legal Issues

The Argument part of the brief, usually the longest portion and often regarded as the principal one, is for arguing. This truism differentiates it from the Statement of Facts, although, as stated in Sec. 7.20, *supra,* the way in which facts are arranged and emphasized may well have a persuasive effect similar to an argument.

To regard the Statement as the factual part of the brief and the Argument as the legal section is, however, only a half-truth and a dangerous one. For factual issues are *argued* in the Argument, not the Statement. In many cases the only issues or the most important issues are factual.

The place to pull together the items in the record which demonstrate that the findings of the lower court or administrative agency are or are not supported by the evidence is the Argument, not the Statement, which usually summarizes the facts in the order in which they occur. Thus, the reasons why the oral testimony of a witness is or is not sufficient to support a verdict or decision should appear in the Argument, not the Statement, even though they may be purely factual.

When a fact in the record is referred to in the Argument, the record reference is to be cited whether or not the same citation for the same fact appears in the Statement of Facts. The judge will not be likely to remember the earlier citation or go back to the earlier page even if you refer to it. If you want him to have confidence in your factual statements by enabling him to verify them when he feels the need to, make that as easy for him as possible.

Some state constitutions limit appellate courts to consideration of questions of law. But whether evidence is substantial enough to satisfy the appropriate legal test—any, or a scintilla, or a preponderance, or no reasonable doubt, or what would satisfy the ordinary reasonable man—is, or can reasonably be said to be, a question of law. In any event, it is the type of question appellate courts should and do decide, even though the only "law" which may be cited on the point is the scope of appellate review, which the appellate judges, of course, already know. A sentence with no more than one or two cases would then be sufficient before the Argument turns to an argumentative analysis of the facts.

(b)   Selection of Points to Argue

Judges and other authorities on appellate practice have often said that appellant should not argue too many questions, and that most cases present only a small number of issues worth presenting to the appellate court. To argue too many, particularly if some are weak, or at least weaker than others, will unfavorably impress the judges and be likely to dilute the effect of the strong points. All this is generally true. See Sec. 7.18, *supra.*

But like most generalizations, this is often easier to say than to apply to the particular case. For example, if the lower court has supported an adverse ruling on a number of alternative grounds, or one's adversary can be expected to do so, the appellant will have to refute each of them or lose his appeal if he does not. In that situation, for him to follow the principle that weak points should be avoided could be disastrous.

On the other hand, if the lawyer is appearing on the other side of the same question, so that he will win if any one part of his argument is accepted, he can concentrate on his strongest points and even omit those which he doubts the appellate court will accept, in part on the theory that if he cannot win on the former, he will not win on the latter.

Another exceptional situation is where the effect of a number of errors, usually at trial, must be cumulated to establish overall prejudice. To avoid the appearance of arguing a number of picayune points, the various separate arguments can be combined as subdivisions under a single heading, prefaced by an introductory statement explaining how the cumulative effect of the unfavorable erroneous rulings deprived appellant of a fair trial.[100]

Apart from that, the determination of which points should not be argued is frequently very difficult. Most lawyers can cite examples where judges surprised them and decided cases on grounds which the lawyer thought to be much weaker than others. Indeed, supreme courts have sometimes decided cases on a ground which the lawyer did not mention in his brief at all, either because it did not occur to him or because he deemed it too weak to raise.

Rosenberg v. *United States,* 346 U.S. 273 (1953), proves the

---

[100]See the chapter on briefs written by Judge Philip W. Tone and Jonathan T. Howe, *Briefs,* ILLINOIS CIVIL PRACTICE AFTER TRIAL, p. 8–33 (Illinois Institute for Continuing Legal Education, 1976), quoting Judge Goodrich, *supra* note 4, at 7.

point in the context of a death sentence. Counsel for the defendants, during a series of appeals, omitted the argument that the capital punishment provisions of the Atomic Energy Act of 1946, which were more restrictive than those of the Espionage Act of 1917 under which defendants had been indicted, should have been applied to a conspiracy most of which (except for the efforts to conceal the prior theft of atomic secrets) had occurred before the 1946 Act was passed. Outside lawyers had suggested that such a point should be argued, but defendants' counsel did not think it had enough merit to be raised. After the Supreme Court had denied review on a number of occasions, the outside counsel, on behalf of a "best friend" who had no connection with the Rosenbergs, went to Mr. Justice Douglas, convinced him that the point was substantial and obtained a stay of execution. During the subsequent oral argument before the Supreme Court, defendants' own lawyer candidly admitted that he had believed the point not worth making, but submitted that his original judgment was wrong, as Justice Douglas' reaction to the point had demonstrated. The full Supreme Court overturned Justice Douglas' order by a vote of six to three. As a matter of hindsight, it is obvious that the point should have been raised, whether it succeeded or failed. Fortunately, most appellate lawyers are not faced with problems of selectivity in the context of a capital offense.

Obviously only a minute proportion of counsel's mistakes (or near mistakes) in judgment are disclosed in published material. The above illustration demonstrates that even very good lawyers cannot always be entirely confident as to their ability to select the best and reject the weakest arguments. Mr. Carson gives another example:

> "[I]n *Russell* v. *Todd,* 309 U.S. 280 (1940), the successful respondent's attorney told me that he inserted in his brief in the Supreme Court the winning point of the 10-year equitable statute of limitations only at the last moment; it was not originally his intention to argue the point in that Court."[101]

Perhaps criminal cases are an exception to the general rule. Defense counsel, including and perhaps particularly appointed counsel, deem it their obligation to raise every possible contention, in part to avoid being charged with not having fulfilled their duty to an indigent client.

---

[101]Carson, *supra* note 34, at 38–39.

Nevertheless, in most cases in which a large number of points can be raised, counsel must decide whether some should be omitted. One reason for this, that weak arguments, particularly if they come first, dilute the force of the strong ones, has already been mentioned. Another reason is that most jurisdictions now limit the length of briefs as well as of oral arguments, thereby not leaving enough space or time to cover persuasively more than a few points.

The treatment of this subject by my former colleague on the Illinois Supreme Court Rules Committee, Philip W. Tone (until recently a member of the United States Court of Appeals for the Seventh Circuit), and Jonathan T. Howe in an Illinois symposium on appellate practice is enlightening, both because of their own suggestions and those of the renowned judges they quote:[102]

> "Normally it is best to narrow the argument to a few of the strongest points available. The shotgun approach, arguing all points that may conceivably be argued on the theory that it is impossible to predict which one will appeal to the court, is favored by some lawyers, but a shotgun brief is almost never an effective brief. In writing the brief, a lawyer should be able to select from among the possible arguments those that have merit, and the brief should be limited to those arguments.
>
> "Narrowing the issues serves to emphasize those remaining and fosters effective presentation. Experienced appellate lawyers will accordingly sometimes omit arguments having merit, in the interest of effective presentation of even stronger arguments. Such pruning is painful and difficult but sometimes desirable.
>
> "Judge Herbert F. Goodrich has said:
>
>> " 'There should not be too many points on appeal. A case with two or three points clearly stated and vigorously argued is much better than one filled with a dozen bases of complaint. If a court goes through a half dozen points which it regards too small to be material it is likely to become a little impatient concerning the possibilities of the rest. Furthermore, a long, long list of points to be urged on appeal is in danger of creating the impression in the judges' minds that "the trial couldn't possibly have been so bad as that." Goodrich, *A Case on Appeal—A Judge's View*, A CASE ON APPEAL 7 (ALI-ABA).'
>
> . . .
>
> "Judge Learned Hand said in a tribute to a deceased lawyer:

---

[102]Tone and Howe, *supra* note 100, at 8–32, 8–33.

" 'With the courage which only comes of justified self-confidence, he dared to rest his case upon its strongest point, and so avoided that appearance of weakness and uncertainty which comes of a clutter of arguments. Few lawyers are willing to do this; it is the mark of the most distinguished talent. Hand, *In Memory of Charles Neave,* THE SPIRIT OF LIBERTY 127–28 (Dilliard's 3d ed. 1951).' "

In the same vein, former Attorney General and Solicitor General William D. Mitchell wrote:

"Some lawyers, of course, do not have enough confidence in their own judgment or are not competent to select weak points, but the most effective advocate is one who has the courage to eliminate such arguments."[103]

Frederick Bernays Wiener added:

"Indeed, it may safely be laid down as a proposition of general application that to include a weak point is virtually certain to dilute every strong one."[104]

More recently, then Louisiana Supreme Court Justice Albert Tate, Jr., has urged that appellate counsel

"should repeatedly select and discard—*select* essential issues, facts, and authorities; *discard* and winnow others ruthlessly, along with excess words and repetitious argument. Counsel's worry, of course, is that what he winnows as superfluous might, if left, somehow catch the court's eye. Hence, he errs unwisely on the side of inclusion. Unless there is particular reason to believe otherwise, however, a safe rule is to assume that appellate judges will have the same good sense as counsel in concluding that the winnowable issue or fact is indeed non-contributory. Part of the craft of counseling is the ability to balance the *possible* contribution of the issue or fact against the undoubted loss of impact and persuasion of a brief that wastes the court's time on side trails that lead nowhere." (Emphasis in original.)[105]

"Only truly arguable points should be selected and relied upon; unessential or diversionary points rarely affect the result, and normally they should be discarded."[106]

All of the foregoing writers emphasize the need for selectivity—for having the confidence and courage to eliminate weak

---

[103]Book Review, 64 Harv. L. Rev. 350, 351 (1950), quoted in F. Wiener, BRIEFING AND ARGUING FEDERAL APPEALS, p. 96 (1967).

[104]*Id.* at 97.

[105]A. Tate, *The Art of Brief Writing: What a Judge Wants to Read,* LITIGATION, Vol. 4, No. 2, pp. 11–12 (American Bar Association Section of Litigation, 1978).

[106]*Id.* at 14.

points, except perhaps in the exceptional situations referred to above.

For the trial lawyer objectively to appraise the effect on appellate judges of abandoning his challenges to rulings which he vigorously opposed below may be difficult. It may be advisable to obtain the assistance of a colleague less personally involved in order to obtain a more objective viewpoint which will more clearly approximate the reactions of appellate judges. What is needed is judgment which melds the self-confidence and courage referred to by Judge Hand, General Mitchell and Colonel Wiener, and the humility taught by the experience of counsel in the *Rosenberg* case.

(c)   The Arrangement of Points

Once appellant has decided what points to argue, he must determine the most effective order of presentation.[107] That, of course, means most effective for his client, not necessarily the order which might otherwise appear most logical. Nor need he follow the order of the points as they appear in the adverse opinion below, or, if he is appellee, in the appellant's brief. He should adopt the arrangement most persuasive for him.[108]

The advice usually given to brief writers is to start off with the strongest argument, if possible. As stated by Justice Tate:

> "Generally, a point that goes to the very heart of the case should be argued first. An experienced judge will usually select the strongest issue for study first. But the judge initially may not know what is counsel's strongest issue, unless counsel, based on his knowledge of the facts and his legal research, so directs the court. . . .
>
> "As a psychological matter, appellant's counsel should force the court early to face head-on his strongest argument; otherwise, the judicial impression of its forcefulness may be lessened, if its study is not reached until after the judge has half-decided on affirmance, having rejected counsel's previous arguments.
>
> "In many instances, of course, counsel cannot argue his strongest point first because of reasons of logical priority. He

---

[107]South Carolina Rule 8.10 requires that a party wishing to challenge a prior decision of the South Carolina Supreme Court must file a petition at least four days before the case is called for argument asking permission to do so, and specifying the reasons why the prior decision should be modified or overruled. Arguing the point in the brief is not enough. *Jones* v. *Dague*, 252 S.C. 261, 166 S.E.2d 99, 103 (1969).

[108]In North Carolina and Oregon each point must begin with the pertinent assignment of error or exception, in Oregon followed by the verbatim instruction or relevant testimony.

must then set forth his arguments in a logical step-by-step progression, relying upon placement, emphasis, and the 'Statement
of the Issues' to indicate the greater importance of a particular
point."[109]

Judge Tone and Mr. Howe and the authorities they quote
support the same position:

> "It is usually best to place the strongest point at or near the
> beginning. Finishing strong is usually not as important as avoiding
> the risk that the reader's attention will flag before the strong point
> can be made.
> "Impressive authority urges presentation of the strongest
> point first. Judge Herbert F. Goodrich counseled:

>> " 'For the appellant the best rule is to bring up the strongest
>> point first and hit it as hard as it can be hit. It is the first point
>> which necessarily gets first the attention of the men in the
>> black robes while their attention is at its highest. If unimpres-
>> sive and small points are discussed before the biggest ones
>> are taken up, the impression will be that this case does not
>> amount to much. But if a good strong point is effectively
>> presented, the smaller ones may fall into place as clinching
>> arguments to support the conclusion already indicated by the
>> strong first point. Goodrich, *A Case on Appeal—The Judge's View,*
>> A CASE ON APPEAL 7–8 (ALI-ABA).'

> "See also Carson, *Conduct of the Appeal—The Lawyer's View,* A
> CASE ON APPEAL 64 (ALI-ABA):

>> " 'The early part of the argument is that in which you strike the
>> mind of the court at its freshest and most attentive. Hence,
>> unless the result be to distort the order of your presentation
>> or otherwise produce an unnatural effect, you should put
>> your strongest point or your weightiest grievance first in the
>> order of argument. The later portion of your brief will be
>> read by the court with a mind influenced by what it has first
>> read. That influence you should seek to have produced by the
>> stronger rather than the weaker part of your argument.' "[110]

Eugene Gressman and I have similarly stated:

> "It is probably wiser to start off with the strongest argument. The
> Court may never reach it if it comes too late in the brief, or it may
> be repelled by the weaker arguments at the beginning."[111]

Others have urged that one should first get to "the heart"
of the case (see Judge Tate, *supra*), possibly without recognizing

---

[109]Tate, *supra* note 105, at 14.
[110]Tone and Howe, *supra* note 100, at 8–34.
[111]R. Stern and E. Gressman, SUPREME COURT PRACTICE, p. 718 (5th ed., 1978).
See also F. Wiener, BRIEFING AND ARGUING FEDERAL APPEALS, p. 143 (1967);
Carson, *supra* note 34, at 61.

that the heart of the argument may not be the same as appellant's strongest point. Indeed, the "strongest point" might be a relatively unimportant one. To place it at the beginning might give the accurate impression that appellant was seeking to postpone the discussion of issues of greater consequence and difficulty. The "heart of the case" is the issue most likely to be dispositive or decisive.

In some cases the sequence of thought, the way the arguments fit together, will dictate a logical arrangement, not beginning with appellant's strongest argument or, for that matter, with the "heart of the case." For example, judges often expect jurisdictional points to be discussed at the beginning.

It is thus apparent that here again no single generalization can always control. The reasons for different arrangements must be taken into account. Perhaps the best advice is to start with one's strongest point or the heart of the case unless there is a better reason for following a more logical or other order.

Counsel for appellant must decide whether to anticipate the appellee's arguments in appellant's opening brief or to hold off until his reply. Waiting has the advantage of enabling appellant to know exactly what appellee intends to say. On the other hand, appellant will know the arguments that appellee has made in the trial court or lower appellate court. Unless appellant has reason to doubt that appellee will make them again, he should deal with such points in his opening brief. For if the points can be met, it is better for appellant to have the court first hear about them from him in a contextual setting which demonstrates their weakness or inapplicability and thus draws their sting. Of course, points relied upon by the court below should be countered, whether appellee has presented them or not.

When appellant's counsel is aware of an opposing argument which neither appellee nor the court below has mentioned, he will normally hold off discussing the point until his reply brief, to see whether and how appellee presents it. He will not want to give appellee a new idea or to set up and demolish a straw man. He still must consider, however, the possibility that the appellate judges will think of it themselves. For if appellee does not raise the question in his brief, the appellant cannot legitimately deal with it in his reply. He will not know at that time, of course, whether the point may occur to the judges at or around the time of the oral argument. In such circumstances appellant's counsel must make an educated guess as to how likely it is that the point will occur to and trouble the court if appellee does not raise it. If he thinks that may occur, and he has a good answer to the argument, he should deal with it in his opening brief.[112] This problem often arises with respect to jurisdictional questions which may bother the judges more than counsel for either litigant.

7.23 Putting Yourself in the Position of the Judge

In John W. Davis' famous article, *The Argument of an Appeal,*[113] his first maxim was that, at least in his imagination, the lawyer "should change places with the court." That will enable the lawyer to understand and appreciate what is most likely to inform and convince the brief's judicial reader. This applies to the written argument as well as to the oral. Since the purpose of the brief is to persuade judges, the writer should consciously have in mind what kind of presentation will be most helpful to the members of the court.

This tenet of common sense does not relate solely to the Argument portion of the brief. It underlies what has been said above as to beginning the brief with the Nature of the Case and the Jurisdictional Facts, as to how the Statement of Facts should be organized and written, and as to the advantage as well as the necessity of being fair and candid.

The guiding principle is what counsel wants a judge to learn from a brief. This depends in part on what a judge is likely to know before he reads it.

This does not mean that the brief should be written with any particular judge or judges in mind. Sometimes, as when an entire supreme court hears all appeals, counsel will know who his judges will be, unless a new judge joins the court before the oral argument. Often, and particularly in the intermediate appellate courts, the identity of the judges will not be known until long after the brief is written, and perhaps not even until the morning of the argument. In either event, it is difficult to tailor a brief to the presumed taste of individual judges even if one

---

[112]Judge Tone and Mr. Howe concluded as to this: "In general, if the appellant has a good counter-argument and if he believes it likely the point will occur to the court if it does not to the appellee's counsel, the point should be discussed. This does not mean that strawmen should be created and then demolished. The kind of point under consideration is one that would be likely to prove troublesome unless properly answered." Tone and Howe, *supra* note 100, at 8-36.

[113]26 A.B.A.J. 895, 896 (1940).

knows a good deal about them. For appellate courts are composed of at least three judges, and often more, and different judges react differently to all kinds of things. What will appeal to some may well not appeal to others. Of course, a brief writer should try to accommodate his work to what sitting judges have said in their opinions, but that relates more to the handling of cases as precedents than to the predilections of individual judges.

My experience is that even for as well-known a court as the Supreme Court of the United States, one should write not for the individuals as such but for an intelligent body of lawyers knowledgeable in what that group of judges would be expected to know. What you know about the philosophies and predilections of the individuals should be kept in mind, but it will not be as helpful as you might expect unless you know that a majority of the judges are of the same mind.

The key question is what will they be likely to know about the case or the law when they first look at the brief, and what will they expect the brief to tell them. Clearly they will know little about the facts of the case, as indicated in Sec. 7.20, *supra.* The same principle, however, applies to the treatment of legal matters. Most obviously, appellate judges are likely to be familiar with subjects which come before them recently and frequently, or which are familiar to experienced lawyers generally. A short reference to a recent decision or accepted doctrine will suffice without elaboration. Subjects such as the principles governing the construction of statutes and other documents, the scope of appellate review, the court's jurisdiction and well known rules of evidence or procedure fall in this category.

Conversely, when there is reason to doubt that some of the judges are familiar with the law to be applied in the case, a treatment in depth is essential. New laws or parts of laws which have not come before the court at all or in recent years, the history of particular bills, and case law in other jurisdictions fall within this category.

What judges will want to know also will depend on their status in the judicial hierarchy. A lower court is bound by precedent to a much greater extent than a supreme court; it will give the higher court's decisions greater weight. See Sec. 7.3(a), *supra.*

Federal judges can be expected to be more familiar with federal than with state law, except in such well-known fields as automobile accident and product liability which often come before them in diversity cases. Apart from that, federal judges may need considerably more education in state law than state judges. The same would be true in reverse when a state court is called upon to decide a federal question.

7.24 Inaccuracy, Overstatement, Lack of Candor, Personalities

What has been said in Sec. 7.20, *supra,* as to the need for playing fair with the court in the Statement of Facts applies equally to the Argument. Arguments and references to law as well as facts can be misleadingly stated. Misstatement or overstatement of what a case holds will certainly come to a court's attention, and its effect may be as disastrous as a misstatement of facts. It may discredit not only other arguments but a lawyer's reputation with the judges. As stated by then Justice Floyd E. Thompson of the Illinois Supreme Court in a speech before the Chicago Bar Association in 1934:

> "Every statement should be carefully weighed and considered before it is printed in the brief. Frequent misstatements cause the court to lose confidence in the brief and in its author. Whether made inadvertently or wilfully, misstatements are inexcusable. . . . Briefs should not contain extravagant statements nor immaterial and heated discussion. The court wants light, not heat."

The problem of half-truths, exaggerations and misleading omissions is not merely a concern of the small proportion of the bar who cannot be trusted to be honest. Lawyers of complete integrity may as advocates develop blind spots as they submerge themselves in one side of a case. The very effort of preparing an argument in support of one position often makes them overlook or undervalue the way facts or cases may look to an outsider, such as a judge, not to mention the lawyer on the other side. Probably most lawyers are aware of this advocate's bias, or would be if they think about it. The best lawyers attempt to retain their objectivity, or at least their ability to foresee how adversaries and judges will react. But even with awareness of the problem, completely overcoming advocate's bias is very difficult, as most lawyers recognize.

Having your arguments reviewed by a member of your firm who is not immersed in the case can be very helpful in this respect, as I can attest from participation both as the advocate and the objective, and also ignorant, reviewer. I have quoted what I thought were all the pertinent parts of a statute only to have an adversary charge that my omission of a sentence I had deemed immaterial distorted the statutory language. On reading the passage again in the light of his disturbing criticism, I saw how he might reasonably have interpreted the sentence as more significant than I had. If I had noticed this in the first place, I would have included the omitted sentence to avoid even the possibility of being charged with trying to mislead the court. For counsel should "take care not only to avoid garbling the quotation but to avoid the least appearance of doing so."[114]

I have also read a draft of a brief written by a distinguished tax lawyer of indubitable integrity which began by describing a section of the Internal Revenue Code as stating so and so. In my ignorance of the subject, I read the statute and found that it didn't say that, though arguably that was what it meant. I had considerable difficulty in getting my learned friend, who had been living with the case for several years, even to reread the statute, as well as in persuading him to modify his previous characterization of it, though he finally did both. Over the years he had convinced himself that the law said what he thought it meant, an error which many of us make.

In reviewing a treatise on constitutional law a number of years ago, I found an old case quoted in support of a startling and novel constitutional theory. I was intrigued enough to read the case. The quotation was accurate, of course, but a passage in the same opinion several pages away showed that the opinion was entirely consistent with the general, and also the Supreme Court's, understanding of what the Constitution meant. To charge the author, who was highly regarded as a scholar, with lack of integrity or with inability to read a case accurately would have been absurd. Obviously he had become too obsessed with his own theory to appreciate, or perhaps even to notice, passages which more objective readers would find significant as well as inconsistent with his basic position.

These illustrations are not intended to justify exaggerations or distortions or inaccuracies by showing that they can occur innocently. My purpose is to show that even the purest of heart,

---

[114]Stated by Justice Wilkins of the Supreme Judicial Court of Massachusetts in *The Argument of an Appeal*, 33 Cornell L.Q. 40, 43 (1947).

the lawyer who would be horrified to be accused of an intention to mislead, must be conscious of the effect of advocate's bias and be very careful both himself and in training his younger colleagues. For this reason as well as those mentioned above, the importance of obtaining a more objective reviewer of a draft of a brief cannot be overestimated, even though sometimes it may be difficult.

I add that the above and other experiences should teach humility, or at least understanding. I am much less ready than my younger colleagues to charge an adversary, whom I think I have caught red-handed, with deliberate misrepresentation or intent to deceive. Those are fighting words which impute bad faith. The argument will be just as strong if your brief merely states that "appellant's brief is misleading in this respect," or "appellant fails to mention" this significant fact, or that "appellant's argument overlooks this portion" of a statute or opinion.

Judges, of course, see many examples of advocate's bias. I am sure they are used to it, though they do not like it. More important, they deplore it as ineffective advocacy. But they know that all of it does not flow from dishonest lawyers who are reckless with the truth. Accordingly, they react very unfavorably to personal attacks upon the opposing lawyer as distinct from his arguments. As the Court of Appeals for the Ninth Circuit once declared:

> "It should be noted the counsel for both sides in their briefs would have made more effective presentations had they devoted less attention to each other's shortcomings as lawyers. They should know that this is the sort of thing of which a court gets tired."[115]

Accordingly, "[b]riefs should never contain disrespectful statements concerning opposing counsel or the trial court." As stated by Colonel Wiener, such indulgence in personalities "like all the other faults . . . fails of its purpose." If you really believe that your opponent's conduct was "shameful and thoroughly unprofessional"—and you will not be so sure after you have cooled down a bit—you should take it up with the appropriate grievance committee but not inject it into your brief.[116]

What has been said applies with geometrically greater force to attacks upon judges, and particularly the judge below who had the temerity to decide against your client. The judi-

---

[115]*Tele-King Distributing Co.* v. *Wyle*, 218 F.2d 940, 943 (CA 9, 1958).
[116]F. Wiener, BRIEFING AND ARGUING FEDERAL APPEALS, p. 258 (1967).

ciary is a brotherhood; its members resist attacks on even inferior members of inferior courts. Appellate judges know that lower court judges are trying to do a difficult job which inevitably leaves half the litigating lawyers unhappy. The appellate judges become aware of the peculiarities of each other and of the trial judges in their areas.[117] But they don't want counsel to dwell on judges' disabilities or inabilities, or worse. If a brief can accurately state that "nothing in the record supports the finding below," or that "the decision below completely disregards six decisions of the Supreme Court," naming them, the appellate court will, if persuaded by the material cited that you are right, get the message without reference to the ignorance or bias of the judge.[118]

A number of rules (including United States Supreme Court Rule 34.6) warn that briefs must be "free from burdensome, irrelevant, immaterial, and scandalous matter"[119] and that briefs not complying "may be disregarded and stricken by the Court." In recent years a brief was stricken for failure to comply with the rules "with respect to conciseness, statement of questions without unnecessary detail, and printing of appendices thereto." *Huffman* v. *Pursue, Ltd.,* 419 U.S. 892 (1974). Georgia Supreme Court Rule 5 (Georgia Code §24–4505) not only forbids arguments "discourteous or disparaging to opposing counsel or to any judge," but adds that "counsel must not indulge in denunciation of any branch of the Government, State or Federal, nor call in question the integrity or impugn the motives of any official, unless he is on trial or otherwise is a party to the record, and his official conduct is properly the subject of scrutiny and adjudication." Louisiana Supreme Court Rule VII, Sec. 7, provides that:

> "The language used in any brief or document filed in this court must be courteous, and free from insulting criticism of any person, individually or officially, or of any class or association of persons, or of any court of justice, or other institution. Any violation of this rule shall subject the author or authors of the brief or document to the humiliation of having the brief or document

---

[117]See *Chandler* v. *Judicial Council,* 398 U.S. 74 (1970).

[118]The Supreme Court once informally rebuked the Solicitor General's Office for stating accurately at the time in a petition for certiorari that only in the named court of appeals were NLRB decisions almost always overturned, thereby impugning antilabor bias to the judges. I am still inclined to believe that this was legitimate advocacy, but the Supreme Court's disagreement is of greater consequence.

[119]"Scandalous" in this context is not limited to the sexual indiscretions of opposing lawyers and judges but extends to any imputation of improper conduct.

returned, and to punishment for contempt of the authority of the court."

Rule IX, Sec. 6, of the Louisiana Courts of Appeal contains even stronger language. Briefs have on rare occasions been returned to the author under these rules, but the contempt sanction does not appear to have been invoked. Whether or not these strongly worded rules are entirely consistent with the First Amendment, they still serve as a guide to the kinds of expressions in briefs which will not make a favorable impression on appellate judges.

7.25 The Handling of Cases—The Importance of "Why"

Judges want to know whether a decision one way or the other will be fair and just, not only to the parties but to the public or the public interest, and what the general consequences of the ruling will be. Decisions of supreme courts are often controlled by such considerations. Such courts have great adeptness in distinguishing, avoiding or even ignoring cases which might lead to conclusions they deem unfair or unwise. This is true, though to a lesser extent, of intermediate appellate courts even though they are bound by prior supreme court authority. As the percentage of decisions accepted for supreme court review gets smaller and smaller, judges and lawyers recognize that most of their decisions will, as a practical matter, be final. They are much less likely to strain to avoid or distinguish a prior decision of their own court or the higher court when the result comports with their sense of justice, common sense and the public interest.

As Mr. Justice Rutledge, while a member of the Court of Appeals for the District of Columbia Circuit, stated with respect to briefs in that court:

> "Perhaps my own major criticism of briefs, apart from that relating to analysis, would be the lack of discussion on principle. Some cases are ruled so clearly by authority, directly in point and controlling, that discussion of principle is superfluous. But these are not many. It has been surprising to find how many appealed cases present issues not directly or exactly ruled by precedent."[120]

The last statement is even more true in the Supreme Court.

Former Chief Justice Schaefer of the Illinois Supreme

---

[120]W. Rutledge, *The Appellate Brief*, 28 A.B.A.J. 251, 253 (1942).

Court, speaking from a supreme court perspective, has expressed the same idea more broadly:

> "[T]he law does not live in black letter rules. It lives in the conditions of actual life that have given birth to those rules. It is on that plane that cases are actually decided. [Since the Court wants to know why the rule has evolved and why it should apply to your particular case, counsel should shape both his brief and his argument] in terms of the consideration[s] from which the rules of law actually stem. That is, it seems to me, the characteristic as I have been able to analyze it, that separates the great argument and the great lawyer from the mediocre one."[121]

Furthermore, too many lawyers seem to believe that it is sufficient to cite a case, to summarize its facts or holding or to quote it. But that merely gives the court the raw material. It does not tell why the case, or what you have said about it, should lead the court to decide in your favor. As stated by Mr. Justice Rutledge:

> "What judges want to know is why this case, or line of cases, should apply to these facts rather than that other line on which the opponent relies with equal certitude, if not certainty. Too often the 'why' is left out. The discussion stops with assertion that this case or line of cases rules the present one. Assertion is not demonstration . . . . The argument which stops at this point may give judges the lead it is desired they follow. But it is bobtailed, nevertheless. The lead may be the wrong one, or the judge may think it such. The attorney's reasons for thinking it the right one may keep the judge out of error, if he can be saved. In a close case, where the authorities pertinent by analogy are conflicting and especially when they are equally pertinent and numerous on both sides, the discussion of the underlying principles as related to the present application counts heavily to swing the scales."[122]

See also Sec. 8.16(a), *infra*, as to the similar importance of reason and principles, and not merely authorities, in oral argument.

This means that your treatment of a case or line of cases you think closely in point or analogous should begin or end, or both, with an explanation of how it supports the conclusion you want the court to adopt. Even if this conclusion is, in your opinion, self-evident, point it out, though without the elaboration that might be necessary when the connection is not so obvious.

How many cases should be cited for a proposition? Many

---

[121]W. Schaefer, *Appellate Advocacy*, 23 Tenn. L. Rev. 471, 476 (1954); *The Appellate Court*, 3 U. Chi. L. S. Rec. 1 (No. 2, 1954).
[122]W. Rutledge, *The Appellate Brief*, 28 A.B.A.J. 251, 253 (1942).

judges and writers say "very few," and that is often correct. Lawyers too often cite as many cases as they can in support of a position, or in any event a large number. Usually no more than two or three are necessary, particularly if those cases cite others.[123] That is clearly enough for well established propositions for which no citations at all are really necessary,[124] and usually enough even for points not familiar to the judges. If a long string of cases is cited, the judges will seldom look beyond the first few, if they support what is said. Even worse than a string of citations is a string of abstracts of cases or of quotations, especially long ones.

How much is said about a case depends, of course, upon its relationship to the court and to your case. A decision of the same or of a higher appellate court on similar facts, particularly if recent, should be driven home, if necessary by detailed analysis and comparison of facts to show that they are indistinguishable from yours. As the court becomes less authoritative the justification for such treatment lessens. Often a citation followed by a parenthetical phrase or clause indicating what the case holds is sufficient.

Of course, in the absence of close cases in the same jurisdiction, reliance upon decisions of other courts is appropriate and may require explanation. But then the emphasis should be on the reasoning of the other cases, not merely upon their force as authorities.

Precedents which counsel knows to be opposed to his position should normally be dealt with in the main briefs. As Mr. Carson has stated:

> "[I]t seems ill-advised not to do so. In the first place you can never be sure that your adversary will not bring up the inconvenient authorities at a time when it is harder to deal with them. In the second place as an officer of the court you owe it to the court to call attention to any pertinent authority. Who knows that the court of its own knowledge or by its own research will not turn up the authority anyhow? In that event your voluntary treatment of the case may have been your only chance to distinguish it."[125]

This admonition extends to dicta and reasoning as well as to direct holdings, at least for courts of the same jurisdiction.

---

[123]Goodrich, *supra* note 4, at 17.
[124]Iowa Rule 14(f) lists 17 propositions of law which are deemed to be so well established that authority need not be cited for them.
[125]Carson, *supra* note 34, at 62.

These practical reasons are reinforced by the duty of lawyers to be candid with courts, even to the extent of mentioning opposing cases not cited by the opposition.

The more difficult question is the extent to which this obligation applies to cases from other jurisdictions which are not controlling, or to cases which are arguably analogous but which are not directly to the point. As to the former, if cases from other states are referred to at all, counsel should not cite merely the favorable ones as representing the law elsewhere. But if only cases within the jurisdiction are cited, there may be no obligation to go outside.[126] The Code of Professional Responsibility states that:

> "Where a lawyer knows of legal authority *in the controlling jurisdiction* directly adverse to the position of his client, he should inform the tribunal of its existence unless his adversary has done so; but, having made such disclosure, he may challenge its soundness in whole or in part." (Emphasis supplied.)[127]

How to handle outside cases containing adverse dicta, reasoning or analogies calls for an exercise of judgment depending on how close they are to the case on appeal. One need not strain to refute or distinguish the reasoning of another jurisdiction, or every possible analogy, particularly if it is quite a distance off the point. Of course, if the case or its reasoning has been referred to by one's adversary or the court below, or in other decisions in the jurisdiction, one must deal with it.

Despite the generally accepted proposition that a brief should not be overloaded with citations, in various situations citing a large number of cases is warranted. To convince a federal court of appeals (or the Supreme Court for that matter) that 10 out of 11 circuits have ruled your way on a point, or a state court that 40 other states have done so, 10 or 40 cases should be cited, though probably in a footnote and after an introductory statement giving the number, so that the judges will not have to count them. And, of course, you must be sure that each case stands for what you say it does.

In order to persuade the Supreme Court that language in several then-recent cases supporting a presumption of insepara-

---

[126]Federal decisions applying the law of the same state should not be treated as "outside."

[127]EC 7–23. See also DR 7–106(B)(1).

bility in construing statutes was inconsistent with a mass of other Supreme Court cases, I once cited 47 decisions.[128] In such circumstances, when the case law is not uniform or "the court below has disregarded settled law," the sheer weight of numbers has significance.[129]

There are also cases of such magnitude that citation of many authorities is justified. In an interesting interchange between two of the foremost masters of appellate practice, John W. Davis and Colonel Frederick Bernays Wiener, with respect to a case in which they were opponents, Davis referred to the "horrible example" of 304 cases cited in Wiener's 295-page brief for the Government in *United States* v. *Northern Pacific Ry. Co.,* 311 U.S. 317 (1940).[130] Wiener countered by pointing out that the case involved a large number of questions relating to title to 40,000,000 acres of land grants to the railway, that the Supreme Court had ordered reargument on a number of specified questions and twice heard six hours of argument. The Court's opinion covered 53 pages of the United States Reports. The number of cases, Wiener insisted, was necessary, *inter alia,* to demonstrate the lower court's "disregard of settled principles of law" and "the number of decisions which . . . the decree below ignored." Wiener concluded:

> "Having regard to all of these factors—the complexity of the issues, the circumstance that the Court was obviously in doubt and frankly seeking guidance, and the number of subsidiary points and principles that needed to be explored and developed—I still think now, as I thought in 1940, that the number of citations was not excessive . . . ."

I agree with Wiener, and not because he won the case. Extraordinary situations call for extraordinary treatment.

The order of citations should, as between cases equally in point, start with the highest court in the jurisdiction, followed by cases in the intermediate appellate court hearing the appeal, then other courts of equal authority and finally other courts. The most recent case in each court should be cited first, and then others in reverse chronological order. The strongest case

---

[128]See *United States* v. *Petrillo,* 330 U.S. 1 (1947), Brief for the United States, p. 143. The Court did not find it necessary to decide the point.

[129]See F. Wiener, BRIEFING AND ARGUING FEDERAL APPEALS, p. 210 (1967).

[130]The story is told in Wiener, *id.* at 205–207. This case was briefed, of course, long before the 1980 Supreme Court rule limiting briefs to 50 pages.

or cases, which normally would be those most closely in point, should come first, even if not from the highest court. Obviously this should also be true in cases coming from different states, despite the Bluebook[131] instruction that cases from different states be cited alphabetically by states.

I recall reviewing a brief drafted by one of my bright young colleagues which included footnotes citing cases from a number of states. After reading the cases cited in one long footnote, I could not resist inquiring why those which most weakly supported the point for which they were cited came first; a judge checking the cases in the order in which they appeared might not be strongly impressed. When he said that he was merely following the Bluebook, I thought he was jesting, but found that the Bluebook states that the proper "order and system" in citing cases from different states is "alphabetically by state" (§2:5). (He had not noticed the caveat three paragraphs earlier that the order specified was "subject to alteration for any good reason.") This led me to comment that such an arrangement might be entirely appropriate for treatises, general digests such as *Corpus Juris, American Jurisprudence* and *American Law Reports,* and law review articles, but not for argumentative writing designed to persuade. Since judges might not read beyond the first one or two cases cited for a proposition, the strongest should obviously come first. The alphabetical order of states might be acceptable if all the cases unquestionably supported the proposition, and if the object was to show that all or almost all states were in accord.

In Sec. 7.39, *infra,* the importance of checking all citations, quotations and record references in briefs is emphasized. But cases also require a different sort of verification. In order to determine whether they have been overruled, discredited or distinguished—or for that matter reaffirmed and broadened— by subsequent authorities, they must be Shepardized (in the customary way or through Westlaw) or now Lexicized, up to the latest possible date. Although it does not often occur that a case is discredited between the date of the brief writer's original research on a point and the filing of a brief, it does happen sometimes. And nothing makes a lawyer so ineffective and embarrassed as when it happens to him.

---

[131]The Bluebook, published by the Harvard Law Review Association, is more formally known as A UNIFORM SYSTEM OF CITATIONS (12th ed., 1978). See Sec. 7.29, *infra.*

7.26 Authorities Other Than Cases

Briefs often cite non-case material in support of legal propositions.[132]

Constitutions and statutes are, of course, direct sources of law, usually of greater stature than case law. Analysis of the current and controlling statutory language should often be supplemented by reference to other provisions of the same statute or related ones, or to changes in statutes over the years, or to the language of the frequently numerous bills or amendments thereto through which the law as enacted evolved.

Official publications manifesting legislative intention, such as committee reports, legislative debates and, to a lesser extent, committee hearings, are also important aids to the determination of statutory meaning, although, in theory at least, they become relevant only when statutory language is ambiguous.[133] These are frequently used in interpreting federal statutes, but since many states do not publish such material, it is often not available to aid in the interpretation of state law.

Light may also be cast on legislative and constitutional meaning by the common law background of a provision and the interrelationship between its history and judicial decisions. History is also frequently important in cases involving the meaning of constitutional provisions. E.g., *United States* v. *Wood,* 299 U.S. 123 (1936), and *Haupt* v. *United States,* 330 U.S. 631 (1947), in each of which old English statutes and cases were examined.

Administrative regulations authorized by statute may have the force of law. Assistance in determining the meaning of statutes, regulations and administrative decisions may also be found in other materials published by administrative agencies. Courts often give substantial weight to various sorts of administrative rulings or interpretations, down to the informal letters and memoranda of government officials, such as opinions of Attorneys General and Treasury Decisions. Such material may be difficult to find away from the seat of government, or by persons who are not or have not been connected with the governmental agency involved.

---

[132]See F. Wiener, BRIEFING AND ARGUING FEDERAL APPEALS, pp. 168–200 (1967). As to the use of non-record material for factual matters, see Sec. 7.30, *infra.*

[133]See *Cass* v. *United States,* 417 U.S. 72, 76–79 (1974), and cases cited therein; *United States* v. *American Trucking Associations,* 310 U.S. 534, 543–44 (1940); *United States* v. *Dickerson,* 310 U.S. 554, 562 (1940).

Writings about the law by those who do not make it are regarded as secondary authorities. They may be valuable either because they collect and summarize cases and other primary material, or because of the weight to be accorded their own reasoning and analysis.

The American Law Institute's *Restatement of the Law,* prepared by prominent representatives of the bench, bar and law schools most familiar with the subject, probably constitutes the highest ranking of the secondary authorities. Next would come the treatises or other writings of recognized authorities in a field.[134] The authority of such a work, and for that matter of any legal writing, depends in the first instance upon the renown of its author. An article by a prominent member of the judiciary or an administrative body or a professor well known in his field would carry more authority than a better reasoned paper of an unknown practicing lawyer or law student. The writings of others gain stature from their own intrinsic quality. This applies to articles and student work in law reviews as well as to books.

The time has long since passed when such material was thought not to be significant enough to cite.[135] Judge Goodrich, a former law school professor and dean, wrote that

> "[s]tudent notes are worth citing; considered articles by scholarly writers are almost a must."[136]

This undoubtedly is an unduly generous generalization, not meant to cover *all* students' work, or for that matter all articles which might perhaps be characterized as "considered" or "scholarly." Much of such work is undoubtedly not worth citing. It may be superficial, biased, badly reasoned or written, and add nothing to what is already known. But references to well-reasoned articles, including student work, are entirely appropriate, particularly if there is little else to cite.[137]

---

[134]Treatises, books, handbooks and articles would seem to differ more in their length than in their quality.

[135]B. Cardozo, *Introduction* to SELECTED READINGS ON THE LAW OF CONTRACTS, pp. vii, ix (1931) ("Certain, in any event, it is that the old prejudice is vanishing"); see also Goodrich, *supra* note 4, at 17.

[136]Goodrich, *supra* note 4, at 17.

[137]Colonel Wiener, however, "would urge that, except in rare instances, student notes should not be cited as authority." "[T]he brief-writer will, by and large, be well advised to use them as case-finders and as sources for his own ideas, rather than as expressions of authority to be cited to the courts. A little reflection will show the reason why. After all, your task as an advocate is to persuade a court of more or less learned and more rather than less elderly judges to decide your case in your favor. They are not likely to be persuaded by what some lads on a law review have said." F. Wiener, BRIEFING AND ARGUING FEDERAL APPEALS, pp. 198, 197 (1967), citing several judicial remarks which took the same view.

Articles have on numerous occasions contributed to the establishment of the law. Perhaps the most prominent examples are the articles by Samuel D. Warren, Jr., and Louis D. Brandeis, *The Right to Privacy*, 4 Harv. L. Rev. 193 (1890), and Charles Warren's *New Light on the History of the Federal Judiciary Act of 1789*, 37 Harv. L. Rev. 49 (1923), which was in part responsible for *Erie R. Co.* v. *Tompkins*, 304 U.S. 64 (1938).[138]

Legal encyclopedias and collections of cases, such as *Corpus Juris Secundum, American Jurisprudence, American Law Reports* and *Lawyers Reports Annotated,* "should be used primarily to orient the lawyer in unfamiliar fields of law, or to supply him with citations to cases and with leads to further research."[139] They are, of course, very valuable for those purposes. In the main, however, they do not purport to do more than summarize what the cases hold, and the cases cited, or other cases, are much more authoritative. They may properly be cited for such summations, or to say that the cases are there collected. And, of course, if counsel does not have easy access to law libraries with other material, he must make do with what he has.

7.27 Overruling; Dissenting and Concurring Opinions

How to deal with dissenting and concurring opinions and cases which you believe ripe for overruling presents delicate and difficult problems.

Insofar as overruling is concerned, the answer is "don't ask for it if you can possibly avoid doing so." Courts are reluctant to admit error even on the part of their deceased brethren if they can avoid it. And usually they can, and you can, by distinguishing the prior authority on some ground, even a flimsy one. It is much better to say, if you honestly can, that the prior case differs from yours in several respects, and that in any event its reasoning should not be extended beyond the facts upon which it was based. Overruling can be requested as a final alternative.

Caution in this respect is even more essential if the presently sitting judges or a number of them participated in the decision you wish to have disapproved. Very rarely can judges be convinced that they were wrong, though it occasionally happens, as the small proportion of successful petitions for rehearing demonstrates. The United States Supreme Court in recent

---

[138]These and other examples are cited in Wiener, *id.* at 199.
[139]*Id.* at 196.

years has been more willing than most courts openly to disapprove prior decisions, even those of recent vintage. But more often than not, that Court as well as most others will use the technique of distinguishing or limiting a case to its own facts, or even ignoring it.

With respect to relatively recent cases which you believe a court might be willing to overrule, parsing the judges in advance may be more important than logical analysis of the issues. To what extent has the personnel of the court changed? Do the new members plus prior dissenters constitute a majority? Is there reason to believe the new members will join the dissenters? If these questions cannot be answered in the affirmative, your chances are thin but better than if the entire original panel is still sitting.

The judges themselves will be fully aware of such factors, but it would be imprudent for counsel to mention them. As an example, some students of Supreme Court history, including this one, surmised that the election of 1936 and President Roosevelt's unsuccessful court-packing proposition of 1937 had something to do with the 180 degree turn in the Supreme Court's interpretation of the Commerce and Due Process Clauses by the same Justices, or at least the two who had the balance of power, a few months later.[140] But those perhaps decisive political factors were not mentioned in the government's briefs. In many situations the court will determine for itself whether it wants to overrule irrespective of what counsel does.

Counsel should accordingly search for factual differences which might be not only technical distinctions but good reasons for persuading judges to change their minds.

Whether dissenting or concurring opinions can usefully be cited also depends on the circumstances and on the judges. No difficulty arises, of course, if the point for which you want to use such an opinion was not disputed by the majority, as sometimes happens. The fact that the majority did not express its agreement will, of course, lessen the authority of the separate opinion but not devastatingly in the absence of disagreement.

Apart from that, dissenting opinions may be expected to carry weight only if the majority by that time has become openminded on the subject, or includes new personnel who are will-

---

[140]See R. Stern, *The Commerce Clause and the National Economy (1933–1946)*, 59 Harv. L. Rev. 645, 883 (1947).

ing to consider overruling the prior decision. If the case or line of cases is old or out of line with the modern trend of authority, or has been undermined by subsequent cases, there may be some basis for optimism. A change in the court's membership can be significant if it is substantial enough to produce a possible new majority and if there is reason to believe that the new judges will vote differently from the old. Except in such rare instances, reliance on dissents is dangerous business to be undertaken only as a last resort.[141]

Concurring opinions can also be relied upon when the majority has neither agreed upon any position nor rejected that taken in the concurrence. In that situation the position of the judges may have to be cumulated to discern any majority view.

7.28 Quotations

Don't overload a brief with a number of long quotations from judicial opinions or anything else. As stated by Judge Tone and Mr. Howe:

> "Quotations from authorities should be used sparingly. Those used should be as short as circumstances permit. What and how much to quote 'is essentially a matter of judgment and proportion.' Wiener, BRIEFING AND ARGUING FEDERAL APPEALS 242 (1961). Of course, quotation should not be made out of context, and an omission that would change the meaning of a quotation should never be made."[142]

One manual on brief writing has gone so far as to suggest that unless "the exact language is vital or helps to clinch the argument," quotations should be avoided; counsel should summarize or paraphrase, since "the court can always read the original quotation," presumably by going to the library.[143] This seems to me to be the wrong approach.

What judges dislike is not quotation per se, but a long series of quotations, even when interlarded with explanatory descriptions of what each case is about. Judges have noted that after a while the reader tends to skip at least the last part of a long quotation—and that reaction is not limited to judges, as I can personally attest.

This does not mean that a brief should never quote, even

---

[141]If the opinion writer is well known, a concurring or dissenting opinion in another court may, on occasion, be worth citing.

[142]Tone and Howe, *supra* note 100, at 8–15.

[143]M. Pittoni, BRIEF WRITING AND ARGUMENTATION, p. 39 (3d ed., 1967).

at length. Colonel Wiener, and I agree, suggests a number of situations in which long quotations may be useful and should not be treated as undesirable per se:

> "It is a good, sound rule of thumb that quotations from opinions should be included only when they add something, and that, whenever possible, they should be short rather than long. . . .
>
> "After all, a good many judges read briefs while sitting in easy chairs, and it is therefore going to advance your case if you quote enough pat matter to satisfy their curiosity without discommoding them and making them get up—particularly if their reading takes place where they do not have ready access to the law library."[144]

A judge is more likely to read what you want him to read if, to use Colonel Wiener's illustration, he can do so without getting out of his chair. It is the function of the brief, so far as page limitations permit, to place everything important for the resolution of disputed matters before the judge so that he need not turn to anything else, or at least not beyond the record or appendix which should also be conveniently available.

What should be quoted? Obviously, any court will want to know what it or a higher court has said on the subject, particularly if it is directly in point, unless, of course, it is hornbook law or otherwise well known to the judge. On doubtful or critical or unfamiliar matters, the court will want to know exactly what other courts have said, and particularly those whose decisions are binding or must be given important weight. The same will often be true as to older but important authorities with which the court is unfamiliar. For the lawyer to paraphrase will force the judge reading the brief back to the opinion itself to find out what it actually said. Sometimes lawyers have been known to give their own flavor to judicial language which they paraphrase, even though they may well believe that they are accurately reflecting what the court wrote. Judges, of course, know that.

It would seem obvious that if a judge has expressed an idea as well as or better than you can, it will carry more persuasive force than even the same words of counsel not surrounded by quotation marks. If I had been able to say that the above paragraph had been written by the Chief Justice of the United States or of your state, would you not have given it greater weight? Whenever, in reviewing a brief, I find that the writer has substituted his own words for the similar language of a judge or

---

[144]F. Wiener, BRIEFING AND ARGUING FEDERAL APPEALS, p. 242 (1967).

other authority, I not only go back to the original quotation but try to make sure that my colleague will not make the same error again.

The same treatment should be accorded to any material of significance not readily accessible to the court, including the writings of scholars and, even more clearly, legislative material. If the reasons why a statute should be interpreted in a certain way appear from the committee report or congressional debates, the court will and should be more impressed by what they say than if the same idea appears to emanate from the brief writer. The judge may not be able or willing to attempt to find the legislative sources if you do not quote them for him.

A solution to the apparent dilemma of not quoting lengthily or too often, and at the same time of providing the judges with what they would normally want to read, is to vary your pace. Quoted language may often be fitted into your own textual paragraph, without indentation but in quotation marks,[145] followed by the proper citation in text or in footnote. This will not have the distracting effect of long indented passages. Obviously this technique will be of no avail if your brief still consists of a series of long quotations from cases or other sources, particularly if the connection to your case is not explained. The mere change in form will not fool the reader if that is all it is. But fitting a quoted passage into your text will give it more authority than your own similar language followed only by the citation, and will not have the effect of a long, psychologically discouraging indented quotation.

This effect will be lost if repeated too often, but it can be

---

[145]The Bluebook (A UNIFORM SYSTEM OF CITATION, Rule 5(a), p. 20 (12th ed., 1976)) mandates that quotations of up to 49 words should not be indented, but that quotations of 50 words or more should be indented. That may be a reasonable guide for students writing for law reviews, though I doubt the wisdom of any such arbitrary line even for writers without prior experience. Briefs should be written in the manner which will be most attractive and persuasive to the judges to whom they are addressed. Not the number of words in a quoted passage but whether it fits more appropriately as a part of the sentence or paragraph to which it is attached, whether it will be more effective standing apart from the text, and whether one has the feel that the judges will be more likely to give it more attention if it is not indented should be the guiding criteria.

The same paragraph of the Bluebook says that indented quotations should not be in quotation marks. On occasion, however, a quotation may end with a citation. This may leave it unclear to the reader, who may not have memorized the Bluebook, whether or not this final citation is in the quotation or to the quotation's source, even though the Bluebook also says that the citation for the quotation should follow the quotation but be unindented. Accordingly, I always insist that quotations, indented or not, be in quotation marks. Even in the few states in which the appellate court rules refer to the Bluebook for matters of form, such a clarifying modification is not likely to result in disciplinary action.

effectively employed along with occasional short indented quotations in a manner which will keep the reader's attention.

An effective technique may be both to paraphrase a holding and then to quote language which demonstrates the accuracy of your interpretation. This may help persuade a reader who tends to skim long quotations by establishing your credibility on the spot.

Applying the same standard of making readily available to the judges what they do not know and would want to know about the case, the brief writer may also quote, if necessary at some length, from testimony or exhibits in the record when the exact language is important.[146] Such matter may appear, however, in the Statement of Facts or Appendix, in which case more summary treatment in the Argument should be sufficient.

With respect to legislative history materials, or other sources that may not readily be available and that are lengthy but also important to the argument, reproduction in an appendix or addendum to the brief may be appropriate.

All of the above leads back to the conclusion that in the ordinary case quotations should neither be numerous nor long. But this generalization, like most others in this field, must yield when the reasons underlying it are outweighed by the greater importance of making readily available to the court exact language which the judges will want to see for themselves.

The desirability, indeed necessity under most rules of court, of limiting the length of a brief is, of course, a factor which must be considered in determining how much should be quoted. The brief writer's judgment and common sense as applied to the needs of the particular case, not any absolute rule, must ultimately control. Thus, while quotations should not be overdone, they should not be underdone either.[147]

Counsel should be aware that judges may not be as impressed by the words of other judges or even of themselves as lawyers might suspect. Former Chief Justice Schaefer of Illinois has cautioned in this respect:

> "Both in the oral argument and in the written brief be wary of how you use the court's own language. A man does not sit very long on an appellate court before he becomes extremely cautious as to the meaning of what some judge, including himself, has said

---

[146]See F. Wiener, BRIEFING AND ARGUING FEDERAL APPEALS, p. 244 (1967).
[147]*Accord, id.* at 242–245.

in some earlier case. Your naivete about that when you are a judge lasts just until the first time somebody quotes back at you something you have written yourself. After that experience, your guard is eternally up. Having seen how what you wrote with a particular situation in mind and confined to that really—and perhaps you were a little careless, even though you tried not to be—can be quoted as applicable in quite different circumstances, you are going to be cautious about taking the words at their sheer face value, whether it be your language or some other judge's."[148]

Chief Judge Prettyman, formerly of the Court of Appeals for the District of Columbia Circuit, also emphasized the need for judicial language to be read in the light of the facts and issues in a particular case:

"Sentences out of context rarely mean what they seem to say, and nobody in the whole world knows that better than the appellate judge. He has learned it by the torturing experience of hearing his own sentences read back to him."[149]

Judges are aware of their own shortcomings in this respect. It is important that counsel know that the judges are aware. Words addressed to a particular problem may not have been meant to cover another. Counsel can convince the court that they do only if for other reasons he can show that they should.

7.29 Forms of Citation

Most court rules do not specify the forms of citations though a few do in some respects. But the forms approved in those rules are substantially the same as the forms recommended in the few recognized form manuals and used by knowledgeable lawyers. The leading works on the subject are *Effective Legal Research* (1969), a treatise by Miles O. Price and Harry Bitner, Librarians for the Columbia and Yale University Law School libraries; Price's *A Practical Manual of Standard Legal Citations* (2d ed., 1958), which is incorporated in the Price and Bitner work; and *A Uniform System of Citation* (12th ed., 1978), published by the Harvard Law Review Association but sponsored by the Columbia, Harvard, Pennsylvania and Yale law reviews, commonly known as the Bluebook, and so referred to herein.

[148]W. Schaefer, *The Appellate Court,* 3 U. Chi. L. S. Rec. 1, 11 (No. 2, 1954).
[149]E. B. Prettyman, *Some Observations Concerning Appellate Advocacy,* 39 Va. L. Rev. 285, 295 (1953).

This book will not attempt to cover a subject to which others have devoted entire volumes. The text of the latest edition of the Bluebook covers 170 pages, Price and Bitner's treatise, 620 pages, and Price's *Practical Manual,* 101. Nevertheless, suggestions as to the desirable practice in a number of common situations may be helpful.

As to a number of items, the usage in the courts and the secondary authorities, including those cited above, is not always uniform. The rules of Florida, Indiana, Oregon and Wisconsin refer to the Bluebook as the official guide to correct form. The Bluebook, however, seems to have been prepared primarily, and understandably, from the viewpoint and for the use of law review and other scholarly writers, not for briefs. That this makes a difference is occasionally noted in the Price and Bitner work.[150] For illustrations, see Secs. 7.25, p. 300, and 7.28, note 145, *supra.* Although usually it will be helpful, the Bluebook should therefore not be automatically followed by brief writers.

(a) United States Supreme Court Cases

United States Supreme Court decisions need only be cited to the official United States Reports. The bound volumes of the Supreme Court Reporter and the Lawyers Edition contain the official pagination as well as their own. They may be cited, however, as a convenience to counsel in offices which save space by not having the official reports.[151] Those unofficial reporters, and the *United States Law Week,* published by The Bureau of National Affairs, Inc., the publisher of this book, and the Commerce Clearing House *U.S. Supreme Court Bulletin,* should be cited for recent cases not yet reported in the Preliminary Prints of the United States Reports, which contain the final official pagination. These Prints customarily arrive a number of months after the decisions reported are rendered.[152] The *Law Week* and the *Bulletin* are ordinarily mailed out no later than the next day, several days before the slip opinions are available for public distribution; the Supreme Court Reporter and the Lawyers Edition advance sheets arrive a few weeks later.

---

[150]See also F. Wiener, BRIEFING AND ARGUING FEDERAL APPEALS, pp. 222–249 (1967).

[151]Florida requires that all three Supreme Court reports be cited, as "380 U.S. 343, 85 S. Ct. 1004, 13 L.Ed.2d 882 (1965)." Florida Appellate Rule 9.800(j).

[152]The Preliminary Print received in my office October 8, 1980, contained cases decided on March 17, 1980.

There is a divergence of view as to how to cite the first 90 volumes of the Supreme Court Reports. Like their English counterparts, as originally published they bore volume numbers attached to the name of the Reporters who published them for the years 1790 to 1874—Dallas, Cranch, Wheaton, Peters, Howard, Black and Wallace. Each Reporter published his own series of reports, running from Black's two volumes to Howard's 24. These volumes were cited simply as 4 Wheat. or 21 Wall., for example. The first volume of the Dallas Reports contained no Supreme Court opinions, but the decisions of other state and federal courts then sitting in Philadelphia for which Mr. Dallas was also the Reporter. Those decisions also were bound in with the United States Supreme Court decisions up to 1800 in 2, 3 and 4 Dallas.

More recent publishers of the bound volumes have put "U.S." numbers upon them, from 1 to 90 U.S. In 1954 the Bluebook, in the words of Colonel Wiener, "introduced the thoroughly abominable system of using the numerical numbers plus a parenthetical citation to the Reporter: e.g., 5 U.S. (1 Cranch) 137,"[153] which he regarded as a misuse of "one of youth's inalienable privileges to be . . . wrong" and a "perverse innovation." Giving primary emphasis in this way to the retrospectively established United States volume number has the advantage of putting the volume in overall chronological sequence and showing to the uninitiated that the volumes are a part of the United States Reports. Using the original numbers of the volumes, however, not only provides the historical flavor but is historically accurate, as the citing of the Dallas volumes as "U.S." certainly is not. The Supreme Court itself adheres to the original numbers and names,[154] and, for what it is worth, Colonel Wiener and Messrs. Price, Bitner, Stern and Gressman (though without Colonel Wiener's vehemence or certainty as to a matter of perhaps not world-shaking importance) agree,[155] the Bluebook to the contrary notwithstanding.

Price and Bitner (p. 339) suggest that the presently preferred method of citation should be, for example:

---

[153]F. Wiener, BRIEFING AND ARGUING FEDERAL APPEALS, pp. 228–229 (1967).

[154]E.g., "*McNutt* v. *Bland*, 2 How. 9 (1844)" and many other cases cited in *Navarro Savings Ass'n* v. *Lee*, 446 U.S. 458, 460–461 (1980).

[155]See F. Wiener, BRIEFING AND ARGUING FEDERAL APPEALS, pp. 228-229 (1967), and R. Stern and E. Gressman, SUPREME COURT PRACTICE, p. 700 (5th ed., 1978).

Smith v. *Orton,* 21 How. 241 (U.S. 1858).

This is a reasonable compromise, but including the U.S. volume number in parentheses would be even better:

Smith v. *Orton,* 21 How. (88 U.S.) 241 (1858).

This would give all the information needed by judges and lawyers not aware of the names of the first seven Supreme Court Reporters, and still retain historical accuracy.

(b) Other Federal Court Cases

In citing cases in the lower federal courts, the identity of the court and the year should appear following the volume and page numbers.

As to federal district court cases reported in the Federal Supplement, there is agreement that they should be cited as, for example:

Barber v. *Seville,* 295 F. Supp. 477 (N.D. Cal. 1974).[156]

In citing cases in the United States courts of appeals, the courts were often formerly identified as "C.C.A. 3d" or "C.A. 3d" preceding the date, but West Publishing Company has long used "3d Cir." instead. The current Bluebook (p. 29) goes along with the latter usage, and most lawyers now defer to the Bluebook. The presently prevalent form used in the United States Supreme Court, "CA6" without any spaces or periods, more closely follows the form previously used.[157] The Supreme Court's present version—perhaps with a space before the number—is simpler and easier to write, and takes three or four typed or printed spaces instead of eight. The Supreme Court form should be at least as authoritative as the Bluebook or the West Publishing Company, particularly when its form is simpler and more economical in space. Take your choice. Of course, none of the above methods of citation can be labeled "wrong."

Cases in the United States Court of Appeals for the District of Columbia Circuit can be cited as

CA DC or D.C. Cir.

---

[156]In a court martial hearing many years ago I heard such a citation orally rendered as "North Dakota California," which all the other non-lawyer judges and advocates present thought was entirely appropriate.

[157]See, for example, 428 U.S. 404, 455, 479.

That court is to be distinguished from the local District of Columbia Court of Appeals, which is cited as

D.C. App.

The old federal cases, before the beginning of the Federal Reporter System in 1880, are collected in alphabetical order in the Federal Cases. They may be cited by volume and case or page number, preferably both, as follows:

Wiener v. *Bluebook, Inc.*, 8 F.Cas.No. 4733, p. 923 (C.C.W.D. N.Y. 1859).

The page number may, if you prefer, precede the case number. For those who do not remember, the "C.C." stands for circuit court.

(c) State Court Decisions

In general, state courts want their own cases cited to the state's official reports, with West's National Reporter System citations added as a convenience to counsel who may only have the West unofficial reports in their libraries. In some states, only the official reports are required to be cited,[158] leaving optional citations to the National Reporter System. In others, both reports must be cited.[159] A number of states, in the interest of economy, have abandoned their separate reports and now use only the National Reporter System[160] for their region, though perhaps with the cases from their particular state bound together in a local edition as well as in the regional reporter.

Conversely, when cases from other states are cited, the Reporter System should be preferred over the official edition, for a great many law offices and court libraries will have the regional reporters covering other states but not the official reports of those states. Both should be cited if available. Some states so require,[161] while others leave it optional.[162] The official

---

[158]Illinois, Massachusetts, New Jersey, New York, Tennessee, Virginia.

[159]Indiana, Iowa, Oregon, Pennsylvania, South Carolina, Washington.

[160]Official state reports were abandoned, in the years indicated, in: Alabama, 1975; Alaska, 1959; Arizona, 1973; Delaware, 1962; Florida, 1948; Idaho, 1978; Iowa, 1968; Kentucky, 1951; Louisiana, 1972; Maine, 1965; Massachusetts, 1975; Minnesota, 1977; Mississippi, 1965; Missouri, 1956; New Mexico, 1975; North Dakota, 1953; Oklahoma, 1953; Tennessee, 1971; Texas, 1962; Utah, 1974; Wisconsin, 1975; Wyoming, 1959.

[161]Indiana, Iowa, New Jersey, New York, Oregon, Pennsylvania, South Carolina, Washington.

[162]Illinois.

citations of other jurisdictions can be obtained by using Shepard's, but as a practical matter this may not be worth the effort where not required.

When only the National Reporter System is cited, the names of the state and court, if they do not otherwise appear, should be given, such as:

> *Brown* v. *Platt,* 249 N.E.2d 762 (Ill. 1963).

For a case in a state intermediate appellate court, the parenthetical expression should be:

> (Fla., 3d DCA 1978).

Presumably all lawyers know that the name of the state or country standing alone signifies the highest court of that jurisdiction.

(d) Dates

The date should always appear, although some courts do not give dates for their own cases. Customarily the dates should appear at the end of the citation; in a few state reports,[163] however, the date directly follows the name of the case, and Indiana so requires for briefs. When both lower and higher appellate courts are cited for the same case, the dates should follow both citations if the dates differ, but only the last if they are the same. For example,

> *Gressman* v. *Grossman,* 525 F.2d 211 (CA 4, 1972), cert. denied, 424 U.S. 926 (1973).

If both rulings had been in 1973, no date need be shown for the court of appeals decision.

(e) Words Showing Case History

The Bluebook would italicize such words as "certiorari denied," "affirmed" or "reversed." The Supreme Court does not, and I see no reason for it. Both abbreviate "cert." in "cert. denied," and also "aff'd" and "rev'd." These are reasonable space-saving devices, despite Colonel Wiener's contrary preference.[164]

---

[163]E.g., California, Illinois, Indiana, Ohio.
[164]Cf. 428 U.S. 433, 455, n. 30 (1976), with F. Wiener, BRIEFING AND ARGUING FEDERAL APPEALS, pp. 232–233 (1967).

It is customary to note that certiorari was denied to show the complete history of a case, even though the Supreme Court has often said that the denial of certiorari cannot be taken to mean anything except that four Justices did not vote to review the case.[165] For that reason Mr. Justice Frankfurter at one time reprimanded me, as Acting Solicitor General, for adding "cert. denied" to citations.[166] Nevertheless, the Solicitor General's Office did not alter its practice.

(f) Names of Cases

Usually cases should be cited by the name appearing at the beginning of the opinion. But if the name is long, it can be abbreviated, often by using the running head at the top of the later pages of the reported opinion. The first names of individuals need not be included, but, apart from that, the first name in the caption should always be written out in full, except for familiar initials like NLRB, SEC and NAACP. "United States" should be spelled out.

When the name of a case changes from one court to another, this is indicated as follows (in an extreme hypothetical example):

> *Elman* v. *United States,* 497 F. Supp. 222 (E.D. Pa. 1971), affirmed *sub nom. Davis* v. *United States,* 540 F.2d 471 (CA 3, 1972), cert. denied *sub nom. Frankel* v. *Commission,* 404 U.S. 943 (1973).

If the only change is to reverse the order of the same names, as often occurs when a case is taken to the United States Supreme Court, the difference in names need not be shown.[167]

The Bluebook italicizes names of cases in the text but not in footnotes; the Supreme Court, the West reporters and I do in both places. There seems to be no sense to the differentiation. Traditionally, the "v." in the title of a case was italicized if the names of the parties were not, and vice versa. This is still the Supreme Court's practice and that used in this book, but the

---

[165]Cf. Mr. Justice Frankfurter in *Maryland* v. *Baltimore Radio Show,* 338 U.S. 912, 917–920 (1950), with Mr. Justice Jackson in *Brown* v. *Allen,* 344 U.S. 443, 542–543 (1953). See also R. Stern and E. Gressman, SUPREME COURT PRACTICE, Sec. 5.7 (5th ed., 1978).

[166]See *Elgin, Joliet and Eastern Ry.* v. *Gibson,* 355 U.S. 897 (1957) (Frankfurter, J., and Harlan, J.); F. Wiener, BRIEFING AND ARGUING FEDERAL APPEALS, p. 233 (1967).

[167]See Bluebook, pp. 46–47.

Bluebook and West now print the names and the "v." in the same type. Since the difference is hardly noticeable, I remain neutral.

(g)   Rehearings

Citations to decisions on petitions for rehearing are unnecessary if all that results is a simple denial. If the court does anything else, even if only to change the opinion but not the result, that should be noted.[168]

(h)   Statutes

Federal statutes may be cited in one or more of four different ways, often in combination:

(1) as "Section 4 of the Act of March 4, 1971";
(2) as "P.L. (for Public Law) 89–4";
(3) as "55 Stat. 976";
(4) as "41 U.S.C. §242."

State laws often appear in equivalent forms. The first and second methods may be necessary for recent unreported statutes. Some court rules require use of both the third and fourth methods, referring to the annual session laws of the legislature, for which "Stat." is the federal equivalent, and also the codification of laws customarily used in the jurisdiction, official or unofficial. Most often the latter is sufficient by itself, except when tracing a law through various changes is material. The practice in your jurisdiction as to this should be determined and followed.

(i)   Legislative Material

Federal legislative material should be cited by committee report, bill or document number, with the Congress, session, page and date also shown, as: "S. Rep. 321, 96th Cong., 2d Sess. 36 (1978)." The Congressional Record should be cited by volume, page and date. Be aware that the Record first appears in the "daily editions," and that the final edition has different pagination. Always cite the latter if it is available. If the daily edition

---

[168]F. Wiener, BRIEFING AND ARGUING FEDERAL APPEALS, pp. 233–234 (1967).

is used, that should be specifically indicated, with the precise date, as:

110 Cong. Rec. 1049 (daily ed., May 15, 1975).

In many states legislative material equivalent to the Congressional Record and other federal documents is nonexistent or hard to find. For those who do not know what is available, state legislators or law librarians should be consulted.

(j) Books and Articles

The names of books and periodicals have been cited in various ways, none of which can be called incorrect so long as the name of the author and of the book or article and periodical are shown, along with the date. The edition should also be indicated, if there has been more than one. The names of books and articles in periodicals are to be italicized in briefs, but not names of the authors or the periodicals. (Solid capital letters are used for the names of books and their authors, and of periodicals, in law review footnotes; the use of different typefaces for text and footnotes seems unnecessarily confusing.) Any reasonable variation should be acceptable.

The Bluebook adds the initial of the author's first name to the last name for authors of books, presumably because so many persons have the same last name. The Bluebook omits the initial for the authors of articles, leaving only the last name, although the above good reasoning would apply to them as well. I recommend initials in both instances.

7.30   Facts Outside the Record—Mootness, Brandeis Briefs and Judicial Notice

That parties and courts, including appellate courts, are limited to reliance upon facts in the record is an accepted principle which, like most principles, is generally true but not invariably. See Sec. 6.1, *supra*. The entire system of determining disputes by trial before a court rests on the assumption that decisions must be based on the evidence submitted to (and held admissible by) the court and nothing else. In the normal situation, attempts to present non-record facts to courts are "unprofessional conduct."[169]

---

[169]*ABA Standards Relating to the Administration of Criminal Justice, Compilation,* pp. 98, 135-136 (1974).

Facts which are subject to judicial notice, however, constitute a well recognized exception to the general rule. "The taking
of judicial notice of a fact outside of the record is part of the
inherent power and function of every court, whether a trial or
appellate tribunal."[170] This does not play a large part in most
litigation, and thus does not to any significant extent undermine
the general principle as to staying within the record.

The definition in the Federal Rules of Evidence (Rule
201(b)), which is in substance declaratory of the preexisting
general law, is that

> "A judicially noticed fact must be one not subject to reasonable
> dispute in that it is either (1) generally known within the territorial
> jurisdiction of the trial court or (2) capable of accurate and ready
> determination by resort to sources whose accuracy cannot reason-
> ably be questioned."[171]

The federal rule further provides in paragraph (e) that any
party is entitled to be heard as to the propriety of taking judicial notice of a particular fact, even after notice has initially
been taken. But there has been disagreement as to whether
evidence can be admitted to disprove a fact a court has found
indisputable. Professors Davis and Thayer and Dean Wigmore
favor admissibility, but Professors Morgan and McNaughton
and Dean McCormick oppose it. The federal rule, the Model
Code and the Uniform Rule are predicated upon indisputability once the court has determined that a fact is judicially noticeable.[172]

Federal Rule 201(a) "governs only judicial notice of adjudicative facts." The Advisory Committee's Note elaborates:

> "Adjudicative facts are simply the facts of the particular case.
> Legislative facts, on the other hand, are those which have rele-
> vance to legal reasoning and the lawmaking process, whether in
> the formulation of a legal principle or ruling by a judge or court
> or in the enactment of a legislative body."

---

[170]*Ibid.*; Wisconsin Supreme Court Justice George R. Currie, *Appellate Courts Use of Facts Outside of the Record by Resort to Judicial Notice and Independent Investigation,* 1960 Wis. L. Rev. 39.

[171]See also Advisory Committee Note to Federal Rule of Evidence 201; UNIFORM RULES OF EVIDENCE, Rule 201(b) (1974); P. Rothstein, RULES OF EVIDENCE FOR THE UNITED STATES COURTS AND MAGISTRATES, pp. 35–47 (2d ed., 1978); 2 K. Davis, ADMINISTRATIVE LAW TREATISE, Chap. 15 (1958 and 1965 pocket parts), §§10.3–10.4 (2d ed., 1978); K. Davis, *Judicial Notice,* 55 Colum. L. Rev. 945 (1955); 9 J. Wigmore, EVIDENCE, §§2565–2583 (3d ed., 1940); C. McCormick, EVIDENCE, §325 (1954); MODEL CODE OF EVIDENCE, Rule 802(c) (1949).

[172]See Advisory Committee Note to Federal Rule of Evidence 201(g), which collects the authorities.

The "terminology was coined by Professor Kenneth Davis" in his writings on the subject; but Professor Davis himself points out that the distinction, though not its formulation, reflected what courts had done "long before." "No rule deals with judicial notice of 'legislative' facts." With respect to legislative facts "the judge is unrestricted in his investigation and conclusion." This

> "renders inappropriate any limitation in the form of indisputability, any formal requirements of notice other than those already inherent in affording opportunities to hear or be heard and exchanging briefs, and any requirement of formal findings at any level. It should, however, leave open the possibility of introducing evidence through regular channels in appropriate situations."[173]

The scope of the doctrine of judicial notice is a matter of the substantive law of evidence, treated at length in the authorities cited above. Two aspects of the problem which often occur in appellate courts are, however, considered here. Although both are subject to analysis and justification in terms of judicial notice theory, the appellate courts seldom refer to them in that context.

(1) The first is the use of an appellate brief to demonstrate that legislation challenged under the Due Process clause was reasonable and therefore constitutional, or, more precisely, that a reasonable legislature could have determined that the statute reasonably served the public interest. In what came to be known as the Brandeis brief technique, Louis D. Brandeis, then a practicing attorney, devoted almost his entire brief in support of the validity of an Oregon law fixing maximum working hours for women to scientific writings establishing that overly long hours were detrimental to women's health. The Supreme Court, relying on this material and stating that it took "judicial cognizance of all matters of general knowledge," upheld the statute. *Muller* v. *Oregon*, 208 U.S. 412, 421 (1908). This was in substance applying the doctrine of judicial notice to legislative facts. Whether or not it was true in *Muller* v. *Oregon*, facts not of record which one party might call to a court's attention might not necessarily be indisputable on their face or by resort to sources whose accuracy cannot be reasonably questioned.

---

[173]Advisory Committee Note to Federal Rule of Evidence 201(a), quoting Professors Davis and Morgan; 2 K. Davis, ADMINISTRATIVE LAW TREATISE, §10.3 (2d ed., 1978); Currie, *supra* note 170, at 50.

Just when in a particular litigation legislative facts can be so established, or whether the safer course would be to include them in a trial record, is a matter for the judgment of the litigating lawyer. If facts really are indisputable, the party relying on them might gain by including them in the record before the trial court, either in the form of affidavits or through expert witnesses, even though preparing such testimony may be more of an effort and more costly than merely referring to one or more authoritative volumes. Often, however, affidavits or documents could be submitted in support of a motion for a summary judgment or a temporary injunction without the need of calling live witnesses. Facts stated should not be challenged if they are indisputable. Proving the facts in the trial court will bring them to the attention of all the judges—and jurors—hearing the case and eliminate any question as to their noticeability or indisputability.

If the dissenting party does dispute the accuracy of the facts or does not believe that they can be verified, he should make sure to advise the court as promptly as possible and, if feasible, to request some kind of hearing on whether the facts are adjudicative or legislative, or indisputable.

I suspect that the Brandeis brief technique is often employed by lawyers newly brought in on appeal, after it is too late to introduce the facts into the trial court record.

(2) The second class of facts which should be called to an appellate court's attention are usually indisputable facts which may change the status of the case, often by making it moot. Common examples are that a party has died, an election been held, a strike terminated, a statute or regulation repealed or modified, a case settled or decided, or a criminal sentence served. Facts of this sort occurring after a case has been instituted may terminate the controversy between the parties. Since Article III, Section 2, of the United States Constitution limits the judicial power to cases and controversies, mooting of the controversy for this reason will make the case nonjusticiable in the federal courts. The same principle governs in many state courts as well.

Usually counsel will as a matter of course call such matters to the appellate court's attention, either in the appropriate brief or in a special submission—by motion or even letter—before or after a brief is filed, depending upon when the fact becomes known to counsel. Facts of this sort are seldom disputable. They thus fall within the accepted scope of judicial notice, even though that is seldom mentioned.

The need for bringing such matters to a court's attention was dramatically demonstrated in *Fusari* v. *Steinberg,* 419 U.S. 379 (1974), where important amendments to the statutes under attack were not mentioned by any party until the oral argument. The Court found "it difficult to understand the failure of counsel fully to inform the Court of these amendments to Connecticut law" (p. 387, n. 12). Chief Justice Burger, concurring, put it more strongly (pp. 390–391):

> "It is disconcerting to this Court to learn of relevant and important developments in a case after the entire Court has come to the Bench to hear arguments.
>
> "Even at oral argument we were not informed of the changes in state law although both parties filed their briefs after the new statute was passed. . . . All parties had an obligation to inform the Court that the system which the District Court had enjoined had been changed; . . .
>
> "This Court must rely on counsel to present issues fully and fairly, and counsel have a continuing duty to inform the Court of any development which may conceivably affect an outcome."

How does a court know what it should judicially notice? The judges may know a fact personally, presumably because every intelligent person is aware of it. They may take notice without the help of or a request by counsel. Federal Evidence Rule 201(c) and (f) provides that "a court may take judicial notice, whether requested or not" and "at any stage of the proceeding."

A member of the Wisconsin Supreme Court has stated that

> "for many years (to the writer's knowledge since 1913) it has been the practice of the members of this court to refresh their recollection upon matters of which courts take judicial notice, by calling upon any department in the State Capitol for information necessary for an intelligent understanding of matters and issues pending before the court, as well as for assistance on the part of those familiar with voluminous records in locating matters therein contained."

Members of that Court

> "do on occasion make a personal search in the files of the state legislative reference library to obtain the legislative history of a particular bill enacted into statute. This is done in situations where it is believed that such legislative history might be material with respect to legislative intent. . . .
>
> ". . . No member of the court feels that in calling for, or in

accepting this assistance the proprieties of the judicial position have been infringed."[174]

"It is of course proper for counsel on appeal to set forth" similar material in their briefs "and request the court to take judicial notice thereof."[175]

Tennessee has embodied the principles of judicial notice with respect to facts occurring after judgment in the 1979 revision of its Rules of Appellate Procedure. Rule 14 provides that the appellate court in its discretion may consider facts "capable of ready demonstration" affecting the position of the parties or the subject matter of the action with respect to such matters as "mootness, bankruptcy, divorce, death, other judgments or proceedings [or] relief from the judgment." Such facts are usually not "genuinely" disputable. See Advisory Comment. They may come to the court's attention by motion of a party or on its own motion. Under the rule, the court "shall direct that the facts be presented in such manner and pursuant to such reasonable notice and opportunity to be heard as it deems fair."[176]

Tennessee thus provides a sensible procedural framework for applying the principles of judicial notice in this context. It enables appellate courts to take into account noncontroversial postjudgment facts for which a retrial in either the trial or appellate court would not be warranted.

Since counsel cannot be sure what a court will notice, he should by motion or in his brief call to the court's attention the facts which he desires the court to notice. If the fact is well known or obvious, no citations may be necessary. If counsel is not certain that the judges know the fact, or will accept it on his bare statement, supporting authorities should be cited or quoted. In the legal area the new fact might appear in a statute or administrative document, or in judicial files. Such documents are conclusive, at least as to what they contain, and what they contain, not its external truth, is what is significant. With respect to facts stated in scientific treatises, historical works or even a

---

[174]Currie, *supra* note 170, at 44–45.

[175]*Ibid.*

[176]The rule "is not intended to permit a retrial in the appellate court" or to replace or limit other means of obtaining post-judgment relief in the trial court. "Since appellate courts are ill-equipped to receive lengthy testimony, postjudgment facts will typically be presented in properly authenticated documents, public records, or affidavits or other sworn statements, any or all of which may accompany the motion." And the rule does not prevent the appellate court from remanding to the trial court for preparation of a supplemental record. J. Sobieski, *The Procedural Details of the Proposed Tennessee Rules of Appellate Procedure*, 46 Tenn. L. Rev. 1, 66–67 (1978).

reliable newspaper the question may be whether the fact is true. The nature of the fact will determine whether judicial notice can be taken merely of what the document says, or whether the document establishes the truth of the fact stated.

For example, a death certificate could be accepted as proof of a person's death. On the other hand, judicial notice of an administrative decision containing findings of fact may establish that the agency rendered the decision, but normally not that the facts found were true.

A court record could establish that a point was raised in a case, and this might suffice for purposes of collateral estoppel, but not necessarily to establish the truth of what the record said.

7.31 *Supra's, Infra's* and Footnotes

Supra's, *infra*'s and footnotes are frowned upon by appellate judges.[177] That does not mean they should never be used, but does mean that they should be used sparingly, and much less than some lawyers use them.

(1) The Latin words *"supra"* and *"infra"* are useful symbols for referring the reader to the page of the brief where a point was or will be discussed in greater depth or length. No English word seems to fit as well. "Above" and "below" also have vertical connotations, "earlier" and "later," temporal. Thus to say that the facts relating to this part of the argument appear "at pp. 9–16, *supra*" or that the legal authorities on a subject are discussed "at pp. 37–40, *infra*" is entirely appropriate.

The frequent use of these symbols in relation to case citations is, however, another matter. To follow the name of a case previously cited with *"supra"* alone, as courts and lawyers often do, either strains a reader's memory, usually unduly, or requires him to turn through a number of preceding pages, to his exasperation. The sin is not so grave if the prior page also is noted, as *"supra,* p. 14." That much of a clue, at least, should be compulsory, as it is in Tennessee Rule 27(h). Nevertheless, even that requires the reader to turn back to another page in order to find out where and when the case is reported.

In either event, judges are likely to search for or go back to the prior page only with great reluctance. Justice Wilkins of the Supreme Judicial Court of Massachusetts has referred to

---

[177]E.g., Iowa Rule 14.

"those disconsolate inadequacies, *supra* and *infra,* [which] border on the discourteous unless the [case] referred to is but a few lines away, and in that event they are not needed."[178] In other words, unless the proposed *supra* is within a page of the prior citation, repeat the citation; if it is within a page, you don't need it.

If counsel wants the court to know that the case was discussed earlier in the brief, as he properly may, abbreviating the name or giving only a part of the citation, such as the precise page, may be sufficient, such as

"*Stone* v. *Powell,* 428 U.S. at 490, *supra,*" or, preferably,
"discussed *supra* at 37," or
"*Detroit Edison,* 428 U.S. 579, *supra* at 37."

So long as enough of the citation is given for the judges to identify and, if necessary, find the case without turning the page, a "*supra*" is not objectionable. Generally, however, repeating the citation without any "*supra*" will be simpler unless there is good reason to let the court know that the same case is cited elsewhere. If the full name of the case or article is too long to keep repeating it, abbreviate it, as in the *Detroit Edison* example above, or as "Sobieski, *Procedural Details,* 46 Tenn. L. Rev. at 66."

(2) Footnotes overly used are an abomination. This will be evident from a reading of almost any recent Supreme Court opinion or law review article or note. Glancing at the bottom of a page whenever a footnote mark appears—particularly in the middle of a sentence or clause—interrupts the train of thought of the textual material; if it occurs as often as it seems to in the above types of legal writing, staying on the train is very difficult indeed. And the smaller print of the footnotes makes them harder to read.

I have sinned as much as other writers for law reviews in this respect, although at the beginning I may not have known any better and thought footnotes a mark of erudition.[179] The further I get from law school, the more my addiction to footnotes diminishes, as I hope this book demonstrates. "There may be some

---

[178]R. Wilkins, *The Argument of an Appeal,* 33 Cornell L.Q. 40, 43 (1947).
[179]A short search revealed I had written articles with 217 and 451 footnotes, but the latter was published in two installments totalling 113 pages. Law review writing accentuates the number of footnotes, since the numerical portion of every citation is required to appear in a footnote.

justification in the manifold areas of the academic world for that formidable display of learning and industry, the thin stream of text meandering in a vale of footnotes, but such a technique is quite self-defeating in [a brief]: it makes the writer's thoughts more difficult to follow—and hence far less likely to persuade the judicial reader."[180]

In short, one should not use footnotes for material which can as well fit in the textual part of the argument. Judges are much more likely to see and read what you write if it appears in the text; they will not be persuaded by what they do not read. And judges have often said that footnotes are disfavored.

A brief writer is trying to persuade judges; he is not working for a community of scholars. And although Supreme Court opinion writers may also be attempting to write persuasively, their need to persuade and convince is markedly less than the need of those who are trying to persuade them. The citation to a single case or a few cases should accompany the substantive proposition in the text. Footnotes may appropriately be used for citing a string of cases, particularly on a point of secondary importance. On a major issue, when a large number of cases may appropriately be cited, which is seldom (but see pp. 298–299, *supra*), the court may be more impressed if the cases appear in the text. If many cases in other state or federal courts are to be cited, as happens more often in treatises, legal encyclopedias and articles than in briefs, footnotes may be better than a long interruption in the flow of the argument.

The other legitimate use of footnotes is to express ideas which are off the main track of or collateral to the argument in the text. Footnote 179, *supra,* is an apt illustration. How many footnotes appear in several of my own articles is of incidental, if any, interest, and well off the main track of discussion of why footnoting should not be overdone.

Occasionally lawyers and judges use footnotes to meet opposing arguments. Supreme Court Justices frequently tuck into long footnotes their replies to dissenting or other opinions in the case, possibly because the other opinion reached them after the body of the opinion was first written. A brief writer may appropriately resort to this technique if the opposing argument must be met.but is weak, off the track of his argument and not very important.

---

[180]F. Wiener, BRIEFING AND ARGUING FEDERAL APPEALS, p. 245 (1967).

7.32   The Conclusion

The Conclusion of a brief performs one useful function. It tells the court what relief is wanted, what the brief writer wants the court to do. Federal Rule of Appellate Procedure 28(a)(5) requires "a short conclusion stating the precise relief sought," and United States Supreme Court Rule 34.1(j) calls for "a conclusion, specifying with particularity the relief to which the party believes himself entitled." In general, the state rules are identical or similar. E.g., Illinois Rule 341(e)(8).

Normally a single sentence is enough. It is sufficient to say that the judgment below should be affirmed or reversed or modified in a particular way, a criminal sentence reduced, or specified injunctive relief granted. If the injunctive relief is complicated, a paragraph may be needed instead of a sentence. If the reasons for the relief sought call for explanation, they should appear in a separate point before the Conclusion.

That may seem like an unimpressive way to end a brief. If not a peroration, such as many lawyers would enjoy inflicting on their readers, at least a short summary of the Argument, or of the reasons for the relief you seek, would appear to rise to a higher finishing note. But what persuades the judges is your reasoning, which should appear earlier in the brief. A summary may be helpful to them, and to you, at the beginning of the brief. That is why the rules often require a Summary of Argument, Points and Authorities or a Table of Headings at the beginning of the brief, not the end. They need not be repeated.

Judges tell us that repetition in briefs unnecessarily prolongs their reading matter and is to be avoided. The page limitations upon the brief writer convey the same message. In short, a summary conclusion or a fighting conclusion will not help you win your case, although, of course, it might convince your client that you are really on his side. You would not, however, want the court to surmise that that was its motivation.

The short text of the Conclusion should end with "Respectfully submitted," and the names and addresses of counsel. These are almost invariably the same as on the cover of the brief, although Oregon permits only the name of one lawyer, presumably lead counsel on the cover, but the names of other lawyers at the conclusion. See Sec. 7.12, *supra.* The name of a member of the bar of the appellate court should ordinarily come first, unless leave for a non-member to handle the appeal has been granted. In only a few jurisdictions (e.g., New Hampshire) must a member of the bar actually sign the brief next to or above his typed or printed name. Usually typing or printing the names is sufficient; the lawyer will be held fully responsible for a brief to which his name is thus attached. New Hampshire also wants a waiver of or request for oral argument, a designation of the lawyer who will argue, and an estimate of the time of argument (not exceeding 20 minutes). In Alabama, the request for argument should also appear after the names of counsel as well as on the front cover.

For the reasons indicated in the discussion of covers of briefs, the phone numbers of counsel and the date the brief was completed or filed should follow the names and addresses of counsel. Often, though unpredictably, these items turn out to be useful, particularly to the clerk.

The certificate of service will generally appear at the very end, on a separate page, unless the clerk prefers it to be filed separately (as in the United States Supreme Court).

If a member of the bar is brought into a case which has been briefed by other lawyers or merely asked to allow his name to be used, he should be aware that the court will hold him responsible if the brief is scandalous, misleading or inadequate in other respects, or even if it is just not very good. If he is not in a position to rewrite the brief or to check its contents, he should at least read it and inquire of the brief writer as to whether the usual means of checking and verifying the contents have been employed. If anything in the argument arouses his suspicion, skepticism or other doubt, he should inquire into it to the extent necessary. For the court will regard the brief as his. A bad or sloppy brief, as well as a good one, will affect his reputation with the court.

7.33 Answering Briefs

The main brief for an appellee or respondent is in general governed by the same rules and principles as the main brief for an appellant or petitioner. There is, of course, one important invariable difference: apart from the Table of Contents, Index, Summary of Argument and Points and Authorities, all of the sections of the brief preliminary to the Argument may either be omitted completely or limited to what is deemed necessary to correct the inadequacies or omissions in the appellant's brief.[181]

This means that the appellee's brief need not include the statements of the Nature of the Case and the Jurisdictional Facts, the citations to the Opinions Below, the Questions Presented and the Statutes Involved. A Statement of Facts may also be omitted, but this will occur only in the rare instance in which the statement in the appellant's brief is entirely satisfactory to the appellee. Even in that situation, the better course is for appellee not to omit the heading, but to say that the facts are undisputed, and that he accepts the statement in appellant's brief or, sometimes, in the opinion below.

The rules in some jurisdictions require the appellee's brief to state the extent to which it disagrees with appellant's Statement if it does not wish the court to accept appellant's Statement of Facts as correct.[182] Pennsylvania Appellate Rule 2112 similarly requires appellee to challenge the appellant's Questions Presented if not satisfied with them. But the court would be likely to draw such a conclusion even without such a rule. Delaware requires that appellee's Summary of Argument admit or deny the propositions stated in appellant's Summary.

As a practical matter the appellee usually has the choice of supplementing and correcting the appellant's statement of issues and of facts, or of restating those parts of the brief in his own language. Courts prefer the first technique, as that enables them readily to focus on the questions and facts as to which the parties disagree, and also makes for a shorter brief. Not infrequently, however, appellee's counsel may come to the conclusion that appellant's Statement of Facts is so prejudicial to appellee, by reason of its emphasis, organization and selection of material, and not merely because of erroneous statements, that a complete restatement by appellee is essential. Appellee's counsel will have to determine the method of presentation of the facts which will be most persuasive in his particular case. I have done it both ways.

If appellee chooses to make a complete Statement of Facts of his own, he should be exceptionally careful not to omit the harmful facts stressed by his adversary. He should face up to them, presumably with less or different emphasis, and, if possi-

---

[181]E.g., United States Supreme Court Rule 34.2; Federal Rule of Appellate Procedure 28(b); Illinois Rule 341(f).

[182]Georgia, Michigan, Oregon, Pennsylvania, Utah.

ble, with a minimizing explanation, or by denying or refuting them. Since the appellate judges will already have read them in appellant's brief, ignoring them will be of no avail.

It is more likely that the appellant's statement of the Questions Presented may be satisfactory to appellee—or at least not harmful enough to call for a restatement. But often the phrasing of the questions will be loaded in the appellant's direction, so that a restatement may give an impression more sympathetic to the appellee's position.

Appellee may wish to present questions in addition to those raised by the appellant. So long as he is not seeking a change in a judgment in his favor, he can make such additional arguments without taking a cross-appeal. (See Sec. 4.7, *supra.*) If he has taken a cross-appeal, the points for which the cross-appeal was taken should be stated in the Questions Presented in appellee's brief, and argued in the Argument.

Appellee may and should organize both his Statement of Facts and Argument in the manner most advantageous to his position. Except in Georgia,[183] he need not follow his opponent's arrangement, although in the course of his argument he should indicate which of appellant's arguments he is meeting, citing the pages of appellant's brief. Normally appellee, like appellant, will want to begin with his own strongest point, but sometimes the argument will not fit into such an organization. Or it may seem essential to refute the appellant's principal argument at the beginning.

The page limitations are usually the same for the principal briefs for appellant and appellee. See Sec. 7.6, *supra.* As shown in Sec. 7.4, *supra,* appellee also usually is allowed the same time to prepare his brief as is the appellant, though in some state courts and the United States Supreme Court his time is substantially less. This difference is presumably justified on the ground that appellee can start his preparation before receiving appellant's brief. He can and should familiarize himself with the record and authorities and engage in whatever research he anticipates to be necessary during the period in which appellant's brief is being written. Often appellee can even prepare drafts of the parts of his brief which he is sure will be necessary without waiting to see what appellant says.

---

[183]Georgia Rule 24-3618(c)(1) provides that appellee's brief should follow the questions in appellant's Enumeration of Errors.

Appellee must also recognize that his main brief will be his only shot at the court, except in the rare instance in which newly discovered authorities will justify the submission of a supplemental memorandum. See Sec. 7.35, *infra*. He is not entitled to surrebuttal to appellant's reply brief.[184] That means that any arguments he anticipates that appellant may make in the reply brief or that the court will think of must be answered in the only brief he will be permitted to file.

The one situation in which a fourth brief is allowed in most jurisdictions as a matter of course is where the appellee has taken a cross-appeal and argued additional points in his own brief. His main brief is regarded as his opening brief on such matters, and the appellant's reply brief as the principal answering brief with respect to them. Appellee will then have a chance to submit a reply brief of his own, which is the equivalent of the reply which an appellant is usually permitted to make.

Usually appellee will have one major advantage over appellant. He has won in the court below. Appellant faces a heavy burden in overturning a jury's verdict or the factual findings of a trial court. The trial court's analysis of the facts in particular is always accorded great weight, both because the trial judge has had the opportunity to see and hear the witnesses, and because, as the appellate court well knows, the trial judge generally has been able to devote much more time to the case than it can.

Appellee should make the most of these advantages, such as by quoting the findings below or by showing that the case turns on the credibility of witnesses, as to which the conclusions of the jury or the trial judge are regarded as almost completely controlling except where the most obvious error appears on the face of the record. These factors, as well as the fact that trial judges are more often right than wrong, result in the affirmance of the decisions below in the large majority of appeals.

A recent study indicates that "16 state supreme courts over a 100-year period . . . had a reversal rate of 38.5%."[185] The rate of reversal was substantially greater—50 percent—in cases heard by supreme courts after exercising discretion to grant leave to appeal.[186]

---

[184]In some states appellant is not entitled to file a reply brief. See Sec. 7.34, *infra*.

[185]*Godfrey* v. *Georgia*, 446 U.S. 420, 453 (1980) (dissenting opinion of Mr. Justice White). Cf. Note, *Courting Reversal: The Supervisory Role of State Supreme Courts*, 87 Yale L.J. 1191, 1198, 1215 (1978).

[186]*Courting Reversal*, *supra* note 185, at 1201.

7.34 Reply Briefs

The appellant is usually accorded a short period of time to answer appellee's brief,[187] in most jurisdictions from 10 to 20 days after that brief is filed, served or received (see Sec. 7.4, *supra*). The rules of a few states seem to make no provision for a reply brief at all.[188] North Carolina's Rule 28(h) prohibits a reply brief except in response to additional questions presented in appellee's brief, as permitted under paragraph (c). Wisconsin Rule 809.19(4) provides that appellant shall file either a reply brief or a statement that none will be filed.

The time for the reply is in some courts, including the federal, measured backward from the date the court's argument session begins. Replies may be filed in the United States Supreme Court up to one week before the date of oral argument and only by leave of Court thereafter. United States Supreme Court Rule 35.3. In the United States courts of appeals the reply brief is due 14 days after service of appellee's brief, but at least three days before the argument. Federal Rule of Appellate Procedure 31(a).

If appellee has cross-appealed, the place for appellant to answer appellee's new contentions is in his reply brief.[189] Seventh Circuit Rule 9(f) (1980) sensibly provides that an appellant's brief as cross-appellee shall be combined with his reply brief and be subject to the same page and time limitations as an appellee's principal brief. Only in such situations does appellee have a chance to file his own rebuttal to the appellant's answer.[190]

The reply brief must be "confined strictly to replying to arguments presented in the brief of the appellee" (Illinois Rule 341(g)). This language of the Illinois rule is typical of a universal limitation.

In contrast to the main briefs, the reply need not be divided into major sections like Statement of Facts or Argument. The reply may nonetheless counter errors in any part of appellee's

---

[187]In California the reply brief is entitled "Appellant's Closing Brief."
[188]Georgia, Louisiana, Nebraska, North Carolina, Texas, Utah. In Oregon, replies may be filed without leave of court except in criminal, habeas corpus, post-conviction, workmen's compensation and domestic relations cases. The Louisiana rules do not provide expressly for reply briefs, but supplemental briefs may be filed without leave in the Supreme Court, though not in the courts of appeals.
[189]If necessary, permission to write a longer reply brief than is permitted by the rules should be requested for that reason.
[190]E.g., 14 days under both Federal Appellate Rule 28(c) and Illinois Rule 343(b).

brief, whether factual, legal or even in the Questions Presented if they are significant enough to merit comment. The answers to different points should be numbered, and, if the brief is of any length, or if it makes a number of separate points, headings for each point will be helpful to the court. They can be merely italicized headings run in at the beginning of the opening paragraph of the point. United States Supreme Court Rule 34.4 states that a reply brief "need not contain a summary of argument, if appropriately divided by topical headings." A table of contents is required if the brief exceeds five pages, unless there is only one item; if over three pages, there must be a table of authorities. Rule 33.5.

Most jurisdictions limit the length of reply briefs, commonly to no more than 20 to 25 pages. New Mexico and South Dakota fix no page limit. (See Sec. 7.6, *supra.*)

A reply brief should seek only to meet the points in appellee's brief not adequately covered in appellant's main brief. If the latter has successfully anticipated the opposing arguments, as it should if possible, no reply may be necessary.

The reply should not attempt to deal with every conceivable error or omission in the appellee's brief which appellant is in a position to criticize. Nothing is more boring and less persuasive than a page-by-page, or point-by-point, attempt to rebut every inaccuracy, no matter how inconsequential. The reply should concentrate on what is significant. Errors or omissions relating to a single subject should be brought together, not only as a matter of logical organization but for the cumulative effect.

If an opposing brief contains a mass of minor errors, emphasis on a few as illustrative may be sufficient to discredit the brief as a whole.

Don't try to quibble about unimportant errors in a way which proves only that you are more careful than your adversary but not necessarily more persuasive. Courts do not enjoy wasting valuable reading time on insignificant items, particularly at the end of a long siege of brief reading.

If space is available, a reply may conclude effectively by pulling the essential elements of a case together in the context of meeting the opposing arguments, such as:

> Appellee's brief makes no effort to meet our arguments that
> _____. And, as we have shown herein, appellee's contention that _____ does not comport with the legislative his-

tory of the statute or the cases construing it. Furthermore, appellee's version of the facts fails to take into consideration that _____. Accordingly, for the reasons stated in our main brief and in this brief, the judgment below should be reversed.

7.35 Supplemental Briefs and Statements

Briefing usually terminates with the reply brief of the appellant, or of the appellee when he has filed a cross-appeal which the appellant answers in *his* reply brief. Occasionally, however, either party may desire to bring additional facts or authorities to the court's attention.

This can always be done by leave of court, whether or not there is a rule providing specifically for supplemental submissions. A party may also wish to correct errors in his own brief. This can usually be done by having the brief corrected in the clerk's office by counsel, not the clerk, substituting pages or copies if the brief has not yet been distributed.

In the most common situations, the problem is how to bring to the court's attention intervening facts of consequence, frequently new cases and statutes. Many jurisdictions provide for the filing of supplemental briefs in such situations without leave of court.[191] Indeed, the Supreme Court of the United States has rebuked counsel for not calling to its attention supplemental facts affecting the justiciability or possible mootness of the issues covered in the main briefs. *Fusari* v. *Steinberg,* 419 U.S. 379 (1975). See Sec. 7.30, p. 321, *supra.*

Such supplemental material may be called to the appellate court's attention in two ways without the making of a formal motion:

(1) Some rules of court, such as United States Supreme Court Rule 35.5, permit the filing without special leave of a supplemental brief restricted to the new matter, but otherwise conforming to the rules as to briefs. The reference to the new matter may include an argument pointing out its relevance. Nevada Rule 31 permits the filing of supplemental authorities up to 15 days before oral argument; other parties have 5 days to respond.

(2) The rules of other courts permit counsel to file only a

---

[191]Seventh Circuit, Georgia, Louisiana, Oregon, Tennessee.

letter (or similar informal memorandum) citing the additional authority and indicating the part of the prior brief or the issue argued orally to which the authority pertains, often without any supporting argument. Such a provision was incorporated in the 1979 amendments to the Federal Rules of Appellate Procedure. Rule 28(j) provides:

> "When pertinent and significant authorities come to the attention of a party after his brief has been filed, or after oral argument but before decision, a party may promptly advise the clerk of the court, by letter, with a copy to all counsel, setting forth the citations. There shall be a reference either to the page of the brief or to a point argued orally to which the citations pertain, but the letter shall without argument state the reasons for the supplemental citations. Any response shall be made promptly and shall be similarly limited."

Under Seventh Circuit Rule 11, counsel is permitted to state "in a single brief sentence the proposition the authority supports." Whether the rule so requires (as the Seventh Circuit rule does) or not, a copy of the new material should be attached if it is not yet published and readily available to the court.

Pennsylvania Appellate Rule 2501(b) similarly provides that if the status of an authority is affected by a subsequent authority "any counsel having knowledge thereof shall file a letter" without argument, enclosing a copy of the later opinion or document.

In some jurisdictions, like those just referred to, such a statement may be filed before or after oral argument, up to the date of the decision. Under United States Supreme Court Rule 35.5, however, a supplemental brief as to new matter may be submitted without further leave only "up to the time the case is called for hearing, or, by leave of Court, thereafter."

In some jurisdictions, authorities not cited in the briefs are not to be referred to in oral argument without giving advance notice in writing to the court and opposing counsel. E.g., Ohio Court of Appeals Rule 21(H), Ohio Supreme Court Rule V-4.

In most jurisdictions permission to file is necessary after oral argument. Often the need for filing an additional memorandum comes to light during the course of the argument, as a result of judicial questioning or the opponent's argument. The court itself will sometimes request the filing of a supplemental memorandum at that time. If not, and counsel is forced to the conclusion that neither his brief nor his argument has adequately covered a point with which the court appears to be concerned, or if a new unanswered argument is presented by his adversary, he should ask orally for leave to file an additional memorandum on the question.

A sufficient number of copies for all members of the court, as well as one for the clerk's office, should be filed. If the document is a brief, the rule governing the number of briefs to be filed would presumably apply. The Seventh Circuit's rule referred to above calls for filing the original plus six copies of the supplemental letter.

The principal justification for a supplemental brief is the need to call attention to new facts or authorities or to respond to questions raised during the course of argument. On occasion, the opponent's reply brief, to which counsel has no right to respond, will contain "a whopping misstatement."[192] If the statement is not only grossly inaccurate but of substantial significance to the appeal, a motion for leave to reply to it in a supplemental memorandum or an equivalent letter will be the only available remedy. The reply should be included in or attached to the motion. And it had better be right!

In general, except for calling attention to *new* cases or statutes, supplemental briefing should be avoided, unless it is vital that new information be brought to the attention of the appellate court. Such a drastic procedure should not be invoked to deal with statements which may be objectionable but are not likely to be of major significance to the deciding court.

7.36 *Amicus* Briefs

Amicus curiae means "friend of the court." Historically, and that means way back in English history,[193] the *amicus* was a lawyer or bystander not participating in a case who would call the judge's attention to a new case or statute or critical fact, such as death of a party.[194]

Courts would occasionally request a lawyer to act as an

---

[192]F. Wiener, BRIEFING AND ARGUING FEDERAL APPEALS, p. 267 (1967).

[193]S. Krislov, *The Amicus Curiae Brief: From Friendship to Advocacy,* 72 Yale L.J. 694 (1963).

[194]A member of Parliament even volunteered to inform a court as to the meaning of a law passed while he was present. *Id.* at 695.

amicus, or to present an argument in support of a position which the court deemed inadequately represented.[195] Most frequently, such requests were, and still are, made to an Attorney General. Even without a request an Attorney General or other public official might appear as *amicus* to present views on behalf of the Government or public interest, which may or may not be the same.

Although attorneys acting as *amici* still appear in the above capacities, in most cases they represent private clients, either interested individuals or companies that have problems or cases similar to those involved in the appeal or organizations of various sorts that are interested in the case or in what the court may say about it.

The lawyer himself was originally the *amicus,* even when he was openly speaking on behalf of a client. Now it is not entirely clear who is the *amicus.* In 1935, the Supreme Court Reporter noted that two lawyers "filed a brief for American Farm Bureau Federation as *amici curiae,* " which would seem to mean that the lawyers were regarded as the *amici.* [196] In 1976, the United States Reports noted that three lawyers "filed a brief for the American Civil Liberties Union as amicus curiae."[197] In 1979 the Court granted a motion of the Chamber of Commerce "to file a brief, as *amicus curiae,* " without reference to any lawyers.[198] These recent examples suggest that the client organization is the *amicus.* These grammatical niceties of the Reporter of Decisions for the United States Supreme Court do not, of course, have the authority of judicial rulings, but they accurately recognize that the *amicus* brief now customarily states the position of the client and not necessarily that of the lawyer personally, though most often they probably do not disagree.

The rules governing the filing of *amicus* briefs commonly require that movant state "the nature of the applicant's interest" and why the *amicus* brief is "desirable" or "will assist the appellate court."[199] The interest factor seems to assume that the brief is filed on behalf of someone having a personal interest in the

---

[195]E.g., *Williams* v. *Georgia,* 348 U.S. 957 (1955); *United States* v. *12 200-ft. Reels,* 404 U.S. 813 (1971); *Mathews* v. *Weber,* 423 U.S. 261, 265, n. 2 (1976).

[196]*United States* v. *Butler,* 297 U.S. 1, 80 L.Ed. 477, 481 (1936).

[197]*Stone* v. *Powell,* 428 U.S. 465, 468, n. (1976).

[198]*Carbon Fuel Co.* v. *United Mine Workers,* 442 U.S. 939 (1979).

[199]E.g., United States Supreme Court Rule 36.3; Federal Appellate Rule 29; Alabama Rule 29; Colorado Rule 29; Illinois Rule 345; Maine Rule 75A(f)(1); Massachusetts Rule 17; New Mexico Rule 9; Ohio Rule 17; Tennessee Rule 31(a); Wisconsin Rule 809.19(7). Georgia requires a "direct interest." Sec. 24–3617.

case, and not merely a lawyer's intellectual interest in a legal question. Indeed, it is questionable whether a practicing lawyer or academician or law review board may properly file an *amicus* brief merely to state his or its own views on a matter before the court,[200] although such a presentation would seem to come closer to the *amicus'* historical function.

In most jurisdictions a brief as *amicus* may be filed only by leave of court, obtainable on motion.[201] In Pennsylvania and Nebraska an *amicus* brief may be filed without leave of court. In Pennsylvania, unless otherwise ordered, the brief shall be filed within the time of the party whose position is being supported, or of the appellant if no party is supported. Appellate Rule 531. In Nebraska the brief must be filed before the case "is placed upon the Call"; after that leave must be obtained. Rule 11(d).

In the United States Supreme Court and the federal courts of appeals[202] and also in some state courts, leave of court is unnecessary if (1) all parties consent in writing, and the brief is accompanied by copies of the consent;[203] or (2) the brief is presented by the appropriate law officer of such governmental agencies as the United States, or a state, or (under United States Supreme Court Rule 36.4) a political subdivision thereof.[204]

The United States Supreme Court for briefs on the merits and the federal courts of appeals unless the parties otherwise consent[205] require that the brief be "presented within the time allowed for the filing of the brief of the party supported." That enables the other party to answer the *amicus* in his own brief. Many states have similar provisions.[206] Most denials of leave to file an *amicus* brief in the United States Supreme Court are for failure to comply with this requirement. For *amicus* briefs relating to petitions for certiorari, Supreme Court Rule 36.1 requires

---

[200]Cf. *Rosenberg* v. *United States*, 346 U.S. 273, 291 (1953).

[201]E.g., Alabama, Colorado, Georgia, Illinois, Tennessee. Hawaii Rule 3(h) provides that in the absence of consent, "the order shall issue only after hearing."

[202]Supreme Court Rule 36; Federal Rule of Appellate Procedure 29.

[203]E.g., Alaska, Florida, Iowa, Maine, Montana, Nevada, New Mexico, Ohio, Washington. The Committee Comments to Alabama Rule 29 state:

"The provision of FRAP Rule 29 permitting the filing of an amicus brief by consent of all the parties has been deleted, since it is felt that such consent would so rarely be granted as to make such a provision meaningless.

"The elimination of the process of consent to amicus briefs is based upon the reality that most amicus briefs are in fact a type of adversary intervention rather than objective assistance to the court."

[204]Massachusetts, Nevada, New Mexico, Rhode Island, Virginia.

[205]Supreme Court Rule 36.2; Federal Appellate Rule 29.

[206]E.g., Florida, Indiana, Iowa, Massachusetts, Virginia. The Illinois Supreme Court is considering a recommendation that it add such a provision to Rule 345.

that the brief be submitted within the time allowed for the opposing brief and states that "such motions are not favored." Distribution to the Court of the petition and brief in opposition will not be delayed pending the receipt of a motion for leave to file an *amicus* brief, or the brief itself.

Other rules provide that the appellate court will fix the time and conditions for filing *amicus* briefs.[207] Often the court will select the same date as that for the brief of the party whom the *amicus* is supporting. If that is not feasible, an appropriate condition would specify a date for filing, usually well before the oral argument, and also, either in the same order or on request, give the opponent time to reply. Wisconsin Rule 809.19(7) requires that the brief be filed no later than 10 days before the oral argument.

The rules of the Supreme Court and the United States courts of appeals attempt to spell out what the *amicus* must show in order to obtain leave to file. Federal Appellate Rule 29 states merely that the motion "shall identify the interest of the applicant and shall state the reasons why a brief of an *amicus curiae* is desirable." Supreme Court Rule 36.3 goes into more detail. The motion, which "shall in no event exceed five pages in length," "shall concisely state the nature of the applicant's interest, set forth facts or questions of law that have not been, or reasons for believing that they will not adequately be, presented by the parties, and their relevancy to the disposition of the case."

The Supreme Court's rule sounds considerably tougher than it is in practice. Although during the 1950s the Supreme Court was quite stringent in granting leave to file *amicus* briefs, that is no longer the case. Most motions are now granted unless the brief will not be filed on time.[208]

Some of the state rules contain similar provisions. Washington Rule 10.6(b) requires the motion to state, in addition to the applicant's interest and the issues to which the brief will be directed, "applicant's familiarity with the issues involved . . . and with the scope of the argument presented or to be presented by the parties, . . . and applicant's reason for believing that additional argument is necessary on these specific issues."

---

[207]E.g., Tennessee, Washington.

[208]S. Krislov, *The Amicus Curiae Brief: From Friendship to Advocacy*, 72 Yale L.J. 694, 713–717 (1963); R. Stern and G. Gressman, SUPREME COURT PRACTICE, pp. 726–728 (5th ed., 1978).

The New York Court of Appeals, in Rule 500.9(e), requires a motion to appear as *amicus curiae* to satisfy

"at least one of the following criteria:
"(1) a showing that the parties are not capable of a full and adequate presentation and that movants could remedy this deficiency, or
"(2) that movants would invite the court's attention to law or arguments which might otherwise escape its consideration, or
"(3) that amici curiae briefs would otherwise be of special assistance to the court."

It often would be difficult or impossible honestly to say that the briefs for the parties have not dealt with the facts or questions to be presented in the *amicus* brief, or that there is reason to believe that the counsel for the parties will not do so adequately. In most instances, the lawyer preparing the *amicus* brief will not have seen the brief for the party whom he is supporting, since his own brief will be filed at approximately the same time or later. And he would normally be unwilling to state, except in most unusual circumstances, that the counsel for the party he is supporting will do an inadequate job. All he can usually say is that the *amicus* has a special interest in the case for given reasons and that his interest in some respects differs from that of the party supported. This will often enable the *amicus* brief to state or emphasize different facts better known to the *amicus* than to the party. The purpose of an *amicus* brief may be to apprise the court of the somewhat different circumstances of the *amicus,* both for the purpose of persuading the court to decide in the manner suggested and also to obtain or avoid language in the opinion which might affect the *amicus* differently from the party.

These facts will often not be in the record of the case. The admonition in the United States Supreme Court rule quoted above that the motion for leave to file "set forth facts . . . that have not been, or . . . will not adequately be, presented by the parties" would seem to so assume, and indeed almost to so suggest.[209] Such facts, which describe the effect of deciding the case a particular way upon persons who are not parties, would not ordinarily be of such common knowledge as to be judicially noticeable. Nevertheless, they may be of value to a court prop-

---

[209]Examples of the Supreme Court's reliance upon such extra record material appear in *Regents* v. *Bakke,* 438 U.S. 265, 316–317, 321–324 (1978); *San Antonio School District* v. *Rodriguez,* 411 U.S. 1, 56–57, n. 111 (1973).

erly concerned as to the effect of a decision beyond the immediate parties to the case.

On the other hand, courts should not rely on non-record facts which are disputable or disputed, and opposing parties or even other *amici* should have an opportunity to advise the court as to that.[210] If the presentation by the *amicus* is to be given weight by the court, the non-record facts relied upon should have the ring of truth on their face. They should not relate to the facts of the particular case as between the parties, but should resemble the "legislative facts" having "relevance to legal reasoning and the law making process" described by the Advisory Committee on the Federal Rules of Evidence in its treatment of the subject of judicial notice. See Sec. 7.30, *supra.*

It is difficult to be more precise in defining the standard to be applied in resolving the tension created by the desirability of permitting outsiders to bring such materials to a court's attention and the general principle that an appellate court is restricted to facts of record or judicially noticeable. In general, an *amicus* brief should lose credibility with the court (with or without an opposing presentation) if it goes too far in setting forth non-record material as indisputably true. The good sense of the court should enable it to recognize when this occurs. A good lawyer should be aware of this danger of overstatement and avoid it.

A rule recently adopted by the Court of Appeals for the Seventh Circuit is designed to prevent *amicus* briefs from merely repeating arguments made by the parties. Seventh Circuit Rule 10(a) (1980) states:

> "Before completing the preparation of an amicus brief, counsel for an amicus curiae shall attempt to ascertain the arguments that will be made in the brief of any party whose position the amicus is supporting, with a view to avoiding any unnecessary repetition or restatement of those arguments in the amicus brief."

This would appear to be a more realistic approach to the problem than that of the United States Supreme Court's rule; it recognizes that at the time the *amicus* brief must be written the *amicus* may often be unable to examine the brief of the party being supported. California and Washington have similar re-

---

[210]If the regular briefing schedule does not afford a party or *amicus* time to reply, he should move for leave to respond to disputed factual statements, preferably with his answer attached.

quirements. Washington Rule 10.3(e) states more bluntly: "Amicus must review all briefs on file and avoid repetition of matters in other briefs." The California applicant for permission to file must specify "the points to be argued" and state "that he is familiar with the questions involved in the case and the scope of their presentation, and believes there is a necessity for additional argument on the points specified."

It is believed, though I have not been able to verify the fact as to many of them, that most of the federal courts of appeals and the state appellate courts are reasonably liberal in allowing *amicus* briefs to be filed. North Carolina is an exception. Its Rule 28(i) provides that an application for leave to file an *amicus* brief must be filed with the brief attached within five days after the appellant dockets his appeal. This would normally be impossible. As might be expected, very few such briefs are filed in North Carolina. Why the circumstances in that state differ so greatly from those elsewhere in the nation as to justify a rule which in substance bars the filing of all *amicus* briefs is not apparent. The courts in that state should be able to protect themselves against a mass of unwarranted *amicus* briefs by a procedure which would not have the effect of precluding the filing of unobjectionable and often helpful *amicus* briefs.

In general, the motion for leave to file an *amicus* brief may be filed with or without the brief being attached. Probably the most common practice is to submit the brief at the same time as the motion, and some states so require,[211] while others specifically so permit.[212] If such motions are customarily granted, however, filing the motion and brief together may bring the brief before the court more promptly, and more easily satisfy the rules specifying when *amicus* briefs must be filed. The United States Supreme Court at one time required that the application for leave to file be "independent of the brief," but this language was eliminated in 1954. The brief may therefore now be submitted along with, and even bound in with, the motion.[213]

Despite the substantial change in the character of *amicus* briefs, their function is still to aid the court in reaching correct decisions. That purpose is not served if the brief adds nothing to the arguments of the party being supported. Merely to say, directly or by implication, that the *amicus* agrees with that party

---

[211]Alabama, California, Iowa.
[212]Washington Rule 10.6(b).
[213]R. Stern and E. Gressman, SUPREME COURT PRACTICE, p. 726 (5th ed., 1978).

is not a legitimate matter to call to the attention of the court. Undoubtedly many *amicus* briefs are filed principally for that reason. Only an appellate judge knows whether such briefs help to persuade the court. Nevertheless, a lawsuit is not a referendum, and the number of persons or organizations which wish to be counted in favor of a particular outcome is not a factor which a court may properly consider. Apart from the irrelevancy of the fact of filing, the number of persons or organizations filing briefs does not reflect the size of their constituency. Some organizations may represent relatively few persons, even though enthusiastic ones. On the other hand, a single large organization may represent a great many more, and the portion of the public not represented by any organization may be vastly greater.

In cases of great public interest, large numbers of organizations file briefs without any real pretense that they are presenting arguments not advanced by the party supported. In *Regents of University of California* v. *Bakke,* 438 U.S. 265 (1978), over 50 *amicus* briefs were filed; how much attention the Court gave to each can only be conjectured, but my guess would be that to say "not much" would be an understatement.

It is not improper, however, to advise the court of the consequences of deciding the case one way or the other, with particular emphasis on the effects upon others than the immediate parties. Consequences may properly be taken into account in interpreting the language of laws or documents. If a party does not go into that in a manner which the *amicus* regards as adequate, the *amicus* appropriately may.

Furthermore, it is proper and often desirable for an *amicus* to present facts or arguments in a different context from those presented by the parties. Thus in a tax case involving depletion allowances for one type of mineral product, an *amicus* brief setting forth different considerations relating to other minerals affected by the same statute could be helpful to the court.[214]

Amicus briefs must conform to the rules governing other briefs both as to their content and form. The *amicus* brief may, however, limit its presentation to an opening statement explaining why the *amicus* has an interest in the case, and an Argument (preceded by a Summary of Argument or Points and Authorities if the court rules so require for briefs generally). See Secs. 7.13,

---

[214]Cf. *United States* v. *Cannelton Sewer Pipe Co.,* 364 U.S. 76 (1960); see F. Wiener, BRIEFING AND ARGUING FEDERAL APPEALS, p. 272 (1967).

7.21, *supra.* The introductory statement may include facts relating to the *amicus'* position which the parties may not be expected to set out. The *amicus,* like an appellee, may also comment on the Questions Presented and the facts, though this usually will be unnecessary. The statement of interest should appear in the motion for leave to file and also at the beginning of the *amicus* brief itself if filed separately. If, as often occurs, the motion and the brief are bound together and filed simultaneously, the statement need not be repeated.

The rules governing the length of briefs will also apply to *amicus* briefs in the absence of a different limitation. In the United States Supreme Court *amicus* briefs prior to the granting of review may not exceed 20 pages; *amicus* briefs in cases before the Court for oral argument may not exceed 30 pages. Rule 36.1 and .2. The Seventh and Eighth Circuits limit *amicus* briefs to 20 pages.

Although *amicus* briefs resemble briefs by the parties, the *amicus* is not a party. He is not entitled to file more than the one brief stating his position; thus he may not file reply or supplemental briefs to meet contentions raised by a party.[215] If the *amicus* has information on such subjects which he feels should be submitted to the court, he should give it to counsel for the party he is supporting.

This does not mean that an *amicus* may not properly seek both to support a petition for certiorari or leave to appeal and then, if the petition is granted, also submit an *amicus* brief on the merits. But the latter brief must stand on its own feet, with separate consents from the parties or leave of court obtained on a separate motion subsequently filed. *Amicus* briefs may be helpful in supporting a petition for review, inasmuch as they add force to a petitioner's contention that the case has public importance extending beyond the interests of the parties. For the converse reason, the filing of an *amicus* brief in opposition to a petition for review will often be unwise. A better time to file an *amicus* brief in support of the respondent is after the petition is granted, if it is.

Amici are hardly ever permitted to argue orally. See Sec. 8.2, *infra.* Thus, if they cannot assert their views in writing, they cannot do so at all.

---

[215]*Connell Construction* v. *Plumbers & Steamfitters Local Union,* 419 U.S. 1030 (1974); *Kewanee Oil Co.* v. *Bicron Corp.,* 416 U.S. 965 (1974).

7.37   Physical Form—Methods of Reproduction

The physical form of briefs is specified in the rules of most jurisdictions. Since these rules prescribe minutiae not described herein, they should be examined by counsel. In the main, however, they reflect a general pattern; the similarities are much more impressive than the differences.

Not too many years ago, most rules required that briefs be printed, except in special circumstances. Since the Xerox revolution, the rules of all but a few jurisdictions provide, in substantially the same language as Federal Appellate Rule 32(a), that

> "[b]riefs and appendices may be produced by standard typographic printing or by any duplicating or copying process which produces a clear black image on white paper."

Carbon copies, however, are not permitted except for proceedings *in forma pauperis* or by special leave of court. Double spacing is usually required.

Only Arkansas Rule 8, Minnesota Rule 132.01, Nebraska Rule 9(a), Connecticut Sec. 3060M, Kentucky Rule 76.12(4) and Michigan Rule 857 still require that briefs be printed, and the last three states only for their supreme courts, not their intermediate appellate courts.[216] Alabama, Georgia, North Carolina and Washington, on the other hand, seem to dispense with printing altogether.

As a result, in the vast majority of jurisdictions most briefs are no longer printed.[217] Other methods of duplication are much less expensive,[218] and also less time consuming because the typed material need not first be set in gallery proof and then page proof, each of which must be proofread and checked before the final brief is printed. The brief as typed in the lawyer's office can be photocopied there or by an outside concern.[219]

---

[216]Compare the smaller number of states requiring abstracts and appendices to be printed. Sec. 6.10, *supra.* These states may allow briefs for indigent parties to be typed. Arkansas also permits briefs in appeals from the Workmen's Compensation Commission to be typed and photocopied.

[217]Vermont Rule 32 requires printing of briefs over 20 pages unless the Supreme Court orders otherwise, but the court does not require printing if photocopying is clear and nonsmudgeable. Although the Oklahoma rule is not clear as to whether briefs must be printed, most briefs submitted to the Oklahoma Supreme Court are duplicated by photocopying and not printed.

[218]In 1980 printing charges in Chicago ranged from $14 to $35 a page, without allowing for corrections; photocopying would cost something like $3 for 30 copies but the number of pages would be larger. See Sec. 6.9, *supra.*

[219]North Carolina and Washington are unusual in that the clerk arranges for duplication of the number of copies required.

Briefs reproduced by such processes are not difficult to read, as their authorization by most appellate courts attests. Indeed, Eighth Circuit Rule 11B(1) provides that all briefs may be typewritten and reproduced by a photocopy or similar process. No good reason, apart perhaps from inertia, would seem to justify the failure of a few jurisdictions to permit the use of less costly and more efficient duplicating processes.

The rules of the various jurisdictions customarily specify the size of pages, the portion of each page which can be used (or, conversely, the margins), and sometimes even the kind of binding and type of paper. Several states permit typing on both sides of the paper. Washington permits lines to be "double or one and one-half spaced." If 1 1/2 is used, the allowable number of pages is approximately 3/4 as much as for double spaced. Although quotations may be single spaced almost everywhere, Georgia requires that they be double spaced. In general, the requirements for briefs are the same as for duplicated records or appendices, as to which see Sec. 6.10, *supra;* the special requirements of the United States Supreme Court are there described.

The relationship between the methods of duplication and typing and the number of pages in the brief is considered in Sec. 7.6, *supra.*

7.38 Number of Copies of Briefs

The number of copies of briefs required to be filed varies widely among the federal and state appellate courts. No general pattern or consensus can be detected. The number is usually, though not invariably, the same as for appendices to briefs, which are considered in Sec. 6.9, *supra.*

The number to be filed in various state appellate courts is shown in the following table. Readers are admonished, however, to look to the current rules governing the appellate court with which they are concerned. They should also be aware that many courts accept a smaller number for indigent parties, particularly in criminal cases. North Carolina and Washington require only one copy because the clerks' offices supervise the reproduction of the number needed, which is not specified in the rules. The cost, which the parties pay to the clerk, is believed to be less than that of private duplication.

Number of Copies of Briefs to Be Filed	States
1	North Carolina; Washington
3	Alabama Court of Civil Appeals; Georgia Court of Appeals; Texas Court of Civil Appeals
4	Florida Third District Court of Appeals;* Michigan Court of Appeals; Mississippi; Ohio Court of Appeals; Tennessee Court of Appeals
5	Alabama Court of Criminal Appeals; Kentucky Court of Appeals; New Jersey Appellate Division; New Mexico Court of Appeals
6	Arizona Court of Appeals; Connecticut Appellate Session; Tennessee Supreme Court
7	Georgia Supreme Court; Nevada; Wyoming
8	Delaware; Florida Supreme Court; North Dakota
9	Alabama Supreme Court; Illinois Appellate Court; Indiana; Mississippi (for rehearings); New Jersey Supreme Court; Rhode Island
10	Arizona Supreme Court; Idaho; Kentucky Supreme Court; Missouri; Montana; Utah
11	California;† Hawaii; New Mexico Supreme Court
12	Maine; Texas Supreme Court; Vermont
15	Colorado; Illinois Supreme Court; Nebraska; South Carolina; South Dakota; West Virginia
16	Louisiana Supreme Court; New Hampshire
17	Arkansas
18	Iowa; Ohio Supreme Court
20	Alaska (civil); Kansas; Minnesota; New Jersey; New York; Oklahoma; Virginia
24	Michigan Supreme Court
25	Massachusetts
26	Oregon
27	Pennsylvania Commonwealth Court
30	Alaska (criminal); Maryland; Pennsylvania (Supreme Court, Superior Court); Wisconsin
55	Connecticut Supreme Court

---

*Only five copies of jurisdictional briefs need be filed.

†Under California Rule 44, 11 copies of briefs on the merits are to be filed in the Supreme Court. In appeals to the Court of Appeal, four copies are to be filed in that court and seven in the Supreme Court. Fifteen copies of a petition for hearing and the response thereto must be filed in the Supreme Court.

As would be expected, the diversity is not as great in the federal courts as among the states, although there is less uniformity than the Federal Rules of Appellate Procedure seem to have contemplated. Federal Rule of Appellate Procedure 31(b) specifies that 25 copies of briefs should be filed in the courts of appeals "unless the court by order in a particular case shall direct a lesser number." A number of the circuits have stretched the quoted language to decrease the number to be filed. The First Circuit thus requires only 10 copies; the Fifth, 7; the Seventh and District of Columbia, 15; the Eighth, 5 "in cases heard on the original record."[220] The Court of Claims requires 16 copies.

The United States Supreme Court still requires 40 copies of all briefs (Rule 35), except that 60 copies must be filed in cases within the Court's original jurisdiction (Rule 9). Over half of these are distributed to historically selected law libraries throughout the country, even though microfiche copies of Supreme Court briefs have been available through commercial publishers for a number of years and are now found in over 155 libraries.[221]

In all courts the number of copies which must be duplicated (if any) is larger than the number required to be filed. Counsel should not overlook the need for making additional copies for all other counsel (or parties not represented by counsel) as well as for themselves. Court rules require from one to five copies for counsel for each other party separately represented; two is the most common number. See Sec. 7.40, *infra*. A lawyer will also usually want at least as many copies for his own office or other lawyers who have assisted or shown an interest in the case, formally or informally, as well as for his client, particularly if the latter has house counsel who supervised or otherwise was active in or closely followed the litigation. In cases of obvious importance, a demand from interested outsiders, or even the press, may be anticipated. Thus, at a minimum four and usually a few more copies should be made in addition to those required for the court.

Except at the lower levels, the explanations for the number specified by each jurisdiction are certainly not apparent, and may well be historical rather than logical. Alabama sensibly specifies one copy for each judge of the appellate court, which means three for the Court of Civil Appeals, five for the Court of Criminal Appeals and nine for the Supreme Court. Tennes-

---

[220]First Circuit Rule 11(f); Fifth Circuit Rule 13.5; Seventh Circuit Rule 9(g); Eighth Circuit Rule 11; D.C. Circuit Rule 8(j).

[221]R. Stern and E. Gressman, SUPREME COURT PRACTICE, Sec. 1.12 and Appendix C (5th ed., 1978).

see has a similar provision but even more sensibly adds one for the clerk, which comes to four for the Courts of Appeals and six for the Supreme Court. Georgia also requires a number equal to the number of judges on the particular court, three for the Court of Appeals and seven for the Supreme Court. California divides the 11 copies required, seven for the Supreme Court and four for the Court of Appeal.

As the table shows, a number of intermediate appellate courts require three, four or five copies which comes close to one for each judge and one for the clerk. Two for each judge, to allow for simultaneous reading by the judge and his law clerk, is also understandable. This explains the 15 copies required for the Colorado, Illinois and South Dakota supreme courts. Beyond that, the numbers, on the surface at least, are inexplicable unless the object is to supply law libraries throughout the state.

When all briefs were required to be printed, additional copies could be run off at little extra cost once the type was set. This is not true under photocopying processes, for which the charges, though substantially less (see Sec. 7.37, *supra*), are proportional to the number of pages copied. Only a few of the additional briefs distributed to libraries are likely ever to be examined by lawyers in subsequent litigation,[222] and this would not seem to justify requiring the clients in all appeals to pay the cost of supplying briefs to the various libraries in a state, or, for that matter, beyond the number needed by the appellate judges and the parties themselves. Certainly the burden of 55 copies imposed by Connecticut would appear to be way out of line.

7.39 Checking for Errors in Text and Citations

An often overlooked but essential element of brief writing is the need for checking for clerical accuracy the text of what has been written. This is different from and in addition to the need for assuring substantive accuracy and for verifying the substantive validity of citations by Shepardizing or similar processes. Those indispensable elements of brief writing have been discussed elsewhere. See Sec. 7.5, *supra*.

Most brief writers know that citations must be accurate, and that at some stage of the brief-writing process the citations must

---

[222]*Ibid.* United States Supreme Court cases may be different in this respect, but the briefs in those cases are now available in many libraries throughout the country.

be checked with respect to title, volume and page number. If possible, the checking should be to the original sources. If the citations in an early draft are so checked, the process of assuring the accuracy of citations thereafter merges with the process of insuring the accuracy of the textual composition. The later draft must be checked against the earlier. That is probably the most common practice. Citation errors in the final draft or printer's proof of a brief can, however, best be avoided by having the citations checked against the original sources at that stage, even though they may have been verified previously. If, to avoid repetition, checking the citations is left to the penultimate state, be sure to allow time for it—and then don't forget to do it. Preferably, the checking should be by a lawyer, or by an experienced paralegal or secretary.

Clerical errors are unintentional mistakes made by anyone participating in the composition of a brief. They are made by stenographers, typists, printers and lawyers. But whoever makes the error in the first place, the lawyer is responsible if it is not discovered and corrected before the brief is filed.

No doubt every writer of a brief or any other document has observed that clerical errors appear in preliminary drafts and frequently slip through into the final copy. Such errors result from inevitable human failures. If a typist's or printer's finger slips a fraction of an inch once in approximately 2,000 times, that would amount to one error per page. Even a good stenographer may not hear a word correctly or may err in interpreting identical sounds which may be differently spelled, such as "to," "too" and "two." In at least one well known system of shorthand, the symbols for those words are identical. The symbols for "not" and "in" are also so similar as to be occasionally confused, sometimes to the writer's great distress.

Lawyers may accidentally dictate or scribble the wrong word or number. Numbers and letters can easily be transposed by anyone, including lawyers. A lawyer may dictate inaccurately from his own illegible notes, as I often do. Words as simple as "the" and "and" can be misspelled, as well as words whose spelling is not so easy.

I have often been horrified to find a "not" or an "un-" omitted. "Not" can appear as "now" and "and" as "an." Words which are often misspelled or misused include "principal" and "principle," "elicit" and "illicit," "waiver" and "waver," "precedents" and "precedence," "complimentary" and "complementary," and "eminent" and "imminent."[223] See Sec. 7.8(9), *supra*. Usually flagrant errors will be caught before the final draft, but not always.

Printers sometimes omit entire lines. The most modern computerized typing equipment once reproduced a brief for me at an incredible rate of speed, but with six pages missing; fortunately they were still somehow retrievable from the innards of the machine.

The persons who read over drafts, whether the lawyer-writer, other lawyers or proofreaders, often do not detect all of the errors. The difficulty is that the human mind, which operates miraculously in many respects in its thought processes, memory and invention of mechanical devices, does not always operate perfectly as to clerical details. Everybody makes mistakes of this sort, no matter how great his intellectual capacity. Indeed, the rapid thinker who reads a passage he has himself written, and perhaps rewritten several times, may be more likely to read it as saying what he knows it is supposed to say and not to notice a mistaken word or letter.

The means of eliminating clerical errors are well known, though none are infallible. Often manpower or womanpower needed to make a document as error-proof as possible is not available. Each draft of a brief should be read over not only by its draftsman but also, if possible, by other persons as well, preferably two or three. Different persons are unlikely to overlook the same errors. Time and again I have observed that each reader of a brief or other writing has discovered errors which no one else noticed. I have been chagrined at the items which I missed but my colleagues uncovered. Their failure to detect some items that I did find was only partially compensatory to my ego.

If possible, one of the readers should not have been a writer of the brief. Such a reader may be more likely to notice mistakes because he does not have in mind a preconceived notion of how the passage was supposed to read. Usually brief writers feel free to inflict their drafts only on colleagues who have participated in the case. Inclusion among the readers of a stranger to the case will often be advantageous, though it is not always feasible.

---

[223]These examples appear in an article by Judge Wilbur F. Pell, Jr., of the Seventh Circuit, who also has seen references to a "writ of quorum nobis" and Judge "Leonard Hand" of the Second Circuit. W. Pell, *Read Before Signing*, 66 A.B.A.J. 977, 978–979 (1980).

Brief writers often rely on proofreading by clerical assistants who compare a draft against a prior draft. That is likely to catch missing or wrong words or letters, but proofreaders also make mistakes.[224]

Apart from clerical proofreaders, I do not think it is necessary to go beyond lawyers in a search for readers not too close to the case. Some familiarity with at least the lingo of brief writing will be conducive to intelligent reading. And frequently a lawyer not in the case will not only detect clerical errors but also come up with a new thought of substantive value.

The checking should, of course, extend to the final draft. Often, however, it ends with semifinal copy such as corrected page proof. Since the printer is not supposed to change any lines or words the lawyer has not marked as needing correction, the lawyer often assumes that pages or paragraphs not modified in the first proof need not be reread. That is correct most of the time. But occasionally, unpredictably and incomprehensibly, new errors occur at that stage. The lawyer should be aware that a change in printed proof requires resetting of the entire line, and, if anything is added or deleted, of subsequent lines in the paragraph. Lines are sometimes transposed or omitted by the printer.[225] For all of these reasons, the final brief should be read before it is filed.

If not read before filing, it should be read immediately thereafter, and any significant errors corrected in the filed copies; often that will necessitate sending someone to the clerk's office to make the corrections, or to substitute corrected copies for those initially filed. Some clerks will help make very simple corrections for you. Otherwise do not leave it to the judges or the clerk's office if you wish to maintain "an amicable relationship with the court."[226] The opposing party should also be notified so that he can correct the copy served upon him.

It is, of course, all very well for outsiders to insist that the

---

[224]I have been told that reading proof backward avoids the misleading influence of the context and is highly accurate. I would regard that as an infliction of cruel and unusual punishment upon the proofreader.

[225]Professor Miller points out:

"You can help the printer by making corrections and alterations of approximately the same length as the original, thereby reducing the number of lines to be reset. If you must add, try to do so near the end of a paragraph and at the galley stage. And always mark all changes out into the margin; otherwise the printer will miss them, and the fault is yours. If you can learn as few as a dozen proofreader's symbols, so much the better."

G. J. Miller, *On Legal Style*, 43 Kentucky L.J. 235, 250 (1955).

[226]W. Pell, *Read Before Signing*, 66 A.B.A.J. at 977 (1980).

above checking techniques be utilized before a brief is filed. Some law offices, however, may not have the facilities or manpower for all that, and some cases may not warrant the kind of full treatment suggested for the most effective correction of errors. But brief writers should be aware that inaccuracies reflect upon them, and may even affect a judge's overall appraisal of a brief. In the words of Judge Wilbur Pell of the Seventh Circuit:

> "These errors may seem of no great significance. What the brief writer actually meant will ordinarily shine through the obscurantism of possible ineptness, and the distraction is only mild. Yet, there is a gnawing feeling on occasion that the obviousness of the uncorrected errors indicates that the brief, having not been read for these errors, may be equally unreliable in its substantive reasoning or its analysis of authorities."[227]

Avoiding such errors is therefore of substantial importance.

In many a case, brief writers will often end up with not enough time for the desired amount of checking and rechecking. That may and usually will result from failure to begin preparation of the brief soon enough. Brief writers who are often, and indeed usually, writing under the gun of judicially imposed deadlines are likely not to allow enough time for checking. The time needed for adequate checking should not be overlooked when the brief writing schedule is planned in advance.

7.40 Serving and Filing Briefs

It is a universal requirement that briefs be served on the other parties to the case before or at the same time as they are filed.

The number of copies to be served varies with the jurisdiction. Most commonly, two copies must be served on counsel for each party separately represented, but the number ranges from one in California, North Dakota and Tennessee to five in Kansas and Pennsylvania. Two copies are required in the United States courts of appeals (Federal Rule of Appellate Procedure 31(b)) and Arizona, Colorado, Hawaii, Idaho, Iowa, Maryland, Massachusetts, Michigan, Mississippi, New Jersey, Oregon, South Dakota, Vermont, Washington; three in the United States Supreme Court (Rule 28.3), Virginia and Wisconsin. If, as in *in*

---

[227] *Ibid.*

forma pauperis cases, a brief is not printed or duplicated in the usual manner, a single copy should be served on counsel for each party separately represented. California requires a copy to be sent to the trial judge.

The reference to "counsel for each party separately represented" means that if a number of parties are represented by the same law firm or firms, the specified number is to be served on those lawyers jointly. Two or more firms representing the same party or parties are not entitled to more. But as a matter of courtesy, to be reciprocated of course, at least one copy should be sent to each law firm representing a party or parties, even if that comes to more than the specified number.

Indeed, unless counsel knows that the other lawyers have no need for more than one or two copies, as may be true for members of firms containing no more than one or two lawyers, he should as a courtesy serve each other party's lawyer with three copies.

A copy of the brief must be served on counsel for every other party to the case. That means every other party in the court below except perhaps parties known by the brief writer to have no interest in the appeal. For example, if only one of several plaintiffs has appealed, the appellee need not serve those who did not. In case of doubt, the party should be served.

United States Supreme Court Rule 19.6 provides:

> "All parties to the proceeding in the court whose judgment is sought to be reviewed shall be deemed parties in this Court, unless the petitioner shall notify the Clerk of this Court in writing of petitioner's belief that one or more of the parties below has no interest in the outcome of the petition. A copy of such notice shall be served on all parties to the proceeding below and a party noted as no longer interested may remain a party here by notifying the Clerk, with service on the other parties, that he has an interest in the petition."

This provision was adopted in 1967 because service was sometimes not made on all the parties below who still had an interest in the case.

Though other jurisdictions have not felt the need for such a rule, the standard that all parties should be served unless counsel believe that they "have no interest in the outcome" of the appeal is a reasonable one which other courts would be likely to follow if a problem arose. It is suggested that counsel conform to that standard whether or not a particular rule provides that all parties, or all adverse parties, be served, or whether it refers to the parties to the appeal or to the proceeding in the court below. As the Supreme Court rule provides, a party mistakenly not served should be able to remain a party in the appellate court without having to move to reenter the case. It should be sufficient for him to give notice to the other parties, without the need for a court order.

Service may be made upon counsel for the other party, or a party himself if unrepresented by counsel, in person or by mail. Serving in person means delivering the required number of copies to the lawyer or "to a clerk or other responsible person at the office of counsel" (Federal Appellate Rule 25(c); United States Supreme Court Rule 28.3 (to "counsel or an employee")), or, for parties unrepresented by counsel, to the party himself, or (under Illinois Rule 11(b)(2)) to a member of his family at least 10 years old.

Service by mail is to be by first-class mail, postage prepaid, to the correct address, deposited in a United States post office or mailbox.

The best proof of service[228] is formal acknowledgment by the person served that the brief has been received on a particular date. This may appear on a separate page which may be attached or appended to the brief or on the cover of a copy of the brief which is to be filed with the clerk of the appellate court —not, of course, on the copy which is left with the opposing counsel. Where an acknowledgment cannot be obtained, as when service is by mail, service can be proved by a separate certificate or affidavit of service setting forth the date and manner of service (such as by first-class mail, postage prepaid) and the name and address (or names and addresses) of the person or persons served.[229] In some jurisdictions a certificate is sufficient from a member of the bar of the appellate court, but an

---

[228]Vermont Rule 25(c) and Wisconsin Rule 809.80 contain the unusual provision that the filing of any paper by a party's attorney constitutes a representation that a copy has been or will be served upon each of the other parties in the manner prescribed by the rules.

[229]An appropriate form might be:

"I hereby certify that on June 19, 1980, three copies of appellant's brief were mailed first class, postage prepaid, to Joseph J. Doakes, Esq., 23 South LaSalle Street, Chicago, Illinois 60604, counsel for the appellee."

In the United States Supreme Court the statement should be added that "I further certify that all parties required to be served have been served." Rule 28.5. This should be signed by the attorney responsible for the service, and his typed name and address attached. The equivalent text should be incorporated in a sworn affidavit where that is required for service by non-attorneys.

affidavit is required from other persons. E.g., United States Supreme Court Rule 28.5(b), (c); Illinois Rule 12. In other states a certificate by anyone making service suffices.[230] The United States Supreme Court Clerk does not want the proof of service to appear on a copy of the brief served, but the acknowledgment, certificate or affidavit should be typed on a separate page bearing the Supreme Court caption of the case above the text.[231]

In some jurisdictions, if a statute is challenged as unconstitutional, copies of briefs for the party challenging the statute should be served on the Attorney General of the state involved.[232] With respect to the United States Supreme Court, service of all briefs on the United States or an officer or agency thereof is to be made upon the Solicitor General, Department of Justice, Washington, D.C. 20530. Service should also be made on any agency authorized to appear in its own behalf, on any officer or employee of the United States who is a party (Supreme Court Rule 28.4) and, as a matter of courtesy, on the attorney for the government who represented the government in the court below.

Although counsel often assume that their time to respond to a served brief begins to run on the date the brief is received, in many jurisdictions it runs from the date of service, which may be different from the date of receipt if service is by mail. To take account of the time between mailing and delivery, some rules specify that "service by mail is complete on mailing," but add that if service is by mail "3 days shall be added" to the period allowed for any response, such as the filing of an answering brief.[233]

In the United States Supreme Court, the time to file an answer to a brief or petition begins to run on "receipt" of the document, Rules 35.2, 22.1. Since that date will not appear on the proof of service, the recipient should advise the Clerk of the date of receipt, at least if the brief served by mail takes more than the usual time to arrive. Otherwise the Clerk may be concerned if the brief in response appears to be late.

In the absence of a special dispensation in the rules, a brief,

---

[230]E.g., Federal Appellate Rule 25(d), the almost identical Rules 25(d) of Alabama, Colorado and North Dakota, and also similar rules of Arizona, Montana and Tennessee. Massachusetts Rule 13 adds "under the penalties of perjury."

[231]R. Stern and E. Gressman, SUPREME COURT PRACTICE, p. 473 (5th ed., 1978).

[232]Under Illinois Rule 344(a) "if the Attorney General and the State's Attorney both appear for a party, each shall be served with three copies."

[233]Federal Appellate Rules 25(c) and 26(c) and the similar rules of Colorado, Massachusetts, Montana and Tennessee. Rhode Island adds 1 day; Mississippi, 2 days; New York and Tennessee, 3 days; Illinois, 4 days; and Florida and Indiana, 5 days.

like any other document, is not deemed filed until it is actually received in the office of the clerk of the appellate court. Counsel who do not live near the office of the clerk of the appellate court will ordinarily have to file their briefs by mail. They have no control over how long the Postal Service will take to deliver the briefs. It is a common, though fortunately not the usual, experience for letters mailed, even to an address in the same city, to be delivered four or five days later, even without a crippling snowstorm, flood, strike, accident or other misfortune. Neither counsel nor his client should be penalized for unexpectedly slow postal service. The short time difference between the date of mailing and the date of receipt by the clerk's office will not unduly delay an appeal or hamper the functioning of the appellate court.

A number of rules now protect counsel against such risks. The Federal Appellate Rules and those of some of the states provide, as an exception to this general rule, that "briefs and appendices shall be deemed filed on the day of mailing if the most expeditious form of delivery by mail, excepting special delivery, is utilized." E.g., Federal Appellate Rule 25(a); Massachusetts Rule 13.1.

The United States Supreme Court rules were amended in 1980 to add a similar provision. Rule 28.2 provides

> "that any document shall be deemed timely filed if it has been deposited in a United States post office or mailbox, with first-class postage prepaid, and properly addressed to the Clerk of this Court, within the time allowed for filing, and if there is filed with the Clerk a notarized statement by a member of the Bar of this Court, setting forth the details of the mailing, and stating that to his knowledge the mailing took place on a particular date within the permitted time."

Under this provision the member of the Supreme Court bar should execute and send the affidavit immediately after the brief has been mailed if he has reason to believe it will arrive after the due date. He can avoid hearsay problems by mailing the documents personally. If a brief mailed in ample time arrives late, the Clerk will presumably request that an affidavit be sent.[234]

In 1967 Illinois Rule 373 similarly made the time of mailing

---

[234]The United States Supreme Court has interpreted its 1980 rule as not extending to a petition for certiorari delivered mistakenly to a private courier service instead of the United States post office, even though it reached the Court sooner. *Homan & Crimen, Inc.* v. *Schweiker*, March 9, 1981 (motion to direct Clerk to accept and docket petition denied).

the time of filing for papers filed in an appellate court;[235] the time of mailing was to "be evidenced by a post mark affixed in and by the United States Post Office."[236] This "was designed to make it unnecessary for counsel to make sure that briefs and other papers mailed before the filing date actually reached the reviewing court within the time limit. Receipt of the paper in the clerk's office a day or two later will not delay the appeal." Committee Comment, 1980. Experience under this provision revealed that postmarks were often undated, illegible or delayed. As a result, in 1980 the rule was amended to provide that proof of mailing should be by certificate of an attorney, affidavit of any other person, or a United States Postal Service Certificate of Mailing, which can be obtained at any post office and will show the time of mailing. The certificate or affidavit should, of course, be mailed subsequently and separately.

If a brief or other document is to be filed on a Saturday, Sunday or legal holiday, when the clerk's office is closed, the time period extends to the next day on which the clerk's office is open. The Office of the Clerk of the United States Supreme Court, however, is open on Saturday mornings, so that in that Court Saturdays count.

---

[235]This rule does not apply to papers such as a notice of appeal filed in the trial court.
[236]A date stamped by a private postage meter does not count. Such a meter can be adjusted by its owner.

8

Oral Argument

8.1 The Importance of Oral Argument

It has become almost axiomatic for writers on appellate advocacy, many of whom are appellate judges, to emphasize the importance of oral argument. Mr. Justice Brennan of the United States Supreme Court has stated that

> "oral argument is the absolutely indispensable ingredient of appellate advocacy . . . . [O]ften my whole notion of what a case is about crystallizes at oral argument. This happens even though I read the briefs before oral argument; indeed, that is the practice now of all the members of the Supreme Court . . . . Often my idea of how a case shapes up is changed by oral argument. . . . Oral argument with us is a Socratic dialogue between Justices and counsel."[1]

Chief Justice Hughes had previously written that

> "the desirability . . . of a full exposition by oral argument in the highest court is not to be gainsaid, for it is a great saving of time of the court in the examination of extended records and briefs, to obtain the grasp of the case that is made possible by oral discussion and to be able more quickly to separate the wheat from the chaff."[2]

Judge Prentice H. Marshall has put it more bluntly:

> "If the case means a damn to your client—request oral argument."

---

[1]Harvard Law School, Occasional Pamphlet No. 9, pp. 22, 23 (1967).
[2]C. E. Hughes, THE SUPREME COURT OF THE UNITED STATES, pp. 62, 63 (1928).

But he admits that he is speaking only of "substantial" appeals, not "the frivolous, dilatory, or professionally purposeless" which there is no chance to win.[3]

Judge Goodrich, although emphasizing the importance of the briefs (see Sec. 7.2, *supra*), agrees that the oral argument is significant, but in more moderate terms:

> "It may be granted that oral argument seldom settles an appeal. But if it is well done, it can go far in helping a court to understand the case. It can also leave the court with the impression that the side presenting this good argument deserves to win. Of course that impression may be dispelled by subsequent study. But certainly, to start that study with the highly favorable impression of the case thus described is a noteworthy advantage for the man who created that impression."[4]

Justices Jackson and Harlan of the United States Supreme Court and Judges Loughran and Bromley of the New York Court of Appeals have all emphasized the importance of oral argument to the judge.[5] Justice Harlan pointed out that "some judges . . . listen better than they read . . . and are more receptive to the spoken than the written word," that "the first impressions that a judge gets of a case are very tenacious" and "frequently persist into the conference room," and that the judges often vote on the cases immediately or shortly after the arguments.[6] Like Mr. Justice Brennan, he concluded that

> "the oral argument gives an opportunity for interchange between court and counsel which the briefs do not give. For my part, there is no substitute, even within the time limits afforded by the busy calendars of modern appellate courts, for the Socratic method of procedure in getting at the real heart of an issue and in finding out where the truth lies."[7]

---

[3]P. Marshall, *Oral Argument*, in ILLINOIS CIVIL PRACTICE AFTER TRIAL, p. 9-4 (Illinois Institute for Continuing Legal Education, 1976). Other judges, when asked when they would consider submitting a case without oral argument, answered, "in substance, *never*. Others would do so only when they felt that the case was hopeless or when, for one reason or another, oral argument would be a waste of everyone's time." H. Fitzgerald and D. Hartnett, *Effective Oral Argument*, THE PRACTICAL LAWYER, Vol. 18, No. 4, p. 51 (ALI-ABA, April 1972), hereinafter cited as Fitzgerald and Hartnett.

[4]H. Goodrich, *A Case on Appeal—A Judge's View*, in A CASE ON APPEAL, pp. 24–25 (ALI-ABA, 1967).

[5]The views of these judges are quoted or summarized in R. Carson, *Conduct of the Appeal—A Lawyer's View*, in A CASE ON APPEAL, pp. 71–74 (ALI-ABA, 1967).

[6]*Id.* at 73. These judges and others have pointed out that judges form at least a tentative conclusion on the basis of the oral argument which in a large percentage of the cases conforms to the court's final decision. But in most cases the judges would have arrived at the same conclusion after first reading the briefs.

[7]*Id.* at 74.

Many of these and similar comments, though by no means all, relate to the experience of the United States Supreme Court, the New York Court of Appeals and other supreme courts which in the exercise of discretion deny leave to argue in the vast majority of the cases filed (approximately 94 percent in the United States Supreme Court). The cases which they accept for argument are not only the most important but usually the most difficult, in many of which the lower court judges have taken conflicting positions. Those close, difficult cases are obviously the ones in which oral presentation, which permits counsel to be questioned as to their premises and reasons, will be most helpful.

Although the Supreme Court, like other appellate courts, permits cases to be submitted on the briefs, its Rule 38.1 states that the Court "is reluctant to accept" the submission of cases only on briefs after it has accepted them for review, and therefore may "require oral argument by the parties." On occasion, when counsel for a party has advised the Court after review has been granted that he will submit on his brief, the Court has appointed outside counsel to argue as *amicus* in support of that party's position.[8]

The practice of other appellate courts and, indeed, to some extent, of the Supreme Court itself in deciding many appeals summarily without argument demonstrates that oral argument is not, however, always regarded as essential to the rendering of appellate justice. And I have heard appellate judges say that they thought oral argument made a difference in only a small percentage of the cases which come before them. One reason for this view is that the value of oral argument is even more dependent on the skill of counsel than is the brief. While a poor brief may at least acquaint the court with the leading cases and major arguments supporting one side of a case, thus allowing independent research by the judges or their clerks to flesh out the contours of the case, a poor oral presentation is both embarrassing to the advocate and of little help to the judges. Unfortunately, it seems that a large number of oral arguments are perceived to be inadequate. Justice Douglas, for example, reflecting on his 36 years on the United States Supreme Court, opined that "[f]ew truly good advocates have appeared before the Court. In

---

[8]*Granville-Smith* v. *Granville-Smith*, 348 U.S. 885, and 349 U.S. 1, 4 (1955); *Williams* v. *Georgia*, 349 U.S. 375, 380–381, n. 4 (1955); *Mathews* v. *Weber*, 423 U.S. 261, 265, n. 2 (1976).

my time 40 percent were incompetent." W. O. Douglas, THE COURT YEARS, p. 183 (1980). Chief Justice Burger has voiced similar sentiments on many occasions. It is unlikely that the arguments are of higher quality in other appellate courts.

The Arizona Supreme Court seldom hears arguments in cases which were argued in the state Court of Appeals. See Sec. 1.7, n. 59, *supra*. The Fifth Circuit has been deciding over half of its cases on the basis of the briefs alone, after a screening process in which a panel of three judges unanimously determines that oral argument will not be helpful. And a great many appellate courts, including almost all of the United States courts of appeals,[9] screen the appeals preliminarily to determine both whether the court will be aided by oral argument, and, if so, how much time counsel should be allowed. The North Carolina Court of Appeals, for example, can decide a case without hearing argument if all the judges agree that an oral presentation will not be of assistance. North Carolina Rule of Appellate Procedure 30(f). Under Oklahoma Court of Criminal Appeals Rule 1.11, an oral argument is mandatory when the death sentence has been imposed, but otherwise is available only by leave or order of court.

This partial change in judicial attitude in large part stems from the explosive enlargement of appellate dockets in the last 25 years, a subject considered at greater length in Sec. 1.6, *supra*. Before then, oral argument had been regarded as an essential element of an appeal. Over the years, however, the time allowed for argument has dwindled from a number of days per case to as little as 10 minutes per side.

As the appellate courts became overburdened, many of them were forced to the conclusion that in many cases an oral presentation was a waste of judicial time. Prior examination of the briefs would reveal the insubstantiality of the appellant's— or less often, the appellee's—position so convincingly that all members of the court agreed that there was no point to further consideration of the case.

Of course, the same conclusion would doubtless have been reached in most of those cases if the oral argument had preceded the reading of the briefs; whichever process came first would have made the other unnecessary. But brief writing

---

[9]The Second Circuit still hears oral argument in all cases in which counsel request argument.

by its very nature permits a more thorough analysis than a short oral argument; all the significant facts and authorities can be better presented in a comprehensive manner in a brief than in an oral argument of 30 minutes or less, particularly when much of that time may be consumed in answering questions. The present preferred practice is that briefs are submitted to and read by the appellate judges before oral argument, and not vice versa.[10] See Sec. 10.1, *infra.* That leaves the courtroom as the arena in which the essence of the case can be discussed in the light of questions from the court often provoked by the prior reading of the briefs.

The extent to which several of the federal courts of appeals now decide cases without oral argument, though understandable in view of their present work load, has been subjected to criticism on the ground that the value of oral argument is inadequately recognized.[11] Sec. 1.7, *supra.* The *Standards Relating to Appellate Courts*, ABA Commission on Standards of Judicial Administration, Sec. 3.35, pp. 56–57 (1977), recommend:

> "A party to an appeal should have the opportunity for oral argument on the merits of the appeal. . . . Oral argument is normally an essential part of the appellate process. It is a medium of communication that is superior to written expression for many appellate counsel and many judges. It provides a fluid and rapidly moving method of getting at essential issues. It contributes to judicial accountability, enlarges the public visibility of appellate decision-making, and is a safeguard against undue reliance on staff work."

The *Standards* conclude that the practice of denying oral argument

> "should be adopted only as an extreme measure when other means of keeping the court abreast of its caseload are insufficient."

---

[10]Some distinguished judges have expressed the view that to read the briefs first tends to close the judge's mind by the time of the oral argument, but this could be said of whichever process came first.

[11]A resolution adopted by the Board of Regents of the American College of Trial Lawyers on March 9, 1979, "deplores as being contrary to our traditional system of justice and to the essential interests of litigants, the action of certain courts both Federal and State in curtailing or eliminating oral argument in non-frivolous matters," urges that "adequate time" be allowed counsel to argue in such matters when counsel "deems oral argument to be in the client's best interests," and also recommends that Congress and the state legislatures provide an adequate number of judges to achieve this result. See also P. Carrington, *Ceremony and Realism: Demise of Appellate Procedure,* 66 A.B.A.J. 860 (1980).

After extensive inquiry among judges and members of the bar, the Commission on Revision of the Federal Court Appellate System found:

> "Oral argument is an essential part of the appellate process. It contributes to judicial accountability, it guards against undue reliance upon staff work, and it promotes understanding in ways that cannot be matched by written communication. It assures the litigant that his case has been given consideration by those charged with deciding it. The hearing of argument takes a small proportion of any appellate court's time; the saving of time to be achieved by discouraging argument is too small to justify routinely dispensing with oral argument."[12]

The Commission nevertheless concluded:

> "To mandate oral argument in every case would clearly be unwarranted; neither is it appropriate to ignore the risks to the process of appellate adjudication inherent in too-ready a denial of the opportunity orally to present a litigant's cause."[13]

The Commission's recommendation for an appropriate national standard to guide the courts of appeals in determining which cases should be argued orally was subsequently embodied in an amendment to the Federal Rules of Appellate Procedure. The rules had previously assumed that appeals would be argued unless the parties agreed to submit on briefs and the court did not direct that the case be argued. After a number of circuits had departed from that practice, Rule 34(a) was modified in 1979 to read as follows:

> "Oral argument shall be allowed in all cases unless pursuant to local rule a panel of three judges, after examination of the briefs and record, shall be unanimously of the opinion that oral argument is not needed. Any such local rule shall provide any party with an opportunity to file a statement setting forth the reasons why, in his opinion, oral argument should be heard. A general statement of the criteria employed in the administration of such local rule shall be published in or with the rule and such criteria shall conform substantially to the following minimum standard: Oral argument will be allowed unless
> (1) the appeal is frivolous; or
> (2) the dispositive issue or set of issues has been recently authoritatively decided; or

---

[12]Commission on Revision of the Federal Court Appellate System, STRUCTURE AND INTERNAL PROCEDURES: RECOMMENDATIONS FOR CHANGE, p. 48 (1975). Similar views are expressed by P. Carrington, D. Meador and M. Rosenberg, JUSTICE ON APPEAL, pp. 17–18 (1976).
[13]Commission on Revision, *id.* at 48.

(3) the facts and legal arguments are adequately presented in the briefs and record and the decisional process would not be significantly aided by oral argument."

Judge Godbold has characterized this rule as providing "for oral argument as a general proposition but permit[ting] exceptions under what are essentially the criteria in use by the United States Court of Appeals for the Fifth Circuit."[14] Indeed, one would think that most appellate courts would apply these standards if they had authority to determine which cases should be heard orally even in the absence of a rule specifying precise criteria.

As of this writing, all the circuits except the Eighth have amended their rules to incorporate the above provision substantially verbatim, and Eighth Circuit Rule 9(a) comes very close. In response to the second sentence of Rule 34(a), quoted above, the rules of most circuits now provide that parties may or must state the reasons why oral argument should be heard. This is to be done in a brief[15] or seven days after the main brief has been filed (Third Circuit Rule 12(6)), or after receiving notice that the court contemplates dispensing with oral argument (Second Circuit Rule 34(g); Seventh Circuit Rule 14 (f.1)), or within a specified number of days after notice of the court's decision to dispense with argument (First Circuit Rule 13; District of Columbia Circuit Rule 11(d)).

Many states still allow oral argument whenever the parties so request. Indeed, some, like the United States Supreme Court (Rule 38.1), may require argument irrespective of the wishes of the parties. In other states the appellate courts have general discretion to dispense with oral argument. Oklahoma Court of Appeals Rule 3.7; New Jersey Rule 2:11-1(b); Florida Rule of Appellate Procedure 9.320. The Florida Committee Note elaborates that

"there is no right to oral argument. It is contemplated that oral argument will be granted only when the court believes its consideration of the issues raised would be enhanced."

---

[14]J. Godbold, *Improvements in Appellate Procedure: Better Use of Available Facilities,* 66 A.B.A.J. 863, 864 (1980).

[15]Fifth Circuit Rule 13.6.4 requires the statement in a preamble to the brief; Eighth Circuit Rule 12(g) in an addendum to the table of contents; Fourth Circuit Rule 7(c) and Sixth Circuit Rule 9(c) at the end of the Argument section. Tenth Circuit Rule 10(e) leaves it to counsel to determine whether the reasons for arguing orally should be stated in a brief or a memorandum.

Illinois Rule 352(a) provides:

> "After the briefs have been filed, the court may dispose of any case without oral argument if no substantial question is presented, but this power shall be exercised sparingly."

Wisconsin Rule 809.22 is similar to Federal Appellate Rule 34(a); the appellate court may direct a submission on briefs when appellant's arguments are clearly without merit or involve only factual issues and the findings below are adequately supported by the evidence, or briefs are fully adequate so that oral presentation will not be justified. The Comment to the rule notes that

> "[i]t may be appropriate to have an oral argument for the sole purpose of allowing the court to ask questions."[16]

New Hampshire Rule 18(5) is even more restrictive; argument will be permitted only for cases involving broad or novel questions of law.[17] If applied narrowly, this rule would seem to foreclose oral argument in all but a few cases. If so, it would not comport with the recommendations in the American Bar Association *Standards,* the Federal Commission Report and the new Federal Appellate Rule.

These criteria reflect the practice actually followed by many appellate courts, and should serve as guides for state appellate courts as well as federal.

8.2 How to Obtain Oral Argument

What can a litigant do about the fact that many appellate courts no longer hear oral argument as a matter of course in all appeals? Obviously, appellant's counsel does not want a court to classify his case as too insubstantial to warrant oral argument. As a formal matter he can do only two things. He may request oral argument in the first place, or he may ask the appellate

---

[16]This probably does not mean that counsel are told in advance that they need only answer questions. Judges usually find that listening to counsel stimulates questions which might not occur to them otherwise.

[17]"(5) Oral argument may be shortened, or dispensed with, by order of the court. Oral argument will probably be dispensed with if the questions of law are narrow, not novel, and the briefs adequately cover the arguments; if the questions of law involve no more than an application of settled rules of law to a recurring fact situation; if the sole question of law is the sufficiency of the evidence, the adequacy of instructions to the jury or rulings on the admissibility of evidence, and the briefs refer to the record, which will determine the outcome."

court to reconsider if oral argument has been denied, whether or not a request has been made. He can and should also submit the best possible brief in support of his position, in order to convince the court that his argument has substantial merit. The judicial reaction to the substantiality of the questions raised as presented in the briefs and record will, of course, be controlling.

In many states,[18] as well as the Fifth and Tenth Circuits, counsel who wish to argue must advise the court that oral argument is requested, and in a few states (e.g., New Hampshire) they must tell the court it is *not* requested. Usually the request is to appear on the cover of the brief, but in some states (Iowa, New Hampshire) at the end or in a motion or a separate document. Under Michigan Rule 819.1 any party wishing to argue must so state on the title page of his brief or be deemed to have waived the right to argue. In Wisconsin appellant must explain early in his brief why oral argument is necessary. Mississippi Rule 7(e) was amended in 1978 to require a letter to be filed within 10 days after the time for appellant to file his rebuttal brief. The court wants counsel to determine whether argument will be of benefit to the court and the clients *after* all briefs have been filed.

In other federal courts of appeals and the United States Supreme Court, no such notification is necessary, although a party may notify the court that he will submit the case on his brief. In those courts, the cases are scheduled for oral argument unless the court on its own initiative determines not to hear them orally. This may result from the court's own screening process, or from motion of counsel for summary affirmance pursuant to court rules.[19]

As the comments of the judges quoted in Sec. 8.1, *supra,* indicate, an appellant who has confidence in his case and hopes to win it normally should request argument. An adverse decision

---

[18]E.g., Georgia Rule 24-4523 (each party separately); Indiana Rule 10; Iowa Rule 21; Michigan Rule 819. For example, Illinois Rule 352(a) states that "a party shall request oral argument by stating at the bottom of the cover page of his brief that oral argument is requested, or, if he has allowed his petition for leave to appeal or answer to stand as his brief, by mailing to the clerk and to opposing parties, within the time in which he could have filed his further brief, a notice that he requests oral argument. . . . A party who has requested oral argument and who thereafter determines to waive oral argument shall promptly notify the clerk and all other parties. Any other party who has filed a brief without requesting oral argument may then request oral argument upon prompt notice to the clerk and all other parties. After the briefs have been filed, the court may dispose of any case without oral argument if no substantial question is presented, but this power should be exercised sparingly."

[19]See Eighth Circuit Rule 9; Tenth Circuit Rule 9.

below, even if without explanatory findings or opinion, has the practical effect of placing the burden of persuasion on appellant. If the appellate judges, either in their individual minds or in voting, end up in equipoise, they will sustain the decision below. This is apart from the universal doctrines of deference to a jury's verdict or the findings of the trial judge who hears the witnesses and can devote greater time and attention to a case at the trial level than can the judges on appeal.

Only if appellant's counsel is convinced that he will not be able to answer embarrassing or devastating questions should he fail to request oral argument. It is easy to say that if he has such a case he should not appeal it. But as a practical matter he may have to, either because he is representing a criminal defendant and is obligated to assert all possible nonfrivolous arguments, or because he does not want to lose a client. There is also the possibility that opposing counsel has not, so far at least, caught on to a worrisome point that oral argument may be likely to bring to light. Of course, these reasons are not sufficient if every argument to be advanced is frivolous.[20]

This does not mean that counsel should not request oral argument whenever he believes his case is more likely to be lost than won. Appeals that may rationally be decided either way usually turn on the court's choice among competing but sensible arguments or values, not upon the court's discovery of an unanswerable defect in an argument, such as an undiscovered or plainly miscited case or statute, or an obvious logical or factual flaw. In short, when a respectable argument can be made,[21] appellant should opt for oral argument, even though he is aware that there is a good chance the court may not agree with his position.

Appellee may and perhaps should apply the same test in deciding whether he wishes to request argument if appellant has not. But since he has won the case in the lower court, he will seldom lack a rational argument to present in support of it, although, of course, there are cases in which the trial court has simply gone haywire. Appellee may also conclude that the weakness of appellant's case so clearly appears from the briefs or the

---

[20]See Sec. 2.2, *supra; Anders* v. *United States,* 386 U.S. 738, 744 (1967). The Code of Professional Responsibility, in *Ethical Consideration* 7-4, provides in part: "A lawyer is not justified in asserting a position in litigation that is frivolous." See also DR 7-106(B)(1) (lawyer's obligation to disclose known adverse authorities).

[21]This excepts the frivolous and insubstantial appeals referred to by Judge Prentice Marshall. See Marshall, *supra* note 3.

opinion below as to make loss of the case inconceivable, or the possibility so slight as not to warrant the additional cost to his client of having the case argued. But usually in such situations he can be even more confident of success if he is able to call the attention of the judges to the holes in the opposing case.[22] Cases of that sort are quite likely to be disposed of without argument by those overburdened appellate courts which screen out the cases not deemed worth hearing.

8.3 Who Should Argue

The question of who should make the oral argument is not exactly the same as whether new counsel should be brought into the case at the appellate level, discussed in Sec. 2.3, *supra*. As pointed out in that section, there are good reasons in many— but not all—cases for adding an experienced appellate lawyer to the trial team, whether he or the trial lawyer ultimately presents the oral argument.

In the main, however, the treatment of the subject in Sec. 2.3 also covers the question of who should argue. It bears reemphasis that if a lawyer who did not try the case argues the appeal, he must take the time to become fully familiar with the record and the authorities.[23] And this is so whether he is an appellate expert, high public official or senior partner in the firm which handled the case below. With respect to the latter, Judge Goodrich wrote:

> "Who should argue the case? Now we skate on thin ice. If a junior has tried the case below and has written the brief, he is the logical person to make the argument. He knows the record. He knows what happened and where the account of any incident is to be found. He knows the facts of the case and he knows the law of the case. Even if he is not so eloquent an advocate as some members of his firm, his lack of eloquence will largely be compensated for by the plenitude of his knowledge. But if the senior partner wants to argue the case, all these considerations will, presumably, have no weight. It is to be hoped, however, that if a senior partner is

---

[22]When the rules permit, as in the Seventh, Eighth and Tenth Circuits, he may make a preliminary motion to dismiss or affirm, and still reserve the right to argue if the court does not think the appeal insubstantial enough to grant the motion.

[23]Indeed, a lawyer who unsuccessfully handled the case below should also reread the record and the authorities before arguing the appeal, not only to refresh his memory but to attempt to understand why the lower court rejected his arguments. He should be "warned by the result below that a fresh view and approach are needed." Carson, *supra* note 5, at 47. That may help him avoid the same fate in the higher court.

to argue the case which his junior has tried and briefed, he will take the time fully to inform himself about it."[24]

Although Judge Goodrich suggests that "senior partners love" to argue appeals because "that is the most fun,"[25] the senior's ego and rank are often not the controlling factors. Private clients who, of course, deem their own cases very important, particularly when they reach an appellate court, frequently want the case to be handled at that stage by a lawyer of stature and prestige. Or the law firm may anticipate that the client will so react, no matter how talented the younger lawyer who handled the case below.

Perhaps for these reasons, younger lawyers are more likely to argue a large number of appeals when they are employed by a public agency, such as an attorney general, prosecuting attorney, public defender or government agency, which has a great many cases on appeal. Such an employer does not have to be concerned about losing a client if the appeal is not argued by a senior lawyer, particularly if it turns out unsuccessfully, as sometimes happens. Even in such agencies, however, the senior may wish to argue the case, often for the worse, particularly when it reaches the United States Supreme Court.

8.4 The Time Allowed for Oral Argument—Parties and *Amici Curiae*

As shown in Sec. 1.7, *supra,* the time allowed for oral argument has been steadily declining. Even the United States Supreme Court now allows only 30 minutes per side in the ordinary case, and the "ordinary" cases in that Court are almost invariably of great importance to the lawyers and the public.

The vast majority of the state appellate courts now also allow 30 minutes to each party, or in a few states for the opening arguments. See p. 371, *infra.* The following list indicates the number of minutes when it differs from 30; when two numbers are given, the first is for appellant, and the second for appellee:

15 — some Ohio Courts of Appeals;
20 — Florida, Georgia, Louisiana Court of Appeals, New Hampshire, South Dakota;
25–20 — Iowa, Missouri Court of Appeals;

---

[24]Goodrich, *supra* note 4, at 25.
[25]*Id.* at 24.

30–20 — Minnesota Supreme Court (sitting in panels), West Virginia;

40–30 — Missouri Supreme Court, Montana;

45   — New Jersey Supreme Court,[26] New York Appellate Division for Second Department;

45–30 — Minnesota Supreme Court *en banc;*

60   — Connecticut Supreme Court, Oklahoma Court of Criminal Appeals (felonies).

Federal Appellate Rule 34(b) formerly allowed 30 minutes per side unless otherwise provided by court rule. In recognition of the fact that many of the courts of appeals were prescribing the time case by case, the rule was modified as of August 1, 1979, to provide that

> "[t]he clerk shall advise all parties whether oral argument is to be heard, and if so, of the time and place therefor, and the time to be allowed each side."

This, of course, assumes that the court or its staff will determine the time case by case on the basis of the papers already before it.

The courts of Mississippi and Wisconsin also determine the amount of time to be allowed on a case-by-case basis. In the New York Court of Appeals, counsel suggests to the clerk the time deemed necessary, and then negotiates with the clerk the time to be allowed. In the New York Appellate Divisions, 30 minutes are allowed in the First, Third and Fourth Departments, and 45 minutes in the Second for most appeals, but only 15 minutes for less important cases. In Pennsylvania 30 minutes are allowed per side unless the parties agree on 15 minutes. Rule 2315.

The above time limits are for the usual appeal. Less time is often allowed for interlocutory or simple appeals, either by rule or on a case-by-case basis.

Counsel may request additional time for good cause, but judges are less likely than counsel to regard a longer argument as necessary. To warrant extra time a case should be of unusual magnitude, either in the number of issues presented, the complexity of the facts or its public importance. The need for presentation of *different* positions by lawyers for more than the usual two parties may also be a significant reason, but not the inability

---

[26]In the New Jersey Appellate Division, 30 minutes are allowed, but only if a party requests or the court orders oral argument. In the New Jersey Supreme Court cases are argued unless the court orders otherwise. Rule 2:11-1(b).

of different parties on the same side to agree upon a single lawyer to argue for them.

Requests for extra time may be by motion, or in some courts by letter to the clerk, submitted well in advance of the date fixed for argument, preferably before the clerk arranges the calendar on which the case will appear. Prior to the revisions of 1979 and 1980, the rules of both the United States Supreme Court and the United States courts of appeals called only for requests made by letter to the clerk; both now require a motion addressed to the court.[27]

In a few states, as the above tabulation demonstrates, appellants are allowed more time than appellees, presumably in recognition of the appellant's obligation to state the facts and the issues at the beginning of the argument. In most jurisdictions, appellant must divide the time allotted his side between his opening argument and his rebuttal. Illinois, Iowa, Rhode Island, South Carolina and South Dakota, however, allow appellant 10 minutes—Texas, 15—additional in rebuttal, again in seeming recognition of his obligation to state the facts in his opening and of the desirability of insuring that he will have time available for rebuttal. This is a reasonable provision even though it takes a little more time.

Amici curiae are seldom permitted to argue. They may move for leave, but must show, in the language of Federal Rule of Appellate Procedure 29, "extraordinary reasons" for participation in the oral argument. In the United States Supreme Court an *amicus* may, with the consent of the party and leave of Court, share in the time allotted the party he is supporting. See also Washington Rule 11.4(b). This is a privilege which the party's attorney, himself hard pressed to argue in the time available, is unlikely to grant unless he deems it advantageous for the *amicus* to appear orally in support of his position. Otherwise the *amicus* must obtain leave of Court on a motion "particularly setting forth why such argument is thought to provide assistance to the Court not otherwise available." United States Supreme Court Rule 38.7. The rule now states that such a motion "will be granted only in the most extraordinary circumstances," omit-

---

[27]United States Supreme Court Rule 38.3 now provides that the motion must be presented "not later than 15 days after service of appellant's or petitioner's brief on the merits, and shall set forth with specificity and conciseness why the case cannot be presented within the half-hour limitation." Federal Appellate Rule 34(b) now provides that "[a] request . . . for allowance of additional time must be made by motion filed reasonably in advance of the date fixed for hearing."

ting the prior exception for the United States and other governments. The Supreme Court rule probably expresses the policy of most other appellate courts.

Counsel dare not assume that they can prepare arguments which will take all of the allotted time. See Sec. 8.16(e), *infra.* The time taken by questioning from the bench and the answers thereto comes out of counsel's allotment, unless the judge is thoughtful enough, as Mr. Justice Black often was, to hold his questioning until counsel's time had expired; counsel may, of course, continue to reply to questions asked after his time is up. If the questioning takes a substantial portion of the allotted time, and clearly prevents him from getting to his prepared argument, he may ask the presiding judge or the court for additional time to complete his argument unless he knows this will be fruitless in the particular court.[28] How successful such a request will be may depend on whether the presiding judge believes that counsel has been unduly harassed or that further argument will be helpful, on how rushed the court is that day to keep up with its calendar, and, of course, on the subjective attitude of the judge or judges toward such requests. Sometimes they are granted. Indeed, sometimes a court, even without a request, will allow a few minutes extra to counsel who has been questioned at length by the court or whose opponent has previously been allowed to go overtime.

Counsel is not required, of course, to consume the entire period allowed him under the rules. Often at the opening of the calendar for the day, counsel will be asked how much time he will need and encouraged to use less than the time allowed by the rule. The court will be grateful if counsel takes less time, at least if he makes an adequate argument. Indeed, many courts reduce the time allowed when they think a case can be argued in less than the customary period. This should be, and usually is, done in advance.

The lawyer arguing is responsible for keeping track of his own time. Often a clock will be on the rostrum or in plain sight on the courtroom wall. Otherwise counsel will be dependent on his watch. In any event, the burden of remembering to look at the clock or watch, and also of noting the exact time when his argument began, is upon him. Often that is difficult in the heat

---

[28]Missouri Rule 84.12 contains the unusually reasonable provision that "[t]ime may be extended by the presiding judge to the extent of time taken by questions from the bench and answers thereto."

of an argument. I try to remember to jot down the time my argument begins at the top of my argument notes. Use of a stopwatch or setting a watch to an even hour at the beginning of the argument has been suggested as a useful means of aiding the lawyer who might otherwise have difficulty in calculating how much time he has left to argue.[29]

Some courts, like the United States Supreme Court, provide assistance by having a warning white light go on five minutes before counsel's time expires, as well as a red light when time is up. When the red light goes on, or counsel is otherwise notified that his time has expired, counsel may assume that he can finish his sentence but not much more without leave of court. The story that Chief Justice Hughes "called time on a leader of the New York Bar in the middle of the word 'if' " may be only slightly apocryphal.[30]

8.5 When the Case Will Be Heard and When Counsel Should Arrive

The clerk's office will normally notify counsel when a case is to be argued, sometimes long in advance but often only two or three weeks ahead of time.[31]

The order in which cases are scheduled will usually depend upon when the last brief or the appellee's brief is filed or due to be filed. Other factors, such as the docket number of the case and the kind of case, may be taken into account. Certain types of cases, such as criminal appeals, may be given priority as a matter of course, and others because of the obvious public or private importance of expediting the appeal. How long a period elapses between the briefing and the arguments will also depend on the court's backlog and on how lenient it is in granting extensions of time for filing the briefs.

Some courts, particularly intermediate courts with rotating panels, sit every day, or every week, or every month. Other courts, particularly supreme courts, will sit for a week or two every month or two months, depending on the number of cases to be argued. In many courts, the arguments will be heard within

---

[29]Fitzgerald and Hartnett, *supra* note 3, at 62.

[30]E. McElwain, *The Business of the Supreme Court as Conducted by Chief Justice Hughes,* 63 Harv. L. Rev. 5, 17 (1949).

[31]In New Hampshire the scheduling order designates the month in which the case will be heard. Supreme Court Rule 12.

a month or two after the appellee's brief or the reply brief is received. In others, the time is much longer.

Counsel can usually ascertain from the clerk when his case is likely to be heard before notification is received. In some courts the clerk, and in others the chief justice or the court, determines the order in which cases will be argued.

Whoever makes up the calendar, requests to advance or postpone arguments should be submitted to the clerk by way of motion or letter as the local practice permits. Judges and clerks will usually attempt to accommodate counsel, even for such personal factors as the taking of a scheduled vacation, if the request is a reasonable one which will not cause undue delay *and* if the request is received before the argument calendar has been formally set up. Seventh Circuit Rule 14(b) (3), (4) may be typical of the general practice. It provides:

> "(3) Requests by counsel, made in advance of the scheduling of an appeal for oral argument, that the court avoid scheduling the oral argument for a particular day or week will be respected, if possible.
> "(4) Once an appeal has been scheduled for oral argument, the court will not ordinarily reschedule it. Requests . . . should therefore be made as early as possible."

Conflict or overlap with other litigation, particularly in the same or a higher court, is, of course, an obvious reason for requesting a change in the scheduled date of argument. If the conflict is with a trial of long duration, however, and if a number of lawyers have worked on the appeal, the appellate court might reasonably believe that another lawyer can argue the appeal and accordingly decline to modify its schedule.

After the argument calendar has been fixed by the court and notices have gone out to counsel, a request to change the date of argument is less likely to be successful. Unforeseeable emergencies such as death or illness will presumably be adequate reasons, but not mere personal convenience of counsel.

Either a number of days in advance of the argument or earlier on the same day, counsel must notify the clerk's office who is to argue; registration on the day of argument also informs the clerk that counsel is present and prepared to argue. The clerk's office informs the judges of the names of the lawyers who are to appear in each case. When the court sits in rotating panels not identified in advance to counsel, the clerk's office will advise counsel of the names of the judges on the morning of argument; the names may also appear on the rostrum or in front of the bench. Some courts identify the judges a few days ahead of time.

Arguing counsel should be aware of the fact that he should be in the courtroom or at least the court building well in advance of the time his case will be called for argument, unless his is the first to be called on a particular day and he is assured that he will not be called the day before if that day's calendar breaks down. Some courts require counsel to be present when the court opens on the day of argument; in others counsel must be present at a particular scheduled time during the day, or a certain number of cases before his case is scheduled to be reached. The United States Supreme Court wants counsel in or close to the courtroom when the second preceding argument on that day begins, and in the courtroom when the preceding argument begins. In the absence of more specific advice from the clerk of a particular court, that is a good policy for counsel to follow in other courts as well. This has the advantage of giving counsel time to get his notes and other material out of his brief case and arrange them on the counsel table so that he can conveniently take what is needed—notes, briefs, record—to the lectern when he rises to argue, or before the court enters if he will be the first person to argue.

Listening to the preceding case has the additional advantage of enabling lawyers not previously experienced in that court to obtain some feel for arguing before it. This is important enough to make it advisable for counsel lacking such experience, and even more so for a lawyer with little prior appellate experience, to listen to a few arguments ahead of his own. If necessary for this purpose, a lawyer from outside the city should arrive early enough on the day before to hear cases argued that day if the court is then sitting.

Indeed, out-of-town lawyers should normally plan to arrive no later than the night before the argument for the additional purpose of obtaining a good night's sleep instead of traveling the next morning. My fortunate adherence to that policy for several arguments in Elgin, Illinois, only 40 miles from my home near Chicago, also had the beneficial effect of avoiding a long ride on icy roads the morning of the argument.

In short, find out when the clerk wants counsel to be present, and allow ample time both to observe the court and to get a good night's sleep.

Lawyers not familiar with the courthouse and its vicinity should also use their pre-argument time to learn:

(1) If they are traveling by private automobile, whether parking areas are available near the courthouse, as they seldom are in cities such as Washington, New York and Chicago. If necessary, call the clerk's office in advance and find out.

(2) If lunch time is likely to occur close to, or even worse in the middle of, the argument, where lunch can quickly and conveniently be obtained. If necessary, ask local counsel or the clerk's office, or look around when you first arrive.[32]

(3) Of even greater importance, when you arrive at the courthouse, long before your case will be reached, where the restroom nearest the courtroom is located. Judges have long recognized the importance of being prepared for a long session in court, and so should the lawyers.

8.6   The Order of Argument—Opening and Closing

Almost invariably the appellant or petitioner has the right to open and close the argument.[33] He can divide his time between the opening and closing as he sees fit, subject to the restriction that the opening contain "a fair statement" or "fair opening" of the case.[34] That sounds as if describing the nature of the case, the issues and the facts might be all that is required. But, of course, the appellant is expected by the court to make his principal argument in his opening, and it is to his advantage to do so, anticipating in advance the opposing arguments rather than rebutting them after they have been made. United States Supreme Court Rule 38.5, as revised in 1980, is more explicit in stating what is expected: "In any case, and regardless of the number of counsel participating, counsel having the opening

---

[32]The United States Supreme Court building has a cafeteria on the ground floor to which counsel in the midst of argument or about to argue will be guided by officers of the Court. Few other courthouses have similar facilities.

[33]Pennsylvania Rule 2321 permits appellant to conclude the argument by way of rebuttal only "if permitted by the court." The accompanying Note explains that "this rule is intended to make clear that the appellant does not have the right at the commencement of argument to reserve a portion of his argument until after the argument of appellee."

[34]E.g., Federal Appellate Rule 34(c).

will present his case fairly and completely and not reserve points of substance for rebuttal." Usually only a few minutes—5 or at most 10—can be reserved for reply, and counsel will be lucky if he has that much time left when his opening is concluded no matter how much he prepares.

To some extent, however, appellant's counsel can attempt to determine in advance how his argument should be divided. The length of the opening argument he prepares, verified by rehearsal (see Sec. 8.8(d), *infra*), will obviously affect how much time he will have left for the closing. He can even prepare to leave for the closing points which are not essential to his affirmative case, which can best be handled after hearing what his opponent has to say on the subject, which he is quite sure his opponent will argue, or which he need not discuss unless his opponent does.

Even though an attempt to determine how much time shall be kept for the closing may be useful, in most cases what occurs during the opening argument—and that is largely unpredictable—will determine how much time remains. Questioning may be light or heavy; it may take all of counsel's time or none, or anything in between. Lawyers on their feet are likely to enlarge on what they intended to say, no matter how carefully they have prepared a concise argument. Many find it difficult to stop talking once they are going, until the court stops them. Occasionally, if the judges seldom interrupt, counsel may even have more time left than expected.

In the main, therefore, the time left for the closing will depend upon the vagaries of the opening. That means that counsel will not know how much time he has left until his opening is concluded. He will then have to decide while his opponent is arguing what to say in reply. Advance preparation of the answers to everything he thinks his opponent may argue is essential, but the decision as to what and how much to say in closing will necessarily be made at the last minute, just before or even after counsel gets up to reply. As to the contents of the closing argument, see Sec. 8.18, *infra.*

As indicated in Sec. 8.4, p. 371, *supra,* a few jurisdictions allow the appellant or petitioner an additional 10 or 15 minutes for rebuttal. That means that he need not reserve part of his opening time for rebuttal. He can accordingly prepare a longer opening argument, although he will still have to anticipate that a portion of his time may be consumed by questioning.

Which side should open and close when both sides appeal or petition for review? Such cases are always required to be argued together as a single case in the time for a single appeal unless extra time is allowed.

There is no necessary relationship between which party appeals first and which as a matter of logical division of the argument should argue first in the appellate court. Perhaps in most cases the first appellant is the party principally aggrieved by the decision below, while the cross-appeal relates to incidental aspects of the case. But this is not necessarily so; the cross-appeal might present more important, or at least equally important, issues.

In a few jurisdictions the appellant who has first noticed his appeal or filed his petition automatically secures the right to open and close. E.g., New Jersey Rule 2:11-1(b). The rules of some states and Federal Rule of Appellate Procedure 34(d) provide that where there are cross-appeals the plaintiff below shall be regarded as the appellant. Since this arrangement would be unreasonable when the defendant was the principal loser below and the plaintiff had been unsuccessful only in minor part, the federal rule and many others qualify the priority given the plaintiff below by adding "unless the parties otherwise agree or the court otherwise directs."

Under Oklahoma Rule 1.18 the clerk decides who shall be treated as the principal appellant. The 1979 amendments to Pennsylvania Appellate Rules 2136 and 2322 provide that in cross-appeals the plaintiff or moving party below shall be deemed the appellant unless the parties agree or the court otherwise directs, but that if the "identity of the appellant . . . is not readily apparent the prothonotary [clerk] of the appellate court shall designate the appellant" for purposes of briefing and arguing. Rule 2322 further provides that if the appeals are not cross-appeals, they shall be argued as separate cases, in which the appellant in each case may open.

Other courts face up to the fact that any rule of thumb may operate arbitrarily. United States Supreme Court Rule 38.2 accordingly provides that "the Court will advise the parties which one is to open and close." Some of the states have similar provisions.

In such circumstances, or whenever a party is dissatisfied with the application of the usual rule to his case, the parties should attempt to agree on the order of argument and advise the clerk of the result. If they cannot agree, they should request the clerk to have the court resolve the matter. The party who seems to be the principal loser below should normally be treated as the appellant. If the parties are evenly balanced in that respect, the court might reasonably designate as the appellant the party whose appeal it regards as presenting the more difficult or more important questions. If the court can find no difference as to that, it might rationally treat the plaintiff below as the appellant on the theory that the plaintiff had the burden below of establishing his case and, with all else evenly balanced, starts with the same obligation in the appellate court.

8.7 Number of Counsel—Multiple Parties

Whether or not court rules so require, only one lawyer per side should argue except where different parties on the same side have at least partially different interests and positions which a single lawyer could not be expected to represent.

Some court rules allow only one lawyer per side in the usual case. United States Supreme Court Rule 38.4 thus provides:

> "Only one counsel will be heard for each side, except by special permission granted upon a request presented not later than 15 days after service of the petitioner's or appellant's brief on the merits. . . . Divided arguments are not favored."

The Federal Rules of Appellate Procedure are silent on this point, merely providing in Rule 34(d) that "[i]f separate appellants support the same argument, care shall be taken to avoid duplication of argument." Seventh Circuit Rule 14(c) sensibly adds:

> "Divided arguments on behalf of a single party or multiple parties with the same interests are not favored by the court. When such arguments are nevertheless divided or when more than one counsel argue on the same side for parties with differing interests, the time allowed shall be apportioned between such counsel in their own discretion. If counsel are unable to agree, the court will allocate the time."

Other rules permit two arguers per side, but still manifest a preference for undivided arguments. Thus, Illinois Rule 352(d) provides:

> "No more than two counsel will be heard from each side except by leave of court, which will be granted when there are several parties on the same side with diverse interests. Divided arguments

are not favored and care shall be taken to avoid duplication of arguments."

The common theme of many of these rules, as well as of all judicial and other commentators on the subject, is that "divided arguments are not favored." Justice Robert H. Jackson, who as Solicitor General was perhaps the most effective oral advocate in my experience, has explained why a divided argument is likely to be less helpful to the court, and even worse for the client:

> "If my experiences at the bar and on the bench unite in dictating one imperative, it is: Never divide between two or more counsel the argument on behalf of a single interest. Sometimes conflicting interests are joined on one side and division is compelled, but otherwise it should not be risked.
> "When two lawyers undertake to share a single presentation, their two arguments at best will be somewhat overlapping, repetitious and incomplete and, at worst, contradictory, inconsistent and confusing. I recall one misadventure in division in which I was to open the case and expound the statute involved, while counsel for a government agency was to follow and explain the agency's regulations. This seemed a natural place to sunder the argument. But the Court perversely refused to honor the division. So long as I was on my feet, the Justices were intensely interested in the regulations, which I had not expected to discuss. By the time my associate took over, they had developed a lively interest in the statute, which was not his part of the case. No counsel should be permitted to take the floor in any case who is not willing to master and able to present every aspect of it. If I had my way, the Court rules would permit only one counsel to argue for a single interest. But while my colleagues think such a rule would be too drastic, I think they all agree that an argument almost invariably is less helpful to us for being parceled out to several counsel."[35]

Illinois Supreme Court Justice Walter V. Schaefer similarly observed: "Judges of reviewing courts have a highly developed perverse instinct for putting the questions" to the lawyer prepared to argue the other parts of the case.[36]

Of course both counsel can come fully prepared to argue all phases of the case, but then there is no good reason for having two of them argue. The first to speak almost always, under questioning or not but in all good faith, will run over into the time which he had agreed should be reserved for his colleague. How much time should be spent on each point, a diffi-

---

[35]R. Jackson, *Advocacy Before the Supreme Court: Suggestions for Effective Case Presentations,* 37 A.B.A.J. 801–802 (1951).
[36]W. Schaefer, *Appellate Advocacy,* 23 Tenn. L. Rev. 471, 473 (1954).

cult decision often subject to instant change under fire, should not be affected by the obligation to share the argument with another lawyer.

Often counsel for different parties with the same interest are unable to agree upon who should argue, either because of personal pride, subjective evaluation of their respective abilities, or differences of opinion as to which points should be emphasized or omitted. These are insufficient reasons for dividing the argument among two or more lawyers.[37]

Division of an argument in order to give another lawyer a chance to appear in the high court or to impress the court or client by involving a senior partner or ranking government attorney is a dangerous tactic, both for the above reasons and because the court will be aware of the reason for his participation. If both lawyers are equally competent and prepared to cover the whole case and if it is thought that the senior's experience requires his participation, he should make the entire argument. Often, however, the junior will be more familiar with the record and the authorities and will be better able to make the major contribution, particularly if the court asks questions.

The major exception to the above general principle is for cases in which parties who in general are on the same side have different interests which require different arguments, as Mr. Justice Jackson and the court rules quoted above recognize. But unless extra time is allowed, so that each party can make an adequate presentation, division of the argument even in such circumstances may be inadvisable. Over-division can be disastrous. When, in a case I overheard, five parties insisted on separate representation in a 30-minute argument before the Illinois Supreme Court, the court rejected the efforts of the lawyers to exceed six minutes each because it resulted from their own inability to agree on less numerous representation. That, of course, was an extreme example.

The other circumstance in which argument by several lawyers on a side is permissible is the giant case of great public interest, often involving numerous parties with different positions. In such cases courts should allow substantial additional

---

[37] I once suggested, partially facetiously, when such a problem arose among a number of lawyers, all of whom had made good arguments in the court below, that if agreement could not otherwise be reached the matter should be decided by lot. I later learned that in at least one case in the Supreme Court of the United States counsel who were unable to agree as to who should argue finally did agree to decide the matter by lot.

time and argument by a number of counsel. In the *Permian Basin Area Rate Cases,* 390 U.S. 747 (1968), the United States Supreme Court allowed 16 lawyers to argue eight hours. But such cases are few and far between.

If leave of court is necessary for additional counsel to appear, as it is in the United States Supreme Court for more than one lawyer per side, and in other courts for more than two counsel per side, application should normally be made by motion submitted in accordance with the court's rules. Particularly if additional time is also being requested, the motion should be submitted well in advance of the argument so that the clerk can be aware of how much time is being allowed when he prepares the calendar. But even if the request is only to permit another lawyer to argue, it should be submitted some time in advance both so that the court may be adequately informed and, more importantly, so that arguing counsel will have adequate time to prepare, and, if necessary, to determine how the argument shall be divided.

On rare occasions, when counsel are unable to agree on who should argue, or on how the time should be divided, the problem is submitted to the court for determination. In some courts the clerk may attempt to work the matter out with counsel, impressing upon them the importance of limiting the number of arguers. If the clerk is unsuccessful in obtaining an agreement among the lawyers, or if it is not his policy to attempt to negotiate an agreement, he submits the matter to the court or to a justice who enters an appropriate order. Counsel should make every effort to accommodate their differences without submitting the matter to the court, which may reach a result unsatisfactory to all of them.

On occasion the United States Supreme Court and other appellate courts may consolidate separate cases which present the same or similar questions for argument. This may mean that the cases will be argued consecutively or in tandem, or that they must be treated and argued in the time allotted one case. In the Supreme Court, the consolidated cases are allowed only the 30 minutes per side for a single case, and only one counsel will be heard on each side. That means that if counsel in different cases each wish to argue, because their interests or positions are somewhat different or otherwise, they must obtain leave of court to do so under Supreme Court Rule 38.4. A court should be lenient in allowing counsel in each case to argue in such circumstances, granting additional time when necessary.

8.8 How to Prepare for Argument and Argue

As a preliminary matter, each party should bring the research upon the basis of which his brief was prepared up-to-date, utilizing the Shepards, Lexis or Westlaw system. If additional authorities of significance are discovered at the last minute,[38] this may be stated during the argument. Some court rules require that such authorities be brought to the attention of the court and opposing counsel beforehand in an explanatory letter or supplemental memorandum, enclosing a copy of the authority if it is not reported. If there is time, this is the most reasonable procedure since it enables the judges and opposing counsel to examine the new authority before the argument and makes unnecessary a more extensive oral analysis than it would otherwise warrant.[39] This would be a good procedure to follow unless something different is prescribed by the rules of the court to which the appeal is taken.

The steps to be followed in preparing for oral argument may be, and usually have been, simply stated: The arguer should read and become fully familiar with the record, the authorities cited by all parties, and the briefs. He should prepare an outline or notes, but not write out his argument, and argue from the notes or outline. He should be aware that questioning is likely to interrupt him and disrupt what he had intended to say, realize that answering the questions is his most important function, and accordingly be prepared to rearrange the argument on the fly.

Observations of other lawyers and my own experience, however, have convinced me that while many and perhaps most able advocates follow the above pattern, many others do not, and that a more detailed and critical exposition of the different techniques of preparation would be helpful. For the methods most suited to the personalities and abilities of some lawyers may not be best for others.

---

[38]Unreported Supreme Court cases are printed within a day in the *United States Law Week*, published by The Bureau of National Affairs, Inc., and in the Commerce Clearing House *Supreme Court Bulletin.* Summaries of some lower court opinions also appear in *U.S. Law Week.* Recent unreported cases in specialized appeals often appear in the special services covering those subjects.

[39]Seventh Circuit Rule 11, for example, requires a letter to the court citing the authority, referring to the pertinent page of the brief and stating "in a single brief sentence the proposition the authority supports" but with "no other argument or explanation." If the authority cited is not yet published, a copy shall accompany the letter. The original and six copies shall be sent to the court, with a copy to opposing counsel. The same procedure is to be followed if the authority is discovered after argument.

In order to enlarge my knowledge of how others prepare their arguments, I addressed a questionnaire to approximately one hundred lawyers who I had reason to believe were able appellate advocates.[40] Ninety-six responded, and I am indebted to them for a substantial enlargement of my knowledge of the variations in how good lawyers prepare and argue their appeals. The following discussion is based upon these responses, as well as upon what others have written on the subject and my own experience.

As indicated, no single method of preparation is utilized by all lawyers. The differences in individual techniques may conform to personal qualities or preferences, or to ignorance of the various methods which are available and which other lawyers use. Furthermore, different cases and circumstances call for different approaches. How to handle a record may depend on whether it has 100 or 10,000 pages, on whether the arguing attorney tried the case, was the brief writer, or neither, on whether he heard or read the testimony, on whether he wrote the brief two years or two months before the oral argument and on how well he can recall the details. How much written preparation for argument by way of sparse or detailed notes or text is called for may depend on whether the argument can be limited to a few minutes on one point—and some can—or must cover a number of facts and points which can only with difficulty be crammed into the time allowed.

The following steps, or most of them, are those followed by most arguers, although a few halt their preparations at each of the stages.

(a)　Becoming Familiar With the Material

The first step in preparation is for the arguer to thoroughly familiarize himself with the case, that is, with the briefs, the record and the authorities. How he does that will depend on the factors mentioned above. If he wrote the brief himself, he will need much less time than if he did not. That would normally mean that he had previously read the record and authorities, and that he may have made notes or a digest as he did so. His recollection, recorded or not, may make it less necessary for him

---

[40] The selections were based on my own knowledge and the suggestions of others, including some judges.

to repeat the entire process, unless the passage of time has dimmed his memory too greatly. That may, of course, happen, since in some overloaded courts the time lag between the last brief and the oral argument may be many months and sometimes even years.

Seldom will a lawyer, even one who did not try a case, come into it after the briefs are completed (although that occasionally happens as it has to me). Thus he will have either written the brief or carefully reviewed it. Accordingly, even a lawyer brought into the case newly for the appeal normally will have studied the briefs and other material while the briefs were being prepared. If he did not, he certainly should when he begins his preparation for the oral argument.

Even the lawyer previously familiar with the case should reread that material if he possibly can. He will usually study the briefs first, as they already represent the distilling of the record and the authorities into the arguments on the issues to be presented.

If possible, the record should be read or reread in full. In some cases where an appendix, excerpts, abstract or the like contains the items which the parties have designated as the significant portions of the record, and where there is reason to believe that other parts of the record are of no consequence, reliance on the designated material may be sufficient. If the record is too voluminous to read in full—and in some kinds of cases records containing thousands of pages are not uncommon —and if the pertinent passages have not already been designated, the arguer must at a minimum read the passages which the record references in the briefs indicate to be important. He should concentrate, of course, on the portions of the record which relate to points in dispute, not facts as to which the briefs agree. Thus, although the desirability of knowing the entire record is generally proclaimed to be essential, many arguers admit that they limit themselves to the items which they believe to be significant or in dispute.

The arguer should, of course, read the record or the significant portions himself, and if they are of any length, digest them himself. A digest prepared by someone else will not impress itself on his mind. With modern dictating equipment now available and not merely pencils and paper, preparing a digest is no longer as tedious as it was in the past.

Reading all of the authorities cited in the briefs, or discovered thereafter, is often also said to be a "must." But the experienced lawyer knows that only a few cases are likely to be mentioned by counsel or the judges during oral argument, and that as a practical matter familiarity with every case cited may not be important. Selecting the crucial cases is usually not difficult. Briefs are full of citations supporting propositions not in dispute, such as the scope of review or the principles of construction of statutes or contracts.

If he does not read them all, the arguer must lean over backward to be sure that he will be familiar with any authority which may possibly be mentioned by his adversary or a judge. He must not take the "ostrich approach to the cases cited against him."[41] "Authority" in this context means not just case citations but any material—legislative, scholarly or even scientific—upon which the court or counsel might rely. The arguer must read this material himself and, if necessary, digest it. If he cannot count on remembering them, the digests should be close at hand during the argument.

In addition to reading authorities cited in briefs, counsel not already generally familiar with the field of law involved will benefit by educating himself through reading more broadly so as to fit the case into its legal perspective and to become aware of the policy considerations which may influence the judges. Such knowledge may be very comforting if the judges probe deeply during the argument.[42]

Merely to have a young lawyer read and digest masses of cases for the senior who is to argue is a horrible practice and a waste of time. Unless he has read the cases himself, the senior will not recall enough from his young associate's notes to handle the cases during the argument. He must read the principal authorities, which can usually be identified from the briefs. If the senior cannot or does not read *all* the cited authorities himself, he should at least know what they stand for. If this is not apparent from the brief, a memorandum from a colleague may be sufficient for relatively unimportant or noncontroversial authorities.

The precise order in which briefs, authorities and record are studied at the beginning of the preparation is not of vital importance. Most lawyers reasonably begin with the briefs,

---

[41]Fitzgerald and Hartnett, *supra* note 3, at 53.
[42]*Id.* at 54.

which identify the issues and put the relevant parts of the record and the authorities in the same argumentative context as will be required for the argument. The record and the authorities each acquire greater meaning from knowledge of the other, but obviously both cannot be read first or at the same time. Reading the record or the significant portions thereof probably should precede reading the cases, at least for counsel unfamiliar with either, since a fresh lawyer coming into the case is likely to know less about its facts than about the law. If he already knows a good deal about both from prior familiarity with the case, which is reread first is immaterial.

(b)   Rough Outline of Points—The Process of Selection

After counsel has determined that he is sufficiently familiar with the facts, the authorities and the arguments presented by both sides, he should prepare a rough outline of the points which might be argued.

This is the time for appraisal and selection, not necessarily for working out details. Which points should be omitted from the argument because they are too weak or too vulnerable, because other points are stronger, because they do not lend themselves to oral presentation, or simply because all the points cannot be covered in the time allotted? Inherent in the process of determining the points to be argued is an evaluation of the merits of each. The opposing arguments, as presented below, as well as any holes in one's own reasoning, whether previously noted by the opposition or not, must be candidly appraised— and sometimes that is hard to do. This process need not be performed in solitude. Discussions with colleagues or co-counsel familiar with the case and also with others not familiar are not only helpful but often essential. The effort should be to make an educated guess as to how the appellate judges will react to each argument, and to choose the arguments which are most likely to be persuasive to the ear.

Points which because of their complexity or their dependence upon figures or detailed analysis of evidence or authorities can better be understood through reading and study should be left to the briefs. If such a point is important, the oral arguer cannot ignore it, but its substance should be summarized with a statement that it can best be understood from examination of the detailed analysis in the brief. See Sec. 8.11, p. 404, *infra.*

In sum, this is the time for thinking more than writing, although usually it will result in a written outline of points to be covered. It may take anything from a few minutes to a number of days depending upon the magnitude and difficulty of the case.

This process of selection and evaluation never ceases until the end of the argument itself. The preparation of the argument in further detail often focuses attention on different facts and authorities and produces new ideas, both favorable and unfavorable, which must then be fed into one's mental computer and the prior thinking rearranged to take them into account.

(c) Preparing in Detail

At this point individual methods of preparation diverge. Only a few brilliant and audacious advocates have the temerity to argue without having in front of them notes of any sort (except perhaps a reference to what they may want to quote), and most of them will prepare and study written notes prior to appearing in court. They do not memorize the argument in advance, but have good enough memories and ability to speak fluently to be able to proceed on the basis of this preparation without more. Everyone else, so far as I know, uses an outline or notes of some sort, and that includes many lawyers of great ability and experience who have good memories but would regard relying on memory alone as completely foolhardy. No one should try it unless in other contexts he has proved his ability to undertake such a performance successfully. For anyone else, an argument prepared in that way would almost certainly sound inadequate.[43]

Memorizing is dangerous, even if one's memory is up to it. For any interruption by the court may throw the memorizer off his stride, and determining just what to come back to or how to rearrange may be difficult without notes. Furthermore, memo-

---

[43]The advice of Fitzgerald and Hartnett is that arguing without notes, even if you can do it, has serious drawbacks. "[E]ven good memories can play tricks, and in the pressure of an oral argument, a significant point may be overlooked if notes are not available. Counsel who have felt themselves to be impervious to nervousness during oral argument can receive just the unsuspected jolt that rattles their mental poise and drives from their minds the carefully memorized outline of argument. As a result, an important point may be overlooked."

You may "discover—too late—that your logical sequence has been destroyed" and you are "not going to impress anybody very much, because the court will recognize it as a rather ostentatious demonstration or stunt, while at the same time, you will be flirting with real trouble for your client's case." *Id.* at 60.

rizing is not worth the mental strain. Writing detailed notes or a text, inserting catchwords, and reviewing and revising several times will make both the thoughts and the key phrases so familiar that only an occasional glance at the notes or outline should be necessary. Having them before you, however, is very comforting in case your memory fails or the need to reply to questions or to your opponent requires a switch to another subject or other rearrangement.

A few lawyers have nothing before them while arguing except a short outline noting the points to be covered.[44] Many prepare notes or an outline in detail, using either descriptive headings for the points to be discussed or catchwords which will jog the memory. Almost as many, either after preparing an outline or in lieu of doing so, write out a draft of argument. A substantial number of lawyers do it sometimes one way and sometimes the other depending on the magnitude of the case. Many prepare different parts of the argument in different ways, relying on notes for items easy to explain and written sentences where careful expression is essential.

Most, but by no means all, of those who write drafts of their arguments then annotate the text with notes, catchwords, underscoring or other emphasis, either in the text itself, in the margin or at the beginning of each paragraph. Some then argue with the text thus annotated before them, making sure that the notes and catchwords are in some emphatic form which can easily be read, such as solid capitals or underscoring or placement in the margin. Others have the paragraph headings or catchwords copied separately from the text, and have only those notes before them during the course of the argument. Others have before them only the full text of the prepared argument, while a few rely on separately prepared notes without the text.

Whichever of these techniques is followed, the argument should not be read. The rules of many courts specifically so state,[45] while others declare that the court looks upon it with disfavor.[46] Judge Goodrich has advised that counsel

---

[44]Mr. Carson favored having "before you during the argument [only] a page in the nature of a table of contents to refresh your memory and give you assurance . . . although the briefs and records should be within reach to be referred to if a question calls for them." Carson, *supra* note 5, at 75.

[45]Illinois Rule 352(c) provides: "Reading at length from the record, briefs, or authorities cited will not be permitted." To the same effect, see New Jersey Rule 2:11-1(b).

[46]United States Supreme Court Rule 38.1 provides, in italics added for emphasis when the rule was recently revised: *"The Court looks with disfavor on any oral argument that is read from a prepared text."*

"should not read his brief to the court. Over and over again one may hear it said from the appellate bench: 'Please do not read us your brief, Counsel. The court may not be able to think but it certainly can read.' . . . The protest against brief reading goes also to a somewhat lesser extent to the reading of any prepared manuscript. Surely a lawyer doing court work can learn to talk to a court from notes without having to put a paper between himself and his judicial audience."[47]

Able advocates who write their arguments are perfectly aware that reading of the argument is not only disfavored by judges but also unhelpful to clients. Most of those who have prepared a text use it or the annotations based upon it just as others use an outline, glancing down when necessary as they shift from one point to another. Some say they do not stick close to the prepared language, and others that they do in the absence of questioning. But that does not mean that they are reading. For, as I can personally attest, the process of preparing a text, annotating it with headnotes and catchwords, and continually reviewing and revising up to the last moment enables one to stick pretty close to the prepared language without reading it or appearing to read it, and without having memorized it.

I have tried all of these methods except having no notes at all or relying on sparse notes which merely indicate the topics to be covered. At the end of my preparation even the latter probably would have been sufficient, but since the catchwords and more detailed notes could better refresh my memory and since they had already been prepared, I preferred to use them.

When I first began to argue I would prepare only a detailed outline. But as I wrote the outline I found that I was thinking in actual sentences, though merely writing down the topical or key words for each thought. This led me to write the full sentence instead, though with no intention of reading it. I would leave ample space between paragraphs. After revising the text for clarity and substance, keeping in mind that it must flow simply enough for oral presentation, I would then insert in the space between the paragraphs the catchwords which would best remind me of the substance of what followed. These words and phrases[48] in solid capital letters would seldom exceed one line which could be seen easily at a glance during the argument.

---

[47]Goodrich, *supra* note 4, at 26.
[48]Persons whose handwriting is as bad as mine must rely on typed notes. Persons who can always read their own handwriting may find that sufficient, but even for them typing would almost certainly be easier to follow.

More often, however, a day or two before the argument I would have the headings typed separately from the text and use them alone as the argument notes. In order to make such notes entirely self-sufficient, I would insert at the appropriate place any short passages which I might wish to quote from statutes, authorities, documents or testimony, so that I would not have to interrupt the argument by turning to the briefs or record. I would also include in the notes or the margin the record references or case citations which I might wish to mention orally in answer to questions or otherwise.

This technique, which I found was also used by a few of the other persons who responded to my questionnaire, has a number of advantages. The process of preparing in this manner gets the material into my head, not memorized but firmly enough so that occasionally glancing at either the annotated text or the annotations is sufficient to keep the argument flowing.

Writing the text in words and phrases which I have time to think about and improve converts the ideas or topics into the form in which they can be best expressed without having to think of the words completely extemporaneously as the argument proceeds. Usually a method of expression carefully worked out in advance will be superior analytically to what I can produce off the cuff. If during the argument I think of something better, either because of questioning or a sudden inspiration, I am free to use it. I have learned from experience, however, that more often than not it would have been better to stick to the previously prepared version.[49]

It is, of course, true that effective oral speech is not necessarily the same as written. The arguer who writes out a textual draft must keep that at the front of his mind, and take advantage of colloquialisms and informality not appropriate for a written presentation. Homey, down-to-earth words and common metaphors may be effective orally though not suitable in formal writing. He can and should insure that his argument will not sound like a written or memorized draft. Going through the argument aloud on the basis of the headnotes or text, a subject treated in the next subsection, enables the arguer to eliminate passages which would not sound right when expressed orally. Hearing

---

[49]To the same effect, see Fitzgerald and Hartnett, *supra* note 3, at 67, quoted at p. 430, note 111, *infra.*

oneself recite will usually be sufficient for this, although critical listeners can be even more helpful.

Many able advocates believe that writing the argument in advance will reduce or eliminate spontaneity, interfere with the desired maintenance of eye contact with the judges and result in a stilted presentation. Both in other writings and in comments on my questionnaire, they have expressed strong disapproval of writing an argument in advance. The advantages of not writing an argument should be stated in their own words.

Colonel Wiener has declared that

> "an oral argument loses much of its spontaneity if it is written out in advance. It is more natural—and hence more effective—if it is delivered from notes."[50]

In his usual firm fashion, he elaborates:

> "I have no hesitation at all in saying 'No,' emphatically 'No,' to the suggestion that an argument be written out in full. If your argument is fully written out, you will read it, and reading one's argument is high on the list of Things Not to Be Done."[51]

Judge Prentice Marshall agrees:

> "Do not write a manuscript of your oral argument; you are going to speak it, not read it."[52]

Others have said that a prepared text is incompatible with the need for adaptability to questioning, and that more of a variable structure for the argument is required; that the most effective argument is one in which the advocate looks at the judges and speaks directly to them with infrequent glances at his notes, except when a short quotation is necessary.

An experienced lawyer from Florida has stated:

> "I never write a full draft of the proposed argument. I consider this to be a very bad way to prepare for argument, since it tends to delude the lawyer into the notion that he will be able to make an uninterrupted presentation to the court. The appellate advocate should recognize that he is liable to be interrupted at any time and diverted from his normal course of argument, and the lawyer who attempts to argue as if he were delivering a speech is likely to be confused by questions from the court, and to have difficulty in regaining his balance. In other words, the temptation would be to return to the prepared text and resume argument as if no

---

[50]F. Wiener, BRIEFING AND ARGUING FEDERAL APPEALS, p. 283 (1967).
[51]*Id.* at 310.
[52]Marshall, *supra* note 3, at 9–13.

questions had intervened, which more often than not results in a clumsy argument and a waste of time in rearguing matters which have already been discussed in the question and answer period with the judges. . . . I think it is most important for the advocate to be looking at the judges, rather than at his notes, during most of the course of his argument. Appellate argument, after all, is a stylized form of persuasion and I think it is the advocate's job to try to capture and hold the attention of each judge, as if engaged in a private discourse. The lawyer who primarily reads from his notes or texts removes himself from this personal interaction with the judges on the court, who simply become an audience rather than individuals who are engaged in intellectual exercise."

In the main, these experienced advocates are correctly describing the effects of arguments which are read to the court. They often assume, or seem to assume, that a previously prepared written argument will be read, or will sound as if it is being read. That does not follow, and is not necessarily so.

A distinguished California lawyer who always writes out a draft of the argument states:

"The advantage of this to me is that writing out the argument tends to make for brevity and a logical progression of the points, and, equally important, gives the arguer an assurance that what he has in mind can be succinctly expressed in language that makes sense. It helps to guard against fuzzy thinking and gaps in logic."

He further states that after then using the text to fill in notes in his outline, he uses only the revised outline. Although he reviews the text, outline and the notes a number of times in advance of the argument,

"I never-never-never read it to the court or even have it before me at the podium. . . . However, having written out the argument, one tends to use the same phraseology in arguing from the notes that has been previously written into the draft, and this makes for a facility in statement which would be lacking if the argument had not been written out."

An advocate of renown declares:

"The manner in which I prepared for argument always depended on the time available, and to some extent upon my familiarity with the subject. If time permitted, I would write and rewrite and rewrite and rewrite the oral argument. The process clarifies one's thoughts. It provides sentences and phrases which can be drawn spontaneously from one's mind during the course of the argument and in answering questions. . . . I cannot believe that I have really made my thoughts precise until I have written them down on a piece of paper and rewritten them seven or eight times in order to remove the lack of precision. I keep up the process until the case is called."

He has the argument before him but does not read it.

"[I]f one has worked and reworked the prepared text, what he says will correspond to the text pretty closely even though he neither memorizes nor reads it."

Another lawyer who has been on both sides of the bench states that though he frequently writes his arguments he never reads them but only refers to them as often as necessary to maintain an orderly sequence. When questions require him to depart from the prepared arrangement, he must be able to resume at whatever point then seems appropriate. "The discipline of writing out the argument," he adds, "helps to point up any flaws and occasionally yields a felicitous locution."

Mr. Justice Jackson's comments on various arguing techniques contain perhaps the best summation of what should and should not be done:

"The manner of delivery must express the talents and habits of the advocate. No one method is indispensable to success, and practice varies widely. Few lawyers are gifted with memory and composure to argue a case without papers of any kind before them. It is not necessary to try. The memorized oration, or anything stilted and inflexible, is not appropriate. Equally objectionable is the opposite extreme—an unorganized, rambling discourse, relying on the inspiration of the moment. If one's oral argument is simply reading his printed brief aloud, he could as well stay at home. Almost as unsatisfying is any argument that has been written out and is read off to us, page after page. We like to meet the eye of the advocate, and sometimes when one starts reading his argument from a manuscript he will be interrupted to wean him from his essay; but it does not often succeed. If you have confidence to address the Court only by reading to it, you really should not argue there."[53]

Justice Jackson's own practice as an advocate

"was to prepare notes, consisting of headings and catch-words rather than of details, to guide the order of argument and prevent important items from being overlooked. Such notes help to get back on the track if one is thrown off by interruptions. They will tend to limit rambling and irrelevance, give you some measure of confidence, and at the same time let you frequently meet your judges eye to eye."[54]

---

[53]R. Jackson, *Advocacy Before the Supreme Court: Suggestions for Effective Case Presentations,* 37 A.B.A.J. 801, 804, 861 (1951).
[54]*Id.* at 861.

Although Justice Jackson frowned upon reading or memorizing an argument, his analysis does not preclude the use of a written draft during the course of preparation if the argument eventually given is not read.

Those who do prepare a written draft, as I now do, find that it provides a more concise and logical organization which can be compressed more easily into the short periods of time now allowed than can a presentation based upon notes or an outline alone. It tends to keep the speaker from rambling.

Fewer pages of notes will be needed, of course, if only the key or catchwords—in substance, an outline—typed apart from the text are before counsel while he argues. Using large legal size pages also helps keep the number of pages down. The smaller the number of pages before counsel when he argues, the less turning or discarding of pages during the argument will be required.

My own personal practice is to have the headings or catchwords typed in capital letters on such large pages. The process of thinking out the key or catchwords, attaching them to, and separating them from, each paragraph of the text and then reviewing both together insures that the notes based upon such catchwords will sufficiently remind me of what I want to say without tying me to the exact text.

Enough has been said to show that there is no single right way to prepare an oral argument, though there are some wrong ways. The latter include failure to master all aspects of the case, including the record and the authorities, failure to take into account the time limitation, failure to think out the best organization and select the few points which can and should be covered orally, and reading an argument to the court. Whatever the nature of the final stage of preparation, it should not be regarded as a single step, but as a continuum which does not terminate until the argument has been completed. For the arguer should leave ample time before the argument for review and revision, both for the improvement in substance which accompanies rethinking, whether in the mind or on paper, and for greater familiarity with the contents, which will reduce the need for reliance on either notes or text.

Counsel should be aware that different methods of arguing have been utilized by able lawyers and select the technique with which he is the most comfortable. This may require experimentation and change, as it has with me. What is required is a mastery of the subject, and a combination of a well-organized presentation prepared in advance with the ability to be completely flexible in the light of questions from the court and the argument of one's adversary.

(d)　Rehearsing

An essential part of the process of improving the argument once it has been prepared, in any form, is rehearsal in advance. To my surprise, the majority of those responding to the questionnaire stated that they rehearsed, sometimes several times, some before a moot court of lawyers, some before their wives, but most to themselves, either aloud or silently. The reasons for this have been eloquently stated by Mr. Justice Jackson:

> "Do not think it beneath you to rehearse for an argument. Not even Caruso, at the height of his artistic career, felt above rehearsing for a hundredth performance, although he and the whole cast were guided and confined by a libretto and a score. Of course, I do not suggest that you should declaim and gesture before a mirror. But, if you have an associate, try out different approaches and thrash out every point with him. Answer the questions that occur to another mind. See what sequence of facts is most effective. Accustom yourself to your materials in different arrangements. Argue the case to yourself, your client, your secretary, your friend, and your wife if she is patient. Use every available anvil on which to hammer out your argument."[55]

Judge Prentice Marshall suggests speaking the argument to yourself several times with the door closed, then "test-marketing" the product on a "partner, secretary or spouse . . . . The lawyer, hopefully, will react as a judge. If your (non-lawyer) spouse understands the argument, certainly the court will. The point is to perform at least once to an audience, and get the audience's reaction."[56]

Colonel Wiener has explained:

> "No lawyer would dream of filing with the clerk the first rough draft of his brief. Why then present to the court the first draft of your oral argument? Many lawyers, too many of them, do just that —which is why such a lot of sorry oral arguments are heard in Federal appellate courts throughout the land.
>
> "There are, of course, some virtuosos, some people who have a flair for the extemporaneous. If you are one of those fortunate

---

[55]*Id.* at 861.
[56]Marshall, *supra* note 3, at 9–12.

few, the paragraphs that follow are not for you. But if you are a simple, run-of-the-mill fellow, like the rest of us, a carefully rehearsed and prepared and revised presentation will always be better than one that is just rolled off the cuff.

"Preparation and rehearsal will save you from going off on unprofitable or even untenable side issues, will spare you the waste of precious minutes on nonessentials, and will substantially assist you in eliminating unhappy turns of phrase."[57]

Rehearsals permit the arguer to time his "remarks, to smooth out infelicities, to ascertain where to expand and what to eliminate."[58] I add that Colonel Wiener, who was my colleague in the Solicitor General's office for several years, is by no means "a simple, run-of-the-mill" lawyer, but a sophisticated legal scholar with an exceptional memory. If *his* arguments benefited from prior rehearsals, others should benefit by his example.

Most appellate advocates do not rehearse very many times, or before an outside audience at all. Undoubtedly a dress rehearsal, so to speak, under the fire of questioning by colleagues who are likely to be much more contentious than the actual judges, is the most effective and helpful technique. Those who rehearse but not to that extent either do not think that necessary or hesitate to inflict themselves upon innocent, though usually interested, bystanders. They may benefit by the use of tape recorders which can be replayed for persons not shocked by the sound of their own voices.[59] Videotape may even be better, though looking at oneself could be distracting, and the incremental improvement not worth the additional cost.

Almost every lawyer who rehearses does so in part to ascertain approximately how many minutes the prepared argument will take. Most measure it on the clock—and this is so whether they mutter or read or improvise from a written draft or outline or nothing at all, to themselves or to colleagues who interrupt with questions. A few have learned by experience how long an oral presentation of one page of text or outline takes; if they are sufficiently skilled at arithmetic, they can then determine the total time by multiplying this factor by the number of pages. These processes will provide only a minimum approximation, as the lawyer, of course, knows, but this nevertheless provides the

---

[57]F. Wiener, BRIEFING AND ARGUING FEDERAL APPEALS, pp. 295–296 (1967).
[58]*Id.* at 307. These objectives can be attained even more fully, in my view, with which Colonel Wiener disagrees, if the argument has been written out and reduced to notes before the rehearsal.
[59]Fitzgerald and Hartnett, *supra* note 3, at 60.

best possible basis for ascertaining in advance the length of the prepared argument and thus knowing how much may have to be eliminated.

Even reading aloud to himself a prepared first draft of a text which he does not intend to read in court enables counsel to know roughly whether slicing is necessary, and how much. I have found that when questioning has not been intense, as sometimes happens, the argument given comes pretty close to the rehearsal time. When the rehearsals persuade me that the argument has not been sufficiently curtailed to permit its presentation in substantially less than the time allowed, I prepare for the anticipated questioning by eliminating items or by using brackets or other marks to identify the materials which can be discarded if necessary.

8.9 Style of Speaking—and Dressing

The oral argument is a combination of a speech and a conversation. The precise proportion of each will not be known in advance and will vary from case to case. The atmosphere, however, is more conducive to a conversational tone than to oratory. Since the audience—or at least the part you care about—is small and not very far away, resounding oratory would not be proper even if there were time for it. On the other hand, the distance is often too great for an ordinary conversational tone, and the lawyer is expected to keep going on his own when the judges choose not to initiate a colloquy. Thus, the argument has ingredients both of formal presentation and informal discussion.

The first essential obviously is that the arguer must be heard. That requires speaking more loudly than in a normal conversation, but not very much more. The judges will seldom be more than 15 feet away, and they will not appreciate a voice which seems to be addressed to persons in the back of the courtroom. Some courtrooms have amplifiers, but most do not. Find out whether yours does, and if it does, remember to stay near the microphone.[60] Whether it does or not, do not wander from the lectern.

If you have a knack for good public speaking so much the better, so long as it does not carry with it a public speaker's

---

[60]The microphone may be for the benefit of the court, not the audience, and may be connected with a recording machine which will enable the judges to play back the argument.

frequent inability to select and stick to a few critical points. But do not worry if you are not an experienced speaker. Knowledge of the subject will carry you through, and one or two arguments should provide enough confidence that you can make an argument which gets across.

In order to be understood, you should not talk too rapidly. On the other hand, in order to cover the substance of your argument in the time available, except in the simplest of cases you dare not talk too slowly. The desirable intermediate pace need not be too deliberate. Judges can keep up with a reasonably rapid presentation and will not appreciate counsel who dawdles. Avoid both extremes.

Don't seek to provide emphasis by persistently waving eyeglasses or other articles at the court. Such mannerisms may be annoying. If inability both to read your notes and see the judges impels you to keep putting on and taking off your glasses, "admit to the ravages of time and buy bifocals, or use larger type."[61]

Of course, you should look at the judges. But the usual advice as to the importance of maintaining eye contact[62] is difficult to follow for the multi-judge court, except when a judge is asking questions. One must not concentrate on the eyes of one judge, even the chief, so as not to appear to be disregarding the others. The effort should be to look at the various judges from time to time. I believe this is a matter which lawyers adequately handle naturally without consciously worrying about it.

Also avoid too monotonous a tone, or, conversely, emphases which are unnecessarily dramatic. Some emphasis, of course, is desirable. Persuasive advocacy resembles persuasive conversation more than play acting. "Uh's," "uh-uh's" and "ah's" obviously interrupt the flow of an argument. A few will not matter much, but a great many will, and some speakers are unaware that what they say is so tainted. Preparation which makes it unnecessary to grope for the best phrasing as one proceeds can be helpful in this respect. Persons who are not naturally fluent extemporaneously may benefit by thinking of the key words and catchwords in advance, and including them in the argument notes.

Nervousness at the commencement of an argument is largely unavoidable. It decreases with experience, but seldom

---

[61]Fitzgerald and Hartnett, *supra* note 3, at 65–66.
[62]*Ibid.;* Carson, *supra* note 5, at 89.

disappears altogether, at least until the argument is under way.[63] Writing out your first sentence and having it before you in large letters can help get you through the first few seconds. So don't be nervous about being nervous. Remember that you know more about your case than the judges do. They don't want you to be or act in awe of them, but will best appreciate an attitude of "intellectual equality"[64]—or at least as much equality as is consistent with respect and deference.[65] Almost all appellate judges will be friendly and courteous unless they discern a lack of candor or integrity. They may, of course, press counsel who make weak arguments, but the cure for that is not to take an appeal where questions cannot be met with at least a respectable answer. See Sec. 8.2, p. 367, *supra*.

The proper method of opening your argument is "May it please the Court," perhaps preceded by "Mr. Chief Justice." Members of the Court should be addressed as "Your Honor," "Mr. Chief Justice," "Mr. Justice," "Mr. Chief Judge" or "Judge," depending upon the correct title, but not as "Judge" where "Justice" is correct. As to female judges the elimination of the "Mr." seems the simplest course, since neither "Madam," "Mrs.," "Miss" nor "Ms." sounds quite right, apart from the difficulty of determining which is correct for a particular judge. The best solution is probably to eliminate the "Mr." for all justices, as the United States Supreme Court did in November 1980 with respect to its own orders and opinions. Counsel should also give his or her name and identify his client unless he knows or is apprised by the clerk's office that the judges have that information.

Dress in appellate courts no longer need be formal, even in the United States Supreme Court. Conservative—which means reasonably dark, or at least not too light—business suits for men and the equivalent for women are the most satisfactory, though many lawyers seem to consider any combination of coat and trousers adequate without suffering any dire consequences. Coats and ties should be worn even in hot weather, unless (presumably when air conditioning is not available or effective) the presiding judge takes pity on the members of the bar, or perhaps

---

[63]Marshall, *supra* note 3, at 9–14.

[64]The phrase is Colonel Wiener's, BRIEFING AND ARGUING FEDERAL APPEALS, p. 299 (1967).

[65]Examples which approach the borderline from both directions, successfully and unsuccessfully, appear in Carson, *supra* note 5, at 83–85.

sets an informal example himself. In the words of Mr. Justice Jackson: "You will not be stopped from arguing if you wear a race-track suit or sport a rainbow necktie. You will just create a first impression that you have strayed in at the wrong bar."[66]

8.10 Physical Arrangements for Arguing

Lawyers organize their papers for argument in various ways. Their argument notes—whether an outline, catchwords or a text—can appear on large legal size paper, ordinary letter size or cards. Notes should be readable at a downward glance. If necessary, they should be typed in solid capital letters, or on a typewriter with extra large characters. If handwritten, they should be large and absolutely legible.

The notes and other material, such as case digests, answers to anticipated questions and quotations from the record, can be assembled in loose-leaf notebooks or on separate sheets of paper. Citation and record references can be placed alongside or in the notes or text, or after the headings or paragraphs. So should quotations. In addition to the notes or other material to be used in presenting the argument, counsel should bring with him to the podium copies of the briefs, statutes, record or appendix which he may possibly want to refer to in answering questions.

There is general agreement that marked tabs should be attached to the pages of the record or briefs—yours or your opponent's—which you may wish to refer to during the argument, since that will enable you to turn to the page much more quickly.[67] But one experienced advocate finds tabs unmanageable if the record is "immense":

> "A number of advocates favor the use of tabs in the record to allow them to locate immediately any key sections of interest to the Court. This is satisfactory if the record is relatively small but becomes virtually unmanageable if the record is immense, and it often is in the complex cases before the Supreme Court. I favor

---

[66]R. Jackson, *Advocacy Before the Supreme Court: Suggestions for Effective Case Presentations,* 37 A.B.A.J. 801, 862 (1951). Chief Justice Arthur T. Vanderbilt of New Jersey would have included "colored shirts," but that advice would probably now apply only to exceptionally bright or dark colors. He also favored "the wearing of vests by practitioners with an undistributed middle." See Carson, *supra* note 5, at 75–76.

[67]"When tabbing the record and other documents, be sure that you affix your tab in such a way that it opens the record to the place where you want it opened. For example, if you wanted to open a book to page 51, you would not affix your tab to page 51, but to the preceding page." Fitzgerald and Hartnett, *supra* note 3, at 55.

an index of key words and phrases which I prepare myself. The index appears entirely on one page, if possible. Next to each word or phrase is the place in the record or the case citation relevant to the subject in question."[68]

I would think that manageability would depend not on the size of the record but on the number of tabs needed.

Mr. Prettyman uses a notebook, with his argument notes on the right-hand page but citations (and I assume quotations) from the record and cases on the left-hand facing page.[69] Colonel Wiener, however, does not believe in using a notebook:

> "I never put my notes for argument in a binder, because I feel that this interferes with flexibility. If, for example, the court asks a question about a topic I had originally planned to cover later on, so that I must now turn to it earlier than I had planned, it is much easier to have unbound notes that enable me to discuss the topic inquired about by pulling out the appropriate pages, and then to resume where I left off when diverted. Ideally, the notes on each topic can be clipped together. At any rate, notes not clamped into a binder will be easier to handle. More than that, because they are not physically rigid, they will be more conducive to a flexible presentation that adjusts the arguments to the reception they evoke."[70]

I agree with the latter view, and would add that even for detailed notes or a textual draft the fewer pages the better. Large legal size pages (8 1/2 by 13 or 14 inches) leave fewer pages to shuffle and look through, and more material that can be seen at a glance without turning a page.

For the same reasons, placing each point on a separate card has disadvantages, even though the cards are easy to shuffle and are regarded by some as an easy way of accommodating the argument to questioning. But there may be too many cards, and cards easily slip to the bottom of the lectern where they may be more difficult to see or even find.

8.11 The Substance of the Oral Argument—In General

(1) In many important respects the strictures applicable to good brief writing govern oral argument, only more so. The

---

[68]E. B. Prettyman, Jr., *Supreme Court Advocacy: Random Thoughts in a Day of Time Restrictions*, LITIGATION, Vol. 4, No. 2, p. 17 (American Bar Association Section of Litigation, 1978).

[69]*Ibid.*

[70]F. Wiener, BRIEFING AND ARGUING FEDERAL APPEALS, p. 314 (1967).

brief writer must determine which points to emphasize and omit from a presentation now customarily limited to 50 pages. But only about one third of that can be spoken in 30 minutes, according to my rough calculations. The result is that not as many points can be covered orally, and that those which are must be treated in less depth. The difference is not slight, but tremendous, as anyone can attest who first cuts his argument to the bone to meet the page limits for briefs and then realizes that only a small portion of that can be presented orally.

Similarly, brief writers are uniformly advised to go easy on quotations and citations and detailed case analyses. Compare Secs. 7.25, 7.28, *supra.* Omitting all quotations has even been recommended, although that goes too far. But even critical passages which survive that paring process must be decimated—or so it seems—in preparing the oral argument. Not only is there not enough time for them, for the reasons stated above, but reading either words or numbers aloud will often not get across or through to the listener.

Candor and clarity are also even more vital in an oral presentation than a written one. Compare Sec. 7.24, *supra.* A lawyer who is caught in a half-truth or misleading remark, either by his opponent or a judge, is in serious trouble, and so is his client. Attempting to explain in answer to searching and possibly even nasty questions can be very unpleasant indeed. Failure to make full disclosure in an opening argument, thus keeping the court inaccurately informed for as much as 30 minutes more until your opponent points out your misstatement, leaves neither your case nor your reputation in good condition.

The need for honesty extends to conceding weaknesses in an argument if that is the only honest reply to a question. Alternatives which preserve your case should be presented at the same time, if possible. If an honest answer means that you cannot win, the case should have been disposed of at an earlier stage.

Avoiding sarcasm or other personal attacks on your adversary is even more essential during the oral argument than in writing a brief, as to which see Sec. 7.24, *supra.* Attacks of this sort make a bad impression on the judges, who expect the argument to be conducted as a polite intellectual discussion among gentlemen. Most lawyers have sense enough to be courteous toward the judges to whom they are arguing. They should also remember to be courteous toward the judge or judges below. A line must be drawn between polite criticism of the judge's reasoning and personal criticism of the judge.

If your opponent has sinned, as by misstating or omitting facts, or misciting or misquoting cases, say so without getting personal. The facts will speak for themselves, and the court will understand and subjectively and silently supply its own adjectives. Do not minimize your gain by transferring some of their ire to you. I still recall a not so subtle challenge to my integrity by an opposing lawyer, not because of what he said but because he was sharply rebuked by Chief Justice Stone.

As for clarity, a brief can be reread, restated and reanalyzed if its meaning is not clear on first reading. Oral argument, on the other hand, does not get across unless it can be caught on the fly. It must therefore be expressed so simply that listeners can readily follow it on first hearing.

(2) Another tenet of oral advocacy is that counsel must recognize which points are susceptible of effective oral explanation and which are not. "[T]here are many points that do not lend themselves at all well to oral presentation and are much better handled in the briefs."[71] Even if the latter are important to the case, the advocate should advise the court of the issue, make any argument which can be readily understood, and tell the court that the details are not adaptable to oral exposition and, accordingly, are left to the brief. Points which depend upon detailed analysis of statutes, technical facts or even cases are likely to fall in this category.

Since the details are often significant, the lawyer must make a judgment whether he can formulate an argument which will come across orally. Rehearsing the argument before others, as suggested in Sec. 8.8(d), *supra,* is probably the best way of determining that in advance.

(3) The arguer, like the brief writer, must attempt to accommodate himself to what appellate judges know and don't know, at least so far as he can surmise. Since the arguer has much less time than the brief writer, not wasting it telling judges what they already know is even more imperative. Legal principles with which judges probably are familiar should be tossed off in a sentence without reference to supporting citations. The court's own recent decisions, which are obviously of the greatest impor-

---

[71]Fitzgerald and Hartnett, *supra* note 3, at 56.

tance, nevertheless need not be described in detail, even though the analogy to, or distinction from, the case at bar may require explanation.

How much the judges know about a case will often depend upon whether they have read the briefs before the oral argument and, to some extent, how long before. As to this, former Chief Judge E. Barrett Prettyman of the United States Court of Appeals for the District of Columbia Circuit has observed:

> "Sometimes the judges read the briefs before the oral argument. Sometimes they do not. To the lawyer preparing and making an oral argument the difference is a material one. If the briefs have been read he can proceed immediately to the point or points in dispute and devote his allotted time to an argument at the nub of the controversy. If the briefs have not been read, he must spend a large part of his time informing the court of the nature of the case, the disputed points, the facts, and the prior proceedings. It is my firm conviction that every appellate court should have an announced custom in this phase of its proceeding. Counsel should be allowed and expected to assume that the announced custom has been followed. If perchance one judge is out of step, through misadventure in the particular case, that judge should let the customary course of argument be followed without interruption for his individual benefit."[72]

Counsel should ascertain the practice of the particular appellate court in this respect; it usually is not confidential, though sometimes all that can be said is that the judges have no common practice. Many courts, including most of the federal courts of appeals, let it be known that they always read the briefs in advance. United States Supreme Court Rule 38.1, as revised in 1980, declares that "[c]ounsel should assume that all Members of the Court have read the briefs in advance of argument." I have heard presiding judges notify counsel that the court has read the briefs and that he need not spend time stating the facts.

Judges nevertheless warn that counsel should not assume that every judge, even on courts which customarily read briefs, remembers the details of what they contain. He may have read the briefs in a number of cases in a short period of time, or several weeks ahead of the argument. He may have been ill or otherwise engaged the night before, when he expected to read the briefs, or the number of briefs taken home might have been

---

[72]E. B. Prettyman, *Some Observations Concerning Appellate Advocacy*, 39 Va. L. Rev. 285, 301 (1953).

too many to permit careful study. These possibilities present a problem to the lawyer who must address himself to the unknown least common denominator on the court in order to make sure that each judge understands his argument. That tactic may displease those members of the court who are better prepared. Nevertheless, unless guided by remarks from the bench, an argument addressed to a probably unidentifiable judge who may not be familiar with the case may be the only safe way to proceed.

One possible approach, particularly with regard to the factual background, is to prepare two versions—a long form which goes into some detail and a short form which does not.[73] Counsel is then prepared for an announcement that the court has read the briefs and does not want a detailed factual discussion.

Often a judge's prior reading of briefs will leave an initial faint recollection which is easily refreshed by counsel's opening summary of the facts and issues. This may stimulate provocative questioning by judges who, understandably, with many other cases before them, need such assistance.

The above examples illustrate the wisdom of the first maxim in John W. Davis' famous article on *The Argument of an Appeal:*

> "Change places with the court.
> "... If the places were reversed and you sat where they do, think what it is you would want first to know about the case. How and in what order would you want the story told? How would you want the skein unravelled? What would make easier your approach to the true solution? These are questions the advocate must unsparingly put to himself."[74]

That means that you should try to put yourself in the position of an experienced lawyer of intelligence who knows little or nothing about the case and is not predisposed to decide it for, or against, your client. (Indeed, it may even be more helpful if counsel tries to put himself in the position of a judge who will be hostile to his position.) This is easier to say than to do, since advocates' bias is likely to color your thinking even when you try to fight it. But you must be aware that your argument will be addressed to such a target and aim accordingly.

---

[73]Cf. Sec. 8.16(e), *infra,* and Prettyman, Jr., *supra* note 68, at 16.

[74]26 A.B.A.J. 895, 896 (1940). For an irreverent treatment of Davis' maxims, see M. Gould, *Mr. Davis' View Out of Date: Oral Argument Losing Its Appeal,* Nat. L.J. March 23, 1981, p. 15.

8.12   Selection of Points to Argue and Omit— Arrangement of the Argument

The predominant fact to keep in mind in selecting the points to argue orally is that, except in cases of very short compass, the argument cannot cover the whole case. In the usual 30 minutes, even without interruption by questioning, you can cover no more than the approximate equivalent of 15 typed pages. Thus, unless there are very few, you cannot deal with all the pertinent facts, all the questions of law or all the details of the points that you do attempt to discuss orally. The more points you try to cover, the less persuasive your reasoning may be as to each. As Mr. Justice Harlan has stated:

> "[I]t often happens that lawyers who attempt to cover *all* of the issues in the case find themselves left with the uncomfortable feeling that they have failed to deal with any of the issues adequately."[75]

The appellant is obligated to tell the court at the beginning what the case is about—to state the nature of the case, the issues, what happened below and the basic factual structure. See Secs. 8.13–8.14, *infra.* This will reduce the time available for discussing the issues. If there are a number of issues which should be argued, the problem is similar to that of the brief writer, but the answer is not necessarily the same. In the first place, counsel cannot cover orally as many points as he can in a brief. Second, points which do not lend themselves to oral exposition, or perhaps, more precisely, to aural understanding, should be left to the brief. See Sec. 8.11(2), *supra.*

Advice commonly given is that appellant should start with his strongest point, and also that he should quickly get to the heart of the case, the "jugular vein." If they are the same, that presents no difficulty. But often they are not. Your strongest point or points may be very easy for you to win, but they may not be sufficient to win the case.

The issue or issues on which you must concentrate in the short time available are those which, in the words of Judge Godbold of the Fifth Circuit, "are likely to be dispositive. [Counsel] must reject other issues or give them short treatment. For oral argument counsel may have to be even more selective

---

[75]J. Harlan, *What Part Does the Oral Argument Play in the Conduct of an Appeal?*, 41 Cornell L.Q. 6, 8 (1955).

than in writing his brief. There is simply no way to present eight or ten issues in twenty or thirty minutes."[76] I would reduce the "eight or ten" to "four or more."

Obviously the points which will be dispositive must be dealt with as effectively as you can, whether they are your strongest points or not. They are the "jugular vein," the "nub" or "heart" of the case, the "cardinal point around which lesser points revolve like planets around the sun," to use figures of speech employed by John W. Davis.[77]

The criterion should be: What points must you win to win your case. If there is more than one point of equal stature in that respect, get to your strongest first, unless logic calls for a different arrangement. Arguments may be dependent on each other, so that taking them out of logical order would be confusing or an obvious indication of lack of confidence in some of them.

Furthermore, you shouldn't waste valuable time even on a dispositive point which you are reasonably sure to win if tougher ones must also be met. In baseball lingo, you must meet your opponent's best pitch if you can't win the game otherwise.

There may, of course, be several such points. You cannot deal with very many, as Judge Godbold pointed out, in less than 30 minutes. Other points *must* be left to the brief. Unless your time is enlarged, there is no choice as to that, particularly if some of your time is consumed answering questions, as it almost invariably will be.

Frequently, when cases contain a number of issues, one side will prevail if one issue is decided in its favor, while the other side must win all. For example, a defendant raising a number of alternative defenses can concentrate on his strongest, while the plaintiff, who must defeat each of them, may reasonably believe that he must deal with all. With the time limits as they are, he will have to choose—and the only rational choice is to devote most or all of his time to the most dangerous points, that is, those which he is most likely to lose, not his strongest.

By now you should have the impression that the process of selecting points to argue is often not simple at all, and that none of the pat phrases or formulas, each of which is entirely reasonable as a general matter, can uniformly be relied on as decisive. That is correct. The advocate must have all of these considera-

---

[76]J. Godbold, *Twenty Pages and Twenty Minutes—Effective Advocacy on Appeal,* 30 Southwestern L.J. 801, 809 (1976).

[77]J. W. Davis, *The Argument of an Appeal,* 26 A.B.A.J. 895, 897 (1940).

tions in mind and exercise his own best judgment in applying them to the circumstances of his case. The process of rehearsal discussed in Sec. 8.8(d), *supra,* can help determine which points can be, and which cannot be, most persuasively presented orally.

Furthermore, the subject is one upon which the arguer might well confer with his colleagues, including some not immersed in the case. For their reaction to the strength and weaknesses of particular arguments may be more objective than his, since they are better able to put themselves in the position of the judge. I have often found that my first reaction to a case comes much closer to the ultimate judicial decision than my views after I have achieved an advocate's frame of mind.

The above treatment of the problem of choosing what points to argue and omit focuses on the dilemma facing appellant's counsel in a case involving more points than can be argued in the time allowed. The appellee has it a lot easier. He need not spend as much time stating the issues or the facts, but need only correct or improve upon what appellant has said. He can also usually concentrate on the legal points covered in the appellant's oral argument, as well as upon the reactions of the judges. If he can win on any of a number of alternative grounds, he should, of course, emphasize his strongest, irrespective of the points which appellant has stressed, for this would be adhering, from his point of view, to the principle that counsel should argue the issues which "are likely to be dispositive."

In other respects, the appellee's judgment as to what to argue should be based on the same considerations as the appellant's. As to appellee's arguments generally, see Sec. 8.19, *infra.*

8.13 Opening the Argument—The Nature of the Case and the Issues

Appellate courts want to know at the beginning of the appellant's argument what the case is about. Only a few sentences are usually needed to show the nature of the case, to state the issues very generally, to tell how the lower courts disposed of them and, if there is any question about it or if it is at all unusual, to tell how the case reached the appellate court.

The precise order of these items is of little consequence, but the opening should arouse the interest of the court. To begin by stating that

> "this case came here on appeal from the Circuit Court of Sangamon County, which set aside a jury verdict for the plaintiff"

or that

> "the case comes here on certiorari to the Court of Appeals for the Tenth Circuit"

will hardly stop the judges from shuffling their papers, though it will answer Mr. Justice Holmes' perhaps apocryphal question, "How did you get here," to which counsel supposedly answered, "On the Baltimore & Ohio."

An opening which might hold the court's attention would begin with a short description of the nature of the case, followed by a summary of the issues, stated generally. How the court below decided these questions is of more interest and concern to the appellate court than a bare statement of the procedural facts. For example:

> "Plaintiff is suing to repossess bowling equipment sold to the defendant under a conditional sales contract under which almost $400,000 remains unpaid. The court below dismissed the complaint on the basis of the statute of frauds, and the question presented is whether all of the essential elements of the contract were set out in writing."

In some cases a slightly longer factual introduction may not only bring the case in sharper focus but suggest the justice of your position. Thus:

> "Plaintiff and defendant are the two leading producers of competitive outboard racing motors. Plaintiff's engineering department headed by Mr. X over a two-year period was able to develop a better motor which won a long series of races. Defendant then hired X, and within three months produced an equally good motor. Two years before that, Mr. Y, another former employee of plaintiff, had disclosed to defendant the external but not internal features of plaintiff's engine.
>
> "Plaintiff is here suing to enjoin defendant from making use of any trade secrets disclosed by X. The trial court held that the earlier disclosures by Y barred plaintiff from recovery, and the question is whether that ruling was correct under the law of Illinois."

When the case turns upon technical details, the nature of the issues should be indicated only broadly, leaving the details to the subsequent statement of facts. Even though not very precise, the following would be sufficient in a proceeding to review a highly technical administrative order:

> "This is a proceeding under the federal Water Pollution Control Act to review a regulation of the EPA prescribing limits on the quantities of specified pollutants which meat slaughterhouses and packing plants can discharge into waterways. Such regulations are directly reviewable in the courts of appeals.
>
> "The overall question is whether the standards prescribed by EPA are arbitrary and capricious because they are not rationally supported by the record material upon which they purport to be based. I will discuss two of these points orally and leave the remainder to our brief."

Some cases may appropriately begin with the question presented, such as:

> "The questions in this suit for breach of a sales contract are whether the contract contained a condition precedent requiring prior purchases of goods to have first been accepted, and whether the contract was defective for lack of mutuality. The trial court granted defendant's motion for summary judgment on both counts. Plaintiff's position is that these rulings were erroneous both in fact and in law."

The opening should seldom take more than about 30 seconds, but it will provide a background which enables the judges to understand what follows.

Short openings of this sort are desirable even for a court which reads the briefs prior to the oral argument. Whether more detail is necessary may depend upon whether the court, through the briefs or otherwise, has previously become familiar with the case.

As the above illustrations suggest, the opening should contain a statement of the issues in the case and perhaps the order in which counsel will argue them. If some of the issues are not to be covered orally, counsel should advise the court which he will argue and which he will not. The latter is important for the purpose of informing the court that you are still relying on those points, as argued in your brief. In addition, judges who wish to ask questions about such points will be put on notice that they may have to break in on the argument of another subject, or wait until the end of the argument.

Reference to the manner in which the case comes before the appellate court or how that court acquired jurisdiction is not necessary if the case comes up by the usual route, such as a direct appeal from a trial court to the initial appellate court or a petition for certiorari, or its equivalent, to a supreme court. Otherwise the jurisdictional basis should be stated, in brief form, such as for an interlocutory order:

> "The trial court certified the question to this court under 28 U.S.C. §1292(b), and this court has granted leave to appeal."

Or:

> "This is an appeal from an order denying a temporary injunction."

For a direct appeal to a supreme court, the following would be sufficient:

> "Since the trial court held that the statute [describing it] violated the constitution of [the state or the United States], direct appeal has been taken to this court pursuant to Section ____ of the Code."

If there is a problem as to the court's jurisdiction important enough to discuss, it should be mentioned at this point, or as one of the issues in the case, and argued either immediately before or after the statement of facts, depending on whether the jurisdictional issue can better be understood in the factual context of the case.

As in writing the brief (as to which see Sec. 7.9, *supra*), throughout the argument counsel should be sure to identify the parties clearly. Such terms as "plaintiff in error" or "defendant in error" are confusing. "Appellant" and "appellee" sound alike and are easily transposed. A petitioner in one court may be a respondent in another in the same case. Actual names or descriptive words, such as the "buyer," the "government," the "employer," or even "plaintiff" and "defendant," are easier to follow.[78]

---

[78]Fitzgerald and Hartnett, *supra* note 3, at 66.

In some cases counsel will have to call the court's attention to the statutory or regulatory provisions upon which the case turns. The reference to these provisions may come at the end of the opening of the argument, or in connection with the discussion of the substantive point to which the language in question relates. More often than not, the latter approach is likely to make the statutory point clearer and avoid repetition.

The appellee, of course, is not called upon to make an opening similar to appellant's or, indeed, any at all. The differences between appellant's and appellee's arguments are considered in Sec. 8.19, *infra.*

8.14 The Statement of Facts

In order to decide an appeal, the appellate court must know the significant facts, either because they provide the foundation upon which the legal questions are based, or because factual issues themselves are presented. For either purpose, the facts should usually be stated before the argument on the legal issues. Even if the court has already read the briefs, "a refreshing of the court's mind on the most important facts is called for" even if it takes "a good part of the time allotted for argument."[79] Whether all of the facts need be stated at that time depends, however, upon the nature of the case and the relation of the facts to the issues presented.

In cases in which the facts are not in issue but provide the background or framework for the questions which are, the facts should be stated first, after the preliminary matters referred to in the preceding section. The same is true where there is only a single issue of a factual nature, such as whether there was sufficient evidence to support a finding, and where counsel can proceed immediately from the statement of the facts into the discussion of that issue.

But where there are several issues to be argued involving facts which are in controversy, treating the factual and legal components of each point together during the argument may both save time and be more persuasive than stating the facts pertinent to all questions at the beginning and then arguing each point of law separately. In this respect oral arguments

---

[79]Goodrich, *supra* note 4, at 27.

differ from briefs. Courts want statements of facts in briefs to be unargumentative, with the argument of factual issues reserved for the argument section. But there is usually not time for such dual treatment of factual issues orally. And it could be confusing for counsel to state the facts as to issues I and II initially, and then to have to return to each separately when arguing those points subsequently. Accordingly, in appropriate cases, counsel must decide whether the background facts, which should still come at the beginning of the argument, should be followed immediately by the facts pertaining to questions in issue, or whether the latter should be combined with the related legal argument. If counsel intends to postpone discussion of the facts relating to the issues to the argument of the issues, the court should be so advised.

If the court tells counsel it is familiar with the facts and that he need not restate them, he should omit the opening description of the factual background, but not the argumentative treatment of the facts in connection with a substantive issue.

Even if the facts are not in controversy, counsel should not regard them as secondary or subsidiary to other parts of the argument. In a great many cases the facts are what the judges know the least about; "it is the education of Justices on the facts of the case that is the essential function of the appellate lawyer."[80] Accordingly, the advocate should not only draw from the facts the material pertinent to the issues on appeal but also try to arrange them as persuasively as he can.

If possible, the facts should be so stated that they march in your direction. Lord Mansfield was said to be "able to give the statement of facts in a case in such a manner that in the end it seemed quite unnecessary to argue the law."[81] I did not hear Lord Mansfield, but I can attest to Mr. Justice Black's oral summaries of his opinions in the Supreme Court, which had the same quality. His statements of facts made it obvious that the result he was supporting was the only conceivably rational one, even though sometimes as many as eight of his colleagues disagreed.

In reciting the facts counsel's first obligation is to be clear

---

[80]Mr. Justice Douglas, THE COURT YEARS, p. 180 (1980); Mr. Justice Jackson, *Advocacy Before the Supreme Court: Suggestions for Effective Case Presentations*, 37 A.B.A.J. 801, 803 (1951).

[81]Carson, *supra* note 5, at 77, which relies upon Chief Judge Vanderbilt's recollection.

and understandable. This seems obvious, but frequently counsel cannot, or does not, put himself in the position of a judge unfamiliar with the case. Counsel often cannot appreciate that a version of the facts which is clear to him after living with the case for months or years will not get across to a newcomer. Since persons frequently are unable to diagnose their own ailments, a rehearsal before outsiders to the case is the recommended remedy. If the subject is one which cannot be clearly explained orally in the time available, counsel should advise the court that his brief covers the matter more fully—and hope that it can be understood.

As in a written brief, facts are usually more clearly understood if the story is told in chronological order. In some cases, however, a topical presentation bringing together all the facts and even the arguments on a particular subject may take less time and also be more persuasive.

Except for judicially noticeable matters (as to which see Sec. 7.30, *supra*), the facts to be recited must appear in the record. Counsel should have the record reference to any fact of significance in his notes in case the court inquires.

Telling facts accurately does not mean just facts favorable to your side. Unfavorable facts are not to be omitted. The argument provides counsel's last opportunity to face up to them and explain why they are not harmful to his case. Judges are unanimous that there is "no way of meeting a weak point except to face up to it. . . . Attempted evasion in an oral argument is a cardinal sin."[82] Accurate statement does not permit describing inferences "as though they were facts,"[83] or references to facts outside the record (unless the court is so informed), misstatements, overstatements or exaggerations, or misleading omissions. Reference to evidence without indicating that there is conflicting testimony, or that the trier of facts drew contrary inferences from other testimony, or did not regard the witnesses as credible would be misleading.

"[T]he attorney who is inaccurate or less than candid interferes with the objective of persuasion. He comes to the court saying 'please believe me and be persuaded.' If it is revealed that what he says or writes cannot be believed, he forfeits the confi-

---

[82]Mr. Justice Harlan, *What Part Does the Oral Argument Play in the Conduct of an Appeal?*, 41 Cornell L.Q. 6, 9 (1955).

[83]J. Godbold, *Twenty Pages and Twenty Minutes—Effective Advocacy on Appeal*, 30 Southwestern L.J. 801, 816–817 (1976).

dence which he seeks to create. The court's distrust of him may taint his next appeal as well."[84]

"Accordingly, every appellate advocate must state facts and law candidly and accurately. This is an uncompromising absolute. 'The mark of really able advocacy is the ability to set forth the facts most favorably within the limits of utter and unswerving accuracy.' "[85] The skillful advocate is the lawyer who refers to opposing facts with complete candor and honesty and at the same time leaves the court with a favorable impression of his case.

Of course, counsel must make do with what he has in the record. Often the sting of facts relied upon by his adversary can be lessened if they are placed in full context, or in the context of other evidence. But there are occasions when this cannot be done, where counsel must accept the fact that on certain matters the record is against him. If counsel cannot on the record expect to overturn the determination of a jury or judge that his client had acted fraudulently, but has other good arguments, he should not waste time denying the fraud or asserting the moral virtues of his client. Many such cases have been won on such grounds as no evidence of damages or the statute of limitations.

Straining to mention irrelevant facts which it is hoped will arouse the court's sympathy will be more likely to produce an adverse reaction, with questions such as "How is that relevant to anything here?" or "Why do you mention that?" Inability to provide any answer except that you hope that the irrelevant fact might nevertheless make the court sympathize with your client is likely to discredit both you and your argument.

That means that the relevant facts must speak for themselves. Able opposing counsel may present them so that they speak in different ways. For example, in a replevin case brought by a conditional seller of goods not fully paid for, where plaintiff had posted a bond based on a valuation of the goods much lower than the contract price, counsel for the defendant should stress the fact of undervaluation and assert that the seller should recover not the goods but the low value he had placed upon them in order to reduce the cost of the bond; the seller, on the other hand, should emphasize the language of the contract and the buyer's obligation to pay the full contract price for the goods if he was to keep them.

---

[84]*Ibid.*
[85]*Id.* at 816, quoting F. Wiener, BRIEFING AND ARGUING FEDERAL APPEALS, p. 49 (1967).

A danger, particularly for the lawyer who tried the case, is that he will let the facts get out of control and run away with the argument, or at least with much of his arguing time.[86] He may be so full of the factual details that he does not want to omit any which prove that justice is on his side or that his client is in the right. I have seen a good trial lawyer, after devoting 27 of his 30 minutes to proving that the defendant had defrauded his client, shocked to discover that he had not gotten to the only issue which the defendant-appellant was urging, that no damages had been proved. Such a predicament can be avoided only by very careful advance preparation, in which the arguer includes only the significant facts he has time for and actually measures the time the factual statement will take to insure that enough will be left for the remainder of the argument.

In their excellent paper on *Effective Oral Argument,* published in *The Practical Lawyer,* Henry St. John Fitzgerald and Daniel Hartnett, of the Virginia Bar, recommend that you

> "[s]et down exactly what facts ought to be included in your factual statement and then draft phrases and even whole sentences that will express them for the best effect—bearing in mind always that they are to be expressed orally, not in writing.
> "Then this very detailed 'outline' of the facts, including the particular 'high impact' phrases and sentences, should be rehearsed for the purpose of timing the delivery, hearing how it sounds out loud, and further polishing and compressing it. When you have improved on it in this manner and delivered it a number of times aloud, it will as closely approach a 'set' piece as can be done, and still preserve the essential spark of good oral presentation."[87]

Although they do not favor writing out a "set" statement, they admit that "in practice it will very closely approach this":

> "It is essential to prepare in advance virtually a 'canned' factual statement, so that it will include precisely the facts you want to include, state them in just the way they should be stated, and in exactly the time you allotted for them."[88]

I add only that there is no reason to shy away from writing it out in the first instance, for the reasons and in the manner described in Sec. 8.8(c), pp. 390–395, *supra,* so long as you do not read it in the courtroom or memorize it.

---

[86]Fitzgerald and Hartnett, *supra* note 3, at 57.
[87]Fitzgerald and Hartnett, *supra* note 3, at 58.
[88]*Id.* at 57–58.

8.15   Charts, Maps, Diagrams, Pictures, Physical Evidence

Some types of facts may be more easily understood if the oral presentation is supported by visible—which usually means enlarged—charts, graphs, maps, models or pictures, even motion pictures. Common examples are pictures or maps of the scene of an accident, maps of real estate boundaries, graphs or tables based on accountant's figures, and diagrams or pictures in patent and trade secret or product liability cases.

Motion pictures may be useful in various types of cases, including personal injury, product liability, patent and obscenity. In some cases, machines themselves, particularly if they have been exhibits, may be brought before the appellate court. Charts may even be useful for outlining family trees and the key words of complicated documents, such as statutes, wills, contracts or charges to a jury.[89]

Whatever the form of what you are asking the court to look at, it must either be in the trial court record, be based directly upon something in that record, be an appropriate subject of judicial notice, or be a combination of these elements.[90] If the document is compiled from material found in different parts of a record, all the page or exhibit numbers must be shown, as well as where the document appears in the brief, if it does. If not in the brief, this information should appear on or be attached to the enlargement itself.

Mr. Justice Schaefer has emphasized that

> "if you are going to use charts, make them big enough. Among the other deficiencies of judges, they tend to be nearsighted. Most of us do not confess to a weakness like that publicly, but, if you watch us lean forward squinting in an effort to follow where counsel says we should look in the brief, you will know it is true."[91]

You should also use a pointer and stand to the side of the chart so that the judges can see what you are pointing to. And if you want the judges to follow your explanation on the chart as you proceed, you should not give them smaller copies, or refer them to copies in the record or brief.[92]

---

[89]W. Schaefer, *The Appellate Court*, 3 U. of Chi. L.S. Rec. 1, 12–13 (No. 2, 1954); W. Schaefer, *Appellate Advocacy*, 23 Tenn. L. Rev. 471, 473–474 (1954); Marshall, *supra* note 3, at 9–26.

[90]O. Rall, *The Use of Visual Aids in Courts of Review*, 52 Northwestern L. Rev. 90, 97 (1957).

[91]W. Schaefer, *The Appellate Court*, 3 U. of Chi. L.S. Rec. 1, 13 (No. 2, 1954).

[92]Fitzgerald and Hartnett, *supra* note 3, at 67.

The burden of bringing such material or physical evidence to the appellate courtroom and of providing related equipment, such as a motion picture projector, falls on counsel, not the officers of the trial or appellate courts, and this is true even if the physical items were exhibits at the trial. The officers of the appellate court will advise counsel as to where such material should be taken, and how and where it should be shown to the judges if that cannot be conveniently done in the courtroom itself. If out-of-town counsel cannot personally bring such material to the courthouse sufficiently in advance of the argument to consult with the court officials, or handle the matter with them adequately over the telephone, he should have local counsel act in his behalf. Counsel should also arrange to have the exhibits removed from the courtroom after the argument unless the court otherwise directs.[93]

8.16 Argument of the Issues

The Argument portion of an oral argument includes argument of factual as well as legal questions, just as was true for the briefs. As indicated above, a great many of the principles applicable to writing the Argument portion of a brief apply to oral arguments as well. Since they are even more essential to an oral presentation, they are worth repeating, at least in part.

(a) The Importance of Reasons and Principles

The oral advocate, like the brief writer, must emphasize the reasons supporting his position, and not merely cite cases. Compare Sec. 7.25, *supra*. Supreme courts usually try to fit decisions into established lines of authority, but they are not bound to do so. Often the issue is which of two different lines governs the case. Prior decisions do not tell the court which line is the closest, or, more to the point, which is the most reasonable for the court to follow. The court must be persuaded to select one line of authorities rather than another by arguments going beyond what the prior cases have held or said. Mr. Justice Douglas has written:

---

[93]E.g., Federal Rule of Appellate Procedure 34(g).

"The pre-eminent appellate advocate makes a distillation of the facts to show why the case fits neatly between two opposed precedents [if it does], and why this particular case should follow one rather than the other."[94]

To repeat the words of Mr. Justice Rutledge, which apply as strongly to oral arguments as to briefs:

"What judges want to know is why this case, or line of cases, should apply to these facts rather than that other line on which the opponent relies with equal certitude, if not certainty. Too often the 'why' is left out. . . . the discussion of the underlying principles as related to the present application counts heavily to swing the scales."[95]

Mr. Justice Rutledge admitted that "[s]ome cases are so clearly ruled by authority, directly in point and controlling, that discussion of principle is superfluous," "but," he added, "these are not many."

This is, of course, particularly true for courts of last resort. But at the time Justice Rutledge was writing, he was a member of a court of appeals, not of the Supreme Court. Intermediate appellate court decisions are subject to further review, but in the vast majority of cases their rulings are final, both because in most review in the higher court is not requested and because the vast majority of requests is denied.[96] The judges are of course fully aware of this fact, and, accordingly, unless the decision of a higher court is clearly controlling, they will be concerned to decide justly in accordance with principle when that path is open, and, as Mr. Justice Rutledge recognized, it usually is. All appellate courts are adept at distinguishing cases which might impel them to reach an unjust or unreasonable conclusion.

That does not mean that courts feel free to impose their own views of policy and morality. They endeavor to fit a case into the body of existing precedent, taking into account the considerations of policy behind the rules. Counsel may properly and effectively rely on the reasoning and principles expressed in earlier decisions, which are likely to be highly persuasive. He should not argue policy blatantly or *in vacuo,* but policy consid-

---

[94]Mr. Justice Douglas, THE COURT YEARS, p. 180 (1980).
[95]W. Rutledge, *The Appellate Brief,* 28 A.B.A.J. 251, 253 (1942).
[96]In the federal system, less than 1 percent of the decisions of the United States courts of appeals are reviewed on the merits by the Supreme Court. Applications for review are filed in only about 10 percent of the cases, and only about 6 percent of these are granted. In the states, the percentages are somewhat higher. See Sec. 5.7(c), *supra.*

erations often underlie judges' choices between different rules and accordingly should be woven into the argument.[97]

In areas governed by legislation, courts search for the intent of the legislature. Counsel should therefore refer to the material manifesting legislative intent and the purposes underlying statutory and constitutional provisions.

(b) The Use of Cases

The need for emphasizing principles and reasons does not mean that cases can or should be disregarded, although many lawyers have stated that in most oral arguments they refer to a few at most. Oral argument is not the occasion for citing many cases or for reciting their factual details. Some cases, particularly in intermediate courts, are governed by controlling authority. Controlling cases should, of course, be driven home by showing how close their facts are to those at bar. The critical issue may be whether such cases are in point or distinguishable.

Arguments based on factual analogy may also justify reference to the facts of other cases. But, in general, oral argument does not lend itself to detailed analysis of that sort, which often is hard to follow. Justice Wilkins of the Supreme Judicial Court of Massachusetts has said in this connection: "Do not relate the facts of cited cases in painful detail. They are too many to be absorbed from oral presentation. It wastes time that can be utilized to better advantage. In the average case it is sufficient to announce that you rely on such and such cases. The court, before deciding the case, will read them just as carefully as have counsel if they are even remotely material to the reasoning of the opinion."[98]

A general statement of what cases hold, mentioning perhaps one or two preferably of recent date, will usually be more

---

[97]As stated by Mr. Justice Schaefer in a lecture sponsored by the Illinois Appellate Lawyers Association. Unless the law is clear, the reviewing court is properly "concerned with policy in the broadest sense"; though not acting like a legislature, it should search for "the underlying principle" and whether it can be applied generally, for "what makes the most sense, most of the time, for most people in the long run." F. Coffin, THE WAYS OF A JUDGE, pp. 106, 132 (1980).

[98]R. Wilkins, *The Argument of an Appeal,* 33 Cornell L.Q. 40, 47 (1947). Judge Goodrich wrote in the same vein: "But for a counsel in oral argument to talk about ten or fifteen different cases is a waste of time. The court cannot possibly remember the distinctions made and the argument gets duller and duller. If the advocate will tell the court why the result he argues for is right and then just point to the authorities in his brief, the argument will be much more interesting and the impression he makes much more lasting." Goodrich, *supra* note 4, at 28.

422 *Appellate Practice in the United States*

appropriate, with details left to the brief. If a proposition for which the cases stand will be familiar to the court, don't cite any cases at all except perhaps a very recent one in the same court. And you need not elaborate on that. Mr. Justice Jackson, after recognizing that if the controlling authority "is a decision, of course you must make clear its meaning and application," has noted "how frequently counsel undertake to expound a recent decision to the very men who made it. If the exposition is accurate, it adds nothing to the court's knowledge, and if it is not," —'nuf said.[99] Just refer to the doctrine or principle as an established one, and proceed to show why it applies or doesn't apply to your case.

If you rely on a substantial number of cases, say so, but do not cite any but the closest in point or the most recent or most authoritative. Merely refer to the "line of decisions of the state supreme court cited on p. 17 of my brief, of which *Oswald* v. *Jones,* decided in 1977, is the most recent." Or say that "decisions in four federal circuits cited on p. 42 of my brief support this position." Name the closest or leading case, or the most recent in the same court. But do not recite a string of names of cases or, even worse, the citations. They should be in your brief, but would be impossible to follow orally.

When you do refer to a specific case, do not give the full formal citation. Use the first name or the entire name if it is short. Unless it is a recent decision of the same court, or a well-known one from a higher court, the court will appreciate your indicating the date or approximate date of the decision by specific reference to the year or the volume number of the report. For example, the *"Kremens* case decided by the Supreme Court in 1977," or "in 431 U.S." is sufficient. *"Kremens* v. *Bartley,* 431 U.S. 119 (1977)" is unnecessarily long. And a string of such citations would merely lose the court's attention. However, the full citation should be readily available because sometimes judges will ask for it, especially if the case is one with which the judge is not familiar. In a number of jurisdictions counsel who intends to refer orally to cases not cited in his brief should give written advance notice to the court and opposing counsel.[100]

For the reason indicated in the preceding subsection, it is appropriate and desirable to refer to the reasoning of cases

---

[99]R. Jackson, *Advocacy Before the Supreme Court,* 37 A.B.A.J. 801, 804 (1951).
[100]E.g., Ohio Court of Appeals Rule 21(H); Ohio Supreme Court Rule 5-4.

which support your position. Say, "The reasoning of this court in the *Swift* case applies equally to the case at bar"—and then explain why. A short quotation directly on the point may also be helpful. That is all you will have time for.

(c) Other Types of Authorities

The extent to which authorities other than cases should be referred to during the oral argument depends upon their nature. The discussion of the same subject in relation to briefs in Sec. 7.26, *supra,* also applies to oral arguments, subject to the factors which distinguish the two methods of arguing described in the preceding pages of this chapter.

The language of a constitution or statute or regulation may be significant enough to require discussion, analysis and, often, quotation, even though all that may be difficult to present orally. If that is the heart of the case, the argument must deal with it, often in depth.

The same may be true of legislative material throwing light on the legislative intent. That often should be summarized orally, with references to more detailed treatment in the brief and an occasional short quotation.

Whether other types of secondary authorities should be mentioned depends on the extent to which primary authorities such as cases and statutes leave the issue open, and the stature of the author or work to be cited. The *Restatements of the Law,* published by the American Law Institute, are more authoritative than other non-case material because they represent the combined efforts and views of many lawyers, usually including the foremost authorities on a particular subject. When the point is not foreclosed by direct authority, treatises by recognized authors also may be relied on for their discussion of the principles which should govern. Other secondary authorities, even if cited in the briefs, will seldom be worth mentioning orally. Courts don't pay enough attention to them to warrant the use of valuable time.

(d) Reading and Quoting

The undesirability of reading an argument, whether from a written draft or, even worse, a brief, is generally recognized. Court rules frequently discourage or even prohibit it. See Sec.

8.8(c), *supra.* Reading long quotations from cases has a similar effect. "Regardless of what is read, the very act of reading draws an iron curtain between counsel and the sympathetic attention of the Court."[101]

Nevertheless, no court has gone so far as to say that all reading of quoted language is disfavored. A case may turn upon a court's analysis or understanding of the words of a statute, contract or other document, upon precisely what a witness has testified, or upon the language of a prior decision. To paraphrase would leave the court in doubt as to the exact language and not be nearly as effective as to quote. In such circumstances, quotation is not only justified but essential.

But if you must read a quotation, keep it short so as not to lose the attention of the court, and don't quote too often. Use the short quotation which is most apt or most recent, or from the most authoritative court. In particular, don't quote long passages from judicial opinions, or from a series of opinions, even if interspersed with descriptions of the cases. The judges will quickly lose interest and not follow, or even try to. If no short passage is to the point, briefly paraphrase or summarize the judicial reasoning and refer to your brief or the opinion itself for the complete text. Then say, for example, "that the numerous other authorities to the same effect are cited and discussed on pp. 33–35 of our brief."

If only parts of a long passage are significant, quote only that much, but tell the court you are quoting only the pertinent language, and where the entire passage appears in your brief or elsewhere. Giving a wrong impression by selective inclusion or exclusion is, of course, both improper and dangerous, as it was for the brief writer. But in an oral presentation, I would lean further toward the omission of material on the borderline of irrelevance or prejudice than in the brief, where I would lean in the opposite direction when there was any doubt. The judges will understand the reasons for keeping oral quotations short, and that you have no intent to mislead when the entire passage is quoted in your brief.

Wasting time finding the passage to be quoted both disturbs the court and interrupts the flow of your argument. If you wish to quote from a brief, record or any other volume, tab the

---

[101]Massachusetts Justice R. Wilkins, *The Argument of an Appeal,* 33 Cornell L.Q. 40, 47 (1947). See also Chief Justice Schaefer, *The Appellate Court,* 3 U. of Chi. L.S. Rec. I, 11–12 (No. 2, 1954); and *Appellate Advocacy,* 23 Tenn. L. Rev. 471, 473 (1954).

page so that you can find it quickly without fumbling. Tabs should also be used for passages to which you anticipate you may need to refer in answering questions from the bench or rebutting what your adversaries will say.

A better technique for what you expect to quote in the course of your argument is to include the language to be quoted in your notes or outline no matter how skimpy it may otherwise be. It takes time to find even marked or tabbed pages in a brief or record. You can proceed more evenly, and waste less time, if you can read such passages without having to look for them. Even the few temerarious enough to argue without notes should have the text of whatever they will quote before them.

Whether it is as helpful as one would normally expect to slow down so that the judges can follow in the brief the passage you are quoting is not clear. Judges who begin reading along with you may continue when you would like them to stop and begin listening to you again. How often this happens is anyone's guess. Its likelihood must be weighed against the equally plausible possibility that a judge will better understand and remember what he both sees and hears simultaneously than what he merely hears.

My own suggestion is that short passages of no more than several lines—and most quoting should be of no more than that —should be read without reference to pages to be followed, but that the judges should be asked to follow, in the brief or elsewhere, longer quotations such as sometimes are unavoidable when dealing with complex statutes or regulations. The judges will better be able to follow if they can use their eyes as well as their ears. Some lawyers think it advantageous to present such material to the court in blown-up form on an enlarged chart so that the judges can follow it with their eyes as the lawyer proceeds with a verbal analysis. Others have presented different versions of statutory language in appendices to briefs.[102] I have not tried those techniques, but able lawyers recommend them.

Whichever technique you use, always have at hand in your notes or on the margin or a facing page the reference to the pages of the document in which the judges can find the passage if they want to see it.

Quoting from *majority* opinions written or joined in by one of the judges before whom you are appearing is appropriate, but

---

[102]Carson, *supra* note 5, at 96.

not with overly complimentary adjectives which would be in bad taste. The same would also be true of quoting from a judge's non-judicial writings.[103] And if you quote a judge, be "doubly sure" to quote accurately and in context.[104] Concurring and dissenting opinions may be relied upon if you have nothing better.

(e) Answering Questions

Appellate advocates know, of course, that oral arguments are subject to interruption by questions from the bench. The natural tendency is to deplore such intrusions upon the prepared argument, which contains what counsel thought would present his case most effectively. But "from the standpoint of the bench, the desirability of questions is quite obvious, as the judges are not there to listen to speeches but to decide the case."[105] Chief Justice Hughes, writing in 1928 when he was a practicing lawyer between his two terms on the Supreme Court, added:

> "Well-prepared and experienced counsel, however, do not object to inquiries from the bench, if the time allowed for argument is not unduly curtailed,[106] as they would much prefer to have the opportunity of knowing the difficulties in the minds of the court and of attempting to meet them rather than to have them concealed and presented in conference when counsel are not present."

Chief Justice Schaefer of Illinois made the same point. In the absence of questions, he said:

> "You have no notion as to whether you are meeting the problem that is in the court's mind," "whether you are shooting wide of the mark or hitting where you ought."[107]

In short, "[r]ejoice when the Court asks questions. . . . A question affords you your only chance to penetrate the mind of

---

103Id. at 88.
104*Ibid.;* R. Jackson, *Advocacy Before the Supreme Court,* 37 A.B.A.J. 801, 804 (1951).
105C. E. Hughes, THE SUPREME COURT OF THE UNITED STATES, p. 62 (1928).
106The qualification "if the time allowed for argument is not unduly curtailed" suggests that in 1928 it usually was not. The reductions in argument time since then have been so drastic that many lawyers now regard at least prolonged questioning as a substantial curtailment, unless the court is lenient in allowing additional time because of it, as occasionally happens. The great expansion of the work load of appellate judges requires counsel to accommodate their arguments to the practical needs of the judiciary.
107W. Schaefer, *The Appellate Court,* 3 U. of Chi. L.S. Rec. 1, 12 (No. 2, 1954); *Appellate Advocacy,* 23 Tenn. L. Rev. 471, 475 (1954).

the court. . . . and to dispel a doubt as soon as it arises."[108] For these reasons, counsel should regard answering questions as the most important part of the argument, not as an incidental interruption which must be tolerated. Time spent in responding to questions should therefore nongrudgingly be accorded first priority over whatever parts of the prepared argument may have to be omitted as a result.

To my surprise, many judicial commentators find it necessary to reiterate that counsel should always answer a question when it is asked, and not reply that he will reach the point later in his argument. I would have thought that few advocates would have been so foolhardy as not to answer a judge's question directly and immediately. If the reply will be more meaningful later on, perhaps after facts or legal prerequisites upon which it is based have been brought to the court's attention, it may be permissible to answer "in short form" and elaborate when the context makes the complete answer more understandable and persuasive, as Justices Jackson and Wilkins have suggested:

> "I advise you never to postpone answer to a question, for that always gives an impression of evasion. It is better immediately to answer the question, even though you do so in short form and suggest that you expect to amplify and support your answer later."[109]

> "It often happens that a question is asked which relates to a matter which counsel intends to consider at a later point in his argument. The best way to handle the situation is for counsel to state briefly what the answer is to be and say that he will cover the matter more fully before he closes. But should he follow this course, or should he feel that to give an answer on the spot would require too long a digression and that he wishes to be excused temporarily from answering, under no circumstances should he omit to carry out his promise."[110]

---

[108]J. W. Davis, *The Argument of an Appeal,* 26 A.B.A.J. 895, 897 (1940). Chief Justice Horace Stern of Pennsylvania, in his letters to his fictitious son Robert, similarly emphasizes, partly in identical words, the importance of responding to questioning:

"Rejoice when the Court asks you questions. It indicates that you are arguing, not before morons, but before judges eager to be informed. Do not shuffle, evade, or . . . seek to postpone your answers. It is not a crime on the part of the Court to have jumped ahead of your progress in the argument. It has been well said that the Judge knows where his doubts lie, at which point he wishes to be enlightened; it is he whose mind must be made up, no one can do it for him, and he must take his own course of thought to accomplish it." H. Stern, *Letters From a Judge to His Lawyer Son,* 21 Temple L.Q. 1, 22 (1947).

[109]R. Jackson, *Advocacy Before the Supreme Court: Suggestions for Effective Case Presentations,* 37 A.B.A.J. 801, 862 (1951).

[110]R. Wilkins, *The Argument of an Appeal,* 33 Cornell L.Q. 40, 46 (1947).

A better course is to rearrange the argument so as to bring up whatever relates to the question and deal with that immediately. If you can weave a portion—even a substantial portion—of your prepared argument into your reply, you will not have to repeat it thereafter, and the answer will not unduly reduce the time available for other points you intended to cover. Such a rearrangement in response to a question will also have the advantage of focusing the argument on what troubles at least one member of the court, and therefore may be more persuasive. This may be awkward in certain situations, as when a complete response to a question asked when counsel first begins to speak requires knowledge of facts which have not yet been stated. Although weaving them into the answer to the question may be possible, that may also be one of the rare occasions for invoking the technique suggested by Justices Jackson and Wilkins.

If counsel is not sure he understands the question, he may rephrase it as he does understand it, or ask the judge for clarification; all of this, of course, must be done very delicately and politely so as not to offend the questioner, such as:

> "As I understand your question, Mr. Justice—and if I don't, I hope you will tell me—the point is whether . . . ."

That may be better than blundering ahead; some judges become distressed if they think counsel is not being responsive, and sometimes counsel's nonresponsiveness is an innocent consequence of failure to perceive exactly what the questioner had in mind.

Counsel should be aware that what he says in oral argument may be treated as an admission or concession, particularly in courts in which the argument is taped or transcribed. This may often seem unfair to a lawyer forced to answer off-the-cuff. The Supreme Court of the United States, which frequently relies on what counsel says, has also stated:

> "We are loath to attach conclusive weight to the relatively spontaneous responses of counsel to equally spontaneous questioning from the Court during oral argument." *Moose Lodge No. 107* v. *Irvis*, 407 U.S. 163, 170 (1972); *Carey* v. *Brown*, 447 U.S. 455 (1980) (Mr. Justice Rehnquist dissenting, n. 1).

But counsel cannot count on that Court or any other being so considerate. If he is uncertain as to his answer and does not wish the court to treat it as conclusive, he should candidly say that he has not really thought about the point and hopes that the court will evaluate his answer with that in mind. Such a response, of course, would not be helpful if it related to a question which a fully prepared lawyer should have anticipated.

There may be questions to which counsel does not know the answer, perhaps because they could not have been anticipated. If he does not know, he should say so without fumbling around. If the point is at all significant, he should ask for an opportunity to reply in a supplemental memorandum after a short time for cogitation and research. Since counsel should be prepared to answer questions which relate directly to the issues before the court, inquiries to which he cannot respond are likely to be collateral to the issues, so that leaving the questions unanswered without a supplemental memorandum may not be too dangerous.

In answering questions, counsel is on his own. Any lawyer qualified to argue will know that notes passed to him during an argument by a colleague will usually be more distractive than helpful. The colleague, be he partner or junior, will know it too, but often he cannot resist the temptation, particularly when the advocate is not doing well in answering inquiries from the court. The only advice that can be given is "don't," except in dire emergencies. Even if the arguer is doing badly, the note seldom will help. Of course, if he realizes that he needs assistance, as when a judge inquires as to factual details which he does not recall but which a colleague is more likely to know, he should openly turn to his colleague without shame, since even a prepared advocate cannot always foresee or remember everything.

How can an advocate prepare for questioning? Most important is to attain complete knowledge of all the factual and legal aspects of the case. Furthermore, most of those responding to my questionnaire stated that they made a conscious effort to predict what questions might be asked and to work out the answers in advance. Some even would put the questions and answers in writing. A rehearsal before lawyers who will ask all questions which occur to them may be very helpful, although it may or may not result in the same inquiries as are asked by the appellate judges thereafter.

The advocate can—and indeed must—take questioning into account in preparing and timing his argument. As stated in Sec. 8.4, *supra*, instead of shortening the prepared argument in advance because of the possibility that questions will take the amount of time they do on the average in that court—if anybody really knows how much that is—counsel can prepare an argument which may take most of the time allowed. He should place at the beginning the essential points which must be reached, but leave the points which can be omitted if necessary to the end, or mention them summarily as points he was unable to cover for which the court is referred to his brief. He can also mark them, as by putting in brackets the points to be omitted if time runs short.

All of the above demonstrates that no matter how thoroughly he prepares, an appellate advocate must remain flexible.[111] He must be able to rearrange, completely if necessary, in response to the judges' reactions. He must know his case in sufficient depth to be able to switch from the points he intended to cover to those in which the judges express an interest. He must be willing and able to rely on his brief as to other issues, and fully understand that the oral argument will seldom be able to cover all of them.

No one can tell in advance how many questions will be asked during any lawyer's argument. The quantity will vary for different courts and judges, and in any court from one case or argument to another. Counsel should prepare with maximum and minimum possibilities in mind.[112] He should learn what he

---

[111]Fitzgerald and Hartnett suggest that extemporaneous flexibility can be overdone, although they obviously were not referring to the need for adjusting an argument to judicial questioning or unexpected statements by the opposition. They observe (*supra* note 3, at 67):

"While you are actually engaged in delivering your argument before the court, you may suddenly think of a new idea, quotable quotation, analogy, or other point that seems very telling as it bursts into your mind. Avoid these sudden inspirations like the plague.

"They obviously have not been carefully considered, as everything else in your oral argument has; they have not been tested by your own contemplation and oral delivery at rehearsal on several occasions; you have not had time to reflect on their applicability and their serviceability for the purpose they seem to serve; and if you proceed to deliver yourself of them, they could lead to trouble.

"If they seem to fit, they cannot add that much more to the oral argument to which you have already devoted so much time and effort. If they fall flat—or worse, backfire —when you hear them aloud, you will be disconcerted, and the court will be thrown off the track you have devoted so much effort to get them on."

[112]E. Barrett Prettyman, Jr., has gone so far as to suggest that counsel allowed the usual 30 minutes to argue should "prepare two arguments," one of 20 minutes and one of 10 minutes. The former is to be used when the questioning is not intense; it also enables counsel to preserve up to 10 minutes for rebuttal (I would limit that to 5). The shorter argument is to be used when counsel is "bombarded with questions." The difficulty is that the questioning may not always take such round numbers of minutes; there is a practical limit to the number of alternative arguments counsel can prepare in advance. But Mr. Prettyman's advice that counsel should determine in advance what overriding points must be driven home, no matter how much time the questioning leaves, should be kept in mind during the course of preparation as well as while speaking. See E. B. Prettyman, Jr., *Supreme Court Advocacy: Random Thoughts in a Day of Time Restrictions*, LITIGATION, Vol. 4, No. 2, p. 16 (American Bar Association Section of Litigation, 1978).

can as to the habits of the court before which he is to appear, although this may be difficult when the court sits in rotating panels not identified in advance. Some courts, like the United States Supreme Court, are likely to ask a great many questions. Others sometimes, but by no means always, ask very few. In the former, there is little point to preparing an argument which would take more than two thirds of the allotted time. In the latter, there is a fair chance that an argument planned to take almost all of the time will be completed, with the few questions likely to relate to subjects which would have been covered in any event. Preparation of a 28-minute argument, where 30 minutes is allowed, would not be unreasonable in such a court, although counsel should still have in mind, and prepare for, the need for omitting the less important points if necessary.

In general, as has been indicated, the questions and the answers thereto come out of the time allotted to counsel under the rules. Even if appellant's lawyer has announced that he will reserve a few minutes for rebuttal, that time will be lost if the questioning causes his opening argument to use some or all of the time reserved.

Counsel normally will be permitted to complete his answer to a question after his time expires, if he sticks to the point and is not unduly long-winded, although he may have to explain that he would like to finish his answer to the question. If the judges continue to ask questions after his time is up, he may, of course, continue to answer.

If the questioning is so intense as to consume a large part of counsel's time or all of his rebuttal time—and if it has prevented him from getting to points which he deems it essential to argue—he can request the presiding judge to grant him additional time. Indeed even without a request some judges may invite him to continue in such circumstances. Some are more willing than others to grant such requests. Liberality in that respect would seem to be appropriate as the time allowed counsel becomes shorter and shorter. Often now it is substantially less than 30 minutes. If questioning seriously cuts into such short periods, courts should be more lenient in allowing counsel additional time to cover at least the principal features of his case.

Another technique both fair to counsel and helpful to the court is for the judges to hold their questions, or at least some of them, until counsel's time is about to expire. This enables him to cover the principal parts of the case and at the same time enables the questioning to perform its valuable function in aiding the court. This is not always feasible, since what counsel says at a particular moment often stimulates or provokes a judge to inquire, but it is a technique which some judges (including Mr. Justice Black) have used and which might well be utilized more.

8.17 Concluding Peroration

That an oral argument should conclude with an appropriate peroration would seem axiomatic to any student of public speaking. In the past, leaders of the bar in famous cases have concluded their arguments most persuasively, often in a manner which could not fail to stir the emotions of the listener.[113]

The trouble is that now there is hardly ever time for a peroration. I do not recall hearing one in years, and have long since abandoned any attempt to include one in arguments of my own.

With only 30 minutes or less to argue and answer questions, the appellant seldom will have time to say more than:

"I would like to reserve my remaining few minutes for rebuttal."

And then he will need those few minutes, if he still has them, to rebut. In Judge Goodrich's words: "If the appellant has a choice between a fervent peroration and a brief opportunity for rebuttal, he had better choose the latter."[114]

Of greater importance, however, is the fact that a conclusion which does not add anything of substance to what previously has been said will seldom have any persuasive effect. There rarely will be time to summarize at any length what one has said before, and to attempt to do so in a few sentences or in a punchy short conclusion, resounding as it may be, is not likely to convince judges who have not already reacted favorably to the reasoning in the substantive argument.

If there is any question as to what you want the court to order, a formal explanation or statement may be desirable, although that is not very likely to be persuasive. Often such a statement is unnecessary, for the substance of your argument will leave the court in no doubt as to the relief you are asking.

---

[113]For examples, see F. Wiener, BRIEFING AND ARGUING FEDERAL APPEALS, Sec. 126, pp. 332–337 (1967).

[114]Goodrich, *supra* note 4, at 30.

In some cases it may be helpful to state, for example, that you are seeking a new trial or reconsideration by the court below of specified issues, or that instructions to the jury should be revised in specified ways when the case is retried.

More often than not, you will find that your time has run out before you have finished all of the points you intended to make, or while you are engaged in answering the court's questions. If that is so, don't worry about the absence of a formal conclusion; just stop. It is more important to make as much of the substantive argument as you have time for than to attempt to summarize or repeat at the end.

Of course, in what now must be the rare situation in which counsel has ample time, there is no reason not to end with a short persuasive bang, which probably should be prepared in advance. But you shouldn't really expect to get to it, or be perturbed if you don't.

8.18 Appellant's Rebuttal

In most jurisdictions appellant is entitled to rebuttal at the close of appellee's argument, and an appellee who has cross-appealed has a similar right to the last word on the issues which he is appealing. New Hampshire Rule 18(4) allows the opening party to close, but adds that the court "does not favor a closing argument [not] limited to unexpected matters." Pennsylvania Rule 2321, however, allows rebuttal only with permission of the court. Whether or not rebuttal is allowed, however, counsel must realize that he may not interrupt his opponent's argument, and keep that in mind in preparing his own opening.

The practice in most state courts, as in the federal appellate courts, is to allow appellant to exercise his own discretion in allocating a portion of his total time to rebuttal. The Missouri Supreme Court permits a reply to be no longer than one quarter of the time consumed in the principal argument. Rule 84.12. Five minutes is allowed in the Missouri Court of Appeals. As a practical matter, usually little time is reserved. Because courts expect them to, because it is to their own strategic advantage, and because lawyers find it difficult to stop talking once they get going, appellants honor their obligation to use the opening for their principal argument, usually to such an extent that it is difficult to break off to save time for rebuttal. See Sec. 8.6, *supra.*

As pointed out in Sec. 8.6, *supra,* a few states—Illinois,

Iowa, South Carolina, South Dakota and Texas—specify the maximum time for appellant's opening argument (20 or 30 minutes) and also grant him 10 minutes to rebut (15 minutes in Texas). This is usually more than he would be able to reserve if the allocation were left to him. This system gives appellant more leeway as to what can and should be said in rebuttal. As a result, some of the restrictions on rebuttal in other jurisdictions do not apply to the same degree in those states.

In general, rebuttal should be undertaken to correct errors or misstatements in or misleading omissions from appellee's argument or to answer arguments made by appellee not met by appellant in his opening. Rebuttal also provides an opportunity for appellant to comment upon questions asked by the court during the appellee's argument and upon appellee's answers thereto. It should not be used merely to repeat and emphasize what has already been covered in appellant's opening, or even to improve upon it unless that can be accomplished in the course of refuting something said by appellee.

Rebuttal also should not be wasted on insignificant errors by one's opponent. "An insipid, note-cluttered, nit-picking rebuttal statement is far worse than none at all."[115] The court will reasonably expect appellant's last few minutes to concentrate on matters which might significantly affect the court's decision.

There is a difference of opinion among experienced advocates as to whether rebuttal is overdone. Former Attorney General and Solicitor General William D. Mitchell, disagreeing with Colonel Wiener, thought it "a rare case where . . . reply argument is justified," since in his brief and opening argument "an appellant should be able to cover adequately his own case and anticipate his adversary's."[116] Mr. Justice Jackson, though recognizing the desirability of supplying "important and definite corrections," added that "the most experienced advocates make least use of the privilege. Many inexperienced ones get into trouble by attempting to renew the principal argument."[117]

Judge Prentice H. Marshall and E. Barrett Prettyman, Jr.,

---

[115]Marshall, *supra* note 3, at 9–25.

[116]W. Mitchell, *Book Review*, 64 Harv. L. Rev. 350, 351 (1950). At that time, however, longer oral arguments were often allowed, such as one hour under United States Supreme Court Rule 28 (as of 1950).

[117]R. Jackson, *Advocacy Before the Supreme Court: Suggestions for Effective Case Presentations*, 37 A.B.A.J. 801, 804 (1951). But compare the position of New Jersey's Chief Justice Vanderbilt, who could not "understand the ineptness of counsel who failed to reserve a few minutes for possible rebuttal." Carson, *supra* note 5, at 89.

believe that rebuttal concentrating on crucial points is generally helpful. If they mean, as they probably do, that critical errors in appellee's presentation should be corrected, I would agree. Certainly they do not advocate rehashing what has already been said. But some time for rebuttal should always be reserved.

Correcting an adversary's version of the record on significant matters may be essential, since the court may not detect such errors itself. Nothing can be more effective than for appellant emphatically to point out at the beginning of rebuttal that, for example:

> "Appellee's argument [or answer to the Chief Justice's question] that witness Brown had told defendant everything he knew about the engine long before the disclosure of trade secrets here complained of should be read with Mr. Brown's undisputed testimony, on p. 47 of the appendix, that he knew nothing about the internal characteristics of the engine but only about external features visible to anyone."

Such an answer could destroy the premise upon which appellee's principal argument rests.

Appellant should attempt to meet in his opening argument the points which he expects appellee to make; defusing them in advance is to his advantage. Since appellee will have tried to put his best foot forward in his brief, appellant is unlikely to be seriously surprised by many new arguments. Often, however, appellee will improve the formulation of an argument in a way appellant could not foresee. If the improved version has not been adequately answered in the opening argument, appellant should deal with it in the rebuttal if he has enough time.

And, of course, if by design or shortage of time or inadvertence appellant failed to deal at all with a point argued by appellee, he can do so in the rebuttal if time permits, which often it won't. Deliberate postponement to the rebuttal of an answer to a contention which you are sure appellee will make runs the risk that you will never be able to get to it, except perhaps in the states in which you are guaranteed 10 minutes to reply.

There is disagreement between Judge Prentice Marshall and Mr. Prettyman, as well as among those responding to my questionnaire, as to whether any effort should be made to prepare a rebuttal argument in advance. Most responses agreed with Mr. Prettyman that "rebuttal should never be prepared in advance,"[118] but given entirely extemporaneously on the basis of memory or notes as to what appellee said. Mr. Prettyman (and I believe most arguers) relies on notes made during appellee's argument of any points which might warrant correction or explanation. I try to add a catchword suggesting the answer, and mark the points which seem specially important with a red mark or a large asterisk in the margin of the page. When the time for rebuttal comes, I usually stick to the marked items in deciding which points to make and which to omit.

Judge Marshall and other responders, with whom I agree, believe that to some extent a rebuttal can be prepared. Judge Marshall has stated:

> "There are many who say that rebuttal can never be planned or rehearsed since it is always extemporaneous. I disagree. If the appellant will give some thought to the arguments he would make were he the appellee and if he will give some thought to the questions he would raise during the appellee's argument if he were on the court, then he can prepare his rebuttal argument. And he should."[119]

I add that he should not expect to make such an argument just as he prepared it. He must adapt it to what appellee, and perhaps the court, actually said. He may have guessed completely wrong. On some occasions all of the available time will need to be spent in replying to misstatements, damaging omissions or arguments not anticipated.

The careful advocate will avail himself of both methods of preparing for rebuttal, knowing full well that he will have to choose at the last minute—indeed, as he gets up to speak— between the product of his advance preparation and the notes hurriedly written during appellee's argument. The latter are almost certainly entitled to priority, since they are directly responsive to the opposing argument, but the advance preparation will often prove to be very helpful; it will often relate to the same points.

In the states permitting a 10-minute rebuttal, appellant can more confidently omit from his opening argument replies to points he does not think require mention unless appellee advances them orally. If appellant is hard pressed for time, he can

---

[118]E. B. Prettyman, Jr., *Supreme Court Advocacy: Random Thoughts in a Day of Time Restrictions,* LITIGATION, Vol. 4, No. 2, p. 19 (American Bar Association Section of Litigation, 1978).

[119]Marshall, *supra* note 3, at 9–25.

even forego attempting to meet in advance some of the points he expects appellee to argue and leave them for rebuttal. This is a perfectly proper use of rebuttal so long as appellee does orally argue the point in question. But when rebuttal time is not guaranteed, this tactic is likely to backfire when questioning leaves little or no time for rebuttal.

Counsel should have the good sense not to bother rebutting arguments which have been demolished by questions from the court. In many cases there is always the possibility that the judges may tee off on the attorney "who returns to his feet" with "an accumulation of questions."[120]

8.19 Appellee's Answering Argument

Most of what has been said about the arguments by appellant (or petitioner) also applies to arguments by appellee (or respondent). Appellee's job, however, is intrinsically easier than appellant's, for he has won below and has the advantage of a favorable verdict, finding or opinion which appellant has the burden of overturning.

The appellee's argument must combine the attributes of a principal argument and a rebuttal. It must present appellee's affirmative argument and also meet the opponent's anticipated contentions as reflected in his briefs. That much can be prepared in advance. It must also deal orally with unexpected contentions or assertions in the opposing arguments, as well as with any significant questions or comments by members of the court.

Often the refutation of the appellant's oral argument or the discussion of judges' comments can be merged into the appropriate part of the argument which appellee has previously prepared. This can be done by inserting a written or mental addition into the appellee's argument notes during the course of appellant's argument.

Frequently, however, it may be advantageous for appellee to begin by immediately challenging the accuracy of something appellant has said, particularly at the end of his argument, or by correcting appellant's answer to a question from the bench. Such an opening may hold the court's attention and undermine appellant's prior presentation. In most instances, though not

---

[120]R. Jackson, *Advocacy Before the Supreme Court: Suggestions for Effective Case Presentations,* 37 A.B.A.J. 801, 804 (1951).

necessarily, it will relate to an argument not made in appellant's brief or answered in appellee's. As with appellant's rebuttal, such an opening will lose its effect unless it relates to errors of some consequence to the disposition of the case. Correction of an inadequate reply to a question from the court should not, however, be regarded as of no significance. At least one judge wants to know the answer, and it may help to straighten him out right away.

Apart from the opportunity to begin with a discrediting rebuttal, the principal difference between the main arguments for an appellant and appellee is that an appellee need not, and indeed should not, redo the introductory portions of appellant's argument or his statement of facts except to the extent that they require correction and supplementation. As in writing briefs, appellee will seldom have any reason for disputing appellant's statement of the nature of the case, of the basis for the court's jurisdiction or of the statutes involved, although occasionally there may be differences as to the last two items.

The same will usually, though not invariably, be true of appellant's statement of the issues. An appellee may be presenting issues of his own, as alternative arguments supporting his position or by way of cross-appeal, and appellant may not have mentioned them. In some cases appellee may be in a position to establish that an issue which appellant purports to raise is really not before the court, either because it was not properly raised and presented below or because appellant's question rests on an incomplete or inaccurate factual premise. It may be possible to demolish all or part of appellant's case by asserting, for example, that:

> "All the questions raised by appellant rest on the mistaken premise that the information as to plaintiff's trade secrets disclosed to defendant by Mr. X was the same as the information disclosed years before by Mr. Y. Undisputed evidence shows that Mr. Y knew nothing about and was in no position to disclose the internal functioning of plaintiff's machine which had been designed and installed by Mr. X. The question of law as to the effect of an identical earlier disclosure is therefore not presented."

Just as there is no point to restating the issues if appellant's statement is reasonably accurate and not misleading, there is no reason to restate facts which appellant has stated accurately.

There is every reason, of course, to correct significant errors or to remedy material omissions, but not to nitpick.

Appellee, like appellant, has the option of dealing with factual matters separately at or near the beginning of his argument or of combining the discussion of different facts with the argument on the substantive issues to which they relate.

In some cases, a point-by-point correction of appellant's factual statements, even limited to matters of importance, would be disjointed, hard to follow and ineffective. When appellant's version gives what appellee believes to be a misleading, unfair or too unfavorable impression, it may be preferable for appellee's counsel to restate in full the facts, or a part of the facts, or the facts as to a particular point. The object is to create a general picture more favorable to his client, in part by placing the facts emphasized by appellant in a broader context which minimizes their significance.

Such a full restatement of facts may take more time, but may be well worth it. Since the court will not assume that all the facts stated by appellant are wrong or misleading, its inclination may be to inquire why appellee doesn't merely stick to correcting appellant's statement. Your restatement should therefore not sound like appellant's opening with merely a few differences which could have been mentioned more briefly.

If you think you can tell from appellant's briefs and prior position in the case how he will present the facts orally, you can prepare your own version of the facts in advance, perhaps trying it both ways—correcting the misstatements or a full statement of your own—to see if the shorter one will do the job. It may be advisable to keep notes in both forms, in case you cannot tell which to use until you hear what he says.

If you do not believe an attempt to predict what he is likely to argue is feasible, you will have to determine during the course of his argument how extensively to go into the facts in the light of what he has said and the court's questions, if any. If you think that there is any possibility that a full statement will be desirable, you should include it in your outline or notes. You can then mark off the items which should and should not be covered orally as your opponent proceeds, leaving to the end, perhaps when you get up, the ultimate decision whether to restate the whole or to cover only items requiring comment or correction.

With respect to meeting appellant's arguments, some persons advocate that the appellee take up the points argued by appellant in the order in which appellant presented them. As in writing a brief, however, appellant's arrangement of facts is likely not to be the best for appellee. Appellee can almost certainly be more persuasive if he prepares his argument in the way most suitable for his client's position, as was also true for his brief, though, of course, he may have to change it if appellant does not say what was expected, or if the judges have asked questions.

Appellee should not only present his argument in the way which most effectively answers his opponent's points. He must take into account that this will be his last chance to meet them. He must recognize that he cannot interrupt his opponent's argument later. Accordingly, it is essential that he listen carefully during the opposing argument and determine what he must say to meet it and how that can best be integrated into his own argument.

Appellee may also wish to present contentions not mentioned by appellant orally but argued in appellant's brief. Appellee is, of course, not bound by appellant's judgment as to what points should be argued orally. Some might be more suitable for appellee than for appellant, as when appellee can give a simple answer to a complicated contention of appellant's. Normally, however, appellee's argument should reply to the points appellant made orally.

In the main, appellee should prepare his affirmative argument just as appellant does, using any of the methods of preparing and arguing discussed in Sec. 8.8, *supra.* Except to the extent required by what appellant and the judges have said before he gets up, appellee should normally endeavor to stick pretty close to his own outline of his affirmative case. On the whole, substituting extemporaneous improvisation for what has been carefully thought out in advance is not an improvement.[121]

Though an appellee should prepare in advance, he must be aware that he may be forced to adapt or even abandon the prepared argument by reason of what his opponent or the court has said, which he can seldom fully foresee. This causes some lawyers who write out full drafts of arguments when they are appellants to rely on notes when they are appellees.

Appellee may find it unnecessary to make a full reply on points the weaknesses of which have been demonstrated by the

---

[121]See Fitzgerald and Hartnett, quoted at p. 430, note 111, *supra.*

judges. That may show that the court fully understands the point and needs no further help from him.

When all is said and done, the key to an effective appellee's argument is flexibility. Either on his feet or immediately before rising, appellee must weigh the advantages and disadvantages of the various alternative approaches available and decide which will be most effective. To do so requires complete knowledge of the case, good judgment and confidence in his judgment. It also presupposes the natural ability or agility which is indispensable for any appellate lawyer.

8.20 Client in the Courtroom

Occasionally clients wish to attend the arguments of appeals. It would seldom occur to most lawyers to try to dissuade them, though a few do. More are likely to encourage them to be present. Corporate house counsel, who are familiar with the case and may have employed litigating counsel, frequently attend.

Nevertheless a number of distinguished judges and lawyers, including Mr. Justice Jackson and Judge Prentice H. Marshall, have advised, in the blunt words of Judge Marshall: "Leave your client at home."[122] The fear is that counsel will tend to tailor his argument to what the client rather than the court wants to hear. A client may expect a polished oration containing flattering treatment of the good guy—himself, of course—and the opposite for the bad guy. Owen Rall, a distinguished Illinois lawyer, has written:

> "Every judge knows that a lawyer is very likely to deliver a different oral argument if his client is in the courtroom than if he is not. I am even told that sometimes judges play a little game among themselves called 'Find the Client.'"[123]

Mr. Justice Jackson had previously taken the same position:

> "I doubt whether it is wise to have clients or parties in interest attend the argument if it can be avoided. Clients unfortunately desire, and their presence is apt to encourage, qualities in an

---

[122]R. Jackson, *Advocacy Before the Supreme Court: Suggestions for Effective Case Presentations,* 37 A.B.A.J. 801, 861 (1951); Marshall, *supra* note 3, at 9-25–9-26; F. Wiener, BRIEFING AND ARGUING FEDERAL APPEALS, pp. 344–346 (1967); O. Rall, *Effective Oral Argument on Appeal,* 48 Ill. Bar J. 572, 574 (1960); Fitzgerald and Hartnett, *supra* note 3, at 64.

[123]O. Rall, *Effective Oral Argument on Appeal,* 48 Ill. Bar J. 572, 574 (1960).

argument that are least admired by judges. When I hear counsel launch into personal attacks on the opposition or praise of a client, I instinctively look about to see if I can identify the client in the room—and often succeed. . . . The case that is argued to please a client . . . will not often make a favorable impression on the Bench."[124]

I suspect that most good lawyers do not take the matter that seriously, and that they would not feel impelled to alter their argument because of the presence of their client. Particularly in criminal cases, however, a client's presence may be an embarrassment and should be avoided; the same may be true of civil litigation in which the client's integrity or morality is in issue.

How far counsel should go to discourage or prevent a client's attendance may well depend upon the nature of the case and of the client. The lawyer is in a position to recognize when these circumstances might combine to present a delicate problem affecting what he might otherwise say. In such a case, if a non-lawyer client wants to be present, counsel may try to discourage him, though most lawyers would not go even that far.[125] If the client does insist upon being present, and, of course, you cannot stop him, counsel should explain what the argument will be like, the reasons for his argument strategy and why fervid pronouncements of his client's innocence or virtue would not be very helpful.

---

[124]R. Jackson, *Advocacy Before the Supreme Court: Suggestions for Effective Case Presentations,* 37 A.B.A.J. 801, 861 (1951).

[125]Mr. Rall recognized in the article cited in note 123, *supra,* pp. 574–575, that: "The advice to leave your client at home is more readily given than acted upon. After all, he is paying the bill—or at least you hope he will pay it—and he thinks that the oral argument will win or lose his case and he wants to be there. As a matter of fact, if you were to try to forbid him to be there he would be downright suspicious of you and he would probably be fully convinced that you are ashamed to have him listen to you."

9

Rehearings and Mandates

9.1 Rehearings in General

Petitions for rehearings are the losing lawyers' last gasp and, most often, little more than that. The vast majority has no chance of success and little reason for being filed except for the belief that nothing will be lost by a final effort to avoid defeat. Although it may cost the client or the lawyer money and time, and the court a little time (usually very little), this is usually not enough in relation to the amount previously expended on the litigation to be a significant deterrent.

There are situations in which a petition for rehearing is justifiable. Most obvious is a new controlling judicial decision or statute calling for a different result.[1] Appellate courts occasionally overlook facts of record which refute a fact stated in or underlying the decision, or misapprehend a citation or other authority. And appellate judges may just change their minds.

The rules allowing petitions for rehearing in almost every American jurisdiction reflect general judicial recognition that appellate courts may make mistakes, and that they should be accorded an opportunity to correct them by permitting losing counsel to call the alleged errors to their attention. Although Maine has no rule or statute expressly authorizing petitions for rehearing, its Supreme Judicial Court has inherent power to correct errors in its opinions and has modified opinions on

---

[1] A new statute applicable only in the future would not fall in this category.

motions for reconsideration submitted by a party.[2] Wisconsin Rules 809.24 and 809.64 permit a party to move for reconsideration of a decision of the Supreme Court but not of the Court of Appeals. The latter, however, may reconsider "on its own motion," and "requests" for reconsideration will be submitted to the court which will enter an order only if on its own motion it then decides to change its ruling.

The basic problem confronting the unsuccessful litigant is that the judges who have decided a case and the lawyers who have lost it approach the matter in different frames of mind. The judges who approach the case objectively have now considered it and reached a conclusion. To convince them that they were wrong is very difficult. The lawyer must submit his petition for rehearing to these judges who have already made up their minds in the first instance.

The lawyer, of course, knows this, but often has difficulty in accommodating his thinking to the judge's mental track. Since he has already presented the best arguments he could think of, he is hard pressed to come up with something different. The judges erred, he believes, in rejecting the arguments previously made. To present the same arguments again, perhaps in more vehement form, to demonstrate the judges' stupidity is much more likely to antagonize than to persuade them.

If counsel is imaginative enough to think of an argument not previously presented, he is confronted by the principle that points not raised in the court below or in the briefs or oral argument in the appellate court cannot be raised for the first time in the petition for rehearing. This dilemma was described by Professors Louisell and Degnan, in what seems to be the only thorough analysis of the problems presented by petitions for rehearing, as follows:

> "There is general agreement that rehearing will not be granted merely for the purpose of again debating matters on which the court has once deliberated and spoken—on this rules, cases, and justices speak with one voice. Nor is there much disposition to grant a petition which raises for the first time a question of law or a legal theory which was not raised on the first argument, especially when that question has not been raised in the trial court and appears for the first time in the petition. The latter principle is

---

[2]*Summit Thread Co.* v. *Corthell,* 132 Me. 336, 341, 171 A. 254, 256 (1934); *Hann* v. *Merrill,* 305 A.2d 545 (Me., 1972–1973); *Maine Central Railroad Co.* v. *Halperin,* 379 A.2d 980 (Me., 1977).

really a corollary of the common appellate rule which bars consideration, except under exceptional circumstances, of matters not raised in the trial court. The simultaneous preclusion from rehearing of certain matters which have been previously raised, on the one hand, and matters which have not been previously raised, on the other, superficially suggests an impasse based on inconsistency in the philosophy of rehearing. Actually, however, there are sound policy reasons for excluding both types—the former because they have had their day in court, the latter because the parties did not see fit seasonably to bring them to court."[3]

This leaves "as the legitimate subject of rehearing matters seasonably presented by the parties but neglected by the appellate court itself in the first decision,"[4] which is a very narrow opening. To it should be added, since it is probably the basis for rehearing most likely to be successful, subsequent cases or other sources of law which the court can properly consider and which counsel could not previously have called to its attention.

Judges have stated that "if the court is persuaded it has or may have blundered, it will grant rehearing to avoid an unjust result or to correct material error."[5] Lawyers would not challenge the appropriateness of such a test; indeed, it is the standard which each would say he is invoking. But each lawyer applies it subjectively to his own case. The result is that most "lawyers who have lost a case on appeal are genuinely convinced that the court has blundered, that the error is material, and that the result is grossly unjust."[6] Although the lapse of time may restore perspective, that will not occur until long after the petition for rehearing must be filed.

The result of applying such a test, which appears to be reasonable both to judges and unsuccessful litigants but which has different meanings to each, has been a "deluge of quite useless and objectively hopeless petitions."[7]

Although the petition for reconsideration by the appellate court is customarily called a petition for rehearing or reargument, those are misnomers. Petition for reconsideration and

---

[3]D. Louisell and R. Degnan, *Rehearing in American Appellate Courts,* 44 Cal. L. Rev. 627, 635 (1956).
[4]*Ibid.*
[5]*Id.* at 634. Judge Goodrich puts it somewhat more narrowly: "Every once in a while a case appears where the court has mistaken the facts or misconstrued the point of a case. In that sort of a situation it may grant petition for reargument." H. Goodrich, *A Case on Appeal—A Judge's View,* in A CASE ON APPEAL, p. 31 (ALI-ABA, 1967).
[6]D. Louisell and R. Degnan, *Rehearing in American Appellate Courts,* 44 Cal. L. Rev. 627, 634 (1956).
[7]*Ibid.*

modification or vacation of judgment would be a more accurate description. Either as a matter of rule or practice, oral arguments of petitions for rehearing are not permitted unless the court so orders, which it hardly ever does. And very often no new argument is ordered even if the petition is granted. What the petitioner is seeking is a change in the judgment previously entered, not necessarily a second oral argument.

The courts dispose of the petitions on that assumption. If the petition is not simply denied, as most are, the courts issue whatever type of order seems appropriate. Most rules so permit. Federal Rule of Appellate Procedure 40(a), which is typical, provides:

> "If a petition for rehearing is granted the court may make a final disposition of the cause without reargument or may restore it to the calendar for reargument or resubmission or may make such other orders as are deemed appropriate under the circumstances of the particular case."

Pennsylvania Appellate Rule 2546 is very similar.

Not infrequently a court merely changes its opinion, sometimes by correcting an error called to its attention but without affecting the result of the case or changing the judgment. The court may reaffirm its prior judgment but explain more fully what it meant; usually this serves to strengthen the opinion and make it less vulnerable in a higher court. Occasionally the revision may completely alter the effect of the first opinion and in substance give petitioner the relief which he had sought or part of it. E.g., *Elgin, Joliet and Eastern Ry.* v. *Burley,* 327 U.S. 661 (1946), in which the United States and a number of other *amici* joined petitioners in urging that the Court should not have construed the Railway Labor Act in a manner which severely disrupted the machinery for handling employee grievances. On rehearing, the Court, purporting to reaffirm its prior decision, concluded that its opinion need not be so interpreted, to everyone's surprise.

Which of these procedures is utilized depends on the court's reaction to the petition for rehearing and the opposing response, if any is filed. If the court is completely persuaded that it has erred, perhaps because of an intervening controlling decision, it might vacate its prior order and substitute a new one without further argument. If the intervening act creates doubt in its mind, a new argument may be ordered.

9.2 Reasons for Granting Rehearing

Reasons for granting rehearing are sometimes specified in appellate rules and sometimes not. The United States Supreme Court rules set no standards for granting rehearing after decisions on the merits, but are quite specific as to petitions seeking rehearings for orders denying petitions for certiorari.[8] Some states[9] which do not specify the criteria for granting rehearing merely state generally that the grounds should be set forth in the petition.

Federal Appellate Rule 40(a) and the rules of many states[10] simply declare that "[t]he petition shall state with particularity the points of law or fact which in the opinion of the petitioner the court has overlooked or misapprehended." The Georgia rules[11] in more detail provide:

> "A rehearing will be granted, on motion of the losing party, only when it appears that the court has overlooked a material fact in the record, a statute, or a decision which is controlling as authority and which would require a different judgment from that rendered, or has erroneously construed or misapplied a provision of law or a controlling authority. No motion for a rehearing will be entertained which does not expressly point out what material fact in the record, or controlling statute or decision, has been overlooked by the court, or what provision of law or controlling authority has been erroneously construed or misapplied."

The words "overlooked or misapprehended" or their equivalents, which appear in many of the rules, obviously do not constitute a very helpful standard. Most unsuccessful advocates honestly believe that the court has either misapprehended or overlooked some of their arguments.

A few states are more specific. Tennessee Rule 39(a), adopted in 1979, which reflects "the current law,"[12] defines the "character of reasons that will be considered," without "controlling nor fully measuring the court's discretion," as follows:

---

[8]United States Supreme Court Rule 51.1, which relates to petitions for rehearing other than those denying or granting certiorari, merely states that "such petition must briefly and distinctly state its grounds." Rule 51.2, which relates to petitions for rehearing of orders on petitions for certiorari, provides that the grounds must be limited "to intervening circumstances of substantial or controlling effect, or to other substantial grounds not previously presented."

[9]Connecticut, Delaware, Hawaii, Wisconsin.

[10]E.g., Colorado, Illinois, Iowa, Nevada, New Mexico, North Dakota.

[11]Georgia Court of Appeals Rule 33 (Georgia Code, §24–3633); Georgia Supreme Court Rule 32 (Georgia Code, §24–4532).

[12]Advisory Committee Comment to Tennessee Appellate Rule 39.

"(1) the court's opinion incorrectly states the material facts established by the evidence and set forth in the record; (2) the court's opinion is in conflict with a statute, prior decision, or other principle of law; (3) the court's opinion overlooks or misapprehends a material fact or proposition of law; and (4) the court's opinion relies upon matters of fact or law upon which the parties have not been heard and that are open to reasonable dispute."

The Pennsylvania standards, which are contained in a Note attached to Rule 2543, are similar. The rule and the Note read as follows:

"Reargument before an appellate court is not a matter of right, but of sound judicial discretion, and reargument will be allowed only when there are compelling reasons therefor.
    Note: The following, while neither controlling nor fully measuring the discretion of the court, indicate the character of the reasons which will be considered:
    (1) Where the decision is by a panel of the court and it appears that the decision may be inconsistent with a decision of a different panel of the same court on the same subject.
    (2) Where the court has overlooked or misapprehended a fact of record material to the outcome of the case.
    (3) Where the court has overlooked or misapprehended (as by misquotation of text or misstatement of result) a controlling or directly relevant authority.
    (4) Where a controlling or directly relevant authority relied upon by the court has been expressly reversed, modified, overruled or otherwise materially affected during the pendency of the matter sub judice, and no notice thereof was given to the court pursuant to Rule 2501(b) (change in status of authorities)."

These standards are more specific, but they include the phrase which is the sole criterion under the federal and many other rules—"overlooked or misapprehended." This still leaves the matter very open-ended.

In 1956 Professors Louisell and Degnan wrote:

"The following are typical of the grounds regarded as sufficient by those [courts] which attempt to specify:
    a. The court has overlooked, misapplied, or failed to consider a statute, decision, or principle directly controlling.
    b. The court has overlooked or misconceived some material fact.
    c. The court has overlooked or misconceived a material question in the case.
    d. There is serious doubt as to the validity, correctness, or

adequacy of precedent relied upon and the case itself is of great precedent potential or of grave public concern."[13]

The first three of these clauses represent efforts to tie down the general "overlooked or misapprehended" standard to particular facts or events of legal consequence. The last invites counsel in important cases to use petitions for rehearing to question prior decisions when he has "serious doubt" as to their soundness, which is again quite open-ended.

These efforts to provide intelligible guidelines "tell little to an attorney who must determine whether his petition has a chance for favorable reception."[14] It may be that no rule which reflects the criteria courts actually apply can be precise enough to cut off the flow of hopeless petitions. For none of these standards are much more definite than that the judges unpredictably have concluded that they have blundered or overlooked or misapprehended something. Counsel can seldom guess the cases in which a court will react in this way.

Surprisingly few of the formulations of good grounds for rehearing include a new judicial decision or other supervening change in the law. Such a decision by a higher court or the same court in conflict with either the holding or reasoning of the case under consideration may provide good cause for reversal without reargument. If the application of the new decision to the case is not entirely clear, reargument would be appropriate. If the conflicting decision is by a court of the same rank as that which rendered the original decision, the conflict may provide grounds for review by a supreme court which did not previously exist. This is the first and principal ground for seeking rehearing after denial of certiorari set out in United States Supreme Court Rule 51.2. Other supreme courts presumably would react in the same way in similar circumstances.

A respectable ground for a petition for rehearing is also presented by a new conflicting decision of another court of equal rank, or even from another jurisdiction, unless the court had previously been aware of and rejected similar outside authorities. "A decent respect for conformity and the stature of a coordinate court justifies such action, whether failure in the first instance to acknowledge the decision is caused by its non-exis-

---

[13]D. Louisell and R. Degnan, *Rehearing in American Appellate Courts,* 44 Cal. L. Rev. 627, 633 (1956).
[14]*Ibid.*

tence at the time of the original hearing or by the failure of counsel for the parties to call it to the attention of the court."[15] A court may grant a petition on such a ground if the judges thought the decision close at the time of the first ruling, although that probably will not appear on the face of the decision. For judges attempt to write persuasive opinions even though in their own minds they are only 51 percent convinced.[16]

The pendency before the same court of other cases presenting the same or a related question is also an appropriate ground for granting rehearing. E.g., *Forgett* v. *United States,* 390 U.S. 203 (1968); *Pickett* v. *Union Terminal Co.,* 315 U.S. 386, 394 (1942). A change in legislation may also constitute "intervening circumstances of substantial or controlling effect" under Supreme Court Rule 51.2. *Massey* v. *United States,* 291 U.S. 608 (1934); *Sioux Tribe* v. *United States,* 329 U.S. 684 (1946).

An unusual provision in the Louisiana constitution (Art. V, Sec. 8B) provides that when a three-judge panel of a court of appeal modifies or reverses a trial court and one of the appellate judges dissents, the case must be reargued before a panel of at least five judges.[17] The theory is that when a trial judge is joined by a dissenting member of the appellate court, the four judges who have heard the case have divided evenly, and that submission to a larger appellate court is therefore appropriate. This reasoning is plausible, but could apply to any reversal where a majority of one overturns the lower court's ruling or, for that matter, when the majority of a supreme court exceeds the minority by less than the difference in the vote of the intermediate appellate court.[18] Adherence to the general principle that only the votes of the judges of the higher court should be counted recognizes their higher rank in the judicial structure which presumably, though not, of course, invariably, is justified by their greater legal stature or ability and not merely because there are more of them.[19]

---

[15]*Id.* at 640.

[16]Chief Justice Schaefer, *Appellate Advocacy,* 23 Tenn. L. Rev. 471, 475 (1954), cites Mr. Justice Cardozo for the statement that a judge's "job is to convince himself to a degree of 51% and then later write an opinion indicating 99% conviction."

[17]See Note, *Right to Appellate Reargument,* 36 Louisiana L. Rev. 844 (1976).

[18]For example, a five-to-four vote in the supreme court and a contrary two-to-one or three-to-two vote below; or six-to-three in the supreme court and four-to-one or three-to-zero below.

[19]The higher court may not be composed of more judges, as when the United States Supreme Court reviews a decision *en banc* of a court of appeals composed of nine or more judges.

The United States Supreme Court and some state courts require certificates that a petition for rehearing is presented "in good faith and not for delay." See Supreme Court Rule 51.1 and .2; Delaware Rule 18; Hawaii Rule 5.[20] Paragraph (f) of Arkansas Rule 20 requires a "certificate of belief that there is merit in the petition and that it is not filed for the purpose of delay," and paragraph (k) adds that "litigants will not be permitted to substitute new counsel for the purpose of filing a petition for rehearing," although such counsel may participate by joining with original counsel with their consent or with permission of the court. The object presumably is to prevent the losing party from shopping around for a new lawyer at that late stage. Most of the United States courts of appeals used to require a certificate, but its omission from the superseding Federal Rules of Appellate Procedure probably reflected the "common view that such certificates are meaningless formalities" not worth the effort.[21] Lawyers who desire to petition for rehearing have little difficulty in attesting to their own good faith, and there is little likelihood that they will be subject to judicial discipline. Whether such limitations are effective is doubtful.

North Carolina and South Carolina go further and require certificates from outside lawyers of experience not professionally connected with the case. North Carolina requires such certificates from two lawyers, and South Carolina from one.[22] At

---

[20]Georgia requires that "[t]here shall be attached to the motion a certificate of counsel that upon careful examination of the opinion of the court he believes that the fact, statute, or decision has been overlooked, or the provision of law or controlling authority has been erroneously construed or misapplied." Georgia Court of Appeals Rule 33(g), Supreme Court Rule 32(g) (Georgia Code, §§3633(g), 4532(g)).

[21]See C. Wright, A. Miller, E. Cooper and E. Gressman, 16 FEDERAL PRACTICE AND PROCEDURE, p. 472 (1977). See also D. Louisell and R. Degnan, *Rehearing in American Appellate Courts*, 44 Cal. L. Rev. 627, 642 (1956).

[22]In 1933 the South Carolina Supreme Court commented on the latter provision as follows:

"We especially call attention to the provision in the rule that the petition for rehearing must be accompanied by 'a certificate from some counsel not concerned in the case that there is merit in such grounds' on which the rehearing is asked. We fear that too often 'counsel not concerned in the case,' out of the goodness of their hearts, as a favor to a brother of the bar, and without examination of the full record in the case, certifies 'that there is merit in such grounds.' The counsel who signs a certificate of that nature should not simply read the petition for rehearing. He should go further and study the transcript of record, the briefs of counsel, the decisions of the court cited therein, the opinion of the court, and the decisions referred to in the opinion. Counsel signing such a certificate should remember that the members of this court, usually consisting of five justices, have read all these records and decisions, and together have considered in conference, often in many conferences, all of them, and that the sole purpose of the court is to decide a case correctly. If 'counsel not concerned in the case,' after the court has rendered its

least in North Carolina these restrictions have had the desired effect of substantially reducing the number of petitions for rehearing. Very few are filed there. Whether this diminution of the burden on the court warrants the imposition on the bar and on the client (if the new attorneys are to be paid by him) is doubtful. The judges who are familiar with the case can dispose of an unmeritorious petition for rehearing in a few minutes. As the South Carolina Supreme Court opinion referred to in footnote 22, *supra*, declares, the outside lawyers should study not merely the petition for rehearing but also the court's opinion, the briefs below, the pertinent parts of the record and also the critical authorities if their certificates are to be meaningful.

Second Circuit Rule 40 attempts to discourage frivolous petitions for rehearing by providing that taxable costs of up to $250 payable to the adversary may be imposed "if a petition for rehearing be found to be wholly without merit, vexatious and for delay." But this is not likely to have much effect except in cases involving small sums and a nonindigent party.

A few states make a petition for rehearing a prerequisite to filing a petition for review in the state supreme court.[23] And in Arizona, as has been pointed out in Sec. 5.7, pp. 131, 134, *supra*, the petition for rehearing constitutes the only argument which can be submitted in support of a petition for review to the state Supreme Court. One purpose of these provisions is to make sure that the courts of appeals have the opportunity either to modify their rulings or to comment on the questions raised before they come to the state supreme court. But the object of a petition requesting review by a supreme court is mainly to convince the court that the issues are of importance or that there is a conflict in the courts of appeals. The former is irrelevant in the courts of appeals, and the conflict will undoubtedly already have been called to the court's attention if counsel was aware of

---

decision, asks the court to review again the entire record and briefs in a cause, then, in fairness to the court, that counsel should do once at least what he asks the court to do twice.

"What we have said is a simple desire to aid the court in expediting its work, and to end as early as reasonably possible litigation. Many hours, uselessly spent in the consideration of petitions for rehearing, could be well spent in disposing of cases pending for decision. We feel assured that by calling the attention of the bar to these matters, about which, perhaps, they have not thought heretofore, we will obtain their co-operation, for we are confident that the lawyers of South Carolina, as a whole, sympathize with the court in its efforts to expedite the business coming before it."

Arnold v. *Carolina Power & Light Co.*, 168 S.C. 163, 167 S.E. 234, 238 (1933).

[23]Alabama, Arizona, Colorado, Georgia, Indiana, Missouri, Oklahoma, Texas, Washington.

it. It is therefore highly doubtful that the compulsory petition for rehearing, which unnecessarily burdens counsel and to a lesser extent the court of appeals, is of any value.

Oregon has an unusual provision (Rule 10.10) whereby the petition for leave to appeal filed in the Supreme Court "serve[s] as the petition for reconsideration in the Court of Appeals." If the Court of Appeals fails to take any action within 10 days, the Supreme Court will proceed to determine whether to grant review. This is the converse of the Arizona practice in which the petition for rehearing in the Court of Appeals in substance serves as the petition for review in the Supreme Court. The Oregon practice would seem to be superior, since it enables counsel to write a petition addressed primarily to the Supreme Court and thus to concentrate on the factors which might induce that court to grant review. These are not necessarily the same as would be appropriate for a petition for rehearing in the court below, which experience shows is much less likely to be granted. The obvious purpose is to give the Court of Appeals the first opportunity to correct its own errors. This advantage must be weighed against the additional burden imposed on the Court of Appeals and the short lengthening of the litigation.

In general, a majority of the voting judges is needed to grant a petition for rehearing. Under New Mexico Rule 19(b), however, two out of five votes are sufficient.

Rule 51.1 of the United States Supreme Court, which applies to rehearings after decisions on the merits, states that a petition for rehearing "will not be granted except at the instance of a Justice who concurred in the judgment or decision and with the concurrence of a majority of the Court." This embodies the rule the Court had described as "well settled" in 1874. *Ambler v. Whipple,* 23 Wall. (90 U.S.) 278, 281–282. New Jersey Rule 2:11–7 is similar. This provision has no effect when the personnel of the Court has not changed after the decision as to which rehearing is sought, for a majority favoring rehearing cannot be obtained unless a member of the previous majority concurs. The obviously intended effect was to prevent the granting of rehearing from turning entirely on the votes of newly appointed Justices, and the encouragement that would give to petitioning whenever a close division of the Court was followed by a change in the Court's membership. The increased likelihood that decisions might be good only for that long would diminish the precedential effect of Supreme Court rulings generally, and give more force to the not entirely inaccurate impression that Supreme Court decisions reflect the position of the Court's membership at any particular time.

This self-imposed restriction has not precluded review on rehearing when the Court has divided four-to-four and a new Justice has been appointed. This is perhaps the largest class of cases in which the Supreme Court grants hearings after decisions on the merits.[24] That means that in such cases five out of the original eight judges joined in recognizing that in such circumstances an authoritative decision is desirable. Similarly, the state supreme courts which sit in divisions frequently rehear when the division is closely divided, even without a petition for rehearing.

9.3   Time for Filing Petitions for Rehearing

The rules or statutes of all states but Maine prescribe the number of days after the entry of the original decision or judgment within which a petition for a rehearing must be filed. Except for five days in Rhode Island, the time ranges from 10 to 30 days. As shown in the following list, all but a few states have chosen 10, 14, 15, 20 or 30 days:

5 days — Rhode Island;

10 days — Alaska, Connecticut, Georgia (and during the same term), Hawaii, Kansas Court of Appeals, Massachusetts, Minnesota, Montana, New Hampshire, New Jersey, New Mexico, Ohio, South Carolina, Tennessee, Virginia (10 days to file notice of intention, 30 to file petition);

14 days — Alabama, Colorado, Iowa, Louisiana Supreme Court, North Dakota, Pennsylvania, Vermont;

15 days — Arizona, California, Delaware, Florida, Mississippi, Missouri, Nevada, Oklahoma, Texas, Wyoming;

17 days — Arkansas;

20 days — Indiana, Kansas Supreme Court, Kentucky, Michigan, Nebraska, North Carolina, South Dakota, Utah, Washington, Wisconsin;

---

[24]E.g., *Gray* v. *Powell,* 312 U.S. 666, 313 U.S. 596 (1941); *Halliburton* v. *Walker,* 326 U.S. 696, 327 U.S. 812 (1946).

21 days — Idaho, Illinois;[25]

30 days — Louisiana Court of Appeals, Maryland, New York, Oregon, Virginia, West Virginia.

Fourteen days are allowed in the United States courts of appeals, and 25 days in the United States Supreme Court.[26]

Ten days should be long enough to prepare a petition for rehearing, but that overlooks the fact that by happenstance 10 days may include either two or four weekend days when printers and at least clerical staffs of law offices may not be at work. Fourteen days or any period consisting of a multiple of seven provides the same number of working days for all cases and is therefore more equitable. Several states now fix all of their time limitations in multiples of seven for this reason.[27] Virginia requires that notice of intent to file a petition for rehearing be filed in 10 days but the actual petition in 30. If a period longer than 14 or 15 days is allowed for filing a petition, requiring earlier notice to be given a successful party and the court has the advantage of not keeping them in uncertainty for too long as to the finality of the judgment.

The number of days for filing a petition for rehearing runs from the "entry of judgment" below,[28] the "judgment or decision,"[29] the "filing of the opinion,"[30] the "decision"[31] or "order,"[32] or similar phrase. In general, these are likely to be the same day, but counsel should verify what the practice is in his jurisdiction. He should note, however, that the time does not run from the date the party or lawyer learns of the judgment, opinion or order, which is likely to be several days after entry if the clerk notifies the parties by mail. The result is that in actuality less time is allowed for preparing the petition than the number of days mentioned in the rule.

In most but not all jurisdictions, the time for filing a petition for rehearing may be extended or shortened by order of the court or a single judge. Extensions of time are not, however, favored or granted without good reason.

---

[25]The Illinois Supreme Court Rules Committee has recommended that this be reduced to 14 days.

[26]Federal Rule of Appellate Procedure 40(a); United States Supreme Court Rule 51.1.

[27]Alabama, Colorado, Illinois, Iowa, Pennsylvania, Vermont, Washington.

[28]Federal Appellate Rule 40; Colorado Appellate Rule 40; Pennsylvania Appellate Rule 2542.

[29]United States Supreme Court Rule 51.1.

[30]Hawaii Rule 5(a); Illinois Rule 367(a).

[31]Oregon Rule 10.20.

[32]Florida Rule 9.330.

Historically, courts had power to modify their judgments or orders up to the end of the term, even in the absence of a timely petition for rehearing. And a timely petition filed but not acted upon within the term or at the beginning of a new term would vest the court with power to change the judgment during the remainder of the term. With the "term" (as distinct from a session) in some courts, including the United States Supreme Court, extending for a year, the result was that judgments could be modified or vacated during periods much longer than the short times in which the rules permitted petitions for rehearing to be filed, plus the usually short additional time for their disposition.

In order to eliminate the fortuitous effect of the end of a term upon a court's power to act in various respects, the Federal Judicial Code was amended in the 1948 recodification to provide that United States courts should be deemed always open for the purpose of filing papers, and that

> "The continued existence or expiration of a term of court in no way affects the power of the court to do any act or take any proceeding." 28 U.S.C. §452.

Thereafter in 1963 Congress, when abolishing terms in the district courts, substituted the word "session" for "term."

This would seem to have left only the time limits prescribed by statute or rule, extendible only as specifically provided. The abolition of terms can, however, also be interpreted as leaving the time in which judgments can be modified without any limit except the court's good judgment. That anyone intended such a result is highly unlikely.

Nevertheless, in 1957, the Supreme Court of the United States, by a vote of four-to-three, without mentioning the term rule or any other limitation, declared that "[w]e have consistently ruled that the interest in finality of litigation must yield where the interest of justice would make unfair the strict application of our rules." *United States* v. *Ohio Power Co.*, 353 U.S. 98, 99 (1957). Mr. Justice Harlan, in dissent, urged that

> "Rule 58, by marking the end of a case in this Court, is intended to further the law's deep-rooted policy that adjudication must at some time become final. I think we should follow it."

The effect of the abolition of the end of term rule by §452, he believed, "was to leave the federal courts untrammeled in establishing their own rules of finality."

Justice Harlan concluded that the history of that provision, which was modeled upon Rule 6(c) of the Federal Rules of Civil Procedure, demonstrated that its

"purpose was 'to prevent reliance upon the continued existence of a term as a source of power to disturb the finality of a judgment upon grounds other than those stated in these rules.' "[33]

In 1965, the Supreme Court reaffirmed the approach taken in *Ohio Power*, with only Mr. Justice Harlan dissenting. *Gondeck* v. *Pan American World Airways*, 382 U.S. 25 (1965).[34]

That "the interests of justice" were served by the Court's action in the *Ohio Power* and *Gondeck* cases cannot be doubted, at least if the public interest in having litigation come to a definite final conclusion is not in itself deemed an important "interest of justice." After the Supreme Court had denied certiorari in *Ohio Power*, a tax case, it granted certiorari in subsequent decisions conflicting with *Ohio Power* below, decided them on the merits in a manner inconsistent with that decision and then reversed *Ohio Power* to insure "uniformity in the application of the principles announced" in those cases. *Gondeck* presented an even more compelling demand for uniformity: subsequent litigation in a different court of appeals (with which the Supreme Court agreed) had established that a survivor of another identically situated employee killed in the same accident was entitled to the compensation denied to *Gondeck's* survivor, although more than three years had elapsed since the denial of Gondeck's petition for certiorari and timely petition for rehearing.

However, in 1970 and 1977 the Court refused review in situations substantially indistinguishable from *Ohio Power* and *Gondeck*, and equally compelling from the standpoint of the unfairness of different treatment for persons in identical situations. *Weed* v. *Bilbrey*, 400 U.S. 982 (1970); *Economy Finance Corp.* v. *United States*, 431 U.S. 926 (1977).[35] This may well indicate that a somewhat differently constituted Supreme Court has now adopted Mr. Justice Harlan's approach; but the majority has given no explanation for its action.

---

[33]The quotation was from the Advisory Committee Report which explained the amendment to the Committee Rule which subsequently "was taken bodily into §452."
[34]A more detailed analysis of these and related Supreme Court decisions appears in R. Stern and E. Gressman, SUPREME COURT PRACTICE, Sec. 15.3 (5th ed., 1978).
[35]In *Weed*, only Justices Douglas and Black dissented, and in *Economy Finance*, no one.

The extent to which state courts stick to the time limits specified in their rules and statutes governing rehearings is difficult to determine, in part because the judicial disposition of petitions for rehearings is often not shown in the reports or indexed. (As indicated in the Introduction, *supra,* state case law is beyond the scope of this book.) It is to be doubted, however, that many of the states are as liberal as the United States Supreme Court in disregarding time limits prescribed by rule or statute.[36]

A change in decisional law will always produce a lack of uniformity in the treatment of those who litigated before and after the change occurred. Certainly in general, "every plaintiff who loses his claim cannot reinstate his action when a rule of law favorable to him is declared, either by the legislature or the court," as Mr. Justice Douglas admitted in his dissent in *Weed* v. *Bilbrey* (400 U.S. at 984). There will be few cases in which the resulting lack of uniformity would produce results which would seem as unjust as those in *Gondeck* and *Weed.* On the whole, the pervasive interest in making all judgments final after a definite date, which applies to all litigation, would seem to outweigh the occasional injustice which may result from adherence to fixed time limitations.[37] Litigation takes long enough as it is, and courts should not create routes which enable parties to prolong uncertainty for perhaps years after the final appellate court has taken what anyone reading the rules would think was the final step.

9.4 The Contents of the Petition

A petition for rehearing should not be a full-scale brief, divided into the same sections as a brief. It should not reargue what was presented to the court in the briefs previously filed. That would be a waste of time both for counsel and the court, would be of no avail and would usually be impossible since court rules often limit the length of petitions for rehearing.

The Federal Rules of Appellate Procedure now allow 15 pages;[38] Alaska, 3; New Hampshire, 10; Mississippi, 25; New Jersey, 20 printed and 25 typed; Illinois, 20 printed and 27

---

[36]Cf. D. Louisell and R. Degnan, *Rehearing in American Appellate Courts,* 44 Cal. L. Rev. 627, 645–646 (1956).

[37]Professors Louisell and Degnan, writing in 1956, concluded that the few decisions which relied upon the term rule instead of the time limits prescribed by court rules "are not surprising," but "are deplorable." *Id.* at 646, n. 78.

[38]Rule 40(b).

typed. Nevada, Pennsylvania, Utah and Vermont adhere to the 10-printed and 15-typed limit previously found in the Federal Appellate Rules.

Court rules prescribe what a petition for rehearing should contain in various degrees of detail. United States Supreme Court Rule 51.1 merely states that

"[s]uch petition must briefly and distinctly state its grounds."

Federal Appellate Rule 40(a) and a number of the state rules (e.g., Illinois Rule 367(b)) require, substantially in the words of the federal rule:

"The petition shall state with particularity the points of law or fact which in the opinion of the petitioner the court has overlooked or misapprehended and shall contain such argument in support of the petition as the petitioner desires to present."

Pennsylvania Appellate Rule 2544(a) is more precise:

"(a) General rule. The application for reargument need not be set forth in numbered paragraphs in the manner of a pleading, and shall contain the following (which shall, insofar as practicable, be set forth in the order stated):

(1) A reference to the order in question or the portions thereof sought to be reargued, and the date of its entry in the appellate court. If the order is voluminous, it may, if more convenient, be appended to the application.

(2) A specification with particularity of the points of law or fact supposed to have been overlooked or misapprehended by the court.

(3) A concise statement of the reasons relied upon for allowance of reargument. See Rule 2543 (considerations governing allowance of reargument) [quoted at p. 448, *supra*].

(4) There shall be appended to the application a copy of any opinions delivered relating to the order with respect to which reargument is sought, and, if reference thereto is necessary to ascertain the grounds of the application for reargument, slip opinions in related cases. If whatever is required by this paragraph to be appended to the application is voluminous, it may, if more convenient, be separately presented."

The Pennsylvania form would seem to be highly suitable for any court which does not prescribe a different form of its own.

Pennsylvania Rule 2544(b) also provides that the application itself shall be the only document filed by petitioner; no separate brief will be accepted. This is the practice in the federal appellate courts and in most of the states, where the rules refer only to the filing of a petition (or application or motion) without more. A few states require or permit a separate short petition stating the points and a supporting memorandum or brief containing the supporting argument.[39] There is no good reason, however, for submitting two documents. A single memorandum (entitled petition, motion or application) which first states briefly the basis of the request for rehearing and is followed by the supporting argument is adequate, and may be shorter and simpler to prepare.

The petition or supporting brief should emphasize the new factors which justify a rehearing, not reargue the case or the reasons why the court was wrong. It has been suggested[40] that the petition should be limited to the reasons why the court should reconsider, and not include the reasons why the court should change its decision in the manner requested by the petition. That may be true in some situations, as where the ground for rehearing is availability of a tie-breaking judge after an equal division of the court. Similarly, a new conflicting decision by a higher court will speak for itself, and the same may be true when a new conflict among courts of equal or lower rank provides a new reason for review. But in most cases the court will want to know why the new or overlooked fact or authority should or might lead to a change in result. Merely to inform a court of appeals that a court of equal stature has reached a contrary result might not persuade it to reconsider without a supporting comparative analysis of the two opinions.

Merely to establish reason to reconsider might also be sufficient if the court's only option was to order a reargument. But frequently courts will determine what should be done, and do it, upon the basis of the petition and response without more. In Illinois, for example, the reconsideration is ordinarily based upon the petition, answer and reply, if any, and is more likely to result in a modified opinion than a second oral argument.[41] Accordingly, it is advisable for the petition to point out why the

---

[39]In Idaho and Utah the supporting memorandum is to be separate from the petition, which is a pleading or statement of points. Idaho Rule 42 and APPELLATE ADVO-CACY HANDBOOK FOR THE UTAH SUPREME COURT, p. 25. New Mexico Rule 19 provides that the motion shall state the points "with particularity" but "shall not contain argument"; the filing of a supporting brief is optional. Under Alabama Rule 40 "the application for rehearing may be made separately or may be included at the beginning of applicant's brief."

[40]D. Louisell and R. Degnan, *Rehearing in American Appellate Courts*, 44 Cal. L. Rev. 627, 644 (1956).

[41]E. Kionka, PRACTITIONER'S HANDBOOK FOR APPEALS TO THE ILLINOIS SUPREME AND APPELLATE COURTS, p. 31 (Illinois Law Enforcement Commission and Illinois Institute for Continuing Legal Education, 1978).

new or overlooked or misunderstood factor requires a change in the initial decision.

A petition for rehearing need not be divided into various sections in the manner required for briefs. The grounds advanced should be set forth at the beginning, and then the argument which justifies them. Whether headings should be supplied should depend upon the number of points raised and their length. Often this will have to be done very briefly, where the rules limit petitions to a small number of pages.

The physical form of the petition and response otherwise should be the same as for briefs in the same jurisdiction. (See Sec. 7.37, *supra.*) That would apply to the method of printing or duplicating and the content of the cover. Some rules prescribe the color of the covers for petitions for rehearing.[42] Others do not, in which case, if possible, colors not previously used for the briefs should be chosen.

The number of copies to be filed and served will usually be the same as for briefs in the same court, although sometimes more copies of the petition may be needed for submission to a larger number of judges. The petition and response should, of course, be served on opposing counsel.

Illinois has an unusual but reasonable provision for petitions filed in its Supreme Court: "a copy of the petition and any order changing the time for filing the petition shall be delivered or mailed to the official reporter." Rule 367(c). This enables him to withhold printing the original opinion until the court acts on the petition for rehearing.

9.5 Responses to Petitions for Rehearing

In the normal course, a party is entitled to meet the arguments submitted to a court by his adversary, particularly when the effort may be to overturn a judgment in his favor. The trend with respect to petitions for rehearing has been in the opposite direction.

Many states specify the time in which responses to petitions for rehearing must be filed, as shown in the following list:

5 days — Florida, Minnesota, Rhode Island, Texas;
7 days — Missouri, Montana;

---

[42]E.g., light green in Illinois (Rule 344(c)); tan in the United States Supreme Court (Rule 33.2).

8 days — California;
10 days — Michigan, Nevada, Ohio, South Dakota;
14 days — Alabama (2 weeks optional);
15 days — Arizona;
20 days — Indiana, Kentucky, Nebraska, Utah;
21 days — Virginia.

Arkansas Rule 20(b) (1979) allows respondent to file his brief "on the following Monday (in the Supreme Court) or Wednesday (in the Court of Appeals) or may on that day obtain further extension of one week."

The rules governing the United States Supreme Court, the federal courts of appeals and most of the states now provide, in the words of Federal Appellate Rule 40(a):

"No answer to a petition for rehearing will be received unless requested by the court, but a petition for rehearing will ordinarily not be granted in the absence of such a request."

See also United States Supreme Court Rule 51.3. A number of the state rules are substantially identical.[43]

The reason why most jurisdictions do not authorize a response as a matter of course is that in most cases a response is unnecessary. A quick perusal of the vast majority of petitions for rehearing is sufficient to convince the courts that no basis for reconsideration is presented. For the courts to wait for an answer in those cases would unnecessarily prolong the litigation, and for the victorious attorney to prepare one would be a waste of his time and his client's money.

Counsel could not be certain, however, that this would be the court's reaction in his case. If the court's rules left the matter open, he would accordingly feel that his duty to his client required him to reply. For the court to re-open the case or, worse, reverse its original decision because the contentions in the petition for rehearing remained unchallenged could be disastrous. The rules prohibiting responses not requested by the court take the attorney off the spot of having to decide for himself whether a response is necessary. He is adequately protected by the provision in most rules that a petition will not be granted without giving him an opportunity to submit a reply.

Some of the rules which so provide, like Federal Appellate

---

[43]Colorado, Delaware, Hawaii, Idaho, Illinois, Iowa, Maryland, Massachusetts, Mississippi, New Hampshire, New Jersey, New Mexico, North Dakota, Oklahoma, Pennsylvania, Tennessee, Vermont, Washington.

Rule 40(a) quoted above, contain the qualifying word "ordinarily," while others, like United States Supreme Court Rule 51.3, do not. But the Supreme Court has held that it has power to waive limitations imposed by its own rules. It has granted rehearing without requesting an answer when the Court has divided equally and a new Justice was available to break the tie,[44] and when a subsequent decision of the Court while rehearing was pending required reversal.[45] In such circumstances the granting of the rehearing rests on considerations with which the Court is fully familiar and can evaluate for itself; what counsel could contribute would be of little effect. The Court's present position, however, seems to call for a reply in virtually all situations where a grant would be likely.[46]

Thus, whether the rule is mandatory in text or not, courts may on occasion proceed without responses in situations of that sort. But they are not likely to do so in other circumstances when a response would be helpful to the court as well as to the respondent. Since respondent will be supporting the court's initial decision, the judges will normally want to know what he has to say with respect to points they have allegedly overlooked, misapprehended or otherwise mishandled before they change their position.

Several states provide for a response only if the rehearing is granted. E.g., Wyoming. The theory is that granting the rehearing does not decide anything except that the matter will be reconsidered. So long as the courts go no further, and do not change the decision in any way before hearing the opposing party, this procedure in substance is similar to requiring a response only on request from the court.

Illinois Rule 367(d) gives the court the option of requiring a response before or after granting the rehearing. In either event, the party opposing the petition has 21 days from the court's request or the granting of rehearing to file an answer, and the petitioner has 14 days after the due date of the answer to file his reply.

Like the petition for rehearing, the response, if one is called for, also should not reargue the case. The court will already have

---

[44]See R. Stern and E. Gressman, SUPREME COURT PRACTICE, p. 778, n. 3 (5th ed., 1978).

[45]E.g., *Forgett* v. *United States*, 390 U.S. 203 (1968). A copy of the essential portion of the *Forgett* petition appears in Stern and Gressman, *id.* at 966–969.

[46]Stern and Gressman, *id.* at 778–779.

manifested its acceptance of the respondent's position in its initial decision. The response should therefore be limited to correcting or otherwise dealing with the new matter referred to in the petition, such as by showing that the alleged conflicting authority is really distinguishable, or that the alleged overlooked fact did not appear in the record, or in any event, would not lead to a different result.

9.6 Rehearings in Banc[47]

Rehearings in banc are possible when cases are originally heard or decided by less than the full appellate court. This occurs in a few state supreme courts which usually or sometimes sit in divisions or departments, such as Missouri and Washington, or in panels of less than a full bench in order to conserve judicial manpower. See Sec. 1.3, *supra.* Subsequent review by the entire court can be ordered if a case results in less than a majority of a full court concurring in the decision, or if a justice who heard the case so requests, or if a majority of the court so orders on its own motion or petition of a party. Which of the above conditions governs depends upon the rules and practices of each court; to allow rehearing in any or all of the above circumstances would be entirely reasonable. Indeed, the combination of all might be the most appropriate. Perhaps the most likely to be successful (though still not very likely) is a request when there has been a dissent, and there is good reason to believe that a majority of the full bench will agree with it.

Whether intermediate appellate courts can rehear in banc depends on how they are organized. In some states, each division or district is a separate court consisting of three judges.[48] In other states some of the divisions have three judges, while others in the more populous areas often have more.[49] Other intermediate courts are regarded as a single appellate court.[50]

---

[47]I would have thought that the correct spelling of this French phrase was *en banc,* and many courts so spell it; but Federal Appellate Rule 35 uses "in banc" unitalicized. Webster's Dictionary has it both ways. Since the federal rule, despite its conversion of one word but not the other into English, has nationwide scope, I follow its fractured French here.

[48]Oklahoma, Wisconsin.

[49]Intermediate courts sit in divisions some of which include more than three judges in California, Florida, Illinois, Louisiana, Missouri, New Jersey, New York, Ohio, Pennsylvania, Tennessee, Texas, Washington. The New York Appellate Division usually sits in panels of five.

[50]Georgia, Iowa, Kansas, Kentucky, Maryland, Michigan, New Mexico, North Carolina, Oregon.

Most of these courts usually sit in panels of three, although a number of them can and occasionally do sit in banc, or at least in larger panels than the usual three. In Iowa, the five-judge court of appeals always sits in banc, as does the six-judge court of appeals in Arkansas.[51] In some jurisdictions the rules provide that a greater number of judges than three shall sit when different panels are in conflict, or when there has been a dissent. In general, however, the state intermediate courts do not sit in banc.[52]

Each of the United States courts of appeals is a separate court. Although they hear cases in panels of three, they are allowed to sit in banc, both to hear an appeal in the first instance, which they do very infrequently, or on rehearing.

A court of appeals hears an appeal in banc initially, usually on its own motion, when it regards a case as of exceptional importance, or perhaps is aware of a conflict.[53] Rule 35(c) of the Federal Rules of Appellate Procedure, as amended in 1979, permits a party to suggest that an appeal be heard initially in banc no later than the date on which appellee's brief is filed. Such a hearing is also required in suits under the Federal Election Campaign Act challenging the constitutionality of the statute[54] upon certification of the constitutional questions by the district court to the court of appeals. Initial hearings in banc are very rare.

In the more usual situations, which are still not very usual, a court will consider whether to grant a rehearing in banc. Such rehearings impose a heavy burden on the appellate court. The Second Circuit has said that the in banc procedure is "often an unwieldy and cumbersome device generating little more than delay, costs and continuing uncertainty that can ill be afforded at a time of burgeoning calendars." *Green* v. *Santa Fe Industries, Inc.,* 533 F.2d 1309, 1310 (1976), reversed (on other grounds), 430 U.S. 462 (1977). The Fifth and Ninth Circuit courts of appeals, prior to the Act of October 20, 1978, were composed

---

[51]Iowa Appellate Operating Procedures, Sec. 3 (1977). As to Arkansas, see Sec. 1.3, note 25, *supra*.

[52]The Pennsylvania Commonwealth Court, which usually sits in panels of three, may hear argument in banc "on the initiative of the Court, or at the request of either party and approved by the assigned judge." (Pennsylvania Rule 3713.) It may hear argument in banc in cases originally argued before a single judge. (Rule 3723.)

[53]For example, *Radiant Burners, Inc.* v. *American Gas Association,* 320 F.2d 314 (CA 7), cert. denied, 375 U.S. 929 (1963).

[54]2 U.S.C. §437(h), discussed in R. Stern and E. Gressman, SUPREME COURT PRACTICE, pp. 128–129 (5th ed., 1978).

of 15 and 13 judges, all of whom would sit in banc unless unable to for individual reasons. Under the 1978 statute, which enlarged those courts by 11 and 10 judges, respectively, a court composed of over 15 judges may "constitute itself into administrative units," and "perform its en banc function by such number of members of its en banc courts as may be prescribed by rule of the court of appeals." Act of October 20, 1978, §6, P.L. 95–486, 92 Stat. 1633.[55] New Ninth Circuit Rule 25 (1980) provides for in banc courts composed of the chief judge and 10 other circuit judges drawn by lot, with the court reserving the right to order a rehearing by the full court "in appropriate cases." In October 1980 the Fifth Circuit was divided into two parts, with Alabama, Florida and Georgia assigned to a new Eleventh Circuit. Act of October 14, 1980, P.L. 96–452, 94 Stat. 1994. Neither part now has over 15 judges.

The Supreme Court of the United States does not regard an intra-circuit conflict as a ground for certiorari[56] since such differences can be resolved by each court of appeals by itself. Sometimes, however, it has taken an intracircuit conflict into account.[57] How the Court will regard the randomly chosen in banc courts composed of less than half of the Ninth Circuit judges remains to be determined. A conflict among them should be sufficient. To require such conflicts to be first resolved by a full circuit bench of over 20 judges would be both impracticable and inconsistent with the theory and purpose of the statute authorizing such a large court to prescribe its own in banc procedure.

The Second Circuit, which seldom hears a case in banc, has found it unnecessary to hear cases "of such extraordinary importance that we are confident that the Supreme Court will accept these matters under its certiorari jurisdiction."[58]

In the United States courts of appeals under Federal Appellate Rule 35(b), no party has the right to move for a rehearing or hearing in banc; he may only *suggest* that such a hearing is

---

[55]The Ninth Circuit has established three administrative units, but with all of the judges rotating among all three units. Ninth Circuit Rule 23 (1980). The Ninth Circuit was not divided because of the problems which might have resulted from allocating the northern and southern portions of California (which has the bulk of the population) to two different circuits.

[56]*Davis* v. *United States*, 417 U.S. 333, 340 (1974); and Mr. Justice Harlan, *Manning the Dikes*, 13 Rec. of N.Y.C. Bar Assoc. 541, 552 (1958).

[57]Cases are collected in R. Stern and E. Gressman, SUPREME COURT PRACTICE, p. 276 (5th ed., 1978).

[58]*Green* v. *Santa Fe Industries, Inc.*, 533 F.2d 1309, 1310 (CA 2, 1976), reversed (on other grounds), 430 U.S. 462 (1977).

appropriate. The difference is that the court need not vote or enter an order on a suggestion. The clerk submits a copy of the suggestion to all members of the court in regular active service and to the members of the panel which decided the case; that may include judges from other circuit or district courts or senior district or circuit judges. Only if any one of those judges so requests will a vote be taken as to whether a rehearing shall be held. Only the judges in regular active service in the circuit may vote, and rehearing will not be allowed unless a majority of those judges vote for it.

The substance of the suggestion for a rehearing in banc should not be the same as that of an ordinary petition for rehearing by the panel which decided the case. The emphasis must be upon the two grounds specified in Federal Appellate Rule 35 for in banc rehearing:

> "Such a hearing or rehearing is not favored and ordinarily will not be ordered except (1) when consideration by the full court is necessary to secure or maintain uniformity of its decisions, or (2) when the proceeding involves a question of exceptional importance."

Because counsel frequently file suggestions without conforming to these requirements, Seventh Circuit Rule 16(b) now requires that

> "Suggestions that an appeal be reheard in banc shall state in a concise sentence at the beginning of the petition why the appeal is of exceptional importance or with what decision of the United States Supreme Court, this court, or another court of appeals, the panel decision is claimed to be in conflict."

The Third, Fifth and Sixth Circuit rules go even farther; they provide[59] that a lawyer petitioning for rehearing must file a statement in substantially the following form:

> "(Designate one or both relied on)
> "I express a belief, based on a reasoned and studied professional judgment, that the panel decision is contrary to the following decision(s) of the United States Court of Appeals for the Sixth Circuit, [or the Supreme Court of the United States] and that consideration by the full Court is necessary to secure and maintain uniformity of decisions in this Court: [citing specifically the case or cases].

---

[59]Third Circuit Rule 22; Fifth Circuit Rule 16.2.2; Sixth Circuit Rule 14(b). The rules of the three circuits differ in minor particulars. The Sixth Circuit requires that the statement be contained "on the first page of the petition."

"I express a belief, based on a reasoned and studied professional judgment, that this appeal involves one or more questions of exceptional importance: [set forth each question in one sentence].

. . . .
"Attorney of record for . . . .
"Counsel are reminded that *en banc* consideration of a case is an extraordinary measure, and that in every case the duty of counsel is fully discharged without filing a suggestion for rehearing *en banc* unless the case meets the rigid standards of Rule 35(a) of the Federal Rules of Appellate Procedure. Counsel are further reminded that the filing of a petition for rehearing or suggestion for rehearing *en banc* are not prerequisites to the filing of a petition for certiorari."

The suggestion may but need not be included in or bound with a petition for rehearing to the panel which heard the case. In either event it must be filed within the time limits prescribed for such a petition, 14 days. The panel will vote on the petition, but suggestions will be treated in the manner described above. Most often the petition for rehearing and suggestion for rehearing in banc are joined in a single document which bears both titles, to wit, "Petition for Rehearing and Suggestion for Rehearing in Banc." To entitle it a "Petition for Rehearing in Banc," which is often done, is to betray one's ignorance; there is no such thing.

The petition and the suggestion, however, should not automatically be joined. The suggestion is appropriate only in the two circumstances set forth in Rule 35 and in the separate circuit rules which are intended to convince counsel that they must strictly conform to that rule. To impose the suggestion upon all of the judges of a court of appeals is a waste of valuable judicial time which should be reserved for cases which warrant it. Other grounds for rehearing should be submitted in a petition addressed only to the panel. Although the grounds may overlap, as when a conflict arises after the panel's initial ruling, they often will not. If the panel was aware of the conflict and refused to follow the conflicting decision, rehearing before the panel because of it would be fruitless, for it had neither overlooked nor misapprehended the ground for reconsideration. Such a conflict might, however, be a good reason for suggesting a rehearing in banc which would be considered in part by different judges who had not previously made up their minds. But if the panel had not been aware of the conflict, that would be a ground for requesting both a rehearing by a panel and argument in banc.

The Seventh Circuit has adopted a practice designed to call to the full court's attention the existence of an intracircuit or intercircuit conflict before a panel's decision becomes final. That court's Rule 16(e) requires that a proposed decision which would overrule a prior decision of the court or create a conflict between or among circuits not be published unless it is first circulated among the other active members of the court, and a majority do not vote to hear in banc.[60] When no rehearing is ordered by the full court, and the panel adheres to its published position, the opinion is to contain a footnote stating that it was circulated and that no judge, or no majority, favored a rehearing in banc on the question (describing it). The Fourth Circuit's practice is similar.

The question has arisen as to whether the order setting a case for rehearing in banc in itself vacates the prior decision of the three-judge panel. This becomes significant if the panel has reversed the trial court and the court sitting in banc then divides evenly, as has occasionally happened. If the panel's order is vacated, the decision of the trial court stands affirmed by an equally divided court; otherwise the panel's reversal remains in effect.

The courts are divided as to the correct solution of this problem; the Supreme Court recently denied a petition to review an equally divided Fourth Circuit's affirmance of the trial court, not the appellate panel.[61] The Fifth and Sixth Circuits provide by rule that "the effect of the granting of a hearing *en banc* shall be to vacate the previous opinion and judgment of this court."[62] The Third and Seventh Circuits have similarly determined that "an order granting rehearing in banc vacates the panel decision, so if the court in banc should be equally divided, judgment of the district court and not the judgment of the panel will be affirmed."[63] The Second Circuit reached the same result by a four-to-two vote in *Drake Bakeries* v. *Local 50,* 294 F.2d 399, 400 (CA 2, 1961), affirmed on other grounds, 370 U.S. 254, 255, n. 1 (1962). The Court of Appeals for the District of Columbia

---

[60]A panel may in its discretion similarly circulate a proposed opinion "which would establish a new rule of procedure."

[61]*United States* v. *Mandel,* 591 F.2d 1347, 602 F.2d 653, 609 F.2d 1076 (CA 4, 1979), cert. denied, 445 U.S. 961 (1980).

[62]Fifth Circuit Rule 17; Sixth Circuit Rule 14a.

[63]PRACTITIONER'S HANDBOOK FOR APPEALS TO THE UNITED STATES COURT OF APPEALS FOR THE SEVENTH CIRCUIT, p. 48 (1979), prepared by the circuit executive and clerk in consultation with Circuit Judge Tone; Third Circuit, INTERNAL OPERATING PROCEDURES, Part O(3)(f).

Circuit, however, sitting in banc in *Bulluck* v. *Washington,* 468 F.2d 1096, 1122 (1972), declared that the order "granting rehearing *en banc* did not vacate the judgment of the Division"; accordingly, the equally divided in banc court vacated its order granting rehearing, leaving the panel's judgment of affirmance in effect. Since in that case the panel had affirmed the district court, whether the panel's or the district court's decision remained in effect made no difference.

In 1900 the Supreme Court had construed a decision of an equally divided Supreme Court of the Territory of New Mexico as letting stand the prior decision of that court and not of the lower court. *Carmichael* v. *Eberle,* 177 U.S. 63 (1900). The supreme courts of Florida and North Carolina have also concluded that the first appellate decision stands and not the judgment below.[64] The language of Rule 35 of the Federal Rules of Appellate Procedure throws no light on this question, which may lie within the discretion of each court of appeals and be dependent upon the precise words of the order granting the rehearing in banc in the particular case or the court's own rules.

9.7 Successive Petitions for Rehearing

The rules of some courts explicitly prohibit successive petitions for rehearing. Thus, United States Supreme Court Rule 51.4 states flatly that

> "Consecutive petitions for rehearings, and petitions for rehearing that are out of time under this Rule, will not be received."

Even without a rule, a request for a court to rehear its prior denial of rehearing would almost invariably be summarily denied. It would, of course, not be within the time limits for a petition for rehearing challenging the original decision.

As with other time limits imposed by its own rules, however, the Supreme Court does not regard this defect as jurisdictional, which means that it retains the power to grant leave to file successive petitions for rehearing or petitions filed out of time. As shown in Sec. 9.3, *supra,* it has occasionally done so when an intervening conflicting decision was called to its attention, al-

---

[64]*Pitton* v. *Atlantic Coast Line Railroad,* 144 Fla. 462, 198 So. 503 (1940); 131 ALR 1003 (to which an Annotation on the subject is attached); *Carolina Power and Light Co.* v. *Merrimack Mutual Fire Insurance Co.,* 240 N.C. 196, 81 S.E.2d 404 (1954).

though it may have changed its policy in this respect. The procedure for a party seeking such relief is to file a motion for leave to file a second or out-of-time petition for rehearing, with the petition attached. The reasons for requesting leave to file out of time or successively should be stated in summary form in the motion for leave to file and be explained further in the petition.

The rule on rehearings in the federal courts of appeals (Federal Rule of Appellate Procedure 40) contains no prohibition against successive petitions. Rule 2 authorizes those courts to suspend the provisions "of any of these rules in a particular case on application of a party, or on its own motion . . . in the interest of expediting the decision, or for other good cause shown." Courts of appeals could rely on this provision to allow the filing of late or successive petitions for rehearing by the same party. They would be likely to do so, if at all, only in compelling circumstances, such as an intervening controlling or conflicting decision. These are the usual reasons for granting timely applications for rehearing.

A few states provide specifically that a second application for rehearing may be filed if the original opinion was modified or reversed. Alabama Rule 40; Idaho Rule 42; Oklahoma Court of Appeals Rule 3.12. Texas Rule 458 permits a further motion for rehearing "if the Court of Civil Appeals hands down an opinion in connection with the overruling of a motion for rehearing."

A petition for rehearing filed by the original successful party who then loses on his opponent's petition for rehearing should not be regarded as a second[65] or consecutive petition. This is his first time to challenge an entirely different judgment which is adverse to him, and it is conceivable that the court may have blundered the second time instead of the first. The court is unlikely to be willing to consider a matter a third time, but such cases have occurred.[66] Only if a rule is specific in this respect should such a petition be barred.

Illinois Rule 367(e) does contain such a bar to more than one rehearing in the state's Appellate Court, but not the Su-

---

[65]Oklahoma Court of Appeals Rule 3.12 so specifies, but Oklahoma Supreme Court Rule 29 does not.

[66]*Droste* v. *Kerner,* 34 Ill.2d 495, 217 N.E.2d 73 (1966), in which the Supreme Court of Illinois first reversed itself on appellant's petition for rehearing and then again on appellee's petition (those facts do not appear in the final opinion, which alone is reported); *Atkins* v. *Schmutz Mfg. Co.,* 401 F.2d 731 (CA 4, 1968), reheard in banc twice, 435 F.2d 527 (CA 4, 1970).

preme Court.[67] The Committee Comment to this provision explains that

> "This new provision is applicable only to the Appellate Court. When that Court has twice considered a case, once initially, and a second time on rehearing, there would seem to be no need for further consideration, especially when there is a higher court from which relief can be sought."

It is likely that the same principles govern practice in other state courts with respect to successive petitions for rehearing. This can be determined by examining the law of the particular state.

9.8 Issuance of the Mandate

The mandate of an appellate court—in some states called the remittitur, rescript, procedendo or remand of record[68]—is its order formally advising the lower court of its decision. The mandate customarily consists of certified copies of the judgment and opinion, in some jurisdictions accompanied by an additional formal order. In the federal courts of appeals, the judgment and opinion suffice "unless the court directs that a formal mandate issue." (Federal Appellate Rule 41(a).) A formal mandate is seldom needed to compel a lower court to comply with the judgment of the higher court. Supreme Court Rule 52.3 contains a similar provision for cases coming from federal courts, but provides for the issuance of a traditional formal order to state courts in the name of the President of the United States.

The rules of the various courts prescribe the time for the issuance of mandates. To allow for the filing of a timely petition for rehearing before the decision becomes final, the time is frequently the same as, or slightly longer than, the time for petitioning for rehearing. In the Illinois appellate courts and the United States Supreme Court, the time is the same. Under the Federal Rules of Appellate Procedure, 14 days is allowed for petitioning for rehearing, but 21 days for sending down the mandate. These times may be enlarged or shortened by the court; either party may move for such an order.

---

[67]Illinois Rule 367(e) provides: "When the Appellate Court has granted a petition for rehearing and entered judgment on the rehearing, no further petitions for rehearing shall be filed in that court."

[68]Remittitur—California, Georgia, Nevada, New York, South Carolina, Wisconsin; rescript—Massachusetts; procedendo—Iowa; remand of record—Pennsylvania.

The issuance of a mandate is normally stayed as of course by the filing of a timely petition for rehearing. If rehearing is denied, the mandate issues forthwith (United States Supreme Court Rule 52.2), or shortly thereafter. (Federal Rule of Appellate Procedure 41(a) and Illinois Rule 368(a)—7 days.)

In order to prevent the issuance of mandates from being automatically stayed during its three months' summer recess, the United States Supreme Court provides in Rule 52.2 that

> "When, however, a petition for rehearing is not acted upon prior to adjournment, or is filed after the Court adjourns, the judgment or mandate of the Court will not be stayed unless specifically ordered by the Court or a Justice."

The practical effect of this is to require a motion for a stay to accompany a petition for rehearing which will not be acted upon prior to adjournment. The motion should show good reason for believing that the petition will be granted, as well as for granting a stay for that long a period. This procedure might well be utilized by other courts in which petitions for rehearing might stay mandates for an excessively long time.

The Federal Rules of Appellate Procedure provide that stays of mandate "may be granted" by the court of appeals pending application to the United States Supreme Court for certiorari, but that the stay shall not exceed 30 days unless the time is "extended for cause shown." Rule 41(b). If the Clerk of the Supreme Court notifies the clerk of the court of appeals that the petition has been filed, the stay will continue in effect until final disposition of the case by the Supreme Court. As a practical matter, this means that the applicant for a stay must file his petition for certiorari in 30 days instead of the 90 days allowed by statute or rule. The rationale is that a petitioner who wishes to delay the enforcement of the order of the lower court may reasonably be expected to expedite the litigation by not taking the full time otherwise allowable by law.

A number of the courts of appeals have gone further by providing in their circuit rules that either in all cases or in criminal cases the motion for a stay of mandate must show that "the petition for certiorari would not be frivolous or filed merely for delay."[69] This requirement was added because of the interest in "minimizing unnecessary delay in the administration of jus-

---

[69]See First Circuit Rule 16; Fifth Circuit Rule 17; Sixth Circuit Rule 15(a); Seventh Circuit Rule 17; Eighth Circuit Rule 18; Ninth Circuit Rule 17; Tenth Circuit Rule 16.

tice,"[70] and "the increasingly large percentage of unsuccessful petitions" for certiorari filed in criminal cases in recent years.[71] The Supreme Court itself will not grant a stay unless there is "a reasonable probability that four members of the Court will consider the issue sufficiently meritorious to grant certiorari."[72] The absence of such restrictions would give losers in the courts below a strong incentive to resort to petitions for certiorari with no chance of success primarily for the purpose of postponing the enforcement of the judgment below. The applicant for a stay of mandate in such circumstances should thus attempt to establish that there is a reasonable chance that certiorari will be granted.

Many state courts have similar rules for stays of mandate pending review by a higher state court or the Supreme Court of the United States. E.g., Pennsylvania Appellate Rule 2572. Under Illinois Rule 368 the mandate of the Appellate Court is automatically stayed (except in injunction cases) by filing a petition for review in the Supreme Court of Illinois or an affidavit of intent to seek such review; the stay is effective until expiration of the time to seek review or of disposition of the case by the Supreme Court. A stay or recall of mandate may also be granted pending review in the Supreme Court of Illinois or the Supreme Court of the United States by the Appellate Court or the Supreme Court of Illinois or the United States Supreme Court or a judge of any of them.[73] The practice elsewhere is generally the same.

---

[70]See First Circuit Rule 16; Sixth Circuit Rule 15(a); Seventh Circuit Rule 17(a); Tenth Circuit Rule 16.

[71]First Circuit Rule 16; Tenth Circuit Rule 16.

[72]*Wise* v. *Lipscomb*, 434 U.S. 1329, 1333–1334 (1977), and other cases quoted in R. Stern and E. Gressman, SUPREME COURT PRACTICE, pp. 871–873 (5th ed., 1978).

[73]See Illinois Rule 368; R. Stern and E. Gressman, SUPREME COURT PRACTICE, Secs. 17.16–17.22 (5th ed., 1978).

10

The Decisional Process

The process of deciding a case may take various forms and be handled in a number of ways. Some of the steps which affect appellate lawyers are discussed in this chapter.[1]

10.1 Reading Briefs in Advance of Argument

Although the question whether appellate judges should read briefs before argument "produced vigorous differences of opinion in the past [it] now has a clear answer: briefs should be studied by all the sitting judges before the case is submitted. If there is to be oral argument, each judge should know enough about the case in advance to be able to ask intelligent questions concerning it, avoid asking questions that would waste the time

---

[1]The subject has been treated in depth in five recent enlightening publications upon which this analysis is to a large extent based: American Bar Association Commission on Standards of Judicial Administration, STANDARDS RELATING TO APPELLATE COURTS (1977); Robert A. Leflar, INTERNAL OPERATING PROCEDURES OF APPELLATE COURTS (American Bar Foundation, 1976); P. Carrington, D. Meador and M. Rosenberg, JUSTICE ON APPEAL (1976); Commission on Revision of the Federal Court Appellate System, STRUCTURE AND INTERNAL PROCEDURES: RECOMMENDATIONS FOR CHANGE (1975); American Bar Association Task Force on Appellate Procedure, EFFICIENCY AND JUSTICE IN APPEALS: METHODS AND SELECTED MATERIALS (1977). These publications will be hereinafter cited respectively as APPELLATE STANDARDS, Leflar, JUSTICE ON APPEAL, APPELLATE COMMISSION, and EFFICIENCY AND JUSTICE. The American Bar Association Commission and Task Force and the Commission on Revision of the Federal Court Appellate System were composed of a number of members of the judiciary as well as of the bar, and the latter also included members of Congress. Professor Leflar has been a member of the Arkansas Supreme Court, and Messrs. Carrington, Meador and Rosenberg were at the time professors at the law schools of the University of Michigan, University of Virginia and Columbia University.

of court and counsel, and listen to the argument with understanding. In addition, any inadequacy of the brief not discovered in advance screening could be noted in time to do something about it. If there is to be no oral argument (and there may be less need for it, or it could be shorter, if all judges have read the briefs in advance), the judge must read the briefs before the case is discussed in conference in order to be able to participate intelligently in the decision. A judge who is unfamiliar with the case or who has not had time to think about the issues is apt to play a negligible or uninformed part in the decision conference."[2]

Some courts publicly announce that the judges will have read the briefs before argument, and many judges say that that is the practice on their courts. United States Supreme Court Rule 38.1 advises counsel to "assume" that the Justices have all read the briefs. That is also the practice in the United States courts of appeals. Nevertheless, it cannot be said that all judges do, particularly on courts where each case is assigned to a single judge soon after it is filed or docketed. See Sec. 8.11(c), *supra.* And even judges who generally read the briefs prior to argument may be distracted in particular cases or at certain times by personal circumstances of various sorts, such as illness, a heavy opinion load, or social or professional engagements.

Professor Leflar notes that "[i]t has been said that judges on an extremely busy court do not have time to read all briefs in advance."[3] He doubts whether this saves time in the long run if the judges read the briefs eventually. Undoubtedly judicial time would be saved if some, or all but one, of the appellate judges did not read the briefs at all, relying either on their colleagues or their staff lawyers or law clerks for oral or written explanations of the case. But such judges would not be fully participating in the formulation of the collegial decision of the court as a whole. "Failure to read [the briefs] would be a betrayal of judicial obligation, an improper delegation of his duty to participate independently in the collegial process of decision in each case on which he sits."[4]

As noted in Sec. 8.11(c), *supra,* each court should make public its practice as to reading briefs before argument. Knowl-

---

[2]Leflar, *supra* note 1, at 29.
[3]*Ibid.*
[4]*Id.* at 30.

edge as to this will aid lawyers preparing to argue; if they knew that the judges did read the briefs in advance of argument, their arguments could be shorter. Counsel would even be helped if all that could be said is that judges are irregular as to the reading of briefs in advance, or that some do and some don't, which some judges might find it embarrassing to admit.

10.2 Conferences Before Argument

The judicial decision-making process often begins before the oral argument. In some courts memoranda summarizing the case are prepared in advance of argument by one or more of the judges or their law clerks or central staff attorneys.

A number of courts have conferences before argument; they "have found that they gain the most from argument when the participating judges have a pre-argument conference to identify for themselves the issues on which they wish counsel to concentrate. If such conferences are held sufficiently in advance of argument, the questions identified can be submitted to counsel to prepare argument accordingly. In other courts, the presiding judge states the issues on which the court wishes argument to focus."[5]

Advising counsel a few days before they come to court of the issues or questions which concern the judges would be highly desirable, for it would enable counsel to prepare in advance to deal with those questions and to allocate their time accordingly. Such a preplanned presentation would usually be superior to the hurried extemporaneous rearrangement that would occur if the questions of interest to the bench were not identified until the commencement of the argument.

Some appellate courts provide for prehearing conferences with counsel either before a judge (who should not thereafter sit on the case) or a member of the court's staff.[6] Rule 33 of the Federal Rules of Appellate Procedure authorizes the courts of appeals to "direct the attorneys . . . to appear before the court or a judge thereof for a prehearing conference to consider the simplification of the issues and such other matters as may aid in

---

[5]APPELLATE STANDARDS, *supra* note 1, at 55. See also EFFICIENCY AND JUSTICE, *supra* note 1, at 95.

[6]Leflar, *supra* note 1, at 30–31; I. Kaufman, *The Pre-Argument Conference: An Appellate Procedural Reform,* 74 Colum. L. Rev. 1094 (1974); J. Hopkins, *The Winds of Change: New Styles in the Appellate Process,* 3 Hofstra L. Rev. 649, 656 (1975).

the disposition of the proceeding . . . ." An appropriate order reciting the action and any agreements made is binding on the parties. A number of states have similar rules.

Such conferences may produce agreement upon schedules for briefing and argument and the length of briefs, may identify, limit or qualify the issues on appeal before briefs are written, or may endeavor to settle the litigation. Whether the conference procedure substantially increases the number of settlements and thereby diminishes the burden on appellate courts is uncertain. Professor Leflar, writing in 1976, reports that experience in a few courts (including the Second Circuit) is that "cases including money damages have the highest probability of being settled," and that "more than one-third of the preheard cases are settled or withdrawn."[7] A 1977 report on the Second Circuit's experience, published by the Federal Judicial Center, and a subsequent article by its author,[8] based upon a comparison of cases in which settlement conferences were and were not held, concluded that the results in the two groups of cases differed only slightly, and that it could not be said that the experience was, or was not, worth the effort.

The Minnesota Supreme Court has ordered prehearing conferences to be held in all civil cases by a justice (who will not thereafter hear the appeal) or hearing officer. The appellant must serve copies of the prescribed prehearing conference statement with his notice of appeal. Counsel are to have authority to settle, and their clients are to be either available or present.[9] New Hampshire Rule 12(2) is similar. Washington Rule 5.5(e)(j) provides that the Chief Justice of the Court of Appeals will determine if a settlement conference will be appropriate for each civil appeal. If so, counsel is notified, and the normal time schedule is stayed. The settlement conference judge is not barred from hearing the case on the merits unless he recuses himself in the interest of justice, or any party objects to his sitting.

---

[7]Leflar, *supra* note 1, at 31.

[8]Professor Jerry Goldman of Northwestern University. See AN EVALUATION OF THE CIVIL APPEALS MANAGEMENT PLAN: AN EXPERIMENT IN JUDICIAL ADMINISTRATION, pp. 89–100 (Federal Judicial Center, 1977); J. Goldman, *The Civil Appeals Management Plan: An Experiment in Appellate Procedural Reform*, 78 Colum. L. Rev. 1209 (1978). The Second Circuit conferences were conducted by a senior staff attorney, not a judge. Possibly judges might be more successful in inducing parties to settle. But query whether such psychological pressure is proper.

[9]See Minnesota Rule of Civil Appellate Procedure 133.02 and Minnesota Supreme Court order of September 10, 1976, attached thereto.

The American Bar Association Task Force on Appellate Procedure commented that

> "On the pro side, if the system does accelerate dispositions without briefing, argument, or opinions, then it has achieved a distinct benefit. . . . On the other hand, if all that happens is that an extra time-consuming step is injected into the process, or if undue pressure to settle is being forced on the parties, or if the only cases being settled are those which would be settled anyway, then the achievement is, at best, minimal."[10]

Whether inducing the parties to settle is an appropriate function of an appellate court is doubtful, even though it does result in a reduction of the judicial work load. Apart from that, the benefit of a prehearing conference does not seem to be worth any substantial effort, such as calling in lawyers from out of town. Agreement upon scheduling, which might expedite appeals to a slight extent as well as be convenient for the lawyers, should be possible without a formal conference. If a "conference" for that purpose is regarded as helpful, a short meeting or telephonic discussion (long distance if necessary) with a circuit executive, staff attorney or member of the clerk's office would often suffice.[11]

The Second Circuit seems to be satisfied with its plan and is continuing with it, but there can as yet be no certainty that such a program should be generally adopted.

The Court of Appeals for the District of Columbia Circuit has a Civil Appeals Management Plan, approved June 6, 1978, which concentrates not on settlement conferences but on the simplification and expedition of appeals by Chief Staff Counsel through informal contacts with the attorneys in person or by letter or telephone. The object is not only to agree on the scheduling of briefs and arguments but to decrease the number of briefs filed by numerous parties in complex cases. Thus, if the position of the government or other principal party is supported by other parties, they can be given a prescribed number of days after the filing of the principal brief on their side to file a brief limited to what they want to add, without repeating what they agree with. This may lengthen the total briefing time somewhat, but it greatly reduces the quantity of reading matter submitted

---

[10]EFFICIENCY AND JUSTICE, *supra* note 1, at 50–51.
[11]My own impression is that a conference for the purpose of limiting the issues would seldom be of much value to either counsel or the court. See J. Goldman, *The Civil Appeals Management Plan: An Experiment in Appellate Procedural Reform*, 78 Colum. L. Rev. 1209, 1234–1235 (1978).

to the court. The parties may be encouraged to agree on joint briefs or division of the issues for briefing. They may also be able to arrange through staff counsel for the filing of briefs longer than the rules ordinarily permit, and for the length and allocation of oral argument time. These administrative matters are usually worked out amicably without bothering the court with a number of motions, although resort to the court or a judge is possible if necessary.

The District of Columbia Plan, either on the initiative of a party's counsel or of Staff Counsel, also enables "the court to identify and resolve appeals which should not proceed to full briefing and submission to a merits panel."[12] These include not only cases so insubstantial that they can be decided summarily on the merits without argument but also those in which the appeal is untimely, or in the wrong court, or beyond the court's jurisdiction for a number of reasons. The preliminary screening also identifies cases in which further proceedings or additional findings in the trial court or administrative agency before review on the merits would be beneficial, or in which subsequent decisions or statutes or other acts might justify reconsideration of the ruling below or even a determination that the controversy has become moot.

The Report of the Court's Advisory Committee on Procedures at the end of the first year under the plan was "overwhelmingly" favorable.[13] Other appellate courts might well consider emulating it.

10.3   Conferences After Argument

Most courts confer after argument (or submission of briefs if there is no oral argument), either on the same day or shortly thereafter. "It is important that the decision conference be held as soon as possible after oral argument, assuming that briefs have been read and that appropriate memoranda have been prepared before argument. Thus, all the judges deciding the case have it fresh in mind. Each sitting judge will then, presumably, have his own memorandum or notes on the case. The best time to hold the conference would be in the afternoon, after arguments have been heard in the morning. If there is no free

---

[12]Civil Appeals Management Plan for the District of Columbia, p. 2 (1978).
[13]Report of the Advisory Committee on Procedures on the Operations of the Civil Appeals Management Plan for the District of Columbia Circuit, p. 4 (May 21, 1979).

time then, it should be held at the earliest time available there-after."[14] As time passes, and particularly if the court hears a substantial number of cases before conferring, "cases and analyses become blurred and confused; they must be reviewed before intelligent discussion can take place. The review takes additional time and may not bring back as clear an understanding of the case as was present when the original study and argument were fresh in the minds of the judges. Time is saved and analysis is better when consideration is prompt."[15]

At the conferences the judges tentatively agree upon decisions, unless any of them asks for more time and consideration at a subsequent conference. This process assures that each judge will have the benefit of the views of his colleagues and of the interchange between all of the judges which is the heart of collegial decision-making before even a tentative conclusion is reached. Appellate Standard 3.36 declares:

> "The judges who are to decide a case should confer after argument is completed and before a decision is formulated. The process by which an opinion is prepared may appropriately vary but all participating judges should join in formulating the opinion." (p. 58.)

> "Group deliberation not only affords the proper measure of appellate justice in each case but also helps maintain the consistency of decisional law." (p. 59.)

"Where the judges cannot assemble in one place to hear oral argument, the court should consider the alternative of a conference [after argument] by telephone."[16]

10.4 The Assignment of Opinions

Cases are assigned for the writing of opinions by either of two methods. In the federal appellate courts and a number of state courts, assignment is made after the conference by the presiding judge.[17] Since no judge will know before then to whom any case will be assigned, each will have equal responsi-

---

[14]Leflar, *supra* note 1, at 36. The practice of the Ninth Circuit in discussing every case in conference, usually shortly after the oral argument, but even if the case is not heard orally, is described in A. Hellman, *Central Staff in Appellate Courts: The Experience of the Ninth Circuit,* 68 Cal. L. Rev. 937, 1000–1001 (1980).

[15]Leflar, *supra* note 1, at 36–37.

[16]EFFICIENCY AND JUSTICE, *supra* note 1, at 99.

[17]Leflar, *supra* note 1, at 39. In some courts, the assignment may come from the chief judge of the court and not the judge presiding over the bench which heard the case, or from both after consultation.

bility for participating in the decisional process up to the time when the decision is tentatively reached.

In most state appellate courts, however, the cases are assigned by rotation, or by lot, either when the appeal is filed or docketed or some time before argument.[18] The inevitable result is that the assigned judge has special responsibility for the case. Indeed, that would seem to be the purpose of the system. Professor Leflar has described the effect as follows:

> "A judge is expected to make special preparation before argument on his cases. He is usually expected not only to study the briefs but to check the record as well. Because he is better prepared than the other judges to ask questions of counsel, counsel might be able to guess which judge has his case and concentrate his argument on that judge, who would lead off in discussion of the case in conference. Each preassigned judge would normally spend much more time on the case assigned to him than on the cases of the other judges. In an ordinary case that had not attracted the special interest of the other judges, the preassigned judge would exert more influence than any of the others in determining how the case should be dealt with. This does not mean that a one-judge decision or a one-man opinion would inevitably ensue. That would not happen if the case were an important or interesting one that attracted the attention of all the judges, or even of several of them. In ordinary cases, however, the advance rotation system tends toward one-judge emphasis to a degree that is not present if the entire study-and-decision process precedes the assignment."[19]

In a few of these states, the assigned judge "is expected to write an opinion for his court without any decision conference and therefore without knowing beforehand the views of the other judges on what the significant issues are."[20] The opinion he drafts will represent only his own position without the benefit of collective discussion and analysis. "[I]t is unlikely that the writer will have written the opinion in the same way he would have written it had he known the views of his colleagues in advance. He cannot express views of which he is unaware."[21] "Worse yet, after a substantial lapse of time—perhaps weeks—during which he was preparing his unguided opinion, the other judges may have become vague about facts and principles they considered important when the case was submitted; they may be

---

[18]*Id.* at 39–40.
[19]*Id.* at 40.
[20]*Id.* at 37.
[21]*Ibid.*

more disposed to forego views that might have proved to be controlling if developed earlier. The one-man opinion, the very opposite of what should be produced by a multi-judge court, must too frequently be the natural result."[22]

Assignment in advance will save judicial time, but only to the extent that other judges do less work on a case than the assigned judge because to some extent they rely on his judgment instead of thinking the case through themselves. A multi-judge court, however, is likely to possess wisdom superior to that of a single judge because it represents the interworkings of the minds of all of the judges. To the extent that the consideration of each case rests largely on the preparation and thought of a single member of the court, this advantage is dissipated.

10.5 Types of Decision

A decision may be an oral ruling from the bench at the close of argument. A substantial proportion of cases are disposed of in this way by the Second Circuit,[23] and a lesser number by the Seventh, which subsequently provides a short written statement of the reasons for the court's action. Other cases in many courts are disposed of by short orders, which merely say "affirmed." E.g., Fifth Circuit Rule 21, Eighth Circuit Rule 14, Tenth Circuit Rule 17(b), which are substantially identical.[24] Many decisions take the form of short opinions, often a single paragraph, stating the court's reasons summarily. Most decisions in the Texas Court of Criminal Appeals (81 percent), the New York Court of Appeals (52 percent), the Florida and New Mexico Courts of Appeals (56 percent), and about 90 percent of the decisions in the New Jersey and New York Appellate Divisions are decided in this manner, as are lesser proportions of the cases in a num-

---

[22]*Ibid.*
[23]EFFICIENCY AND JUSTICE, *supra* note 1, at 97.
[24]Fifth Circuit Rule 21 reads as follows:

"Rule 21. Affirmance Without Opinion

"When the Court determines that any one or more of the following circumstances exists and is dispositive of a matter submitted to the Court for decision: (1) that a judgment of the District Court is based on findings of fact which are not clearly erroneous, (2) that the evidence in support of a jury verdict is not insufficient, or (3) that the order of an administrative agency is supported by substantial evidence on the record as a whole; and the Court also determines that no error of law appears and an opinion would have no precedential value, the judgment or order may be affirmed or enforced without opinion.

"In such case, the Court may in its discretion enter either of the following orders: 'AFFIRMED. See Local Rule 21,' or 'ENFORCED. See Local Rule 21.'"

ber of other appellate courts.[25] These opinions are customarily *per curiam,* which means that they do not appear as the work of any one of the judges. And then, of course, there are the cases decided by full explanatory opinion.

These different techniques of deciding cases present a number of problems. A recent study by three leaders in the field of appellate court administration has declared that announcing the reasons for decisions is an "imperative" of the judicial process; this is essential to "the integrity of the process."[26] "Conclusions easily reached without setting down the reasons sometimes undergo revision when the decider sets out to justify the decision. Furthermore, litigants and the public are reassured when they can see that the determination emerged at the end of a reasoning process that is explicitly stated, rather than as an imperious ukase without a nod to law or a need to justify. Especially in a case in which there is no oral argument, the opinion is an essential demonstration that the court has in fact considered the case. In many circumstances, appellate courts have required administrative agencies to write opinions. It is paradoxical for appellate courts to claim the power now to do without them."[27]

The Commission on Revision of the Federal Court Appellate System, taking the same position, recommended "that the Federal Rules of Appellate Procedure require that in every case there be some record, however brief, and whatever the form, of the reasoning which impelled the decision. In an appropriate case, citation to a single precedent would suffice. In other cases informal memoranda, intended for the parties themselves, would serve the purpose intended. Opinions can be signed or unsigned, published or unpublished, but in each case the litigants and their attorneys would be apprised of the reasoning which underlies the conclusion of the court. The decision would be available to the public."[28]

"The pressures of heavy workloads have, [however], led some appellate courts to overreact by curtailing too sharply the explanation that accompanies the decision."[29] The practice of

---

[25]T. Marvell and M. Kuykendall, *Appellate Courts—Facts and Figures,* 4 State Court J. 9, 14, 36 (Spring 1980).
[26]JUSTICE ON APPEAL, *supra* note 1, at 8–10.
[27]*Id.* at 31–32.
[28]APPELLATE COMMISSION, *supra* note 1, at 50–51.
[29]JUSTICE ON APPEAL, *supra* note 1, at 32. See also EFFICIENCY AND JUSTICE, *supra* note 1, at 115.

those federal courts which "have adopted the practice of issuing curt or perfunctory rulings that say nothing more than 'Judgment affirmed' "[30] falls in that category.

Such a drastic departure from the fundamental principle that appellate courts should state the reasons for their decisions is not necessary. As indicated above, in many cases reasons can be stated without long explanation. Possible alternatives are set out in the *Standards Relating to Appellate Courts* (p. 58):

> "The court should give its decision and opinion in a form appropriate to the complexity and importance of the issues presented in the case. A full written opinion reciting the facts, the questions presented, and analysis of pertinent authorities and principles, should be rendered in cases involving new or unsettled questions of general importance. Cases not involving such questions should be decided by memorandum opinion. Every decision should be supported, at minimum, by a citation of the authority or statement of grounds upon which it is based. When the lower court decision was based on a written opinion that adequately expresses the appellate court's view of the law, the reviewing court should incorporate that opinion or such portions of it as are deemed pertinent, or, if it has been published, affirm on the basis of that opinion."[31]

As the above indicates, a sentence or even a phrase will often suffice, such as by saying merely "affirmed," and adding a reference to the authority or authorities relied upon, or "affirmed on the authority of the opinion below." "Affirmed substantially for the reasons stated in the court below" would also be adequate; that would mean that the court does not necessarily endorse in *haec verba* everything stated by the court below. If the case is a factual one and the sole question is whether there are sufficient facts to support the verdict of a jury, or the findings of a judge or administrative body, a statement that the verdict or findings are adequately supported by the evidence might suffice. More satisfactory and only slightly more burdensome would be something like:

> "The finding that defendant was driving unreasonably fast is amply supported by the evidence."

Or better yet

> "The finding that defendant was driving unreasonably fast is supported by the evidence as to the length of his skid

---

[30]JUSTICE ON APPEAL, *supra* note 1, at 32.
[31]To the same effect, see APPELLATE COMMISSION, *supra* note 1, at 50–51.

marks at the scene of the accident as well as by oral testimony."

Or

"The finding that plaintiff was an employee of defendant corporation is adequately supported by evidence that defendant's superintendent frequently gave him orders as to the details of his work and that he obeyed them."

An oral statement of reasons at the close of argument satisfies this imperative of judicial decision-making, particularly if it is taken down in some way and either transcribed or made available for transcription. The Seventh Circuit's practice of following the oral pronouncement with a short written version of the same reasons is certainly appropriate and helpful, but it may go further than necessary.

An increasingly large category of decisions now consists of short explanatory memoranda stating the reasons for the court's ruling. These are addressed primarily to the parties—or to their lawyers—who are familiar with the case, not to the outsiders who read reported decisions.

10.6 Publication of Opinions

There is no good reason why a cryptic phrase, sentence, paragraph or short memorandum which adequately explains the court's decision to the parties should be published in the law reports. Nonpublication saves a great deal of judicial time. An unpublished opinion addressed to the parties need not contain a statement of facts. It may be written less formally and with less rewriting and polishing. It can often be written in several hours or less, while a published opinion more often takes a number of days.

Moreover, limiting publication to opinions which contribute something to an understanding of the law will save substantial sums. The saving in judges' time will ultimately translate into a reduction to the public of the cost of judicial administration. And the publication of fewer opinions will mean that lawyers and law libraries will need to purchase fewer law books. "Routine publication of all opinions involves substantial expense and results in publication of many decisions that are of little interest or use to anyone other than the immediate parties.

The total cost includes not only printing, distribution, and storage, but also, ultimately, the rapidly increasing expense of legal research resulting from the proliferation of published reports. Where the point is reached in an individual jurisdiction that these costs outweigh the value of routine publication of all appellate opinions, procedures should be adopted that limit publication to those opinions having some apparent precedential significance."[32]

There is general agreement as to what the criteria for publication should be, although the various formulations differ in detail. The standards proposed in a number of the recent studies of appellate court administration and in the rules of some courts[33] have been incorporated in a recent rule of the Seventh Circuit, as follows:

"Circuit Rule 35(c). Guidelines for Method of Disposition

"(1) Published opinions.
A published opinion will be filed when the decision

(i)	establishes a new, or changes an existing, rule of law;
(ii)	involves an issue of continuing public interest;
(iii)	criticizes or questions existing law;
(iv)	constitutes a significant and non-duplicative contribution to legal literature "(A) by a historical review of law, "(B) by describing legislative history, or "(C) by resolving or creating a conflict in the law;
(v)	reverses a judgment or denies enforcement of an order when the lower court or agency has published an opinion supporting the judgment or order; or
(vi)	is pursuant to an order or remand from the Supreme Court and is not rendered merely in ministerial obedience to specific directions of that Court.

"(2) Unpublished orders.
When the decision does not satisfy the criteria for publication, as stated above, it will be filed as an unpublished order. The order will ordinarily contain reasons for the judgment, but may not do

---

[32]APPELLATE STANDARDS, *supra* note 1, at 63–64.
[33]Cf. APPELLATE STANDARDS, p. 62, and Leflar, pp. 57–58, both at *supra* note 1; Fourth Circuit Rule 18; Sixth Circuit Rule 11; Ninth Circuit Rule 21(b). The First Circuit describes the "test, broadly phrased," as "whether the district courts, future litigants, or we ourselves would be likely to benefit from the opportunity to read or cite the opinion, having in mind that only published opinions may be cited." See Plan for the Publication of Opinion, Statement of Policy, attached as an appendix to the First Circuit rules.

so if the court has announced its decision and reasons from the bench. A statement of facts may be omitted from the order or may not be complete or detailed."

A majority of the judges participating in the decision usually determine whether it shall be published. Seventh Circuit Rule 35(d), for example, provides:

"(1) The determination to dispose of an appeal by unpublished order shall be made by a majority of the panel rendering the decision.

"(2) The requirement of a majority represents the policy of this circuit. Notwithstanding the right of a single federal judge to make an opinion available for publication, it is expected that a single judge will ordinarily respect and abide by the opinion of the majority in determining whether to publish."

An alternative is the proposal in *Appellate Standards* that

"A concurring or dissenting opinion should be published if its author believes it should be; if such an opinion is published, the majority opinion should be published as well."[34]

In several states the responsibility of determining which court of appeals decisions shall be published is given to committees of judges. Under Colorado Rule 35(f) the committee consists of a Supreme Court justice, a Court of Appeals judge and the reporter of decisions. Under Wisconsin Rule 809.23(2), the judges who join in a Court of Appeals opinion are to make a recommendation as to publication to a committee consisting of the Chief Judge of that court and one judge from each district. The rules of those states provide that unpublished opinions do not have precedential value. In Oklahoma the Supreme Court and the Court of Criminal Appeals determine which of their opinions shall be published. Although Court of Appeals opinions will be published on request of the presiding judge of the division handing down the opinion, the opinion shall not have "precedential effect but may be considered persuasive" unless the Supreme Court specifically authorizes the publication.[35] The published opinion shall bear a notation disclosing whether publication was approved by the Supreme Court or ordered by the Court of Appeals.

Some of the nonpublication rules allow parties or others to

---

[34]APPELLATE STANDARD 3.37, supra note 1, at 63.

[35]See Oklahoma Supreme Court Memorandum of Policy, West's Oklahoma Court Rules, Civil Appeals Procedure, p. 904 (1978–1979).

request that an opinion be published. Ninth Circuit Rule 21(f) permits such a request to be made by letter within 60 days of the issuance of the opinion. Seventh Circuit Rule 35(d)(3) permits "any person [to] request by motion that a decision by unpublished order be issued as a published opinion," giving "the reasons why the publication would be consistent with the guidelines for method of disposition set forth in this rule." See also Wisconsin Rule 809.23(4). It should be noted that this provision is not limited to parties or even lawyers, though presumably requests would normally emanate from them. Such requests, in which both parties may join, have been granted when the importance of the opinion to the public has been shown.

10.7 Ability to Cite Unpublished Opinions

In most courts a corollary of having some opinions unpublished is that the nonpublished opinions are not to be cited. The principal reasons are that such opinions are not of general significance and also that they would be unknown and unavailable to all but a few members of the bar. "Allowing citation of unpublished opinions would [create] pressures to make such opinions generally available, resulting in a secondary system of unofficial publication which to some extent [would frustrate] the purpose of the non-publication rule."[36] The Wisconsin Judicial Council Committee Note to Rule 809.23 adds that "the type of opinion written for the benefit of the parties is different from an opinion written for publication and often should not be published without substantial revision; . . . an unpublished opinion is not new authority but only a repeated application of a settled rule for which there is ample published authority." The rule does not, of course, preclude use of the decision in the same or a related case. Seventh Circuit Rule 35(b)(2)(iv) is typical:[37]

> "Except to support a claim of *res judicata,* collateral estoppel or law of the case, [unpublished orders] shall not be cited or used as precedent (a) in any federal court within the circuit in any written document or in oral argument or (b) by any such court for any purpose."

---

[36] APPELLATE STANDARDS, *supra* note 1, at 64; see also APPELLATE COMMISSION, *supra* note 1, at 51–52.

[37] See also Wisconsin Rule of Appellate Procedure 809.23(3); First Circuit Rule 14; Fourth Circuit Rule 18(d)(ii); Ninth Circuit Rule 21(c). Sixth Circuit Rule 11 contains no exceptions for related cases.

There has been a substantial difference of opinion as to the wisdom of a noncitability rule.[38]

After first favoring a nonpublication and noncitability rule, the authors of *Justice on Appeal* came to a contrary conclusion after greater reflection. Such rules in combination have the advantage of enabling appellate judges to save time by writing shorter opinions. But noncitability still leaves in a favored position the lawyers who know about the case, particularly institutional or governmental law offices which will keep up even with unpublished opinions in a particular field. They "retain access to the court's reasoning and can direct their arguments accordingly."[39] Such a rule might leave multipanel courts in "a state of disarray that is hard to cure because counsel are prevented by the rule from calling attention to contradictory or chaotic decisions."[40] The authors' conclusion is that the efficiency gained by the practice is outweighed by the disadvantages to the attainment of rational, uniform and informed justice.

A compromise endorsed by a majority of the Commission on Standards of Judicial Administration would permit citation of unpublished material "only if a person making reference to it provides the court and opposing parties with a copy of the opinion or otherwise gives them reasonable advance notice of its contents." Some court rules so state.[41]

The judicial trend at the present time is in the direction of both nonpublication and noncitability, and counsel will have to learn to put up with it. Experience may perhaps throw light on whether those requirements can and should be modified.

---

[38]The opposing arguments are summarized in EFFICIENCY AND JUSTICE, *supra* note 1, at 107–113.

[39]S. Wasby, T. Marvell and A. Aikman, VOLUME AND DELAY IN STATE APPELLATE COURTS, p. 99 (National Center for State Courts, 1979).

[40]JUSTICE ON APPEAL, pp. 37, 38, 39, and EFFICIENCY AND JUSTICE, p. 111, both at *supra* note 1.

[41]E.g., Tenth Circuit Rule 17(c).

11

Motion Practice

11.1 In General—Emergencies

A motion is an application for an order or other relief,
unless another form or title such as petition for rehearing or
petition for leave to appeal is prescribed by the rules of the
jurisdiction. Relief relating to the merits of an appeal is not
usually sought by motion, except for motions to dismiss or
affirm or other summary disposition.

There is not a great divergence in the rules of the various
jurisdictions dealing with motions, and the practice would probably be very much the same in the absence of a specific rule on
the subject. Many of the state rules closely follow Rule 27 of the
Federal Rules of Appellate Procedure.[1] The variations in motion practice in the various jurisdictions, though slight on the
whole, require that counsel examine the rules of the appellate
court with which he is concerned.

Motions can request a great many kinds of relief. Thirty
categories of motions "expressly or implicitly authorized by various rules" are listed in the Illinois Practitioner's Handbook,[2]
and these do not purport to be exclusive. Among the most
common are motions relating to extensions of time, stays or

---

[1]E.g., Massachusetts Appellate Rule 15; Nevada Rule 27; Tennessee Rule 22; Wisconsin Rule 809.14. The motions practice in the Ninth Circuit is described in detail in A.
Hellman, *Central Staff in Appellate Courts: The Experience of the Ninth Circuit,* 68 Cal. L. Rev.
937, 952–957 (1980).
[2]PRACTITIONER'S HANDBOOK FOR APPEALS TO THE ILLINOIS SUPREME
AND APPELLATE COURTS, p. 18 (1978).

bail, the record, the length of briefs, and the length and date of oral argument.

The motion practice may also be utilized when special expedition is essential in an emergency. Appellate courts can and do act very speedily when convinced that is necessary. This occurs not only in capital punishment situations but also when an immediate stay is needed to prevent serious irreparable injury, as when collection of a major state tax has been enjoined or an unreversible and allegedly illegal corporate act will occur. Emergency relief may be obtainable in a few days or even hours, and sometimes the entire appeal can be compressed into a very short period. Federal Appellate Rule 2 provides:

> "In the interest of expediting decision, or for other good cause shown, a court of appeals may, except as otherwise provided in Rule 26(b), suspend the requirements or provisions of any of these rules in a particular case on application of a party or on its own motion and may order proceedings in accordance with its direction."

Ninth Circuit Rule 6(h) provides expressly for "Emergency Motions," which are to be labeled as such. Such a motion is to include telephone numbers and addresses of all counsel, state whether the grounds in support were submitted to the district court, and, if not, why the motion should not be remanded, and be accompanied by an affidavit stating the facts showing the nature of the emergency. Opposing counsel should, of course, be notified, if necessary by telephone, so as to permit him to respond. An affidavit is to be attached stating when and how opposing counsel was notified or, if not, why that was not practicable. See also note 16, *infra.*

This sensible procedure probably comes close to what other courts may require in similar circumstances with or without a rule. Embodying it in a rule, however, has the advantage of making it unnecessary for counsel to make a hurried phone call to the clerk's office to find out what to do.

In the absence of such a rule, counsel should consult the clerk immediately, and also give prompt notice to the opposition. An application for a prehearing conference, such as is permitted under Federal Appellate Rule 33 and Illinois Rule 310, may enable the court quickly to prescribe an expedited schedule.

11.2 Classes of Motions

Most motions fall into three classes, although they are usually not so divided in rules of court:

(1) Procedural motions, for such things as extensions of time to file records, briefs or other papers (but not a notice of appeal), or for additional time to argue, which usually do not seriously prejudice the opposition;

(2) Substantive motions not going to the merits of the appeal but which nevertheless are important to both parties, such as motions for stay or bail or security, or to file papers after the due date;

(3) Motions which may dispose of all or part of the merits of the appeal, such as motions to dismiss or affirm or otherwise dispose of the case without oral argument.

These three categories are often treated in different ways. Motions in Class 3, which may be dispositive of the appeal, must always be decided by the full court, or a panel of the size which would decide the case in normal course. E.g., Federal Rule of Appellate Procedure 27(c). The other motions can be decided by the court or a single judge,[3] with procedural motions usually being submitted to a single judge. Such motions may also often be acted on without awaiting expiration of the opposing party's time to respond, but "any party adversely affected by such action may request reconsideration, vacation, or modification of such action." Federal Rule of Appellate Procedure 27(b).

A number of jurisdictions delegate to the clerk or court administrator the authority to decide in the first instance uncontested or procedural motions, or both. A 1979 amendment to Federal Appellate Rule 27(b) provides that "pursuant to rule or order of the court, motions for specified types of procedural orders may be disposed of by the clerk," subject of course to reconsideration by the court if requested. This recognized the prior practice of some of the circuits. Tennessee's 1979 Rule 22(b) similarly permits the appellate court by rule or order to

---

[3]In the United States Supreme Court, a motion denied by one Justice may be renewed before another. Rule 43.5. This unusual practice, which has little to commend it and which the rule itself says "is not favored," does not apply to motions to extend time. When the Court is in session, such renewed motions are customarily referred to the entire Court.

specify the types of procedural motions which may be disposed of by the clerk. It was expected that this delegation would "be limited to routine and unopposed motions that do not immediately affect the outcome of the appeal."[4] Fifth Circuit Rule 10.1 authorizes the clerk to act for the court on 18 different types of "unopposed procedural motions."[5] Rule 6(f) of the United States Court of Appeals for the District of Columbia Circuit permits the clerk to grant motions to stay the mandate in appropriate circumstances, but procedural motions only if timely and consented to or unopposed and if the granting "would not procedurally delay the working of the court." In the Third and Sixth Circuits the clerks may decide unopposed *or* procedural motions, in civil cases in the Ninth Circuit unopposed motions for extensions of time of not more than 28 days, and in the Tenth, specified types of procedural motions.[6] Eighth Circuit Rule 2(d) also authorizes the clerk to act on procedural matters, including 16 specified types of motions, and adds that "if any of the above motions are opposed, the clerk is authorized to submit the matter for ruling to a single judge of the court."

United States Supreme Court Rule 29.4 provides that all applications for extensions of time (except for filing petitions for certiorari or for rehearing, docketing appeals or issuing mandates) "shall in the first instance be acted upon by the Clerk, whether addressed to him, to the Court, or to a Justice."

Washington Rule 17.2 provides that all but a few major types of motions may be determined initially by a commissioner or clerk of the appellate court. Oral argument of up to 10 minutes per side may be authorized by those officials, and such an argument may be made by "conference telephone call" if the court so directs. (Rule 17.5.) Kansas Rule 5.01 provides that the clerk may pass, *inter alia*, upon unopposed motions for extensions of time. In Minnesota, motions with respect to the time for filing the transcript of record or for extending the time for the filing of briefs and appendices are to be first heard and considered by the Court Administrator of the Supreme Court as ref-

---

[4]J. Sobieski, *The Procedural Details of the Proposed Tennessee Rules of Appellate Procedure,* 46 Tenn. L. Rev. 1, 111–112 (1978).

[5]Fifth Circuit Rule 10.2 authorizes a single judge, subject to review by the court, to act on 12 categories of procedural motions, one of which consists of those delegated to the clerk of court when such motions are *unopposed.*

[6]Third Circuit Rule 11.5; Sixth Circuit Rule 8(c); Ninth Circuit Rule 13(h); Tenth Circuit Rule 13. As to the Ninth Circuit's reliance on the clerk and staff attorneys to dispose of certain motions, see A. Hellman, *Central Staff in Appellate Courts: The Experience of the Ninth Circuit,* 68 Cal. L. Rev. 937, 952–957 (1980).

eree; he then submits his recommendation to a justice of the court who must sign the order.[7]

Such procedural motions, and particularly motions for extensions of time, probably comprise the most numerous items of business for appellate courts. Transferring the burden of passing upon such applications initially, even only for those which are unopposed, to a clerk or administrator should substantially relieve the appellate judges of a burden which may be both annoying and time-consuming. In almost all cases, such matters can be worked out with the clerk or administrator, who will accommodate counsel's requests, if reasonable, with the public interest in not delaying the progress of the court's calendar. A wise staff official will know when disputes as to such matters should be transferred to a court or a judge.

This procedure should be time-saving and helpful if the court has confidence in the official to whom it delegates the authority—and it should not delegate to anyone else. The fact that it has such confidence and does not want to be bothered with such details makes successful appeal from the official to the court very unlikely—and thus gives the bar a strong incentive to work out such problems at staff level. Although review of the decision of the clerk or administrator by the court or a judge is always available, seldom should it be necessary.

11.3 What Must Be Filed; Contents of Motion

In the federal appellate courts and most state courts, the motion itself may and usually should contain the supporting arguments, factual or legal. If facts are asserted which are not found in the record, they should appear in a supporting affidavit, or the motion itself should be verified. This is obviously necessary for facts which are likely to be disputed. Courts also desire such verification of facts supporting requests for extension of time.

Usually the reasons for granting the motion, both factual and legal, can be presented and argued in the motion itself. That is the usual practice. If such argument is the equivalent of a long full-scale brief, it may be preferable to submit it in a separate memorandum along with the motion. Most jurisdictions permit

---

[7]Minnesota Rules of Civil Appellate Procedure 110.02(3), 131.011; letter from Supreme Court Administrator.

counsel to determine whether or not to file a separate memorandum. Federal Rule of Appellate Procedure 27(a) gives counsel the option of presenting his argument in the motion or a supporting brief. United States Supreme Court Rule 42.1 requires that the argument appear in the motion itself. Some states, like Tennessee (Rule 22(a)), require both that the motion "state the grounds on which it is based and the order or other relief requested," and that "each copy . . . shall be accompanied by a memorandum of law." This requires two documents which will overlap to a substantial extent when one will normally do.

Alaska Rule 14 requires that there shall be filed with the motion "a brief, complete statement of the reasons in support," "the points and authorities on which the moving party relies," and affidavits where necessary, as well as an appropriate order. On its face this would seem to preclude combining into a single document the motion, the reasons, and the points and authorities, or even the last two items. Attorneys are, however, encouraged to consolidate as much as possible to save paper and space but still comply with the rule.[8]

In some jurisdictions a motion should be prefaced by a separate "notice of motion," stating that the motion attached will be filed or presented at a specified time. A general reference in the notice to the character of the motion will be sufficient. The purpose is to inform other parties when they should file their responses, or appear personally if oral argument is allowed. A court rule specifying the time to respond is simpler and fairer than leaving it to movant's counsel or making it depend upon the court's calendar.

A few kinds of motions must be prefaced with a formal motion for leave to file. Motions filed after the expiration of the permissible time fall in this category. A second motion for rehearing based upon an intervening decision is an example. A motion for leave to file must often accompany the pleading in a case filed originally in a supreme court or, in some jurisdictions, a request for an original writ. The 1980 revision of the United States Supreme Court rules retained the preliminary motion for leave to file a case falling within the Court's original jurisdiction (Rule 9.3), but abolished the motion for leave to file a petition for a writ. Cf. 1980 Rule 27 with 1970 Rule 31(1). Whether the traditional motion for leave serves a useful purpose

---

[8]Letter from Chief Deputy Clerk of Supreme Court of Alaska.

is doubtful. The Court must examine the attached petition in any event, and can just as speedily exercise its discretion to dismiss a proceeding it deems not worthy of further consideration.

In Illinois, Alaska and some other jurisdictions, a copy of a proposed order should accompany each motion.[9]

A motion should bear the usual caption of the case in the appellate court, ending with a description of the motion itself, such as:

MOTION FOR EXTENSION OF TIME TO FILE APPELLANT'S BRIEF

If the caption of the motion is on a separate cover page, the name, address and telephone number of the attorney, and the date, should appear at the bottom of the page, and also at the end of the motion with the attorney's signature.

Motions should begin with a formal request for the relief sought. An explanation of the factual and legal basis for granting the relief should follow unless because of its length or the rules of the particular jurisdiction it appears in a separate memorandum. The relevant facts should usually come first, and then the reasons why the facts justify the relief requested. The relief should also be stated at the end. Few motions, and this includes those which contain the grounds for relief, should exceed two or three pages. In Delaware three is the maximum. In all jurisdictions proof of service should be attached, as well as affidavits, copies of pertinent parts of the record or other material where necessary.

11.4 Filing and Service of Motions

Motion papers must be filed with the clerk of the appellate court. Some courts, including the federal courts of appeals, also permit motions allowable by a single judge to be filed with him; this is usually done when his chambers and the clerk's office are in different cities.[10] He transmits the motion to the clerk after

---

[9]See Alaska Appellate Rule 14(a)(4); PRACTITIONER'S HANDBOOK FOR APPEALS TO THE ILLINOIS SUPREME AND APPELLATE COURTS, p. 19 (1978).

[10]E.g., Federal Rule of Appellate Procedure 25(a); Tennessee Rule 20(a). Motions in the Illinois Supreme Court are to be filed with the clerk when the court is in session, but may be filed with the clerk or the "justice of the judicial district involved" when the court is not in session and the justices are back in their districts. If the motion will require action by all the justices, copies should be sent to the clerk in Springfield and to each justice at his district chambers. Illinois Rule 361(b), (c).

he acts upon it. Every motion in an adversary proceeding should be served on all other parties to the case. This covers almost all motions except motions for admission to the bar, withdrawal of counsel and perhaps a few others of no concern to opposing counsel. As with other documents, service may be in person or by mail. The motion filed should be accompanied by proof of service consisting of an acknowledgment of service by the attorney or party served, or a certificate or affidavit by the person effecting the service.[11]

Some courts, like the United States Supreme Court, want the proof of service to appear on a separate sheet of paper for separate filing.[12] In other courts the proof may appear at the end of the motion, usually on a separate page. An admission of service by the served party may also appear on the cover.

In some courts a backing sheet in blue or some other color should be attached to the back of the motion, with the caption typed thereon; other courts, such as the United States Supreme Court, will tear off such a backing.[13] A court's preference may depend upon its system of filing. If necessary, counsel should ascertain from the clerk's office what the particular court prefers.

11.5 Form and Number of Copies

In general, the form of a motion should be the same as for a brief. See Sec. 7.37, *supra*. Motions normally may be typed, usually on pages 8 1/2 by 11 inches in size, unless the court rules otherwise specify. A few courts, including the United States Supreme Court (Rule 39) but not the federal courts of appeals, require legal-size paper 8 1/2 by 13 inches. A motion need be printed in the few courts which still require that a brief be printed only if it goes to the full court and is the equivalent of a brief on the merits. That usually means that only motions to the appellate court raising controversial questions of substance which might affect the disposition of the entire case should be printed.

If the motion goes to the merits and must be decided by the

---

[11]In some courts, certificates are sufficient from members of the bar, but affidavits are required from other persons. E.g., United States Supreme Court Rule 28.5; Illinois Rule 12. In other courts certificates are sufficient from all persons. Federal Rule of Appellate Procedure 25(d).

[12]R. Stern and E. Gressman, SUPREME COURT PRACTICE, p. 473 (5th ed., 1978).

[13]*Id.* at 801.

full court, the number of copies should normally be the same as for a brief. Otherwise, the number of copies to be filed usually conforms to the number of judges to whom the motion is to be submitted, often with an additional copy for the clerk. The United States Supreme Court requires one unprinted copy if the motion goes to a single Justice, and one plus nine if it goes to the entire Court, but 40 for certain kinds of motions or if a motion to the Court is longer than five pages. Rule 42.2. The latter types of motions are to be duplicated in the manner described in Supreme Court Rule 33, which in practical effect means printed.[14]

Federal Rule of Appellate Procedure 27(d), however, requires an original plus three copies for all motions unless the court requests more. Illinois requires the same number for its Appellate Court, which also sits in panels of three, but only the original plus one in the Supreme Court, presumably because in that court motions customarily go to a single justice. Illinois Rule 361(e). New Jersey requires nine for its Supreme Court and five for the Appellate Division. Alaska requires one copy; Tennessee and Wisconsin, two; Iowa, three; Idaho and Nevada, an original plus six; Utah, six; and Connecticut, ten.

11.6 Responses to Motions

The rules of court usually specify the number of days other parties have to oppose, object to or comment on a motion. Seven days is allowed by Federal Rule of Appellate Procedure Rule 27(a) and by a number of states.[15] The United States Supreme Court,[16] Arizona, Connecticut, Delaware and Ohio allow 10 days; Tennessee, Missouri and Minnesota, five. Illinois allows two days after personal service or four days after service by mail (Rule 361(b)(2)). A court may, of course, specify a different period in any particular case.

---

[14]Sixty copies are required in original cases (Rule 9.3). As to the peculiar meaning of printing in the United States Supreme Court and the difficulties which that Court's rules pose for counsel, see Sec. 6.10, *supra;* R. Stern and E. Gressman, SUPREME COURT PRACTICE, Sec. 6.23 (5th ed., 1978). The 1980 rule revision makes no change in this respect.

[15]E.g., Massachusetts, Minnesota, Nevada, Wisconsin.

[16]United States Supreme Court Rule 42.4 provides for 10 days to respond, but further states that the response "shall be made as promptly as possible considering the nature of the relief asked and any asserted need for emergency action," and also that the time limitation may be "otherwise ordered by the Court or a Justice, or by the Clerk" in the first instance under Rule 29.4.

In some states the court will not act on any motion until the opponent's time to respond has expired or the response has been filed. If the movant wishes the court to act expeditiously and believes his opponent will not object, he should ask the opponent so to notify the clerk immediately or to authorize him so to state. If immediate action on a contested motion is essential, the movant should consult the clerk's office in person or by telephone and also notify the opposition in the same way. See Sec. 11.1, *supra.*

In many jurisdictions, including the federal, procedural motions may be acted on without waiting for a response, although, as noted above, other parties may then request reconsideration. Wisconsin allows seven days for this. If a party wishes to object, he should therefore immediately advise the clerk, preferably by telephone, so that the court or motion judge may promptly be informed, and either take the fact of opposition into account or delay the decision until the objector may file a response stating his reasons.

The rules of some jurisdictions prohibit the filing of a reply to the response to the motion,[17] while others do not. District of Columbia Circuit Rule 6(c) permits a reply to be filed within three days after service of the response. Minnesota allows two days; Arizona allows five; Delaware allows seven.

11.7 Oral Argument

Most appellate courts do not allow oral argument on motions, unless special permission is granted.[18] A few do on special application. Some rules are specific as to this and others are not. Argument is more likely to be allowed for motions of substantive importance affecting the merits of the case or such matters as a stay pending appeal or bail. The Second Circuit will allow oral argument, if requested, on certain kinds of motions when the court is in session. (Second Circuit Rule 27(b).)

The chief judge of the Spokane Division of the Washington Court of Appeals has reported that "approximately 50 percent

---

[17]E.g., Alaska Rule 14(b).

[18]The Federal Rules of Appellate Procedure say nothing about oral argument. But the rules of many of the circuits and states provide that oral argument will not be heard on any motion unless ordered by the court. First Circuit Rule 10; Third Circuit Rule 11.1; Fifth Circuit Rule 10.3; Seventh Circuit Rule 6(a); Eighth Circuit Rule 3; Ninth Circuit Rule 6(f); Minnesota Rule 127; Illinois Rule 361(b)(2); Alabama Rule 27(c).

of all motions in his court use telephone conferences."[19] This technique may well be used to dispose of reasonably simple motions, saving counsel both time and travel expense in getting to a court where they often must wait a considerable time before being heard. The American Bar Association's Action Commission to Reduce Court Costs and Delay hopes to experiment with such "telemotions" in a variety of courts.[20]

---

[19]Seth Hufstedler and P. Nejelski, *A.B.A. Action Committee Challenges Litigation Cost and Delay,* 66 A.B.A.J. 965, 967 (1980). Whether this figure relates to all motions, a small proportion heard orally or only those heard by a commissioner or clerk under Washington Rule 17.5 (see Sec. 11.2, *supra*) is not clear.

[20]*Ibid.*

Appendix

Forms

No single form of any appellate document would satisfy the requirements for all of the appellate courts in the United States. Counsel must familiarize himself with the rules, as well as relevant statutes and cases, which govern the court in which his appeal is filed. The following forms of petition for review to a state supreme court, answer to such a petition, and brief on the merits are in the form which this book recommends when permissible under the rules of the particular court. In the main they conform to the practice in most jurisdictions and contain the items most appellate courts want in the order which will be most useful to the judges who read them.

The forms are taken from documents submitted to the Illinois Supreme Court. Illinois Rule 341(d) requires Illinois cases to be cited to the official reports (Ill. or Ill. App.), with additional citations to the North Eastern Reporter optional. Cases from other jurisdictions may be cited from either the official reports, the National Reporter System or both.

Appendix A

Petition for Leave to Appeal From State Intermediate Appellate Court to State Supreme Court

No. 47308

IN THE
SUPREME COURT OF ILLINOIS

LOSS, LEADER & RICH, et al.,
    Plaintiffs-Respondents
    v.
SIXTEENTH NATIONAL BANK, et al.,
    Defendants-Petitioners

Petition for Leave to Appeal from
Appellate Court of Illinois,
First District

There Heard on Appeal from the
Circuit Court of Cook County, Illinois

Honorable Daniel A. Covelli, Judge Presiding

PETITION FOR LEAVE TO APPEAL

LOTTA DOE
SHAD ROE
Attorneys for Defendants-
Petitioners

Of Counsel:

ROE, DOE and NOE
462 S. LaSalle Street
Chicago, Illinois 60604
782-0600

February 10, 1975

504

[Here insert Table of Contents and Index of Authorities
unless contrary to the rules in the jurisdiction.]

IN THE
SUPREME COURT OF ILLINOIS

No. 47308

LOSS, LEADER & RICH, et al.,
Plaintiffs-Respondents

v.

SIXTEENTH NATIONAL BANK, et al.,
Defendants-Petitioners

Petition for Leave to Appeal from
Appellate Court of Illinois,
First District

There Heard on Appeal from the
Circuit Court of Cook County, Illinois

Honorable Daniel A. Covelli, Judge Presiding

PETITION FOR LEAVE TO APPEAL

Petitioners Sixteenth National Bank of Chicago, Alstor, Inc., Like Company, and Never Inn, Inc., pray that they be granted leave to appeal from the judgment of the Illinois Appellate Court, First District, heretofore entered in this cause, and that said judgment be reversed. The respondent-plaintiff law firms are Loss, Leader & Rich, Humpty & Dumpty, and Ruth, Gehrig & Mantle.

The judgment and opinion of the Appellate Court was entered on December 16, 1974. Defendants' petition for rehearing, filed December 30, 1974, was denied January 16, 1975.

POINTS RELIED UPON FOR REVERSAL

I. Whether the courts below erred in awarding to attorneys of certain taxpayers who successfully challenged the constitutionality of a legislative enactment fees out of tax payments made, pending appeal, by other taxpayers not parties to the litigation?

II. Whether the courts below applied erroneous standards in awarding attorneys' fees giving little or no consideration to the time expended by the attorneys and as a result required the payment of exorbitant amounts far beyond the sums to which the attorneys were fairly entitled?

STATEMENT OF FACTS

This matter involves the propriety of an award of attorneys' fees to three law firms, the plaintiffs-respondents.

These attorneys representing various clients brought two actions, later consolidated, in the Circuit Court of Cook County challenging the constitutionality of the 1969 amendment to Section 26 of the Revenue Act of 1939 (*Ill. Rev. Stats.* 1969, Ch. 120 §507) and praying to enjoin its enforcement. (C57–59; C92–95).* Subsequently, an original action was brought before the Supreme Court (by other counsel) also challenging the constitutionality of this 1969 amendment (*Dee-El Garage, Inc.* v. *Korzen,* Case No. 44455).

On June 28, 1971, the Circuit Court of Cook County, by the Honorable Daniel A. Covelli, Chancellor, entered two identical decrees in these two actions which held Section 26, as amended, unconstitutional but did not enjoin the collection of the controverted tax pending appeal. The decrees, however, required any tax moneys collected to be segregated in a "special fund" subject to the jurisdiction of the court for the purpose of awarding costs, expenses, and reasonable attorneys' fees as well as ordering the refund of the collected moneys if the decrees were affirmed on appeal. (C58–59).

Thereafter, assessment notices in the amount of $16,762,349.96 were sent out by the Assessor's office (C187–C210). Only 70 taxpayers, including present petitioners, chose to pay their tax obligations, with the result that only $4,785,883.25 in taxes were collected and segregated in accordance with the Court's decrees. (T. 859–870). No tax moneys were paid by any of the named plaintiffs in the Circuit Court actions.

The appeal by the taxing authorities from the decrees in the Circuit Court actions was consolidated by the Supreme Court for argument with the *Dee-El* action. On October 2, 1972 the Supreme Court issued its opinion finding Section 26, as amended, unconstitutional. (53 Ill. 2d 1). The decrees of the Circuit Court were affirmed and the cause remanded for determination of the disposition of the accumulated fund. (C61–C72).

Upon remand, on December 13, 1972, a joint petition was filed in the Circuit Court on behalf of the attorneys for the named plaintiffs in the Circuit Court actions, seeking as attorneys' fees a sum "not less than" twenty-five percent of the segregated fund. (C79–C148).

---

*All page references refer to Volume I of the Record on Appeal. The Clerk's record is cited as C.——, the transcript as T.——.

During the hearing on the Joint Petition the following facts emerged:

a) The total time spent by the three firms of attorneys from the filing of the original complaint in March, 1970 until the filing of the Joint Petition for fees aggregated 1,661 hours. (T. 68, 345, 415).

b) The normal billing rate for the first firm was stated to be $100 per hour for "a wealthy client" in a tax matter. (T. 71).

c) The normal billing rate at the second firm—apparently without regard to nature of matter or wealth of client—was stated to range between $30 and $75 per hour (T. 271), while that of partners at the third firm ranged between $60 and $75 per hour. (T. 651).

On April 27, 1973, Judge Covelli entered a Final Judgment Decree (C483–C490), ordering that fifteen percent (15%) of the assessed taxes paid into the special fund, a total of $717,882.49, be divided equally among the three sets of attorneys. (C488). The clients of these firms had already paid them $138,263.35.

Thus, the recovery for each of the three sets of attorneys from the order here appealed is as follows:

(a) First firm—276 hours (T. 68)—total recovery $239,294.16; resulting rate of $867.52 per hour.

(b) Second firm—886 hours (T. 345)—total recovery $304,093.-25; resulting rate of $343.22 per hour.

(c) Third firm—499 hours (T. 415)—total recovery $312,758.41; resulting rate of $626.77 per hour.

The aggregate recovery awarded is $856,145.84 at a rate of $515.44 per hour.

Petitioners are taxpayers who, during the pendency of the appeal in the Circuit Court actions, paid under protest a total of $2,852,401.78 of the controverted tax pursuant to assessment notices. Under the Circuit Court decree, petitioners have been charged the following amounts in attorneys' fees.

Sixteenth National Bank	—$278,264.46
Alstor, Inc.	—$ 81,017.68
Like Co.	—$ 14,283.77
Never Inn	—$ 54,294.34
Total	$427,860.25

Petitioners appealed the Circuit Court's allowance of fees to the Illinois Appellate Court, First Division, contending (1) that Illinois law precludes the award of fees in the circumstances here presented, and (2) that even if fees could be appropriately awarded, the fees here were excessive in amount. The attorneys cross-appealed on the ground that the record justified an award of 25% of the fund or an amount of $1,196,470.81 at an average rate of $720.33 per hour.

On December 16, 1974, the Illinois Appellate Court affirmed the lower court's allowance of fees at an average rate of $515.44 per hour. This petition requests leave to appeal from that decision.

REASONS FOR GRANTING THE PETITION

This case presents two questions which are of sufficient importance, both to taxpayers and to members of the bar, to require a resolution by this court. On both, we submit, the decision below is in conflict with other decisions of this court and is plainly wrong.

A. The first question is whether in the circumstances here presented attorneys for certain taxpayers who successfully challenged the constitutionality of a legislative enactment are entitled to be paid legal fees by other taxpayers who were not parties to the litigation. This Court has previously directed itself to this question, holding that attorneys' fees should not be awarded in a class action, apparently irrespective of the involvement of a fund, "wherein the plaintiff seeks a declaratory judgment that a legislative enactment is unconstitutional." *Rosemont Building Supply, Inc., et al.* v. *Illinois Highway Trust Authority, et al.*, 51 Ill. 2d 126, 130 (1972). Cf. *Hoffman* v. *Lehnhausen*, 48 Ill. 2d 323 (1971); *Doran* v. *Cullerton*, 51 Ill. 2d 553 (1972).*

In the recent decision of *Flynn* v. *Kucharski*, 59 Ill. 2d 61 (1974), this Court allowed an award of attorneys' fees in a dispute involving the legality of a diversion of collected tax moneys. Despite the apparent distinction between *Flynn* and the prior Supreme Court decisions controlling in the instant matter, the Illinois Appellate Court for the First District has erroneously interpreted the *Flynn* decision as holding the earlier cases to apply only when no fund was in existence.

It is true that a so-called fund exists in the present matter. However, whereas in *Flynn* and other typical fund situations the plaintiff had forced defendants to establish a fund for the benefit of other class members with money defendants were unlawfully retaining, in the present matter the fund is comprised of payments of tax obligations by petitioners and other taxpayers, not parties to the litigation, made after the Circuit Court judgment of unconstitutionality with such payments being segregated as a protective device to ensure the return of these moneys if the tax was held invalid.

---

*In the *Rosemont, Hoffman* and *Flynn* cases, as here, the complaints seem to have requested both declaratory and injunctive relief, but in *Rosemont* and the instant case the prayer for a declaration of constitutionality received predominant attention.

Furthermore the precise scope of the *Flynn* decision in relation to this Court's holdings in *Hoffman, Rosemont,* and *Doran* is presently before the Court in *City of East Peoria et al.* v. *Tazewell County et al.* (No. 46704) in which the Appellate Court for the Third District, following the prior Supreme Court decisions, held that fees should not be awarded in litigation wherein the plaintiff seeks a declaratory judgment that a legislative enactment is unconstitutional. 17 Ill. App. 3d 943 (1974).

We respectfully submit that the public interest in the clarification of the law on this subject would be served if this Court considered the instant matter as well as the *East Peoria* case, so as to make clear the circumstances in which third persons who benefit from litigation involving others are required to pay attorneys' fees.

B. The second question, which assumes that the Court resolves the point just discussed in favor of the allowance of attorneys' fees, is whether the court below applied erroneous standards in fixing the fees for the attorneys here, and as a result required the payment of exorbitant amounts far beyond the sums to which the attorneys were fairly entitled.

Judge Covelli in the Circuit Court made it clear that his award of attorneys' fees in the amount of 15% of the taxes assessed and paid* by present petitioners and other taxpayers did not in any way take into account the time and labor expended by the attorneys. On the contrary, in answer to the contention that time and labor were the primary factors to be considered, he stated:

> "This is not a quantum meruit procedure. . . . This being a contingent fee basis, if they put in 25 minutes they still want 25 percent. So I think we're wasting time when we are talking about hours."

In so holding, Judge Covelli's decision was clearly contrary to this Court's subsequent ruling in *Flynn* v. *Kucharski, supra,* wherein the Court, reducing the fee award to $75.00 per hour, stated (59 Ill. 2d at 66–67):

> "In a case of this kind the fee is not, as it is in the usual contingent-fee case, an amount that has been fixed by voluntary agreement between the client and his attorney. Rather, it is an amount taken, by order of the court, from money that belongs to others. The rights of those others must be carefully considered as well as those of the attorneys. In our opinion the time expended in such a case *is not to be relegated to a secondary or minor*

---

*The inappropriateness of using a percentage standard which bears no relation to the efforts expended by the attorneys is further demonstrated by the fact that out of assessment notices in the amount of $16,762,349.96 only the $4,785,883.25 paid by taxpayers, including present petitioners, into the special fund created by Judge Covelli has been charged with a 15% attorneys' fee. If all the persons assessed had timely paid their taxes, under Judge Covelli's decree the attorneys would have received over $2.5 million in fees.

position; it is a highly significant factor in determining the fee." (Emphasis supplied.)*

Judge Covelli's decree required the payment of fees of a total of $717,882.49 to be divided equally among the three sets of attorneys. The clients of the three law firms had already paid them $138,263.35. The aggregate recovery thus amounted to $856,145.84 for 1,661 hours of work, or an average of $515.44 per hour.

The Appellate Court stated that (p. 8):

"The normal billing rate for the three law firms ranged from $60 to $100 per hour."

Clearly neither Court below gave weight at all to the time expended by the lawyers involved, as *Flynn* requires they should.

We do not suggest that time is the only factor to be considered. As enumerated in *Flynn,* other factors commonly taken into account in awarding fees include (59 Ill. 2d at 66):

"a) The novelty, complexity and difficulty of the case.
"b) The contingent nature of the fee.
"c) The benefit to the class and to the public.
"d) The skills and qualification of counsel."

In considering these various factors in *Flynn* where "the fee was entirely contingent" (59 Ill. 2d at 66), this Court held that the amount awarded to the lawyers should not exceed $75 per hour.

We do not question the skills and qualifications of counsel here, nor the novelty and difficulty of the litigation, though it may be noted that it was determined on summary judgment without the need for trial. However, the apparent benefit to the class† as a result of the nullification of the 1969 amendment to Section 26 of the Revenue Act of 1939 (*Ill. Rev. Stat.* 1969, Ch. 120 §507) will be substantially diminished by the back tax assessments for which present petitioners will be liable due to the automatic reinstatement of the former Section 26.‡

---

*The Appellate Court here sought to distinguish the *Flynn* case on the ground that the attorneys there had failed "to keep records of the amount of time they spent on the case." This Court did mention that fact, but it does not justify awarding attorneys who did keep records approximately seven times as much per hour as the attorneys in the *Flynn* case.

†Whatever benefits were derived as a result of this litigation were shared by all taxpayers subject to the law in question. Ironically those taxpayers who chose to ignore tax assessment notices (in the amount of $11,976,466.71) and not pay their tax obligations when due received the "benefits" at no charge whatsoever.

‡In holding the 1969 amendment unconstitutional in *Dee-El Garage* v. *Korzen,* 53 Ill. 2d 1 (1972), this Court stated:

"The effect of enacting an invalid amendment to a statute is to leave the law in force as it was prior to the adoption of the amendment (citing cases). Accordingly, the provision for taxing leasehold interests in tax exempt property as contained in Section 26 before the 1969 amendment remains in force and, in fact, was never repealed or replaced by the invalid amendment."

And although in a contingent fee case attorneys are properly entitled to additional amounts for the risk they are taking of not recovering any fees if their clients do not prevail, the firms here were not proceeding on a contingent basis, as they were being compensated by their clients for their time.

In perhaps the best reasoned recent federal appellate decisions on the subject, *Lindy Bros. Builders* v. *American Radiator & Standard Sanitary Corp.*, 487 F.2d 161 (3rd Cir. 1973) and *City of Detroit* v. *Grinnell Corporation*, 495 F.2d 448 (2nd Cir. 1974), the Courts of Appeals, approaching the problem in the same way as this Court did in *Flynn*, stressed the primary importance of first determining the time spent on the case and the reasonable hourly rates for such time. After that the contingent nature of any recovery (only partly present here), the quality of the attorneys' work, the complexity and novelty of the issues, and the amount of the recovery were also to be taken into account. In *Lindy* the Third Circuit significantly added (487 F.2d at 168):

> "In making allowance for the quality of work, the court must keep in mind that the attorney will receive an otherwise reasonable compensation for his time under the figure arrived at from the hourly rate. Any increase or decrease in fees to adjust for the quality of work is designed to take account of an unusual degree of skill."

In the *Detroit* case the Second Circuit reversed a fee award where the District Court, though "eschewing any reliance upon a percentage fee approach" (p. 470), had awarded a fee which amounted to exactly fifteen per cent of the settlement recovery, just as did the courts below here. In holding that the "only legitimate starting point" in determining fees in a class action is the amount of time actually spent by the attorneys multiplied by "typical hourly rates" (p. 471), the Court emphasized that any other standard, particularly a percentage award, is inherently improper—a windfall at the expense of the members of the class the attorneys purportedly represent. The Court stated (495 F.2d at 469, 470):

> "For the sake of their own integrity [and] the integrity of the legal profession, . . . it is important that the courts should avoid awarding 'windfall fees' and that they should likewise avoid every appearance of having done so."

> "Anchoring the analysis to this concept [the amount of time the attorney has expended on the case] is the only way of approaching the problem that can claim objectivity, a claim which is obviously vital to the prestige of the bar and the courts."

In attempting to justify the District Court's award which compensated him at a rate of $635 per hour, the petitioning attorney had directed the Court's attention to other cases where awards were even greater. To this the Court replied (495 F.2d at 473, n. 13):

> ". . . these observations merely illustrate the results that accrue when a fee is awarded on a contingency basis without reference to the labor actually expended on the client's behalf."

The same can be said of many of the cases upon which appellees here relied in the courts below.

While in the ordinary contingent class action case it may well be that the attorneys are entitled to more than their normal hourly rates for time spent, nevertheless it should be kept in mind that in the ordinary case the fees are charged proportionately to each and all members of the class represented, whereas in this case the entire fee is being assessed against only a small portion of the class which paid the taxes segregated pursuant to the Circuit Court's orders. The other two-thirds of the class are receiving all of the "benefits" without any expense whatsoever. In any event in *Flynn* only $75 per hour was allowed—not $515—and in two antitrust cases in the United States District Court in Chicago cited by both parties below, counsel were allowed $90 and $152 per hour.* The need for considering other factors thus clearly does not justify a flat percentage award which will give counsel the amounts per hour allowed here.

The Appellate Court in the instant matter suggested that if the trial court had considered time spent, the judge "should have given them more than the 15% awarded". We have difficulty in following this reasoning. It fails to start out with time spent as the most significant factor, and instead builds up from an amount based upon the element of contingency, contrary to the standards prescribed in *Flynn* v. *Kucharski* and the other authorities cited above.

The Appellate Court also stated that in the exercise of its "independent judgment" it found that the 15% of the fund "represents an equitable fee". We submit that the Appellate Court also did not observe this Court's standards requiring that time and labor be treated as "highly significant" and not secondary. Its decision also represents an abuse of discretion.†

The question here presented far transcends in importance the facts of this case. It is highly important to the public, which includes

---

Illinois v. *Harper & Row Publishers, Inc.,* 55 F.R.D. 221 (N.D. Ill. 1972, Decker, J.); *Colson* v. *Hilton Hotels,* 59 F.R.D. 324 (N.D. Ill. 1972, Marovitz, J.). See also *Liebman* v. *J. W. Peterson Coal & Oil Co.* (N.D. Ill., April 5, 1974, Will, J.) in which Judge Will, adopting the same approach, fixed reasonable fees at the attorneys' normal hourly rates, none of which exceeded $90 per hour.

†We are not unmindful of the fact that three lawyers, unaffiliated with the present proceeding, testified in support of the Joint Petition for fees. (T. 76–143; 507–554; 557–627.) It should be noted that their opinion was based upon practices in Federal Courts with respect to class actions in the securities field and with respect to bankruptcy proceedings. These are precisely the areas where abuses are most apparent with respect to a contingent fee system applied against unrepresented members of a class.

This Court has expressed justifiable skepticism as to the value of such testimony (*Lee* v. *Lomax,* 219 Ill. 218, 221 (1905)). See also *Richheimer* v. *Richheimer,* 59 Ill. App. 2d 354, 365 (1st Dist. 1965).

large taxpayers as well as small, and also persons in other types of class litigation, that they not be charged legal fees over five times as much as attorneys paid on a time basis. It is also important to the Bar that the standards which the courts of Illinois should follow in fixing attorneys' fees should be clarified, so that lawyers cannot be charged with mulcting their clients or—as here—a large body of persons who are not their clients. We submit that these considerations should induce this Court to review and reverse the decisions of the courts below.

CONCLUSION

For the above reasons, petitioners submit that they should be granted leave to appeal and that the judgment of the Appellate Court should be reversed.

Respectfully submitted,

LOTTA DOE
SHAD ROE

Attorneys for
Defendants-
    Petitioners

Of Counsel:
ROE, DOE and NOE
462 South LaSalle Street
Chicago, Illinois 60604
STate 2-0600

February 10, 1975

APPENDIX

OPINION OF THE APPELLATE COURT
[Quote in Full]

[LEAVE TO APPEAL WAS GRANTED AND THE JUDGMENT BELOW REVERSED. 62 Ill. 2d 483]

Appendix B

Answer to Petition for Leave to Appeal From State Intermediate Appellate Court to State Supreme Court

No. 46226

IN THE
SUPREME COURT OF ILLINOIS

EVAN STEPHEN

Plaintiff-Petitioner,

vs.

EQUIPMENT, INC., an Illinois corporation

Defendant-Respondent.

On Petition for Leave to Appeal from the Appellate Court of Illinois, Second Appellate District. There Heard on Appeal from the Circuit Court of Kane County.

ANSWER TO PETITION FOR LEAVE TO APPEAL

O. O. NOE
LOTTA DOE
462 South LaSalle Street
Chicago, Illinois 60604
STate 2-0600
Attorney for Defendant-
Respondent

Of Counsel:
ROE, DOE and NOE
462 South LaSalle Street
Chicago, Illinois 60604

October 30, 1973

[Here insert Table of Contents and
Index of Authorities unless contrary
to the rules in the jurisdiction.]

IN THE

SUPREME COURT OF ILLINOIS

EVAN STEVEN

Plaintiff-Petitioner,

vs.

EQUIPMENT, INC., an Illinois corporation

Defendant-Respondent.

On Petition for Leave to Appeal from the Appellate Court of Illinois, Second Appellate District. There Heard on Appeal from the Circuit Court of Kane County.

ANSWER TO PETITION FOR LEAVE TO APPEAL

THE ISSUES

As the Court will discover when it compares the Petition for Leave to Appeal with the opinion of the Appellate Court (set forth in the Appendix to the Petition, hereinafter cited as App.), the questions which petitioner seeks to present here do not pertain to the principal grounds upon which the Appellate Court decided the case.

The questions actually presented by the decision below are:

1. Whether there was insufficient evidence of damages to go to the jury on Counts II, III and IV of the complaint.

2. Whether confusion as to the theory on which the case was pleaded, tried, submitted to the jury, and appealed required a retrial as to Count I.

THE FACTS

The facts as stated in the Petition for Leave to Appeal contain exaggerations and inaccuracies, but since they do not relate to the ground of the Appellate Court decision, there is no good reason to go into detailed factual matters here.

The facts with respect to plaintiff's alleged damages are fully reviewed in the Appellate Court opinion. See also pp. 6–8, *infra.* The opinion painstakingly sets out the testimony of plaintiff himself, which the defendant has always conceded must be taken to be true in determining whether there was evidence to support the verdict of the jury. As noted above, petitioner does not assert error as to any of this, or even refer to it. The evidence relating to the alleged fraud, which the petition does purport to summarize, would not warrant reversal of the Appellate Court, since plaintiff is not entitled to recover in the absence of adequate proof of damages.

[Alternative methods of introducing the statement of facts are:

The facts as stated in the Petition for Leave to Appeal can be accepted for purposes of the petition before the Court.

[OR

The facts as stated in the Petition for Leave to Appeal contain exaggerations and inaccuracies in a number of important respects.

[OR

The selection of facts in the Petition for Leave to Appeal is sufficiently inaccurate or misleading so as to require a complete and accurate statement of the material facts here.

Then, if necessary, correct or amplify the statement of facts in the petition or restate the facts, whichever seems more appropriate.]

REASONS FOR NOT GRANTING THE PETITION

The decision of the Appellate Court turned on the evidence and the record in this case. The rulings that there was insufficient evidence of damages to go to the jury on Counts II, III and IV, and that on Count I a new trial was necessary because of confusion as to the instructions and as to the theory on which the Count was tried will not affect any case but this one. These rulings are not challenged in the Petition and, as we shall show, were clearly correct. Indeed, the unchallenged reasoning of the Appellate Court as to the insufficiency of plaintiff's evidence as to damages with respect to Counts II, III and IV, would, as the opinion strongly suggests (App. 17), probably be dispositive of Count I on the remand.

The only points which are raised in the Petition would not lead to a reversal of the Appellate Court's judgment. Thus the Appellate Court's general discussion of the circumstances in which a promise as to future conduct may constitute fraud (App. 12–14)—which is the only portion of the opinion below which the Petition seeks to have reviewed—is at most an alternative holding not essential to the disposition of the case.

Clearly the case in no way satisfies the standards set out in Rule

315(a) for granting petitions for leave to appeal. The issues turning on the facts of record in the particular case are not of "general importance" and do not involve conflicts with other decisions of this Court or the Appellate Court. Rule 315(a), though not limiting this Court's exercise of discretion was, like Rule 19 of the United States Supreme Court on which it was modeled, designed to permit this Court to keep up with its caseload by limiting itself to the disposition of "cases which present questions whose resolution will have immediate importance far beyond the particular facts and parties involved."* The United States Supreme Court does not "grant certiorari to review evidence and discuss specific facts" (*United States* v. *Johnston*, 268 U.S. 220, 227 (1925)), except in extraordinary circumstances. The criteria in this Court should be the same.

In any event the decision of the Appellate Court was correct, and there is no good reason to overturn it. We deal with the Counts in the same order as did the Appellate Court.

Count II. Count II charged that defendant fraudulently failed to carry out an agreement to provide a merchandise outlet for plaintiff's line of liquid tight fittings for one year, causing plaintiff to forego negotiating with other companies. Plaintiff claimed that he was entitled to the profits he would have made if he had manufactured and sold the fittings, which he estimated would range from $18,650 to $56,250 (App. 19). The jury awarded him $100,000 as prayed for in the complaint. The Appellate Court found that the evidence as to damages not only did not support the verdict but was "purely speculative" (App. 9, 15).

A consistent course of Illinois decisions, including the decision of this Court in 1969 in *Weiland Tool & Mfg. Co.* v. *Whitney*, 44 Ill.2d 105, 117, 251 N.E.2d 242, 249 (1969), has uniformly held that "profits cannot be recovered as an element of damages where they are speculative, contingent or uncertain," particularly when based entirely upon the testimony of a highly "interested witness". *Salaban* v. *East St. Louis and Interurban Water Co.*, 284 Ill. App. 358, 361–362, 1 N.E.2d 731, 733 (1936). The *Weiland* case reiterated that profits must be proved with some "definiteness".

The cases differentiate between "a long established business" the owner of which "generally has it in his power to prove the amount of the expenses of operation and the income he has derived from it for a long time before, and for the time during the interruption of which he complains" (*Roseland* v. *Phister Mfg. Co.*, 125 F.2d 417, 420 (7th Cir., 1942)), and a " 'new venture' as to which it may be an estimated loss of profits would be improper, because of uncertainty and speculation"

---

*Chief Justice Vinson, *Work of the Federal Courts*, 69 S. Ct. vi (1949).

(*Meyer* v. *Buckman,* 7 Ill. App.2d 385, 406, 129 N.E.2d 603 (2d Dist., 1955)).*

Here the profits which plaintiff was claiming were for a new enterprise which had not even risen to the status of a "venture". Plaintiff was hoping to manufacture a product which he had never made before except in prototype form. The record does not show that he had acquired the necessary equipment or any facilities for manufacturing. And if he had been able to commence production, he would have had to compete with established companies. His estimated prices were the same as theirs, but whether he would have obtained customers without selling at a lower price is purely speculative. Profitability would depend upon costs, prices and the volume of business, all of which were completely conjectural. Volume would, of course, depend upon price which would in turn depend both upon cost and competitors' prices. His estimate of volume and profits in such circumstances could thus be nothing more than a prophecy or guess. Here, as in *Weiland Tool & Mfg. Co.* v. *Whitney, supra,* even if plaintiff had sold his fittings there is no proof that volume would have been adequate to produce a profit or that a profit was attainable at any volume.

To clinch the matter, it should be sufficient to point out, as did the Appellate Court (App. 10), that although defendants' alleged agreement to merchandise plaintiff's liquid tight fittings was only for one year, plaintiff "never sold any of his liquid tight fittings to the industry" during the approximately five years from July, 1965, when he and defendant came to the parting of the ways, to the date of trial. Defendant was not restricting him during that period.

Count III. In this Count plaintiff alleged that defendant had failed to carry out an agreement to fill unfilled orders of BMFC. Although plaintiff would not have profited personally from those orders and was not personally liable for BMFC's failure to complete them, the jury awarded him the $50,000 prayed for under this Count. His argument was that the damages were for injury to his reputation, but, as the Appellate Court said (App. 11), there is absolutely no evidence in the record to show that there was any such damage. Though challenged repeatedly to do so, plaintiff has been unable to point to any such evidence either in his brief below or his Petition to this Court.

Count IV. Under Count IV plaintiff claimed and was awarded $50,000 for defendant's failure to make available to him the same facilities as BMFC had for work in the development of liquid tight fittings. Although plaintiff testified that the value of these facilities was $900 per month, "the somewhat incongruous situation," as the court below noted, is that he "had testified that by the summer of 1965 he had for all practical purposes completed the work on the fittings." (App. 12.)

---

*Plaintiff's brief below (pp. 76–77) conceded that it is a "horn book proposition that anticipated profits are not recoverable when the claimant is not an established business".

There was "no evidence whatsoever as to time deemed necessary even by the selfserving testimony of plaintiff himself." (App. 12.) Since there was no evidence that these facilities were needed for *any* time, there was no evidence to show that Steven was entitled to any damages under this Count.

In any event, the evidence that plaintiff suffered any damage from not having such facilities available to him was completely speculative. There was no evidence that he did, or attempted to do, any development work on the fittings after July 1965, that he needed such or similar facilities to do this or other work at that time or for any time thereafter or, for the reasons stated above with respect to Count II, that he would have profited from the use of such facilities. In the absence of proof of damages, the Count was properly dismissed.

Count I. In this Count plaintiff claimed that defendant had agreed to employ him part-time for $15,000 per year and the jury brought in a verdict for $140,000, the amount prayed for. Plaintiff's testimony as quoted in the Appellate Court's opinion (App. 16–17) is all that is relied on to show an agreement and damages for this Count, and, as the Appellate Court said, "It is difficult to perceive how plaintiff arrived at that amount and even more difficult to determine how the jury reached that figure from the evidence presented." (App. 17.)

Indeed, the conversation upon which plaintiff relied in Count I was so vague and indefinite that it is doubtful whether it constituted a contract at all. If this Court should grant leave to appeal, we will contend that plaintiff was not entitled to any damages under this Count, and that therefore the verdict as to it too should have been reversed without a remand. See Rule 318(a).

In any event, the Appellate Court was clearly correct in finding that the proceedings as to Count I were too confusing for the verdict to stand. On its face the Count pleads a breach of contract (C. 903). Plaintiff tried his case on the theory of fraud, as appears from his counsel's statements to the Court when the instructions were being prepared and his argument to the jury. The instruction to the jury on Count I was clearly on a fraud theory: it required the plaintiff to prove "that the representation was knowingly and intentionally false" (R. 1366). Plaintiff's counsel had stated that "We have no objection to Defendant's 3", the instruction in question (R. 1226). Only in the Appellate Court did plaintiff try to shift back to the contract theory.

At the conference on instructions, it appeared, as the Appellate Court found (App. 18), that counsel for both parties were unclear as to whether the Count was based on fraud or breach of contract, and that the trial judge was also confused as to this (R. 1247–1254). The Appellate Court admitted that it could not tell, and reasonably concluded that the jury also could not have been certain.

[Discussion of record facts omitted.]

There was thus ample basis for the Appellate Court to find that the whole course of the litigation showed confusion and inconsistency on the part of plaintiff's counsel as to the theory under which Count I was tried, as well as for the basis for the jury verdict.

The remand for a new trial on Count I was therefore more than plaintiff was entitled to. The Count should have been dismissed, since there was no evidence to support an award of damages under a charge to the jury to which all parties had agreed, or indeed on any other rational theory.

The only part of the opinion below challenged in the Petition is the Appellate Court's recognition that, as an alternative basis for its decision, fraud cannot be predicated on "mere oral promises concerning future performance," which are not regarded as misrepresentations of fact. This Court has often so held, most recently in *Sinclair* v. *Sullivan Chevrolet Co.*, 31 Ill.2d 507, 510, 202 N.E.2d 516, 518 (1964) and *Illinois Rockford Corp.* v. *Kulp*, 41 Ill.2d 215, 224, 242 N.E.2d 228, 323 (1968). See also *Brodsky* v. *Frank,* 342 Ill. 110, 117–118, 173 N.E. 775, 778 (1930); *Hayes* v. *Disque,* 401 Ill. 479, 488, 82 N.E.2d 350, 355 (1948); *Miller* v. *Sutliff,* 241 Ill. 521, 526, 89 N.E. 651, 652 (1909); *Gage* v. *Lewis,* 68 Ill. 604, 615–616 (1873). Indeed, plaintiff does not dispute that the "general rule" in Illinois is "that a failure to comply with a future promise, without more, does not constitute fraud" (Pet., p. 15). This was recognized in a jury instruction (R. 1376). Nor does plaintiff deny that the alleged "oral agreement of February 2nd is the linchpin of plaintiff's action" (Pet., p. 13).

Plaintiff contends, however, that the *Illinois Rockford* and other cases* establish that a fraud action may be sustained when the false representation of intent is part of a scheme or device to defraud. But those cases were totally different from the case at bar because they involved parties to fiduciary relationships or other factors which indicated that they had not dealt at arm's length. In the *Illinois Rockford* case, in addition, this Court found not merely a false promise but misrepresentation in failure to reveal the fact of prior negotiation in which it had been agreed that defendant would be paid more than plaintiff for a company they owned equally. The instant case, in which the parties dealt at arm's length under the guidance of counsel, clearly does not fall in that category. The Appellate Court has not disputed the authority of such cases, and whether the facts of a case fall within one category or another does not present an issue of general importance.

The Appellate Court held that since plaintiff had not shown that he was entitled to actual damages, he was not entitled to punitive

---

Roda v. *Berko,* 401 Ill. 335, 339–341, 81 N.E.2d 912, 915 (1948); *Willis v. Atkins,* 412 Ill. 245, 259–261, 106 N.E.2d 370, 377–378 (1952).

damages, citing authorities so holding.* Petitioner does not assert error as to this.

Moreover, recent decisions of this Court establish that plaintiff was not entitled to punitive damages in any event. *Herman* v. *Prudence Mutual Casualty Co.*, 41 Ill.2d 468, 480, 244 N.E.2d 809, 815 (1969); *Knierim* v. *Izzo*, 22 Ill.2d 73, 87–88, 174 N.E.2d 157, 165 (1961) (proof of more than basic ingredients of cause of action necessary). In *Herman* a deliberate misrepresentation in order to induce a plaintiff to sign a release without consulting a lawyer was held not sufficiently wanton or malicious to justify punitive damages. Here, on the contrary, plaintiff and defendant were business people dealing at arm's length, both represented and assisted throughout by able counsel, in a dispute which in perspective turned upon the existence and performance of unusually unspecific oral understandings. Since the claim here also is that plaintiff was induced to sign a release of his claim against defendant, the *Herman* case is closely in point.

CONCLUSION

The Appellate Court has ordered a new trial as to Count I. The points which plaintiff requests this Court to review are not dispositive of the case. For the above reasons—and particularly because the Petition does not and cannot challenge the clearly correct rulings of the Appellate Court which in themselves support its decision—the Petition for Leave to Appeal should be denied.

Respectfully submitted,
O. O. NOE
LOTTA DOE
462 South LaSalle Street
Chicago, Illinois 60604
STate 2-0600
Attorney for Defendant-Respondent

---

*In *Madison* v. *Wigal*, 18 Ill.App.2d 564, 576–577, 153 N.E.2d 90, 97 (2d Dist., 1958), the Court stated:

". . . Actual damages must be proven and awarded in order to substantiate awarding punitive damages, while punitive damages are not compensatory they cannot be awarded unless actual damages are shown, *Fentz* v. *Meadows*, 72 Ill. 540. . . ."

The abstract opinion of the Appellate Court in *Shrout* v. *McDonald's System, Inc.*, 90 Ill.App.2d 60, 234 N.E.2d 45 (1968), stated on this point (Abst. Op., p. 5):

". . . Where actual damages are not recoverable, there can be no award of punitive damages. *Reeda* v. *The Tribune Co.*, 218 Ill. App. 45; *Madison* v. *Wigal*, 18 Ill.App.2d 564, 153 N.E. 2d 90. . . ."

Of Counsel

ROE, DOE and NOE
462 South LaSalle Street
Chicago, Illinois 60604

October 30, 1973

[LEAVE TO APPEAL WAS DENIED. 54 Ill. 2d 599 (1973).]

Appendix C

Brief on the Merits in a State Supreme Court

No. 45844

IN THE
SUPREME COURT OF ILLINOIS

BRUNSWICK CORPORATION,
      Plaintiff-Petitioner,

vs.

THUNDERBIRD, INC., et al.,
      Defendants-Respondents.

On Petition For Leave To Appeal From Appellate Court
Of Illinois, First District, Fourth Division.

BRIEF FOR PETITIONER BRUNSWICK

SHAD ROE
O. O. NOE
462 South LaSalle Street
Chicago, Illinois 60604
STate 2-0600
Attorneys for Brunswick Corporation

Of Counsel:

ROE, DOE and NOE
462 South LaSalle Street
Chicago, Illinois 60604

October 30, 1973

[Most jurisdictions require a Table of Contents and alphabetical Index of Authorities at this point. A few others (including Illinois since December 1980) require that the Points and Authorities (see pp. 526–527, *infra*), with page numbers added, appear at this point instead of the table and index.]

TABLE OF CONTENTS

PAGE

Nature of the Proceedings 525
Jurisdiction 525
Issues Presented for Review 526
Statutory Provisions Involved 526
Points and Authorities 526
Statement of Facts 528
Argument 529
I. Brunswick Had Both Substantive And Procedural Rights To Repossess The Equipment 530
   A. Brunswick was Entitled to Repossess the Property Under its Contract and the Commercial Code 530
   B. Brunswick was Entitled to Repossess the Property Under the Replevin Act 531
   C. Brunswick is not Limited to Recovering the $74,000 at Which the Bowling Equipment was Valued in the Replevin Complaint 535
II. Thunderbird Is Not Entitled To Enjoin Brunswick's Repossession Of The Property From It 540
Conclusion 540
Appendix—Illinois Replevin Act . . . . .App. 540

[Here insert Index of Authorities if the rules of the jurisdiction so require.]

IN THE
SUPREME COURT OF ILLINOIS
No. 45844

BRUNSWICK CORPORATION,
Plaintiff-Petitioner,

vs.

THUNDERBIRD, INC., et al.,
Defendants-Respondents

On Petition For Leave To Appeal From Appellate Court
Of Illinois, First District, Fourth Division

BRIEF FOR PETITIONER BRUNSWICK

NATURE OF THE PROCEEDINGS

This case involves Brunswick's attempt to repossess in a replevin proceeding bowling equipment on which respondents in possession had defaulted under a conditional sales contract, leaving $379,690 in principal unpaid. The circuit court entered judgment for plaintiff after trial, but the Appellate Court reversed on condition that plaintiff be paid $74,000.00, the value placed upon the equipment in its replevin complaint, plus the interest on that amount during the period the equipment was wrongfully retained by defendants.

On November 14, 1972, this Court granted Brunswick's petition for leave to appeal.

JURISDICTION

This appeal is from a final judgment dismissing plaintiff's complaint. The Appellate Court's jurisdiction rested on Rule 301, and this Court's on Rule 315.

The judgment of the Appellate Court was entered on September 3, 1972. A petition for rehearing filed on September 16 was denied October 3. Plaintiff's petition for leave to appeal to this Court, filed on October 30, was granted November 14, 1972.

ISSUES PRESENTED FOR REVIEW

1. Whether a plaintiff who has established its right to property has the right in a replevin action to repossess the property irrespective of its value, or whether the defendant or Appellate Court may require the plaintiff to accept the value of the property as stated in the replevin complaint and affidavit.

2. Whether a plaintiff in replevin in entitled, in addition to repossession, to damages based on the deterioration of the property while it was wrongfully detained by the defendant.

STATUTORY PROVISIONS INVOLVED

The provisions of the Replevin Act, Ill. Rev. Stat., Ch. 119, §§ 1–26, are set forth in the Appendix to this brief. The pertinent provisions of the Commercial Code (Ill. Rev. Stat. (1971), Ch. 26, §§ 306, 501–506) are quoted at pp. 18–19, *infra.* [If these provisions were short, they could be quoted here.]

[Only a few states require Points and Authorities, some at this point and others at the beginning of the brief with page references in lieu of the table of contents and index of authorities. Since December 1980, Illinois Rule 341(e) requires the Points and Authorities to appear at the beginning of the brief, with page references.]

POINTS AND AUTHORITIES

I.

BRUNSWICK HAD BOTH SUBSTANTIVE AND PROCEDURAL RIGHTS TO REPOSSESS THE EQUIPMENT.

A. Brunswick was Entitled to Repossess the Property Under its Contract and the Commercial Code.
    Commercial Code (Ill. Rev. Stat. (1971), Ch. 26 §§ 306, 501–506)

B. Brunswick was Entitled to Repossess the Property Under the Replevin Act.
    When property has been found a plaintiff in replevin is entitled to the property and not merely to a judgment for its value.

Replevin Act (Ill. Rev. Stat. (1971), Ch. 119, §§ 1–26)
Kehoe v. Rounds, 69 Ill. 351, 353 (1873)
O'Toole v. Klimek Boat and Engine Works, 24 Ill.App.2d 111, 115
(1st Dist., 1960)
Annotation, 170 A.L.R. 122 (1947)
77 C.J.S. Replevin, Section 131
Schwantz v. *Pillow,* 7 S.W. 167, 169 (Ark., 1888)
Charlotte Barber Supply Co. v. *Branham,* 191 S.E. 891, 893 (S.C.,
1937)
Kunz v. *Nelson,* 76 P.2d 577, 582 (Utah, 1938)
Brook v. *James A. Cullimore & Co.,* 436 P.2d 32, 34 (Okla., 1967)

Cases distinguished

Cottrell v. *Gerson,* 371 Ill. 174 (1939)
James B. Clow & Sons v. *Yount,* 93 Ill. App. 112 (1st Dist., 1900).

C. Brunswick is not Limited to Recovering the $74,000 at Which the
Bowling Equipment was Valued in the Replevin Complaint.
Snydacker v. *Brosse,* 51 Ill. 357 (1869)
Peters for use of Keenon v. *Brown,* 245 Ill. App. 570 (1st Dist.,
1927)
Farson v. *Gilbert,* 85 Ill. App. 364 (1st Dist., 1898)
Martin v. *Hertz,* 224 Ill. 84 (1906)
Brook v. *James A. Cullimore & Co.,* 436 P.2d 32 (Okla., 1967)
Respondents cannot invoke an estoppel since they did not
change their position in reliance upon the alleged representation
by Brunswick.
Levin v. *Civil Service Commission,* 52 Ill.2d 516, 524 (1972)
Malloy v. *City of Chicago,* 369 Ill. 97, 104 (1938)
Hickey v. *Illinois Central R.R. Co.,* 35 Ill.2d 427, 447 (1966)
Dill v. *Widman,* 413 Ill. 448, 456 (1953)
The trial court may enter the judgment which is correct as a matter
of law, and is not bound by pleadings or prayers for relief.
Ill. Rev. Stat. (1971), Ch. 110, §§ 34, 46, ¶ (3)
Pope v. *Speiser,* 7 Ill.2d 231, 243 (1955)

II.

DEFENDANT IS NOT ENTITLED TO ENJOIN BRUNSWICK'S RE-
POSSESSION OF THE PROPERTY FROM IT.
Lewis v. *Blumenthal,* 395 Ill. 588, 593 (1947)
People ex rel. American National Bank v. *Smith,* 110 Ill.App.2d 354,
362 (1st Dist., 4th Div., 1969)

STATEMENT OF FACTS

The facts insofar as relevant to the issues before the Court are as follows:

On February 28, 1962, Thunderbird, Inc. placed an order with Brunswick for bowling equipment, of which the principal items were 36 bowling lanes and pinsetting machines to be installed in a bowling establishment to be built on Rand Road in Mount Prospect, Illinois. The specified price was $610,042.70 (including $127,025.10 for interest), of which $45,000 was paid at the time and $565,042.70 was to be paid over eight years (R. 22–23). The cash price of the equipment was $483,017.60, of which $303,264 was for the automatic pinsetters.

The equipment was delivered and installed by Brunswick, which under the contract and note retained a security interest in the property. The contract provided that title "shall not pass to Buyer until the total amount payable as herein provided is actually paid" (Para. 3), and that if "the Buyer defaults . . . the Seller . . . may take immediate possession of said property" (Para. 10) (R. 24–25).

The bowling operation, managed by Thunderbird, was not successful.* In February, 1964 Brunswick agreed to rearrange and extend the schedule of payments, but in February, 1966 payments were discontinued (R. 181), and none have been made since. $379,690 of the original purchase price thus remains unpaid.

On April 17, 1967, Brunswick filed its "Complaint in Replevin" (R. 45–46), alleging that on October 11, 1966 it had demanded possession of the property and been refused, that Thunderbird was wrongfully detaining the property and that Brunswick was lawfully entitled to it. The complaint averred that the value of the property was $74,000, and alleged "that in the event that said property is not returned plaintiff will be damaged in the sum of $74,000 for the value thereof and in the sum of $305,690 for damages sustained by such wrongful damage and use thereof" (R. 46, ¶ 5). The complaint prayed (R. 46):

> ". . . judgment that said property be returned or that defendants be required to pay the value thereof, $74,000, and that defendants pay to the plaintiff damages in the sum of $305,690 for said wrongful detention."

The bond attached was in the amount of $148,000, twice the stated value of the property, as required by Section 10 of the Replevin Act (Ill. Rev. Stat. (1971), Ch. 119, § 10).

The sheriff thereupon served the writ of replevin at the premises containing the property, and respondent Thunderbird executed a redelivery bond in the same amount pursuant to Section 14 of the

---

*Evidence summarized in the opinion of the Appellate Court (App. 7–8) indicated that Thunderbird's losses resulted from inefficiency in its management.

Replevin Act. As a result it and its successors in interest have retained the property pending determination of the litigation (R. 175).

In September, 1971, the circuit court found after trial (R. 176, ¶ 7):

". . . The Court finds that Brunswick is entitled to have possession of the goods and chattels together with damages for detention from October 11, 1966. Said damages are for depreciation in value during the period of detention computed on the straight line method based on a 15 year life."

The judgment of the court as to the replevin count of Brunswick's complaint was that:

"It Is Ordered, Adjudged, Determined And Decreed As Follows (R. 184):

"A. Plaintiff Brunswick Corporation is, and at all times since the making of its demand for possession on October 11, 1966, has been entitled to the possession of all of the goods and chattels described in paragraph one of its original complaint for replevin herein; and is entitled to have and recover of and from defendant Thunderbird Bowl, Inc., possession of the property described in paragraph 3 hereof and judgment is entered in accordance therewith. (R. 186).

"B. Defendant Thunderbird Bowl, Inc., from and after October 11, 1966, has wrongfully detained from plaintiff Brunswick Corporation the goods and chattels referred to in Paragraph 'A' preceding.

"C. Defendant Thunderbird Bowl, Inc., is obliged to pay said plaintiff the damages sustained by said plaintiff on account of the wrongful detention of said goods and chattels, by said defendant, from and after October 11, 1966, to the present time, and said plaintiff shall have judgment therefor against said defendant in the amount of $157,456.80." (R. 184).

The Appellate Court modified the relief granted, saying simply that since Brunswick's prayer was "that the property be returned or that defendants be required to pay the value thereof, $74,000," plus damages for wrongful detention, defendants were entitled to retain the equipment on payment to Brunswick of $74,000 plus interest of $18,243.05 for the period that the property was wrongfully detained. (No. 45844, App. to Pet. 14.)

[A few jurisdictions require a Summary of Argument at this point.]

ARGUMENT

The effect of the decision of the Appellate Court has been to deprive a supposedly secured creditor of any effective means of recovering either the equipment to which it retained title or more than a small proportion of the price for which the equipment was sold. This result was reached only by disregarding the long understood meaning of the replevin statute as well as Brunswick's rights under the conditional sales contract and the Commercial Code.

I.

BRUNSWICK HAD BOTH SUBSTANTIVE AND PROCEDURAL RIGHTS TO REPOSSESS THE EQUIPMENT.

A. Brunswick was Entitled to Repossess the Property Under its Contract and the Commercial Code.

The terms of the conditional sales contract and the provisions of the Commercial Code (Ill. Rev. Stat. (1971), Ch. 26, §§ 306, 501–506) plainly establish that as a matter of substantive law Brunswick was entitled to repossess the bowling equipment after the purchaser discontinued payment of the required installments.

As shown at p. 8, *supra,* the contract provided that title did not pass from the seller to the buyer "until the total amount payable . . . is actually paid" and that if "the Buyer defaults . . . the Seller . . . may take immediate possession of the property."

These rights are confirmed by the Commercial Code. Section 9–501 of the Code* states that "when a debtor is in default under a security agreement, a secured party has the rights and remedies provided in this Part and except as limited by subsection (3) those provided in the security agreement." He may "foreclose or otherwise enforce the security interest by any available judicial procedure." Section 9–503 further provides, in substantially the language of the contract here, that a "secured party has on default the right to take possession of the collateral"—either without judicial process if that can be done peacefully or by action.

Under Section 9–506 the debtor may "redeem the collateral by tendering fulfillment of all obligations secured by the collateral as well as the expenses reasonably incurred by the secured party" in repossessing and selling it. This means that the purchasers here have the right to recover the goods upon *payment in full of the indebtedness,* not the value of the goods at any particular time, plus the creditor's costs in retaking and selling it.

Section 9–306(2) provides that "a security interest continues in collateral notwithstanding sale, exchange or other disposition thereof by the debtor," with exceptions irrelevant here. This means that Brunswick's right to the property continued notwithstanding the various transfers or other dispositions of it through the line of other respondents in these actions.

Under the contract and these provisions of the Commercial Code Brunswick clearly has the right to the property, and the purchasers have no right to interfere with Brunswick's repossession and retention of it except by payment of the total amount due, as Section 9–506 in particular makes clear.

---

*All of the Code provisions are contained in Ill. Rev. Stat. Ch. 26.

The decision of the Appellate Court deprives Brunswick of this basic right, in contravention both of the agreement freely entered into and of the provisions of the Commercial Code. Although $379,690 plus interest remained unpaid under the contract at the time of default, the decision of the Appellate Court requires Brunswick to accept $74,-000 plus interest of $18,243.05 on that amount in place of the property.

The value of the property undoubtedly has fluctuated with the fortunes of the bowling business since the time of the original sale. The record shows that the original purchase price for a new pinsetting machine in 1962 was $8,100 (R. 64) and that at the time of the trial used machines were sold by Brunswick after reconditioning for $6,350 (R. 410). For a period in the 1960's the supply exceeded the demand, but this is no longer so. (The separate prices for the other items of equipment do not appear in the record.) The value of the equipment in place was estimated at $74,000 for purposes of Brunswick's replevin bond (R. 438–440); respondent's answer denied the accuracy of the estimate, which it characterized "as a matter of opinion" (R. 50).

These differences in value or in estimates of value for various purposes and at various times do not affect Brunswick's right to possession of the property. Indeed, the very fact that the value of the property is both disputable and continually changing is good reason for allowing the owner-seller to insist upon enforcement of his contractual right to repossession of the property itself, so long as the amount specified in the contract of sale, which presumably represented its value at the time of sale, remains unpaid.

B. Brunswick was Entitled to Repossess the Property Under the Replevin Act.

The basic concept of the Illinois Replevin Act (Ill. Rev. Stat. (1971), Ch. 119), is to provide a remedy for the recovery of property by the person who has the right to possession, not merely a judgment for whatever the Court finds to be the value of the property. Other remedies are available for securing a money judgment. Only if the physical property cannot be found can the plaintiff having a right to repossess it be remitted to a recovery of its value. Here, of course, no one is claiming that the bowling equipment cannot be found. It has remained on the same premises since it was first sold by Brunswick in 1962.

The Appellate Court has held that if the wrongful possessor of the property pays the person with the right to possess the value placed on the goods in the replevin affidavit, he is entitled to retain possession. This ruling is inconsistent with the statute and the controlling authorities, as well as with the rights vested in a conditional seller by his contract and the Commercial Code.

The Replevin Act provides for the recovery "by the owner or person entitled to their possession" of goods "wrongfully detained" (§ 1). Section 4 provides that the complaint shall describe the property, and state that plaintiff "is the owner . . . or that he is then lawfully entitled to the possession thereof" and that "the property is wrongfully detained by the defendant." Nothing is required to be said about actual value. Under Section 7 the sheriff or other appropriate officer is directed to take the property from the defendant "and deliver the same to the plaintiff," unless the defendant executes the bond referred to in Section 14.

The statute then provides for bonds to protect the parties and the sheriff or officer against injury if it turns out that the wrong party has possession of the property before the proceeding is finally concluded. The plaintiff must first provide the officer with a bond "in double the value of the property" to insure return of the property to the defendant and to pay all costs and damages resulting from the wrongful suing out of the writ if the Court so orders; the bond also serves the function of protecting and saving harmless the officer who has seized the property if the Court finds that defendant was entitled to keep it (§ 10). Upon receipt of this bond the officer is to take and deliver the property to the plaintiff unless the defendant executes a bond in the same amount to guarantee delivery of the property "in as good condition as it was when the action was commenced" if the plaintiff prevails in the action (§ 14).

The only reference in the statute to paying the plaintiff the *value* of the property is in Section 18, which gives the plaintiff the option of proceeding to judgment for the value of the property and damages for the property or any part of it which "has not been found or delivered." This Section reads as follows:

> "§ 18. *When the property* or any part thereof *has not been found or delivered* as aforesaid, and the defendant is summoned or enters his appearance, the plaintiff may proceed, under original or amended complaint, as in an action for the wrongful taking and detention of such property or so much thereof as is not found and delivered to the sheriff or other officer, and *as to the property not found and delivered,* the plaintiff, if he shall recover, shall be entitled to judgment for the value thereof or his interest therein, and such damages as he shall have sustained by reason of the wrongful taking and detention." (Emphasis supplied.)

This provision for recovery of value "when the property or any part thereof has not been found or delivered" means clearly that no such judgment is to be entered for property which can be found, as is also apparent from the remainder of the statute. The Act obviously does not mean that the defendant has the option of limiting the plaintiff to recovery of the value of the property by refusing to deliver the property to the seizing officer. The argument accepted by the court below would mean that a debtor could force his creditor to sell secured property to him at a value fixed by the Court. This would convert the replevin statute into a device for compulsory condemnation for private purposes, which it clearly was never intended to be.

The cases confirm that neither in Illinois or elsewhere has the law of replevin been so distorted.

It has long been settled in this state that when the property has been "found" a plaintiff in replevin is not entitled to a judgment for the value of the property. Thus in *Kehoe* v. *Rounds,* 69 Ill. 351, 353–354 (1873), the Court held:

> "There is no authority, under the statute, for the court to render judgment for the value of the property, as in an action of trover, except in cases where it shall appear the officer was unable to obtain it on the replevin writ. This fact does not appear in the case, and hence the judgment is unwarranted."

A more recent decision, which followed *Kehoe,* is *O'Toole* v. *Klimek Boat and Engine Works,* 24 Ill.App.2d 111, 115 (1st Dist., 1960). That was a replevin case in which the goods were "found" and defendant kept possession by posting a redelivery bond. The Appellate Court held that a judgment for plaintiff for the value of the goods was void, saying (p. 115):

> *"There is no authority under the statute to render judgment for the value of the property in a replevin action where the writ has been returned 'property found.'* If the legislature had so intended it would have so stated. (*Kehoe* v. *Rounds,* 69 Ill. 351.) Ill. Rev. Stat. 1957, Sec. 18, provides that when 'property is not found' the plaintiff shall be entitled to 'Judgment for the value thereof' or his interest therein; and such damages as he shall have sustained by reason of the wrongful taking and detention.
>
> "We find that the judgment entered on July 1, 1958 is void in that it transcended the statutory authority specifically given and was directly contrary to the statute. . . ." (Emphasis supplied.)

The law in other jurisdictions is the same. The general rule is stated in 77 C.J.S. Replevin, Section 131:

> "In general, a redelivery bond stands in place of the property as security for the payment of the value thereof, so that plaintiff may rely on it exclusively, but *not so as to entitle defendant, after judgment against him, to pay the assessed value and retain the property.* Thus the effect of defendant's re-bonding is to turn the suit into an action for damages for the value of the property or for the return of the goods to plaintiff, at his option. *However, the redelivery bond in replevin is a substitute for the property only in those cases where a delivery of the property cannot be had on final judgment.* A redelivery bond which is conditioned on defendant's performance of the judgment of the court in the action is not in a strict sense a substitute for the property released in pursuance thereof, and does not give the surety on the bond the option to return the property." (Emphasis supplied.)

An Annotation in 170 A.L.R. 122 (1947), notes that modern statutes provide for an alternative judgment for money in a replevin action, and deals with the problem presented when the judgment may or must be in the alternative, as was prayed in the complaint here. The cases are there summarized as holding (*id.* at pp. 123, 124):

> "Where an alternative judgment is entered in a replevin action, it is practically the universal rule that the successful party to the action has the right to retain or obtain possession of the disputed property, and that the party wrongfully in possession does not have the right to retain the property and pay the alternative money judgment, if the property can be returned to the party entitled to possession thereof.
> "The cases (see Whetmore v. Rupe (1884) 65 Cal 237, 3 P 851) point out that to permit the defendant to make an election would be to give him, because of his wrongdoing, the privilege of restoring the article to its owner or paying instead its value as fixed by a jury."*

The reasons for requiring return of the property, not merely of its value, have been elaborated in several of the decisions in other states. In *Schwantz* v. *Pillow,* 7 S.W. 167, 169 (Ark., 1888), the Supreme Court of Arkansas, in holding that a plaintiff need not accept the alternative valuation of the mule there involved, stated:

> ". . . The appellant's contention that the bond required to enable a defendant in replevin to retain the property, stands for all purposes, in lieu of the property itself, would lead to this: that a party without color of right acquires an absolute title, against the true owner who sues him for the possession of specific articles of personal property, by the execution of a bond to retain the possession. If that result had been contemplated by the legislative, the provision directing delivery of the property to the plaintiff, in case the verdict is in his favor, would not have been added. . . . If the plaintiff recovers, the judgment of the court in the first instance is for the delivery of the property. . . ."

Similarly, in *Charlotte Barber Supply Co.* v. *Branham,* 191 S.E. 891, 893 (S.C., 1937), which involved the replevin of certain barber chairs and related equipment, the Court stated:

> "There is no merit in the contention made by the appellant that he may, at his option, deliver the property in dispute, or pay the value thereof as assessed by the jury. *The appellant overlooks the vital point that he may pay the value only in the event possession of the property cannot be had.* This claim advanced by the defendant, under the admitted facts, is arresting and

---

*The Annotation further points out that there is a difference of view among the authorities as to whether the *successful* party has the option of requiring payment of the value instead of taking repossession of the property, but states that (170 A.L.R. 124):

> "The most generally accepted view is that the successful party to a replevin action is not entitled to recover the value of the property unless the other party is unable to return the property taken, and that the unsuccessful litigant is entitled to satisfy an alternative judgment by delivery of the property for which the action is brought."

startling in its implications. The principle involved is utterly untenable, and contrary to the statute.

"In such actions, the prevailing party, under the law, and under a verdict of this character, should have the right and opportunity to first exhaust every available and appropriate remedy known to the law, in the effort to locate and gain possession of the property in dispute, before he should be required or forced to accept the alternative verdict, the value assessed by the jury." (Emphasis supplied.)

To the same effect see *Kunz* v. *Nelson,* 76 P.2d 577, 582 (Utah, 1938); *Brook* v. *James A. Cullimore & Co.,* 436 P.2d 32, 34 (Okla., 1967), *infra,* pp. 33–34.

It is thus clear that under the authorities which have interpreted the Illinois Replevin statute and similar laws in other states Brunswick had a right to repossess the physical property to which it was entitled, and that respondents-defendants had no right to insist that they retain the property upon payment to Brunswick of its value.

C. Brunswick is not Limited to Recovering the $74,000 at Which the Bowling Equipment was Valued in the Replevin Complaint.

The opinion of the Appellate Court does not mention any of the statutory provisions, principles and authorities referred to above. It relies entirely on the fact that Brunswick valued the property at $74,-000 for bonding purposes, and prayed in the alternative for the return of the property or payment of its value, adding that "to permit Brunswick to recover damages in excess of the value stated by it in its affidavit would work a serious injustice" (Op., p. 13).

Respondents had contended that Brunswick was barred from recovery under the doctrines of estoppel and judicial admission.

The fundamental error of the Appellate Court in finding the value placed on the property conclusive is that the value is relevant for two purposes neither of which is present here. If a defendant's property is seized, the amount of the plaintiff's bond, if unduly low, might be inadequate to protect the defendant if plaintiff obtains the property but defendant ultimately is held entitled to it and sues to collect on the bond. When, however, the defendant retains the property by executing his own forthcoming bond in the same amount, the lower the plaintiff's evaluation the smaller the bond the defendant must provide. In that circumstance defendant benefits if the plaintiff has placed a low evaluation on the property.

The principal effect of the evaluation is upon the amount which a plaintiff may recover if the property is not found. In that situation alone, as we have shown, is plaintiff entitled under Section 18 of the Replevin Act to judgment for the value of the property plus any damage sustained by reason of the wrongful intention. Even then, the plaintiff's valuation is only *prima facie* evidence of the value of the property; it is not conclusive, as the cases discussed at pp. 29–31, *infra,* attest. But where the property is available, plaintiff is entitled to recover possession, not the value of the property, and the valuation in such case is irrelevant. That is the situation here.

Accordingly, even if the allegation and affidavit of value be regarded as a judicial admission, it is the admission of a fact irrelevant to the relief to which Brunswick is entitled, and therefore cannot be deemed controlling as it was by the Appellate Court.

Moreover, the circumstances clearly make the law of estoppel inapplicable. For it is well established that the party invoking an estoppel "must have changed his position for the worse, upon a representation concerning a material fact to a party ignorant of the matter, with the intention that it be acted upon, and which has been acted upon." *Malloy* v. *City of Chicago*, 369 Ill. 97, 104 (1938). "Whether the principle of estoppel is sought to be applied against a public body as in this case or against a private individual, the one claiming the benefit of the principle must have relied upon the actions or representations of the other and must have had no knowledge or convenient means of knowing the true facts. (*Hickey* v. *Illinois Central R.R. Co.*, 35 Ill.2d 427, 447; *Dill* v. *Widman*, 413 Ill. 448, 456.)" *Levin* v. *Civil Service Commission*, 52 Ill.2d 516, 524 (1972).

Here all parties were familiar with the relevant facts, and the respondents' only reliance upon Brunswick's valuation of the bowling equipment was in determining the size of its own redelivery bond. Indeed, respondents' answer to Brunswick's complaint *denied* the allegation of value and averred "that the value alleged for said property is a matter of opinion" (R. 50). Brunswick was not attempting to induce respondents to act upon the valuation to their detriment; the only pertinent action which respondents could take was the posting of their own bond in the same amount in order to retain the property, as they did. A low value worked to respondents' advantage in this respect, not the contrary. Furthermore, respondents were obviously not "ignorant of the matter". They knew that the cash price of the equipment in 1962 had been $483,000. Finally, so long as the property could be found and physically repossessed, the valuation was not "material", except for purposes indicated above with respect to which the representation has not been harmful to the respondents. Thus for almost every significant fact the requisites for establishing an estoppel are absent here.

The decisions of this Court and of the Appellate Courts (although the latter are not entirely harmonious) do not treat the statements in replevin bonds as conclusive upon the party making them.

In *Snydacker v. Brosse*, 51 Ill. 357 (1869), an action for replevin, the Court stated (p. 363):

> "It is urged, that appellee, having sworn, in her affidavit, that the property was her husband's when she commenced the replevin suit, is

estopped from now suing for any damage to it. Such an affidavit is, no doubt, strong evidence to prove that the property belonged to her husband, but at the same time it is not conclusive. She might, if she could, explain the affidavit, and show that the property belonged to her; and it is for the jury to say, from all the circumstances, whether she succeeded in the proof."

Subsequently in *Farson* v. *Gilbert,* 85 Ill.App. 364 (1st Dist., 1898), the Appellate Court rejected the contention "that the plaintiff in replevin, who has fixed the value of the property by his statement in his affidavit for the writ, is estopped from afterward asserting a different value when sued upon his bond" (pp. 365–366). The Court reasoned that (p. 366):

> "But such a rule would many times operate very harshly and unreasonably. It is common knowledge that such statement of value is usually made without a very nice attention to the real value of the property, but is made largely as an estimate, based somewhat upon the amount of the plaintiff's claim, lest under some circumstances the jury might not, perhaps, be at liberty to give him more than the value he had himself estimated.
>
> "The effect of a rule that the amount set out in the replevin affidavit is conclusive evidence of the value of the property, in a suit upon the bond, would often be liable to work serious injustice, and such would be especially true in cases like the present, between lien holders. Upon careful consideration, we regard the better rule to be as stated in *Gibbs* v. *Bartlett,* 2 Watts & Serg. 29, viz.: 'It (the amount stated in the replevin affidavit) has ever been considered as *prima facie,* but not conclusive evidence.'
>
> "In accordance with such rule, either party should, in a suit upon the replevin bond, be permitted to show by parol evidence the actual value of the property the defendant has failed to return."

The *Farson* case was cited approvingly by this Court in *Martin* v. *Hertz,* 224 Ill. 84 (1906), where the Court stated that "the value stated in the replevin affidavit is at least *prima facie* evidence of value in a suit upon the replevin bond." The *Martin* and *Farson* cases were in turn followed by the Appellate Court in *Peters for use of Keenon* v. *Brown,* 245 Ill. App. 570 (1st Dist., 1927), where the Court, after quoting from both of those cases and commenting disapprovingly on two Appellate Court cases which it believed not to be in accord with them, concluded (245 Ill. App. at 574–575):

> "On principle we are not disposed to approve of a rule which would prevent the actual facts from being disclosed in an action of this kind. Value is very often a mere matter of opinion. We see no good reason why the actual facts should not be permitted to be shown by competent testimony. The statement in *Cermak* v. *Cable Piano Co., supra,* [211 Ill. App. 219] to the effect that a witness who signed the affidavit in replevin may not qualify or modify the statements therein made when afterwards called as

a witness, must be regarded as inadvertently made. See 23 R. C.L. § 57, p. 898; *Maguire* v. *Pan-American Amusement Co.,* 205 Mass. 64.

"We hold that the defendant Surety Company in this case was not concluded or estopped on the question of value by the statement of Mrs. Brown in her affidavit as to the value of the goods or by the value stated in the writ which issued."

In its opinion (App. 12–13) the Appellate Court attempts to distinguish the *Snydacker* and *Farson* cases on their facts, but it does not mention the more recent *Martin* or *Peters* cases, or indicate why the refusal of the courts to give conclusive effect to the affidavits in the *Snydacker* and *Farson* cases, whether or not factually distinguishable, should be distinguished in principle from the other cases or the case at bar.

Here if the value of the property was relevant to the relief to which Brunwick was entitled—and we have already shown that it was not—the value stated in the complaint (and denied in respondents' answer) was at most *prima facie* evidence, which was outweighed by the actual contract price of $305,833 agreed upon between the respondents and S.T. in 1967, the year in which the complaint in replevin was filed (see pp. 10–12, *supra*), and also by oral testimony that a reconditioned pinsetter was priced at $6,350 (R. 410).

The Appellate Court's decision rested to a substantial extent on the fact that Brunswick's prayer for relief was in the alternative, for the return of the property or payment of its value. The court overlooked the inclusion in the second alternative of $305,690 damages for wrongful detention, in addition to the $74,000. (R. 46, quoted at p. 9, *supra*). Moreover, the Court gave undue emphasis to the prayer; Section 34 of the Civil Practice Act (Ill. Rev. Stat. (1971), Ch. 110, § 34) provides that "except in cases of default, the prayer for relief does not limit the relief obtainable", so long as the other party is protected from prejudice resulting from surprise.

The prayer here was in accord with Illinois practice; it conforms to the form for complaints in replevin set forth in 9 Nichols, *Illinois Civil Practice,* § 7461. This form undoubtedly reflects the fact that the plaintiff may recover the value of any portion of the property not found. It does not signify that when the property can be found plaintiff is giving *the defendant* the option, which he would not have under the law, of deciding whether plaintiff shall be allowed to repossess the property or instead be paid a sum of money in substitution therefor.

The authorities discussed at pp. 22–26, *supra,* are decisive as to this. In particular, the Annotation in 170 A.L.R. 122 collects the authorities on the precise problem. Indeed, it was "concerned only with those cases in which it affirmatively appears that an alternative judgment was actually entered." Even when the judgment—and not merely the complaint—is in the alternative, the cases there summarized hold that the successful party either takes the property, if it can be found, or has the option of deciding whether to accept its value instead. It is clear, however, that the unsuccessful defendant wrongfully in possession is not given this election. See pp. 23–26, *supra.* It is precisely this right to elect which respondents are demanding here.

The A.L.R. Annotation was cited with approval quite recently in *Brook v. James A. Cullimore & Co.,* 436 P.2d 32 (Okla., 1967). The plaintiff there sued in replevin for property covered by a chattel mortgage to secure a note for $8,147.26. The petition and affidavit for replevin valued the property at $2,500, and the complaint sought judgment in the alternative for the possession of the property or for $2,500 plus costs and an attorney's fee, "in the event delivery cannot be had in substantially the same condition as at the time of the filing of this action" (436 P.2d at 33). Defendant offered to confess judgment and to satisfy the judgment by paying the amount prayed for, which plaintiff refused. The Court held that defendant has no right to compel plaintiff to accept a payment of the value of the property in lieu of repossession. Its reasoning is so pertinent that we quote it at length (*Id.* at pp. 34, 35):

> "If a return of the property sought by replevin is possible, it *must* be returned. *Leeper, Graves & Co.* v. *First Nat. Bank of Hobart,* 26 Okl. 707, 110 P. 655, 29 L.R.A., N.S., 747. *The defeated litigant is not granted an option to either relinquish possession or pay the value of the property. This rule applies with equal force when, as here, the successful plaintiff prays judgment for possession of the property or for its value as set forth in the affidavit. The alternative prayer is not to be treated as an election to accept money damages in lieu of the return of the property. It does not confer upon the defeated defendant a power to pay the value of the property and retain it as his own.* The alternative remedy of a money judgment in replevin is extended solely for the benefit of the wronged party and affords a measure of relief only when the property cannot be returned. . . .
>
> "Here, the law did not afford Brook an option to pay the value of the property and retain it as his own, against Cullimore's will. Cullimore did not elect to accept a money judgment in lieu of the property sought to be recovered. . . . The unsuccessful litigant in replevin has no right to the cumulative remedy of an alternative money judgment since, we reiterate, that remedy avails to the wronged party only. . . ." (Emphasis supplied.)

The many cases cited from many states in the A.L.R. Annotation as holding that the successful party has the right to repossess the property if he so elects, even where the *judgment,* and not merely the complaint, as here, is in the alternative are *a fortiori* in point.

Here the judgment of the Circuit Court was not in the alternative. It merely found that Brunswick was entitled to possession. Under the above authorities this was correct as a matter of law, so long as the property could be found. Indeed, these cases establish that even if the judgment had been in the alternative pursuant to the prayer for relief, the successful party with the right to possession, not the wrongful detainer, has the right to elect which alternative should be chosen.

II.

THUNDERBIRD IS NOT ENTITLED TO ENJOIN BRUNSWICK'S REPOSSESSION OF THE PROPERTY FROM IT

[Remainder of Argument omitted.]

CONCLUSION

For the foregoing reasons Brunswick submits that the judgment of the Appellate Court should be reversed and the judgment of the Circuit Court affirmed.

Respectfully submitted,

SHAD ROE
O. O. NOE
462 South LaSalle Street
Chicago, Illinois 60604
STate 2-0600

Of Counsel
ROE, DOE and NOE
462 South LaSalle Street
Chicago, Illinois 60604

Attorneys for
Brunswick Corporation

October 30, 1973

APPENDIX

Ill. Rev. Stat. (1971)
(Chapter 119 before 1973 Amendments.)
Chapter 119

REPLEVIN

An Act to revise the law in relation to replevin. Approved February 9, 1874. R. S. 1874, p. 851.

[Statute Quoted]

[JUDGMENT WAS REVERSED. 57 Ill. 2d 461 (1974)]

Index

A

Abney v. *U.S.* 70, 71
Abstracts 178, 190–197
Adams; U.S. v. 96
Adickes v. *Kress & Co.* 269
Agreed statement of facts 172
Alabama
    certiorari petition and brief, simultaneous filing 131, 215
    deferred appendix system 177
    electronic transcript recording 167–168
Alaska
    electronic transcript recording 167
    interlocutory appeals 62
Allen, W. 228
Allied Chemical Corp. v. *Daiflon, Inc.* 75
Ambler v. *Whipple* 453
American Bar Association, reports of 479, 481, 488, 490
American Jurisprudence 303
American Law Reports 303
Amici curiae
    briefs of 51, 249, 335–343
    oral argument denial to 343, 371–372
Anders v. *California* 43
Answering argument 437–441
Answering briefs
    color of cover 249
    contents of 245–246, 327–330
    filing time 220, 222
    page limitation for duplicated briefs 229
Answering questions in oral argument 426–432
Antitrust cases 117–118

Appeal as of right
    and discretionary review 152–154
    interlocutory appeals 56–57
    from intermediate to supreme court 119–122
    overview of 18–22
    from trial court to supreme court 116–119
Appellant briefs
    color of cover 249
    contents of 244–245
    filing time 219–220, 222
    page limitation for duplicated briefs 229
    statement of facts in 274
Appellants
    in courtroom 441–442
    identifying terms for 240–243, 412
    rebuttal in oral argument 433–437
    standing to appeal 49–51
Appellate courts
    administration, relation to appellate practice 5–6
    appellate jurisdiction 14–15
    case load increases 22–24
    conferences
        post-hearing 480–481
        prehearing 477–480
    historical background 6–7
    law clerks 28
    original jurisdiction 12–14
    staff attorneys 27–30
    structure 7–12
Appellate procedures
    appealing a decision, guidelines for 41–44
    new counsel 44–49

Appellate procedures—*Contd.*
  for original jurisdiction cases 15–18
  raising of issues in lower court 37–41
  standing to appeal 49–51
Appellee briefs (*See* Answering briefs)
Appellees
  answering argument of 437–441
  identifying terms for 240–243, 412
  requesting of oral argument 367–368
Appendix
  color of cover 249
  content of 158
    reduction of 179–183
  deferred appendix system 179, 200–205
  filing with certiorari petition 132
  as narration or verbatim quotation 190–197
  need for 176–179
  number of copies 183–187, 208
  preparation standards 197–200
  reproduction standards 187–190
  what constitutes 41, 157, 179, 197
Argument
  in *amicus* brief 342
  in answering brief 329
  in brief 280–289
  in petition for certiorari 146–148
  summary of argument 276–280, 328
Arizona
  interlocutory appeals 55, 63–64
  oral argument 25n, 213
  rehearing petition as supreme court review petition 32n, 134–135, 217–218, 452–453
Arkansas
  narrative abstract required 194–195
  panel and *en banc* sitting by appeals court 12n
  records, reproduction requirements 198
  supreme court original jurisdiction 13
Articles, citation of 317
Assignment of errors 89–90, 262
Authorities (*See* Cases)

B

Banks v. *Chicago Trimmers* 50
Barnett; U.S. v. 128
Bell, Griffin 79
Bitner, Harry 309, 311
Black, Hugo 372, 414, 432
Blonder-Tongue Laboratories, Inc. v. *University of Illinois Foundation* 270
Bluebook 309, 310, 312, 314–317

Bonds
  for costs on appeal 88, 107–109
  supersedeas 109–111
Books, citation of 317
Brandeis, Louis D. 303, 319
Brandeis briefs 319–320
Brennan, William J. 358
Briefs
  amicus briefs 335–343
  answering briefs 327–330
  argument 280–289
  argument summary 276–280
  arrangement of preliminary items 251–256
  Brandeis briefs 319–320
  briefs below, use in supreme courts 30–33, 216–219
  checking for errors 226, 348–352
  citation of cases 296–300
    format 309–317
    supra and *infra* 323–324
  conclusion 326–327
  concurring and dissenting opinions, citation of 304–305
  contents 244–246
  covers 246–249
  and docketing 105
  filing times 219–224
  footnotes in 324–325
  headings 243–244
  identification of parties 240–243
  importance of 210–214
  inaccurate or disparaging statements in 291–295
  judges' reading of before oral argument 475–477
  judicial notice and 317–323
  jurisdictional statement 257–259
  nature of proceeding 256–257
  non-case material as authority 301–303
  number of copies 345–348, 352–354
  in opposition to certiorari petitions 148–150
  overruling decisions, guidelines for obtaining 303–304
  page limitation 226–230
  petitions distinguished from 214–216
  points and authorities 250–251
  preparation for writing of 230–233
  questions presented 261–270
  quotations in 305–309, 345
  in rehearings 460
  reply briefs 331–333
  reproduction standards 344–345
  revising of 224–226
  sample form 523–540

serving and filing of 222–223, 352–357
statement of facts 270–276
statutes involved 259–260
supplemental briefs and statements 333–335
table of contents in 249–250
time for filing 219–224
types of 209–210
use in preparing oral argument 384–385
writing guidelines 233–240, 289–291, 295–300
Brunswick Corp. v. *Sheridan* 58
Bryant v. *Yellen* 50
Bulluck v. *Washington* 470
Burger, Warren 123, 158, 321, 361

C

California, interlocutory appeals 75–76
Captions in briefs 252
  identification of parties in 240–241
Cardozo, B. 302n
Carmichael v. *Eberle* 470
Carolina, Clinchfield & Ohio Ry. v. *U.S.* 129
Carrington, P. 362n
Carson, R. 283, 297, 359
Case load increases 22–24
Cases
  in briefs, purpose 295–300
  citation format 309–317
  in oral argument 421–423
  points and authorities, brief requirements 250–251
  supra and *infra* use 323–324
  use in preparing oral argument 385–386
Certification
  in interlocutory appeals 59–61, 65–68
  to supreme courts
    by courts of other jurisdictions 154–155
    by intermediate courts 126–130, 151–152
Certiorari petition (*See* Petition for certiorari)
Certiorari writ 73–78
Charts, in oral argument 418–419
Checking of briefs 226, 348–352
Chrysler Corporation v. *Brown* 239
Circuit courts of appeals (*See also* specific circuits)
  appendices and briefs, number of copies 185n
  case load 22–23

cases, citation format for 312–313
certification to Supreme Court 126
establishment 8–9
oral argument 364
rehearings *en banc* 465–470
Citation of cases (*See* Cases)
Clark, Charles E. 210
Clients, in courtroom 441–442
Closing right in oral argument 376–379
Code of Professional Responsibility 44
Cohen v. *Beneficial Industrial Loan Corp.* 70–72
Colorado, oral argument 213
Colors
  of brief covers 249
  of certiorari petition covers 143
  of petition for rehearing 461
Commission on Revision of the Federal Court Appellate System 363, 484
Commission on Standards of Judicial Administration 490
Common law, citation in briefs 301
Conclusion
  of brief 326–327
  of oral argument 432–433
Concurring opinions, use
  in briefs 304–305
  in oral argument 426
Congressional Record 316–317
Connecticut
  arrangement of preliminary items in briefs 254
  briefs and records, number of copies required 185, 346, 348
Consolidation of cases 382
Constitutional law, citation in briefs 301
Constitutional questions
  direct appeal to supreme courts 116–117, 119–120, 152–153
  notification to government 106–107
Contempt as means of interlocutory appeal 78–79
Coopers & Lybrand v. *Livesay* 60, 65, 67, 69, 71, 72
Copies, number of
  appendices 183–187, 208
  briefs 345–348, 352–354
  motions 498–499
  notices of appeal 83
  petitions for certiorari 131
  petitions for rehearing 461
  supplemental briefs and statements 335
Corpus Juris Secundum 303
Costello v. *U.S.* 269

Costs of appealing 42–43
  bond requirement 67, 83, 88, 107–109
  docketing fees 87–88
  payment of filing fee 133
Counsel
  arguer, selection of 368–369
  courtroom arrival time 375–376
  dress style 400–401
  new counsel for appeals 44–49
  number of in oral argument 379–382
  speaking style 398–400
Covers (*See also* Colors)
  of appendices 197
  briefs, information required on 240, 246–249
  of certiorari petitions 143
  of petitions for rehearing 461
Cox Broadcasting Corp. v. *Cohn* 70, 71, 78
Criminal cases
  argument section of brief 283
  filing time for briefs 221
  interlocutory appeal 56, 72
  new counsel in 44–45
  notice of appeal, serving of 85, 87
  supplemental brief by defendant 210n
  time to appeal 94
Cross-appeals
  appellee's reply brief in 330
  brief covers 249
  and fee payment 88
  filing times 97–99
  necessity for 99–102
  opening and closing right 378–379
  questions presented in 329
Curtiss-Wright Corp. v. *General Electric Co.* 58
Cuyler v. *Sullivan* 270

D

Dates
  on brief covers 248
  in case citations 314
Davis, John W. 289, 299, 406, 408
Davis, Kenneth C. 318, 319
D.C. Circuit
  briefs, preliminary items in 252–254
  Civil Appeals Management Plan 479–480
Decisions
  statement of reasons for 484–486
  types of 483–484
Deferred appendix 179, 200–205
Degnan, R. 444–445, 448–449

Delaware
  interlocutory appeals 63, 68
  oral argument 213
Designation of record (*See also* Appendix; Record) 41, 88–89, 111, 157, 160
Diagrams, in oral argument 418–419
Discretionary review (*See also* Interlocutory review)
  and appeal as of right 152–154
  and briefs in opposition 148–150
  and certification
    by courts of other jurisdictions 154–155
    by intermediate court 126–130
  documents required 130–135
    contents of 142–148
  filing time 135–137
  granting of
    grounds for 137–142
    before judgment below 122–126
    by majority or minority vote 114–116
  means of exercising, overview 20–22, 112–114, 150–154
  refusal to grant, significance 113, 116
Disparaging statements in briefs 291–295
Dissenting opinions, use of
  in briefs 304–305
  in oral argument 426
Divided argument 379–382
Docketing
  fees 87–88
  procedures 103–105, 176
Douglas, William O. 115, 154, 283, 360–361, 419–420, 458
Drake Bakeries v. *Local 50* 469
Dress style for courtroom 400–401
Duplicated record (*See* Appendix)
Duplication (*See* Reproduction standards)

E

Economy Finance Corp. v. *U.S.* 457
Effective Legal Research 309
Eighth Circuit, briefs, preliminary items in 254
Electronic recording of proceedings 167–170
Elements of Style 225
Elgin, Joliet and Eastern Ry. v. *Burley* 446
Erie R. Co. v. *Tomkins* 154, 214, 270, 303
Estelle v. *Gamble* 69
Evidence outside the record 317–323
Exhibits 159, 161, 273

F

Factual determinations, review of 216
Federal Election Campaign Act 465
Federal Interlocutory Appeals Act of 1958
    59–60
Federal questions
    raising in state court 38–39
    Supreme Court review of state decisions
      on 71
Federal Radio Commission v. *Nelson Bros.*
    B.&M. Co. 15
Federal Rules of Appellate Procedure 7
    amicus briefs 338
    appendices
      deferred appendix system 203
      number of copies 185
    brief requirements
      arrangement of preliminary items 255
      conclusion 326
      cover colors 249
      filing times 219
      number of copies 185, 346–347, 352
      page limitation 228–229
      record references 272–273
      reproduction standards 344
      serving 222–223, 354, 356
      statement of facts 272
    disposition of motions 493
    docketing 104
    emergency motions 492
    oral argument 363–364, 370
      by *amici* 371
      number of counsel 379
    prehearing conferences 477–478
    record requirements 161, 165
    rehearings
      answer to petition for 462
      en banc 465–467
      petitions for 446, 447, 459
      stays of mandate 473
    reply briefs 331
    statutes involved, inclusion in brief 260
    stays of judgment 110–111
    supersedeas bonds 110
    supplemental briefs and statements 334
    transcript completion by reporter 166
Federal Rules of Evidence, judicial notice
    318, 321
Federal Trade Commission v. *Minneapolis*
    Honeywell Co. 96
Fees (*See* Costs of appealing)
Ferguson v. *Moore-McCormack Lines* 114
Fifth Circuit, briefs, preliminary items in
    252–253

Filing time (*See* Time limitations)
Finality doctrine (*See also* Interlocutory re-
    view)
    application to some claims or parties
      58–59
    exceptions 54–56
    and extraordinary writs 73–78
    judge-made exceptions 69–73
    overview 52–54
Firestone Tire and Rubber Co. v. *Risjord* 71
Fitzgerald, Henry St. John 359n, 417
Florida
    discretionary review policy 139–141
    interlocutory appeals 57
Footnotes in briefs 324–325
Forgett v. *U.S.* 450
Frankfurter, Felix 53, 115, 315
Fry v. *U.S.* 270
Fusari v. *Steinberg* 321, 333

G

General Motors Corp.; U.S. v. 69
Georgia
    answering briefs 329
    assignment of errors 89, 262
    interlocutory appeals 62–63
    rehearings 447
Gideon v. *Wainwright* 87
Godbold, J. 203–204, 364, 407–408
Gondeck v. *Pan American World Airways*
    457
Goodrich, Herbert F. 177, 211, 302, 359,
    368–369, 389–390, 432
Government briefs 249
Green v. *Santa Fe Industries, Inc.* 465
Gressman, Eugene 227, 287, 311
Gutierrez v. *Waterman S.S. Corp.* 269

H

Harlan, John Marshall 114, 359, 407, 456–
    457
Harris v. *Pennsylvania R. Co.* 115
Hartnett, Daniel 359n, 417
Haupt v. *U.S.* 301
Hawaii, screening of appeals by supreme
    court 33
Hazard, G. 67
Headings in briefs 243–244
Helstoski v. *Meanor* 74, 101
Howe, Jonathan T. 284–285, 287, 289,
    305
Huffman v. *Pursue, Ltd.* 294

Hughes, Charles Evans 358, 373, 426
Hunter v. *Ohio ex rel. Miller* 50

I

Idaho, screening of appeals by supreme
    court 33, 34n
Identification of parties
  in briefs 240–243
  in oral argument 412
Illinois
  briefs, arrangement of preliminary
    items 255
  discretionary interlocutory review 61
  reconstruction of nontranscribed pro-
    ceedings 171
  record on appeal, what constitutes
    162n
  rehearing petition, filing of 461
  reproduced record
    making understandable 198–199
    narrative abstract 191–193
  supreme court review of judgments
    below 115–116
  transcripts, certificate of correctness for
    166
Imperial Irrigation Dist.; U.S. v. 50
Inaccurate statements
  in briefs 291–295
  in oral argument 415–416
Indexes in briefs 249
Indiana, interlocutory appeals 62
Information statement 90–93
Infra symbol, use of 323
Injunctions 110
Interlocutory review
  application procedures 66–67, 258
  briefs, filing time for 221
  certification by trial court 65–68
  and contempt 78–79
  and extraordinary writs 73–78
  federal standards 59–60
  highest court's review 69
  as matter of discretion 59
  as matter of right 56–57
  state standards 61–65
Intermediate appellate courts (*See* Circuit
    courts of appeals; State inter-
    mediate appellate courts)
Intervention 49–51
Iowa
  interlocutory appeals 63
  screening of appeals by supreme court
    33, 35, 36, 118
Irvine v. *California* 269

Island Creek Coal Co. v. *Local Union No. 1827*
  165
Issuance of mandates 472–474

J

Jackson, Robert H. 269, 271, 359, 380,
    394, 396, 401, 422, 427, 434,
    441–442
Jacobson, E., and Schroeder, M. 213n
James, F. 67
Jay, John 8
Judicial decisions (*See* Decisions; Opin-
    ions)
Judicial notice 317–323
Jurisdiction
  appellate 14–15
  original 12–14
Jurisdictional statement
  in answering briefs 328
  in briefs 257–259
  and petition for certiorari 118, 144
  and questions presented 263

K

Kentucky, supreme court review of judg-
    ments below 116
Kerr v. *U.S. District Court* 74, 77
Kozinski, A. 228

L

Law clerks 28
Lawyers Reports Annotated 303
Leave to appeal (*See also* Petition for certi-
    orari) 106
Lederer v. *McGarvey* 129
Leflar, Robert A. 476, 478, 482
Legislative material, citation of 316–317
Lehman Brothers v. *Schein* 155
Louisell, D. 444–445, 448–449
Louisiana
  electronic transcript recording 167
  rehearings 450

M

MacDonald; U.S. v. 69, 71
Maine, interlocutory appeals 63
Majority opinions, use in oral argument
    425–426

Mandamus writ 73–78
Mandate, issuance of 472–474
Maness v. *Meyers* 78
Maps, in oral argument 418–419
Marbury v. *Madison* 15
Marshall, John 8
Marshall, Prentice H. 358–359, 392, 396, 434–436, 441
Massachusetts
    interlocutory appeals 63
    screening of appeals by supreme court 34–36, 118–119
Massey v. *U.S.* 450
Masters 17–18
McCormick, C. 318
Mendenhall; U.S. v. 270
Michigan, interlocutory appeals 62
Miller, G.J. 234
Mississippi, narrative abstract required 194–195
Mitchell, William D. 285, 434
Moody v. *Albemarle Paper Co.* 128
Mootness 320–321
Moragne v. *States Marine Lines* 270
Motions
    contents and accompanying documents 495–497
    disposition of 493–495
    emergency motions 492
    filing and serving 497–498
    form 498
    leave to file 496–497
    number of copies 498–499
    oral argument for 494, 500–501
    as relief 491–492
    responses to 499–500
    types of 493
Muller v. *Oregon* 319
Multiple parties 379–382

docketing 105
interlocutory appeals 64
notice of appeal 82–83
oral argument 365, 366
transmission of record 174n
New Jersey, briefs, arrangement of preliminary items 254
New Light on the History of the Federal Judiciary Act of 1789 303
New Mexico, electronic transcript recording 167
New York
    briefs, filing schedules 221
    interlocutory appeals 55
    oral argument 370
Ninth Circuit, briefs, preliminary items in 252–253
Non-case material, citation in briefs 301–303
North Carolina
    amicus briefs 341
    narrative abstract 194
    rehearings 451–452
    reply briefs 331
Northern Pacific Ry. Co.; U.S. v. 299
Notes, use in oral argument 388–396, 401–402
Notice of appeal
    accompanying documents 88–93
    for appeals as of right 117, 118, 121
    copies, number required 83
    and cross-appeals 101–102
    and docketing 103–105
    filing requirements 83–85
    filing times 93–97
    procedures, pre-1954 80–81
    serving of 85–87
    what constitutes 81–83
Number of copies (*See* Copies, number of)

N

O

Names of cases, citation form 315–316
Narrative abstract 178, 190–197
National Reporter System, West's 313, 315, 316
Nature of proceeding
    in answering briefs 328
    in briefs 256–257
    in oral argument 409–413
Nebraska, *amicus* briefs 337
Nevada, interlocutory appeals 57
New counsel 44–49
New Hampshire
    appeal petition procedures 19, 20

Objections when necessary below 38
Ohio, electronic transcript recording 168
Ohio ex rel. Eaton v. *Price* 115
Ohio Power; U.S. v. 456, 457
Oklahoma
    discretionary interlocutory review 61
    screening of appeals by supreme court 33, 35, 36, 118
Opening right in oral argument 376–379
Opinions
    citation of unpublished opinions 489–490
    publication criteria 486–489

Opinions—*Contd.*
  use in briefs and oral argument 304–
    305, 425–426
  writing, assignment of 481–483
Oral argument
  answering questions 426–432
  appellant's rebuttal 433–437
  appellee's answering argument 437–
    441
  arguer, selection of 368–369
  cases and authorities, use of 421–423
  client in courtroom 441–442
  concluding peroration 432–433
  consolidated cases 382
  courtroom arrival time for counsel 375–
    376
  denial to *amici* 343, 371–372
  discretionary review for 113, 115
  divided argument 379–382
  dress style 400–401
  hearing, scheduling for 373–374
  identification of parties 412
  importance and use of 23, 25–26, 211–
    214, 358–365
  judges' reading of briefs beforehand
    475–477
  for motions 494, 500–501
  notes, use of 388–396, 401–402
  opening and closing right 376–379
  preparation for 383–388, 396–398
  quotations in 423–426
  rebuttal 433–437
  in rehearings 446
  rehearsing 396–398
  requesting of 365–368
  selection and arrangement of points
    407–409
  speaking style 398–400
  statement of facts 413–417
  statement of issues 409–413
  substance of argument, general princi-
    ples regarding 402–406, 419–
    421
  time allowances 369–373
  visible evidence, use of 418–419
Oregon
  electronic transcript recording 167
  supreme court review petition as ap-
    peals court rehearing petition
    133–134, 453
Organization of briefs 244–246
  arrangement of preliminary items 251–
    256
Original jurisdiction 12–14
  procedures in 15–18
Overruling decisions 303–304

P

Page limitations
  amicus briefs 343
  answering briefs 329
  certiorari petitions 147
  principal briefs 226–229
  rehearing petitions 458–459
  reply briefs 229–230, 332
Parties, identification of
  in briefs 240–243
  in oral argument 412
Patent cases 56
Pell, Wilbur 352
Pennsylvania
  amicus briefs 337
  briefs, arrangement of preliminary
    items 255
  rehearings 448, 459
  transcripts, trial judge responsibility for
    169, 176
Periodicals, citation of 317
Permian Basin Area Rate Cases 382
Petition for certiorari
  answer to, sample form 514–522
  brief in opposition to 148–150
  briefs distinguished from 214–216
  common law writ distinguished from
    73–74
  content and accompanying documents
    130–133, 142–148, 263
  filing times 135–137
  grounds for granting review 137–142
  percentage granted, decrease in 26–27
  rehearing petition as 133–135
  sample form 504–513
  situations requiring 106
Pickett v. *Union Terminal Co.* 450
Pictures, in oral argument 418–419
Points and authorities 250–251
Pollard v. *U.S.* 269
*Practical Manual of Standard Legal Citations,
  A* 309
Prentis v. *Atlantic Coast Line Co.* 15
Prettyman, E. Barrett 242
Prettyman, E. Barrett, Jr. 242, 309, 402,
    405, 434–436
Price, Miles O. 309, 311
Printing, when required
  briefs 344–345
  records 187–190
Prohibition writ 73–78
Publication of opinions 486–489
Publications, citation in briefs 301

Q

Questions, answering of in oral argument
426–432
Questions presented
in *amicus* briefs 343
in answering briefs 328, 329
in appellee briefs 246
brief requirements 261–268
in petitions for certiorari 144–145
restrictive effect 268–270
Quotations
in briefs 305–309, 345
in oral argument 423–426

R

Rall, Owen 441, 442
Reapportionment cases 153
Rebuttal in oral argument 433–437
Record (*See also* Appendix)
agreed statement of facts 172
in brief preparation 230–232
completeness requirement 40–41
content of 159–161
designation of 41, 88–89, 111, 161–162
filing with certiorari petition 132
highest court requirements 205–207
number of copies 207
omissions from 162–163
in oral argument preparation 385
page numbering 172–173
preparation, overview 156–158
preparation and transmission 161, 173–
176
reconstruction of nontranscribed proceedings 170–172
retention in trial court 174–175
time for filing 161, 163, 173–174
transcript 163–170
Regents of University of California v. *Bakke*
342
Regulations, citation in briefs 301
Rehearing
contents of petition 458–461
decisions, citation of in briefs 316
en banc 10–12, 464–470
filing times 454–455
mandate, issuance of 472–474
nature of decisions in 445–446
page limitation of petition 458–459
petition for as prerequisite to supreme
court review 133–135
reasons for granting 443–445, 447–454
responses to petitions for 461–464

successive petitions for 470–472
and term rule 456–458
Rehearing for oral argument 396–398
Rehnquist, William 239
Reply briefs
color of cover 249
filing time 221, 222
page limitation for duplicated briefs
229–230
requirements, overview 246, 331–333
Reporters, transcript preparation duty
166, 168–170
Reproduced record (*See* Appendix)
Reproduction standards
briefs 344–345
petition for rehearing 461
records 187–190
Responses to motions 499–500
Responses to rehearing petitions 461–464
Restatement of the Law 302, 423
Revision of briefs 224–226
Rhode Island, electronic transcript re-
cording 167
Right to Privacy, The 303
Rosenberg v. *U.S.* 282–283
Rutledge, W. 295, 296, 420

S

Schaefer, Walter V. 295–296, 308–309,
380, 418, 426
Scheduling of oral arguments 373–374
Screening of appeals 33–36, 118–119
Sears Roebuck & Co. v. *Mackey* 58
Secondary authorities, citation in briefs
302–303
Serving of briefs 222–223, 352–357
Seventh Circuit
briefs, preliminary items in 243, 255–
256
opinions, publication criteria for 487–
488
Sioux Tribe v. *U.S.* 450
Snider v. *All State Administrators* 189
Sobieski, J. 65, 101, 102, 165–166, 171
South Carolina
briefs, arrangement of preliminary
items 254
challenging prior decisions 286
narrative abstract 194
rehearings 451–452
South Dakota
briefs, arrangement of preliminary
items 254
interlocutory appeals 63

South-Eastern Underwriters Association; U.S.
v. 267
Speaking style for oral argument 398–400
Specification of errors 262
Staff attorneys 27–30
Standards Relating to Appellate Courts 64, 67–
68, 90–92, 362, 485
Standing to appeal 49–51
State ex rel. Riley v. *Martin* 11
State intermediate appellate courts
cases, citation format 313–314
certification to highest court 21, 126–
130, 151–152
establishment 9–10
panel and *en banc* sitting 12
rehearings *en banc* 464–465
State supreme courts
briefs below, use of 30–33
cases, citation format for 313–314
discretionary review 21
jurisdiction 13–14
panel and *en banc* sitting 11–12
rehearings *en banc* 464
screening of appeals 33–36
Statement of facts
in answering briefs 328, 329
in appellee briefs 246
brief requirements 270–276
headings in 244
in oral argument 413–417
in petitions for certiorari 145–146
Statutes involved 259–260, 328
Statutory law, citation in briefs 301,
316
Stays
of judgment 109–111
of mandate 473–474
Stevens, John Paul 60, 71
Storer Broadcasting Co.; U.S. v. 269
Strunk, W., Jr., and White, E. B. 225
Summary of argument 276–280, 328
Sun Insurance Office, Ltd. v. *Clay* 155
Supersedeas bonds 109–111
Supplemental briefs and statements 333–
335
Supra symbol, use of 323–324
Supreme courts (*See* State supreme courts;
U.S. Supreme Court)

T

Table of contents
in appendices 187
in briefs 249–250
of oral testimony 198

Tate, Albert, Jr. 271–272, 285–287
Tennessee
cross-appeals, notice in 101–102
interlocutory appeals 64–65
reconstruction of nontranscribed proceedings 171
rehearings 447–448
transcripts, certificate of correctness for
166
Term rule, and rehearings 456–457
Terrazas; U.S. v. 269
Texas
briefs, preliminary items in 252
supreme court review of judgments
below 113
timely transcript preparation 168
Thompson, Floyd E. 291
Time limitations
briefs 219–224, 329, 331
briefs in opposition to certiorari petitions 148
certiorari petitions 135–137
cross-appeals 97–99
interlocutory appeals 66, 68
issuance of mandates 472–473
notice of appeal 93–97
oral argument 369–373
petition for supreme court review before judgment below 124
records 161, 163, 173–174
rehearing petitions 454–458
responses to 461–464
responses to motions 499–500
transcripts 163–166
Tone, Philip W. 284–285, 287, 289, 305
Transcript
certificate of correctness for 166–167
completeness requirement 40–41
designation of 88–89, 111, 163–165
electronic recording 167–168
filing times 165–166
reporter's timely preparation of 168–
170
what constitutes 159
Trice v. *Moyers* 171

U

Uniform System of Citation, A (Bluebook)
309, 310, 312, 314–317
United Mine Workers; U.S. v. 78
United States Law Week 310
Unpublished opinions, citation of 489–
490
U.S. Government briefs 249

U.S. Supreme Court
  appeal procedures 117–118
  appeals as of right to 120
  case load 22
  cases, citation format for 310–312
  certification before decision below 126–129
  discretionary review 113–115
  findings of fact, non-review of 216
  jurisdiction 13
  rehearing, and term rule 456–457
  stays of mandate 474
U.S. Supreme Court Bulletin 310
U.S. Supreme Court Rules
  amicus briefs 337–339, 341, 343
  appendices, number of copies 185
  brief requirements
    arrangement of preliminary items 252–255
    conclusion 326
    cover colors 249
    filing time 219
    inaccurate or disparaging statements 294
    jurisdictional statement 258
    number of copies 185, 347, 352
    page limitation 227–228
    questions presented 261, 263
    record references 273
    serving 353, 357
    statement of facts 272
    summary of argument 276, 277, 279–280
  docketing 105
  granting of certiorari before judgment below 51, 123–126
  notice of appeal, filing time 94–95
  oral argument 113, 360, 364
    by *amici* 371
    consolidation of cases 382
    number of counsel 379
    opening and closing 376–377
  original jurisdiction procedures 16, 18
  record, printing requirements 188, 189
  rehearing
    filing time 455
    issuance of mandates 473
    petition, contents of 459
    standards for granting 447, 449, 453–454
    successive petitions for 470–471

without requesting answer 463
reply briefs 331, 332
supplemental briefs and statements 333, 334

V

Vachon v. *New Hampshire* 270
Vance v. *Terrazas* 266
Verbatim testimony 190–197
Virginia, appeal petition procedures 19–20
Visible evidence in oral argument 418–419

W

Walker v. *Birmingham* 78
Wallace, J. Clifford 212
Warren, Charles 303
Warren, Samuel D., Jr. 303
Washington
  briefs in criminal cases 210n
  interlocutory appeals 63
Washington v. *Confederated Tribes* 96
Weed v. *Bilbrey* 457, 458
West Virginia, appeal petition procedures 19–20
Wiener, Frederick Bernays 285, 293, 299, 306, 311, 314, 392, 396–397, 402, 434
Wigmore, J. 318
Wilkins, R. 323–324, 421, 427
Will v. *Calvert Fire Insurance Co.* 75
Will v. *U.S.* 74–75
Wisconsin
  briefs, arrangement of preliminary items 254
  interlocutory appeals 64
  transcript preparation, reporter's obligation 168–169
Wisniewski v. *U.S.* 128
Wood; U.S. v. 301
Writing of briefs
  grammar and style guidelines 233–240, 289–291
  preparation for 230–233
Writs
  and appellate jurisdiction 14–15
  and interlocutory appeal 73–78

ublic

kes no bribes from that interest.
ly corrupting in this sense. I
a fact.

pt your definitions, but there
is it corrupt for a member of
a special interest and then, on
that interest as its lawyer in

he agrees to the retainer while
retainer comes to him in due

n policy in Congress with full
from that special interest?
ting into what Dr. Smyth calls
t going to chop logic. Out of
has been, relatively speaking,
ue sense of the word.

ory incline me to confirm that
ere is such a person, appears
imself, follows a special inter-
tion is false and the public is
ess and politics.

litical scandals in connection
er accompanied by corruption
tive Department, not in the
some deals bordering on cor-
Congresses were occasionally
scandal of the Civil War and
nal scandal.

als in the Executive Depart-
Route Fraud, the Whiskey
al resources through the Fed-
the Harding scandals. They
We have grounds for believ-
Harding, knew little, if any-
der their respective adminis-
know, they were derelict in
ere so heavy that they could
r high subordinates, then our

and unreasonably disparaged. . . . The truth is, the Senate is just
what the mode of election and the conditions of public life in this
country make it.

BEARD: I dissent from that.

SENATOR TESSELL: You would dissent from the Ten Command-
ments.

BEARD: I regard Mr. Wilson's statement as lacking in exactness,
as largely rhetorical. The methods by which members of Congress
are elected certainly have a considerable, if immeasurable, influence
on the quality of the persons chosen. The same may be said of 'the
conditions of public life in this country.' Neither the Senate nor the
House is *just what* the methods of election and the conditions of
public life make it. Taken in its plain sense, if it has any, Wilson's
statement means that Senators and Representatives are automata,
jumping jacks, going through performances mechanically determined by the methods of election and the conditions of public life.

If Senators and Representatives are dominated by methods of
election and conditions of public life, then they have no free will
to shape their own conduct and procedure. They have no backbone,
no power over their course. They are compelled by something not
themselves to split each house up into thirty or forty tyrannical committees. They are forced by an outside power to waste time day by
day, week after week, month after month, over petty bills, claims,
and disputes. An overriding necessity dictates that they must divide
and diffuse their intelligence, instead of concentrating it on the
great business before them. It drives them into supine dependence
on executive will. It paralyzes their own capacity for constructive
thinking and action. They can develop no leadership in national
affairs. They must continue to abide by the mass of precedents their
forerunners have built up since 1789. They must be as confused,
trivial, or tumultuous as the methods of election and conditions of
public life that are supposed to have lifted them into power and to
dominate them while they are in power.

This idea of Congress I regard as false to fact and to the Constitution of the United States. If members of Congress believe in it,
they are misled and thus help to reduce their own stature; they
avoid their opportunities for creative work and their responsibilities to the nation besides. If millions of intelligent citizens believe
that this must be the situation, if makers of public opinion keep

hammering this idea into the heads of voters everywhere, if Senators and Representatives bow to this measure of their stature, then the national legislature will decline in its own esteem and in the esteem of the public.

In my opinion, individuals and groups rise in stature and power in some relation to their conception of their responsibilities and opportunities. There is no duty of legislators so humble that it does not symbolize some greatness of quality. And the duty of Congress as contemplated by the framers of the Constitution is as great as the greatness of our nation and of all that this nation may be and may accomplish in the coming years.

The framers of the Constitution expected, if some among them did not intend, that Congress should be the dominant branch of the Federal Government. They sought to establish a strong Executive, but, reasoning from past experience in America, they assumed the supremacy of the legislature. They put it first in order in the Constitution, the Executive second, and the judiciary third. They vested in Congress immense legislative powers. They gave it the power of the purse and the power of the sword—the two mighty engines of government. They authorized Congress to determine the structure of the executive department, the powers of all administrative officers, the number of justices in the Supreme Court, the appellate jurisdiction of that Court, and the form and jurisdiction of inferior Federal courts.

And, what is highly important though usually forgotten, they left Congress free to determine the nature and form of its relations to the President and his subordinates. If Congress has largely failed to develop this phase of its responsibility and has allowed the President to assume a dominant position, the fault lies with Congress, not with the Constitution.

The framers of the Constitution intended that Congress should represent the varied and effective interests of the country. The Senate was to represent the states in their corporate capacities; and the House, the multitudinous interests of the people in general—agricultural, commercial, industrial, moral, and intellectual. That the Federal Government might be kept in constant touch with the sentiments and desires of the voters, biennial elections were provided for members of the House.

Senators and Representatives were expected to be mediators be-

commerce or manufacturing, if he t
Lobbies and blocs are not necessa
doubt whether many of them are

BEARD: In general, Senator, I ac
re qualifications. In your opinion
Congress to vote for the measures
tiring, to accept a retainer fro
Washington or before the courts?

SENATOR TESSELL: It is corrupt,
Congress. It is not corrupt if t
rse after he retires.

BEARD: Suppose he follows a ce
ctancy that the retainer will c

SENATOR TESSELL: Now you are
physics, as you tell me. I am
experience, I maintain that t
corruption in Congress in th

BEARD: My studies of American
n. The average American,
k that when anybody, exce
operation is corrupt. The
y by this conception of b
few exceptions, the grea
Federal Government, w
have appeared in the E
ve Department. There w
in the first Congress. L
by them. The Crédit Mo
uction period was a cong
onsider the long list of
specially since 1865—the
he bare-faced stealing of r
nd Office, Teapot Dome,
ll in the Executive Depart
t the Presidents, from Gr
about the scandals going
s; nevertheless, if they di
luty. If their official burd
ep track of such actions b

presidential system is in so far sadly defective. As a rule it has been owing to congressional vigilance that scandals in the Executive Department have been unearthed, investigated, and stamped out. One more argument for Congress.

Mrs. Smyth: I have followed this discussion with deep interest. I had been inclined, for some reason, to regard the connection of special economic interests with politics as corrupt. I see now that it is not necessarily or generally corrupt. Obviously the existence of all kinds of economic and sectional interests is a fact. How could they fail to exist? They have arisen with the economic and political growth of the country. Our ways of working and earning a living create these interests. We cannot abolish them without abolishing the business of getting a living and living. Still I am puzzled by one of Robert's questions that is unanswered. Why didn't the framers of the Constitution provide for the frank representation of economic interests in Congress?

Beard: First let me say that framers of the Constitution were familiar with the idea of class representation which has been talked about recently as if it were an original discovery of modern minds. The parliaments of Europe which arose during the Middle Ages were class parliaments. They were composed of representatives of the great estates, or classes—aristocratic, clerical, burgher, and small landed classes. I have discussed this briefly in my *Economic Basis of Politics*. Framers of the Constitution were familiar with such representation of interests.

Furthermore, the subject was up for consideration at the time the Constitution was adopted. Hamilton, in Number 35 of *The Federalist*, discussed the problem of representing landed, mercantile, and other economic interests directly in Congress. You can quickly read that Number for yourselves and discover the reasons he assigned for opposing any such system for the Congress of the United States.

Meanwhile, I can state that the idea of class representation in Congress was dismissed on four broad grounds:

First, the scheme of congressional elections made possible any representation of economic interests the voters might desire or deem feasible. Certainly agriculture, manufacturing, commerce, and labor have had representation and could have more of it as far as the Constitution is concerned.

Second, men like Madison thought that there was likely to be too much crass representation of powerful economic interests and that unless checked it might easily tear the government and the country apart.

Third, except for slavery, the laws of the United States did not draw legal lines between classes. The fluid nature of social conditions did not make possible a rigid stratification into fixed classes. In old Europe, before 1787, there had been relatively little movement of people across class lines. In the United States such a movement has been one of the striking characteristics of our civilization.

Fourth, framers of the Constitution looked upon human beings as *political* as well as *economic* creatures. They knew that the country confronted problems other than those economic in character—problems of Union, of ambitious leaders, of national defense, of liberty, of justice, of education. They knew that some men were more desirous of sheer power than of riches. They sought, as it were, to have represented in Congress the dawning consciousness of national unity and responsibility, as well as potent economic interests.

I do not say that the two types of human interest are sharply separated in fact, but the political animal may differ substantially from the pecuniary animal in ambitions and talents. How to get a fair working balance among interests so necessary to national life is a continuing problem in the grand strategy of statesmanship. On the whole, I think, the framers of the Constitution were amazingly successful in handling the problem. At least their Constitution has survived hundreds of constitutions drafted since their day by persons presumably more modern and more expert in the problems of the modern age.

DR. SMYTH: Then you are defending the whole rotten borough system of the Senate—the system which gives two Senators to each state, large and small. You favor letting Nevada, with 110,000 inhabitants, have the same weight in the Senate as New York with 13,500,000 inhabitants. I do not see how you can lend any countenance to it. It is simply preposterous.

SENATOR TESSELL: The senatorial rotten boroughs, as you call them, Doctor, are not much worse than the Southern rotten boroughs overrepresented in the House. Some Southern Representatives speak for eight or ten thousand voters, while many Northern representatives speak for more than two hundred thousand voters.

If you propose to clean house, the representation of the South will be reduced along with that of the grasshopper states with a handful of inhabitants. And what is more, if the Constitution as it now stands were enforced by the Senators and Representatives bound by oath to support it, the representation of the Southern states would be reduced.

BEARD: Moreover, the representation of those Northern states which impose literacy, poll taxes, and other qualifications on voters would also be reduced.

DR. SMYTH: I do not quite understand that.

BEARD: The Fourteenth Amendment provides that when 'a state deprives any adult male citizens of the right to vote in the major elections, its representation in Congress shall be proportionately reduced. The general position of the rule has been altered by the adoption of woman suffrage, but the rule is still in the Constitution. It is, however, academic now. Congress never has enforced it and is not likely to enforce it.

Leaving that aside, I should like to go back to your quarrel with the equal representation of the states in the Senate as preposterous. I also want to couple with it Senator Tessell's quarrel with the over-representation of Southern states in Congress. Why, Doctor Smyth, is unequal representation in the Senate preposterous? I take it that you regard it as absurd because it conflicts with the democratic idea that all heads are equal and that every representative in a legislature should represent the same number of heads. Or if you do not make it a matter of democratic logic, I suppose that you think the country would be better off in important respects if Senators were apportioned according to population. Have I caught the drift of your thinking?

DR. SMYTH: You have on both counts, but I begin to scent trouble. The states with small populations are not likely to surrender their equality in the Senate. It cannot be taken away from them without their consent. Nothing short of a revolution would ever get rid of their unfair power in the Senate, and people do not seem inclined to make more revolutions on the logic of democratic theories—one head, one vote, and an equal number of heads in every legislative district. There is not much use in pursuing that further. Would the country be better off if small states were deprived of their equal representation in the Senate? You are going to ask me to prove that it would be; and, to save my soul, I should not know how to go about it.

BEARD: One way to go about proving it would be to examine the Senate votes on bills you favor or condemn. Either. way, you would find that the states with small populations—Rhode Island, Vermont, Delaware, Nevada, Idaho, and so forth—do not vote solidly together for or against bills demanded by the most populous states. According to studies that have been made, the line-up in the Senate on important bills is never strictly one of small states against large states. Similarity of interests, economic and intellectual, principally economic, seems to be more influential than equal numbers of heads in determining the kind of laws the country receives from the Senate.

As to Senator Tessell's proposal for reducing Southern representation in Congress, I am of the opinion that nothing short of a bitter sectional fight could ever effect that change, even though Congress may succeed in abolishing poll taxes by ordinary legislation. What may come we do not know. But it would take a great crisis in national affairs to make that an issue and in a great crisis more will be involved than such tinkering with our legislative machine.

DR. SMYTH, with a gesture indicating that our long session must close: Well, with all due apologies, I am not satisfied. You have let Congress off too easily. Our congressional government or presidential government or whatever you call it is under fire. It is charged by many responsible critics with being incompetent and inefficient in our mechanical and scientific age when government must be competent and efficient or perish. Unequal representation in the Senate and House opens the way for minority dictation. There is something awry somewhere, but I suspect that patching up Congress or the Executive Department is not enough. So I propose that, after we have discussed the Executive and the judiciary, we add a new session to our program—a critique of the congressional-presidential system. What about it?

Your idea is excellent, I replied, as my guests made their way out into the snowstorm.

XV

The Executive as Power

D R. SMYTH, making another dig at my method of analysis: Since, at our last session, you seemed unable to draw a clear line between legislative, executive, and judicial powers, I am prepared to hear you say tonight that since 1933 President Franklin Roosevelt has constitutional warrant for seizing all the power he can get his hands on. The line cannot be drawn; hence he can draw it to suit himself. Furthermore, according to your theory, or whatever you may call it, the opinions of the Supreme Court vary, so that we cannot rely on that body to define and hold positive limits on the executive power. In short, all talk about the division of powers which we heard in grade school and have heard ever after is worse than deceptive; it is nonsense. If I am to take your views at face value, political power is a dark continent that has no external boundary of its own, physical or intellectual; and within this dark continent covered with mist there are no boundaries either—at least no boundaries that we can be sure of. Before we begin I wish that you would tell me in simple words, just what the President of the United States is.

BEARD, slowly: I shall begin by making statements under the head of what the President is. If you hear one you do not like, you may protest against it. First of all, the President is a person chosen indirectly by a majority or a minority of the voters.

MRS. SMYTH: A minority of the voters?

BEARD: Yes, by a minority. Thousands of people entitled to vote do not take the trouble to vote. Sometimes a third or nearly half of them stay away from the polls. But we can rule them out. More than once a President has been elected by a minority of the voters who took the trouble to vote. For example, in 1860 the combined votes against Lincoln amounted to about a million more than his total. Wilson's vote in 1912 was more than a million short of the vote for all the candidates against him. And stranger still, two Presidents, Rutherford Hayes in 1876 and Benjamin Harrison in 1888, did not even get a popular plurality; that is, they stood lower in the scale of votes than their defeated rivals. So all we can truly say is that the President is a person elected according to the rules of the game provided by the Constitution, the laws, and party practices.

Mrs. SMYTH: I was aware that our electoral system is complicated, but I had not realized that a President could be elected by a minority.

DR. SMYTH: Don't mention it or Beard will go to his filing case and show that *no* President has been the choice of a majority of the people. That is more quicksand and I want to get on with what the President *is*.

BEARD: What the President *is* depends in part upon the size and character of the vote cast for him, especially the character of the vote and intensity of the popular resolve behind it.

Now my next statement in reply to your question: The President is not a fixed quantity or quality. As a personality, he may be avid of power or more or less indifferent to it. Like Coolidge he may not want to be great; or like some other Presidents he may be hungry for dominion over others, even suffer from delusions of grandeur.

He is in part his own view of his office. He may believe, with Theodore Roosevelt, that he can do anything that the Constitution and laws do not forbid him to do. Or, Doctor, like your hero, Grover Cleveland, he may take a limited view of his powers, especially respecting matters on which he does not wish to act.

The power of the Executive varies not only according to the personality of the President. It varies according to circumstances. In times of crisis, as during the Civil War, the First World War, the panic of 1933, or the Second World War, executive power is about as great as the President can make it or cares to make it, within physical limits and subject to the restraints imposed by Congress, the Supreme Court, and the temper of the people.

DR. SMYTH: Why don't you say that the power of the President is what he can get away with and let it go at that?

BEARD: For the reason that your statement lacks exactness. You see that I do strive for exactness in political science, as you do, Doctor, in medical science. You wanted to know what the President *is* and I am trying to indicate by making relevant statements. The President is, again in part, all the activities he carries on, under powers conferred upon him by the Constitution and the acts of Congress as understood and contemplated by Congress and the people—or rather as understood and contemplated by his supporters in Congress and among the people. There are a multitude of things he cannot get away with.

DR. SMYTH: Yes. Roosevelt could not get away with his court packing plan in 1937, but he got away with enough, at that. Go ahead with your statements.

BEARD: The President is head of his political party, and has great powers as the dispenser of patronage, jobs, contracts, and other perquisites of his office. He has the prestige of his high office, the office occupied by Washington, Jefferson, and Lincoln. He possesses all the imponderable powers conferred upon him by the traditions of the office, as cherished by the people, even by his opponents. If he possessed only ponderable powers, we could easily dispose of the subject tonight by listing them precisely. But we must, if we are realistic, recognize the imponderables. The President is, in one way, a symbol of national unity and authority; or he is so regarded, or so regards himself, especially when he speaks on foreign affairs to other nations in time of peace and in time of war.

MRS. SMYTH: But what happened to President Wilson when he appeared as the symbol of national unity? He spoke for the nation during the First World War, and nobly, I believed. He presented a plan for putting an end to war. Robert seldom gets enthusiastic over anything political. But we threshed out the question of the Fourteen Points and the League of Nations at home, and we both came to the conclusion that President Wilson did speak for the nation, was right, and ought to be supported by the nation.

Then along came that awful Henry Cabot Lodge, Borah, and Harding—and Theodore Roosevelt, too—and proclaimed from the housetops that President Wilson did not speak for the nation. If it had not been for the rule requiring a two-thirds vote for the ratification of treaties, the Senate would have approved the League of Nations. A minority of the Senators defeated it. A majority of them favored it, and I think that the majority, like President Wilson, really represented the sentiments of the country on the subject. One could almost say that President Wilson, while using his power to speak for the nation in foreign affairs, was destroyed politically and shattered physically, by a minority of obstructionist politicians.

During the First World War, President Wilson seemed to be the most powerful man in the whole world and the man most highly respected. Remember how the masses of England, France, and Italy were thrilled by his ideas and looked upon him as a savior! Then all his power was destroyed by a petulant minority. Remember the spiteful things Lodge and Theodore Roosevelt wrote about Wilson in their letters. Their malice was worse than catty. It was deadly.

DR. SMYTH: I know now what Beard will say to that. He will say that the President is partly times and circumstances; politics is a fight; Wilson had his day and lost the power he had accumulated. In other words, as I should put the case, Wilson simply could not get away with it. I also know Beard's reply to that remark. He will agree that there is something in what I have just said.

BEARD: Let all that you have both just said stand. It will illustrate what I have asserted about the immeasurable powers of the President and the limits imposed on them by his opponents and by that vague thing called public sentiment. There is only one of Mrs. Smyth's remarks that I shall question now. It is her comment that the majority of the Senators who favored approving the League of Nations represented the sentiments of the country. That may be true, but I do not know that it is true.

Only one-third of the Senators who passed upon the League had been elected in November, 1918, that is, *after* President Wilson's general foreign policies respecting a new world order had been announced; and even then the specific terms of a league of nations were not before the country. Two-thirds of the Senators had been elected *before* those specific policies had been proclaimed, even before the United States had entered the war against the Central Powers.

Would President Wilson and Senators in favor of the League of Nations actually have been elected in 1916 if they had presented to the people a program of war and the League of Nations as framed at Versailles in that campaign? I doubt it, although both parties favored some kind of international association against war during the campaign. One of the Democratic slogans in the campaign was that President Wilson had kept us out of war. The Democrats lost in the congressional election of 1916, and at the first congressional election after 1916 they were badly defeated. In 1920, when the country had the first chance to pass on the League of Nations, it swept the Democrats out as if in a fury.

Mrs. Smyth: Then you think that President Wilson was a visionary, not a prophet?

Beard: He was a visionary in the sense that he was utterly mistaken in his belief or expectation that he could induce the Senate and people of the United States to enter the League of Nations as designed at Paris in 1919 by the Peace Conference. What do you mean by calling Wilson a prophet?

Mrs. Smyth: He prophesied that if the United States did not join the League, another big war would come soon. Well, it came. Was he not a prophet in that?

Beard: How do you know that if we had joined the League, another big war would not have come anyway, and sooner?

Mrs. Smyth: Of course, I do not *know* it, but I am convinced of it. If after this war the United States does enter a world league or federation and lasting peace comes, then President Wilson will be vindicated as a prophet.

Beard: How long will your new peace have to last in order to make President Wilson a prophet? A thousand years?

Mrs. Smyth: I see your point and do not wish to press mine any longer just now, for our theme tonight is not the League of Nations.

Beard: Aside from the hazardous business of prophecy, the struggle over the League illustrates my contention that what the President *is* depends in part, in large part, upon his personality—his qualities of mind, his psychological propensities. He is not omnipotent. His power is limited. What he is or can get away with often depends upon his capacity to judge the limits of his own powers. That involves insight, knowledge, and a sense of the possible.

President Wilson evidently thought that he had the power to force the ratification of the Treaty, with perhaps minor reservations respecting the League of Nations, and that the country would support him. His chief opponents in the Senate were belligerent. He chose to make it an open struggle—political battle instead of conciliatory negotiation. Had he made concessions on reservations, the

United States might have entered the League of Nations. President Wilson overestimated his power and was broken in the contest of power. The President *is* power, but limited power. And marvellous is the eye that can discern its strength and its limitations.

DR. SMYTH: But the Constitution intrusts the conduct of foreign affairs to the President, does it not?

BEARD: Before I take up that question, let me ask you a few simple questions by way of preliminary so that we may know what we are talking about when we say foreign affairs. I shall ask you questions and you can give your answers. My first question is, What do you mean by foreign affairs?

DR. SMYTH: I should say, travel, intercourse, and commerce between the people of the United States and the people of other countries and transactions between their governments; making treaties; regulating commerce; declaring the policies of the United States in relation to other nations; exchanging ministers, ambassadors, and consuls; controlling immigration and emigration; deciding upon the size and nature of our armaments; exchanging notes and carrying on negotiations with other governments; declaring war and making peace. There may be other things, but these are the most important that I can recall.

BEARD: They suffice. Now let me put some yes or no questions to you, the kind you like to put to me. Can the President alone regulate intercourse with other countries at his pleasure—that is, tariffs, tonnage duties, financial exchanges, and travel?

No. Congress has that power.

Can the President at his pleasure regulate immigration and emigration?

No. Congress passes immigration acts.

Can the President determine the conditions of naturalization and the rights of aliens in the United States?

No.

Can the President fix the size and nature of our army, navy, and other armed forces?

No.

Can the President alone set up ministries and consulates in other countries and pick his own ministers and consuls?

No. Since Congress must provide the money for them, it could control this branch of foreign business, if it wanted to do so. Besides, the Senate must approve the persons named by the President as ministers or ambassadors.

Can the President make treaties with other countries?

No. A treaty must have the approval of two-thirds of the Senate. But the President can make minor agreements without asking the consent of the Senate.

Can the President declare war?

No. That power is supposed to be in the hands of Congress.

Can the President make peace?

If it takes a treaty, the Senate must approve.

Can the President declare the foreign policy of the United States and impose it upon the country by his own will?

There are two questions. Certainly the President can declare the foreign policy of the United States. But he cannot impose it upon the country by mere declaration. If President Wilson had enjoyed that power, the United States would have been in the League of Nations and the Second World War would not have broken out.

BEARD, in conclusion: Excellent, Doctor. I have only one possible exception to your answers. How do you know that the Second World War would not have occurred, if the United States had joined the League of Nations?

DR. SMYTH, after a long pause: I don't exactly know it. But I believe it. With a strong League, no country would have dared to go to war.

BEARD: What we can say, then, in response to the question raised by the Doctor, may be put this way: The President is power. He has power of knowledge, will, and decision. His decisions, applied through all the agents and material instruments at his command as the Executive, can set in motion actions that deeply affect every aspect of life, liberty, and property, even the very basis of the Republic. But this power is limited by Congress and the Courts; by his own capacities or incapacities; by the amount of popular support he can marshal and maintain; by his own sense of self-restraint —by time and circumstances, by the contingencies and requirements of peace and war.

DR. SMYTH: Your words are plain enough, but the substance covered by them eludes me. At least some of it does. As I comprehend your language, the President may be more powerful in some ways than in others. That is to say, the contingencies or necessities at a given time may be in some branch of domestic affairs like the banking crisis of 1933, and at another time in foreign affairs. Furthermore he can make contingencies himself, bring on crises himself and then take advantage of his own disturbances to enhance his power. This is especially true in foreign affairs. Still, I am under the impression, from things I have read, that the President's power in foreign affairs, to conduct foreign affairs, is for practical purposes unlimited. Is that not true, according to the Constitution?

BEARD: Let me ask you whether you think the Constitution confers upon the President unlimited powers over foreign affairs?

MRS. SMYTH: Since you say that Robert's answers to your questions are correct, it is evident that the President does not have unlimited powers.

DR. SMYTH: Anyway, that follows logically from your constitutional principle that all our agents of government, from the President down, have limited powers. I see that. But this system makes a mess for us, keeps us in an eternal wrangle among the agents of government so that we are seldom sure of anything. It helps to paralyze us for action when action is absolutely necessary. In foreign affairs, at least, the President ought to have a free hand, it seems to me.

The Doctor knitted his brow, as if his own declaration was boiling in his mind. A puzzled look came over his wife's face.

MRS. SMYTH: No, that will not do. According to the definition of foreign affairs or relations we accepted a few minutes ago, there is no positive line between domestic and foreign affairs. If you gave the President the absolute power to fix foreign policy, any policy he adopted would need money for enforcement. Unless he could lay taxes himself, he would have to go to Congress for the money, and that would give Congress supremacy over him. I do not think that the country would want him to have full power to regulate all commerce and immigration, to declare war, to make peace, to fix tariff rates. When you come to think of it, almost anything the President can do in foreign affairs may slash right into our own industry, commerce, life, liberty, property, oh, everything we call domestic! I give it up. There seems to be no easy way to run either domestic or foreign affairs. It is clear that the President has large powers over foreign affairs, and I cannot see why the framers of the Constitution did not intrust him with more powers. Surely they had confidence in the Executive office for which they made provision?

DR. SMYTH: From what we have heard here, I can throw light on that. They didn't trust anybody—too much, at least. I am surprised that they trusted one another enough to sign their own document! However, I suppose that none of them went so far as to fear that the President of a republic might betray his country in dealing with other countries.

BEARD: Your supposition is naïve, Doctor, but don't take offense at the word. In Number 22 of *The Federalist,* Alexander Hamilton said:

> One of the weak sides of republics, among their numerous advantages, is that they afford too easy inlet to foreign corruption. An hereditary monarch, though often disposed to sacrifice his subjects to his ambition, has so great a personal interest in the government and in the external glory of the nation, that it is not easy for a foreign power to give him the equivalent for what he would sacrifice by treachery to the state. . . . In republics, persons elevated from the mass of the community, by the suffrages of their fellow-citizens, to great stations of pre-eminence and power, may find compensations for betraying their trust. . . . Hence it is that history furnishes us with so many mortifying examples of the prevalency of foreign corruption in republican government.

MRS. SMYTH: Was Hamilton mean enough to say that about republics, when the United States was a republic? Still he was talking in general terms. He couldn't have been mean enough to think that of any man chosen to head our Republic.

DR. SMYTH, sardonically: He was mean enough to think it, but not mean enough to say it publicly.

BEARD: You are both hasty in your surmises. I do not concede that Hamilton was mean in taking this view of republics. He was speaking of actual experiences with republics in the past and had evidence to support his contention that there had been foreign corruption in republics. There had been foreign corruption in monarchies also. But let that pass. Hamilton thought and publicly said that the Constitution was so designed as to guard against improper foreign influences in the executive department.

DR. SMYTH, as Mrs. Smyth gasped: Where did Hamilton say that?

BEARD: In Number 75 of *The Federalist* on the treaty-making power. This is what Hamilton wrote:

> However proper and safe it may be in governments where the executive magistrate is an hereditary monarch, to commit to him the entire power of making treaties, it would be utterly unsafe and improper to intrust that power to an elective magistrate of four years' duration. . . . A man raised from the station of a private citizen to the rank of chief magistrate, possessed of a moderate or slender fortune, and looking forward to a period not very remote when he may probably be obliged to return to the station from which he was taken, might sometimes be under temptations to sacrifice his duty to his interest, which it would require superlative virtue to withstand. . . . An ambitious man might make his own aggrandizement, by the aid of a foreign power, the price of his treachery to his constituents. The history of human conduct does not warrant that exalted opinion of human virtue which would make it wise in a nation to commit interests of so delicate and momentous a kind, as those which concern its intercourse with the rest of the world, to the sole disposal of a magistrate created and circumstanced as would be a President of the United States.

DR. SMYTH: That is the worst thing I ever heard. It is as bad as anything old Machiavelli ever wrote. It is an insult to the American people. Surely Hamilton did not spread that around widely as his opinion. If he had, he would have been driven out of politics.

BEARD: You are mistaken again, Doctor. Hamilton's statement was published in *The Federalist*. Let me repeat: This volume is a collection of articles written by Jay, Madison, and Hamilton for newspapers as arguments in favor of the ratification of the Constitution. These articles were published and then widely reprinted for the purpose of inducing the people to support ratification. They are regarded by lawyers and the Supreme Court, and not only by teachers of history and political science, as commentaries of the highest value in discovering the intentions of the men who framed the Constitution and in ascertaining the nature of our national government.

Mark well my words—and his! Hamilton did not say that any President under the Constitution would ever betray our country. He said that an ambitious executive of a republic, *unless restrained in power over foreign affairs as our Constitution provides,* might come under foreign influences and betray his country. He was arguing against conferring upon the President unlimited power over foreign affairs.

DR. SMYTH: Your comments do not help very much. Hamilton's very idea smirches the character of the American people and tends to destroy our confidence in the President as our national leader and the symbol of our national unity, especially in foreign affairs. I am not now defending any President in particular. I am referring to the high office of chief executive and to any person who may be elected by the people to that office.

BEARD: It is my turn now, Doctor, to take you to task. You have objected to my use of symbolism in any form, and at this late hour you speak of the President as the symbol of our national unity. You recognize him as our national leader. Let me ask, What do you mean by symbol of our national unity?

DR. SMYTH: It seems clear to me. When the President speaks as Chief Executive, as head of the nation, all other countries in the world are bound to recognize his voice as the voice of the nation, and we are also bound to regard it as such. In this respect the President is the leader of the nation.

BEARD: You sound like the Justice of the Supreme Court who declared, in the Curtiss-Wright case of 1934: 'In this vast external realm [of foreign affairs], with its important, complicated, delicate, and manifold problems, the President alone has the power to speak or listen as a representative of the nation.'

What law of the land, what provision of the Constitution or any statute, what axiom of our political tradition states that the President's voice is the voice of the nation which all citizens are bound to accept as such? I can answer for you. The answer is, None, absolutely None. The Constitution does not use the term foreign affairs. It does not declare the President to be the symbol of national unity or his voice to be the voice of the nation.

It is true that under custom accepted by Congress and the courts, the official communications of the Government of the United States with foreign governments must be through the President's office or the creature of Congress—the State Department. But it is through an Act of Congress and custom, not through any mandate of the Constitution, that this rule has come into force. When the Department of State was originally instituted, Congress provided that the

Secretary shall perform such duties as the President may intrust to him relative to correspondence and other business connected with our foreign relations. Congress could have required the Secretary of State to report to the legislative department as well as the executive department or to it alone. In the case of the Treasury Department, it did require the Secretary to report to Congress. But in making the Secretary of State the special minister of the President, Congress did not enact that the President's voice in foreign affairs must be regarded as the voice of the nation. Such a law would have been futile, had it been made.

And as a matter of fact, Doctor, you are also in error, when you think that foreign governments must accept anything the President says in the way of foreign policy as binding on the nation. Perhaps it should be so, but it is not so. Foreign *peoples* have been misled by thinking that the President alone can make commitments which the nation must fulfil; but foreign *governments* know that there are constitutional limitations on the power of the President to make treaties and do other things in the way of regulating and controlling our commerce and intercourse with other countries. Other governments have known this since the adoption of our Constitution.

Mrs. Smyth: Why, of course, on second thought, that must be a fact. I know nothing about the law, but I do remember how President Wilson was treated. He prepared and announced a foreign program for us during the First World War. I believe that it was a right program. Still, Clemenceau and Lloyd George and other men at the Paris conference must have known that the President had to get the approval of the Senate for the treaty he signed, including the League of Nations. Anyway, President Wilson's voice was not accepted as the voice of the nation in this important business. I think it should have been, but it was not. So, Robert, that much of your theory goes overboard.

Beard: Two more questions: Would you be willing to give the President an absolute power to commit the nation to any foreign policy he might deem desirable for any reason? And, since it might take all the economic and armed force of the nation to implement his policy, what would become of the power of Congress over domestic affairs?

Dr. Smyth: No, in a pinch, I should not be willing to give the

President an absolute power to bind the nation to a foreign policy. And I get the idea there is no sharp line between foreign affairs and domestic affairs. If the President is absolute in one, he must be absolute in the other also, or at least strong enough in money and arms to make good on any of his foreign commitments. Once more you have got us into a kind of intellectual jam. Power must be limited but there is no way of fixing the limits definitely, once and for all. Like a magician, you fall back on that elusive thing called the exercise of judgment.

Mrs. Smyth: We use judgment every day, or should, and we do not know exactly what it is, except, perhaps, that when we have collected a lot of facts in a given situation and are puzzled about how to act on them, we finally make up our minds, reach a decision in a jump, using our own judgment. Still there is something in the idea that the President is our national leader. Let us explore · that.

Beard: The question then becomes, What and how much is in the idea of presidential leadership? To bring this problem to a focus, let me read you the following propositions taken from Woodrow Wilson's *Constitutional Government:*

　[The President is] the political leader of the nation, or has it in his choice to be.

The nation as a whole has chosen him and is conscious that it has no other political spokesman.

Let him once win the admiration and confidence of the Country, and no other single force can withstand him, no combination of forces will easily overpower him.

His position takes the imagination of the Country.

He is the representative of no constituency, but of the whole people. When he speaks in his true character, he speaks for no special interest.

If he rightly interprets the national thought and boldly insists upon it, he is irresistible; and the country never feels the zest of action so much as when its President is of such insight and calibre. Its instinct is for united action, and it craves a single leader. It is for this reason that it will often prefer to choose a man rather than a party.

A President whom it [the country] trusts cannot only lead it, but form it to his views. . . . If he lead the nation, his party can hardly resist him. *His office is anything he has the sagacity and force to make it* (emphasis mine).

DR. SMYTH: The President certainly has it in his choice to be the political leader of the nation, *if he can be.* It is not true that the nation as a whole has chosen him. As you reminded us a few minutes ago, he is in fact chosen by only a portion of the voters, perhaps even less than a plurality. I am not sure that the country is conscious that it has no other political spokesman. It is conscious that it has no other President at the moment. His position certainly may or may not 'take the imagination of the country,' or even his own party. Look at the way the Democrats utterly repudiated Grover Cleveland during his second term—or rather the Bryan mobster-wing of the Democrats. The President speaks for no special interest, Wilson says. While I wish to God that was always true, I realize it is not always true. A long line of Republican Presidents certainly spoke for the special interests of big business, and Wilson himself said so, somewhere, didn't he?

BEARD: I hesitate to break into your commentary on Wilson's propositions relative to presidential leadership, but I will answer your question by quoting these sentences from *The New Freedom,* a collection of his speeches made during the campaign of 1912: 'Our government has been for the past few years under the control of heads of great corporations. . . . The government of the · United States is a foster child of the special interests.'

I may add that if, as Wilson said, the whole government was controlled by the special interests during the period in question, then the President at that time was no leader; he was a kind of office boy. But let us go on with the propositions from Wilson's *Constitutional Government* published in 1908.

DR. SMYTH: Really, I am through. I want to modify my previous reckless statement that the President is our national leader to run as follows: the President may be an accepted leader of such a large majority of the people that neither Congress nor the courts nor the minority can withstand him and he may have his own way—up to a certain point. I suppose it is another case of great but limited power, on which you are constantly harping. Yes, it must be limited power or the President would have or could have the power of a Hitler or a Stalin. Wasn't it William James who said that it is almost impossible to have any good thing without having too much of it? This political science is beginning to get on my nerves.

I should like to get back to my medicine but, horrible thought, I have to testify tomorrow in a lunacy case. I have to decide whether a man who has been my patient is or is not crazy enough to be deprived of control over his own property and put under a con- servator. I have been trying to make up my mind for two weeks utterly in vain, but at 10:30 in the morning it must be made up and I must swear to the truth of the make-up.

The Doctor sighed as if he were through with everything.

MRS. SMYTH, with flashing eyes: I do not like Wilson's statement that the nation craves a single leader and that the President's office is anything he has the sagacity and force to make of it. Craving for a single leadership sounds to me a lot like Hitler's doctrine. Too much single leadership and too much force add up to totalitarianism. Of course, President Wilson did not mean to put this meaning into his words, but they can be so interpreted.

There is danger in such talk. Perhaps that is just suspicion on my part. People, all of us, do have a tendency to run from responsibility, to crave some authority able to settle tangled problems once and for all. On the other hand we all have a tendency to resent authority when it is established, and to do as we please in spite of it. It is hard to be uncertain about things, to be always making adjustments among conflicting interests and wills, to be tolerant, to take half a loaf instead of a whole loaf. It almost seems as if running politics is in some ways like running a nursery where every child is deter- mined to have its own complete way but never, or seldom, can be allowed to have it. I am just rambling on and must stop it. You can both ignore what I have said if you like. I am no authority on political science.

BEARD: You are more of an authority than you imagine. I do not want to ignore what you have said, for I think it is true. One of the greatest rulers of human beings in all times, one of the thinkers most experienced in the art and science of politics, Marcus Aurelius, soldier, administrator, head of the Roman empire, phi- losopher—a fascinating and tragic figure—once exclaimed that people are like 'little children quarreling, crying, and then straightaway laughing.' The business of government was for him the business of ruling and getting along with such people and, as things go, he was ingenious at least, if not a genius. The nursery, the family, the community is a microcosm of universal politics.

Dr. Smyth, giving me a hard glance that softened into a smile: The Judiciary as Power, according to Marcus Aurelius, is next, isn't it?

XVI

The Judiciary as Power

D R. SMYTH, drawing a piece of paper out of his pocket: I was in Judge Ranyin's chambers this afternoon on some Hospital business and happened to tell him that we were coming here this evening to discuss with you the Judiciary as Power, particularly the Supreme Court of the United States. The Judge broke out in wrath and declared that you didn't know a thing about the Judiciary or the Constitution either, and he cited as authority Justice Holmes' contemptuous disposal of you in the *Holmes-Pollock Letters*. He got still madder when I asked him to come along and hold up his end of the argument. He had no time to waste, he went on; he had given a lifetime to legal business and did not intend to fritter away an evening talking with a man who knew nothing whatever about it

But he sat down and wrote the following proposition, which he asked me to put up to you the first thing on my arrival:

The Supreme Court of the United States exercises no power of its own. Its highest function is to apply knowledge of the Constitution to acts of legislatures and to determine whether those acts square with the Constitution, the supreme law made by all the people. The presumption of the Court is always in favor of the validity of an act of Congress or any legislature, and it sets aside an act only when the act violates the Constitution beyond all reasonable doubt. The Court is not a political department of the Government, and exercises no political power. It does not exercise power at all. It merely gives effect to the superior power of the Constitution.

What do you think of that? It is what I was brought up to believe.

MRS. SMYTH: I can guess your answer. It is that the proposition is a view held in certain quarters but does not wholly conform to various relevant facts in the case. You see I am getting on to your constitutional angles myself.

BEARD: Your statement suits me, though I was not intending to put it that way exactly. I was about to remark that the Judge's memorandum from on high reminded me of the editorials of the *New York Times* written against the appointment of Louis Brandeis to the Supreme Court in 1916. When President Wilson nominated Brandeis, the *Times* was shocked and made a long protest. It said that Brandeis had been an advocate of reforms, a pleader of causes, and had no place on the bench. 'The Supreme Court,' the editor expostulated, 'sits not to expound or advance theories or doctrines, but to judge of the constitutionality of the enactments which Congress may decree. . . . The court needs no advocate [of social justice], can never put itself in the position of pleading for any cause.'

After the Senate committee by a purely party division recommended the confirmation of Brandeis by the Senate, the *Times* continued to deplore the very idea of appointing Brandeis. He was all right, perhaps, in politics, but never in that high tribunal, it said. 'The Supreme Court, by its very nature,' the editor asserted, 'must be a conservative body; it is the conservator of our institutions, it protects the people against the errors of their legislative servants, it is the defender of the Constitution itself.' And more—a whole column in the same vein.

MRS. SMYTH: That is curious. How the *Times* must have reversed itself! When Brandeis resigned from the Court full of honors and praise, the *Times* paid a great tribute to him; or, perhaps, it was when he died. Did it never occur to the editor that the Supreme Court, as well as Congress, could err? Or isn't it really human?

DR. SMYTH: Besides, what was the matter with the editor? Did not he know that many advocates of reforms and pleaders of causes, politicians I mean, have been appointed to the Supreme Court? I am no scholar in history, but am I not right in thinking that many such advocates had been elevated to the Court before Brandeis came on the scene?

BEARD: Suppose we take Judge Ranyin's proposition, Mrs. Smyth's question, and your question as our starting points. The Judge says that the Supreme Court exercises no power of its own and that its highest function is to apply *knowledge* of the Constitution to acts of legislatures and to determine whether those acts square with the Constitution. That is a theory widely held among lawyers. Does it square with the facts? It does not.

Parts of the Constitution are matters of fact and of knowledge about which there can be no difference of opinion. The Constitution fixes the term of the President at four years, not two or six or any other number. In a case involving the issue of the President's term, the Court would apply *knowledge*. It has no power on that issue.

Dr. SMYTH: What would it do if in the midst of great emergency, a social revolution, or war, the President as Commander in Chief should just extend his term? I imagine that the Supreme Court would have small chance to exercise even its knowledge.

BEARD: In such a case the Constitution would be either dead or suspended. But we are speaking of times called normal. There are other parts of the Constitution that are not mere matters of knowledge, parts as to the meaning of which the wisest and best informed judges may and do disagree. For instance, 'No person shall . . . be deprived of life, liberty, or property without due process of law'; and 'Congress shall make no law . . . abridging the freedom of speech, or of the press.' In fact many of the most important clauses of the Constitution are vague and open to various interpretations. The great political controversies that have shaken the country have turned upon or involved these general clauses on which the wisest and best informed have differed, may and do differ. It is right here that the Supreme Court has power. As Justice Stone said somewhere, in effect, in such cases the only restraint on the Justices of the Court is their self-restraint.

Mrs. SMYTH: Then it does have power, that is, a power of negation—to declare laws null and void.

BEARD: A negative power is also positive: its exercise may set in train national emotions and forces which will produce the most extraordinary results. Mere opposition often makes us think carefully and formulate our ideas clearly. Even when the Court declares a law void, the opinions of the Justices may be so framed as to offer an absolute bar to such legislation or so formulated as to indicate other ways by which legislatures may accomplish the same or similar ends under the Constitution. It is within the power of the Justice who holds a law invalid to determine whether his opinion is to be wholly negative or largely constructive in thought. Thought is power. Then, in many cases of high national significance, there are dissenting opinions in which Justices may differ from their brethren and set forth reasons for sustaining the validity of legislative acts; in the Dred Scott case of 1857 or the income tax case of 1895, for example.

Dr. Smyth: The business of dissenting opinions has always troubled me. Of course medical doctors in consultation often disagree but they do not write opinions about their disagreements.

Mrs. Smyth: It might be a good thing if they did. It might make them stop and think if they had to go on record and, besides, it might help to educate the public and the profession.

Dr. Smyth: Not a bad idea, perhaps. However I see that it is risky to bring up medicine again. So I'll bring up Judge Ranyin again. He says in his memorandum that the Supreme Court does not set a piece of legislation aside as invalid unless it violates the Constitution 'beyond all reasonable doubt.' Yet right along the Supreme Court has split three to six or four to five on the validity of acts of Congress. As a casual reader of newspaper headlines, I know that. How on earth can anybody say there is no reasonable doubt, when four out of nine men, all supposed to *know* the law, insist that there is a doubt? As I understand it, the opinion of the Court may hold that an act of Congress is invalid and four dissenters may assert that the exact opposite is true. It seems to me that if lawyers had any sense of humor or of propriety, they would quit talking that way.

Beard: I think the rule that the Court should assume that a law is valid unless it is invalid beyond a reasonable doubt is a good rule. It runs against hasty and ill-considered action by judges. Still, an excellent rule may be made to savor of hypocrisy if too much talked about by persons lacking in discrimination. I think that lawyers and judges ought to remember, also, Justice Stone's dictum that 'Congress and the courts both unhappily may falter or be mistaken in the performance of their constitutional duty.'

At all events, the mere opinions of the Court are a form of power. They help to educate the lawyers and the country at large in matters of constitutional government and public policy . . .

Dr. Smyth: But isn't the opinion of the Court in a case the law of the case, and the dissenting opinions just dead-letter fulminations?

Beard: No, the opinion of the Court is not the law or the decision in the case. The decision is a very definite thing; for instance, in its *decision* in a constitutional case the majority of the Justices agree that an act of government is or is not valid under the Constitution. That is definite. The *opinion* of the Court is the argument or reasoning of the Justice who writes it, designed to show *why* the decision should be as it is. But, of course, all the Justices in the majority group may not agree on this opinion. While agreeing on the decision, they may differ violently as to *why* it should be so decided. Sometimes, the opinion of the Court, as distinct from the decision, is the opinion of only two or three Justices, and two or three other Justices may each write a separate opinion intended to show why the decision is right—an opinion called concurring, which rips into the opinion of the Court and purports to show that its reasoning is bad.

Then there may be one or more dissenting opinions designed to show that the decision and opinion of the Court are both wrong and that the case should have been decided the other way. Moreover, dissenting opinions are not, as you suggest, just dead-letter fulminations. The doctrines of law set forth in dissenting opinions may in time become the law of the land. The Court may reverse itself later and take the view of dissenters at a previous time. This has been true of many great dissenting opinions by Justice Holmes and Justice Brandeis. And don't forget Chief Justice Stone's dissent in the Gobitis case.

In my view, the great decisions and opinions of the ablest Justices are power, a creative or a destructive power, and the Supreme Court Justices should have this power on their own account and exercise it. Not many people read these opinions unless their interests are involved in the litigation. But lawyers often do, even when they have no immediate stake in the cases; and lawyers are very influential in the affairs of the nation. They constitute a kind of governing élite —the aristocracy of the robe, as my old professor, John W. Burgess, used to call them.

In my view, the great decisions and opinions of Chief Justice Marshall between 1801 and 1835 were primary contributions to stabilizing and perpetuating the Republic. Able lawyers everywhere read his opinions and got from them ideas and convictions respecting the nature of the Union. Probably, more people read the speeches of Daniel Webster, but the views of Webster coincided with those of Chief Justice Marshall. As I am given to see things, Marshall was a godsend to the country.

DR. SMYTH: Coming, as you have said, from a long line of Federalists, Whigs, and Republicans, you would think so.

BEARD: Perhaps. Yet if you believe that the establishment of our Republic as indivisible was a good thing for us, then you must think likewise. If you think it would have been better for all of us that the Republic should have been broken to pieces in 1861—1865, then you may conclude that Marshall was not a godsend to America. It all turns on an *if,* not on brute facts.

At this stage in our discussion, Dr. Smyth drew another slip of paper out of his pocket, with the comment that Judge Ranyin had given it to him with instructions to ask me what I had to say about it. The note was copied from Charles Warren's *Congress, the Constitution and the Supreme Court,* and ran as follows:

It is a solemn fact that, even in times of comparative freedom from emergency or excitement, Congress, or one of its branches, has violated the provisions of the Bill of Rights at least ten times since the year 1867; and at least ten times has the Supreme Court saved the individual against Congressional usurpation of power.

DR. SMYTH, commenting: This looks like a pretty serious indictment of Congress and a strong case for the Supreme Court. Judge Ranyin asks, What is your reply to that? I suppose that when Warren holds that the Court has saved the citizens' rights ten times, he cites ten judicial cases to support or prove his contention?

BEARD: I wish Judge Ranyin had come up with you. Since he would not, here is a copy of Warren's book and here are my notes on the ten cases. You are right. He does cite them. But it would take a week for us to go through all the cases. However, here is a copy of an article on the very passage Judge Ranyin cites from Warren—an article by a competent lawyer, Professor Henry W. Edgerton, now a federal judge in the District of Columbia, printed in the *Cornell Law Quarterly* in 1937. Edgerton analyzes Warren's ten cases. Two of the cases involved only action by one branch of Congress, not congressional legislation. The other eight cases boil down to very little liberty saved by the Court, if any. Edgerton, in my judgment, shows that Warren's sweeping statement amounts to a misrepresentation of the situation; that his solemn fact is not a fact, is on a fair estimate less than half a fact.

Judge Ranyin need not get excited on any such score. I am as much in favor of decisions by the Supreme Court upholding the citizens' liberties as he is. Indeed, I regret that the Court has not set aside many acts of Congress which do, in my view, violate the Constitution and yet have received judicial approval. Though Warren is very much excited about the alleged infringements he cites, he apparently is not much disturbed by a long line of Supreme Court decisions upholding state and federal legislation *against* freedom of press, speech, and civil rights generally.

DR. SMYTH: What about Judge Ranyin's statement that Supreme Court Justices are above partisanship? I presume he meant that they ought to be above partisanship, for he has been vociferous in contending that President Franklin D. Roosevelt's Judges are just New Deal judges. Perhaps he thinks that until the New Deal all Justices were above partisanship. If so, that is a question of historical fact which a study of history can answer.

BEARD: If partisanship is taken in the narrow sense to mean that Judges of the Supreme Court have perverted the Constitution and the law to serve some low interests of party managers, I think it would be true to historical facts to maintain that the Supreme Court has been remarkably free from partisanship. There have been a few cases in which traces of political jobbery have appeared, but they are so few that they may be discarded and the Supreme Court acquitted of partisanship in this sense.

But in the larger sense of grand public policies espoused by political parties, the Supreme Court has not been above and indifferent to the great conflicting interests of parties. On the contrary, the Justices on that bench have reflected those interests in the momentous cases of American history—such as the Dred Scott case of 1857, the Legal Tender cases of 1872, the income tax case of 1895, the Insular cases after the Spanish war, and some of the New Deal cases. This is not to say that the Justices of the Court in such cases always divide according to their party labels. They do not. Nor indeed do hot partisans in general divide sharply over such issues. There are Republicans sympathetic to the New Deal, and there are Democrats who have fought it from the beginning.

MRS. SMYTH: I should think that one test would be whether, in selecting Supreme Court Justices, Presidents have been indifferent to party considerations and chosen freely or equally from both parties. If it is just a matter of getting a competent lawyer who knows the Constitution, then Presidents might choose men outside their party about as often as they do men inside. For instance President Roosevelt appointed Harlan Stone Chief Justice after the resignation of Mr. Hughes and Mr. Stone is a Republican. How many such cases of such nonpartisanship have there been in our history?

BEARD: Not many. I recall only two offhand. Let us look at the roll:

President Washington nominated three Chief Justices in his time —Jay, Rutledge, and Ellsworth. All Federalists. Not a Jeffersonian Republican among them.

President Adams nominated John Marshall, an ardent Federalist politician, to succeed Ellsworth; and Marshall held on until his death in 1835, handing down decisions reflecting the great policies of the Federalist party.

The next Chief Justice was Roger B. Taney, a Democratic officeholder chosen by Andrew Jackson. Taney held on to the place until his death in 1864. In none of his great opinions did Taney get far off the Democratic line of policy.

It was Lincoln's lot to select Taney's successor, and he chose Salmon P. Chase, a former Democrat, who had been head of the Treasury Department under Lincoln and wanted the Republican nomination in 1864. A zealous politician if there ever was one.

After Chase came, first, Morrison R. Waite and then Melville Fuller. Waite was a good, sound, though not fierce, Republican, picked by President Grant. Fuller was a good, sound, active Democrat, nominated by President Cleveland.

Then came the first political break in the historic rule. President Taft elevated Edward D. White, of Louisiana, a Democrat, to the place of Chief Justice. White was a good, sound, conservative like Taft, but a party Democrat, no Bryan Democrat.

The next Chief Justice was William H. Taft, nominated by President Harding. As to their party politics, no comment is necessary.

After Taft's resignation, President Hoover selected Charles E. Hughes. No comment on party politics is needed here.

With the elevation of Justice Harlan Stone to the Chief Justiceship by President Roosevelt came the second break. It would seem then that, unless we count Chase as a Democrat, there have been only two departures from the political rule as to Chief Justices since the organization of the Supreme Court under the Constitution.

DR. SMYTH: But all of President Roosevelt's other appointees to the Court were good, sound New-Deal Democrats—Black, Reed, Murphy, Douglas, Frankfurter, Jackson, Byrnes, and Rutledge. Stone had often been favorable to the New Deal in his opinions. President Roosevelt did not make Owen Roberts Chief Justice, for Roberts had been what you call a good, sound Republican. He would scarcely have dared to make Murphy or any of his other appointees Chief Justice. Besides, he needed some age and dignity in the Court. Give me that list of Chief Justices. I want to show it to Judge Ranyin and ask him whether he still thinks that the Supreme Court is above partisanship. As a doctor of medicine I do not know a thing about jurisprudence, but I need only common sense to see through a hole in a millstone.

BEARD: Here is the list and also a list of all the other Supreme Court Justices since the creation of the Court under President Washington, with annotations relative to their politics and their appointments. Look it over.

DR. SMYTH, dryly, after running through the list: This very string of facts indicates to me that there has been a lot of partisanship in the narrow sense of the term.

BEARD: In some appointments, perhaps so, but my rule still holds good, namely, that even partisan judges have seldom, if ever, sunk to the level of petty politics, although they have often sustained or struck at actions involving grand national politics. It is right here that they have displayed their power, for good or ill. Yet I would warn you that the work of the Court is not all on dramatic cases. What it does by decisions and opinions relative to routine matters, in the aggregate may well outweigh in terms of national interest and welfare its actions in highly controversial cases.

As a recognized center of power, places in the Supreme Court have been the objects of ambitious men and a concern of party managers since the early days of the Constitution. It is true that John Jay, first Chief Justice, thought that the Court was of relatively little importance and esteemed more highly the governorship of New York, to which he was elected after serving as minister extraordinary to Great Britain. And in 1801 he refused re-appointment as Chief Justice. That, however, was a temporary and exceptional view. Washington and John Adams, by their appointments, committed the Court to trusted Federalists. But certainly from Marshall's day onward, many ambitious men have looked upon membership in the Court as an opportunity for the exercise of power, as well as a place of honor and dignity, and have sought to attain it by various methods of political maneuvering.

MRS. SMYTH: Innocently no doubt, I have always thought of that membership as an honor which went to great lawyers, with no seeking or political maneuvering on their part.

BEARD: There are of course a number of cases in which the honor has apparently gone to men who have not sought it or perhaps even permitted their friends to seek it for them. But John P. Frank recently published in the Wisconsin *Law Review* articles on "The Appointment of Supreme Court Justices: Prestige, Principles, and Politics," and he conclusively explodes the idea that great lawyers and politicians always wait quietly, without expectancy, until a discerning President, after surveying the geniuses of the country, finds them to be just the right men for the Supreme Court.

Beveridge in his *Life of John Marshall* says that John Adams nominated Marshall as Chief Justice 'without previous notification even to himself.' That may be so but it is the kind of statement that no historian can prove. Marshall was then (and for several weeks after) Adams' Secretary of State, and they were intimately associated in office. It may be that Adams nominated Marshall without asking him whether he would accept.

For many of the later Justices the records are ample and convincing. They permit us to say that ambitious men, usually though not always active politicians, have zealously sought membership on the Court and employed great ingenuity in their own behalf. William Howard Taft's early ambition was to be a Justice of the Supreme Court. After the election of Harding in 1920, as Pringle shows in his *Life and Times of William Howard Taft,* Mr. Taft made a point of visiting Harding, enlisted the interest of Harry Daugherty in his behalf, and, with great trepidation of spirit, pulled wires to secure the Chief Justiceship. His labors were successful, thanks partly to Daugherty's sympathetic co-operation. And no man in the United States was more concerned than Taft with getting the right kind of justices for the Court—that is, good, sound conservatives who held his own views respecting the powers and functions of the Court. From Washington to Franklin D. Roosevelt, Presidents have recognized the fact that the Supreme Court is a center of great power and have tried to select justices in general sympathy with their policies. This rule applies to Republicans and Democrats alike.

And why not? The Supreme Court is not a group of disembodied spirits operating in a vacuum on logical premises that express or affect none of the powerful interests over which party conflicts rage. In a refined but none the less real way, its members express these conflicts of interest. It would be preposterous for a President who believes that his policies are sound and constitutional to nominate judges who hold opposite views—judges who would declare his policies unconstitutional. Presidents are sometimes disappointed in details but in the general run they get what they expect.

Dr. Smyth: I remember hearing that Theodore Roosevelt was disappointed—yes, angry—because Justice Holmes did not decide some cases to suit him.

Beard: That is true. But one of the reasons Theodore Roosevelt assigned for nominating Holmes was the progressive views on labor and social legislation Holmes had expounded as judge in Massachusetts. These views Holmes continued to expound as a Justice of the Supreme Court throughout his entire career in that tribunal. As we have learned in our sessions, there are few rules in politics without exceptions. If there were no rules, however, there would be chaos in government and society.

Dr. Smyth: But Justices of the Supreme Court abstain from politics after they are appointed, however active they have been previously?

Beard: Though in general they abstain from active participation in party politics, here again there have been exceptions. A number of Justices during the past hundred years have actively, if quietly, carried on underground campaigns to get the nomination for the presidency. I know of no evidence that Justice Charles E. Hughes worked to get the Republican nomination in 1916; still he got it and resigned from the Court to run for President. Many Justices while in service on the bench have maintained intimate relations with their party brother in the White House, and have advised him in law, tactics, and strategy. There is some popular resentment at this, but the practice has been common to the latest hour.

Mrs. Smyth: At least they do not make political speeches for their party brother in the White House.

Beard: Campaign speeches, no. At all events I never heard of any case under that head, although Justices have occasionally been accused of injecting campaign speeches into their opinions, sometimes with an eye to their own political prospects. Yet Justices of the Supreme Court have gone around making speeches in support of presidential policies. Speaking more politely, we should perhaps call them addresses. They are usually delivered on ceremonial occasions, such as the Fourth of July, or at commencements when Justices receive honorary degrees from colleges and universities.

Going to my files I brought out an armful of speeches by Supreme Court Justices and judicial opinions savoring of the stump, and spread them out on a table.

MRS. SMYTH: I see a reason for classifying these papers by presidential administrations but what are all these curious underscores and check-marks?

BEARD: The lines underscore the passages in addresses and opinions by Supreme Court Justices that correspond to pertinent presidential or party policies. The check-marks indicate the precise presidential or party statements which correspond to the judicial utterances *seriatim*. Here is a good one. This is an address delivered by a Supreme Court Justice at.a college commencement. In parallel columns you see, on one side, this Justice's declaration of American faith and, on the other side, his President's declaration of 'my policies' to which the Justice's beliefs correspond.

Evidently fascinated by these exhibits, the Smyths examined many of them, folder by folder, commenting with amusement and astonishment as they came across distinguished names with which they were especially familiar.

MRS. SMYTH, taking up one clipping: Why, I heard that address when I went to a college class reunion. I was deeply moved by it. I thought it was magnificent. The Justice looked so grand in his robes and spoke with great fervor. Now I fear that he was merely dishing out White House policies. Here is another one in which the Justice makes a subtle attack on Wilson's New Freedom policies. Here is another one, in which the Justice seems to think that things have not been right since Grover Cleveland's time. This is positively the most entertaining collection of orations I have ever seen.

DR. SMYTH: They may be entertaining, but I think the whole business is a shame. Supreme Court Justices should not be traveling around the country making addresses that are ill-disguised political speeches. I almost think that it is a shame for you to have collected and annotated these papers.

BEARD: In other words, you hold it disgraceful for anyone who is studying a subject to try to find out all he can about it. I do not call it a shame for Justices of the Supreme Court to be running in and out of the White House or making addresses upholding or criticizing presidential policies. I really believe that it is dangerous to the country, in that it impairs the dignity and influence of the Court which gives it power in protecting civil liberties against arbitrary or tyrannical action on the part of Congress and the President.

MRS. SMYTH: It also shows that some of the Justices have been men of small minds or men capable of subordinating their duties as Justices to the policies of other men. They should not be making speeches at all, in my opinion. They ought to attend to their judicial business.

BEARD: Justices are human beings. Some of them have been small men. I have no objection to their being decorated with honorary degrees if they want such baubles, or to their making addresses if they get any satisfaction out of that. I merely think that they should be careful. They do not have the power of the purse or the sword but they have a power of the spirit, not an unlimited power, but an undoubted power associated with their high office. In my judgment they can easily impair that power by indiscretions in public addresses and in judicial opinions. For the sake of civil liberties and self-government throughout the country, they should be everlastingly on guard against every form of utterance that might diminish the respect of the nation for them—for the power of their spirit in matters of liberty, public welfare, and self-government.

DR. SMYTH: That seems sound to me, but, in your care for civil liberties, you are laying stress on the negative power of the Supreme Court—the power to declare legislative and executive acts void. That is power, I admit, yet negative power.

BEARD: But it is not wholly negative. Sometimes the Court holds a state law unconstitutional only as interpreted and applied in the particular case. By its opinion in this instance, it may guide state officials to proper ways of enforcing the act. When the Court does declare a law void as written, it does not necessarily close the door on all legislation of the kind. If it blocks the actions of police officials in a case involving civil liberty, it does by implication, and may often by direct statements of its opinion, tell those police officials how to observe the provisions of the Constitution on human rights.

Negation, as I have said before, may be a form of constructive or creative proposal or suggestion. Whenever the Court deals with the validity of a legislative or executive act, it deals with questions of public policy and private rights, of governmental power and freedom. And we must not forget that in cases properly brought before it the Court influences, if it does not absolutely control, the actions of all inferior judges and courts, federal and state, involving public policies and civil liberties.

It is a tribunal to which the humblest private citizen may appeal through counsel with full confidence that, if the Court finds his plea lawful, he will be decently and respectfully heard, without scorn, browbeating, and contempt.

DR. SMYTH: That reminds me of a case in one of our local courts in which the judge, instead of acting as an impartial arbiter, lectured witnesses and poured both ridicule and contempt on the defendant, right before the jury. He overruled every objection to such abuse that the lawyer for the defendant made. He ordered that lawyer to sit down when he was making what seemed to me to be a fair attempt to dissipate the air of prejudice the judge himself had created.

MRS. SMYTH: I suppose you have a bushel of notes on such incidents.

BEARD: I have a load of them that I could bring in. I'll just show you a copy of an address by Charles E. Hughes to the Harvard Law Alumni in 1920. In this address, Hughes expressed alarm over the way judges, prosecuting attorneys, and juries went to excesses in condemning persons tried under various sedition acts during the First World War; and he wondered whether, in view of the terrible precedents, the Constitution could survive another great war, even if victoriously waged.

The gruesome story is told with quiet eloquence by Zechariah Chafee in his *Free Speech in the United States* (new edition, 1942). In this survey Chafee shows that one of the grave dangers inherent in vaguely phrased sedition laws is the loose and vindictive way judges of the lower courts can interpret and enforce them, with the aid of loud-mouthed prosecutors, often engaged in trying to advance themselves in politics by pandering to the temporary passions of overwrought citizens. It is necessary for us to remember, therefore, the power the Supreme Court has in reviewing and overriding judges, prosecutors, and juries in the lower courts. If, by its own ineptitude and folly, the Court loses its spiritual appeal to the nation, then the last safeguard for civil liberties is shattered. Then the private citizen will be deprived of the one tribunal to which he can now go for relief.

DR. SMYTH: But he always can appeal to his member of Congress and perhaps get a hearing, if not redress, before a congressional committee.

BEARD: A citizen in jail charged with criticizing the Government has a small chance of getting a hearing before a congressional committee. Judging by the experience of the past twenty-five years with congressional committees in charge of bills pertaining to civil liberties, the citizen, even if not accused of any crime, stands a better chance of being browbeaten and ridiculed by one or more committee members than he does of getting a quiet judicial hearing. Some of the worst and most ignorant enemies of constitutional rights have been and are members of Congress. In no case is a citizen who protests against sedition bills likely to obtain from a congressional committee as a whole the kind of solemn, dignified, and even-tempered hearing that the Supreme Court provides.

MRS. SMYTH: You mean, if he can afford a competent lawyer and the expense of getting there to be heard. One evening, not long ago, you referred somewhat caustically off the record to a recent decision of the Supreme Court holding that the right of a man accused of a serious crime to have a counsel assigned to him by the trial court is not a right guaranteed by the Constitution. I remember also your surprise at finding Justices Stone and Frankfurter voting to uphold this inhuman doctrine, as you called it.

BEARD: I was a bit hot about that decision and hotter still about the black-letter sophistry employed by Justice Roberts in the opinion of the Court. I gave thanks that Justices Black, Douglas, and Murphy dissented and fairly blistered their brethren of the majority. Undoubtedly there is a deficiency in this respect. As a general rule federal and state courts do assign counsel to persons unable to employ counsel, but there are exceptions in state courts. In some state and local courts, only poor persons accused of the graver crimes are allowed free counsel.

Lawyers point out, and so did the Supreme Court in the Maryland case, that if free counsel were allowed to paupers in every case, then persons accused of petty violations of the traffic laws should have lawyers assigned to defend them.

But common sense tells us that a distinction may be made between trivial crimes and grave crimes. In the Maryland case, in which the Supreme Court denied the right of counsel, the accused had been condemned to prison for eight years on conviction for robbery. In my view there ought to be a public defender connected even with petty courts for the purpose of affording defense to persons charged with petty crimes and unable to pay for counsel. Great criminals are sometimes made by the mistreatment of petty criminals or of innocent persons. Here is a field for constructive work, and there already are public defenders in a few jurisdictions.

This illustrates the point I have often made, namely, that by its decisions and opinions the Supreme Court of the United States may operate with tremendous effect in the development of grand justice in the United States, filling it with the concreteness of daily and hourly practice. My phrase grand justice acquires real meaning from the action and language of Justice Hugo Black in the case of Chambers et al. *v.* Florida.

Mrs. SMYTH: Oh, tell us about Justice Black. We know only the bitter words exchanged over his nomination to the Court. Do you know him? Have you ever met him personally?

BEARD: I cannot say that I *know* him—or myself either. But I had the curious experience of passing a completely impersonal judgment on him. It happened, in 1934, as I recall the year, that I was invited to speak at a little dinner in Washington attended by several Senators, Representatives, government officials and their wives. I had never met Mr. Black, had never seen him. In the seating arrangement at the dinner, I was placed on the left of a gentleman whose name I did not get when I was introduced to him.

During the dinner, we talked casually about many subjects. My neighbor was evidently interested deeply in history and well versed in it. He asked me a number of questions about land tenure in ancient Rome, in Europe, and in the United States. Out of my slight knowledge of the subject I made the best answers I could and named a number of important books on it. My unknown neighbor's discussion of my answers and of the books I mentioned showed that he had made scholarly searches on his own account. His information and his discernment, the gravity of his spirit, his eagerness to get at the bottom of things, his judicial temper in weighing my objections to some of his views, all awakened in me an extraordinary interest in the nameless personality on my right. In our give and take over hot contemporary questions, about which we differed squarely as to various points, he displayed the same high qualities. As soon as the affair was over, I drew the chairman of the meeting into a corner and asked him to write on my card the name of the man who had sat on my right at the table. Then I learned that this unknown man, on whom I had passed an impersonal judgment, was Senator Hugo Black!

MRS. SMYTH: That *is* a story. It must be a good thing to be deaf sometimes and not know to whom you are talking. It makes your judgment more objective. I am glad to hear this story. Until this moment, I had mere impressions as to Mr. Black's qualities, some rather bad impressions gathered from reading critical editorials during the fight against his confirmation by the Senate. Please tell us now about the Chambers case.

BEARD: The Chambers case was decided in 1940. Justice Black wrote the opinion that sustained the decision. It was a case of four Negroes accused of murder in Florida, arrested, subjected to a third-degree treatment, which wrung vague confessions of guilt from them, and finally condemned to death. They claimed that they had been cruelly treated by Florida officials and that they were about to be deprived of life and liberty without the due process of law guaranteed to all by the Constitution of the United States. Through counsel they applied to the Supreme Court for relief, *in forma pauperum,* as paupers; and the Court, reversing the decision of the Supreme Court of Florida against the Negroes, saved their lives and released them from prison.

In his opinion, which will ring with power as long as liberty and justice are cherished in our country, Justice Black reviewed the third-degree treatment meted out to the Negroes by Florida officials, and asserted, with moderated eloquence, great American principles of civil liberty. The whole document ought to be read by all citizens who care for the perpetuity of the Republic, but we have time for only a few passages:

As assurance against ancient evils, our country, in order to preserve 'the blessings of liberty,' wrote into its basic law the requirement, among others, that the forfeiture of the lives, liberties or property of people accused of crime can only follow if procedural safeguards of due process have been obeyed.

The determination to preserve an accused's right to procedural due process sprang in large part from knowledge of the historical truth that the rights and liberties of people accused of crime could not be safely entrusted to secret inquisitorial processes. The testimony of centuries, in governments of varying kinds over populations of different races and beliefs, stood as proof that physical and mental torture and coercion had brought about the tragically unjust sacrifices of some who were the noblest and most useful of their generations. The rack, the thumbscrew, the wheel, solitary confinement, protracted questioning and cross questioning, and other ingenious forms of entrapment of the helpless or unpopular had left their wake of mutilated bodies and shattered minds along the way to the cross, the guillotine, the stake and the hangman's noose. And they who have suffered most from secret and dictatorial proceedings have almost always been the poor, the ignorant, the numerically weak, the friendless, and the powerless. . . .

For five days petitioners were subjected to interrogations culminating in Saturday's (May 20th) all-night examination. Over a period of five days they steadily refused to confess and disclaimed any guilt. The very circumstances surrounding their confinement and their questioning without any formal charges having been brought, were such as to fill petitioners with terror and frightful misgivings. Some were practical strangers in the community; three were arrested in a one-room farm tenant house which was their home; the haunting fear of mob violence was around them in an atmosphere charged with excitement and public indignation. From virtually the moment of their arrest until their eventual confessions, they never knew just when any one would be called back to the fourth-floor room, and there, surrounded by his accusers and others, interrogated by men who held their very lives—so far as these ignorant petitioners could know—in the balance. The rejection of petitioner Woodward's first 'confession,' given in the early hours of Sunday morning, because it was found wanting, demonstrates the relentless tenacity which 'broke' petitioners' will and rendered them helpless to resist their accusers further. To permit human lives to be forfeited upon confessions thus obtained would make of the constitutional requirement of due process of law a meaningless symbol.

We are not impressed by the argument that law enforcement methods such as those under review are necessary to uphold our laws. The Constitution proscribes such lawless means irrespective of the end. And this argument flouts the basic principle that all people must stand on an equality before the bar of justice in every American Court. Today, as in ages past, we are not without tragic proof that the exalted power of some governments to punish manufactured crime dictatorially is the handmaid of tyranny. Under our constitutional system, courts stand against any winds that blow as havens of refuge for those who might otherwise suffer because they are helpless, weak, outnumbered, or because they are non-conforming victims of prejudice and public excitement. Due process of law, preserved for all by our Constitution, commands that no such practice as that disclosed by this record shall send any accused to his death. No higher duty, no more solemn responsibility, rests upon this Court, than that of translating into living law and maintaining this constitutional shield deliberately planned and inscribed for the benefit of every human being subject to our Constitution—of whatever race, creed or persuasion.

Mrs. Smyth: That is a fitting climax to our study tonight. Now I understand your feeling—may I call it *mental feeling?*—about the Supreme Court, what it is and may be in our national life. I had always thought of it as a mysterious arcanum for lawyers, far beyond comprehension by ordinary mortals like myself. Yet it is really power; it may be grandly human power! I should think that the Justices of the Court would be overwhelmed by the sense of their responsibility. Surely all the people of the United States should know and appreciate its role in the maintenance of our Republic. Vibrating through Justice Black's clear and simple English appears that personality which you have just described to us.

Dr. Smyth himself seemed deeply moved and, as we parted, expressed his feelings in a handgrip tighter than usual.

XVII

Critique of the Federal System

WE were a long time in getting to the agenda for our seventeenth meeting, for a tragic death in our community that morning had stirred the whole town. We found it hard to shake off the pall of private grief and turn our minds to what seemed to be remote—public affairs. After exchanging views on the sad occurrence and wondering over and over again how it happened, we managed to shift our thought to the theme of the evening. In fact, catching myself up short, I realized the futility of dwelling on an incident about which we knew little and could discover no more by exchanging idle guesses. So I deliberately diverted attention from the subject.

BEARD: At our seminar on Congress you expressed the desire to devote a session to what you called a critique of our federal system. It would be helpful to have before us at the outset your ideas on the subject. That would prevent us from just shooting in the dark.

DR. SMYTH: I have tried to conjure up a little competence for this meeting by putting on my thinking cap. You know and I know that 'we, the people' as newspaper readers have gathered from news columns and editorials a number of criticisms, sometimes definite, sometimes vague, to the effect that our federal system is out of date, is not fitted for the times in which we live. Not long ago, while the New Deal battle was on, the Supreme Court was attacked for blocking the will of the people. The President was criticized with equal severity for trying to override the Court rough-shod.

Now Congress is assailed for blocking grand projects proposed by the President, again as a crowd of rubber stamps, or as plain dunderheads and nincompoops. Years ago President Harding was denounced as a weak President who always yielded to the politicians in Congress. Afterward Coolidge was ridiculed as a do-nothing

President and Hoover as a bewildered President. From time to time we have a crop of political scandals which certainly add nothing to the credit of our system of government.

Perhaps the major part of the criticism comes under the caption that our political machinery, made for a small country mainly rural in economy, is not fitted for our industrial age, for managing and regulating an economy that is technological and national in scope. This impression I have gathered from reading and talking with men of affairs. For instance, down at the Union Club not long ago, several of us had a confab with John Shuttleford, a big man in the manufacturing field. Shuttleford is a considerate fellow who refused to join the hate-Roosevelt crowd. He tried to go along with the Roosevelt administration as best he could, and his relations with labor are known to be steady and friendly. So he is no common grouser.

Shuttleford told us that, much to his regret, he doubted whether our eighteenth-century political machine could much longer stand the strain of dealing with complex economic matters, even to the minimum amount necessary to public safety. And he questioned whether it was capable of administering the measures absolutely required to prevent periodical depressions from producing revolutionary discontent. He was of the opinion that many government functions, such as boondoggling, should and could be lopped off, but that it was foolish to expect a return to the few and simple government functions that existed when as a young man he first entered business.

One of our group asked him a question about the tyrannical bureaucracy, and Shuttleford astonished his business companions by saying that there is a great deal of plain bunk in such talk. A lawyer present retorted that it would be all right if Congress would make laws in detail and not enact blanket statutes for bureaucrats to fill in by their harebrained decrees. The lawyer argued that there should be easy appeals to the Courts against all orders and decrees of the bureaucrats. Shuttleford replied that this was all theoretical; that in practice any such reform would hamstring business, at least a lot of manufacturing concerns.

He then gave an example out of his experiences. His concern manufactures machinery for steamships. In the interest of safety at sea there are federal laws regulating construction, he went on to say. Everybody knows that this is absolutely necessary to prevent the use of unseaworthy vessels by owners greedy for profits at all risks. The federal laws in this case occupy only a few printed pages. The details are worked out by engineers who know the shipbuilding business.

Turning to the lawyer, Shuttleford remarked very quietly: 'The orders and regulations issued by what you call the bureaucrats under these few pages of law fill a book of two or three hundred pages of fine print. If Congress enacted all the engineers' specifications into law, the statute would be out of date in a few weeks owing to rapid changes in ship machinery and construction. In this case the law simply *must* be general with the details left to federal administrators.

'In all my years, I have tried to be reasonable and have never had any trouble with the federal steamboat inspectors. Often we have forty or fifty cases in a year to be settled with the inspectors. I should go crazy if I had to prove every technical case in engineering to a committee of Congress. Besides I should be bankrupt if I had to wait on Congress for necessary modifications in legislation.'

Keeping his eyes on the lawyer, Shuttleford continued: 'Now as to your idea of appealing to the Courts every time I have an objection to a ruling by the Steamboat Inspection Service. I did appeal once, on good legal advice. I had to spend precious days in court with my engineers. The lawyers did not know a thing about engineering. The engineers knew nothing about law. The judges knew nothing about engineering. At no time during the trial of the case could I discover whether the wordy disputes were over law or over the type of construction necessary for installing a given type of pumping machinery. What a headache! I won the case at the end of two years and, so help me God, by that time a change in construction and installation made the devices we were disputing about as obsolete as oxcarts. Courts are all right for some things, but henceforward I am going to deal with bureaucrats.'

BEARD, as Dr. Smyth paused: Please go on with Shuttleford. It is like a breath of fresh air from the world of reality. I have always liked him. His exterior is cold but he is always courteous in an even way. Let us hear more from him.

DR. SMYTH: There is not much more to tell. Shuttleford, modestly declaring that he is no statesman, called for reforms in our system of government along the following lines: Congress ought to be smaller; the number of Senators from what he called grasshopper states ought to be reduced; the hullabaloo national party conventions ought to be abolished and the President be elected by Congress; and there ought to be a small legislative council composed of members from both houses, in constant session, working with the President and his administrators in interpreting and enforcing laws. Shuttleford admitted that the chances of effecting these reforms were slight. He closed with the words: 'I am worried. I fear that people will not see the necessity of revamping our old political machinery to fit modern industrial conditions or that such reforms may be delayed until we run into a smash which will make the breakdown of 1933 look like a tea party.'

BEARD: Well, Mrs. Smyth, your husband seems to have gathered in a lot of ideas for a critique of our federal system. Have you other suggestions?

MRS. SMYTH: After the question of a session on criticism came up, I wrote out at home on this sheet of paper a few topics, which I shall 'read into the record':

What about the scandals that constantly rise in our great cities from the operations of bosses and political machines, such as Hague's in Jersey City or the Kelly-Nash crowd in Chicago?

Since the Federal Government is spending so much money in our local cities and communities and building up armies of officeholders and recipients of federal funds, aren't our states and local governments in danger of losing their independence?

If this local independence, this local practice in self-government, is destroyed, what will happen to the spirit of the citizens and to the country at large?

Supposing that this increasing centralization continues, will the states and local units become mere shells and perhaps be abolished?

I realize that our communities depend on industries large and small, which in turn depend on the national and international market. I feel that Mr. Shuttleford is right in insisting upon the necessity of a big federal regulating machine to make constant adjustments in business and finance. So I am wondering, with shuddering horror, whether there is something in fascism or communism. I do not mean in the fantastic and cruel notions associated with these systems, but in the acceptance of strong, centralized, almost dictatorial government. To subject our whole economic life to the changing winds and storms of party politics may well become dangerous—impossible. I hear people who dislike fascism and communism, as heartily as I do, talk this way. How much of our liberty and self-government, how much of constitutionalism can we retain and at the same time keep our national economy going in a way to provide the people with the conditions needed for a decent community and nation?

BEARD: You have given me a large order composed of many specific items, some of them widely scattered from any center I can easily visualize. The best way for me to proceed, I think, is to concentrate your related items under the best formula I can devise, and to consider this covering formula first, leaving the odds and ends of criticisms for separate treatment.

The most exact formula I can hit upon is: *Our federal political machinery, devised for a simple agricultural society, is not competent to resolve efficiently the issues forced upon government by the needs of our great industrial nation.*

That, I take it, is also the substance of the complaint by Mr. Shuttleford.

What is the nature of this inefficiency?

Congress seems powerless to initiate important legislation. There are constant conflicts between Congress and the President and within the branches of the executive department. Hence endless delays and endless bickerings.

If the President and Congress are deadlocked over a vital question, there is no way of compelling them to reach a rational adjustment or of appealing to the voters at a general election; that is, allowing the people to settle the dispute in a short time.

The two Houses of Congress are so organized, with committees and special privileges for senior members, that it often takes months, even years, to get a desirable bill through Congress—if the President does not drive it through.

Perhaps worst of all, or a part of it all, is the utter irresponsibility of executive officials and members of Congress. They can dodge, intrigue underground, or emit clouds of ink like cuttlefish, to obscure the issues and confuse the public.

DR. SMYTH: That is a pretty neat way of putting most of the case in a nutshell.

BEARD: I am not quite through yet. In this criticism it is generally assumed that legal responsibility to the people makes for efficiency.

MRS. SMYTH: I should say that it makes for democracy but not necessarily for efficiency. Many of our corrupt and wasteful political machines in cities are elected by the people, stand in well with the people, and are kept in power for years by the people. In the days when we had prohibition, thousands of Americans were willing to accept the waste of municipal money by politicians as long as they could buy their beer and whisky under the noses of police officials. In other words, they preferred liberty to honesty and efficiency.

BEARD: Your statement is all right, but it is a common assumption that responsibility or accountability to the people works for competence and efficiency in government as well as for democracy. To put it the other way around: democracy is weighted on the side of efficiency, directness, and the exercise of intelligence in the conduct of government. It is on this basis that able critics of our federal system have demanded the abolition of our presidential-congressional system and the adoption of parliamentary government instead. Henry Hazlitt has recently argued persuasively for such a reconstruction of our system in his book *A New Constitution Now* and in special articles on the subject. His book I regard as a clear and effective criticism of our system of checks and balances and, within the logic of his theory, a cogent argument for a parliamentary scheme of government.

Mrs. Smyth wrote the title of Mr. Hazlitt's book on a library card and engaged the Doctor in a conversation as to the best procedure to be followed during the rest of the evening. At the conclusion of their colloquy, MRS. SMYTH reported the upshot:

Our theme tonight is above all a critique of our own system of government, to which the parliamentary form presents certain contrasts. Just what are the features of the parliamentary form which are marked departures from our system—features which critics propose to substitute for specific features of our own type? Suppose that you dwell at length upon this question, taking your time, without interruption from us until we have a fairly complete picture before us.

BEARD: Thus instructed, I list the following essentials of parliamentary government, especially as operated in Great Britain, to be contrasted with the presidential-congressional-judicial system:

1. The chief executive or premier is chosen, not independently by the voters, but by a conference of the majority party in the legislature, thus informally by the legislature. In practice the actual selection of the premier is more devious. There is a higgling among the members of the majority. The choice is usually narrowed to the two or more members of that majority who by long service and talents are marked for the office by a kind of natural selection.

2. The cabinet officers who serve under the premier as a rule come from the same party as the premier and are selected, with his consent, by the same method of higgling within the party conference.

3. A true parliamentary system requires a legislature of one chamber or a legislature in which one chamber, like the House of Commons in Great Britain, is supreme for practical, operating purposes. If there were two chambers of equal powers, deadlocks between them could arise, and thus what are called the evils of the check and balance system would prevent the smooth working of the parliamentary machine.

4. Parliamentary government is a kind of hair-trigger government. The political party which wins a majority in the legislature by that fact wins the indisputable right to choose the premier and all cabinet officers. The executive is in theory a servant of the legislature. The majority in the legislature can resolve to turn the executive out of office at any time by an adverse vote on an important issue. On the other hand the executive in such a cabinet crisis has a certain degree of independence. The whole cabinet may refuse to obey the legislature, resign, and allow the legislature to choose its successor. Or it may advise the Crown to dissolve the legislature, call a new election, appeal to the people. If it wins a majority in the new legislature, it continues to hold office. If it loses, it automatically goes out of power and is supplanted by a cabinet presumed to represent the latest expression of popular will.

Under this system members of the legislature and the executive do not hold office for any fixed term of years as in the case of our Representatives, Senators, and President. According to the theory, the cabinet and the parliament retain power as long as they correctly reflect the most up-to-date sentiment of the country. There may be a law requiring an election at least every five or seven years, but the parliament may repeal that law and extend terms indefinitely. If there are clashes between the cabinet and the legislature, two or more elections may be held in the same year. If no clashes occur, there is supposed to be no need for an election.

The hair-trigger feature of the system lies in this: at any moment the political gun may go off. If, at any moment, on any issue of weight, the legislature breaks with the executive, it may force a resignation of the cabinet or a new election. Or if the executive, in conflict with the legislature, believes that the legislature does not have the confidence of the country, the executive can force a dissolution of that body.

Thus there can be no long deadlocks between the executive and the legislature, such as produce delays, inaction, and confusion under the American system of divided powers. The will of the majority in the election of the legislature immediately prevails, and that will can be discovered at a new election at any time.

5. Under the parliamentary system, the executive is directly and constantly responsible to the legislature and can be held to responsibility by threats of an adverse vote. The executive has the power of initiating the budget—the program of expenditures and taxes. It also has the power of initiating all important measures on legislation. Private members of the legislature have certain rights of initiating legislation, even measures involving expenditures and taxes, but these rights are very limited.

6. The premier and other members of the cabinet in the parliamentary system are as a rule members of the legislature, chosen in the regular course of legislative elections. They have seats in the legislature; they may be heard there at will in support of their measures; they may be questioned there as to matters of administration—law enforcement—large and small. They may force a concentration of the able minds in the legislature on great measures of public interest. Thus they are able to prevent prolix and irrevelant discussions and to bring debates to a focus at any moment on matters of high significance to the nation.

In this way the best minds of the executive serve the legislature in preparing projects of legislation and members of the legislature may constantly scrutinize all acts of the administration.

7. To complete the *logic* of the parliamentary system, the courts

of law have no power to set aside statutes as unconstitutional, for that would introduce deadlocks between the courts on the one side and the executive and the legislature on the other side.

This in brief is my formulation of the parliamentary theory of government. In practice there are many variations of detail. The system works best where there are only two great political parties, fairly equal in popular support. Where there are many political parties, as in France before 1940 or Germany during the Weimar Republic, the hair-trigger system produces almost constant clashes between cabinet and legislature and is likely in any case to paralyze government rather than strengthen it.

The theory of parliamentary government as I have formulated it rests upon certain fundamental assumptions. According to the theory, the legislature fresh from the people is sovereign, that is it can exercise practically all powers over the life, liberty, and property of the people. It is to be immediately and constantly responsive to the sentiments of the people as revealed in legislative elections. The will of the popular majority so disclosed is to be almost instantaneously expressed in the legislation and administration of the government. The responsibility of the executive to the legislature and to the country is clear and definite. The control the legislature has over the administration works for efficiency in administration. The power of the executive over legislation works for a concentration of talents on the business of legislating. In short, as the theory goes, parliamentary government is best adapted to eliminate deadlocks and confusion in government, to meet the needs of government in a complex industrial society, and to assure efficiency in administration.

Mrs. Smyth: So far you have spoken of the theory of parliamentary government. I can see that in fundamental points it is opposed to the features of our constitutional government as we have discussed them in our previous sessions. But what about practice in the long run?

Beard: Ah, practice is another matter, even in Great Britain where the system is supposed to be in effect in its purest form. To go into practice would take months of our time. But I can declare with confidence that the introduction of parliamentary government in many other countries has not automatically worked according to the theory. The present state of France, Italy, Germany, and Yugoslavia, for instance, indicates that it may break down cr may be incompetent to meet the needs of complex societies.

Parliamentary government is not like a good watch which runs regularly in all sorts of conditions. Its actual operation depends on the traditions of the country, on the experience of the people in self-government, on the number and character of the political parties or factions, and on obvious and subtle variations in civilization. Mark well, I do not say that parliamentary government was the cause of Hitler's rise to power in Germany or of France's collapse in 1940. That would be a ridiculous simplification. Nor do I say that our system of constitutional government would have worked as well or any better in Germany or France.

In the eighteenth century, radical political philosophers in Europe had a childlike faith in constitutions. Many believed that it was merely necessary to draw up the right kind of paper constitution in order to establish popular government and assure its success. More than a century's bitter experience has taught the portion of mankind capable of learning that this belief is utopian. No constitution works perfectly. To be workable, even in a limited sense, any form of government must be adapted to the traditions, political experience and habits, the prevailing economic interests, and the intellectual and moral values of the people for whom it is devised.

It is customary to speak of the common bonds of all humanity, of the natural rights all human beings enjoy, of the similarities among nations and peoples. Universal traits of mankind I have no desire to minimize or underestimate. But anybody who has studied the histories of the various nations and has traveled widely and observed closely cannot fail to be struck by fundamental divergences in the experiences, temper, economies, and social institutions of the various nations of the earth.

Civilization in the United States is by no means identical with civilization in Great Britain or any other country, despite similarities in specific features. Our history, our experience, have been in many ways unique. Our form of government has been adapted to our character and circumstances. Latin-American constitutions more or less modeled on our plan have not worked in the same way or encountered similar successes. To expect a common form of government for all nations of the earth is, in my view, a fantasy. To expect that the British parliamentary system, if adopted here, would work as it does in Great Britain, or indeed accomplish here the wonders attributed to it, is in my view also a fantasy.

DR. SMYTH: That is more gloom. You allow validity to many criticisms brought against our system. You picture the theory of parliamentary government as if it would introduce into government competency for dealing with the needs of a complex society, responsibility with reference to all official acts, and efficiency in administration. Then you straightaway declare that theory unworkable here and leave us stuck with our rigid Constitution which is responsible for our deadlocks, confusion, incompetency, and inefficiency. You admit that in a great national crisis it might break down for these very reasons. You offer no hope for adapting our form of government to the real needs of our industrial society. The chances are that in a real national calamity we may see established here a totalitarian government of one kind or another.

BEARD: You have said a great deal in a few words. Before I consider the whole bill of doubts, I want to correct one of your statements. When you say that our Constitution is rigid, you repeat an idea about the Constitution which was not written into the document by the framers. It is an idea created by partisan politicians for their own interests and later repeated by foreign critics like James Bryce and by citizens who pick up their views from conversations and stray bits of news and information.

In some few respects our Constitution is rigid. The number of Senators from each state is *fixed* at two. But in vital respects our Constitution is highly flexible. The elastic clause is not the only thing elastic in it. It was intended to be flexible, adapted, as John Marshall said, to the storms of the ages. It is as flexible as American intelligence and character may make it.

A great deal of the rigidity ascribed to it is not in the Constitution itself. It is in the huge body of congressional and executive practices built up under it—precedents and practices not imposed on the country by the Constitution but self-imposed by politicians, sometimes for the very purpose of escaping responsibility and preventing the introduction of efficiency. Our Constitution is encrusted with the accumulated impediments of one hundred and fifty years. If they were scraped off, and if we seized upon the freedom to which we are entitled under the letter and spirit of the Constitution, we could work wonders without altering a line of the document.

Here I should like to qualify another one of your statements. I do not believe that even in a great national crisis we shall necessarily subject ourselves to what you call a totalitarian government of some kind or other. My guess may be wrong, but that is my belief. We passed through the crisis of the American Revolution and the crisis of the Civil War without falling into a totalitarian system, though it was then freely predicted that we would.

This we have already discussed. We may have in a great national crisis a straight military dictatorship under the President or a joint committee of Congress. But I believe that it will prove to be temporary if it ever comes. The idea of our repeating all the mental imagery, ideas, rhetoric, sentiments, and hocus-pocus of totalitarianism in Germany, Russia, or Italy seems to me so highly fanciful as to be purely speculative, for America has not been and never can be Russia, Germany or Italy, through whatever variety of untried being we may pass in the indefinite future.

I agree with you that our fortunes will depend in some considerable measure upon what we do in the way of making our government competent to meet the needs of society, and at the same time efficient in administration. But competence and efficiency, though necessary for the perdurance of a government, are not the sole ends or guarantees of government. Besides, competence in what? In making laws against liberty of opinion, such as the Alien Registration Act of 1940? Efficiency of political police in suppressing liberty of opinion and action?

The end of government in the United States at least is not mere technical efficiency, nor mere competence in specific matters, nor speed of political action, nor instant responsiveness to the will of the majority, nor the unrestricted rule of simple majorities. For us the ends are not only a more perfect Union, the establishment of justice, provision for common defense and general welfare, but also—and don't forget it—the maintenance of the blessings of liberty and the long-run service of American society. Long-run efficiency, competence, action, and deference to temporary majorities or pluralities are devices we believe necessary to achieve the social ends of government.

The philosophy of parliamentary government presents many forms of contradiction to the American system. If we adopted that type of government, we should have to abolish the Senate or reduce it to the status of a mere advisory body, in order to prevent deadlocks between the two houses of Congress. This, I am convinced, is practically impossible, given the tenacity of underlying interests, and undesirable besides. We should also have to abrogate the power of the Supreme Court to declare void acts of Congress trenching upon personal liberty. This, too, I deem undesirable and dangerous.

Under our system, momentary efficiency, speed, or competence may be sacrificed, more or less, and rightly, in the interest of mature deliberation and civil liberty; but it is long-run efficiency and competence that count in the survival of our nation. Parliamentary government puts the great issues of life, liberty, economy, and the pursuit of happiness at stake in single popular elections and places them at the mercy of a majority of the people who take the trouble to vote after the heats and distempers of a campaign.

Dr. Smyth: That lets me out. I should rather endure the risk of incompetence, inefficiency, and confusion than stake the great values of personal liberty on a single throw of the political dice. I am beginning to see that delays, bickerings, and deadlocks in politics may be the price we have to pay for such liberty, justice, and happiness as we have. I suspect also, in view of our political habits, that parliamentary government here would put a premium on factious opposition tactics. It would spur ambitious men in a restless quest for power to intrigues and maneuvers designed to oust the President and the cabinet chosen by Congress and to put members of the opposition in the vacant places of power and patronage.

There is a fine appeal in the logic of the parliamentary theory. But as you once said here, quoting Madison, it is folly to try by a pure ideal the necessities of practical situations—or something like that. In practice there are objections to any system of government, including our own, and the problem at bottom seems to be a question of balancing advantages and disadvantages. I am beginning to doubt whether Americans could be induced to adopt parliamentary government. If they did adopt it, obstructionism, delays, and incompetence might still continue; they might even be worse. *For forms of government let fools contest,* somebody has said.

Beard: That line about forms of government is from Alexander Pope. The next line is *Whate'er is best administer'd is best*. I do not accept a thing in the couplet. Forms of government are vital to the happiness of the people. Some forms of government are better than others. Our form in general we deem best for us, and efforts to make radical changes in it in the direction of parliamentary or authoritarian government will be and ought to be contested. In my opinion those who lead in that contest would not necessarily be fools, as Pope contends.

While dissenting from Pope's doctrine, I agree with you that there would be obstructionism and factionalism in parliamentary government if it were adopted by the United States. Even Britain is not free from these proclivities of mankind. I have observed it at work in places as far apart as Paris, Berlin, Belgrade, Rome, and Tokyo. I have seen pressing public business delayed for weeks, months, years, while leaders of parties, cliques, and gangs battled and intrigued against the premier and cabinet in power.

You may think that our own factionalism is contemptible: the House fighting the Senate, Congress quarreling with the President, the President lashing out at Congress, the Supreme Court annulling laws duly passed and signed, and all that. Often the way in which these battles are carried on is disgusting. But, suppose that the Supreme Court had no power to annul laws; suppose Congress could at any moment oust the President and his cabinet, would such practices automatically disappear? My answer is, No. And greater evils would probably be added unto these.

Mrs. Smyth: I can well imagine what our Congress would look like and would do, if it had full and constant control over the President and his cabinet and all the jobs in the Executive Department. Add to that putting life, liberty, and the pursuit of happiness at the mercy of mere majorities in single congressional elections. And in such elections the party that polls the most votes does not always get a majority of the seats in the House of Representatives. In 1942 nearly half the voters did not take the trouble to vote, the Republicans received slightly over fifty per cent of the votes cast, and the Democrats got a majority of the seats! As Robert remarked, that lets me out.

Yet the old problems still haunt me. Our Government should be more competent to deal with the needs of our highly industrialized society. It should be more efficient in discharging its duties. The three departments of the Government ought to be engaged in less wrangling, ought to act more responsibly, ought to stick closer to public business.

And it has been pretty well agreed that Congress has, in a dangerous measure, surrendered its legislative function to the President. A limb that is not rightly used withers. Congress seems in peril of the kind of decline that leads to death. If Congress becomes utterly futile, we shall then be in danger of being ruled by the President alone as a sort of Caesar. That would be a sorry outcome for us. So I want to ask this question, Are there not ways of getting more competence, more efficiency, more responsibility in our Government under our Constitution pretty much as it stands now?

BEARD: You have, I think, stated very simply the supreme constitutional issue of our troubled times. I believe that we need again the kind of concentration of talents on this issue that was effected in framing the Constitution in 1787. We ought to return once more to first principles. We ought to clear away in our thought accumulated precedents and practices that hamper the establishment of competence, efficiency, and responsibility in governmental procedure.

But I do not propose to draw up for you a paper scheme for accomplishing these ends. No individual is wise enough to prescribe what is to be done. Such a prescription, like the Constitution itself, should come from the common counsel of experienced and reflective persons. Many paper plans for a new constitution were drawn up before the Convention met in 1787. Various paper plans were presented to the Convention early in its sessions. Those plans were all useful though none of them was adopted as written. The Constitution was a result of the pooling of experiences, the checking and counterchecking of ideas, adjustments, and compromises among realistic interests. So I shall merely list for you a few things which I think *might* be done to make our Government more competent, more efficient, and more responsible. My tentative suggestions are as follows:

There are now great talents in the Senate and the House of Representatives. The organization and procedure of the two bodies should be such as to effect and compel a concentration of those talents on the needs of our society.

For this purpose numerous committees, which disperse talents and waste much time, could be abolished. Some committees could be made joint committees representing both houses, as is done in the Massachusetts Legislature. Thus double hearings could be eliminated.

In each house there could be a grand committee duly elected and put in charge of all the important legislative problems. It might have subcommittees to deal with particular types of bills, but its responsibility for submitting all measures of national significance should be clear and positively fixed in legislative practice and in popular understanding.

This grand committee in each house should have such control over procedure that it could force the due consideration of its proposed measures of law and action.

This grand committee should have at its command a staff of the most competent persons in the country for investigating and reporting on the legislative needs of the nation—the best experts in the several branches of these needs. Thus the outside talents of the nation also could be concentrated on current problems of government. The work of the staff could be supplemented by public hearings on proposed measures—hearings well prepared in advance so as to avoid the meanderings and futilities that mark most of the present hearings and promote a penetrating and comprehensive review of its proposals.

With a view to giving each house ample time to deliberate upon the measures proposed by the grand committee, all petty business and irrelevant airings of opinion should be rigidly excluded by rule. Congress now wastes endless hours on trivial claims against the government, special bills such as pension petitions and other private measures. Such trivial business could all be turned over to appropriate branches of the federal administration, subject, if necessary, to review by Congress under narrow limitations as to verbiage.

There are in ordinary times seldom more than eight or ten great bills of national significance. With the multitude of minor measures out of the way, there would be ample time for full-dress debates on the great bills. By such debates the country, as well as members of Congress, could be interested in and enlightened about public business and talents dedicated to the consideration of it. Thus *competence* could be brought to bear on the issues of our society and on the conduct of government.

Under such a scheme every member of Congress would be free to introduce his own bills dealing with these issues. If he could marshal a majority in favor of his proposals, the grand committee might be compelled to consider and report on them to the house in which they originated.

Some such program would, I believe, squelch windbags in Congress, make necessary a concentration of energies and talents, eliminate the snooping committees, standing and special, and give us a more competent, more efficient, and more responsible Congress.

There remains the question of institutionalizing the relations of Congress and the President; that is making them regular, open, and dignified, instead of irregular, subterranean, and often undignified, vulgar, and capricious.

The hands of the clock on the mantel approach midnight and the subject of legislative-executive relations is as limitless as anybody's realistic imagination. So I shall finish with some mere hints.

A congressional legislative council could be created to conduct relations with the Executive. The council could consist of members chosen from the grand committees of the two houses, or could be otherwise constituted in such a way as to represent the strength of the parties in Congress. The staff of experts associated with the grand committees could also serve the legislative council. The council could sit continuously even between sessions of Congress. Stated days could be set aside for meetings of the council and the President. Apart from the President's formal messages to Congress, his communications with Congress would be through the council. The council would serve as a mediating agency between the Executive and the Legislature, adjusting controversies, working out co-operative measures and projects, and defining issues joined by the council and the President.*

---

* Happy to have support for some of the "theoretical" views I had expressed at our seventeenth seminar and to find a much better statement of the whole case by a Senator of the United States, I wrote to the Smyths as follows:

Hosannah Hill, July 8, 1943.

Dear Dr. and Mrs. Smyth,

If you will look at your current *Atlantic Monthly* you will discover an interesting article by Senator Robert M. La Follette on the very subject of our seventeenth seminar. There he states tersely and comprehensively all that I was fumbling after in our discussion. I enclose a copy of the *Congressional Record* for July 5 which contains an address by Senator La Follette to his colleagues on the need for reform in our federal system and presents a series of concrete resolutions designed to effect such reform. After you have read the article and the address you will see that we were not just wandering around in our own Wonderland.

The recent rains have been bad for hay-making at the farm but I suppose that the roof of your hospital is tight, so that your work goes on without interruption. I saw in the paper that you have fewer automobile accidents to take care of, now that gas is hard to come by.

Sincerely yours,

Charles A. Beard.

Before we begin to tinker with the system established by the Constitution, or talk about borrowing some other system from somewhere, we should have more bold, analytical, creative thought about our Government among members of the Government and the people outside. We should diminish servitude to precedents established under it. The founders of the Republic broke with precedents and set up a highly flexible scheme of government—that is, flexible to informed and daring minds. We should measure up in our times and circumstances, given our changed conditions and needs, to their example.

A great deal might be done by reforming the manners of members of Congress and Presidents—their ways of conducting themselves, using their mouths, and viewing their responsibilities. I should like to see the greatest thinkers in the United States write books on the manners and morals of government in relation to the ends of government and the instruments of efficiency and responsibility. Most of our books on government deal merely with descriptions of political and legal practices. This is the way the subject is usually taught in our institutions of learning. Then we have an abundant literature of abuse, some of which is highly useful.

Unfortunately, we have no truly magnificent works on government comparable to *The Federalist* but adapted to our needs and dealing temperately, realistically, and insistently with all that *ought* to be done to bring our government, in a multitude of ways, closer to the ideal purposes set forth in the Preamble to the Constitution. In this respect our intellectual power seems to have declined. Or has it merely been diverted to specialties such as business, private law or natural science? Can we recover it or return it to this channel?

I could go on indefinitely with the details of proposed ways of increasing competence, efficiency, and responsibility in our system of government. But I have given enough illustrations of what could be done under our Constitution to show that it is wide open to radical changes in the current ways of transacting public business. I put no special value on any of my proposals. I do not advance them as 'solutions' of the problem of competent, efficient, and responsible government. Every one of my suggestions may be fanciful. They indicate, however, that if the talents of the country were concentrated once more on the first principles of such a government, the Constitution as it now stands would give them an almost limitless scope for accomplishing the design of adapting our Government to the needs of our society.

Our troubles lie then, DR. SMYTH concluded, not so much in the rigidity of the Constitution as in our lack of political sagacity.

XVIII

Political Parties as Agencies and Motors

IT was fortunate, DR. SMYTH opened our exchange of greetings, that last Friday evening you gave us the high-sounding title for our discussion tonight. We did not exactly grasp its meaning at the time, but we smelt something unearthly in the air. Otherwise we should have brought up with us Joe Smedge, our town boss, who is supposed to know party politics from A to Z. Joe is a smart man. For all important purposes he runs both parties, allowing small liberties to his vassals in matters that amount to nothing. He keeps all the varieties of racial tribesmen in both parties in such good humor that they never kick over the traces at election time.

He owns, I am told, the majority stock in both of our dailies, attends directors' meetings, and takes an interest in seeing that the right slant is given to the news and in the editorials. The editors of one of the papers told me, however, that while Joe did not worry much about the news stories in themselves, or the editorials, he watched headlines like a hawk, on the theory that most of his precinct captains read only the headlines, if anything. As soon as women got the vote, Joe beat the Democratic boss to the draw by installing two captains in each precinct—one safe man and one safe woman.

Joe combines business with politics and intellectual interests. In fact, he was a shrewd business man before he became our leading statesman. He was strong for Abraham Lincoln and the Grand Old Party until he got two million dollars for public works out of the Democrats in Washington during the big crash. Then he weakened a little, but he has never lost his grip on the business side of politics.

Not long ago one of the state factory inspectors condemned a safety appliance at our factory and blustered a bit. The foreman, who is one of Joe's precinct captains, settled the matter by telling the inspector that the Company had bought the appliance from Joe's machine works. He is, as I said, a smart man. But I left him down at the Theodore Roosevelt Club rooms playing pool with some friends.

Yet before I left him I asked him to tell me in a few words just what a political party is, and this is his definition: 'A political party is a lot of busy men (and women now) who do for the people everything needed in the way of government and do it soon enough to keep them satisfied.'

How's that for a scientific statement of fact?

BEARD: Ingenious, but not accurate and a little too simple. Joe has given an idealized definition of a political party. Often a party is not as bright as Joe imagines it to be. It fails to guess right on what the people need. Its sense of timing may be bad so that it hands out things too soon or too late. In such a case it may be badly defeated or indeed go to smash, like the Federalists and the Whigs long ago. Joe's theory overlooks the fact that parties sometimes come into existence for the purpose of doing things *to* the people as well as *for* them. His theory is unphilosophic in so far as it assumes that the political party is a kind of free-swinging body of persons, free to do things for and to the people at will. I sometimes think that political parties are more often the victims or agents of forces not of their own generating than independent creative motors in political life. Lincoln more than once gave expression to this idea.

MRS. SMYTH: To come right down to cases, take Joe himself. Many a time in our city he has been compelled by outraged public sentiment to do important things for the town which he had publicly and privately sworn he would never do. His vision is keen, but it is short.

BEARD: That is one trouble with politics in the United States. Too many people suppose that running a nation's government is about the same as running a city government or a factory or a business office. That is one reason why we have so many small-time politicians in Washington. Joe's theory also leaves out of account the composition of political parties—the varieties of interests in American society. It does not cover the relation of the parties to the whole of society and to the movement of ideas and interests in society. Above all, it ignores the role of fate in national history, of fate beyond the power of individuals and parties to control.

DR. SMYTH: Now you are going full steam. I knew that you would take a simple proposition like Joe's definition of a political party and run it into metaphysics.

Mrs. Smyth: Robert, I hoped you had overcome your old habit of bringing up metaphysics every time you encounter a statement that seems a little mystifying.

Beard: William James once said in effect that metaphysics is what you have when you think long and hard enough about any subject. One of the world's greatest scientists is reported to have declared that if he could understand a grain of sand, he could understand the universe. What you call my metaphysics merely represents, I suspect, my thought about the accumulated facts I have derived from the study of the history of parties—from the factions of ancient Greece and Rome to the congressional elections of 1942 in the United States. These are facts likely to be missed by persons who confine their time-span to today.

It is owing to such facts that I put into the title for our discussion here tonight the words 'as agencies and motors.' By those words I mean that at times and in certain relations the party seems to act as a fated agency of history, of forces behind, in, and through its operations, of forces beyond its control, of forces compelling it to do things that its leaders did not intend to do, did not want to do, were violently opposed to doing. At other times and in other relations a party, or rather its leaders, seem to defy popular sentiments and to act freely, not as mere agents, but in a creative manner; by this I mean that leaders bring into being new institutions and practices despite all the force of countervailing traditions and majority desires.

Mrs. Smyth: I confess that all you have just said sounds highly abstract to me. Won't you make it more concrete by illustrations out of everyday experience, as you have done in such cases during all our study?

Beard: The history of parties is largely the history of illustrations. I shall offer two examples.

In 1861 the Republican party came to official power in the United States. It represented a minority of the people. In the election of 1860 the Democrats had split, and no party received a majority mandate to do anything. The verdict of the majority was that nothing should be done about slavery in the states where it legally existed. As we have seen, the Republicans with Lincoln's approval were prepared to combine with Democrats and pass a constitutional amendment guaranteeing slavery forever in the South. The Republican party, though expressing some strong anti-slavery sentiments, was in leadership and in rank and file anti-abolitionist and was committed to the policy of letting slavery alone in the Southern states. Then in 1861 came the war.

The voters in the Southern states who voted for secession did not by that act deliberately vote for war. Many—how many we do not know—believed that secession could be peacefully effected and would perpetuate slavery. Whether the majorities in the secessionist states would have voted for secession if they had realized what was coming, that war, defeat and abolition were coming, we do not know. But it seems safe to guess that, if Southern voters had foreseen what was coming, their verdict would have been different.

At all events, in the consciousness of the people in 1860, the issue before the country was not war or peace. Nor was it slavery or abolition of slavery. Relatively few persons then dimly divined the issue in such terms. We now know that war and abolition were to come out of it, but the voters of 1860 did not know it. The joining of issues on war and abolition, it seems to me, took on the character of inexorable fate beyond the intention or understanding of party leaders and party members.

Dr. Smyth: That is all right for ancient history. Give us an illustration of our own time, with which we are more familiar.

Beard: I am not sure that we are more familiar with, or know more about our own time than other times, at least about the fate hidden in our time which will be revealed in coming years. But you can take the Republicans and Herbert Hoover in 1928. Look at their sweeping victory, including the majorities in Southern states. On March 4, 1929, it looked as if the Republicans were in power for an indefinite period, and that their economic policies were rock-founded. In the autumn came the economic crash, which relatively few persons foresaw; and fewer, still, foresaw its devastating course. That crash and its aftermath were in the nature of what I call fate. Had Mr. Hoover and the Republicans in Congress foreseen it, the probabilities are that they could not have prevented it by any measures they could have devised or the country would have sanctioned. The crash came. In the congressional elections of 1930 the Republicans received a terrific beating. I do not have to tell you what happened in 1932 and in the elections since, particularly 1936.

These historical examples show what I mean when I contend that parties may be agencies or victims of fate or forces beyond their knowledge or control.

None of the party programs in 1860 was realized as the outcome of the election. Each proved to be a scrap of paper in a storm which only a few had foreseen as to nature and consequences. No party presented abolition to the voters as a program in 1860. Yet out of the totality of history, including actions taken by voters in that year, came abolition.

DR. SMYTH: That is an awful thought. It is a good thing that you are not uttering it publicly. I suspect that you ought to get hemlock for thinking it privately. You are saying in effect that when our noble voters, all steamed up with patriotism, go to the polls to effect a reform or prevent a reform or save their country, they do not know what they are doing. They think they are plumping for one thing and the consequence is the direct opposite. They are poor boobs and might as well stay at home. According to your statement, Republicans came to power in 1861 promising to guarantee slavery in the South, and ended with destroying slavery throughout the United States. Under that theory the Republicans might now come to power in a landslide of votes on a promise to save the country from the New Deal, or even socialism, and, in an unexpected crash, end in creating a bigger New Deal, or shoving the country into more socialism.

MRS. SMYTH, in unwonted excitement: If what you said about the elections of 1860 is true, if what the Doctor has just said could happen in spite of a majority against it, then elections are a delusion and popular government is also a delusion! If such things are so, then we ought to adopt . . .

BEARD: Adopt what, Mrs. Smyth? And who are we?

MRS. SMYTH: Frankly, I wonder. This brings me to a dead end. I cannot believe it. I have been active in the politics of our precinct and our town. We keep track of what the mayor and council do. We devise programs of municipal reform and we have realized many of our dreams of municipal improvement. Why, the splendid public health program of our city is almost entirely due to the work of public-spirited men and women in an election about ten years ago, when we elected a mayor and a council committed to that program. I have seen the same kind of effective work done in our state, and it was by such hard work that we won national suffrage for women. Now you seem to be saying that we may vote for one thing and get the exact opposite, that fate may compel our elected representatives to do things they never promised or intended to do. You are declaring that things are not what they seem and that the world is turned upside down.

BEARD: Unintentionally, I have led you into some perplexity. Let me rectify my error. Before I make this attempt, let me recall one of your side remarks. In a moment of discouragement you were about to insist that we ought to adopt some other form of government. By we, I suppose, you meant the American people. You gave it up when I asked you what form of government we ought to adopt. You and the Doctor seem to think that I have been introducing a taint of treason into our discussion of popular government by proclaiming the futility of political action through parties. The Doctor implied that such things would be demoralizing if said publicly.

In my opinion, people are not as ignorant as you imagine. Our copybook theory of party politics is that one party offers to the voters its platform of promises, that another party offers another program, that one party receives a majority of votes and, thus victorious at the polls, proceeds to carry that program—and nothing more—into effect. That, I take it, is a theory you both for the moment subscribe to.

DR. SMYTH: I can sing to a harp the words that are on your lips now for the fiftieth time, 'There is something in the theory.'

BEARD: Exactly. There is a great deal in the theory, but on second thought you and all reflective Americans know very well that often you vote for one thing and, though victorious at the polls, get something else and a lot that you did not intend or expect. It is no treason to point out what everybody knows. And it is no condemnation of popular government or popular elections to say it. I believe that Americans are generally aware that sometimes they get what they have voted for, and that sometimes they get things they do not want and have voted against.

Knowing this, they still prefer our system of popular government. I certainly do. I doubt whether we *could* adopt some opposite form of government—whether our spirit and traditions would permit us to do it. Under dictatorial forms of government or any other form that I can visualize, the dominant leaders also are victims of fate and folly and their peoples suffer from the mistakes of leaders. There seems to be no panacea for avoiding such hazards of politics. Americans will do well, I believe, to suffer the ills they have under popular institutions rather than fly to ills they know not of—or know only too well by hearsay.

Under our system, the people have opportunities not offered by other systems. Often by political action they do shape their own fortunes. They are free to work by trial and error to desirable ends and in many cases great and small they do attain these ends. Under our system a pioneer in thought may advance an idea of political or social improvement, gain adherents, do battle for the idea in the forum of politics, and live to see it triumphant through adoption by a political party, and victory at the polls. Sometimes slowly, sometimes rapidly, by straight or devious ways, through our party institutions aspirations of the people are realized. Though, as I believe, many things are fated, are beyond the control of majorities, not all things are fated; and, in the area of freedom, Americans under our system of government work out good fortunes for themselves and their children and children's children. Without quarreling with fate, I rejoice in the freedom.

Mrs. Smyth: Having frightened us by the thought that we may believe in the promises of a party, vote for its candidates, and then get at their hands the exact opposite of what we expect, you owe it to us to give us more fully the other side of the picture if there is one. Of course we are aware on second thought that victorious candidates do not always fulfil their promises after election, but we had been inclined to believe in what you called the copybook theory of American politics. I guess we all like to believe in fairies.

Beard: I thought it good tactics to tell you the worst first. Frankly, I do not see how our system of popular government could work without parties.

Dr. Smyth: There is no fear on that score. Americans take to party politics like ducks to water. They are the greatest joiners in the world, and at the same time they are always disputing among themselves over everything under the sun. I cannot imagine the United States without political parties. They seem to spring up and flourish like prairie grass on the great plains.

BEARD: In the absence of the silence imposed by the sword, wherever there is freedom of expression, differences of interest and opinion will find vent. That seems to be like a historical law. As James Madison said in Number 10 of *The Federalist:*

The latent causes of faction are . . . sown in the nature of man; and we see them everywhere brought into different degrees of activity, according to the different circumstances of civil society. A zeal for different opinions concerning religion, concerning government, and many other points, as well of speculation as of practice; and attachment to different leaders ambitiously contending for pre-eminence and power; or to persons of other descriptions whose fortunes have been interesting to the human passions, have, in turn, divided mankind into parties, inflamed them with mutual animosity, and rendered them more disposed to vex and oppress each other than to co-operate for the common good. So strong is this propensity of mankind to fall into mutual animosities, that where no substantial occasion presents itself, the most frivolous and fanciful distinctions have been sufficient to kindle their unfriendly passions and excite their most violent conflicts. But the most common and durable source of faction has been the various and unequal distribution of property.

Then Madison goes on to say that those who have property and those who have none have ever formed distinct interests in society, and that to these are to be added 'a landed interest, a manufacturing interest, a mercantile interest, a moneyed interest, with many lesser interests,' which 'grow up of necessity in civilized nations, and divide them into different classes, actuated by different sentiments and views.' When the sword of a despot does not enforce silence on a people, these propensities, sentiments, and economic interests will find expression in disputes, parties, and factions.

Liberty includes freedom to express these sentiments and interests and to secure governmental actions favorable or gratifying to them. But we as a people have many common bonds which transcend these conflicting interests and help to hold us together—a common language, various common traditions, a common consciousness of many elementary rights and wrongs, and common institutions, including the system of government provided by the Constitution.

And strange to say, the political party in the United States, while often it intensifies conflicts among the people, also acts as a mediatory or conciliatory institution. Our economy and society are highly intricate in composition and in motion. Our economy does not consist of a mere landlord class and a large body of serfs, tenants, and field hands. It does not consist merely of a small capitalist class and a huge proletariat. There are rich and poor. There are large accumulations of wealth and dire poverty. But the gulf between the extremes is filled with graduations. Roughly, we may say, the larger share of manufacturing and financial wealth is in the hands of the Republicans, but it is not all in their hands. Landed property is divided between Republicans and Democrats. The ranks of the Democratic party are crowded by persons from low-income groups, but many a proletarian is a sound Republican.

We have no party that is a purely class party. Jefferson's early Republican party, as he said, represented principally the landed interests, as against the capitalistic interests. Andrew Jackson's Democratic party appealed especially to farmers and mechanics. But as our economy has grown more complex, the economic composition of our political parties has grown more intricate, complex, and various.

In these circumstances, each party becomes an aggregation of interests. Its large campaign contributions may come from one or more principal interests. But its membership includes representatives of many interests, often conflicting interests, large and small.

Thus the political party, or rather its management, may become a *creative force* by drawing together interests which would otherwise be factional and perhaps vindictive, as often happens in Latin-American countries and in Europe. The party so operating becomes more than the mere *sum* of its interested parts, even though one interest may wield great power in its councils. It becomes in itself a power—a power to mediate among and discipline its members, a power to form patterns of political action which are not mere mosaics of the several interests in its ranks. To alter the figure of speech, it brings many little streams of factional power into a common current, mingles them, and becomes something else than its components.

Democrats, for instance, will grant to a Democratic President of the United States measures which they would fight to the last ditch if proposed by a Republican President. They will yield to the management of their party a control over interests which they would defend to the last gasp against the Republican management.

Out of such party coherence come new ideas, legislation, practices, institutions, which otherwise, it is highly probable, would never have been brought into being.

DR. SMYTH: I can see that all right, but these ideas, laws, and practices so created by a party are not necessarily good for the country. They may be bad. Look at the New Deal, a form of state socialism the Democrats had fought against for more than a hundred years.

BEARD: How do you determine for sure whether a law or institution or practice is good for the country or bad? How do you know that what you call a bad creation by a party may not help educate the country and prepare the way for something good?

DR. SMYTH: Let me pass that up, or leave the questions for you to answer.

BEARD: The New Deal is too close to us in time for us to render a dispassionate judgment upon it. That is why I constantly recur to past experience for guidance. Let us take a new deal more remote in time: the Federalist deal which followed the adoption of the Constitution. It put the finances of the Republic on a firm basis. It stimulated manufacturing interests by a discriminative tariff on imports, and other interests by special favors. It created a national bank which facilitated commercial activities throughout the Union. As a good old-line Democrat, Dr. Smyth, you probably regard all that as bad for the country.

DR. SMYTH: I was brought up to believe that it was injurious to the country but, honestly, I do not know enough about it to decide the question in any way, even one convincing to myself. How would you pass judgment on the issue you have raised?

BEARD: Like you, I have my traditional political belief about the issue. Mine is that the Federalist new deal was an advantage to the country. That program certainly helped to cement the Union, to transform the country from a raw-material province of Europe into an independent industrial nation, to enrich our civilization by the diversification of economic activities. I look upon all this as good for the country. But there is another judgment upon the issue. It is the judgment of the Democratic party which once held Federalism to be an evil.

The Democratic party has often been in full power for long periods of time. It has often cursed the protectionism of the Federalist deal. It has occasionally, once at least as I recall, demanded free trade with the world. But it has never established free trade for a single year in all the history of its power. It has at times abolished one piece of Federalism or another, usually only to restore it later; and the economic policies of the Democratic party in our own time embrace the fundamentals of Federalism: protection for American manufacturing industries, a national banking system, the promotion of some industries by special favors, the diversification of our economy, a big navy, a strong army, and all the rest. While adding many things to the Federalist deal, the Democrats today retain most of its great policies. So, I say, the Democratic party has pronounced the fundamentals of Federalism advantageous for the country. Republicans, of course, so pronounce them. The verdict of history is that they were good for the country at the time, and in many respects are still good.

MRS. SMYTH: From that historical record, I presume you might reason that what Robert calls the bad New Deal will receive a favorable verdict in the long time to come. In the funny mixup of politics, I, the daughter of a Republican father, look upon the New Deal with favor, while Robert, son of a true-blue Democrat, condemns it root and branch.

DR. SMYTH: Wait a minute, Beard, before you render a pontifical judgment on the latest New Deal. All this confusion is due to the fact that we no longer have real party divisions in the United States. There are Democrats in the Republican party, and Republicans in the Democratic party, and Socialists in both of them. If we could clean house and get a real line-up, it would be better for the country and we should all know where we stand. Then all the opponents of the New Deal would be together and we could smash it and get back to sanity. Go ahead, Beard, with your argument that the New Deal has merits.

BEARD: How far back in our history would you have to go to reach sanity?

DR. SMYTH: I might say, to the New Freedom of Woodrow Wilson, but there was too much labor socialism in it. In a strict sense, for sanity we should have to go back to Grover Cleveland.

BEARD: Then the country has been fairly crazy since Grover Cleveland left the White House in 1897? If so, the Democratic party also has been crazy, for it has repudiated in fact about everything that Cleveland stood for.

With that out of my system, I shall merely say this about the New Deal as helpful or harmful to the country. My guess is that if the Republicans come to full power again, they will, despite their promises, keep many fundamentals of the New Deal. Above all they will have to face and will face the great issues President Roosevelt raised and, for a time, grappled with in ways right or wrong—full employment, the elimination of disastrous depressions, social security, and many more. So I propose a paradox as truthful: If the New Deal is as "bad" as you believe it to be, large parts of it may prove to be beneficial to the country. Anyway, America is not going back to Grover Cleveland or Calvin Coolidge or Herbert Hoover. If I know anything, I know that much. But let us return to the thesis respecting parties as creative forces in national life for weal or woe.

DR. SMYTH: First, may I make a little excursion or diversion? After our discussion so far tonight, I confess that there is something in your argument, to use your everlasting maxim, something historically true, if utterly unreasonable. Furthermore, in my present mood, I must declare myself an absolute independent in politics. And there are millions of people like me in the country, millions who have little or no faith, interest, or confidence in any or all of your parties.

BEARD: That is not an excursion or a diversion, Doctor. I was just coming to that myself. As minute studies of political behavior indicate, membership in the two old parties is extensively hereditary. Children in huge numbers inherit party views from their parents and can give no other reasons for the political faith that is in them. But other minute studies seem to indicate that an increasing percentage of our voters is partly or entirely independent.

Party managers, more and more, have to keep their eyes on the independent voters and on third parties that arise from time to time. This necessity is an incentive to creativeness, for party managers want to stay in power or to get into power. Besides running their machines, they act as brokers in opinion, to use a borrowed phrase. The two great party managements, so often evenly balanced, have to bid high for independent votes or lose in campaigns.

DR. SMYTH: How true that is! They would sell their souls rather than get out of office if in, or to get in if out. I say that a party ought to die rather than surrender its principles for mere power and patronage. Party leaders ought to stand squarely on their principles and, win or lose, battle for them to the last ditch.

BEARD: You mean they should stand pat. That is what the Bourbons of old France did, and they lost their heads. If political leaders all stood pat, battling, as you say, for their principles to the bitter end, the country, I have no doubt, would be torn asunder, and the sword would more often be the arbiter in our domestic affairs.

That isn't all. It frequently if not generally happens that men and women who stand pat on what they call their principles are just suffering from mental stagnation in a world which is certainly highly changeful. They may be as dangerous to the civilized way of conducting affairs as the most violent radicals—even the fellows who are willing to meet the test of shooting it out. Standpatters are certain to be outmoded, for our country will change unless it dies. Radicals are likely to be wrong too, but they sometimes have a chance to be vindicated—if they can correctly guess the direction and the velocity of change.

Anyway, it is from the independents, progressives, and radicals that new ideas, inventions, devices, and proposals for the improvement of the individual and society are to be expected. Life is change as well as habit. The spirit of science, so indispensable to our economy, is the spirit of free exploration, free inquiry, and change. From these quarters come the new ideals bidding for acceptance by the American people. Independents take them up first. Sometimes they form third parties, but third parties seldom get very far in the United States. As soon as one of them can muster about a million votes or more, one of the old parties takes the wind out of its sails by adopting more or less of its program.

Thus new ideas work their way up from independents, sometimes through third parties, into the creed of a major party and into the practice of national life. Many of the political ideals and practices now warmly cherished in the United States were once roundly condemned by standpatters, but the ideals rose to power in spite of them. One of the most noteworthy examples is the idea of freedom for chattel slaves. In large part the history of the United States is a story of the rise and progress of ideas. And through the agency of political parties new ideas are often made real in the institutions, practices, and economy of the nation.

DR. SMYTH: The evening draws to a close. As I get the drift of our discussion, we have two broad propositions before us. A party is in some respects an agency of forces outside and inside itself and as such may be driven by fate to actions contrary to the alleged purposes it was elected by the people to accomplish. In the second place, a party may become a kind of creative force or motor, as you call it, by drawing together varieties of ideas and interests and becoming more than the mere sum of these ideas and interests. It seems to me that we have left out of account the role of party leaders, the great figures in history, who inspire and educate their followers. They surely have some effect on the nature and course of parties.

BEARD: There is undoubtedly truth in what you say about leaders, but that involves perhaps the most difficult branch of historical and political thought. Every individual in the world is unique in various respects, however much he may be like other persons in his tribe, clan, or nation. This uniqueness may be a creative force in history. The greater the personality, the more powerful and inventive, the more marked are the qualities of uniqueness. Yet no personality is so unique as to be entirely free from the influence of heredity and environment. The dominating political leader sometimes seems merely to bring to a focus the dominating sentiments of his time and nation.

Jefferson has been called the founder of the Democratic party, and yet he was in many ways an expression of popular forces of discontent and aspiration that existed in the United States independently of his influence. But as a student of history and a thinker gifted in the art of formulating sentiments into striking ideas, he was more than a mere expression of popular tempers and views. In this role, Jefferson developed principles of policy for his party and the nation, which entered into the living heritage of our country.

Yet I am unable to distinguish between what Jefferson was in his uniqueness and what he was as a representative of popular sentiments. I do not agree with Carlyle that history is at bottom merely the work of great men. Nor do I agree with the proposition that history is nothing but the inexorable movement of impersonal forces in which personalities are like pawns in a game or dust in a whirlwind.

MRS. SMYTH: In any case, you leave small fry pretty much out of the picture as more or less futile. We work in the politics of our wards, counties, states, and the nation, hoping to realize our aspirations. A part of the time we are utterly defeated. We win a victory and get the opposite of our expectations and desires. A part of the time we do seem to count, that is, when our views and demands enter into what you call the creative work of a party; but as individuals most of us amount to little or nothing.

BEARD: I fear, Mrs. Smyth, that you are quarreling with the nature of our human world. We are all social beings, not free-swinging beings endowed with independent power. We do our work, such as it is, in society, not upon society. Some, by fate, fortune, and character, achieve greatness of influence in politics. Yet all of us contribute according to our powers to the sum of ideas, sentiments, and aspirations that count in the political government of our country. Sometimes we are defeated even in apparent victory. But a very defeat may become in a larger sense a victory for the nation.

DR. SMYTH: Come, now, how do you make that out?

BEARD: I will repeat an illustration. The majority of the American people certainly voted against the abolition of slavery in 1860. In a few years, in spite of themselves and against their own intentions, they saw slavery abolished. Their expectations were defeated. But nearly all of us now regard this defeat as a victory for our civilization.

MRS. SMYTH: Then politics, small and large, ward or precinct and national, is like life. We strive. We use our powers, or should use them, to the best of our abilities. We often have victories to rejoice in. Sometimes victories turn to sour fruit. Often we have defeats. Some of them are real and terrible. Others in the end happily disappoint us. In politics, by studying the ideas and interests which enter into party conflicts, we may become more and more influential in forming the popular sentiments that do enter into mastery of our national fortunes. As living beings we have to struggle for something or perish. The more we know about the nature of things political and the more we understand what it is we are dealing with, the better equipped we are for our function as citizens. So our evening's debate adds up for me. I feel reassured now.

DR. SMYTH: Sue has a way of trying to bring order out of chaos.

MRS. SMYTH: If I didn't, things would not be so easy for you.

DR. SMYTH: Now you are saying something profoundly true.

BEARD: In the great, the small is often symbolized. Politics is quite a bit like life.

DR. SMYTH, moving rapidly toward the door: If we go on this way we shall soon be like the disputants in Plato's *Republic*. Scholars today cannot tell whether they were concentrating on human justice or headed all the time for a consideration of the immortality of the soul. Your theory of political parties in national life carries me back to my freshman days at college when we discussed freedom of the will and determinism. You brush that scholastic debate aside and say that there are both freedom and fate in politics and everywhere else in human affairs, and you give us a picture of a crazy world in which no sane person would want to live.

BEARD: Come back for a moment, Doctor, and give me your picture of a world not crazy—of a sane world, fashioned to your heart's desire. It is true that I regard debates over either freedom or determinism as futile, and I am convinced that our world is partly free and partly determined and, besides, crowded with what seem to be accidents. Would your sane world be wholly free or wholly determined? Give us your picture of sanity.

Mrs. Smyth looked at her husband intently, as he stood a long time in a meditative mood.

Great God! he burst out. I have never seriously faced that issue. I have gone along through the years calling this or that crazy, criticizing people for being or appearing crazy, without realizing that my words implied some standard or articulate theory of sanity on my own part. Now by demanding my theory of sanity for people and the world, you make it plain to me that I am myself operating on some theory of things. I want to think it over. Give me time.

Before my guests could get their motor started, I shouted from the porch, All the time you want or have.

XIX

The Economic Underwriting of the Constitution

REMEMBERING Dr. Smyth's desire to have Henry Walker, president of the City Trades Union Council, present at our session on the economic underwriting of the Constitution, I took the liberty of bringing John Whiteworth, an industrial magnate, head of a big steel corporation in a neighboring state, into the discussion. Whiteworth built a huge summer mansion on Hilton Mountain overlooking our town, long before he had to pay any federal income tax on his annual earnings. Now he is among what he calls the poor·rich. He closes up.fifteen or twenty rooms in wintertime and lives in the remaining eight or ten rooms when he comes up for cold-weather outings.

Whiteworth is not exactly in my class, and I had come to know him by a kind of sociological accident. A short time before we first met in 1915, ex-President Taft had delivered a tirade against me before the Pennsylvania Society in New York City, taking my book, *An Economic Interpretation of the Constitution,* as his theme. Whiteworth had heard the speech. Shortly afterward he had encountered a town magnate on the street and redelivered Mr. Taft's charges. The local magnate replied that Taft was right, of course, about that book, but that he knew me and that, while I might be a bit off in the head, I was not a bad fellow. He also suggested that the three of us hold a little party, for the fun of it. Owing to that chance affair, I spent an evening at Whiteworth's place on Hilton Mountain. Having felt out his dogmatic spots and his soft spots, I sidestepped useless debate and told him a string of Indiana stories that seemed to amuse him immensely. Ever since we have been good friends, despite our differençes of opinion on many matters.

In introducing Whiteworth to the Smyths and to Henry Walker, I explained to them that I thought we ought to have a man of Whiteworth's experience at our session on economic underwriting, and that he had at first hesitated, but had consented to join us. Incidentally, I added that I had forgotten just why he hesitated. He refreshed my memory.

WHITEWORTH: When you rattled up to my place in your disgraceful old car, Stuttering Kate, and told me that you were going to discuss the economic underwriting of the Constitution, I replied that it was all out of my line. Our law firm, Belton, Holstein, Levy, Antonio and Lasinski, takes care of constitutional matters for us, and as to an economic underwriting of the Constitution, I can't see any sense in it. In the words of our Mr. Belton, it is the business of the Constitution to underwrite economics, that is free business enterprise.

The trouble with you, Beard, is that you get the cart before the horse. Leaders among the framers of the Constitution were, as you have said yourself, businessmen, men of substantial property interests; and they made the Constitution, as you did not say, for the purpose of preventing government interference with business. As our Mr. Belton would put it, they did not think that the Constitution needed any economic underwriting; they thought that free enterprise needed a constitutional underwriting. To quote our Mr. Belton again: 'Until the New Deal dunderheads came along and befuddled the people, everybody in his right mind knew just what the Constitution was for, namely, to protect free enterprise.'

MR. WALKER, labor leader, growing red in the face: I know your Mr. Belton, of Belton, Holstein, Levy, Antonio, and Lasinski very well, Mr. Whiteworth. Away back in 1922, during the railway shopmen's strike, he had a hand in getting the notorious Harry M. Daugherty to extort an injunction from a federal judge. That injunction forbade strikers or their leaders to engage in picketing or to persuade any person to leave work or refrain from going to work, by word of mouth, telegrams, telephone messages, interviews in newspapers, or any other way. . . .

BEARD: The injunction read 'or otherwise in any manner whatsoever.'

WHITEWORTH: Oh, you would remember the very words! But let that go. Daugherty's injunction is a fine example of what I mean by a constitutional underwriting of rights guaranteed by the Constitution, the constitutional underwriting of free economic enterprise.

WALKER: But what about underwriting the rights of labor to organize and bargain with employers on hours, wages, and conditions of work? Doesn't the Constitution underwrite these human rights of labor as much as it does the rights for your Company?

WHITEWORTH: There isn't a word in the Constitution about the rights of labor, not a word about labor. Not a word. Our Mr. Belton, who knows his Constitution from A to Z, keeps repeating that.

WALKER: Your blessed Mr. Belton may be right on that point. I guess the word labor isn't in the Constitution. But I know the word liberty is, and that's what I am talking about—the liberty of labor to organize and get a square deal for industrial workers.

BEARD: You are both misinformed, gentlemen, about the word labor. It is in the Constitution. Mr. Belton has overlooked it. There is a clause in Article IV which reads:

No person held to service or labor in one state, under the laws thereof, escaping into another, shall . . . be discharged from such service or labor, but shall be delivered up on claim of the party to whom such service or labor may be due.

There is the word labor three times.

WHITEWORTH: That's my chief quarrel with you, Beard, you are always bringing up irrelevant matters. You know that the clause you have just cited is the provision for the return of runaway slaves, and is obsolete.

WALKER: Of course it is. It never did have anything to do with white labor.

BEARD: I was just joking. You both thought that the word labor is not in the Constitution, and I merely said it is there three times. You agreed that the clause referred only to runaway slaves. You are both wrong again. When the Constitution was framed, there were thousands of white workers, men and women, indentured or bound to labor for their masters for terms of years. This clause covered white servants as well as Negro slaves.

WHITEWORTH: I never heard of that.

WALKER: I never did either.

BEARD: I am not surprised at that. Nor should I blame you at all for complete ignorance of the Constitution and its history if you were not all the time talking about your rights under the Constitution. But go ahead with your rights.

WALKER: I was saying that labor claims its liberty to organize and bargain under the Constitution. The word liberty is certainly in the Constitution, more than once. It includes the kind of liberty that trade unionists are demanding, the same liberty of organization that manufacturers enjoy.

WHITEWORTH: It means liberty for individual human beings. It isn't liberty for labor to form an organization and, through its walking delegates, dictate hours, wages, and everything else to other laborers and to employers. It means liberty for competition among employers and workers to carry on as they please, to improve their conditions, to make a little more money than they are making. The word labor, may be, as Beard says, in the Constitution three times, but the words trade union certainly are not there at all. Are they, Mr. Walker?

WALKER: I suppose not, but I'll bet a dollar that the word company or corporation is not there either.

WHITEWORTH: I've got you there, Mr. Walker! It is true the words company and corporation are not in the Constitution. Our Mr. Belton has often told us that in our conferences. The word person, however, is there, he says, and a company or corporation is, in the eyes of the law, a person, a legal person. Now, Beard, you cannot deny that. You will have to admit that much.

MRS. SMYTH: Watch your step, gentlemen, or Mr. Beard will go to his records and pull out a ton of notes on the origin, history, and meaning of the word person in law, from the most ancient code of Moses down to the latest utterances of Justice Hugo Black.

WHITEWORTH: God forbid! Just let Beard answer one simple, honest question, Is a corporation or company a person at law and entitled to the rights of human persons under the Constitution? Yes or no.

BEARD: No.

WHITEWORTH: Our Mr. Belton declares that it is, and are you going to pit yourself against the best lawyer in the United States?

BEARD: You wanted a Yes or No and I answered your question correctly with a No. Now let me make my own statement. A company or corporation, if duly organized under law, is a person at law for certain purposes and is entitled to certain rights of natural persons, but is not entitled to all the rights of natural persons or citizens under the Constitution.

DR. SMYTH: Hold right there. Otherwise you will be citing all the law cases—Tubbs *v.* Tubbs, Inc., or Bubbs *v.* Bubbs, Inc., and all the opinions of the judges, the concurring opinions and the dissenting and discriminating opinions, until the crack of doom. I have been through it here in this room. It would serve Mr. Whiteworth and Mr. Walker right to have to endure some of it, but let us move along. They are both talking about the rights of organizations, manufacturing corporations and trade union corporations. . . .

WALKER: Pardon me, but a trade union is not incorporated at law like a business corporation and is not subject to the same rules of law. Labor is not a commodity such as manufacturers turn out. A trade union is a society of human persons for the mutual benefit of its members as human beings with rights.

WHITEWORTH: That is correct in a way, Mr. Walker. Your trade union is not incorporated like our Company. You get your charter from the American Federation of Labor or the Congress of Industrial Organizations. We have to get ours from the state government. Our charter is our constitution, and the directors and managers have to obey it. They have to make an accounting to the stockholders and the public for every dollar received and spent, including the salaries paid to officers. Our Company cannot contribute money to campaign funds for the purpose of getting its friends into office. On the other hand, your trade union can spend all the money it likes on influencing candidates and government job holders.* And it is my opinion that every trade union should be incorporated just like our

---

* Aware that Mr. Whiteworth would be pleased to hear that his desire for restraints on organized labor had been partly realized after the discussion at our seminar, I wrote him the following letter:

Hosannah Hill, June 29, 1943.

Dear Mr. Whiteworth,

Enclosed you will find a copy of the Smith-Connally "War Labor Disputes Act" and a copy of the *Congressional Record* for June 25 which contains President Roosevelt's veto message. Section 9 of the Act prohibits, for the period covered by the Act, political contributions by labor organizations. One newspaper columnist declares the President's message to be of high order and another thinks it is so bad that he could not have written it himself. You will doubtless be much pleased with the Act.

With warm personal regards,
Yours sincerely,
Charles A. Beard.

Company, and that its officers should be compelled to obey its charter and account for all the moneys received and spent.

BEARD: That is another way of stating that your Company does not have all the rights of natural persons and many other forms of human organization under the Constitution.

WHITEWORTH: That's correct. Now I understand what you meant when you said that corporations do not have *all* the rights of natural persons. Come to think about it, they do not have, or at least do not get, all such rights as things are now run by the Government. What I want to know of Mr. Walker is this, Why shouldn't every trade union be incorporated and forced to obey its government charter just like every industrial or business company?

WALKER: I explained that before. A trade union is not organized for profit. It is an organization of human beings for purposes of mutual benefit. This mutual benefit is a standard of living for labor which lifts workers out of poverty and gives them the conditions that make for good and independent citizens. It works for what Mr. Beard calls an economic underwriting of the Constitution. Depressed and poverty-stricken citizens can't stand up, assert their rights, and govern themselves in a democratic way. Only citizens who have some economic strength can get the education and conditions of life which are necessary to self-government. Paupers and beggars are not good materials for citizenship.

WHITEWORTH: I don't want to argue all that—merely to say in passing that one of your trade unions recently wrung out of my Company an increase of wages equal to all the profit paid out in dividends to our stockholders that year, and a lot of companies are making no profits at all on account of the high wages they pay to one of your so-called non-profit-making unions of human beings. I think your union people will have to come around and accept incorporation and responsibility to the public for your funds and the way you do business, just like the business corporations. There have been too many rackets and scandals recently in the labor world for you to escape such regulation much longer. Your labor czars don't let members vote freely in union elections and they run their organizations for their own benefit, not for the benefit of the members. Government has tightened down on business corporations recently and it will bring you fellows to terms along with us, unless I miss my guess.

Mrs. Smyth, displaying some rising temper: After listening to you representatives of labor and big business, I have begun to wonder where the consumers come into the picture. Have they no rights as to the prices of products from which both wages and profits are drawn?

Whiteworth: Competition takes care of prices and keeps them as low as the high wages paid to labor will allow.

Walker: It is really the producer that counts. Pay producers good wages, and they can pay good prices. When you are talking about consumers, you are really talking about white-collar workers. Their salaries are often low. If white-collar workers, who complain as consumers, want to have salaries high enough to meet prices, let them organize the way industrial workers do.

Mrs. Smyth: What about small business people, who run millions of little concerns, all necessary to keep our economy going?

Whiteworth: That's what I ask, too. Trade unions are helping to squeeze them to the wall. A big company like mine can fight back and can pass some of the wage increases on to the public. The little fellow is caught between labor and price-cutting.

Walker: Your little business fellows are out to make money. Most of them fail within a year or two. Then they lay their troubles on trade unions. . . .

Whiteworth: And big business?

Walker: That is your lookout. Organized labor does not propose to be ground down by the price-slashing of little business concerns.

Beard: What about farmers? How do they come into your pictures?

Walker: Let them organize and join industrial workers in upholding national standards of life. The trouble with farmers is that most of them are anarchists who will not organize at all, or even co-operate. As a rule they are against organized labor, even though they know that the prices they get for farm produce depend on the high wages which industrial workers manage to win by collective action. If farmers could only see that they are really workers too, and would join labor, they would get their standard of life raised to a higher level.

Whiteworth: Good Lord, Walker, farmers are so well organized now for their game that they almost boss the Government of the United States. If business men and industrial workers do not get together, they will both be run over by the farm bloc, by wild-eyed populists from the West, sons of the wild jackass, as they really are.

WALKER: For years I have been arguing that if management and labor will get together, they can stabilize business and stop the sniping from farmers and gas-station people and little fellows generally. Management and labor! There's the clue to progress in the future.

DR. SMYTH: What you actually mean, then, is that business managers and labor managers are to get together and run the country for yourselves. I read a review of a book on such a managerial revolution. Do you have the book, Beard?

BEARD: Yes, here it is: James Burnham's *The Managerial Revolution,* published in 1941.

MRS. SMYTH: Why, it is all cluttered up with pencil notes and you have put a question mark on about every page. What is the trouble with it?

BEARD: Oh, I just applied the Socratic elenchus to his major statements.

WHITEWORTH: What, in heaven's name, is the Socratic elenchus?

BEARD: In a general way, the Socratic question, Is it true? Or positively, The exact opposite of what you say is the truth of the matter. I just question Burnham's statements and especially his assumptions.

MRS. SMYTH: His assumptions?

BEARD: Particularly, that economic managers have guts enough to make a revolution and could make good afterward, as against the warrior, the statesman, the saint, or the popular hero. With all due respect to Mr. Walker and Mr. Whiteworth, the economic man, as such, is not cast in a heroic mold. Sacrifice, real or nominal, plus political genius, is the secret of revolutionary heroism.

DR. SMYTH: We are clear off the track of the economic underwriting of the Constitution. Whiteworth and Walker have talked about their class rights under the Constitution and have taken it for granted that, if they had their way, everything would be just fine for everybody and the Constitution. From some remarks you dropped, Beard, as we went away last week, I gathered that you meant by the phrase, economic underwriting, that, while the Constitution guarantees certain rights, it depends for its existence and functioning, in part at least, upon certain underlying economic conditions. Did I get your idea? If so, let us consider those conditions.

WHITEWORTH: That is merely Beard's idea of the economic interpretation of the Constitution. Ex-President Taft demolished that. The leading framers of the Constitution, as Beard wrote, were business men, but he is rattle-brained when he claims that their business interests had material influence on their politics. It was an ideal, not their business, that controlled them. The fathers of our country did not believe in class conflicts. Nor did they believe that economics underwrote the Constitution. They believed that under the Constitution, if the government were run according to it, business would be let alone and get the kind of fair deal that would make the country great. Of course, I forgot to say, labor and farmers too would get the same kind of fair deal. In any event, that is the way ex-President Taft, who ought to know, explained it to us in New York City.

DR. SMYTH: What have you to say on that, Beard?

BEARD: Just what all the fathers thought, I do not know. I have some acquaintance with their writings now available to us, and I have never found a scrap of paper indicating that any of them who supported the finished Constitution said anything that gives the slightest countenance to the theory Mr. Whiteworth has ascribed to them, especially the idea of no government interference with economic enterprise. Judging by the records, the leaders among them held opinions exactly opposite to that. The papers of the convention that framed the Constitution show that the members recognized the tremendous influence of conflicting economic interests in American society. If they had talked in terms of an abstract ideal, they could scarcely have agreed on that. They talked almost constantly in terms of conflicting interests, and their Constitution represented compromises among interests.

Madison, for instance, in more than one speech pointed out that the conflict of interests was inescapable. He told the convention that the greatest conflict of all was between those who had property and those who had none. Leaders among the framers wanted, among other things, first, to hold the Union together; second, to set up a government that would protect, regulate, and promote types of economic enterprise; third, to put brakes on the state legislatures which had been attacking the interests of protected classes. All the framers who listened to the debates must have known that conflicting economic interests existed before the Constitution was adopted and would continue afterward. Some of them feared a plutocracy as much as they feared a propertyless majority.

Madison believed that the Constitution, which he had done so much to design, rested on property interests and would endure only as long as property was widely enough distributed to afford a popular support for it, including the safeguards it furnished to property. Jefferson, who has been called the idealist of the Revolution, was convinced that the American Republic could last only as long as the overwhelming majority of the people were farm owners, engaged in agriculture. He declared that mobs in the great cities were sores on the body politic and inimical to republican institutions.

In this direction Madison went beyond Jefferson. The Sage of Monticello foresaw the coming of industrialism, the rise of a vast class of propertyless proletarians, the relative decline of agriculturalists in numbers and influence, and thus a destruction of the economic underwriting of popular government. But he could see no way out of the doom. He thought that the free land would last longer than it did. He was mistaken about that, but that was an incident. He could discover no plan for avoiding the crash, or, if he did, it is not to be found anywhere in his records.

But Madison, writing in 1829-30, hoped there might be a way out of the calamity that would come when the fairly equal distribution of property had given way to a plutocracy on the one side and a propertyless multitude on the other. He thought that the crisis would arrive in about a hundred years, about 1930—which was not a bad guess. Yet he hoped that the tendency to concentration of wealth might be 'diminished and the permanency defeated by the equalizing tendency of the laws.'

In other words, Madison contemplated the use of government to provide an economic underwriting of the Republic by laws designed to control the concentration of wealth and to force a more equal distribution of wealth. For this, he admitted, experience had as yet provided no sure test by experiment. To accomplish the end so necessary to the maintenance of popular government, he concluded, would require 'all the wisdom of the wisest patriots.'

In 1932, as Madison had foreseen, the Government of the United States, under the leadership of President Hoover, began to wrestle with that problem. Mr. Hoover sponsored and Congress passed legislation designed to underwrite home-owners in danger of losing their property, farmers heavily in debt, and railway and other corporations in financial difficulties. President Franklin D. Roosevelt, his successor, carried the work further by seeking to underwrite the millions of unemployed who had no property to live on and no way of earning their bread. Is there anyone in this room who believes that no economic underwriting of any kind or degree is necessary to the existence and continuance of constitutional government?

It is a kind of double-barreled proposition: Without an appropriate economic underwriting, constitutional government could not come into being; and if a constitutional government cannot assure the continuance of a sufficient economic underwriting it will certainly perish.

WHITEWORTH: It sounds pretty theoretical to me. I suppose that you will now try to show that the big purpose of the men who made the Constitution was *not* to protect free enterprise from government interference.

BEARD: To tell the truth, Mr. Whiteworth, I had not thought it worth discussing, for it is a kind of partial truth that amounts to a misrepresentation of fundamental facts in the case.

WHITEWORTH: Oh, why don't you just call it a falsehood and be done with it?

BEARD: For the reason that I do not regard it as a falsehood. You seem to want everything to be either white or black, and I seldom find such a clear-cut division in history. The framers of the Constitution certainly contemplated a large degree of economic liberty for business, industry, and agriculture, as well as a large amount of intellectual and political liberty for the people of the United States. A majority of them wanted to put brakes on the interference of state governments with financial, business, and commercial transactions. But a majority of them intended that the new Federal Government should do a lot of interfering with business as it had been run up to 1789. I know that many Jeffersonian Democrats dispute this. In my opinion they are mistaken, and I do not think that this is merely my old Republican prejudice.

WHITEWORTH: You don't mean to say that you are a Republican!

BEARD: I was brought up by a rock-ribbed Republican father.

WHITEWORTH: I never would have thought it.

BEARD: Well, not all Republicans are as obtuse to facts as you seem to think. Let's go back. I maintained that a majority of the framers of the Constitution intended the Federal Government to interfere with business as it had been run up to 1789. What is my proof? The first two administrations, under President Washington, were largely directed by men who had been members of the Constitutional Convention. As soon as they got under way, they began to enact laws interfering with business as it had been run. They put protective tariffs on a number of imported manufactures. They gave bounties to New England fisheries. They set up a United States Bank. They made discriminations in tonnage and other duties in behalf of American shipping. I shall not bore you with a long list. I covered this subject in my *Economic Origins of Jeffersonian Democracy*.

WHITEWORTH: But that isn't interference with business. That is promotion of business.

BEARD: Let me ask you a few questions. Doesn't a protective duty on manufactures interfere with the business of importing merchants? Doesn't a United States Bank interfere with the business of state banks? Don't discriminative duties on shipping interfere with the importing and the exporting business? Don't duties on manufactures interfere with the business of producing and exporting agricultural products?

WHITEWORTH: They do in a way, I suppose, but they help business more than they interfere with it.

MRS. SMYTH: The point seems to be: Whose business? But time is passing. Could we now discuss how and by whom the economic underwriting necessary to the continuance of our Republic is going to be effected in the future? Mr. Walker and Mr. Whiteworth seem to agree that if management and labor could get together they could guarantee the underwriting. Most people in the United States, I fancy, believe that a disastrous economic crash would spell ruin all around. Do you think that labor and management could provide that underwriting?

BEARD: Certainly not without government intervention and ultimate control. Certainly not without government.

At this point both Whiteworth and Walker exclaimed together, in effect, that they recognized the necessity of some government intervention and control. I replied that capital and labor could not agree at all on the nature of specific measures of intervention and control. Some wrangling occurred as Whiteworth and Walker tried to formulate a single plank in their platform. I turned the discussion to Mrs. Smyth's question.

• BEARD: In the first place, these labor-management schemes leave American agriculture entirely out of account and all the millions of farmers, tenants, laborers on the land, all the families living by that mode of economic life. Even if managers and labor leaders could get together, they do not have as such the qualities for government, which is a peculiar kind of art and science, partly economic but also very human. Governing a country takes something more than the kind of interests, habits, and experiences developed in factories, at machines, in offices, and in drafting rooms. The qualities required for successful government are, perhaps, best covered by the word statesmanship, which comprises, in addition to direct experience with business and labor, a knowledge of law and history, a keen appreciation of economic forces in history, administrative experience in public undertakings, the intuitive and practical power of discerning what is necessary and possible in great affairs, many with worldwide implications.

WHITEWORTH: On that point I agree with Walter Lippmann, the most brilliant thinker in the United States outside the business world.

BEARD: Which Walter Lippmann?

WHITEWORTH: What do you mean by that?

BEARD: I mean that in the course of his meanderings he has been on nearly every side of nearly every question, in one way or another, from socialism to world salvation.

WHITEWORTH: I refer to his address to businessmen reported in *Time* for December 21, 1942. There he said that American businessmen hold the world's fate in their hands because the United States alone has 'no governing class which has a social position and political power superior to the business community.' He warned American businessmen to study the respective fates of the French and the British aristocracies. The French aristocrats, Lippmann said, perished because they would make no surrender of their privileges; but the British aristocracy made concessions and continued the work of government. American businessmen hold a commanding position in world affairs, and it is their duty now to exercise that power wisely and effectively. What is the matter with that?

BEARD: Lippmann's allocution is merely one of the terrible simplifications of history that he loves to make. It is not his fault, of course. A man who writes on everything with facility has to simplify in order to get on. Besides, English aristocrats received some education during the Puritan revolution in the seventeenth century.

WHITEWORTH: Judging by your remarks on what you call qualities of statesmanship necessary to govern a great country and your criticism of Mr. Lippmann, you evidently think that businessmen don't have sense enough to run the government. It is my opinion that they have more sense than the politicians and that they could carry on the kind of government which is necessary to let business enterprise do the rest for the prosperity and happiness of the people. It takes nothing but good common sense to run the government as it used to be run before it began to interfere with business in every direction. If we could repeal these laws interfering with business and get back to fundamentals in government, running it would be fairly simple.

BEARD: You have expressed an idea, Mr. Whiteworth, which has wide currency among men of your class. I should like to explore it with you. If I could ask you some questions and get your answers, we might bring our opinions to a head and see what it is we agree upon and differ about. You are not an anarchist, are you?

WHITEWORTH: Heavens, No! How did you get that notion? Why do you ask such a foolish question?

BEARD: I just wanted to get that out of the way. I now know that you believe in some kind of government for the United States. Next, I ask, What kind of government?

WHITEWORTH: Our own kind of government. Our form of government. It is all right. It is only the politicians who run it that disturb me.

BEARD: I shall put aside the question of how you are going to keep our form of government and at the same time secure the election of your right kind of men to take the places of politicians. That might give you a headache. As to form, I take it you would keep the President, the Congress, and the Judiciary. Now we come to things you would have government do. You would have it protect private property, of course?

WHITEWORTH: That is another absurd question. To be sure, it is the duty of government to protect private property. If it did not, we certainly should have anarchy.

BEARD: Would you have everything private property?

WHITEWORTH: I suspect that is a trick question. I would keep government out of business absolutely.

BEARD: Would you abolish laws of inheritance which force the division of a man's property among his heirs on his death and prevent the entailment of estates in the line of the eldest sons?

WHITEWORTH: No. I think that would be unfair to the family. I would keep the laws of inheritance which provide for the division of estates.

BEARD: Would you retain taxes on inheritance?

WHITEWORTH: Yes. Moderate taxes.

BEARD: How moderate?

WHITEWORTH: I should want to think it over.

BEARD: You said that you wanted to keep government out of business absolutely, when I asked you whether everything should be private property. Would you have all transportation privately owned and operated?

WHITEWORTH: Absolutely.

BEARD: Our great system of public highways representing an outlay greater than the capital value of all the railways? Would you turn the ownership and operation of highways over to private parties?

WHITEWORTH: No, of course not. I had overlooked that.

BEARD: Would you turn all the national domain of forests and lands over to private parties, to do as they please with it?

WHITEWORTH: No. A certain amount of conservation is necessary to protect our watersheds.

BEARD: How much conservation?

WHITEWORTH: I should not want to answer that offhand.

BEARD: What about our waterworks and watersheds owned and managed by the city?

WHITEWORTH: That is all right. I would leave it where it is. It is well managed and our rates are low enough. Let us stop this line. There are a lot of things government does own and ought to own. Wherever possible, however, the government should leave operation in private hands.

BEARD: How do you determine what is possible and what is impossible ?

WHITEWORTH: That is just a professor's quibbling.

BEARD: Very well. Do you think that the public interest should be the principle for determining whether anything should be publicly owned and operated or publicly owned and leased?

WHITEWORTH: As a patriotic citizen, I should regard that as a fair principle, but there is danger in it.

BEARD: Danger from whom and in what sense?

WHITEWORTH: Come back to earth and let us have some sensible questions.

BEARD: Would you repeal the Interstate Commerce Act, abolish the Interstate Commerce Commission, and leave all rail, water and pipe-line transportation uncontrolled?

WHITEWORTH: There is sense in that kind of question. I'll give a concise No. When I started in as a manufacturer long years ago, the railways had a free hand to do about as they pleased. They made discriminations in rates between shippers. They gave rebates on freight rates paid to favorite shippers. They issued stocks and bonds that registered water—no values. No, the railways have to be regulated.

BEARD: Would you abolish the Federal Trade Commission? Repeal all laws defining and regulating unfair trade practices?

WHITEWORTH: Never. If all fair practices laws were repealed, the honest and decent businessman would be penalized if not ruined by unscrupulous adulterators and tricksters. Some of the rulings by the Federal Trade Commission are crazy, but we need some control. You are going to ask, How much? But you may as well omit that.

BEARD: I omit it. Mr. Whiteworth, would you repeal the anti-trust laws and leave private corporations and parties free to make combinations according to their interests and otherwise do as they please in conducting their enterprises?

WHITEWORTH: No, I would not repeal all the antitrust legislation, but I would have the government stop hounding business. There are a lot of illegitimate combinations in restraint of trade, formed for the purpose of enriching insiders and skinning the public. But business men are sick and tired of uncertainty as to what they can and cannot do under the laws. Men in my company, with a lot of others, were indicted not long ago and forced into a long lawsuit, which we won at great expense. It was a damned outrage! One morning I picked up my newspaper and read a headline, 'John Whiteworth Indicted.'

I come from an old family of honorable business men, if I do say so. It made me sick to see my name spread all over the front page as a kind of criminal, along with gangsters recently indicted. I felt as if my neighbors regarded me as a sneak thief when I rode on my suburban train to business that day. It was an infernal outrage! It cost us about $250,000 to go through the trial and win the suit. But that did not wipe out the stain of that accursed headline. That Thurman Arnold, the federal prosecutor, is a relentless persecutor. By the way, someone told me during the trial that he once wrote a book in which he made fun of antitrust legislation. Is that so?

BEARD: Yes. Take the book, *The Folklore of Capitalism,* published in 1937, home with you, Mr. Whiteworth, if you want to read it. It is one of the brilliant books of our time. You ought to read carefully Chapter IX on "The Effect of Antitrust Laws in Encouraging Large Combinations."

WHITEWORTH: You may keep it right here on your shelf, or burn it, for all I care. I repeat that business ought not to be hounded.

BEARD: I heartily concur with you on that, Mr. Whiteworth. It is both a preposterous and an outrageous practice, in my opinion too. But, since you are unwilling to repeal all legislation against trusts and combinations, may I ask, What kind of laws would you keep or substitute for the present laws?

WHITEWORTH: I would forbid all combinations in restraint of trade against the public interest. I would forbid all unfair trade practices directed against the public interest. That is clear, isn't it?

BEARD: In principle, yes; in reality, no, until more precisely defined. Would you, for instance, allow all the big concerns in one line of manufacturing to confer and agree on the price scales of their products?

WHITEWORTH: I would, in reason. Let them compete in quality but not in self-destructive competition. Fair competition is all right. Cut-throat competition does nobody any good, not even the consumer, in the long run. But you are just trying to drive me deeper and deeper into what old Professor Sandifell used to call disturbing speculation. By the way, we boys at college named his course on philosophy 'a damned dim candle over a damned dark abyss.' You just want to make everything so complicated that nobody can understand it.

BEARD: If you think hard about it, Mr. Whiteworth, it is complicated. If it is complicated, then we deceive ourselves and the public by pretending that it is simple. An economic theory is an empty abstraction unless you get down to just what comes under it and what is done and said under it.

WHITEWORTH: Oh, I know that, but why don't you get after Walker and his trade unions? They are combinations in restraint of trade, wages, and prices, and some of them are no better than rackets. I was glad to see Arnold go after them.

BEARD: I am willing, if Mr. Walker is. What about it, Mr. Walker?

WALKER: I'll take my turn.

BEARD: Mr. Walker, a while ago you said that every American citizen has the right to work. I suppose you mean by that a right to a job?

WALKER: I do indeed. Unemployment is a shame. It is degrading to human beings to be jobless and breadless. It is demoralizing to the bodies and souls of men and women, especially if it lasts a long time. If you do not believe that, our minds cannot meet.

BEARD: I believe it, Mr. Walker, as warmly as you do. My only question is how to bring full employment about and keep it. One scheme proposed is to cut wages and divide the work evenly among all the workers. That is, let us say, if there are a hundred jobs in an industry and a hundred men are employed at $10 a day while another hundred are unemployed in that trade, the work should be divided so as to employ two hundred men at $5 a day. What do you think of that scheme?

WALKER: That would be ruinous to the American standard of living which trade unions are organized to uphold and advance. That is what Hitler did. He cut wages and divided the work. I am against all schemes for cutting wages, dividing work, and making longer work days.

BEARD: Then you propose that every person in every trade should be furnished a job at wages which he fixes and for the work day that suits him?

WALKER: No. I put it this way: Every person in a trade should be furnished a job at trade-union wages and on trade-union terms as to hours and other working conditions. Surely you are not opposed to that?

BEARD: Not in principle. But by whom and how is that job to be furnished to every person?

WALKER: That is a problem for management or business and the government to solve. The only right way to divide up work is to shorten the work day and give more workers employment at standard wages.

BEARD: Then neither the American Federation of Labor nor the Congress of Industrial Organizations has a plan for guaranteeing everybody in every trade a job at standard wages and in standard conditions. And one more question while we are on this subject, How would you prevent too many workers from rushing into one trade?

WALKER: We have no plans to guarantee jobs to every person at standard wages. It would be the duty of trade unions by apprenticeship and other rules to keep too many workers from crowding into a trade.

BEARD: So you stand fast on the proposition that it is the duty of management or business and government to provide for full employment, jobs for everybody, on the conditions that trade unions prescribe? That is your idea of the right to work?

WALKER: That is my idea of the right to work. I don't say that all trade unionists have it. It is what I mean by the right to work.

BEARD: But suppose that business and government worked out a plan for full employment, and such a plan meant imposing regulations on trade unions such as those prevailing in Russia, would you be willing to make such a surrender of trade-union liberties in the interest of that full employment?

WALKER: Never!

BEARD: Then you prefer to go along as you do now and take the distresses of unemployment for union members and outsiders, as the American Federation of Labor has in the past?

WALKER: If it is a choice between surrendering trade-union gains and adopting such despotic plans for full employment, we will stick by our gains.

BEARD: In that case, what becomes of your right to work?

WALKER: Since you have got a simple proposition all tangled up in your speculation, as Mr. Whiteworth called it, my right to work goes by the board. Still I stick to it. Don't you recognize any rights for human beings?

MRS. SMYTH: We have constantly had that issue of speculation up before us in other relations, Mr. Walker. Charles Beard insists there is no such thing as a natural right, a right guaranteed by nature. He holds that rights are just abstract theories and that no people have any rights in fact except the rights which they have sense enough and competence enough to bring into being, uphold, and enforce in fact, in reality, in practical life and affairs. At first that seemed to me a hard-hearted view of human nature and our world. Now I am beginning to believe that it is true, just a statement of the facts in the case. Isn't that your position, Mr. Beard?

BEARD: You have put it about as I should want to state it. However, I shall add that I believe there is moral power in many abstract ideas of rights. They may inspire and guide us. They become realities to the extent that we have power, intellectual and moral, to give actual effect to them.

DR. SMYTH: A few minutes ago, Mr. Whiteworth and Mr. Walker seemed to be drawing together on the proposition that management and labor could solve the problem of an economic underwriting, including, I take it, that of full employment. Before we adjourn, let us develop their views on this subject.

BEARD: With reference to Dr. Smyth's suggestion, I propose that Mr. Whiteworth, Mr. Walker, and I have a three-cornered conference on what is in our minds as to the management-labor way out of our economic difficulties, as a way of securing an economic underwriting.

[Assent was given.]

BEARD: Mr. Whiteworth, just how do you see the management-labor organization?

WHITEWORTH: In each plant, all workers would be organized in a single union. Everyone of them would be in the union, with one vote. This union would have a constitution, hold regular and special meetings, and elect a council and chairman empowered to carry on all business with the manager of the plant as to hours, wages, working conditions, complaints, and suggestions. It would be agreed that there are to be no strikes until a certain procedure of negotiation had been followed. I could give more details, but this is the sum and substance of the general proposition.

BEARD: Your corporation has many plants scattered over the country. Would you have a separate management-union arrangement for each plant?

WHITEWORTH: Yes, a separate management for each plant.

BEARD: Where do you stand so far on this proposition, Mr. Walker?

WALKER: Bosh, that is just the old company-union game, by which workers are divided into little isolated bodies and made helpless! It gives no special position to skilled craftsmen. It would disrupt the American Federation of Labor and the Congress of Industrial Organizations alike. Any single company could arrange with its hog-tied union to cut wages and undersell competing companies. Then the whole structure of decent wages would go to pieces. If a company had a strike, its workers would receive no help from other workers organized on the national scale. If I should agree to that, I would agree to the complete destruction of organized labor in the United States. It would be suicide for labor.

BEARD: Then what form of management-labor organization do you propose, Mr. Walker?

WALKER: I would keep the present form of national labor organization. There ought to be a merger of the two big national organizations—the American Federation of Labor and the Congress of Industrial Organizations. It's a pity that the split ever occurred. The workers of each plant would choose their committee and chairman to deal with management, subject to fixed union rules about wages, hours, and working conditions throughout the country. Otherwise there would be local anarchy. Besides, officials of national labor organizations would have to have a veto over any arrangements between the local management and the local union, if those arrangements were out of line with labor standards established by national labor organizations.

BEARD: Would you demand the closed shop in every plant and compel management to collect union dues for you?

WALKER: I would have a closed shop wherever we could get it. In any case I would demand preference for union members in every plant.

BEARD: Well, now Mr. Walker. . . .

WHITEWORTH: You need not go an inch further. What Mr. Walker has proposed is the complete subjection of management to some centralized labor authority as well as to the local labor union. Unless you have federal incorporation of all labor unions and national laws giving the rank and file of labor free election of labor leaders, you would, under the Walker plan, turn all American industry over to an irresponsible labor oligarchy in Washington. Just remember that the management of a plant or a single industry throughout the country does not have a free hand to do as it pleases. There are stockholders to be considered. I suppose you will make the usual crack that stockholders count for nothing. That is a form of New Deal or Communist propaganda.

If all the stockholders were thrown out of the window and management did not have to consider them at all, it could not do as it pleased. It is absolutely subject to the price scales and other conditions of the general market in which it buys raw materials and sells its product. It is also subject absolutely to the introduction of new inventions and to technical changes in patents, machines, and processes. It must either adapt plant operations to these pressures from the outside or go into bankruptcy. And organized labor in the plant generally tries to block these changes in the interest of keeping or getting work for its members.

BEARD: But, Mr. Whiteworth, suppose all industry were organized on a national scale to deal with labor organized on a national scale. If power confronted power, organized industry and organized labor, would not a kind of general and equal bargaining power be created?

WHITEWORTH: It is useless to suppose such a case. Yet I will suppose it. Such a management-labor organization on a national scale would be bigger than the Government. One or the other would have to rule. There would be a fight between Government and the management-labor combination. And the Government would come out on top, or perhaps the United States Army. To get such a combination of management and labor, you would have to force all the millions of little business concerns into it and all the millions of industrial workers who now refuse to join labor unions. We may have to face that some day, but that would be a Bolshevik revolution or a Fascist revolution, not a phony managerial revolution. If management and labor did win out against the Federal Government, they would soon begin to fight it out between themselves.

BEARD: There seem to be some formidable difficulties in the way of providing a national economic underwriting by a management-labor combination. But suppose that all industries and all industrial workers were organized in locals and on a national scale. Suppose they could agree on hours, wages, and everything else of significance to them. Suppose all industries and all labor unions were organized and then united in one big holding company, with a monopoly over all conditions of production established by friendly arrangements. Suppose that government, which you both agree must continue to exist, accepts your set-up. Suppose all this. Then let me ask you this question, What about agriculture, that other branch of economy so vital to the life of our nation; what would you do about that?

This question was greeted by a shrug of the shoulders from Mr. Whiteworth, and another from Mr. Walker. A desultory argument followed, in which they admitted that agriculture was vital to the feeding of managers and industrial workers, that they knew little about it, and that they had no plans in their schemes for organizing and adjusting the relations of agriculture to industry.

Then I put another question.

BEARD: Suppose now that we did have a workable plan for agriculture, your monopoly by management and labor would still be subject to fluctuations in the national market. It would be also subject more or less to fluctuations in the international market, even if you or the Federal Government created a national autarchy, that is, adopted a program of national self-sufficiency. You will still have depressions, less violent, perhaps. Is there anything in your management-labor scheme to provide a real economic underwriting, full employment for all workers all the time, on any level or wages?

Another desultory debate occurred, the Smyths taking part in it. The opinion was expressed that fluctuations in business would be less violent, that the level of employment would be somewhere between the depression bottom and boom top. There was no agreement that anything like full employment or even an approach to that ideal could be guaranteed under any management-labor combination. All conceded that heavy responsibility for dealing with unemployment would still have to be assumed by government.

Thereupon I put my final question: What would you do about *new* ideas as to how industry, labor, agriculture, and government should be run—ideas which would continue to arise unless an iron censorship were imposed on all thinking?

That question encountered impatience on the part of Mr. Whiteworth and Mr. Walker. They appeared to regard it as irrelevant or academic, as having nothing to do with their affairs, either management or labor. They fumbled about with the notion that if fair economic conditions could be maintained, people would be content, and no troublesome ideas in favor of change would come up to bother them. Mr. Whiteworth was not sure that this would prove to be the case. Mr. Walker thought it would be hard to stop agitations in organized labor even under just agreements with employers; that when things were about perfect in this respect, agitators would stir up troubles in their unions and sometimes pull off wildcat strikes on some grounds.

DR. SMYTH: To provide an economic underwriting for the Republic, indeed to keep it going on an even keel, we need a human science more comprehensive than the so-called science of the management-labor combination.

BEARD: I heartily applaud that. So do many of the leading figures in American business, labor organizations, and politics. There is an immense and growing literature on that very subject. Here is a book—George Galloway's *Postwar Planning in the United States*—which gives one hundred and ten pages to listing the organizations and agencies, public and private, engaged in studies and activities connected with economic underwriting; and thirty pages to the titles of books, articles, and other materials bearing on the subject. If you will come into my north library, I will show you groaning shelves full of the books and folders of clippings I have myself collected. For years there has been a striking convergence of American thought on public and associational efforts to provide full employment, expand our productive plant, provide an economic underwriting. The convergence of thought is, in my opinion, an impressive sign of the times—a promise of action to come.

After we had returned to the fireside, Mr. Whiteworth and Mr. Walker soon took their leave, but Dr. and Mrs. Smyth lingered a few moments, evidently impressed by the casual examination of the materials which I had showed them.

MRS. SMYTH, puzzled by the evening's procedure: With all the live, up-to-date books and articles by prominent writers from business, labor, and political circles at your command, why did you wind and twist your way through history and details tonight? Why did you not go right straight at a comprehensive summary of all these plans for getting right down to the work of providing an economic underwriting for the Republic in modern terms?

DR. SMYTH, before I could answer: I suspect Beard of trying to lead us, especially Whiteworth and Walker, all around through the tortuous course of history and petty details for the purpose of tripping us up, tying us in knots, breaking down our assurance, forcing us to define our words, frightening us into believing that something heroic would have to be done to create what he calls an economic underwriting. It is a kind of game borrowed from old Socrates and dressed up in an American garb, that is, with less theory and more facts. Anyway, it worked pretty well.

BEARD: You do me too much honor by associating me with Socrates. I thoroughly appreciate your joke. If I possessed even a hundredth part of his acumen in analyzing ideas, I should be happy. But in another way, I want to steer entirely clear of both Socrates and Plato. In my opinion, Greek metaphysics has done damage, not good, to the Western world and to Christian thought and practice. If modern Europeans had devoted to the study of *The Federalist* the attention they gave to Plato's *Republic,* they would have been far better off in every way.

You ascribe to me far more consciousness of purpose than I was aware of in shaping the direction of our discussion tonight. If I had attacked the subject head-on by summarizing the best contemporary plans for an economic underwriting of our Republic, we should have got into a maze of prejudices and lost sight of the ominous significance of the theme for the future of the nation. At least, I so view the tactics of the occasion.

XX

The Republic in the World of Nations

ON Mrs. Smyth's insistence, to which I bowed with some reluctance, our seminar on foreign policies took the form of a social conclave at her home. I had supposed that she intended to have a small company in for the evening, but when I arrived late, on account of a cold and balky motor, I found her spacious drawing room crowded and a cocktail party in full swing. Already faces were becoming red and voices loud. As I stepped out on the gallery overlooking the scene, I quickly discovered that Mrs. Smyth had deliberately brought together choice members of the intelligentsia from the town and the neighborhood. Some of them I knew personally and others mainly through their writings in the daily papers or their propaganda activities or their lectures to the natives.

Suppressing a lusty desire to escape to my retreat on Hosannah Hill, I slipped into the drawing room by a side door. Mrs. Smyth took me immediately to Professor and Mrs. Tempey, with both of whom I had been acquainted for years. The Professor, who teaches international relations at Berwick University, greeted me a little boisterously and victoriously with: How's the old isolationist? To which Mrs. Tempey added, with a smile intended to be devastating: A bit confused *now*, I suspect?

As I was not selling groceries or peddling intellectual wares at a price, I could express my sentiments freely, and I said: Confused as ever, Mrs. Tempey. I confess that I never have been able to reduce the world and universal history to a simple miniature with no blurred lines in it.

While the Tempeys were profusely commenting on my reply, I secretly turned off my hearing instrument and my mind ran back over the memories of nearly fifty years. The Professor had been an ardent supporter.of President Wilson's League of Nations and put the blame for all the troubles that had befallen the world since 1919 on the people of the United States. With the aid of grants from Peace Foundations he had kept up the battle for the League with never-failing optimism, and combined his teaching at the University with lecturing all over the country to foreign policy associations, women's clubs, and every kind of organization that would lend him ears. Whenever I had seen him, he had told me the peace movement was making rapid progress.

The Washington conference for the reduction of naval armaments he welcomed with enthusiasm as a step toward the pacification of the Far East. The Locarno treaties proved to him that he was on the right line. The Kellogg Pact of 1928, by which the nations of the earth renounced war as an instrument of national policy, brought Tempey's zeal to a boiling point. The defeat of the proposal to enter the World Court, by the United States Senate, discouraged him for a moment, but President Roosevelt's Quarantine Speech at Chicago in 1937 revived his spirits and assured him that what he then called collective security was the key to the salvation of mankind. The Atlantic Charter and President Roosevelt's four freedoms for the world made Tempey's cup of joy run over. After Pearl Harbor he immediately gave the following statement to the press:

> At last national unity has been attained, national confusion has been blown away by Japanese treachery. We are now one people, with one mind, with one resolve, namely, that after the Axis powers have been destroyed a new world order guaranteeing permanent peace and the four freedoms to all peoples will be established.

Mrs. Tempey was not less zealous in the advocacy of internationalism than her husband. They had both spent two summers in Europe, on fellowships from a Peace Foundation, studying international affairs. On her return from the second trip, Mrs. Tempey toured the United States, lecturing on America's Duty in the Present Crisis. She had given a course of six lectures in our city auditorium on: The British Commonwealth of Nations, Western Europe, Central and Eastern Europe, The Balkans, The Communist Menace, and The Far East. One of our dailies which had regularly hammered President Roosevelt's New Deal for pauperizing the United States, while praising his foreign policies after 1937, reported Mrs. Tempey's lectures fully, so that I could read them and discover for myself how wonderful they were.

While the Tempeys were alternately praising the glorious times in which we are living, Frank Brooklin joined us, despite signs of disapproval from the Tempeys. Brooklin is a kind of free lance associated with one of our newspapers. I had known him principally through.his writings. He had an occasional column on Village Gossip which was undoubtedly clever. He also reviewed books with equal facility. Just for my own enlightenment I kept clippings of them for a year and noted that he reviewed one hundred and twenty-five books, ranging from universal history and political philosophy through geopolitics to scientific progress and modernist fiction. Like Mrs. Tempey's lectures, they were wonderful.

It was rumored around town that Brooklin was or had been a communist, or at least a fellow traveler. At all events he had been active in the Popular Front. After Hitler and Stalin made their pact in 1939, he denounced the conflict in Europe as just another imperialist war. During the life of this pact he fraternized with the Peace Mobilization crowd. Once he tried.to enlist my interest in it, but I characterized his proposal as indefensible. As soon as the German army invaded Russia, Brooklin reversed himself as quickly as if he had received commands from a drill sergeant, and blossomed out for 'the people's war' and 'the new democratic world order.'

In a few seconds the Tempeys and Brooklin were deadlocked in a dispute, most of which I managed to miss. Before it closed I heard the Professor tell Brooklin that the United Nations would 'take care of Stalin' 'if he tried to block the right kind of settlement in Eastern Europe and Asia.'

By this time several of Mrs. Smyth's guests had gathered around us. A British professional lecturer and propagandist, who had spent years in scouting in the regions west of the Hudson River, engaged the Tempeys in a discussion over the fate of the British Empire after the war. They favored a liquidation of all empires and a pooling of colonial resources under a system of mandates. He, on his part, insisted that 'it just could not be made to work.'

Another disputant thought that Herbert Agar was the intellectual superman of the times. A young woman, who had read Ely Culbertson's fifty-page plan for organizing the world, explained that it was 'more realistic' than any of the others. One of her companions stoutly maintained that regional organizations throughout the world ought to come first, and that Herbert Hoover should be designated by President Roosevelt as head of a committee to work out the details. 'Of course,' she conceded, 'a world council and a world court would have to be added in order to effect the proper coordination of the several regions.'

From far off on the right came the booming voice of Theodore Laif, chairman of the local Council for Co-operation among Peace Societies. He said that while he approved all the other serious thinkers' ideas, he had, with regret, noted a neglect of the part to be played by the democracy of China in the coming world order. He had been deeply moved, he said, by the profound writings of Pearl Buck and Lin Yu Tang on that point and felt sure that American people, by their neglect, were alienating the affections of the powerful Chinese nation and driving it into the arms of Russia, the arch intriguer on the northwestern frontiers. Just as the Tempeys and Brooklin closed in on Laif, Mrs. Smyth drew me aside and I missed the outcome of the argument.

MRS. SMYTH: I have invited all these people to give colors and tones to our party. Besides yourself, there are to be only four regular · speakers. These four guests have positive plans for the coming world order and I hope our discussion can be made to turn on their projects. I shall try to keep the belligerents now gathered around the Tempeys off on the side lines.

The first of my star performers (said Mrs. Smyth) is Doctor Margaret Farebanks, a Doctor of Philosophy in International Relations, from one of our greatest universities. Dr. Farebanks spent several years at Geneva observing the League of Nations in operation and supports a modified League for the world as the best guarantee of permanent peace.

For a thoroughgoing federation of the world, John Lytelton speaks with confidence. A retired lawyer with a keen mind and wide knowledge of federal principles, Mr. Lytelton has devoted a long time to the study of his chosen subject. He has reached a firm conclusion that a league of sovereign nations is bound to fail and, using the analogy of the American Union, he proposes a world federation on the model of our United States.

The third star, Dr. Ryald Hetherson, is the local representative of a union of Protestant churchmen who are working for the Christianization of international relations. Dr. Hetherson has no fixed plans for a world government or order. He is prepared, he says, to support any plan that offers promise of world peace, though he believes that none will be successful unless the peoples and governments of the world are animated by the Christian spirit.

The fourth leading performer is Professor George Winstanley from Carstairs University, a teacher of economics. He is skeptical of politics and politicians and has developed a project for an economic union of nations to precede a political union. He favors, he says, getting down to bed-rock by starting a union of like-minded nations on principles of reciprocal economic advantages.

Having introduced me to her four stars, Mrs. Smyth gave the signal for a march to the dining table. In the seating arrangement I was placed between Mrs. Tempey and Mr. Brooklin and, while they continued in loud tones the debate on the role to be played by Russia in post-war plans for peace, I enjoyed my victuals, marveling throughout at Mrs. Smyth's skill in the management of household economy. From snatches of conversations around the table I gathered the impression that I was not the only person present who suffered from confusion about the coming "world order."

After the meal was over, the proponents of plans, informed of their role by our hostess in advance, drew bundles of papers out of their portfolios.

Mrs. Smyth opened the conference: Since it is already apparent that many differences of opinion exist among us, I suggest that we discover first the fundamental propositions on which we agree before we take up specific plans for the new world order. I suppose that at the outset we can all consent to this statement: The supreme object of American foreign policy ought to be to bring permanent, or lasting, peace to the nations of the earth.

Dr. Smyth, after a silence that seemed to give consent: If you adopt your usual method, Beard, you will want to ask upon what assumptions respecting the universe of mankind that proposition rests. I first thought that inquiring about basic assumptions was just a quirk on your part, but after nineteen sessions I have come to the conclusion that there is some sense in it. So try it on these new innocents.

Beard: This party belongs to you and your wife, not to me. I prefer to remain a listener, or at least to wait until some definite schemes for attaining the objective are before us.

PROFESSOR WINSTANLEY: Surely you agree that such should be the supreme object of our foreign policy?

BEARD: You ask me a direct question, Professor, and I should like to answer it if I could. But I do not understand two terms used in the proposition as stated by our hostess. Mrs. Smyth, are you using permanent and lasting as synonymous? In my mind they are not. Permanent means forever, for all time. Lasting means for some period of time, not necessarily everlasting. It will not help to introduce that other weasel word, durable. It makes a great difference whether you set out to make a permanent or everlasting peace or a peace that will endure for what we hope will prove to be a long period of time, let us say thirty, forty, or fifty years.

MRS. SMYTH: Frankly, I used the terms rather thoughtlessly, in the current fashion. I meant, of course, a permanent peace, that is, putting a final end to war.

[A chorus of approval greeted this clarification of Mrs. Smyth's proposition, but Mr. Brooklin gave me a wink.]

MRS. TEMPEY: Come now and give us your answer, so that we can divide the sheep and the goats.

BEARD: To save time, I will declare simply that I do not believe that the supreme object of American foreign policy should be to bring permanent peace to the nations of the world.

PROFESSOR TEMPEY: Then, what on earth should it be?

BEARD: In my opinion, the supreme object of American foreign policy should be to protect and promote the interests, spiritual and material, of the American people, and, subject to that mandate, to conduct foreign affairs in such a manner as to contribute to the peace and civilization of mankind. Or, to put it another way, to protect and advance American civilization on this continent, the firm earthly basis of our economic and military power, with due reference to relevant international responsibilities.

In order to get on, I was willing to let Mrs. Smyth's proposition stand. But since the question of underlying presuppositions has been raised, I answer that the proposition rests upon four huge assumptions: First, that *the supreme object of our national life* is to bring permanent peace to all nations; a foreign policy directed to the end of permanent peace would be vain unless unreservedly supported by our domestic economy and moral resources. Second, that world peace is desirable or good for mankind or a majority of mankind. Third, that the constitution of our universe makes it possible to effect and maintain permanent world peace for all mankind. Fourth, that it is possible for the Government of the United States to secure at home adequate and continuous support for making and keeping this world peace, a support that will provide all the military, economic, and other sacrifices which it would entail upon our people.

PROFESSOR WINSTANLEY: Surely, you believe that permanent world peace is desirable.

BEARD: As a human being, I share that aspiration, but as a student of history I do not *know* that it is desirable, that it would be good for all mankind. Mankind has never experienced peace throughout the world for any long period of time. There are many writers on politics, history, and biology who contend that prolonged peace would lead to degeneration among some peoples and overpopulation in many countries, particularly in the Orient. But, as I have said, I share the aspiration for world peace and am willing to assume, to take the risk, that it would be desirable.

DR. FAREBANKS: That is a sour note of skepticism, to begin with. You cannot base effective action on anything less than firm conviction that your ends are *feasible* as well as desirable.

DR. SMYTH: I do not see that at all. When I perform a surgical operation I want to proceed on knowledge, not mere conviction. When I encounter a new problem in surgery I want to get some real knowledge about it before I lay open a living body. Beard did not say that permanent peace is *not* desirable. He said he did not know it *is*, on the basis of human experience. But, in spite of that he consents to let you make the assumption that it is desirable. That is what he calls an act of faith.

PROFESSOR WINSTANLEY: But Beard also struck a second note of skepticism by saying that the possibility of world peace also is a mere assumption. Militarists are constantly insisting that there has always been war and there always will be war, that permanent peace is an impossibility. Now a lot of evils once defended as necessary have been abolished. Executions for witchcraft, for one instance. Chattel slavery for another. Defenders of slavery were always citing history, contending that slavery had always existed and therefore always would and must exist. I for one do not propose to be deceived by that type of historical argument. I believe that world peace is a possibility.

DR. SMYTH: Pardon me. You have just said that you believe that world peace is a possibility. You did not say that you *know* it. That is an act of faith on your part. The fact that many evils have been abolished does not prove that this evil, if it is an evil, can also be abolished. Beard agreed to share your aspiration on that point. What you and Doctor Farebanks call skepticism seems to me to be merely caution. Let us take up the fourth assumption, namely, that it is possible for the Government of the United States to get adequate popular support for making a world peace and for all the military, economic, and other sacrifices which it would entail. This is something on which we all, as citizens, at least have opinions. I am inclined to take the affirmative position on that question.

DR. HETHERSON: I am decidedly of the same opinion. War is a barbaric evil. . . .

MRS. SMYTH: You do not include our war with Japan, Germany, and Italy?

DR. HETHERSON: On the contrary, ours is a righteous war against war. I mean war as an institution is a barbaric evil. I believe that the American people, along with most of the peoples of the earth, are heartily sick of war and want to put a stop to it—want to establish institutions to assure permanent peace. Isolationism is dead as a door-nail in the United States. The American people are ready to make any sacrifice necessary to assure a permanent world order. They were ready for it and in favor of it in 1919. If it had not been for tricky and ambitious Republican politicians, the United States would have joined the League of Nations and the present war would not have come about. The recent Gallup polls all show the American people ready and anxious for a settlement after this war that will put an end to war. They are prepared to make all the sacrifices necessary to gain that great end of humanity.

MRS. SMYTH: Is that your understanding of the American spirit, Mr. Beard?

BEARD: Personally, I am in favor of pushing the war against Germany, Japan, and Italy to a successful conclusion. Whether it is righteous in the sight of God I leave to our theologian, Dr. Hetherson. In my opinion, too, there has been a decline in the sheer love of war among many nations. A lot of people in every country become sick of war after they have been in it for two or three years; but the great nations seem to like a war every generation or two. At least they seem to like it enough to get into it. I suspect that there is something in the old adage that when the devil is sick, he would be a saint. Before I agree to the proposition that isolationism is dead, I should like to hear a definition of the term.

DR. HETHERSON: I volunteer to define it. Isolationism is the creed that America owes nothing to other countries and has no moral responsibilities in the world; that foreign wars are none of our business; that the United States should shrink behind high nationalist walls, let the world go hang, and refuse to co-operate in efforts to maintain peace in the world.

BEARD: If that is a correct definition of isolationism, I must say that I never heard of an American of the slightest importance in public life who favors isolationism. If that is isolationism, it is indeed dead; or rather, it never came to life. At least I approve burying the corpse. However, I have no way of knowing that the overwhelming majority of the American people were in favor of our entrance into the League of Nations in 1919. They did not elect Mr. Wilson President in 1916 on a commitment to make a war, or to take the United States into such a League as was set up at Versailles. Just why they elected him, I do not know, but one of the popular slogans in the campaign was that he kept us out of war.

When, in the congressional campaign of 1918, President Wilson called for the return of Democrats to support his policies, the majority of the voters answered him with an emphatic repudiation of his call. I do not maintain that this was a vote against the League of Nations idea, but certainly it is not to be interpreted as a vote for the League idea. Nor do I agree that it was merely tricky Republican politicians who defeated the ratification of the League covenant. I haven't a word to say in defense of the Republican tactics. But President Wilson, by numerous important actions, especially by rejecting compromise modifications, was partly responsible for his own defeat and the defeat of the League.

In any case, if the American people were warmly in favor of the League, as Dr. Hetherson maintains, they had a chance to show it in the election of 1920. The Democrats promised to join the League. The Republicans equivocated. The voters may have been in favor of the League, but they proved in a landslide that they were more in favor of something else. To put the case in another way, there were not enough in favor of the League to elect the men who squarely pledged themselves to put it into effect. Some Republicans said that Harding favored the League, but he merely spoke vaguely of some kind of international association. The weight of evidence, in my judgment, runs against the contention that the majority of the American people ever favored the League intensely enough to force ratification by the Senate.

What efforts and sacrifices in the interest of permanent peace the American people are willing to make or support now is for me problematical. As to the Gallup polls, cited by Dr. Hetherson, they have often been amazingly correct in predicting election returns, but they missed fire badly in the congressional election of 1942, when more than half of the active voters cast their ballots for Republican candidates, and a lot of so-called pre-Pearl Harbor isolationists were successful at the polls.

Hence I am unwilling to base anything serious on a Gallup poll, even relative to election figures. They are worse than useless on matters of opinion. People who would not actually sacrifice a pin for an opinion will say 'yes' to an abstract proposition. Gallup polls, as critics have pointed out, do not measure the *intensity* of opinions or convictions. Intensity of interest, as well as numbers of heads, counts in determining what the American people will support in the way of labor and sacrifice. A majority of the American people may be for an all-out effort to establish and maintain world peace. Though I have grave doubts about it, they may be.

Mrs. Smyth: At this juncture I should like to read the following statement which I have drawn up:

> We assume or believe that permanent world peace is desirable and possible; that efforts should be made to establish an international agreement or agreements most likely to effect and maintain it; and that the American people will support such agreement or agreements as general propositions.

Suppose we take a Gallup poll here on this and then consider the specific elements which are to fit into the general proposition.

Beard: The vote is unanimous, save for my reservation that I am unwilling to accept the formula without an inspection of the agreement or agreements in detail.

Mrs. Smyth: Since we have here representatives of three definite plans for world organization, I suggest that we now have Dr. Fare-banks' statement for the League of Nations, to be modified by amendments. The League is still in existence, and many people are inclined to start with an institution that is not solely new theory. We know something about the League, how it worked, and what its shortcomings were. Mrs. Farebanks has long been associated with our local League of Nations Society, and has observed the League at work in Geneva.

Dr. Farebanks: Nobody can speak with authority for all sup-porters of the League as to modifications in the League regarded as necessary to make it an effective organization for permanent peace. But after a study of many proposals for changes in the con-stitution of the League, which competent authorities have made, I present the following:

1. The states as members of the League must surrender the idea of enjoying henceforward complete sovereignty, and accept a cur-tailment of their sovereignty.

2. The rule of unanimous decision in the Council of the League must be abrogated and provision made for the application of sanctions and force to aggressors on a two-thirds vote.

3. There must be created for the League an executive department strong enough to enforce the decisions of the Council against peace-breakers.

4. It will be necessary to institute an international armed force at the disposal of the League for police work and for putting down aggressors, including insurrectionists.

5. An international Economic Department must be established in the League on the model of the International Labor Office. The Department should embrace representatives of governments, man-agement, and labor. Its duty would be to administer legislation of the League pertaining to world commerce, finance, migration, and living standards.

That a League so constituted could maintain world peace and promote the economic measures favorable to such peace I have no doubt. I shall merely indicate by a single quotation how easily it could work in case of a crisis threatening peace. It is from the address of Prime Minister Churchill delivered to the Congress of the United States on December 16, 1941. 'Five or six years ago,' Churchill declared, 'it would have been easy, without shedding a drop of blood, for the United States and Great Britain to have insisted on the fulfilment of the disarmament clauses in the treaties Germany signed after the Great War.'

In these few words, Mr. Churchill showed how we could have avoided the Second World War. I could enlarge upon the subject, but this is the substance of my case for the new League. Any questions?

BEARD: Would it not have been possible, without shedding a drop of blood, for Great Britain, France and Russia, all members of the League, to have suppressed Hitler in 1933, or Mussolini in 1936, or both of them in 1939? Could they not have done this without the aid of the United States?

DR. FAREBANKS: Unquestionably they had the physical force, but they could not co-operate.

BEARD: What reason have you for believing that the United States, if it had been a member of the League in 1935 or 1936, would have forced co-operation against Hitler and Mussolini on Great Britain, France, and Russia?

DR. FAREBANKS: I think that the United States, being a democratic country and more impartial in respect of Europe, would have been quicker to see the danger to peace offered by the rise of Mussolini and Hitler, and more likely to have insisted on co-operation against them.

BEARD: Is it not true that Great Britain went behind France's back, in violation of the Versailles Treaty, and made a naval deal with Hitler in 1935?

DR. FAREBANKS: Yes. That, I think, was a mistake.

BEARD: Did not Churchill once declare himself in favor of Fascism for Italy, and praise Mussolini? Did not American bankers and investors help to underwrite Mussolini with the aid of a large loan floated in the United States? Is there not evidence that the Tory government in London before 1939 was more eager to turn Hitler against Russia than to form a combination against him and destroy him?

DR. FAREBANKS: I concede that those are the facts. However, I do not see their relevance to the problem of the reformed League of Nations to prevent the repetition of such mistakes.

BEARD: You have admitted that, if the nations of Europe now united against the Axis had really wanted to suppress Mussolini or Hitler at any time before 1939, they could have done it easily without our aid. You have acknowledged that they did not need the help of the United States to effect that end. Have you any more support than your own opinion for believing that, if the United States had been in the League all along, things would have been any different? As between Russian communism and fascism from 1924 to 1939, on which side did American sentiments lie in the main?

Mrs. Smyth: Pardon me for interrupting. Such a discussion of ancient history could go on indefinitely. I suggest that we now have the federation plan from Mr. Lytelton.

Mr. Lytelton: I shall state my case as briefly as possible. The reformed League, as presented by Dr. Farebanks, in my opinion would not be strong enough to overcome the disruptive force of the national sovereignties, even if diminished. Their conflicts over interests, prestige, commerce, colonies, and special priviliges would go on as before and end in another disruption of the world confederacy so constituted. Instead, I propose a real federation of all the nations on the model of the United States of America.

All nations would be equally represented in the Senate or Council. In the lower house or Assembly, they would be represented more or less on the basis of population. There would be an Executive, perhaps of three members. The federation government would have adequate powers, akin to those of the Congress of the United States, over international commerce and finance, and all other common concerns. It would have the power to aid member governments against insurrections and to suppress conflicts among those governments verging in the direction of war. The various national states in the federation would still possess large powers and discharge local functions as the states do now in the American Union.

Why do I believe that such a federation is feasible? The following are my reasons: The world has achieved an economic unity stronger than that of the United States in 1787. Commerce among the nations of the earth is more active and valuable than commerce among the American states in 1787. Rapid transportation has annihilated space and brought the nations of the earth closer together than the states of the American Union were in 1787. Local industries everywhere are more dependent for their existence upon world trade than the local industries in the American states in 1787 were dependent on national trade. Intercommunication among all parts of the world is instantaneous. Nationalism is dead or dying. The state of the world is ripe for federation. If not, why not?

DR. WINSTANLEY: Despite the economic unity which you mention, Mr. Lytelton, there are still grave conflicts of interest among the nations, especially the industrial and commercial nations. I recognize that these conflicts grow out of misinterpretation of national interests and that they are gross violations of the economic laws of the free world market. They are largely induced by politicians who inflame the sentiments of nations by appeals to prejudices. But they undoubtedly exist. It is for this reason that I propose to attack the problem of world peace from the economic instead of the political end.

At this turn of affairs a lively exchange of views occurred, in which the four world-planners took part. Dr. Farebanks was of the opinion that the independent nations were not ready to surrender as much sovereignty as a federation would require. Dr. Hetherson announced that he was ready to support any world plan that promised a lasting peace, while insisting that, unless the spirit of the several peoples of the earth were ready for it, success could not be expected. All the world-planners agreed, however, that Mr. Lytelton's description of the growing economic unification of the world had a close relation to the growing intellectual and spiritual unification of the world.

DR. SMYTH, looking in my direction: Let's have it.

BEARD: Mr. Lytelton makes a far-fetched analogy between the basic conditions of the thirteen American states in 1787 and the basic conditions of the fifty or more independent nations of the earth so utterly diverse in race, history, sentiments, and economy. All I ask you to do, if you want confirmation of my assertion, is to read the first five numbers of *The Federalist*. In America in 1787 more than ninety percent of the whites were of British origin—had a common historical heritage. A common language and the broad principles of a common civil and criminal law prevailed from New Hampshire to Georgia; most of the people were Christians in religious profession; the traditions of the Revolution united their hearts; fear of foreign aggression against the young Republic was a potent force in overcoming their diversities of interest.

The ancient heritages of Europe and Africa and Asia have not been wholly uprooted by the mere adoption and use of the machines and the gadgets of modern industrialism. Nor does a common use of machines make men, women, and children of all nations alike in traditions, habits, sentiments, and values. Moreover hundreds of millions of the earth's people do not have gadgets or machines and are not likely to have them soon, if ever. Nor is the statement, often repeated, that inventions have annihilated space and brought people closer together anything more than a metaphor. Communications are no doubt quicker but the overwhelming majority of people in all the nations have no money or time for extensive traveling and, in space, are as far apart as ever.

If a world federation were formed, conflicts of national interests would go on inside of it. It took a long and bloody civil war to decide the question as to who was to govern the United States of America. A war is no less a war because it is called civil instead of foreign. There is no reason I can fathom for believing that the closer nations are drawn together by commerce and intercourse, the more alike they become intellectually, morally, and spiritually. I suspect that the exact opposite may often be true, as the present state of the world seems to hint. I do not believe that economic practices and relations determine all political relations and sentiments. I do not believe that the politics which Professor Winstanley scorns is all bad or can ever be subdued to purely economic considerations. I sometimes think that politics is more of a determining force in history than economics.

DR. SMYTH: Whew! That is unmitigated pessimism.

MRS. SMYTH: Let us hear from Dr. Hetherson.

DR. HETHERSON: As I have said, I have no precise plan for the coming world order. Some plan is doubtless necessary, but I prefer to leave that to practical persons, like my colleagues, who have spoken for a reformed League and for a new federation. I start from the proposition that war as an institution is barbaric and unchristian; that economic sacrifices must be made by the American people to usher in permanent peace; that Christians must make these sacrifices; that the brotherhood of man is a fact, is a great truth; and that the Christians of the world, in co-operation with Jews, must spread the spirit of brotherhood throughout the earth. I agree heartily with Herbert Hoover and Hugh Gibson, who say in their *Problems of a Lasting Peace:* 'In the end there can be no trustworthy security except by giving the decent elements in a people a chance to co-operate in the work of peace.' In the domain of the spirit lies our hope. God's law of love must reign throughout the earth. When the spirit is ready all obstacles to a lasting peace will be overcome.

During Dr. Hetherson's discourse, here abridged, shadows of impatience occasionally flickered over the faces of the other world-planners. Only Mrs. Smyth listened steadily, with occasional approving glances. At the end, after a long silence Dr. Smyth looked at me with quizzical eyes and inquired: Well?

BEARD: If the peoples of the earth were animated by Dr. Hetherson's spirit, the problems of a lasting peace would be easy of solution. The Christian world-view has been a powerful force in Western history. Its coming destiny I do not pretend to divine. Where conduct squares with that world-view, peace *does* reign.

Mrs. Smyth relieved the tension by calling for Professor Winstanley's project of an Economic Union.

PROFESSOR WINSTANLEY: At this late hour, I can give you only the barest outline. For details I must refer you to Otto T. Mallery's *Economic Union and Durable Peace* or, if you are cramped for reading time, to his 'Typical Plans for a Postwar World Peace' published in *International Conciliation* for November, 1942. My plan differs from his in some ways, but I accept his basic principles. He states them as follows:

1. If goods cannot cross political frontiers, soldiers will.
2. Unless shackles can be dropped from trade, bombs will drop from the sky.
3. Economic bargains, likely to be kept, are preferable to political agreements likely to be broken.
4. Mass unemployment was not overcome by the trade and economic policies adopted by the principal industrial nations during the period between wars, except while preparing for war. Therefore these policies were failures and must be superseded.

It might be well to stop here and consider these principles advanced by Mr. Mallery before we take up concrete plans.

BEARD, after waiting for other comment: Until I have heard the details of your plan I prefer to reserve my remarks on these principles. To me they are not principles at all, but rhetorical flourishes. They consist of two misleading images, one declaration that is historically untenable, and at the end a grand *non sequitur*.

PROFESSOR WINSTANLEY: Of course, if you reject these principles, you will reject the plan of Economic Union based on them. Still, here are the elements of the plan, in my own words, with modifications of my own making:

1. To get full employment and raise living standards for more people of the earth, the benefits of mass production must be extended over larger and larger geographical areas.

2. This extension of mass production cannot be made by any peace conference or by any sudden introduction of free trade. It must be done gradually and mainly by extension of economic agreements among nations.

3. Such agreements cannot be left to politicians. They should be made by agents of management, labor, and governments representing like-minded nations at first and then all other nations.

4. Equal access to raw materials and to the ever-widening international market must be given to the defeated nations in due time.

5. The Economic Union so formed should be governed by an Economic Board representing managers, workers, and governments.

6. The Economic Board, with a Bank at its service, would promote reciprocal trade agreements, aid in giving equal access to colonial raw materials, enforce international fair trade practices, regulate cartels, and promote joint action against depressions.

7. The Economic Union can exist in, under, or alongside any kind of international organization or institutions which may be established. It is a business proposition appealing to capital and labor. By mediation and action it would seek to promote the welfare of all member nations and adjust economic conflicts among them, thus removing the struggles of interests which constitute the main causes of war.

As Mr. Mallery says: 'Our greatest foe is cynicism and fear that what ought to be can never be. Against this fear all plans and planners should present a united front and avow with a calm vehemence that faith is essential to its own realization.'

If I may speak frankly, the kind of cynicism that Mr. Beard expressed at the beginning of our session, which he shares with too many Americans, is the chief barrier to such economic union among nations and to lasting peace for mankind.

BEARD: I do not see that it helps to bring cynicism into our discussion. You have yourself made cynical references to politicians, but I cannot discover in what way references to cynicism advance our knowledge or understanding. We are trying, I take it, to discover ways and means of bringing peace and well-being to the United States and other nations as far as possible and for as long a period of time as possible. In this quest a testing of details by such historical experience and power of reasoning on probabilities as we have at our command seems to me the more helpful method.

So I will venture to take up a few points in the program which has just been presented. What do you mean, Professor Winstanley, by the phrase, equal access to raw materials for all nations? As I understand the words raw materials, they include, besides mineral and organic substances in their raw state, such as copper and timber, also unfinished agricultural products, such as cotton, rice, and tobacco. Various nations, for example, have neither oil nor cotton.

If the United States should give them equal access to its resources, would that allow capitalists and laborers from those countries to enter the United States and exploit our resources for themselves? Since these resources are largely in private ownership in the United States, who is to fix prices for the privilege of exploitation, and how? If foreign capitalists and their workers are not to enter the United States and get this equal access at first hand, how is the equal access to be obtained? Finally, are foreign nations or nationals to pay for the goods they get in the United States, or are they to have them free of charge? If they are to pay, with which specific types of goods are they to pay?

DR. WINSTANLEY: You have a faulty conception of the whole business, Beard. Equal access to raw materials means: (1) nationals and governments of all nations shall have the same and equal right to buy our raw materials in our markets and export them, not the right to enter this country and develop the materials themselves; (2) there shall be no discrimination in our laws against any nation in respect of buying such raw materials; (3) the prices of such raw materials shall be the same for buyers of all nations; (4) all such raw materials are to be paid for, directly or indirectly. This aboli-

tion of discrimination would make for equality among the nations
—between the haves and the have-nots.

BEARD: That does not differ essentially from the policies historically
pursued by the United States, as I understand them. In peacetime
any foreign governments or nationals can buy here anything they
can pay for, out of cash or credits or money borrowed from American
money-lenders. As a general rule, except in wartime, or war emergencies, all countries of the world have been equal in that sense,
in American markets. If you are going to require foreigners to buy
and pay for the raw materials they want from the United States,
then the countries which have the greatest wealth and facilities for
paying their bills will be best served in American markets. The
have-nots with little or nothing to exchange for our raw materials
will be able to get little or nothing here. Their equality of access
is thus a mere fiction. Their position will be like that of the poorest
people in New York City: they have equal access with the rich to
the furs and jewels of Fifth Avenue; their only trouble is that they
haven't the money to pay for such luxuries. There is one more point.
Suppose the people of the United States wish to conserve their
resources for themselves and sell only limited quantities? If they
do this, then they will have special advantages as against other
nations.

Several years ago, Mary Beard and I had lunch with H. G. Wells
and Frank Simonds in Washington, both advocates of equal access
to raw materials as a preventive of war. We put to them the very
questions which I have put here. When Simonds was asked whether
the have-nots were to pay for the raw materials they got in the
United States, he answered 'Yes'; but he and Wells went on to
argue that an international organization could facilitate exchanges
so that the have-nots could pay for their raw materials.

When I pressed the contention that in the long run the have-nots
would have to produce and send out real wealth to pay for their
raw materials, Simonds admitted that that would be the case. The
only important thing we could agree upon was that possibly by
international commitments the colonies of various imperial powers
might be forced open for the have-nots as well as for the haves to
trade with them on equal terms. And Simonds admitted the fact
that most of the precious raw materials of the world are to be found
in independent countries, not in colonies.

Mr. Wells took the socialist position when Mary Beard asked him where he stood on this issue. He said that, after socialism had supplanted capitalist commercial rivalry, the question of capitalistic trade for profit would disappear and the world brotherhood of man would share and share alike. In his vision, the whole world would be one commonwealth of free people, and goods would flow freely from one part to another. He conceded that there would be exchanges of goods between the parts of the world.

Thereupon Mary Beard asked him whether, for example, the Russian part of the socialist world-commonwealth, having great riches in raw materials, would simply give huge supplies to the Chinese part or the Japanese part, that is, mine or work the raw materials and ship them away free of charge to have-nots of the world commonwealth. At this, Wells threw up the sponge and replied that, when the whole world was operated on socialist principles, such matters as intersocialist trade could be easily arranged. This left me in a fog, and so do Mr. Mallery's specific proposals.

PROFESSOR WINSTANLEY: So you want wars over commerce and raw materials to go on forever? It is generally understood among people who have studied the matter that the struggle for commercial advantages and raw materials is the chief cause of wars, the decisive cause. As Mr. Mallery well says: 'Unless shackles can be dropped from trade, bombs will drop from the sky.'

BEARD: The sentence you have just quoted is, in my opinion, a mere vague metaphor. Men were fighting for centuries before there was any international trade to shackle or unshackle. Recall the endless wars among the ancient Greeks. Were they all on account of shackles on trade? Of course not. Look at the Civil War in the United States. There was free trade from one end of the Union to the other; yet war came, long, bloody, and devastating war. As to what you call the chief cause of wars, or the decisive cause, I confess that I do not know the cause of anything and suspect that you . . .

DR. SMYTH: Hold him, Professor Winstanley! I saw on his desk at his house the other night a manuscript of endless pages, entitled *The Idea of 'Cause' in Natural Science and the Humanistic Sciences.* Come down to earth, Beard.

BEARD: All right, since you seem to think that an effort to be exact in the use of language is unearthly—and futile. What does anybody mean by the metaphor dropping the shackles off trade? I understand, a little bit, the phrase free trade. It means that there shall be no government interference with commerce among nations in the form of protective tariffs, bounties, monetary management, and other discriminative devices. It means that the nationals of all countries shall be free to exchange goods among themselves on terms made by themselves.

Such free trade takes for granted a vast and complicated set of relations respecting property ownership and use and capitalistic production in each nation engaged in this so-called international commerce. It takes for granted also what is called free competition within each nation; that is the absence of private monopolistic controls over resources, patents, and processes in the restraint of trade. It assumes, too, that the United States will not be compelled to safeguard its resources and the devices necessary to the defense of the country or to any wars that it may get into, to say nothing of safeguarding the civilization of the American people.

I am familiar with free trade as promulgated by British industrialists at the middle of the nineteenth century when Britain was the workshop of the world. But I am unable to visualize it as applied to nations, empires, colonies, and protectorates, to the economies of the various nations and empires as now constituted, with all the kinds of government controls and systems of culture and production now in force, from Great Britain to Russia.

Do you actually believe, Professor Winstanley, that countries with managed economies like Russia, or partly managed economies like Great Britain and other first-rate powers, will or can return to the unmanaged economies such as existed fifty or a hundred years ago?

Professor Winstanley: No, I realize that we are in an age of more or less managed economies and that a return to the conditions prevailing in 1850, or even 1914, is out of the question. As Mr. Mallery says, the economic union 'should begin with a few like-minded nations and not with the whole world.' That would include the countries with the largest amount of free enterprise.

Beard: Well, American business men are constantly telling us that enterprise is not free here. But, aside from that, name the countries like-minded enough to form your economic union.

Professor Winstanley: I should say the United States, Great Britain, France, most Latin American countries, Belgium, Holland,

Denmark, Norway, Canada, Australia—in general the democracies.

BEARD: But all the democracies have new deals or managed economies of one kind or another. If any government keeps control over its own currency, it will, in practice, more or less manage its economy and foreign trade. Are you proposing that each country abolish all the controls it has devised to deal with unemployment or to maintain its standards of living? Besides, how do you know what some of those countries will look like after the war?

PROFESSOR WINSTANLEY: I shall reply by repeating Mr. Mallery's words: 'Mass unemployment was not overcome by the trade and economic policies adopted by the principal industrial nations during the period between wars, except while preparing for wars. Therefore these policies were failures and must be superseded.'

I will add on my own account that any country that attempts to raise, or even maintain, its standards of life by managing its domestic economy is doomed to failure and will only end up in lowering its standards. As Cordell Hull has put the argument, no country can lift itself by its bootstraps. If we could get shackles off trade throughout the world, standards of living would automatically rise in all countries enjoying free trade. You would not then have the paradox of one country having shoes to sell and needing wheat, and other countries having wheat to sell and needing shoes—both suffering from unemployment and depressed standards. If they could trade freely, this condition of affairs would not exist.

BEARD: Mr. Mallery is dead right in holding that the measures taken to overcome mass employment by managing economy were not wholly successful, or, for the sake of argument, not successful at all. It does not follow either in logic or historical necessity that therefore these policies *must* be superseded, still less that they be specifically superseded by a world economic union or free trade. Nor does it follow that any expedient of international arrangement will in fact overcome mass unemployment, raise or maintain standards of life for the participating nations.

The very conditions which Professor Winstanley has described as existing between nations now separated by tariff barriers have existed between states of the American Union separated by no tariff barriers. In 1933 there were millions of people with wheat, corn, bacon, and cotton to sell in the West and South and millions of people with shoes, cotton cloth, automobiles, and cooking utensils to sell in the East and North. No trade shackles prevented them from exchanging goods, and yet thousands, nay, millions were suffering in the four sections of the country. What reason is there for believing that unshackling trade throughout the world will do something that unshackling it throughout the United States has not done, does not do? In print and orally I have been asking American economists that question for years and I have got nothing but grunts and contempt from them. One of them took the trouble to write a large pamphlet against me intimating that I am dishonest as well as an ass.

DR. HETHERSON: You are overlooking, in this economic discussion, all ethical questions. The United States is a great power and has the moral responsibilities of a great power. We are a Christian people, besides, and must make all the sacrifices necessary to prevent war and maintain peace and the four freedoms everywhere for everybody. We should not consider these questions in economic terms alone.

BEARD: For years imperialists and internationalists have been asserting that the United States is a great power and must assume the responsibilities of a great power. Of course the United States is a great power, and will be until it has exhausted its oil, coal, and iron, and the morale of the people has degenerated with the exhaustion of economic opportunities at home. Of course it has responsibilities. That is a truism. But what responsibilities? To whom, where, when, and in what form—intellectual, spiritual, and material?

It is not exactly true to say that we are a Christian people. The generalization is too sweeping. There are millions of Jews among us. More than half the population does not belong to any Christian denomination. But, apart from that, do Christians have obligations to help, without limits, Mohammedans, Buddhists, and other pagans that reject the Christian religion and are doing their best to beat back the tide of Christian missionaries?

Since we have been shifted to moral grounds, I want to put up to you a moral question which will test your claims to a higher morality: Are all you world-planners who stand for the brotherhood of man prepared to sweep away all our immigration laws and let your brothers and sisters from every part of the world migrate freely to the United States and settle here?

DR. HETHERSON: Your question is too broad. Some of us would

favor removing many restrictions on immigration and keeping others.

BEARD: Very well, let us take immigration legislation piecemeal. How many would abolish the exclusion of immigrants suffering from loathsome and contagious diseases, advocates of the overthrow of the American system of government, and persons guilty of crimes involving moral turpitude?

A long silence followed. Even Mr. Brooklin did no more than laugh softly.

BEARD: None of you, I take it. How many would abolish the literacy test for immigrants?

More silence.

BEARD: How many would abolish all numerical limits on immigration?

More silence.

BEARD: How many would abolish the quota system which discriminates against the peoples of Southern and Eastern Europe?

Two favored modifying the system at some time in the future. None favored an immediate repeal of the discriminative laws.

BEARD: How many would repeal the exclusion acts directed against the Japanese, Chinese, and millions of other Asiatics?

DR. HETHERSON: I favor putting all Orientals on the quota basis, thus doing away with discriminations, especially the discrimination against the Chinese.

Two others joined Dr. Hetherson in this view. The rest sat mute.

BEARD: The discriminative quota system is still discriminative, a denial of universal equality. How many here believe that it would be possible to induce the Congress of the United States to repeal any of the above laws restricting immigration?

The whole party was mute.

DR. HETHERSON, sadly breaking the stillness: I fear that Congress is more likely to increase the restrictions on immigration than to diminish them, even though such laws stir up ill-will against us in the Orient and in Southern and Eastern Europe.

BEARD: I assume that we all agree on the desirability of maintaining the Republic and our system of self-government and limited liberty. Do any of you think that it would contribute to the strength of the Republic and to the support of popular government, if Congress would admit several million immigrants from countries that have never displayed any zest for self-government and capacity for it?

A desultory discussion followed this question, revealing much difference of opinion. When Mrs. Smyth called for a show of hands, there were only two affirmative votes. One of the two qualified his affirmation by adding: Of course, I should want to apply literacy and other tests, besides that of mere bodily strength.

DR. SMYTH: This immigration question is evidently too hot for us to handle. It is a moral question. From a moral standpoint, from a Christian standpoint, there are objections to our exclusiveness in matters of immigration. Yet I realize that we do have certain precious ways of life which can be kept only by having a population fairly uniform in character. For us these ways are values. If they are values, then it would not help humanity to destroy them by allowing too many unassimilable elements to enter the country. Though I am troubled in my mind about our treatment of immigration, I feel certain of that.

BEARD: The issue is economic as well as moral. At all events organized labor in the United States has for more than fifty years battled for restrictions on immigration, holding the position that free immigration breaks down the standard of life for our industrial workers. Are not Americans in general convinced that a high stand-ard of wages underwrites the good life, or at least works for a better quality of citizenship? Immigration restriction is as much a pro-tective device as a protective tariff on manufactures.

It is, of course, contrary to that free movement of capital, labor and goods usually covered by the term free trade. Once, free immi-gration made it possible for people to get access to raw materials, land, and other resources. The access was not equal, for many per-sons wanted to come to America and yet could not raise the passage money; and many who came got little access to our natural resources, except with the pick and shovel as employees of corporations.

Limitations on immigration certainly bottle up American re-sources against the poor and hungry of other lands, especially those heavily overpopulated, like Italy, China, Japan, and India. Yet it appears that none of you will publicly declare that our responsibilities as a great power include making room for two or three hundred millions of European and Oriental people. Besides, you all know that experience demonstrates the futility of emigration as a solution for the problem of chronic overpopulation where it exists. The issue as I grasp it is one of our having morality without going to such extremes of sentimental sympathy that morality is destroyed in the United States.

Mrs. Smyth: Mr. Beard has played a negative role thus far, on the whole. It certainly would be interesting if not gratifying to learn what the old cynic actually thinks about plans for the post-war world and what he has to offer that is constructive.

Beard: I thought you knew me better by this time, Mrs. Smyth, than to speak of me as a cynic, even jokingly. I am old obviously. But I resent the application of the term cynic to me, for it implies a low and contemptuous view of mankind and its struggles for civilization—a view I do not entertain. I especially resent it when it comes from this congregation, not a single member of which is optimistic enough, despite all the talk about universal union and brotherhood, to favor a total repeal of our immigration laws and the opening of our gates to the unlimited multitudes of hungry and oppressed men, women, and children in Europe, Africa, and Asia. Even the most optimistic among you are not optimistic enough to believe that the American people as represented in the Congress of the United States will in fact authorize any such repeal and such opening of our national gates. That's that for cynicism.

The discussion of what you call plans for the post-war world meets my personal approval, particularly when it is carried on in an equable temper, with due respect for stubborn facts, and without contempt for those who venture to question the workability of such plans. This discussion comports with the democratic process, which I prefer to characterize as the constitutional process of proposal, discussion, and adoption or rejection.

From the aspirations for the peace and happiness of the United States and the other nations of the world, expressed here, I do not dissent. I am sure of this much: I should like to see the world at peace, a world of highly civilized peoples as nations using their talents and resources to make the true, the good, the beautiful, and the useful prevail more widely.

Nevertheless when Mrs. Smyth asks me what I *think* about plans for the post-war world, instead of being moved to make a string of assertions as they come to my lips, I am shocked into inquiring what one thinks one is doing when one thinks, especially about a matter of the future invisible to us. Since I am no scholastic able to spin out propositions indefinitely by a purely logical process, I cannot proceed to the business of thinking without having some knowledge and concrete realities to work on or with. When I am invited to consider such great public policies as are inherent in a world plan, I am oppressed by the thought that they involve nothing less than knowledge and interpretation of mankind's long history on this planet. This alone is enough to give me pause—and pain. It cramps my facility for voluble expression on the subject.

Now you are asking me what I think about plans for a situation— a combination of order and chaos—hidden from us in the veiled future. Judging by past experiences of history (and I have no other resort for criteria), many contingencies and great events now unforeseen will occur in this unfolding future. There may be shifts in the two coalitions now engaged in war. Unities enforced by war may be shattered when war dies down. Great internal explosions may occur within nations now apparently firm in façade. New combinations of powers may arise.

It takes little knowledge of world history to recall how alliances have been broken, coalitions reformed, eternal friendships forsworn, and the grand designs of the highest statesmen and generals shattered by uncalculated events. For instance, few people early in 1917 could foresee the Bolshevik revolution in Russia and realize that before the end of the war Russia's two allies, Great Britain and France, and her associate, the United States, would be waging unofficial wars on the Soviet Union, north, south and far east. Recalling this bit of history, not merely ancient, leads me to wonder what would happen if Hitler and Mussolini were rubbed out of the picture and relatively limited fascist regimes, such as prevailed in Italy when the Black Shirts first came to power, were established in France, Germany, and Italy, as well as Spain, and new insurrections broke out against them. Many other illustrations of possible contingencies may easily be derived from historical experience, but I forbear citing any more.

Coming home to the United States, I confess that I can see in the midst of the multitude of plans, definite and indefinite, put forth

by high officials and eminent citizens and associations, no agreement on fundamentals and details about which to think with any
degree of precision and certitude. Nor am I able now to fathom the
future of our internal economy, or discern clearly the features of
foreign policy which the people of the United States will support
persistently and consistently by taxes, army, regimentation, and other
sacrifices.

Thus it is impossible for me at this point in time to visualize the
complicated situation which you call the post-war world—primary
contours and elements of which are hidden from view and must now
be mere matters of speculation. What I think about a shadow-land
impenetrable to my vision is worthless to me and, I am sure, to
others. I suspect, but I do not know, that if the statesmen or military
leaders, called upon to draw the terms of the settlement at the end
of the war, concentrate on making a durable rather than a permanent peace the results may be more lasting. As to the making of
minute plans for the post-war world, I prefer to leave that operation
to others who feel that they have a competence to which I cannot lay
claim.

Yet I know that someday practical decisions will have to be made
on the settlement at the close of hostilities. Speaking as construc-
tively as I can, I should approve, for the present, an effort to hold
the United Nations together on practical issues, while striving to
adjust grave differences between and within them and to effect
agreements among them on points of continuing co-operation during
the war. As to the military and territorial settlement at the end of
the conflict, I am inclined to the opinion that it should not be accompanied by an elaborate world constitution, full of vague phrases
that could be, and probably would be, twisted and turned by governments competing for power. Instead, the settlement should be
accompanied by a brief and simple treaty. I would limit the treaty to
ten years or more, subject to renewal, and bind the signatory powers
to refrain from resorting to violence during that period, and to abide
by stipulated methods of arbitration and conciliation in case controversies arise under the terms of the treaty.

The shorter this treaty is, the better; the more concise the terms
I have just mentioned, the more likely would be the prospect of
observance; the slighter the strain on human nature, the more probable would be whole-hearted willingness to abide by it.

This proposal, I submit, is constructive. It is supported by no little historical experience, including the extraordinary fortunes of our own Constitution which fills only eight pages of print. This program, I believe, would be more likely to realize aspirations for the good of our country and humanity, which we all cherish, than grandiose plans for settling everything and everybody all at once and for all time and for trying to hold millions of people down by police and propaganda. It leaves, as a French statesman once remarked of a short constitution for France, 'something to Providence.'

Having listened without interruptions, if with some impatience, Mrs. Smyth's guests broke up into groups and engaged in animated contentions over the four elaborate plans for the postwar world that had been presented at the table. Taking this as a signal for flight, I escaped to my study on Hosannah Hill, where, for a few minutes, I tried to compose my troubled mind by reading the fifth-century lines of Rutilius to the future of the Roman Empire.

XXI

The Fate and Fortunes of Our Republic

WHAT was on your mind, I asked the Smyths, when you suggested this additional session of our fireside seminar?

MRS. SMYTH: In the course of our discussions, especially at the session on world relations, we were overpowered by the realization that every proposition involved assumptions unprovable but taken for granted; that by assigning a cause to any event we are required, if thoughtful, to make a futile inquiry into the cause of the cause backward along an infinite chain of causes ending in the darkness of prehistory—silence; that all our schemes for a world order come within the sweep of what you call great history; that our institutions, hopes, and plans run up against fate as well as opportunities for action. For your consent to let us have one more conference, and this one all by ourselves, we are grateful.

DR. SMYTH: That's true, Beard. This time we can go straight to your large historical philosophy and your ways of thinking about history. I shall try to have patience with you, though I have not always been successful at the art. Please have patience with me a little longer.

BEARD: There is no reason or pleasure in any other attitude—at least when we are in our right minds. So be as frank as you wish about your present difficulties. Let us go about the business in the freest possible style.

DR. SMYTH: As we told you on the occasion of our first visit last autumn, we had read Spengler or, perhaps it would be truer to say, tried to read him years ago, and we have been deeply interested in his new theory of history. I mean the theory that every nation moves through a kind of cycle from youth to old age and death—spring, summer, autumn, and winter. Just what happens when winter comes, we could not quite make out from Spengler's words, but it seems that at the end of Winter comes Caesar, the man of blood and iron who conquers the man of gold—our urban civilization.

MRS. SMYTH: If Spengler's theory is valid, then it applies to our Republic, to America; and our Republic is fated to perish, to fall under the empire of a Caesar, when its Winter inevitably comes. This is a dreary outlook and makes futile all our talk about constitutionalism, America's place in the world, and the effort to maintain the ideals of liberty and justice which we have discussed during our many sessions together.

If Spengler's new theory is valid, then all that the advocates of world order said the other night at our house goes overboard also. Their propositions were based on the idea that all nations are growing more alike, better ready for world union; that the same civilization will become common around the world; and that all nations will develop together into a peaceful and prosperous future for all time. Spengler dashes such optimistic hopes to earth. We want to know your views on what we may call the larger historical drama in which everything we have talked about has taken place or will take place.

BEARD: That is a tall order. Spengler's theory is really a deterministic theory of our universe.

DR. SMYTH: A kind of Calvinistic theory, then—a theory that all things, events, and persons have been predestined by God or Nature from the beginning of the universe and none of us can do anything about them. It amounts to a species of theology. You probably will want to sidestep it on the ground that you are a historian, not a theologian, and I cannot blame you. As an Episcopalian, I believe in free will, not predestination. But Spengler's theory bothers us, perhaps partly because I read critics who uphold it so stanchly.

BEARD: Pardon me, a moment, for a digression. I do not call myself a historian, but a *student* of history. It is customary for historians, or economists, or what-have-you, to answer, when such a question is raised, 'Oh, that belongs to theology or sociology, or some other learned discipline.' But such a reply really begs the question. It enables the person who makes it to escape the pain of thought about his own field, for his field, whatever it is, actually comes within the scope of that question, however vociferously he may deny it. I am willing to face Spengler's theory of the Universe. Everyone who tries to think his way through the maze of our world must do it. How shall we proceed?

MRS. SMYTH: Suppose you state the theory in your own words and then we can examine it together.

BEARD: Spengler wrote other books and essays besides *The Decline of the West* to which you refer. One of them, the most important for understanding what he was driving at, was *Preussentum und Sozialismus,* which he said contained the germ of his two volumes on *The Decline of the West.* In this little book, which has not been translated, as far as I know, Spengler displayed the Prussian Junker's hatred for the bourgeoisie and indicated a desire to see a union of Prussian state socialism with the socialism of industrial workers. If this could be effected, he evidently believed, it would redound to the strength, glory, and prosperity of Great Germany. . . .

MRS. SMYTH: Was Spengler himself a Junker?

BEARD: Oh, No! he was a small-time professor or schoolmaster in a German gymnasium or technical high school. He taught mathematics before he retired to write his huge book on *The Decline.* Spengler was not a Junker but a petty bourgeois who had taken on the inveterate dislike the agrarian Junker has for the business classes.

DR. SMYTH: That sounds anti-Semitic.

BEARD: The distrust—indeed we may say the contempt—of the agrarian for the urbanite has nothing to do with anti-Semitism. It is thousands of years old. It appeared strongly in Aristotle's *Politics* written in the fourth century B.C. It was not directed by Aristotle against Jews, but against all business classes. After the rise of Christianity in the West, Jews were excluded from engaging in agriculture and forced to enter business. Then they also got the full shock of the old agrarian distrust of and contempt for business, trading, and finance. Spengler was not an anti-Semite, and members of Hitler's party broke with him over that very point.

MRS. SMYTH: Robert, suppose we do not interrupt for a moment, if we can command that restraint, until we get the case of Spengler before us.

[The Doctor nodded his assent.]

BEARD: About ten years after *The Decline of the West* appeared, Spengler published his *Der Mensch und die Technik,* translated as *Man and Technics.* In his work on Prussianism and Socialism,

Spengler was optimistic in the sense that he regarded as possible a union of Prussianism and Socialism which would prove beneficial for Germany if it could be brought about by the intelligence and will of Junkers and industrial workers. In his book on *The Decline,* Spengler had seemed to be dubious as to what would happen when Winter came and Caesar conquered the man of money.

Would it be the establishment of a great and prosperous Empire like that of Rome after Julius Caesar overthrew the Republic and imperial dominion was founded on the ruins of the old constitutionalism? Would an upthrust of peasants, farmers, and strong peoples from below break the death of Winter and start a new Spring?

It is difficult for me to discover what was in his mind on these crucial questions, although I have studied over and over both the German edition and the English translation. But I am convinced that in *The Decline,* Spengler was not wholly pessimistic, had not completely surrendered to the pessimistic belief that all human beings are caught in a web of cruel fate and are powerless to do anything about it. Perhaps he was a black pessimist even when he wrote *The Decline.* Germans who knew him tell me that he was a pessimist even then, but *The Decline* leaves the door of human hope slightly ajar, as I read the lines and between the lines.

In his *Man and Technics,* however, Spengler leaves no doubt as to where he stood at the time of its publication. There he makes man simply a beast of prey. There what he calls 'machine culture' comes to a black and tragic end. Let me read you his final words:

> We are born into this time and must bravely follow the path to the destined end. There is no other way. Our duty is to hold on to the lost position, without hope, without rescue, like that Roman soldier whose bones were found in front of a door in Pompeii, who, during the eruption of Vesuvius, died at his post because they forgot to relieve him. That is greatness. That is what it means to be a thoroughbred. The honorable end is the one thing that can *not* be taken from a man.

Dr. Smyth: I call that dithyrambic or lyrical rubbish and a contradiction in its own terms. If all is fated, it is nonsense to talk about bravery, greatness, the thoroughbred, and honor—least of all honor. It is just as if a drop of water in the river that flows through our valley to the sea should rise up and say: 'I am brave; I am great;

I am a thoroughbred; I have honor as, inevitably and will-less, I flow, by the law of gravitation, relentlessly to the sea.' I am willing to let a pessimist believe that man is a mere machine, whose every act, word, thought is fated or predestined as the movement of our river to the sea, but I don't want him to get moral on my hands and proclaim his honor in the circumstances. I am willing to have Holy Willie, in Robert Burns' poem, believe that God sends one to heaven and ten to hell, all for His glory and not for any good or ill they have done afore Him; but I object to introducing moral exhortations to human beings into any such argument. Fatalism is beyond good and evil, honor and dishonor.

MRS. SMYTH: I do not quite believe that. A person may believe in a *good* fate; that mankind is fated to make endless progress toward the good. Some of the advocates of a peaceful and happy world order took that stand at our house last Friday evening.

DR. SMYTH: Yes, but they said that it would not turn out that way *unless* all Americans got busy and forced things to that conclusion. There was an if in their argument: *If* Americans will do their part, the beautiful world order will arrive. In determinism or mechanism, correctly understood, there is and can be no if. To the determinist or mechanist, as a physiologist knows, a thing is or will be, inescapable; it is not conditioned by any if. I can get that point all right, without the aid of philosophy.

Of course, a determinist may say that the machine will work for what we call good, and in this sense he may be optimistic. Even so, he rules out moral choices on our part; his system is beyond good and evil. To tell me that nobody can, by persistent effort, improve his technique in surgery is to fly in the face of my experiences.

MRS. SMYTH: If the American Republic is fated to sink into the death of Spengler's Winter, to be transformed from a system of liberty and self-government into a dictatorial empire, then it is futile, it is nonsense, for American citizens to discuss constitutionalism, liberty, justice, or anything else. I do not believe in any such destiny for us, and I want to ask Mr. Beard to consider two questions before he goes on with Spengler and determinism. Does the study of history necessarily lead to pessimism? If not, what is ahead for our Republic?

BEARD: In fact, Mrs. Smyth, Spengler's theory is very old, not new. The ancient Greeks had cyclical theories of political history. In

Aristotle's *Politics*, government moves from one form to another in succession and back again. His was a kind of tread-mill theory of the necessary fates of governments, let us say, from monarchy to aristocracy, from aristocracy to democracy, from democracy to tyranny, and back again, with slight variations. About 1725, Giambattista Vico, an Italian philosopher and sociologist, developed a cyclical theory somewhat vaguely—from barbarism to what we call civilization and back again—all very much in the style adopted by Spengler.

To pass over other examples, I will cite our own Brooks Adams. In his *The Law of Civilization and Decay*, published first in 1895, the cyclical theory re-appears. According to Adams, nations move from the dispersion of barbarism to the concentration of civilization and back again, with a possible re-infusion of barbarian blood after decay reaches or approaches its climax.

DR. SMYTH: How did Adams get a 'possible' into his fate? A thing is fated or it is not. In fate there is nothing possible, no alternative.

BEARD: Adams got a possible into his cyclical theory for the reason that, like Spengler, he was not sure what would happen when Winter came. For the first edition of his book he had one ending. For the second edition, he had another ending. For the French translation, he had still another ending, and an equivocal one. But it would take too long to go into that. My point is that Spengler's theory is not new. In origins it is old, very old, though it keeps cropping up in modern thought.

MRS. SMYTH: How do you account for the emphasis that has been laid on this cyclical theory in comparatively recent times? How did it get the hold it has over contemporary imaginations?

BEARD: The fortunes of ancient Rome have exercised a powerful influence over strong minds for at least fifteen hundred years. With many weak minds the theme has become a disease. Some of the early Church fathers wrote interpretations of Rome's misfortunes, partly with a view to reconciling the terrible events which marked the breakdown of Roman dominion with the Christian theory of Divine Providence. The renaissance, so-called, the wholesale recovery of Greek and Roman learning after the darkness of the Middle Ages, opened a new world of knowledge and thought to men and women long preoccupied with the Christian theology and world-view. For generations this pagan learning helped to fill the vacuum in secular learning, relatively neglected by theologians—many, not all, for I do not want to fall into the error of depreciating the secular wisdom of the Middle Ages. Meanwhile Western Christianity in development—even Protestant and sectarian—stemmed from the Roman system of thought and practice and, despite efforts to escape to primitive Christianity, has never discarded all of the Roman heritage. And of course the Roman Catholic Church has steadily retained its ties with Rome. . . .

DR. SMYTH: I see that a huge book could be written under the title, The Tyranny of the Roman Tradition over the Western Mind. I don't mean the Catholic tradition, but the whole Roman tradition—rise, growth, decline, and fall. I had never before realized its importance for our thinking about history, including our own history. But, fascinating as the subject is, I wish you would connect this tradition with the cyclical theory of history which exercises a kind of tyranny over modern minds. You don't mind my breaking in?

BEARD: Not at all. You know my tendency to go on and on, and round and round, in dealing with every single point of emphasis in our wide-ranging discussions. As far as I know the first systematic cyclical theory of history, from barbarism through civilization and back again, and over again, was formulated by Vico, the Italian scholar whom I mentioned a few minutes ago. He did not use the word civilization but that idea fairly fits the substance of his thought.

For perhaps a thousand years or more, a tragic sense of Rome haunted Italian thinkers and it still haunts them today. There is nothing mysterious about that. It haunted Vico and he worked out his theory of cycle as a new science.

To jump nearly two centuries, the distinguished Egyptologist, W. M. Flinders Petrie, was captured by the theory of cycle and published one of his own in his *Revolution of Civilization*. Petrie's knowledge of Egyptian history was profound. But his knowledge of universal and modern history was certainly sketchy in important spots. Under the tyranny of the ancient tradition, he was rash enough to talk about the course which every civilization follows.

DR. SMYTH: I take it that you don't think much of Petrie's book.

BEARD: I look upon it as a theory of universal history utterly out of harmony with huge bodies of knowledge at the command of students of universal history. What Petrie did not know about civilization in the United States would fill the Encyclopaedia Britannica. For Americans to base any public policy or private judgment on Petrie's theory would be like basing it on moonshine. Shall I go on with the history of the cyclical theory of history?

DR. SMYTH: It scarcely seems worth while. Sue and I will read more about it at home and not use up all the time tonight on it. But tell us this, Does the study of history necessarily lead to pessimism as to the future of humanity—for our intellectual purposes, in the United States?

BEARD: It does not. Max Nordau bears me out when he says that pessimism or optimism is a matter of temperament, not a matter of philosophy or historical knowledge. Mark Twain who, despite his many sorrows, had about everything that optimism could crave, was a pessimist. The crippled telephone operator at your Hospital has endured poverty and suffering, and yet is about the most cheerful person in our city, a genuine optimist.

The study of history does not necessarily lead to pessimism. Among historians who have devoted their lives to the study of history, some are pessimists and some are optimists as to the future of mankind. The same person is optimistic one day and pessimistic the next. Which day is the right one for classifying him? You answer. Certainly many great, good, marvelous, and delightful persons, events, and things have appeared in history; and many horrible things also. Since the records of history are fragmentary, we can never know enough to strike a balance between the good and the evil in history. Anyway, what would such a balance look like? What features would it have?

It is easy for a pessimist to select innumerable facts to *illustrate* his theory that the world is the home of desolation and sorrow for mankind, and to ignore the countervailing facts. It is easy for an optimist to ignore the pessimist's catalogue and to select just as many facts to illustrate a theory that the world is a place of increasing happiness for humanity. But a multiplication of historical illustrations is not proof.

MRS. SMYTH: Please repeat that last sentence.

BEARD: *A multiplication of historical illustrations is not proof.* I imagine that almost any theory of history could be illustrated in some way. As I understand our intellectual processes, we can formulate three types of propositions: a law, a hypothesis, and a fiction.

A law is something known—the law of gravitation, for instance. Or a mathematical law: if a silo is twenty feet in diameter, its circumference is approximately 3.1416 times twenty feet, always and everywhere.

A hypothesis is a theoretical proposition that can be explored, tested, and proved or disproved. If proved, it ceases to be a theory and comes within the denomination of laws or facts.

A fiction is a different type of theoretical proposition. It is not a law. Nor is it a hypothesis to be proved or disproved. If well grounded in imagination, logic, and knowledge, a fiction is a symbol containing workable truth, but not the whole truth of the reality covered by it. It is not fixed, like the law of gravitation, but changes with the coming of creative thought and action, and the increase of knowledge pertaining to that reality. It remains, however, to the end, partly false, in that it does not embrace all the facts necessarily relevant to it, and it is partly a matter of belief and reasoned conviction.

The theory of the infinite extension of space and the theory of the infinite divisibility of matter are fictions beyond proof and beyond our intellectual grasp; but they have been and are useful fictions in mathematics and physics. All our comprehensive ideas or theories that purport to cover universal history including, for our purposes, American history specifically, are in the nature of fictions, that is, interpretations into which enter elements of knowledge, imagination, and conviction or belief.

As Havelock Ellis says:

> Matter is a fiction, just as the fundamental ideas with which the sciences generally operate are mostly fictions, and the scientific materialization of the world has proved a necessary and useful fiction, only harmful when we regard it as hypothesis and therefore possibly true. The representative world is a system of fictions. It is a symbol by the help of which we orient ourselves. The business of science is to make the symbol ever more adequate, but it remains a symbol, a means of action, for action is the last end of thinking.

Dr. Smyth: I could name a lot of fictions in medicine—theories on which a doctor proceeds when he does not know *all* about the disease he is treating. And a doctor is often successful that way. I should like to know more about fictions as applied to history, public affairs, our Republic, and its future. Can you give me the title of a book which would help me?

BEARD: I'll bring one in—Hans Vaihinger's *Philosophie des Als Ob.* Here is an English translation, *The Philosophy of 'As If.'* Havelock Ellis gives a brief treatment of it, and some criticism, in the third chapter of *The Dance of Life.*

DR. SMYTH: The dance of life! What next?

MRS. SMYTH: Never mind. I am willing to drop the subject—for the moment. To come down to hard cases, do you believe that there will always be an America, our America? Do you believe that our Republic will endure forever? Can we master fate? Must the Republic be turned into an empire, like the Roman Republic, and ultimately dissolve to ruins? With these questions all of our smaller questions reviewed this winter are involved.

BEARD: I shall tackle the third question first and dispose of it. We cannot master our fate. What is fated is fated and is beyond our power of control.

Will there always be an America? I believe that there will always be an America, an America with unique characteristics, however great the changes that will come. I believe that, but I do not know any way by which anybody can *demonstrate* the proposition. A China existed before Rome was founded and China still lives. I do not believe that the United States, with all its primary features, will perish from the earth, any more than China has perished in the course of thousands of years. I believe that our Republic, with authority and liberty constantly readjusted under constitutional principles, will long endure; forever, I hope.

You are entitled to ask: What are the grounds for this assurance? Here we come to human ultimates in thinking about our universe and in reaching convictions about it. What I call a conviction is not just a blind faith. It is a calculation based on knowledge of numerous relevant facts well established by a consensus of competence in critical scholarship, and it is formulated with reference to the highest degree of probability that seems warranted by these facts. The possibility of error is by no means excluded from this operation, but if there is a more efficient way of arriving at informed and reasoned assurance, I have never come across it in my years of searching under Pascal's mandate: *chercher en gémissant.*

After the prelude, I give you the grounds of my assurance respecting the fortunes of our Republic. My first is that the analogy of Rome and other societies which have perished is utterly inapplicable to the United States. What is called the fate of Rome, as a prophecy for modern nations, is a fancy of European pessimists—the offspring of their pessimism, not the source of their pessimism; or it is a thesis of special pleaders with a cause of their own to sustain. The serious application of biological, physical and historical analogies to current human affairs as if they were laws is, in my view, a sign of intellectual weakness and displays ignorance of the true nature of history.

Now I come to the second ground of my belief in the future of our Republic: History does not repeat itself. The proposition that it does repeat itself is false to the facts in the case. Rome did not repeat the history of Egypt, Babylonia, or the Alexandrian empire. No European nation has repeated the history of Rome in the course of the last four or five hundred years. America has not repeated and cannot repeat the history of any European nation.

The spring-summer-autumn-winter theory of national histories is nothing but delusive rhetoric. Rome, as a political state, rose, expanded, was transformed, declined, and dissolved. Rome at its height was not a nation, but a congeries of nationalities ruled by Roman officials headed by an emperor, a commander in chief with unlimited power. All along her northern borders were barbarian hordes who could make and use weapons about as destructive as Roman weapons. Rome decayed and the Roman empire dissolved. Never again has the posture of human affairs been identical, even similar. Many nations, still thriving, are old enough to be mature—whatever these words may mean—are old enough to be in their autumn or winter time, if there were anything whatever in the seasonal theory of history.

England as a united nation has existed for nearly nine hundred years and is still full of vitality and promise. When China was a thousand years old, it was still young. It is really rhetorical to speak of nations as young or old. When a man reaches three score and ten he knows very well that he is old. How many years does it take to make a nation old? A hundred years or five hundred years or a thousand years? If so many people did not talk solemnly and pontifically in such terms, it would be silly for us to discuss them. The chief reason for considering the cyclical theory of history is to dismiss it to the limbo of historical lumber.

America is not fated to repeat the history of Rome or any other nation in the world. There is fate—things necessary and inescapable —in our history, I have no doubt, including the fate to be distinguished from the histories of all other countries. America is fated to be America, and all the pulling and hauling of world-planners cannot alter that fact.

But according to my world-view, our universe is not all fate; we have some freedom in it. Besides fate or determinism, there is *creative intelligence* in the world, and there is also *opportunity* to exercise our powers, intellectual and moral. America is well endowed with such powers. I find no evidences of general decline in them, at least of any such decline as marked Rome in the fifth and sixth centuries A.D. Unwise leadership may lead to a sad wastage of these powers. But our resilience is great. The destruction of great cities and vast agricultural equipment during wars, in countries less favorably endowed than the United States, has been followed in modern times by a complete reconstruction on better lines within ten years.

Calamities may come upon America or be brought upon the country by demagogic leadership. Civil storms may shake the United States. Temporary dictatorships may be set up. But the vast accumulation of physical, biological, and social knowledge that distinguishes the modern world from all antiquity, we may be fairly certain, will not be destroyed. Even in the midst of the worst imaginable domestic calamities, it is highly *improbable* that all our sciences, arts, skills, liberties, aspirations, institutions, laboratories, libraries, museums, industries, and farms will be utterly devastated. Enough of our Republic will be kept intact to restore, rebuild, and go ahead. Of this I *feel* sure.

I am not merely dreaming. Nor am I teaching the pleasing theory of the Victorian optimism which believed in straight-line, uninterrupted and everlasting progress. I am allowing for calamities enough to please the sourest pessimists. Yet, I have confidence in the tenacity of civilization, always in conflict with its foe, barbarism, and I hold to the conviction that it will not be extinguished on the earth. While I reject middle-class utopianism, I also reject the utopianism of communism—the spring into endless freedom and peace. I do not expect the United States ever to be as well-ordered as a Sunday

School. Still less do I expect the world of nations ever to be as well-ordered as a Sunday School. The universe does not seem to be "planned that way." But civilization in the United States, I believe, will continue for long centuries to come.

Such is the nature of my faith in the Republic, in American civilization, in the future of America. There are immense and varied opportunities in which we can work for the good, the true, the useful, and the beautiful. For us to belittle or fail to use our intellectual and moral powers for this work is to belie the best in our natures. To depreciate and neglect the exercise of these powers is as great a folly as to overestimate and overstrain them. The little that the strongest of us can do may seem small, but surely the unresting spirit of Americans will endlessly strive to carry on the values in their heritage, to improve upon them, to create new arts and sciences of living, to sustain and make better the Republic.

If this combination of faith and knowledge be not the workable truth of the business before *us,* what is it?

Dr. Smyth: Leave it there. It is the kind of well-seasoned pessimism that I like. Under it I can keep faith in our Republic, discharge my duties as a citizen with more discrimination than hitherto, and work harder than ever in the place where I seem fated to work at preventing and curing human ills with the aids afforded by modern science.

Mrs. Smyth: No! That is the kind of well-reasoned optimism under which I can go on working where I seem fated to work, with renewed strength.

Beard: Have it either way or both ways. You asked for my human ultimates and I have given them to you.

In this mood we shook hands and brought our long student communion to a close.

CONSTITUTION

OF THE

UNITED STATES OF AMERICA

Constitution of the
United States of America

PREAMBLE

We, the People of the United States, in Order to form a more perfect Union, establish Justice, insure domestic Tranquility, provide for the common defence, promote the general Welfare, and secure the Blessings of Liberty to ourselves and our Posterity, do ordain and establish this Constitution for the United States of America.

ARTICLE I.

Section 1. All legislative Powers herein granted shall be vested in a Congress of the United States, which shall consist of a Senate and House of Representatives.

Section 2. The House of Representatives shall be composed of Members chosen every second Year by the People of the several States, and the Electors in each State shall have the Qualifications requisite for Electors of the most numerous Branch of the State Legislature.

No Person shall be a Representative who shall not have attained to the Age of twenty-five Years, and been seven Years a Citizen of the United States, and who shall not, when elected, be an Inhabitant of that State in which he shall be chosen.

Representatives and direct Taxes shall be apportioned among the several States which may be included within this Union, according to their respective Numbers, which shall be determined by adding to the whole Number of free Persons, including those bound to Service for a Term of Years, and excluding Indians not taxed, three-fifths of all other Persons. The actual Enumeration shall be made within three Years after the first Meeting of the Congress of the United States, and within every subsequent Term of ten Years, in such Manner as they shall by Law direct. The Number of Representatives shall not exceed one for every thirty Thousand, but each State shall have at Least one Representative; and until such enumeration shall be made, the State of New Hampshire shall be entitled to choose three, Massachusetts eight, Rhode-Island and Providence Plantations one, Connecticut five, New-York six, New Jersey four, Pennsylvania eight, Delaware one, Maryland six, Virginia ten, North Carolina five, South Carolina five, and Georgia three.

When vacancies happen in the Representation from any State, the Executive Authority thereof shall issue Writs of Election to fill such Vacancies.

The House of Representatives shall choose their Speaker and other Officers; and shall have the sole Power of Impeachment.

Section 3. The Senate of the United States shall be composed of two Senators from each State, chosen by the Legislature thereof, for six Years; and each Senator shall have one Vote.

Immediately after they shall be assembled in Consequence of the first Election, they shall be divided as equally as may be into three Classes. The Seats of the Senators of the first Class shall be vacated at the Expiration of the second Year, of the second Class at the Expiration of the fourth Year, and of the third Class at the Expiration of the sixth Year, so that one-third may be chosen every second Year; and if Vacancies happen by Resignation, or otherwise, during the Recess of the Legislature of any State, the Executive thereof may make temporary Appointment until the next Meeting of the Legislature, which shall then fill such Vacancies.

No Person shall be a Senator who shall not have attained to the Age of thirty Years, and been nine Years a Citizen of the United States, and who shall not, when elected, be an Inhabitant of that State for which he shall be chosen.

The Vice-President of the United States shall be President of the Senate, but shall have no Vote, unless they be equally divided.

The Senate shall choose their other Officers, and also a President pro tempore, in the Absence of the Vice-President, or when he shall exercise the Office of President of the United States.

The Senate shall have the sole Power to try all Impeachments. When sitting for that Purpose, they shall be on Oath or Affirmation. When the President of the United States is tried, the Chief Justice shall preside: And no Person shall be convicted without the Concurrence of two-thirds of the Members present.

Judgment of Cases of Impeachment shall not extend further than to removal from Office, and disqualification to hold and enjoy any Office of honor, Trust or Profit under the United States: but the Party convicted shall nevertheless be liable and subject to Indictment, Trial, Judgment and Punishment, according to Law.

Section 4. The Times, Places and Manner of holding Elections for Senators and Representatives, shall be prescribed in each State by the Legislature thereof; but the Congress may at any time by Law make or alter such Regulations, except as to the Places of choosing Senators.

The Congress shall assemble at least once in every Year, and such Meeting shall be on the first Monday in December, unless they shall by Law appoint a different Day.

Section 5. Each House shall be the Judge of the Elections, Returns and Qualifications of its own Members, and a Majority of each shall constitute a Quorum to do Business; but a smaller Number may adjourn from day to day, and may be authorized to compel the Attendance of absent Members, in such Manner, and under such Penalties as each House may provide.

Each House may determine the Rules of its Proceedings, punish its Members for disorderly Behaviour, and, with the Concurrence of two-thirds, expel a Member.

Each House shall keep a Journal of its Proceedings, and from time to time publish the same, excepting such Parts as may in their Judgment require Secrecy; and the Yeas and Nays of the Members of either House on any question shall, at the Desire of one-fifth of those Present, be entered on the Journal.

Neither House, during the Session of Congress, shall, without the Consent of the other, adjourn for more than three days, nor to any other Place than that in which the two Houses shall be sitting.

Section 6. The Senators and Representatives shall receive a Compensation for their Services, to be ascertained by Law, and paid out of the Treasury of the United States. They shall in all Cases, except Treason, Felony and Breach of the Peace, be privileged from Arrest during their Attendance at the Session of their respective Houses, and in going to and returning from the same; and for any Speech or Debate in either House, they shall not be questioned in any other Place.

No Senator or Representative shall, during the Time for which he was elected, be appointed to any civil Office under the Authority of the United States, which shall have been created, or the Emoluments whereof shall have been increased during such time; and no Person holding any Office under the United States, shall be a Member of either House during his Continuance in Office.

Section 7. All Bills for raising Revenue shall originate in the House of Representatives; but the Senate may propose or concur with Amendments as on other Bills.

Every Bill which shall have passed the House of Representatives and the Senate shall, before it becomes a Law, be presented to the President of the United States; If he approve, he shall sign it, but if not, he shall return it, with his Objections, to that House in which it shall have originated, who shall enter the Objections at large on their Journal, and proceed to reconsider it. If after such Reconsideration two-thirds of the House shall agree to pass the Bill, it shall be sent, together with the Objections, to the other House, by which it shall likewise be reconsidered, and if approved by two-thirds of that House, it shall become a Law. But in all such Cases the Votes of both Houses shall be determined by Yeas and Nays, and the Names of the Persons voting for and against the Bill shall be entered on the Journal of each House respectively. If any Bill shall not be returned by the President within ten Days (Sundays excepted) after it shall have been presented to him, the Same shall be a Law, in like Manner as if he had signed it, unless the Congress by their Adjournment prevent its Return, in which Case it shall not be a Law.

Every Order, Resolution, or Vote to which the Concurrence of the Senate and House of Representatives may be necessary (except on a question of Adjournment) shall be presented to the President of the United States; and before the Same shall take Effect, shall be approved by him, or being disapproved by him, shall be repassed by two-thirds of the Senate and House of Representatives, according to the Rules and Limitations prescribed in the Case of a Bill.

Section 8. The Congress shall have Power: To lay and collect Taxes, Duties, Imposts and Excises, to pay the Debts and provide for the common Defence and general Welfare of the United States; but all Duties, Imposts and Excises shall be uniform throughout the United States;

To borrow Money on the credit of the United States;

To regulate Commerce with foreign Nations, and among the several States, and with the Indian Tribes;

To establish an uniform Rule of Naturalization, and uniform Laws on the subject of Bankruptcies throughout the United States;

To coin Money, regulate the Value thereof, and of foreign Coin, and fix the Standard of Weights and Measures;

To provide for the Punishment of counterfeiting the Securities and current Coin of the United States;

To establish Post Offices and post Roads;

To promote the Progress of Science and useful Arts, by securing for limited Times to Authors and Inventors the exclusive Right to their respective Writings and Discoveries;

To constitute Tribunals inferior to the supreme Court;

To define and punish Piracies and Felonies committed on the high Seas, and Offences against the Law of Nations;

To declare War, grant Letters of Marque and Reprisal, and make Rules concerning captures on Land and Water;

To raise and support Armies, but no Appropriation of Money to that Use shall be for a longer Term than two Years;

To provide and maintain a Navy;

To make Rules for the Government and Regulation of the land and naval Forces;

To provide for calling forth the Militia to execute the Laws of the Union, suppress Insurrections and repel Invasions;

To provide for organizing, arming, and disciplining the Militia, and for governing such Part of them as may be employed in the Service of the United States, reserving to the States respectively, the Appointment of the Officers, and the Authority of training the Militia according to the discipline prescribed by Congress;

To exercise exclusive Legislation in all Cases whatsoever, over such District (not exceeding ten Miles square) as may, by Cession of particular States, and the Acceptance of Congress, become the Seat of Government of the United States, and to exercise like Authority over all Places purchased by the Consent of the Legislature of the State in which the Same shall be, for the Erection of Forts, Magazines, Arsenals, dock-Yards, and other needful Buildings;—And

To make all Laws which shall be necessary and proper for carrying into Execution the foregoing Powers, and all other Powers vested by this Constitution in the Government of the United States, or in any Department or Officer thereof.

Section 9. The Migration or Importation of such Persons as **any**

of the States now existing shall think proper to admit, shall not be prohibited by the Congress prior to the Year one thousand eight hundred and eight, but a Tax or duty may be imposed on such Importation, not exceeding ten dollars for each Person.

The Privilege of the Writ of Habeas Corpus shall not be suspended, unless when in Cases of Rebellion or Invasion the public Safety may require it.

No Bill of Attainder or ex post facto Law shall be passed.

No Capitation, or other direct, Tax shall be laid, unless in Proportion to the Census or Enumeration herein before directed to be taken.

No Tax or Duty shall be laid on Articles exported from any State.

No Preference shall be given by any Regulation of Commerce or Revenue to the Ports of one State over those of another: nor shall Vessels bound to, or from, one State, be obliged to enter, clear, or pay Duties in another.

No Money shall be drawn from the Treasury, but in Consequence of Appropriations made by Law; and a regular Statement and Account of the Receipts and Expenditures of all public Money shall be published from time to time.

No Title of Nobility shall be granted by the United States; And no Person holding any Office of Profit or Trust under them, shall, without the Consent of the Congress, accept of any present, Emolument, Office, or Title, of any kind whatever, from any King, Prince, or foreign State.

Section 10. No State shall enter into any Treaty, Alliance, or Confederation; grant Letters of Marque and Reprisal; coin Money; emit Bills of Credit; make any Thing but gold and silver Coin a Tender in Payment of Debts; pass any Bill of Attainder, ex post facto Law, or Law impairing the Obligation of Contracts, or grant any Title of Nobility.

No State shall, without the Consent of the Congress, lay any Imposts or Duties on Imports or Exports, except what may be absolutely necessary for executing it's inspection Laws: and the net Produce of all Duties and Imposts, laid by any State on Imports or Exports, shall be for the Use of the Treasury of the United States; and all such Laws shall be subject to the Revision and Control of the Congress.

No State shall, without the Consent of Congress, lay any Duty of Tonnage, keep Troops, or Ships of War in time of Peace, enter into any Agreement or Compact with another State, or with a foreign Power, or engage in War, unless actually invaded, or in such imminent Danger as will not admit of delay.

ARTICLE II.

Section 1. The executive Power shall be vested in a President of the United States of America. He shall hold his Office during the Term of four Years, and, together with the Vice-President, chosen for the same Term, be elected, as follows:

Each State shall appoint, in such Manner as the Legislature thereof may direct, a Number of Electors, equal to the whole Number of Senators and Representatives to which the State may be entitled in the Congress: but no Senator or Representative, or Person holding an Office of Trust or Profit under the United States, shall be appointed an Elector.

The Electors shall meet in their respective States, and vote by Ballot for two Persons, of whom one at least shall not be an Inhabitant of the same State with themselves. And they shall make a List of all the Persons voted for, and of the Number of Votes for each; which List they shall sign and certify, and transmit sealed to the Seat of the Government of the United States, directed to the President of the Senate. The President of the Senate shall, in the Presence of the Senate and House of Representatives, open all the Certificates, and the Votes shall then be counted. The Person having the greatest Number of Votes shall be the President, if such Number be a Majority of the whole Number of Electors appointed; and if there be more than one who have such Majority, and have an equal Number of Votes, then the House of Representatives shall immediately choose by Ballot one of them for President; and if no Person have a majority, then from the five highest on the List the said House shall in like Manner choose the President. But in choosing the President, the Votes shall be taken by States, the Representation from each State having one Vote. A quorum for this Purpose shall consist of a Member or Members from two-thirds of the States, and a Majority of all the States shall be necessary to a Choice. In every Case, after the Choice of the President, the Person having the greatest Number of Votes of the Electors shall be the Vice-President. But if there should remain two or more who have equal Votes, the Senate shall choose from them by Ballot the Vice-President.

The Congress may determine the Time of choosing the Electors, and the Day on which they shall give their Votes; which Day shall be the same throughout the United States.

No Person except a natural born Citizen, or a Citizen of the United States, at the time of the Adoption of this Constitution, shall be eligible to the Office of President; neither shall any Person be eligible to that Office who shall not have attained to the Age of thirty-five Years, and been fourteen Years a Resident within the United States.

In Case of the Removal of the President from Office, or of his Death, Resignation, or Inability to discharge the Powers and Duties of the said Office, the Same shall devolve on the Vice-President, and the Congress may by Law provide for the Case of Removal, Death, Resignation or Inability, both of the President and Vice-President, declaring what Officer shall then act as President, and such Officer shall act accordingly, until the Disability be removed, or a President shall be elected.

The President shall, at stated Times, receive for his Services, a Compensation, which shall neither be increased nor diminished during the Period for which he shall have been elected, and he shall not receive within that Period any other Emolument from the United States, or any of them.

Before he enter on the Execution of his Office, he shall take the following Oath or Affirmation:—"I do solemnly swear (or affirm) that I will faithfully execute the office of President of the United States, and will, to the best of my Ability, preserve, protect and defend the Constitution of the United States."

Section 2.   The President shall be Commander-in-Chief of the Army and Navy of the United States, and of the Militia of the several States, when called into the actual Service of the United States; he may require the Opinion, in writing, of the principal Officer in each of the executive Departments, upon any Subject relating to the Duties of their respective Offices, and he shall have Power to grant Reprieves and Pardons for all Offences against the United States, except in Cases of Impeachment.

He shall have Power, by and with the Advice and Consent of the Senate, to make Treaties, provided two-thirds of the Senators present concur; and he shall nominate, and by and with the Advice and Consent of the Senate, shall appoint Ambassadors, other public Ministers and Consuls, Judges of the Supreme Court, and all other Officers of the United States, whose Appointments are not herein otherwise provided for, and which shall be established by Law: but the Congress may by Law vest the Appointment of such inferior Officers, as they think proper, in the President alone, in the Courts of Law, or in the Heads of Departments.

The President shall have Power to fill up all Vacancies that may happen during the Recess of the Senate, by granting Commissions which shall expire at the End of their next Session.

Section 3. He shall from time to time give to the Congress Information of the State of the Union, and recommend to their Consideration such Measures as he shall judge necessary and expedient; he may, on extraordinary Occasions, convene both Houses, or either of them, and in Case of Disagreement between them, with Respect to the Time of Adjournment, he may adjourn them to such Time as he shall think proper; he shall receive Ambassadors and other public Ministers; he shall take Care that the Laws be faithfully executed, and shall Commission all the Officers of the United States.

Section 4. The President, Vice-President and all civil Officers of the United States, shall be removed from Office on Impeachment for, and Conviction of, Treason, Bribery, or other high Crimes and Misdemeanors.

ARTICLE III.

Section 1. The judicial Power of the United States shall be vested in one Supreme Court, and in such inferior Courts as the Congress may from time to time ordain and establish. The Judges, both of the Supreme and inferior Courts, shall hold their Offices during good Behaviour, and shall, at stated Times, receive for their Services, a Compensation, which shall not be diminished during their Continuance in Office.

Section 2. The judicial Power shall extend to all Cases, in Law and Equity, arising under this Constitution, the Laws of the United States, and Treaties made, or which shall be made, under their Authority;—to all Cases affecting Ambassadors, other public Ministers and Consuls;—to all Cases of admiralty and maritime Jurisdiction;—to Controversies to which the United States shall be a Party;—to Controversies between two or more States;—between a State and Citizens of another State;—between Citizens of different States;—between Citizens of the same State claiming Lands under Grants of different States, and between a State, or the Citizens thereof, and foreign States, Citizens or Subjects.

In all Cases affecting Ambassadors, other public Ministers and Consuls, and those in which a State shall be Party, the Supreme Court shall have original Jurisdiction. In all the other Cases before mentioned, the Supreme Court shall have appellate Jurisdiction, both as to Law and Fact, with such Exceptions, and under such Regulations as the Congress shall make.

The Trial of all Crimes, except in Cases of Impeachment, shall be by Jury; and such Trial shall be held in the State where the said Crimes shall have been committed; but when not committed within any State, the Trial shall be at such Place or Places as the Congress may by Law have directed.

Section 3. Treason against the United States, shall consist only in levying War against them, or in adhering to their Enemies, giving them Aid and Comfort. No Person shall be convicted of Treason unless on the Testimony of two Witnesses to the same overt Act, or on Confession in open Court.

The Congress shall have Power to declare the Punishment of Treason, but no Attainder of Treason shall work Corruption of Blood, or Forfeiture except during the Life of the Person attainted.

ARTICLE IV.

Section 1. Full Faith and Credit shall be given in each State to the public Acts, Records and judicial Proceedings of every other State. And the Congress may by general Laws prescribe the Manner in which such Acts, Records and Proceedings shall be proved, and the Effect thereof.

Section 2. The Citizens of each State shall be entitled to all Privileges and Immunities of Citizens in the several States.

A Person charged in any State with Treason, Felony, or other Crime, who shall flee from Justice, and be found in another State, shall on Demand of the executive Authority of the State from which he fled, be delivered up, to be removed to the State having Jurisdiction of the Crime.

No Person held to Service or Labour in one State, under the Laws thereof, escaping into another, shall, in Consequence of any Law or Regulation therein, be discharged from such Service or Labour, but shall be delivered up on Claim of the Party to whom such Service or Labour may be due.

Section 3. New States may be admitted by the Congress into this Union; but no new State shall be formed or erected within the Jurisdiction of any other State; nor any State be formed by the Junction of two or more States, or Parts of States, without the Consent of the Legislatures of the States concerned as well as of the Congress.

The Congress shall have Power to dispose of and make all needful Rules and Regulations respecting the Territory or other Property belonging to the United States; and nothing in this Constitution shall be so construed as to Prejudice any Claims of the United States, or of any particular State.

Section 4. The United States shall guarantee to every State in this Union a Republican Form of Government, and shall protect each of them against Invasion; and on Application of the Legislature, or of the Executive (when the Legislature cannot be convened) against domestic Violence.

ARTICLE V.

The Congress, whenever two-thirds of both Houses shall deem it necessary, shall propose Amendments to this Constitution, or, on the Application of the Legislatures of two-thirds of the several States, shall call a Convention for proposing Amendments, which, in either Case, shall be valid to all Intents and Purposes, as Part of this Constitution, when ratified by the Legislatures of three-fourths of the several States, or by Conventions in three-fourths thereof, as the one or the other Mode of Ratification may be proposed by the Congress; Provided that no Amendment which may be made prior to the Year One thousand eight hundred and eight shall in any Manner affect the first and fourth Clauses in the Ninth Section of the first Article; and that no State, without its Consent, shall be deprived of it's equal Suffrage in the Senate.

ARTICLE VI.

All Debts contracted and Engagements entered into, before the Adoption of this Constitution, shall be as valid against the United States under this Constitution, as under the Confederation.

This Constitution, and the Laws of the United States which shall be made in Pursuance thereof and all Treaties made, or which shall be made, under the Authority of the United States, shall be the supreme Law of the Land; and the Judges in every State shall be bound thereby, any Thing in the Constitution or Laws of any State to the Contrary notwithstanding.

The Senators and Representatives before mentioned, and the Members of the several State Legislatures, and all executive and judicial Officers, both of the United States and of the several States, shall be bound by Oath or Affirmation, to support this Constitution; but no religious Test shall ever be required as a Qualification to any Office or public Trust under the United States.

ARTICLE VII.

The Ratification of the Conventions of nine States, shall be sufficient for the Establishment of this Constitution between the States so ratifying the Same.

done in Convention by the Unanimous Consent of the States present the Seventeenth Day of September in the Year of our Lord one thousand seven hundred and Eighty-seven, and of the Independence of the United States of America the Twelfth. In witness whereof We have hereunto subscribed our Names, Attest

WILLIAM JACKSON
    Secretary

G⁰ WASHINGTON—Presidᵗ
                    and deputy from Virginia

New Hampshire—JOHN LANGDON, NICHOLAS GILMAN.

Massachusetts—NATHANIEL GORHAM, RUFUS KING.

Connecticut—Wᵐ Samˡ JOHNSON, ROGER SHERMAN.

New York—ALEXANDER HAMILTON.

New Jersey—WIL: LIVINGSTON, DAVID BREARLEY, Wᵐ PATERSON, JONA: DAYTON.

Pennsylvania—B. FRANKLIN, THOMAS MIFFLIN, ROBᵗ MORRIS, GEO. CLYMER, THOˢ FITZSIMONS, JARED INGERSOLL, JAMES WILSON, GOUV MORRIS.

Delaware—GEO: READ, GUNNING BEDFORD, jun. JOHN DICKINSON, RICHARD BASSETT, JACO: BROOM.

Maryland—JAMES McHENRY, DAN OF Sᵗ THOˢ JENIFER, DANˡ CARROLL.

Virginia—JOHN BLAIR, JAMES MADISON, Jr.

North Carolina—Wᵐ BLOUNT, RICHᵈ DOBBS SPAIGHT, HU WILLIAMSON.

South Carolina—J. RUTLEDGE, CHARLES COTESWORTH PINCKNEY, CHARLES PINCKNEY, PIERCE BUTLER.

Georgia—WILLIAM FEW, ABR BALDWIN.

In Convention Monday September 17th 1787.

Present The States of New Hampshire, Massachusetts, Connecticut, Mʳ Hamilton from New York, New Jersey, Pennsylvania, Delaware, Maryland, Virginia, North Carolina, South Carolina and Georgia. Resolved,

That the preceeding Constitution be laid before the United States in Congress assembled, and that it is the Opinion of this Convention, that it should afterwards be submitted to a Convention of Delegates, chosen in each State by the People thereof, under the Recommendation of its Legislature, for their Assent and Ratification; and that each Convention assenting to, and ratifying the Same, should give Notice thereof to the United States in Congress assembled.

Resolved, That it is the Opinion of this Convention, that as soon as the Conventions of nine States shall have ratified this Constitution, the United States in Congress assembled should fix a Day on which Electors should be appointed by the States which shall have ratified the same, and a Day on which the Electors should assemble to vote for the President, and the Time and Place for commencing Proceedings under this Constitution. That after such Publication the Electors should be appointed, and the Senators and Representatives elected: That the Electors should meet on the Day fixed for the Election of the President and should transmit their Votes certified, signed, sealed and directed, as the Constitution requires, to the Secretary of the United States in Congress assembled, that the Senators and Representatives should convene at the Time and Place assigned; that the Senators should appoint a President of the Senate, for the sole Purpose of receiving, opening and counting the Votes for President; and, that after he shall be chosen, the Congress, together with the President, should, without Delay, proceed to execute this Constitution.

By the Unanimous Order of the Convention

G° Washington Presid^t

W. Jackson Secretary.

Amendments.

Articles in addition to, and Amendment of the Constitution of the United States of America, proposed by Congress, and ratified by the Legislatures of the several States, pursuant to the fifth Article of the original Constitution.

Article I.

Congress shall make no law respecting an establishment of religion, or prohibiting the free exercise thereof; or abridging the freedom of speech, or of the press; or the right of the people peaceably to assemble, and to petition the Government for a redress of grievances.

Article II.

A well-regulated Militia, being necessary to the security of a free State, the right of the people to keep and bear Arms, shall not be infringed.

Article III.

No Soldier shall, in time of peace be quartered in any house, without the consent of the Owner, nor in time of war, but in a manner to be prescribed by law.

Article IV.

The right of the people to be secure in their persons, houses, papers, and effects, against unreasonable searches and seizures, shall not be violated, and no Warrants shall issue, but upon probable cause, supported by Oath or affirmation, and particularly describing the place to be searched, and the persons or things to be seized.

Article V.

No person shall be held to answer for a capital, or other infamous crime, unless on a presentment or indictment of a Grand Jury, except in cases arising in the land or naval forces, or in the Militia, when in actual service in time of War or public danger; nor shall any person be subject for the same offence to be twice put in jeopardy of life or limb; nor shall be compelled in any criminal case to be a witness against himself, nor be deprived of life, liberty, or property, without due process of law; nor shall private property be taken for public use, without just compensation.

Article VI.

In all criminal prosecutions, the accused shall enjoy the right to a speedy and public trial, by an impartial jury of the State and district wherein the crime shall have been committed, which district shall have been previously ascertained by law, and to be informed of the nature and cause of the accusation; to be confronted with the witnesses against him; to have compulsory process for obtaining witnesses in his favor, and to have the Assistance of Counsel for his defence.

Article VII.

In Suits at common law, where the value in controversy shall exceed twenty dollars, the right of trial by jury shall be preserved, and no fact tried by a jury, shall be otherwise re-examined in any Court of the United States, than according to the rules of the common law.

Article VIII.

Excessive bail shall not be required, nor excessive fines imposed, nor cruel and unusual punishments inflicted.

Article IX.

The enumeration in the Constitution, of certain rights, shall not be be construed to deny or disparage others retained by the people.

Article X.

The powers not delegated to the United States by the Constitution, nor prohibited by it to the States, are reserved to the States respectively, or to the people.

Article XI.

The Judicial power of the United States shall not be construed to extend to any suit in law or equity, commenced or prosecuted against one of the United States by Citizens of another State, or by Citizens or Subjects of any Foreign State.

Article XII.

The Electors shall meet in their respective states, and vote by ballot for President and Vice-President, one of whom, at least, shall not be an inhabitant of the same state with themselves; they shall name in their ballots the person voted for as President, and in distinct ballots the person voted for as Vice-President, and they shall make distinct lists of all persons voted for as President, and of all persons voted for as Vice-President, and of the number of votes for each, which lists they shall sign and certify, and transmit sealed to the seat of the government of the United States, directed to the President of the Senate;—The President of the Senate shall, in the presence of the Senate and House of Representatives, open all the certificates and the votes shall then be counted;—The person having the greatest number of votes for President, shall be the President, if such number be a majority of the whole number of Electors appointed; and if no person have such majority, then from the persons having the highest numbers not exceeding three on the list of those voted for as President, the House of Representatives shall choose immediately, by ballot, the President. But in choosing the

President, the votes shall be taken by states, the representation from each state having one vote; a quorum for this purpose shall consist of a member or members from two-thirds of the states, and a majority of all the states shall be necessary to a choice. And if the House of Representatives shall not choose a President whenever the right of choice shall devolve upon them, before the fourth day of March next following, then the Vice-President shall act as President, as in the case of the death or other constitutional disability of the President.—The person having the greatest number of votes as Vice-President, shall be the Vice-President, if such number be a majority of the whole number of Electors appointed, and if no person have a majority, then from the two highest numbers on the list, the Senate shall choose the Vice-President; a quorum for the purpose shall consist of two-thirds of the whole number of Senators, and a majority of the whole number shall be necessary to a choice. But no person constitutionally ineligible to the office of President shall be eligible to that of Vice-President of the United States.

ARTICLE XIII.

Section 1. Neither slavery nor involuntary servitude, except as a punishment for crime whereof the party shall have been duly convicted, shall exist within the United States, or any place subject to their jurisdiction.

Section 2. Congress shall have power to enforce this article by appropriate legislation.

ARTICLE XIV.

Section 1. All persons born or naturalized in the United States, and subject to the jurisdiction thereof, are citizens of the United States and of the State wherein they reside. No State shall make or enforce any law which shall abridge the privileges or immunities of citizens of the United States; nor shall any State deprive any person of life, liberty, or property, without due process of law; nor deny to any person within its jurisdiction the equal protection of the laws.

Section 2. Representatives shall be apportioned among the several States according to their respective numbers, counting the whole number of persons in each State, excluding Indians not taxed. But when the right to vote at any election for the choice of electors for President and Vice-President of the United States, Representatives in Congress, the Executive and Judicial officers of a State, or the members of the

Legislature thereof, is denied to any of the male members of such State, being twenty-one years of age, and citizens of the United States, or in any way abridged, except for participation in rebellion, or other crime, the basis of representation therein shall be reduced in the proportion which the number of such male citizens shall bear to the whole number of male citizens twenty-one years of age in such State.

Section 3. No person shall be a Senator or Representative in Congress, or elector of President and Vice-President, or holding any office, civil or military, under the United States, or under any State, who, having previously taken an oath, as a member of Congress, or as an officer of the United States, or as a member of any State legislature, or as an executive or judicial officer of any State, to support the Constitution of the United States, shall have engaged in insurrection or rebellion against the same, or given aid and comfort to the enemies thereof. But Congress may by a vote of two-thirds of each House, remove such disability.

Section 4. The validity of the public debt of the United States, authorized by law, including debts incurred for payment of pensions and bounties for services in suppressing insurrection and rebellion, shall not be questioned. But neither the United States nor any State shall assume or pay any debt or obligation incurred in aid of insurrection or rebellion against the United States, or any claim for the loss or emancipation of any slave; but all such debts, obligations and claims shall be held illegal and void.

Section 5. The Congress shall have power to enforce, by appropriate legislation, the provisions of this article.

ARTICLE XV.

Section 1. The right of the citizens of the United States to vote shall not be denied or abridged by the United States or by any State on account of race, color, or previous condition of servitude.——

Section 2. The Congress shall have power to enforce the provisions of this article by appropriate legislation.—

ARTICLE XVI.

The Congress shall have power to lay and collect taxes on incomes, from whatever sources derived, without apportionment among the several States, and without regard to any census or enumeration.

Article XVII.

The Senate of the United States shall be composed of two Senators from each State, elected by the people thereof, for six years; and each Senator shall have one vote. The electors in each State shall have the qualifications requisite for electors of the most numerous branch of the State legislatures.

When vacancies happen in the representation of any State in the Senate, the executive authority of such State shall issue writs of election to fill such vacancies: *Provided,* That the legislature of any State may empower the executive thereof to make temporary appointment until the people fill the vacancies by election as the legislature may direct.

This amendment shall not be so construed as to affect the election or term of any Senator chosen before it becomes valid as part of the Constitution.

Article XVIII.

Section 1. After one year from the ratification of this article the manufacture, sale, or transportation of intoxicating liquors within, the importation thereof into, or the exportation thereof from the United States and all territory subject to the jurisdiction thereof for beverage purposes is hereby prohibited.

Section 2. The Congress and the several States shall have concurrent power to enforce this article by appropriate legislation.

Section 3. This article shall be inoperative unless it shall have been ratified as an amendment to the Constitution by the legislatures of the several States, as provided in the Constitution, within seven years from the date of the submission hereof to the States by the Congress.

Article XIX.

The right of citizens of the United States to vote shall not be denied or abridged by the United States or by any State on account of sex.

Congress shall have power to enforce this article by appropriate legislation.

Article XX

Section 1. The terms of the President and Vice-President shall end at noon on the 20th day of January, and the terms of Senators and Representatives at noon on the 3d day of January, of the years in which such terms would have ended if this article had not been ratified; and the terms of their successors shall then begin.

Section 2. The Congress shall assemble at least once in every year, and such meeting shall begin at noon on the 3d day of January, unless they shall by law appoint a different day.

Section 3. If, at the time fixed for the beginning of the term of the President, the President elect shall have died, the Vice-President elect shall become President. If a President shall not have been chosen before the time fixed for the beginning of his term, or if the President elect shall have failed to qualify, then the Vice-President elect shall act as President until a President shall have qualified; and the Congress may by law provide for the case wherein neither a President elect nor a Vice-President elect shall have qualified, declaring who shall then act as President, or the manner in which one who is to act shall be selected, and such person shall act accordingly until a President or Vice-President shall have qualified.

Section 4. The Congress may by law provide for the case of the death of any of the persons from whom the House of Representatives may choose a President whenever the right of choice shall have devolved upon them, and for the case of the death of any of the persons from whom the Senate may choose a Vice-President whenever the right of choice shall have devolved upon them.

Section 5. Sections 1 and 2 shall take effect on the 15th day of October following the ratification of this article.

Section 6. This article shall be inoperative unless it shall have been ratified as an amendment to the Constitution by the legislatures of three-fourths of the several States within seven years from the date of its submission. [The text followed above is that of the 'Literal Print' edition issued by the Department of State in Washington, D. C., 1933.]

ARTICLE XXI.

Section 1. The eighteenth article of amendment to the Constitution of the United States is hereby repealed.

Section 2. The transportation or importation into any State, Territory, or Possession of the United States for delivery or use therein of intoxicating liquors, in violation of the laws thereof, is hereby prohibited.

Section 3. This article shall be inoperative unless it shall have been ratified as an amendment to the Constitution by conventions in the several States, as provided in the Constitution, within seven years from the date of the submission hereof to the States by the Congress.